Querying XML

XQuery, XPath, and SQL/XML in Context

The Morgan Kaufmann Series in Data Management Systems

Series Editor: Jim Gray, Microsoft Research

Querying XML: XQuery, XPath, and SQL/XML in Context
Jim Melton and Stephen Buxton

Data Mining: Concepts and Techniques, Second Edition
Jiawei Han and Micheline Kamber

Database Modeling and Design: Logical Design, Fourth Edition
Toby J, Teorey, Sam S. Lightstone and Thomas P. Nadeau

Foundations of Multidimensional and Metric Data Structures
Hanan Samet

Joe Celko's SQL for Smarties: Advanced SQL Programming, Third Edition
Joe Celko

Moving Objects Databases
Ralf Hartmut Güting and Markus Schneider

Joe Celko's SQL Programming Style
Joe Celko

Data Mining, Second Edition: Concepts and Techniques
Ian Witten and Eibe Frank

Fuzzy Modeling and Genetic Algorithms for Data Mining and Exploration
Earl Cox

Data Modeling Essentials, Third Edition
Graeme C. Simsion and Graham C. Witt

Location-Based Services
Jochen Schiller and Agnès Voisard

Database Modeling with Microsft" Visio for Enterprise Architects
Terry Halpin, Ken Evans, Patrick Hallock, Bill Maclean

Designing Data-Intensive Web Applications
Stephano Ceri, Piero Fraternali, Aldo Bongio, Marco Brambilla, Sara Comai, and Maristella Matera

Mining the Web: Discovering Knowledge from Hypertext Data
Soumen Chakrabarti

Advanced SQL: 1999—Understanding Object-Relational and Other Advanced Features
Jim Melton

Database Tuning: Principles, Experiments, and Troubleshooting Techniques
Dennis Shasha and Philippe Bonnet

SQL:1999—Understanding Relational Language Components
Jim Melton and Alan R. Simon

Information Visualization in Data Mining and Knowledge Discovery
Edited by Usama Fayyad, Georges G. Grinstein, and Andreas Wierse

Transactional Information Systems: Theory, Algorithms, and Practice of Concurrency Control and Recovery
Gerhard Weikum and Gottfried Vossen

Spatial Databases: With Application to GIS
Philippe Rigaux, Michel Scholl, and Agnes Voisard

Information Modeling and Relational Databases: From Conceptual Analysis to Logical Design
Terry Halpin

Component Database Systems
Edited by Klaus R. Dittrich and Andreas Geppert

Managing Reference Data in Enterprise Databases: Binding Corporate Data to the Wider World
Malcolm Chisholm

Understanding SQL and Java Together: A Guide to SQLJ, JDBC, and Related Technologies
Jim Melton and Andrew Eisenberg

Database: Principles, Programming, and Performance, Second Edition
Patrick and Elizabeth O'Neil

The Object Data Standard: ODMG 3.0
Edited by R. G. G. Cattell and Douglas K. Barry

Data on the Web: From Relations to Semistructured Data and XML
Serge Abiteboul, Peter Buneman, and Dan Suciu

Data Mining: Practical Machine Learning Tools and Techniques with Java Implementations
Ian Witten and Eibe Frank

Joe Celko's SQL for Smarties: Advanced SQL Programming, Second Edition
Joe Celko

Joe Celko's Data and Databases: Concepts in Practice
Joe Celko

Developing Time-Oriented Database Applications in SQL
Richard T. Snodgrass

Web Farming for the Data Warehouse
Richard D. Hackathorn

Management of Heterogeneous and Autonomous Database Systems
Edited by Ahmed Elmagarmid, Marek Rusinkiewicz, and Amit Sheth

Object-Relational DBMSs: Tracking the Next Great Wave, Second Edition
Michael Stonebraker and Paul Brown,with Dorothy Moore

A Complete Guide to DB2 Universal Database
Don Chamberlin

Universal Database Management: A Guide to Object/Relational Technology
Cynthia Maro Saracco

Readings in Database Systems, Third Edition
Edited by Michael Stonebraker and Joseph M. Hellerstein

Understanding SQL's Stored Procedures: A Complete Guide to SQL/PSM
Jim Melton

Principles of Multimedia Database Systems
V. S. Subrahmanian

Principles of Database Query Processing for Advanced Applications
Clement T. Yu and Weiyi Meng

Advanced Database Systems
Carlo Zaniolo, Stefano Ceri, Christos Faloutsos, Richard T. Snodgrass, V. S. Subrahmanian, and Roberto Zicari

Principles of Transaction Processing
Philip A. Bernstein and Eric Newcomer

Using the New DB2: IBMs Object-Relational Database System
Don Chamberlin

Distributed Algorithms
Nancy A. Lynch

Active Database Systems: Triggers and Rules For Advanced Database Processing
Edited by Jennifer Widom and Stefano Ceri

Migrating Legacy Systems: Gateways, Interfaces, & the Incremental Approach
Michael L. Brodie and Michael Stonebraker

Atomic Transactions
Nancy Lynch, Michael Merritt, William Weihl, and Alan Fekete

Query Processing for Advanced Database Systems
Edited by Johann Christoph Freytag, David Maier, and Gottfried Vossen

Transaction Processing: Concepts and Techniques
Jim Gray and Andreas Reuter

Building an Object-Oriented Database System: The Story of O_2
Edited by François Bancilhon, Claude Delobel, and Paris Kanellakis

Database Transaction Models for Advanced Applications
Edited by Ahmed K. Elmagarmid

A Guide to Developing Client/Server SQL Applications
Setrag Khoshafian, Arvola Chan, Anna Wong, and Harry K. T. Wong

The Benchmark Handbook for Database and Transaction Processing Systems, Second Edition
Edited by Jim Gray

Camelot and Avalon: A Distributed Transaction Facility
Edited by Jeffrey L. Eppinger, Lily B. Mummert, and Alfred Z. Spector

Readings in Object-Oriented Database Systems
Edited by Stanley B. Zdonik and David Maier

Querying XML

XQuery, XPath, and SQL/XML in Context

Jim Melton
and
Stephen Buxton

Amsterdam • Boston
Heidelberg • London
New York • Oxford • Paris
San Diego • San Francisco
Singapore • Sydney • Tokyo

Publisher	Diane Cerra
Publishing Services Manager	Simon Crump
Editorial Assistant	Asma Stephan
Cover Design	Ross Carron Design
Cover Image	©Javier Pierini/Digital Images/Getty Images
Composition	Multiscience Press
Technical Illustration	Dartmouth Publishing, Inc.
Copyeditor	Elliot Simon
Proofreader	Jacqui Brownstein
Indexer	Northwind Editorial Services
Interior printer	Maple-Vail Book Manufacturing Group
Cover printer	Phoenix Color

Morgan Kaufmann Publishers is an imprint of Elsevier.
500 Sansome Street, Suite 400, San Francisco, CA 94111

This book is printed on acid-free paper.

Library of Congress Cataloging-in-Publication Data
Application submitted

ISBN 13: 978-1-55860-711-8
ISBN 10: 1-55860-711-0

For information on all Morgan Kaufmann publications,
visit our Web site at www.mkp.com or www.books.elsevier.com

Printed in the United States of America
06 07 08 09 10 5 4 3 2 1

To rescued Shelties, and Shelties in need of rescue, everywhere. Especially to senior Shelties who, after years of devotion to their owners, are cruelly discarded for the most pathetic of reasons: "We're thinking about moving", "She's just in the way", "He's too old to be fun any more", and the worst of all - "We're getting a puppy and, you know…". And to the loving people who welcome these old dogs into their lives, knowing that older Shelties are calmer, settled, cuddly, and devoted — they selflessly deal with medical needs, arthritic limitations, and the piddles of old age. Wonderful karma accrues to these people for giving these seniors love and respect, allowing them to live out their lives in comfort and happiness.

Jim

To my Mum and Dad, for their long, long journey.

Stephen

Contents

Foreword

by Don Chamberlin
IBM Fellow
Almaden Research Center

Companies come and go in the database industry, but one thing remains constant: Jim Melton remains at the center of the database standards community. For more years than anyone cares to remember, Jim has served as editor of the international standard for the SQL database language. Perhaps more importantly, he has translated this standard into terminology that ordinary people can understand and has made it accessible to everyone in a series of successful books.

Now the database world is undergoing its most important transition since the advent of the relational data model in the 1970's. A new self-describing data format, XML, is emerging as the standard format for exchange of semi-structured data on the Web. XML is fundamentally different from relations because it carries descriptive metadata with each data instance rather than storing it in a separate catalog. This new format gives unprecedented flexibility for representing various types of data but at the same time it requires a new approach to query.

A collection of query-related standards is emerging around the XML data format, and as usual Jim Melton is at the center of the action. Jim is co-chair of the W3C XML Query Working Group, which is creating an important new language called XQuery and (together with the XSLT Working Group) is revising the well-known XPath language. Jim is also co-Spec Lead for XQJ, the Java interface to XQuery that is being developed under the Java Community Process. In addition, as editor of the SQL Standard, Jim serves as editor of SQL/XML, the set of SQL extensions that enable relational databases to store and query XML data.

Stephen Buxton is also a long-time member of the W3C XML Query Working Group, and a specialist in full-text search and retrieval. Stephen's expertise in approximate queries on unstructured text complements Jim's long experience with exact queries on structured data.

In short, there is no more authoritative pair of authors on Querying XML than Jim Melton and Stephen Buxton. Best of all, as readers of Jim's other books know, his informal writing style will teach you what you need to know about this complex subject without giving you a headache. If you need a comprehensive and accessible overview of Querying XML, this is the book you have been waiting for.

Don Chamberlin

December 2005

Preface

Why the subject matter is important

In a remarkably short period, XML has arguably become the most important language for marking up documents for the World Wide Web and for industry in general. Equally important, XML is rapidly becoming the *lingua franca* for marking up traditional business data, for exchanging information between business partners and between application programs, and for expressing a host of concepts that improve the usability of computer systems.

While it may be tempting to view XML as a "silver bullet"—a solution to all of our problems—the truth is a bit more prosaic: XML is merely a tool (admittedly a very important one) that can help solve a significant range of problems. Like most tools, XML introduces tradeoffs and complications. Among the difficulties that XML users will increasingly encounter are the ones posed by locating and retrieving information stored in documents marked up using XML.

As you'll learn in this book, there are many approaches to querying XML documents and repositories of such documents. We cannot claim to have addressed every possible approach, or even every approach in use at the time we wrote this book. There are simply too many possibilities and alternatives, too many researchers and practitioners inventing new technologies. Instead, we have focused on the approaches that have the broadest uses, the largest community of adherents, and the greatest promise for economic success.

Before going further, we think that a quick explanation is in order for one key term that crops up repeatedly in this book: *document*. Because of XML's origins, sequences of characters that follow the rules of XML, and are able to stand alone, are properly known as "XML documents", even when they have nothing to do with books, articles, or any kind of textual material. When numeric data or even graphic images are represented in a standalone XML form, that XML is properly called an XML document. XML that cannot stand by itself is sometimes called an XML *fragment*. In general, throughout this book, we use the word "document" or "fragment" when a specific sort of XML is being referenced and we need to be clear about the nature of that XML. Otherwise, we mostly use the raw term "XML" and depend on the context to disambiguate our usage.

Why we wrote this book

"XML" is an enormous topic for any individual to understand. The term has come to imply much more than the markup language of the same name. Due in large part to the versatility of the markup language and the enormous utility of the Internet and the World Wide Web, there are countless computer scientists and software engineers developing specifications, tools, application programs, and even hardware that use or depend on some use of XML.

There are many fine books available that can teach you how to mark up your documents and your data with XML, how to use the eXtensible Stylesheet Language (XSL) to transform documents into other documents, how to use the many tools such as XML parsers and XSL transformation engines, and so forth. There are even several available books focused exclusively on XQuery, the almost-finalized W3C XML Query language.

But we have not seen any books that cover a broader subject that we think is vital: how to locate information in documents that are marked up using XML and how to find and extract that information in repositories of such documents. It is certainly important to mark up your documents and your data to capture the meaning inherent in them, but tremendous additional value is available when you can use powerful query facilities that not only find certain documents in a repository, but also find and extract the fine-grained information contained in those documents.

In this book, we identify and explore several approaches to querying XML documents, concentrating on those that we believe are most likely to be important in the near-to-medium future. We also give you a perspective on some of the other technologies that are closely related to the subject of querying XML. In doing so, we give you not only valuable insights about locating and retrieving information in XML documents, but we put the subject into the contexts in which it will be used.

Who should read this book

We wrote this book primarily to benefit software engineers who have to design and build applications that use XML and to access documents and data presented in an XML form. While the subject is necessarily technical in nature and presentation, we decline to focus exclusively on production of lines of code. Instead, we approach mastery of the subject by ensuring that readers understand the reason a particular topic is important, that they know the context in which the topic is relevant, that the principles of the topic are made clear, *and* that the details of writing code appropriate to the topic are illustrated and exemplified.

The book should be of interest to more than just software developers, though. Architects of software systems that use XML must know how search and retrieval issues are to be handled, while managers and team leaders need an understanding of the relationships between XML markup and storage and future retrieval of documents based on the semantics of the information they contain.

How the book is organized

This book is divided into several parts. Part I, "XML: Documents and Data", starts off with a survey of structured document technology and examines several languages used to produce and/or represent such documents. It continues with an exploration of the problems associated with querying data generally, as well as with searching XML documents, and includes a comparison of querying XML with the use of SQL used to query traditional data.

Part II, "Metadata and XML", introduces the subject of metadata for XML—information that describes XML documents and markup languages. This part covers Document Type Definitions (DTDs) and XML Schemas (with some attention given to competing XML schema definition languages). We discuss the "meaning" of XML markup and survey its use in a number of different XML-related markup languages. This part finishes with a presentation of XML's Information Set (commonly known as the Infoset) and an introduction to several other data models used to describe XML documents in a formal manner.

Part III, "Managing XML for Querying", looks at the different sorts of databases (e.g., relational, object-relational, object-oriented, and so-called "native XML") in which XML documents are being stored. It also examines several other W3C specifications that play a role in XML documents that might be queried. This part of the book includes some information about a number of current products that are used to store, manage, query, and retrieve XML documents.

Part IV, "Querying XML", is the technical heart of the book, describing four ways to query XML. XPath (the XML Path Language) is already an established language for querying within an XML document, so this part begins with a significant discussion of the XPath and its usage for XML querying. XQuery is a brand new language designed specifically for querying XML, so we will spend a lot of time and detail on it, including an analysis of the type system and data model used by that language, an examination of the formal semantics of the language, and a discussion (replete with examples) of the use of XQuery and its companion XQueryX. SQL is the leading query language for structured data today. We explore the ways that SQL can be used to query XML, especially if the XML is "shredded" and stored in an object-relational form. Finally, in this Part we discuss SQL/XML, a set of extensions to SQL that leverage XPath and XQuery to overcome some of SQL's limitations in managing semi-structured data.

Part V, "Querying and the World Wide Web", provides a look at a number of specific XML-based markup languages and responds to the question of whether XPath, XQuery, SQL, and/or SQL/XML are suitable for querying documents that are marked up using such languages or whether other, more specific, query facilities are needed to deal with them. It also looks at the ways in which XML is, and is going to be, used on the Internet, both for casual uses like browsing and for industrial uses such as data interchange between business partners. The impacts of internationalization on XML and related specifications are addressed here as well.

We finish up the book with appendices that give you a glimpse into the way in which open standards like XML, XQuery, and SQL/XML are developed, that contain the complete grammar of XQuery, that list and describe all of the SQL/XML functions, and that provides a lengthy set of examples and a small sample of data against which they have been tested.

The example we're using

We are both avid fans of the cinema—which is illustrated by the fact that, between us, we subscribe to just about every possible movie channel offered by satellite television providers. Continuing the tradition started in earlier books written by Jim, we've chosen to use the subject of *movies* as the basis for our example. We've collected data on a broad range of films and organized it into a sort of "database" that is, in fact, a modestly large XML document. This document - data with XML markup - serves as the foundation for many of our examples. (Note that we do not pretend that our example document is marked up in any sort of optimal way, suitable for industrial use; we chose specific markup styles to illustrate the points we make at various parts of the book.) When the topic demands something a little less data-oriented, we use a smallish textual document that discusses several film-related topics.

Syntax Conventions

In several places in this book, we define the syntax of various language components relevant to XML, XML query languages, and so forth. While we are not particularly fond of the syntax conventions that the W3C has adopted (we find them somewhat less readable than several other conventions), we believe that readers of this book will be best served by consistency of style accompanied by explanations.

Therefore, we have (with slight reluctance) adopted the same style used in the W3C specifications that we reference in the book. You may be familiar with those conventions, but we think that a quick summary will help some readers.

A variation of Backus-Naur Form (BNF) is used for syntax presentation. More specifically, a syntactic symbol (called a *nonterminal symbol* to distinguish it from language components that represent only themselves) is defined using a notation in which the symbol being defined appears to the left of a special operator (`::=`) and the definition of that symbol appears as an expression written following that operator. For example:

```
nonterminal-x ::= nonterminal-y ( ',' nonterminal-y )*
```

That line, called a *BNF production*, defines a nonterminal symbol (`nonterminal-x`) by saying that it is made up of a second nonterminal symbol (`nonterminal-y`), optionally followed by zero or more (that's the meaning of the asterisk, `*`) repetitions of a sequence made up of a literal comma (that's a *terminal symbol*) and another instance of that second nonterminal symbol (`nonterminal-y`).

Therefore, if `nonterminal-y` happens to be defined to be an identifier (in XML, these are either *QNames* or *NCNames*), then an instance of `nonterminal-x` might be:

```
film , cinema , movie
```

One important thing to note is that, in this style of BNF, all terminal symbols are enclosed in quotation marks, which might be single quotation marks (`'...'`) or double quotation marks (`"..."`). Anything, including parentheses, not enclosed in quotation marks is either a nonterminal symbol or a character used in the BNF to specify its meaning.

Here is a complete list of the conventions used in this book by this style of BNF:

- `"string"` — the literal `string` given inside the double quotes
- `'string'` — the literal `string` given inside the single quotes
- `a b` — a single occurrence of `a` followed by a single occurrence of `b`
- `a | b` — a single occurrence of `a` or a single occurrence of `b`, but not both
- `a?` — a single occurrence of `a` or nothing at all; optional `a`
- `a+` — one or more occurrences of `a`
- `a*` — zero or more occurrences of `a`
- `( expression )` — `expression` is treated as a unit; allows subgroups to carry the operators `?`, `*`, or `+`
- `/* ... */` — a comment in the BNF (this is unrelated to comments in languages being defined by the BNF, such as XQuery)

Additional resources

The data and queries in appendix A, plus additional examples and explanations, are available for download from the web site for this book's examples, http://xqzone.marklogic.com/queryingxmlbook/. You may also visit http://www.mkp.com/QueryingXML for more information.

Type conventions

A quick note on the typographical conventions we use in this book seems in order:

- Type in this font is used for all ordinary text.
- *Type in this font* is used for terms that we define or for emphasis.
- `Type in this font` is used for all the examples, syntax presentations, keywords, identifiers, and XML text that appear in ordinary text.

Acknowledgements

Writing a book is an immense task and it consumes enormous quantities of resources such as energy, time for research and for writing, and often patience. A book like this one is quite difficult to produce, but difficult tasks often produce commensurately great rewards (financial rewards very rarely among them!). It's exceedingly rare to do it alone—the help, guidance, and support of others is always appreciated: for ideas, for trying out concepts and wording, for reviewing paragraphs and whole chapters, and just for offering encouragement.

We want to give credit to all of the wonderful, talented people who have helped us create this book, especially the following people (alphabetized by their last names) who gave us extensive reviews, which heavily influenced the content and accuracy of this book.

- James Bean, author of "XML for Data Architects: Designing for Reuse and Integration" and "Engineering Global E-

Commerce Sites", both published by Morgan Kaurmann, and CEO of Relational Logistics Group.

- Alexander Falk, President and CEO of Altova, GmbH in Austria, and Altova, Inc. in the USA, who also generously provided us with licenses for Altova's flagship Enterprise XML Suite.
- Muralidhar Krishnaprasad, our friend and colleague at Oracle, who seems to be an expert at all things related to XQuery, especially its implementation.
- Zhen Hua Liu, also our friend and colleague at Oracle, who is a driving force behind the implementation of SQL/XML and a constant source of valuable information and observations.

Of course, all remaining errors (and we harbor no illusions that we found and eliminated all errors in a subject as complex as this one) are solely our responsibility.

We also offer our deepest gratitude to the wonderful people at Morgan Kaufmann Publishers for their invaluable help and participation in the production of the book. Diane Cerra, our talented and patient editor, who trusted Jim enough to publish his first book, got us started on this book and came back to help us finish it. Two other editors, Lothlórien Homet and Rick Adams, worked with us for several months during the time when we were writing the most difficult chapters.

At various times during the lengthy writing process, Asma Stephan, Corina Derman, Mona Buehler, and Belinda Breyer made themselves available to answer our questions about schedules and production, to track down information that we managed to misplace, to make sure that our chapters were quickly reviewed by the right people, and to give us frequent and friendly reminders of approaching deadlines. Our production manager, Simon Crump, worked closely and patiently with us during the production process, making sure that our drafts were thoroughly copyedited and properly typeset, that our reviews of the galleys were applied to the typeset draft, and that all production errors were promptly handled. Brent dela Cruz, our marketing manager, bears the burden of ensuring that this book is made available to you, our readers. To Diane, Asma, Simon, Brent, and all of the other fantastic people at Morgan Kaufmann, *thanks*!

Credit must also be given to the incredible group of people who make up the various W3C Working Groups responsible for the specifications discussed in this book. The languages and facilities related to querying XML documents include XML Query (co-chaired by Jim's long-time friend and colleague Andrew Eisenberg), XSL (chaired by the delightful Sharon Adler), and XML Schema (first chaired by one of the most generous and smartest people around, Michael Sperberg-McQueen, and now chaired by our good friend David Ezell, who is proving to be remarkably good at herding cats), among others.

We are particularly grateful to our friends who offered suggestions that certainly improved the content and focus of the book. They include Ashok Malhotra, Andrew Eisenberg, Murali Krishnaprasad, and Zhen Hua Liu.

Finally, we want to express our appreciation to Don Chamberlin for writing the Foreword to this book. Don wrote the Foreword for Jim's first SQL book and it feels like we've reached a sort of closure, coming full circle on SQL and starting a new circle for the next major query language.

Jim: I give special thanks to my wonderful partner, best friend, and spouse, Barbara Edelberg. She took up all the slack when I was stuck at the computer 'til all hours of the night, writing. Barbara had to deal with me on the road and unavailable so much of the time. It was Barbara's emotional support and encouragement, as I agonized over every sentence in the book, that got me through it. I also owe a debt of gratitude to my co-author, friend, and backpacking buddy, Stephen Buxton, for stepping in to write the book with me – he joined me just as I was falling into despair at the magnitude of the task and the difficulty of writing this book while doing my "day job".

Stephen: I'd like to say thank you to my family for their support and encouragement – my kids Maria and Samuel, and my other "kids" Jennie and Sarah, and most of all, my lovely wife Veronica ("I thought you said it was finished!"), who has stuck with me through many, many late nights and weekends. I'd also like to thank my co-author, erstwhile colleague, and very good friend Jim Melton for guiding me through my first authoring experience. Thanks Jim!

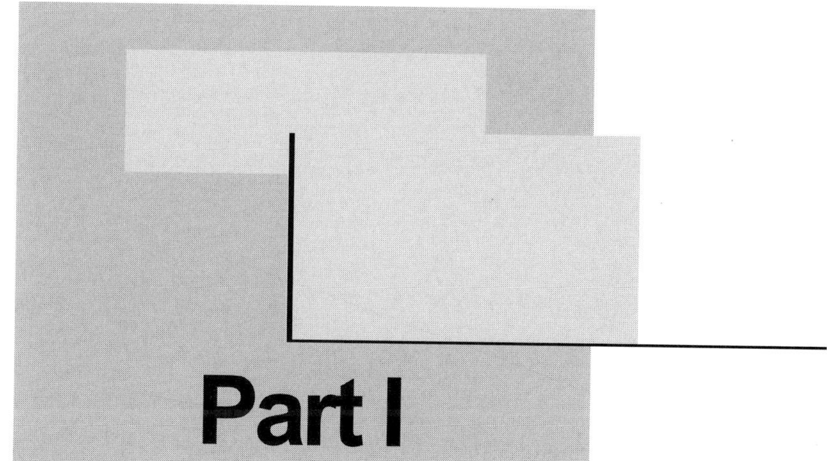

Part I

XML: Documents and Data

Chapter 1

XML

1.1 Introduction

The title of this book is *Querying XML*, so we start by introducing XML, describing what we mean by "querying," and then discussing the special challenges in querying XML.

XML — the Extensible Markup Language — defines a set of rules for adding markup to data. Markup adds structure to data, and gives us a way of talking about the meaning of that data. The family of XML technologies provides a way to standardize the representation of data, so that we can process any data with standard programs, share data across applications, and transfer data from one person or application to another. In this first chapter, we introduce XML by looking at what markup is and what it's good for. Then we look at a number of different uses for XML — a number of different kinds of XML data. Finally, we give examples of other ways to represent data, and compare them with XML.

1.2 Adding Markup to Data

Let's take the movies example (Appendix A: The Example) used throughout this book. We have data describing many of our favorite movies. The data includes the title of the movie, the year it was first released, the names of some of the cast members, and other information about the movie. In this section, we look at the data in its raw form, then discuss how that data might be marked up to make it more useful.

1.2.1 Raw Data

We could represent our movie data in raw form, as in Example 1-1.

Example 1-1 *movie, Raw Data*

```
An American Werewolf in London1981LandisJohnFolseyGeorge,
Jr.GuberPeterPetersJon98NaughtonDavidmaleDavid
KesslerAgutterJennyfemaleAlex Price
```

Example 1-1 is the raw data for one movie – a single record. In this format, the data doesn't tell you much about the movie. You can probably spot the title, and, if you are familiar with "An American Werewolf in London," you may be able to glean some information by means of educated guesswork. But if you wanted to write a program to read this data and do something with it – such as finding the name of the director – you would have to write code specifically for this piece of data (*e.g.*, code that extracts the characters at positions 41 through 44 and 35 through 40 and adds a space in between them). What we need is some way to represent the data so that a program (or person) can process any movie record in the same way.

1.2.2 Separating Fields

A simple way to add some rudimentary structure to this record is to add a comma between each of the data items, or fields.

Example 1-2 *movie, Fields Separated by Commas*

```
An American Werewolf in London,1981,Landis,John,Folsey,George\,
Jr.,Guber,Peter,Peters,Jon,98,Naughton,David,male,David
Kessler,Agutter,Jenny,female,Alex Price
```

Example 1-2 is the same movie data represented as a comma-separated list. Notice that, even with this simple mechanism, we had to introduce the "\" (backslash) character to "escape" a comma that was actually part of the data.

There are other ways to distinguish between fields of a record. In the early days of computing, fixed-length fields were common –

each field might occupy, say, 8 bytes. This method makes access simple — if you want to access the beginning of the third field, you can go directly to the 17th byte. But fields smaller than 8 bytes take up more space than they need to, and fields longer than 8 bytes require some indication that they are spread across more than one field (such as a continuation marker).

Let's continue our discussion with the comma-separated list in Example 1-2. You can spot the fields in this record, but there is no way of knowing which fields go together. For example, the fields "Agutter," "Jenny," "female," and "Alex Price" each describe one aspect of a cast member, but it's not apparent from the comma-separated list that those fields have anything in common. We have a way of delineating fields; now we need some way of grouping fields together.

1.2.3 Grouping Fields Together

Example 1-3 groups fields together. It also introduces a hierarchy of fields and subfields. Fields are separated by one or more commas, and fields that belong together are bounded by "," at the start and "$," at the end.

Example 1-3 *movie, Grouped Fields*

```
,
    ,An American Werewolf in London$,
    ,1981$,
    ,
        ,Landis$,
        ,John$,
    $,
    ,
        ,Folsey$,
        ,George, Jr.$,
    $,
    ,
        ,Guber$,
        ,Peter$,
    $,
    ,
        ,Peters$,
        ,Jon$,
```

```
        $,
        ,98$,
        ,
            ,Agutter$,
            ,Jenny$,
            ,female$,
            ,Alex Price$,
        $,
    $,
```

Example 1-3 is shown with some extra white space — each subfield starts on a new line, and is indented. This is purely for (human) readability.

Now we know that "Agutter,Jenny,female,Alex Price" all belongs together and is all related in some way to "An American Werewolf in London." And if you want to write a program to extract the director of each movie, given that each movie is formatted in the same way as in Example 1-3, you can write some general code that will parse the movie into first, second, and third fields, extract the contents of the third field, and parse that to get the first and last name of the director.

We are making progress! But Example 1-3 still has some shortcomings. There is no indication of what a field represents, other than its position within the record, which makes it difficult for humans to read. This has two implications — first, the data is vulnerable to error. If you (or the program generating the data) make a mistake and leave out the year of release, it's not obvious that anything is missing, and a program processing this data may well return "LandisJohn" when asked for the year of release. Second, it makes it difficult to talk about the data. Most of the time, when we want to "talk about" the data, we want to describe some manipulation to a program — *i.e.*, it's difficult to write a program that says things like "print the second field of the third field of the movie record, then a space, then the first field of the third field of the movie record." Our next step is to *name* the fields and subfields.

1.2.4 Naming Fields

If you read Example 1-3, you can probably guess that "An American Werewolf in London" is the title of the movie, and you may even deduce that Jenny Agutter plays the female lead, a character named Alex Price. But who is Peter Guber? And what does "98" mean?

What we need is a way to name each field, to make it easier to talk about the fields — to write programs that manipulate them — and also to give some clue as to what the fields actually mean. We could devise a way to represent field names as part of our comma-separated list — perhaps each comma would be followed by a field name in double quotes. Fortunately, we don't need to — we have XML.

Example 1-4 *movie, Fields Grouped and Named*

```
<movie>
    <title>An American Werewolf in London</title>
    <yearReleased>1981</yearReleased>
    <director>
        <familyName>Landis</familyName>
        <givenName>John</givenName>
    </director>
    <producer>
        <familyName>Folsey</familyName>
        <givenName>George, Jr.</givenName>
        <otherNames></otherNames>
    </producer>
    <producer>
        <familyName>Guber</familyName>
        <givenName>Peter</givenName>
        <otherNames></otherNames>
    </producer>
    <producer>
        <familyName>Peters</familyName>
        <givenName>Jon</givenName>
        <otherNames></otherNames>
    </producer>
    <runningTime>98</runningTime>
    <cast>
        <familyName>Agutter</familyName>
        <givenName>Jenny</givenName>
        <maleOrFemale>female</maleOrFemale>
        <character>Alex Price</character>
    </cast>
</movie>
```

Example 1-4 is close to the XML representation of movie data that we will use for the rest of this book. The "," and "$," have been replaced by "*<tagname>*" and "*</ tagname>*." Each field in this record – in XML terms, each element in this document – has a name. We can now refer to elements by name and by their position with respect to other named elements. And when the name is something meaningful, such as "producer," it gives a hint to the human reader about what the data means. All we need now is a map of the data – actually two maps, one to tell us what the structure of a movie record (a valid movie document) looks like, the other to tell us what each element actually means.

1.2.5 A Structural Map of the Data

One useful kind of data map tells you something about the structure, or "shape," of the document – which fields are subfields of others and in what order they can appear in the document. Such a map is obviously useful for someone manipulating the data, since she needs to know that the `director` element contains a `familyName` and a `givenName`. It's also useful for error-checking and consistency – every movie has a director, so if the `director` element is missing, then the data is corrupted or at best incomplete. Let's take a look at a couple of structural data maps for XML – DTDs and XML Schemas.[1]

DTD — Document Type Definition

An early attempt at providing a map for XML was the DTD, or Document Type Definition (actually the DTD was inherited from SGML – see Section 1.5.3). A DTD defines what elements and attributes are allowed, where, and in what order. A DTD may also enumerate the values allowed for each attribute (but not for elements), and it may identify some attributes as type ID (meaning they must have a value that is unique across the XML document) or IDREF (meaning they must match some attribute of type ID). Example 1-5 shows a possible DTD for the movie document.[2]

---

1 See also Chapter 5, "Structural Metadata."

2 Example 1-5 is *one possible* DTD that describes the movie document. When you create a DTD based on a sample document, you can't tell which of the elements in the sample are optional or which elements may occur more than once. Some elements may be optionally present in a document but not present in your sample document. If your document includes attributes, you can't tell which are IDs or IDREFs, and you can only guess at attributes' enumerated values.

Example 1-5 *A DTD for movie*

```
<!ELEMENT movie (title, yearReleased, director, producer+,
                runningTime, cast+)>
<!ELEMENT title (#PCDATA)>
<!ELEMENT yearReleased (#PCDATA)>
<!ELEMENT director (familyName, givenName, otherNames?)>
<!ELEMENT producer (familyName, givenName, otherNames?)>
<!ELEMENT runningTime (#PCDATA)>
<!ELEMENT cast (familyName, givenName, otherNames?,
               maleOrFemale, character)>
<!ELEMENT familyName (#PCDATA)>
<!ELEMENT givenName (#PCDATA)>
<!ELEMENT otherNames (#PCDATA)>
<!ELEMENT maleOrFemale (#PCDATA)>
<!ELEMENT character (#PCDATA)>
```

The first line of Example 1-5 says that a movie must contain a `title`, a `yearReleased`, a `director`, at least one `producer`, a `runningTime`, and at least one `cast` (member), in that order. The following lines describe the "shape" of each of these elements. Each simple (leaf) element, though, is described as "#PCDATA" – despite its name (Document *Type* Definition), the DTD does not give us any data type information.[3] For example, it does not distinguish between `runningTime` (which is probably an integer) and `title` (which is probably a string).

XML Schema

DTDs have a couple of drawbacks – they don't include any data type information about fields,[4] and DTDs are not XML documents. XML Schema solves both these problems. Like a DTD, an XML Schema defines where elements may occur in a document, and in what order, in a formal, standard way. But an XML Schema may also describe the data type of the element (integer, string, *etc.*) and give rules about which values are allowed. And an XML Schema docu-

3 Though the DTD does not give us data type information, it does give us the type of the document, in the sense of Schema's Complex Types.

4 A DTD may include some data type information for attributes, such as ID/IDREF type and enumeration.

ment is itself an XML document, with its own XML Schema.[5] Example 1-6 shows a possible XML Schema for the movies document.

Example 1-6 *An XML Schema for movie*

```
<?xml version="1.0" encoding="UTF-8"?>
<xs:schema xmlns:xs="http://www.w3.org/2001/XMLSchema"
           elementFormDefault="qualified">
 <xs:element name="familyName" type="xs:string"/>
 <xs:element name="givenName" type="xs:string"/>
 <xs:element name="movie">
        <xs:complexType>
            <xs:sequence>
                <xs:element name="title" type="xs:string"/>
                <xs:element name="yearReleased">
                    <xs:simpleType>
                        <xs:restriction base="xs:integer">
                            <xs:minInclusive value="1900"/>
                            <xs:maxInclusive value="2100"/>
                        </xs:restriction>
                    </xs:simpleType>
                </xs:element>
                <xs:element name="director">
                    <xs:complexType>
                        <xs:sequence>
                            <xs:element ref="familyName"/>
                            <xs:element ref="givenName"/>
                        </xs:sequence>
                    </xs:complexType>
                </xs:element>
                <xs:element name="producer"
                             maxOccurs="unbounded">
                    <xs:complexType>
                        <xs:sequence>
                            <xs:element ref="familyName"/>
                            <xs:element ref="givenName"/>
                            <xs:element name="otherNames"
                                        type="xs:string"/>
                        </xs:sequence>
```

5 W3C Schema for Schemas, available at: http://www.w3.org/TR/xmlschema-1/#normative-schemaSchema.

```
                </xs:complexType>
            </xs:element>
            <xs:element name="runningTime"
                        type="xs:integer"/>
            <xs:element name="cast"
                        maxOccurs="unbounded">
                <xs:complexType>
                    <xs:sequence>
                        <xs:element ref="familyName"/>
                        <xs:element ref="givenName"/>
                        <xs:element name="maleOrFemale">
                            <xs:simpleType>
                                <xs:restriction
                                    base="xs:string">
                                    <xs:enumeration
                                        value="male"/>
                                    <xs:enumeration
                                       value="female"/>
                                </xs:restriction>
                            </xs:simpleType>
                        </xs:element>
                        <xs:element name="character"
                                    type="xs:string"/>
                    </xs:sequence>
                </xs:complexType>
            </xs:element>
        </xs:sequence>
    </xs:complexType>
  </xs:element>
</xs:schema>
```

In Example 1-6, each element in the XML document is described by an element in the XML Schema called `xs:element`. A simple element such as `title` is modeled with the attributes `xs:name="title" xs:type="xs:string"`. An element that has children (subfields), such as `director`, is described by an `xs:complexType` element — in this case, a sequence of elements. The elements `familyName` and `givenName` occur in several places in the XML document (the *instance* document), so they are defined once at the start of the XML Schema and are pointed to (via the `ref` attribute) whenever needed.

XML Schema has a rich set of data types that can be attributed to elements — we have described `runningTime` as type `xs:integer`, so it is now distinguishable from the `xs:string` elements.

Example 1-6 also illustrates two more capabilities of XML Schema:

1. Bounding — `yearReleased` is an integer and is bounded to be between 1900 and 2100 inclusive.
2. Enumeration — `maleOrFemale` is a string, and it may only have the value `male` or `female`.

DTD, XML Schema, and Others

We have only briefly touched on DTDs and XML Schema, to give a general flavor of each approach. There are other approaches to mapping or modeling data, notably RELAX NG. At the time of writing, DTDs may still be the most common way to describe data. But there seems to be a general move toward XML Schema, with most existing users planning, or at least considering, a move from DTDs to XML Schema and most new users adopting XML Schema. For the rest of this book we will talk in terms of XML Schema, with occasional references to DTDs.

1.2.6 Markup and Meaning

With the XML document in Example 1-4 and the XML Schema in Example 1-6, we know an awful lot about the data.

1. We know how to break it down into meaningful pieces (elements, sub-elements, sub-subelements).
2. Each element and subelement has a meaningful[6] name, to improve readability and to refer to the element easily.
3. We have a Schema that describes rules for the data (such as order, type, scooping, and legal values).

6 A well-thought-out element name does add some meaning for a human reader with some knowledge of the data and/or the domain. But without a defined vocabulary, it's only a very little meaning, and of course that meaning can't be machine-processed.

Have we succeeded in representing the *meaning* of the data? Somewhat. We know a lot more about the data, but we still don't know its meaning.

There are several things we could do to add to what we already know about the data, getting us closer to representing the meaning. First, we could add more tags — for example, we could split the "yearReleased" element into subelements "USA," "Europe," and "Asia." See Chapter 4 for a discussion of semantic markup and metadata. Second, we could use RDF (again, see Chapter 4) to denote which "John Landis" was the producer of this movie and to define relationships to enable inference about the data. But the next logical step is to define an XML-based markup language — *i.e.*, to create a formal definition of the meaning of the data within each of the allowable elements, separate from the actual markup (syntax) definition.

We said at the beginning of this chapter that XML is an Extensible Markup Language — more accurately, it is a language or framework for defining markup languages. This topic is important enough for its own section in this chapter — see Section 1.3.

1.2.7 Why XML?

Before we discuss XML-based markup languages, we want to make sure that you agree that XML is a good thing.

With the movie data marked up as XML and with an XML Schema to describe the data, our movie data is fairly human-readable. Perhaps more important, it is machine-readable. A collection of XML documents plus an XML Schema provide all the information necessary for a program to process the data in a standard way. Any XML parser can parse the document and report errors, any XSLT engine can transform the document (*e.g.*, for display or printing), and any XML-aware query engine can query it.

You could devise your own markup — as we started to do with the comma-separated list. But we recommend using XML instead, for at least the following reasons.

1. Designing a markup strategy is not as simple as it might seem. With our very simple earlier example, we already had to deal with choosing symbols for start and end markers, and escaping marker symbols that appear in actual data. Many man-years of effort have gone into defining XML and its family — why reinvent the wheel?

2. If you use your own markup system for tagging data, you will also need to reinvent a way to describe that data (XML Schema). And you will need to create a suite of tools to process your documents — tools that understand your home-grown tagging system.
3. If you use XML, you can leverage a family of technologies to store, manage, publish, and query data. There is a good chance that your customers, suppliers, and software applications use XML too, so you can share and exchange data with a minimum of effort.

1.3 XML-Based Markup Languages

You read in Section 1.2 that XML defines the *representation* of a piece of data — *e.g.*, a start tag/end tag pair delimits an element. An XML-based markup language defines the *meaning* of that representation.

An XML Schema defines a set of elements and attributes and how they can be put together. An XML-based markup language consists of an XML Schema plus a human-readable description of the meaning of the elements and attributes. In terms of a human language, you can think of XML as the alphabet and vocabulary; an XML Schema[7] adds grammar (syntax); an XML-based markup language builds on the alphabet, vocabulary, and syntax, adding the *semantics* of the language. Let's look at some examples to make these distinctions clear.

MDL — Movie Definition Language

We could create an XML-based markup language for our movie data by taking the XML Schema in Example 1-6 and adding a definition of the semantics of each element. For example:

```
title : the value of the title element is the English-language
title of the first US release of the movie.
givenName : is the first given name of a director, producer or
cast.
familyName : is the family name (in Western cultures, normally
the last name) of a director, producer or cast.
...
```

7 Or a DTD.

These semantic definitions are human-readable, not machine-readable. The Semantic Web[8] is an attempt to make semantics machine-readable (see Chapters 4 and 18). The Semantic Web is still very much a work in progress — in the meantime, let's look at some XML-based markup languages that are already widely used.

XBRL — Extensible Business Reporting Language

XBRL is an XML-based markup language developed by a consortium (XBRL International) to make it easy for businesses to exchange financial reporting data. The definition of XBRL includes a set of XML Schemas, plus additional syntax rules, to define what is legal in an XBRL instance. XBRL also includes a precise definition of the semantics of each element and attribute. For example, the attribute "precision" is defined in the XBRL 2.1 spec[9] like this:

> The precision attribute MUST be a non-negative integer or the string "INF" that conveys the arithmetic precision of a measurement, and, therefore, the utility of that measurement to further calculations. Different software packages may claim different levels of accuracy for the numbers they produce. The precision attribute allows any producer to state the precision of the output in the same way. If a numeric fact has a precision attribute that has the value "n," then it is correct to "n" significant figures (see Section 4.6.1 for the normative definition of 'correct to "n" significant figures'). An application SHOULD ignore any digits after the first "n" decimal digits, counting from the left, starting at the first nonzero digit in the lexical representation of any number for which the value of precision is specified or inferred to be "n."
>
> The meaning of precision="INF" is that the lexical representation of the number is the exact value of the fact being represented.

The first part of this definition — "The precision attribute MUST be a non-negative integer or the string `"INF"`" — can be expressed in XML Schema, and the spec does include an XML Schema for

---

8 See the W3C Semantic Web Activity at: http://www.w3.org/2001/sw/.

9 XBRL specifications and recommendations are available at: http://www.xbrl.org/SpecRecommendations/.

"precision." The rest is semantic and must be defined as part of the markup language.

Dublin Core

Dublin Core[10] defines a markup language for catalog metadata. Dublin Core was initially designed to address the cataloging of books, but it has been extended to cover any kind of information resource, digital or physical. Dublin Core is used extensively in libraries to maintain a rich set of metadata about books, pictures, manuscripts, *etc.* to make it easier for people to find and browse resources.

Table 1-1 *Dublin Core Metadata Definition, Sample*

Element Name: Title		
	Label:	Title
	Definition:	A name given to the resource.
	Comment:	Typically, Title will be a name by which the resource is formally known.
Element Name: Creator		
	Label:	Creator
	Definition:	An entity primarily responsible for making the content of the resource.
	Comment:	Examples of Creator include a person, an organization, and a service. Typically, the name of a Creator should be used to indicate the entity.
Element Name: Subject		
	Label:	Subject and Keywords
	Definition:	A topic of the content of the resource.
	Comment:	Typically, Subject will be expressed as keywords, key phrases, or classification codes that describe a topic of the resource. Recommended best practice is to select a value from a controlled vocabulary or formal classification scheme.

10 *The Dublin Core Metadata Initiative,* http://dublincore.org/.

Dublin Core defines a set of 15 elements that express the core catalog metadata of a resource. For each element there is a single-word, normative name (*e.g.*, Title, Creator, Subject); a descriptive label, meant to convey the meaning of the element to human readers; a definition, giving a more precise semantic definition; and a comment. Table 1-1 shows three of the elements defined by Dublin Core, taken from *DMCI Metadata Terms.*[11]

Dublin Core also includes a set of XML Schemas[12] that define how to express these elements in an XML document. Note that Dublin Core does not define a language for a whole document – Dublin Core elements are meant to be inserted in XML, RDF/XML, or HTML documents.

DocBook

DocBook[13] defines a set of XML tags for use in creating marked-up books, articles, and documentation. Why would anyone write a document using markup (such as XML) instead of a word processor (such as Microsoft Word)? First, it's easier to index (for searching) and categorize (for browsing) a document that has some semantic markup. The semantic markup might be additional metadata – *i.e.*, data that is not part of the printed document, such as the intended audience for each chapter. Or it might mark semantic boundaries – *e.g.*, if you mark up the examples in a document, it's easy to search for examples that feature some term. Careful use of styles in an editor such as Microsoft Word *could* help with searching and browsing, but people rarely use formatting styles so precisely. Second, when you create a document in XML you separate the *content* of the document from its *physical representation*. You can write the content once and then materialize it in a number of formats – paper printed copies, HTML web pages, Braille, audio, and so on. And you can easily present the information in a number of different styles to suit different audiences, such as large type for the sight impaired and highly colorful for teenagers. This is not possible with WYSIWYG editors such as Word, where the author applies specific formatting instructions when creating the content.

---

11 http://dublincore.org/documents/dcmi-terms/

12 In fact, Dublin Core defines an RDF Schema as well as XML Schemas to describe its elements. See http://dublincore.org/schemas/.

13 Norman Walsh and Leonard Muellner, *DocBook: The Definitive Guide* (Sebastopol, CA: O'Reilly, 1999). See http://www.docbook.org/.

DocBook defines its set of tags normatively using a DTD. The DocBook project started in 1999, too early for XML Schema to be used, though there is an "experimental W3C XML Schema" as well as experimental RELAX NG, RELAX, and TREX schemas.[14]

The online DocBook[15] includes a simple sample XML file that conforms to the DocBook DTD; see Example 1-7.

Example 1-7 *DocBook Example Document*

```
<article id="article">
  <title>Article Title</title>
  <indexterm id="foo" class="startofrange">
    <primary>Meaningless</primary>
  </indexterm>
  <para>Some text.<footnote>
      <para>This is a footnote.</para>
    </footnote>
  </para>
  <indexterm startref="foo" class="endofrange"/>
</article>
```

Because this sample is valid according to the DocBook DTD (or Schema), you know that any stylesheets[16] designed to work on DocBook will work on this sample. But if you are writing an article or you are writing a stylesheet to format an article, you need to know what these tags mean. For example, what is an `indexterm`? How should you use this tag in a document? What should a stylesheet do with it? For the *meaning* of the tags, again you need to look at the human language documentation, not just the DTD (or Schema). DocBook describes the semantics of the `indexterm` tag and the "Processing expectations" — *i.e.*, what you can expect a stylesheet to do with an `indexterm` element.

XML-Based Markup Languages — Summary

In Section 1.2 we hope we convinced you that XML is a useful way to represent data. In this section, we convinced you that XML (with XML Schema) must be complemented by some semantic information

14 See http://www.docbook.org/ for details and links.

15 http://www.docbook.org/tdg/index.html

16 A *stylesheet* is a mechanism for programmatically transforming an XML document into another format, such as HTML. See Chapter 7.

to make all those tags actually *mean* something. Everyone who writes an XML document to be shared, exchanged, and/or manipulated by others *must* also define the structure of the document and the semantics of each of its parts (at least, it's hard to imagine an XML document simple enough that it would *not* require any such external definition). That is, every XML author or consumer requires an XML-based markup language definition. Many make up their own for a limited domain of use. The languages we have described in this section are just the better-known standard ones.

1.4 XML Data

There is an old Indian story about six blind men who stumble across an elephant. Each man reaches out and touches a different part of the elephant. One grabs the tail and says he has found a length of string; one touches a leg and declares he has found a tree trunk; a third feels the side of the elephant's body and is convinced he is standing in front of a wall; and so on. Similarly, there are many *kinds* of XML data, each with its own characteristics and uses. When a developer or software user talks about "XML data," often she means just one of these kinds of data. Like the blind men in the story, she may be convinced that hers is the only (important) kind of XML data that exists.

In this book, when we talk about "Querying XML," we will be clear about what applies to all XML (the whole elephant) and how the different kinds of XML (the tail, the trunk, the body) are treated. When we talk about processing (and in particular querying) XML data in this book, we consider three broad categories of XML data: structured, unstructured, and messages.[17]

1.4.1 Structured Data

The movie sample we used in Example 1-4 is an example of structured data. All the data in `movie` is in small, well-defined chunks (`givenName`, `familyName`, . . .), and there are some obvious tree-structure (or parent-child) relationships (*e.g.*, `producer` naturally breaks down into `givenName`, `familyName`, and `otherNames`). Other examples of structured data include purchase orders, library

17 The alert reader might question this breakdown, for it appears to mix two dimensions: structured vs. unstructured and persistent vs. transient data. However, we think this does represent the three main uses of XML — see the following few sections.

catalogs, parts inventories, and payroll records. Structured data is often managed in a persistent store, such as a database.

1.4.2 Unstructured Data

For our purposes, unstructured data is data with significant amounts of text. Examples include a Microsoft Word document, an e-mail, and a technical manual. The term *unstructured* is misleading – all documents have some structure, even if it's just the structure that's implicit in, *e.g.*, punctuation marks.[18] Using XML to represent an unstructured document allows you to add structure and/or formalize the existing structure. You can also employ XML to mark up unstructured data for presentation, but this should be avoided – in general, you should use XML for semantic markup and leave it to a reporting/publishing tool (such as XSLT) to map "meaning" into presentation.

1.4.3 Messages

An XML message is typically a small, well-defined piece of data passed from one application to another, possibly as (or in) a stream. This is an increasingly popular use of XML, enabling application integration and web services. Messages are usually highly structured, but they are different from most structured data because they generally need to be queried one at a time, possibly in a stream, and there is generally a requirement to process many (possibly many thousands) per second. Messages are generally created, consumed, and disposed of on the fly, with no permanent storage and no need for updates.[19]

1.4.4 XML Data — Summary

Table 1-2 summarizes the characteristics of the three kinds of data we have discussed so far.

18 Some people use a third category, "semistructured documents," to refer to documents that mix structured and unstructured elements.

19 This is not always the case. Some messages may be stored for long periods before being consumed, but they are generally not queried many times or updated.

Table 1-2 *XML Data*

	Structured (data)	Messages (data)	Unstructured (documents)
Field	Small, well defined	Small, well defined	Large, mainly text
Record	Large	Small	Large
Storage	Persistent, database	Nonpersistent, memory	Persistent, database or files
Query	Across large numbers, with complex relationships/constraints	Across a single message	Across large numbers of documents, with search for meaning

1.5 Some Other Ways to Represent Data

XML is not the only way to represent structured or unstructured data. In this section, we discuss some other popular ways to represent data and compare them with XML.

First, we discuss SQL, which is currently the most prevalent way of representing structured data. Then we look at some of the presentation markup languages, which describe unstructured and semistructured data with an emphasis on presentation. Last, we look at a couple of XML's closest relatives, SGML and HTML.

1.5.1 SQL — Structure Only

SQL — the SQL Query Language — has been the main way of storing and querying structured data for several decades. More recently, the SQL world has embraced the object-relational data representation and has expanded its scope to include unstructured data such as text, AVI (audio, video, image), and spatial data.

In a relational database, *records* become *rows in a table*, and *fields* become the *cells of the table*. Our movie example might be represented as in Figure 1-1.

Figure 1-1 shows six relational tables. Relational tables are built as columns and rows. Only the rows pertaining to the movie "An American Werewolf in London" are shown.

The first table, `MOVIES`, has a column for each simple, nonrepeating field in the movie record. It also has an `ID` field. It is common to give a relational table an extra column that is a unique identifier, or

Table MOVIES

ID	title	yearReleased	director	runningTime
42	An American Werewolf in London	1981	78	98

Table DIRECTORS

ID	familyName	givenName
78	Landis	John

Table PRODUCERS

ID	familyName	givenName	otherNames
44	Folsey	George, Jr.	
45	Guber	Peter	

Table MOVIES_PRODUCERS

MOVIE	PRODUCER
42	44
42	45

Table CAST

ID	familyName	givenName	maleOrFemale	character
34	Agutter	Jenny	female	Alex Price

Table MOVIES_CAST

MOVIE	CAST
42	34

Figure 1-1 *movie, SQL (Relational) Representation.*

"primary key." With the `ID` column, we can easily refer to any row in the table (any movie). The table `MOVIES` achieves field separation and naming, just as XML does. SQL databases have a data dictionary that maps the data, describing the columns that make up each table and the type of each column. But the traditional relational table is flat – it cannot directly represent the tree structure we saw in the XML examples. How can we represent a field such as `director` – which is made up of several fields – relationally? We create a new table, `DIRECTORS`, with an `ID` column, and we reference the "John Landis" `ID` in the `MOVIES` table. This strategy will not work for `producer`, since there can be more than one producer for a given movie. Creating a PRODUCERS table helps, but we now have two producer IDs for "An American Werewolf in London."[20]

To handle repeating fields we need a join table such as MOVIES-PRODUCERS, which maps records in MOVIES to records in PRODUCERS via their primary key fields. We have handled cast in the same way — although there is only one cast member in our sample fragment, we must be able to represent many cast members per movie. Since cast includes a field called character, it is easy to imagine character as another set of subfields (givenName, familyName), which would require yet more tables.

SQL tables do not represent hierarchical structures as readily as XML. Figure 1-1 represents all the data and relationships that Example 1-4 does, but we needed to create six tables and do some design work to achieve that. The SQL world has addressed the limitations of two-dimensional tables in several ways:

1. Subtables: Many modern relational databases allow "the thing in a cell of a table" to be another table (subtable) or an array.
2. Object-relational: An object-relational database allows "the thing in a cell of a table" to be an object, not just a field. A field is a single value, whereas an object can have a complex type made of several values.

Even with the power of subtables and objects, it is more natural to represent hierarchical structure as XML. And XML can be more flexible — it is not essential to have a DTD or an XML Schema, so you can create complex fields, repeating fields, and arbitrarily deep hierarchical structure on the fly (though some would say this is not a good thing). SQL, on the other hand, can represent more complex relationships quite easily, while XML has to massage everything into a tree structure (not all data is naturally tree-shaped). SQL can handle constraints, such as "every movie must have at least one producer," with which XML is still struggling. And SQL has the notions of transactions and updates, which the XML world (at the time of writing) has only just begun to consider. Add to that the availability and maturity of robust, scalable SQL databases, indexing technology, expertise,

20 We could have movie IDs in the PRODUCERS table, but we assume a producer produces several movies.

and tools, and you can see why SQL is still the preferred way to structure, store, and query data in many applications.

1.5.2 Presentation Languages — Presentation Only

There is a family of markup languages that deal only with presentation and have nothing to say about structure or semantics. These languages allow the creator of the content (generally documents) to dictate exactly how the text should appear, first on a printed page and later on a computer screen.

roff, troff, groff

troff was written in 1973 by Joe Ossana. troff is a typesetting program that takes as input a text file containing a mix of content and markup (in troff format) and outputs a file that can produce a formatted, paginated printed document on a typesetter. Originally the output of troff would drive only a Graphic Systems CAT typesetter; it was modified in 1979 by Brian Kernighan to work with any typesetter.

Example 1-8 gives the flavor of a troff file – it is somewhat verbose, not terribly human-readable, but gives you complete control over the presentation of text. troff was modeled on the earlier roff (run-off). GNU has produced a C++ version of roff called groff.

Example 1-8 *troff Markup to Start a New Paragraph*

```
.de pg \"paragraph
.br \"break
.ft R \"force font,
.ps 10 \"size,
.vs 12p \"spacing,
.in 0 \"and indent
.sp 0.4 \"prespace
.ne 1+\\n(.Vu \"want more than 1 line
.ti 0.2i \"temp indent
```

TeX/LaTeX

TeX[21] is a macro-based text formatting language produced by Donald Knuth. Disappointed with the quality of the typesetting in his *Art of Computer Programming,*[22] Knuth started writing TeX in 1978. It

21 Donald E. Knuth, *The TeXBook* (New York: Addison-Wesley Professional, 1984).

22 Donald E. Knuth, *The Art of Computer Programming,* Volumes 1–3 (New York: Addison-Wesley Professional, 1998).

quickly became popular enough to displace troff in the technical typesetting community. TeX gives the author complete control over typesetting presentation and is especially useful for producing documents with specialized formatting requirements, such as scientific and mathematical journals and textbooks.

In 1984, Leslie Lamport wrote LaTeX,[23] a document-preparation system layered on top of TeX. LaTeX makes TeX more accessible to authors and has been adopted as a standard in many technical publishing houses.

PostScript

PostScript is a page-description language — a programming language for printing graphics and text — developed by Adobe in 1985. Today, PostScript is the de facto standard for communicating with printers. Example 1-9[24] is a PostScript program to print "Hello, world!" in Times-Roman, 20 points, in the lower left corner of the page.

Example 1-9 *PostScript Markup to Print Hello, world!*

```
%!
% Sample of printing text

/Times-Roman findfont   % Get the basic font
20 scalefont            % Scale the font to 20 points
setfont                 % Make it the current font
newpath                 % Start a new path
72 72 move to           % Lower left corner of text at (72, 72)
(Hello, world!) show    % Typeset "Hello, world!"

showpage
```

PDF

PDF — Portable Document Format — is the de facto standard for exchanging electronic documents. The PDF format is owned and developed by Adobe. It is purely a presentation format — like PostScript[25] and troff, PDF files represent text and graphics precisely, but

23 Leslie Lamport, *LaTeX: A Document Preparation System* (New York: Addison-Wesley Professional, 1994).

24 You can find this example in many places on the web, *e.g.*, http://docs.mandragor.org/files/Programming_languages/Forth_And_PostScript/First_Guide_To_PostScript_en/text.htm.

25 Some people even refer to PDF as "smart PostScript."

it makes no attempt to be human-readable or machine-processable. PDF has been called a "paper format" — even though a PDF document is a file, it has many of the characteristics of a printed page. Sometimes this is desirable — *e.g.*, PDF files can be protected by digital signature to preserve the integrity of their contents. Clearly this is an advantage if you are dealing with legal contracts or other critical information. On the other hand, PDF documents are notoriously difficult to manipulate and process — even editing a PDF document is hard. In general, PDF is used as an end format — that is, data is stored, processed, and managed in some other format (such as XML) and converted to PDF for printing and/or publication.

1.5.3 SGML

SGML is the Standard Generalized Markup Language, ISO standard 8879.[26] SGML and XML are closely related — in fact, (almost) every XML document is a valid SGML document, since XML was originally born as an SGML *profile,* or subset.[27]

SGML introduced a number of features that continue to be important in XML:[28]

- Descriptive markup — the idea that markup should not be *procedural* (as in the presentation languages in Section 1.5.2). Rather, markup should be *descriptive.* This distinction is important in the development of SGML (and later XML) as a language that is independent of any platform or application.
- Document type — SGML introduced the notion of a *document type* and was the first language to define a DTD (Document Type Definition). The document type is important for

26 ISO 8879:1986, *Information processing — Text and office systems — Standard Generalized Markup Language (SGML)* (Geneva, Switzerland: International Organization for Standardization, 1986). Available at: http://www.iso.org/iso/en/CatalogueDetailPage.CatalogueDetail?CSNUMBER=16387.

27 For a listing of the SGML declaration for XML and a description of the differences between SGML and XML, see: James Clark, *Comparison of SGML and XML* (Cambridge, MA: World Wide Web Consortium, 1997). Available at: http://www.w3.org/TR/NOTE-sgml-xml.html.

28 C. M. Sperberg-McQueen and Lou Burnard (eds.), *A Gentle Introduction to SGML* (The Text Encoding Initiative, 1994). Available at: http://www.isgmlug.org/sgmlhelp/g-index.htm.

defining the structural constraints on a document. This notion carried over into XML Schema as a *complex type*.

- Data independence — one of the primary goals of SGML was to enable faithful sharing of documents across different hardware and software platforms. One concrete way this was achieved was to introduce the notion of *entities*, to provide "descriptive mappings for nonportable characters."

SGML enjoyed some success in the 1990s, mostly in places with high-end document processing and publishing requirements, such as the aircraft industry (for aircraft maintenance manuals) and the military. But most people agree that SGML is too complicated for more general use.

1.5.4 HTML

HTML is the one standard that needs no introduction. We are confident that everyone that reads this has read HTML, and almost all have written at least some HTML.

HTML contributed to the Internet boom of the late 1990s by providing a simple, *standard* markup language that was, like SGML, independent of hardware and software platforms and that separated content from presentation. We emphasize "standard" because in the early days of the Internet it was important to have a standard way to exchange data that could be presented in a rich format by any browser. Unfortunately, the standard defined by the W3C was contaminated by the proprietary extensions of all the major browser vendors during the so-called "browser wars," leading to the heinous "this page best displayed in . . ." labels on many websites.

At first glance, HTML looks very similar to XML — it consists of start and end tags that delimit elements, optionally with attributes. But HTML differs from XML in two important ways, one technical and the other conceptual.

First, HTML is much more forgiving (some would say "sloppy") than XML. For example, a paragraph tag in HTML starts at a paragraph start tag (`<p>`) and ends at *either* a paragraph end tag (`</p>`) *or* immediately before the next paragraph start tag, whichever comes first. In XML, this construct is not allowed — a start tag with no matching end tag is not valid. Similarly, an empty element in HTML can be represented by a stand-alone start tag (such as the line separator, `<br>`). Again, this kind of stand-alone marker is not valid in XML —

an empty element must be a start tag/end tag pair (`<br></br>`) or the shorthand empty element representation (`<br/>`).

Second, XML is all about marking up the *meaning* of the data, whereas HTML has drifted toward *presentation* markup. There has been much (sometimes heated) debate over the exact line between semantic and presentation markup — is a "heading" semantics or presentation? But HTML, with its tags for purely formatting markup, such as italics and boldface, has definitely crossed over that line into presentation markup.

Fortunately, both of these differences can be resolved. Most HTML can be turned into valid XML (and not lose its validity as HTML) with some simple cleanup, such as making sure all start tags have a matching end tag. And XML is a markup language (or a language for markup languages) — you can use XML to represent any kind of markup, semantic or representation (or syntactic or anything else). XML is particularly effective when used to markup the meaning of data, leaving the presentation aspects to some other step, such as applying an XSL stylesheet. But there is no reason why you should not use XML for the mix of semantic and representation markup that is HTML. XHTML[29] does just that — XHTML defines a variant of HTML that is also valid XML. The XHTML 1.0 spec actually defines several flavors of XHTML. *XHTML transitional* is very close to HTML, but it is also valid XML. *XHTML strict* goes further, eliminating representation markup for fonts, colors, and other formatting (in favor of CSS, Cascading Style Sheets).

Today, all the leading browsers will display not only HTML and XHTML, but also XML with an associated XSL stylesheet. We believe that over the next few years, all new documents on the web will be either XHTML or XML.

1.6 Chapter Summary

In this chapter, we introduced XML, the Extensible Markup Language. XML is common enough that we expect everyone reading this book to have some familiarity with it, so we used this chapter to put XML in some historical and technical context. We discussed what *markup* is and what it's good for. Then we looked at a number of different kinds of XML data, to show where and how XML is use-

29 *XHTML™ 1.0 The Extensible HyperText Markup Language (Second Edition): A Reformulation of HTML 4 in XML 1.0* (Cambridge, MA: World Wide Web Consortium, 2002). Available at: http://www.w3.org/TR/xhtml1/.

ful. And we looked briefly at some of the other ways to represent data and compared them with XML. In the next chapter, we discuss querying. Once we have laid the foundations with discussions of XML and querying, we can introduce the title topic of this book – *querying XML*.

Chapter 2

Querying

2.1 Introduction

In Chapter 1 we discussed the second term of the title of this book – "XML." In this chapter we give some background on "querying," before introducing "querying XML" in Chapter 3. We describe the query problem and some ways that problem is addressed today. In this chapter we focus on the issues that are common to *all* query scenarios, and we focus on SQL as a query solution. In the next chapter you will see how those issues can be addressed when the data is XML, and we will describe some wrinkles that are unique to *querying XML*.

2.1.1 Definitions of Query

Let's start with three definitions of the word *query*. In everyday English, to query means "to ask questions of, especially with a desire for authoritative information."[1] We like this definition because it points up the precise nature of (most) queries – when you query a database, you don't expect to get back an educated guess at, say, the total sales of each movie in the last calendar year. On the contrary, you expect a precise, authoritative answer.

1 Merriam-Webster Online Dictionary. Available at: http://www.merriam-webster.com.

Our second definition talks about querying databases and introduces the notion of a query *language*. "[databases] provide a means of retrieving records or parts of records and performing various calculations before displaying the results. The interface by which such manipulations are specified is called the query language."[2] This definition also brings out the need for a query to not only return a record or set of records but also to bring back parts of records and to manipulate (compare, aggregate, transform, *etc.*) that data.

Finally, here's a more pedantic definition:

> In general, a query (noun) is a question, often required to be expressed in a formal way. The word derives from the Latin *quaere* (the imperative form of *quaerere*, meaning to ask or seek). In computers, what a user of a search engine or database enters is sometimes called the query. To query (verb) means to submit a query (noun). A database query can be either a *select query* or an *action query*. A select query is simply a data retrieval query. An action query can ask for additional operations on the data, such as insertion, updating, or deletion.[3]

This definition emphasizes the importance of update as a part of query (see Chapter 13, "What's Missing?"). It also talks about *query* in terms of both search engines and databases. We discuss the broader notions of *search* (as opposed to *query*) in Chapter 18, "Finding Stuff." In the rest of this book, however, we consider *query* to be the more formal kind of query that you might pose to a database or other query application — finding things that you know exist and/or retrieving information that you need in order to do some task.

2.2 Querying Traditional Data

In this section we discuss querying simple data types, such as integers, dates, and short strings, that can be easily represented in simple structures such as rows and columns in a table. In the rest of this book, we will refer to this as *traditional data*. Section 2.3 discusses querying nontraditional data.

2 Encyclopedia Brittanica Online. Available at: http://www.britannica.com.
3 Whatis.com. Available at: http://www.whatis.com.

For the past two decades the most popular way of querying data has been SQL, the SQL Query Language. Most of the world's critical data is stored in a relational database, and most users and applications employ SQL to find, retrieve, and manipulate that data. So SQL defines the benchmark (or gold standard) for querying data – any new approach to querying data must either do at least all the things that SQL does or provide a good reason for not doing those things. That's why we focus on SQL in this section and the next.

A relational database (a SQL database) stores data in tables and allows search across those tables with SQL. SQL is particularly good at querying traditional data (though you will read in Section 2.3 that SQL has been extended to query nontraditional data, too).

2.2.1 The Relational Model and SQL

We have already seen (Figure 1-1) that the movies data can be stored in a set of tables. The Relational Model,[4] first proposed by Dr. Ted Codd[5] and developed in collaboration with Chris Date and others, includes the notion of tables, columns, and rows (or relations, attributes, and tuples). A table can be viewed as a grid of rows and columns, where each row–column intersection (or *cell*) contains a single data item. Each column has a data type (integer, character, date, *etc.*). The Relational Model also defines a relational algebra, with operations on *tuples* (rows in a table, or intermediate query results).[6] The most important operations are *projection, selection, union*, and *join*.

A *projection* produces only some of the *columns* of the table, by naming those columns in the SELECT clause. See Example 2-1[7] (where the result of the query is the contents of the shaded column).

---

4 Note that the Relational Model is not the only way to organize data in a database. Before the Relational Model was defined, databases were generally implemented using the Hierarchical Model or the Network Model. More recently, some have favored the Object Model of database implementation.

5 E. F. Codd, A relational model of data for large shared data banks, *Communications of the ACM* **13**(6), 377–387 (1970). Available at: http://www.acm.org/classics/nov95/toc.html

6 For an overview of the Relational Model and an in-depth description of SQL:1999, see: Jim Melton and Alan Simon, *SQL:1999 – Understanding Relational Language Components* (San Francisco: Morgan Kaufman: 2001).

7 The data for each of these examples is taken from Chapter 1. We have added some rows to the data so that the examples make sense.

A *selection* produces only some of the *rows* of the table, by filtering the results using some predicate. See Example 2-2 (where the result of the query is the contents of the shaded rows).

Of course, these operations can be composed in an ad hoc way — see Example 2-3 for an example of selection and projection together (where the result of the query is the contents of the shaded cells).

Union and *join* combine data from two or more tables. Union combines data vertically (appends rows from one table onto rows of another), while join combines data horizontally (appends columns from one table onto columns of another, usually on the basis of the value of one of the columns).

Example 2-1 *Projection*

```
SELECT title FROM movies
```

Result:

ID	title	yearReleased	director	runningTime
42	An American Werewolf in London	1981	78	98
43	Animal House	1978	78	109
44	Best in Show	2000	79	90
45	Blade Runner	1982	80	117

Example 2-2 *Selection*

```
SELECT * FROM movies WHERE runningTime < 100
```

Result:

ID	title	yearReleased	director	runningTime
42	An American Werewolf in London	1981	78	98
43	Animal House	1978	78	109
44	Best in Show	2000	79	90
45	Blade Runner	1982	80	117

Example 2-3 *Projection and Selection*

```
SELECT title FROM movies WHERE runningTime < 100
```

Result:

ID	title	yearReleased	director	runningTime
42	An American Werewolf in London	1981	78	98
43	Animal House	1978	78	109
44	Best in Show	2000	79	90
45	Blade Runner	1982	80	117

Example 2-4 *Union*

```
SELECT * FROM directors
  UNION
  SELECT ID, familyName, givenName FROM producers
```

Result:

ID	familyName	givenName
78	Landis	John
79	Christopher	Guest
80	Scott	Ridley
44	Folsey	George, Jr.
45	Guber	Peter
46	Murphy	Karen
47	Simmons	Matty
48	Reitman	Ivan
49	Deeley	Michael

Example 2-5 *Join*

```
SELECT movies.ID, movies.title, movies.yearReleased,
       directors.familyName, directors.givenName
  FROM movies, directors
  WHERE movies.director = directors.id
```

Result:

ID	title	yearReleased	family Name	givenName
42	An American Werewolf in London	1981	Landis	John
43	Animal House	1978	Landis	John
44	Best in Show	2000	Guest	Christopher
45	Blade Runner	1982	Scott	Ridley

Relational databases and the SQL Query Language have been enormously successful. SQL has set the bar for query languages, so that any general-purpose query language for XML will be expected do at least what SQL does for relational data. That said, the Relational Model does have its limitations. Many of these limitations are addressed by object-relational storage and the object extensions to SQL, described in the next section.

2.2.2 Extensions to SQL

One of the major criticisms of the Relational Model is that its data model imposes a rather simplistic structure on the data. The Relational Model represents all data as tables (rows and columns) of cells, where each cell contains a single data item. While much of the world's data fits quite neatly into this model, a lot of data simply does not fit.

Rows and Columns with Single-Value Cells — Too Simplistic

In Figure 1-1 we could not represent all the data about one movie in one row of the MOVIES table. The director, the producer, and arguably the title do not fit into a single relational cell. The director does not fit because the director data consists of two (and possibly many) data items, `firstName` and `givenName`. The producer data also consists of more than one data item, plus there is a many-to-many relationship between producers and movies — not only can there be many movies attributed to the same producer, but there may be many producers associated with each movie. The status of the title data is more controversial — it seems to be a single data item of type string, but if we want to do anything really useful with it we need to consider it as (at least) a sequence of words. We will pursue this further in Chapter 13, "What's Missing?."

Object-Relational Storage

In the 1990s the advent of object-oriented database management systems (OODBMSs) caused a huge stir, with many predicting the end of the road for relational database management systems (RDBMSs). Some said that the Relational Model was so limited that relational databases would disappear entirely in favor of object-oriented databases. What has happened instead is that all the major relational database vendors have implemented object extensions, so they are now object-relational[8] database management systems (ORDBMSs).[9]

In an object-relational database, we can represent complex structure as an object type, or class. An object type may include simple types, and it also includes *methods* — operations that can be performed on that type. Now, instead of a single data item appearing in a cell, we can have an instance of an object type.

In our movie example, we might add a `director` object type, with methods that return the director's name (familyName + givenName) as a single string in some natural format. Stonebraker's book on ORDBMSs (mentioned earlier) gives more compelling examples of much more complex object types, to represent data defining two-dimensional spatial objects, image files in many formats, and time series data (which is used by stock traders to analyze trends in stock prices). Since Stonebraker's book was published, life sciences has emerged as an important field, where complex objects representing such things as DNA are needed. There are, of course, a lot of usage

---

8 For further reading on the benefits of object-relational databases, see Michael Stonebraker, *Object-Relational DBMSs, The Next Great Wave* (San Francisco: Morgan Kaufmann, 1996).

9 There is an obvious analogy here with XML databases. Just a few years ago, some pundits were rash enough to forecast the demise of RDBMSs in favor of XML databases — instead, the major RDBMS vendors are adding XML and XQuery capabilities, so their products might be called ORXDBMSs (object-relational-XML database management systems).

scenarios that fall in between these extremes of complexity – many applications today model real-world things like "customers" and "purchase orders" as objects. And in the XML world, the DOM (Document Object Model) is an object representation of an XML document (see Chapter 6, "The XML Information Set (Infoset) and Beyond," for a brief description of the DOM).

Object Extensions to SQL

With SQL:1999[10] (formerly referred to as SQL3), the SQL standard embraced object-oriented technology with a set of extensions to SQL-92. Extensions include support for:

- user-defined types
- type constructors for row types, reference types, and collection types
- user-defined functions and procedures
- LOBs (large objects)

With these extensions, a SQL:1999 database user can define, manipulate, and query objects in SQL. Database vendors have also implemented their own object extensions, in addition to those defined in the SQL:1999 standard.

2.2.3 Querying Traditional Data — Summary

In this section we introduced the notion of traditional data, defined informally as "numbers, dates, and short strings." We introduced the Relational Model and SQL, which are still the gold standard for storing, representing, manipulating, and querying this kind of data. Then we introduced object-relational technology, which allows traditional data with a rich structure, and briefly summarized the SQL object extensions in SQL:1999.

A lot of the data that is stored and represented as XML today is traditional data. Interestingly, some of the major database vendors' first forays into XML and XQuery support are based on an object-ori-

10 For an in-depth discussion of the object-relational extensions in SQL:1999, see Jim Melton, *Advanced SQL:1999 – Understanding Object-Relational and Other Advanced Features* (San Francisco: Morgan Kaufmann, 2002).

ented approach, presumably leveraging their existing object infrastructure and capabilities.

2.3 Querying Nontraditional Data

At least 90% of the data in the world is nontraditional data, and a great deal of valuable information is locked up in Word files,[11] PowerPoint presentations, PDF documents, diagrams, and so on. In the last 10 years or so, as the problems of storing and querying traditional data have been largely solved by SQL and its object extensions, the database industry has turned to solving the problem of querying nontraditional data. We define *nontraditional data* informally as data that cannot be represented naturally as numbers and dates and strings, such as documents and pictures and movie clips. We hesitate to call it "unstructured," since everything has some structure. And it is not always binary (though it often has some binary component).

In this section, we describe three approaches to querying nontraditional data — metadata, objects, and markup. Let's assume that the movie *American Werewolf in London* has:

- a preview clip, AmericanWerewolfInLondon-preview.mpg
- a radio ad, AmericanWerewolfInLondon-RadioAd.mp3
- a poster, AmericanWerewolfInLondon-Poster.jpg
- a review, AmericanWerewolfInLondon-review.pdf

Let's also assume that we want to be able to store and query all that nontraditional data, along with the movies data we already have.

11 Microsoft plans to make XML the default format in the next version of Microsoft Office (see: Microsoft Office Open XML Formats Overview, June 2005. Available at: http://www.microsoft.com/office/preview/fileoverview.mspx). And Adobe is moving toward an XML format for (some) PDF files (see: The Adobe XML architecture. Available at: http://www.adobe.com/enterprise/xml.html). So there's a real prospect that XML will open up the most common document formats, making them accessible to XQuery.

2.3.1 Metadata

One approach is to store the nontraditional data as an opaque chunk of data and add metadata. In a database this opaque chunk is often called a BLOB, or binary large object. Despite its name, a LOB has none of the useful attributes of an object. LOB storage just means that the data item is stored as a single item in one place. A binary LOB is a LOB that contains data that is not character-based, as opposed to a character LOB, or CLOB, which contains data that is in the character set of the database. A LOB is handled in a special way by the database to cope with its potentially large size – typically two or four gigabytes. But the data is opaque; *i.e.*, nothing is known about a LOB instance except that it may be large.

Once we have the data in a LOB, we can store it in a database table and add metadata in other columns in the table. Then we can query the metadata to find a particular instance of a LOB or to find out information about an instance of a LOB.

There are several ways to create the metadata:

- Some formats have metadata embedded in them. Text formats (PDF, Microsoft Word) generally contain some automatically generated metadata – the author's name, document title, last modified date, *etc.* – and some metadata that can be added by the author. This metadata can be extracted programmatically and written into database columns as the data is inserted. For example, Oracle's *inter*Media product will extract metadata from most common document, audio, video, and image formats and make that metadata available for query in columns of a table. But the LOB is still opaque – some processing needs to be done to "decorate" it with metadata, even if that metadata exists in the LOB.
- Whoever publishes the data – inserts the data into a database – can add metadata via an application. A CMS (content management system) will allow the publisher to add all kinds of metadata at various stages of the publishing process.[12]

12 But beware of GIGO – garbage in, garbage out. Manual metadata systems are notorious for producing minimal or useless metadata. When was the last time you filled out the Properties sheet on a Microsoft Word document you were writing?

- Some interesting programs[13] can produce meaningful metadata for text documents automatically, even when that metadata does not exist explicitly in the document. They work by recognizing names of people and companies and so on and possibly checking those names against an internal dictionary or a web service. At the time of writing, this technology — automatic entity extraction — is still in its infancy.

Once the metadata columns have been populated, you can query the metadata to find, or find out about, the LOB data — *e.g.*, think of the movie example as metadata for the actual movie.

2.3.2 Objects

Object technology offers the potential of storing nontraditional data items in a nonopaque way — to "open the box" and treat, say, a PDF document as a PDF document rather than as an opaque LOB. All we need to do is define an object type to represent the PDF-formatted data, and some methods that make sense for PDF. Then we can query the actual document instead of querying its metadata.

In Section 2.3.1 we said that Oracle's *inter*Media can extract metadata that is embedded in, *e.g.*, a picture. *inter*Media does that by creating an object type for the picture format and querying that object to extract useful metadata.

2.3.3 Markup

We have discussed decorating nontraditional data with metadata and querying nontraditional data directly using object technology. Both approaches require some special, nonstandard effort. The metadata approach requires manual or programmatic effort to produce the metadata, then some design to figure out how to store the metadata, and finally some programming to create an application that will query the metadata in an application-specific way. The objects approach requires the definition of an object type, with methods, for each kind of data to be queried, plus an application to query that data.

---

13 Some examples of companies that offer entity-extraction technology:
Basis — http://www.basistech.com/entity-extraction/
Inxight — http://www.inxight.com/products/smartdiscovery/ee/
ClearForest — http://www.clearforest.com/Products/Tags.asp

You can achieve similar results with markup, but you end up with an XML document that can be described and queried with standard tools. That means you can leverage existing tools and skills and communicate your efforts easily to other companies, institutions, or software programs.

You can, of course, use markup to represent metadata that has been created or extracted as described in Section 2.3.1. Adobe has taken this approach with their XML Data Packet Specification, part of the Adobe XML Architecture.[14] The specification defines a format for wrapping a PDF document in XML tags to make a *data packet* that can be consumed by anything that understands XML. Any XML that is embedded in the PDF document can be extracted and packaged as a separate packet, while the bulk of the PDF document is encoded in base 64.

A bolder approach is to define an XML markup language that will allow you to represent the nontraditional data "natively" as XML. In the document world, the de facto standard way of representing a technical paper or article as XML is DocBook (though of course there are many XML languages that are regarded as standard in some domain). Microsoft has made a lot of progress in this area – with Microsoft Office 2003, you can save any Office document as XML. Microsoft have introduced several markup languages, including WordML and ExcelML, to describe the XML structure of Office documents that are represented as XML.[15]

Even more adventurous are the attempts to define markup languages for other media types. Probably the most advanced is scalable vector graphics (SVG),[16] which became a W3C recommendation in January of 2003. SVG defines a way of representing rich graphical content (consisting of vector graphic shapes, images, and text) in XML.

---

14 Adobe XML Architecture, XML Data Packet Specification, Version 2.0 (2003). Available at: http://partners.adobe.com/public/developer/en/xml/xdp_2.0.pdf.

15 Microsoft's website has many articles on Office 2003 XML support, *e.g.*, Dave Beauchemin, *Exploring XML in the Microsoft Office System* (Redmond, WA: Microsoft, 2003). Available at: http://www.microsoft.com/office/previous/xp/columns/column21.asp.

16 *Scalable Vector Graphics (SVG) 1.1* (Cambridge, MA: World Wide Web Consortium, 2003). Available at: http://www.w3.org/TR/SVG11/.

2.3.4 Querying Content

So far in this section on querying nontraditional data we have described ways to extract (or at least *surface*) traditional, structured data that tells us something about the nontraditional content so that we can query that traditional data. There is another approach – to query the nontraditional data directly, in a way that is appropriate to that *kind* of data.

The obvious example is to query text data using full-text queries. We discuss full-text querying in Chapter 13, "What's Missing?" There are analogous query mechanisms for other kinds of nontraditional data. For example, if you want to query across images, you can extract some metadata (size, date, exposure, *etc.*); represent that metadata in a database column or an object attribute or as markup; and query that metadata. Or you can directly query images according to their similarity to some given image (a query by example) or potentially by giving a verbal description of the image you are looking for. You might compare images along several dimensions – texture, colors, shapes, *etc.* – so that an example image of a brown cow might bring back other cows, other brown things, or other brown cows. This kind of multimedia search, looking for aspects of audio, video, and image, has enormous potential – think of matching a face on the CCTV screen at an airport, or looking for close matches to the chorus of "My Sweet Lord" to check for possible copyright infringement, or sorting movies by the number of car chases. But direct multimedia search is outside the scope of this book, except for full-text search.

2.4 Chapter Summary

In this chapter we discussed the meaning of *query* and *query language*. We described what a query is and what it needs to be able to do, and we introduced SQL, the SQL Query Language, as the gold standard for any query language. We also discussed the different challenges in querying traditional and nontraditional data. Now that we know what XML is and what querying is, the next chapter will discuss the challenges of "*querying XML*."

Chapter

3

Querying XML

3.1 Introduction

In Chapter 2 we looked at what it means to query data in general and described SQL as a language for querying relational data. In this chapter we discuss the notion of *querying XML* (which, after all, is why you're reading this book). XML is quite different from relational data, and it offers its own special challenges and opportunities for the query writer.

We start with the assumption that it is necessary to query the XML representation of data. You could, of course, convert XML data to some other representation (say, relational) and query that representation using some language (such as SQL). Sometimes that is the most appropriate strategy — for example, if the XML data is highly regular and will be queried many times in the same way, you may be able to query it more efficiently in a purely relational context. Often, though, you want to store and represent the data as XML throughout its life (or at least preserve the XML abstraction over your data when querying).

We also assume that you want to do all the things described in Chapter 2 and at least all the things that SQL can do on relational data. Querying XML data is different from querying relational data — it requires navigating around a tree structure that may or may not be well defined (in structure and in type). Also, XML arbitrarily mixes data, metadata, and representational annotation (though the latter is frowned on).

We give some examples of queries in XPath, but this chapter is intended for discussion of querying XML in general terms. As you read the examples, we invite you to map the simple example data onto your own data and to decide how useful the query constructs are in your own environment. After the examples, we introduce some other languages in use today for querying XML. We argue that knowledge of document structure and data types is a good thing and that XQuery 1.0 and XPath 2.0 will be the most important languages for querying XML.

3.2 Navigating an XML Document

Since an XML document is by nature hierarchical, it can be represented easily in a tree diagram. The movie document we introduced in Chapter 1 is represented as a tree diagram in Figure 3-1. The figure is incomplete, but it should give you an idea of what the XML tree looks like.

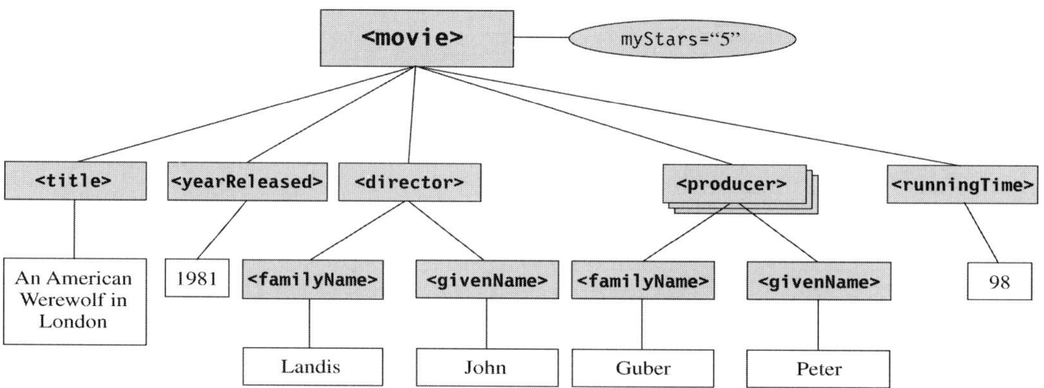

Figure 3-1 *movie Document.*

What kinds of questions might you ask about the data represented in Figure 3-1? First, you might want to know the title of this movie. If the data were stored in a relational database and you were querying with SQL, you'd need to know which cell represented the title of this movie (which table, column, row). With an XML document, you can find the title of the movie in two ways.

First, you can ask for the value of the title by name. In English, "return the value of the `title` element." That's fine if the XML document is as simple as this one, but what if there are `title` elements in more than one place in the tree? For example, a director or producer or cast member might have a title (Mr., Ms., Dr., etc.). What if there is more than one title — say, an English title and a French title?

The second way to ask for the title of the movie is to *walk the tree* — that is, give explicit instructions on how to navigate from the top of the tree (if this is an XML document, we know that the tree has a single "top" since it's a *rooted tree*)[1] to the element you are interested in. In English, "start at the top of the tree, move down to the first child element, and return its value." You could simply walk the structure (if you knew where to go to get the data you want), but it would be useful to be able to apply conditions (predicates) along the way — at least check the names of nodes and, better yet, check the contents of elements and the values of attributes.

As you will read in later chapters, the popular languages for querying XML offer both methods. In XPath, for example, `//title` returns the element named "title" (actually a sequence of all title elements) anywhere in the document, while `/movie/title` returns the title by starting at the root node and navigating to the `title` element that is a child of the `movie` element. XPath is described in detail in Chapter 9, "XPath 1.0 and XPath 2.0" — in this introductory chapter we give just enough explanation about XPath to understand the examples. `//` can be read as "at any point in the XML tree," so that `//title` means quite simply "at any point in the XML tree, return all nodes with the name `title`." In the second example, the leading "`/`" means "start at the top of the tree." Any other "`/`" in the XPath can be read as "go down one level in the tree, i.e., select the children of the current node." After each "`/`" (after each *step*), the result is filtered so that it contains only elements whose names match the name in the XPath expression, i.e., "movie" and then "title." Note that the "top of the tree" is not the element named "movie," it's a notional node[2] *above* the element named "movie." For more on this notional top node, see Chapter 6, "The XML Information Set (Infoset) and Beyond," and Chapter 10, "Introduction to XQuery 1.0."

In the rest of this section, we look in more detail at walking the XML tree.

---

1 See Chapter 6, "The XML Information Set (Infoset) and Beyond."

2 The top node is *notional,* in the sense that it doesn't map to anything in the serialized XML document. When looking at an XML document on a page (or on a screen), you have to imagine this top node.

3.2.1 Walking the XML Tree

Let's consider the XML document purely as an abstract tree. To traverse or walk a tree, you need to be able to express the following:

- The top node — in XPath, this is called the *root node* (an imaginary node that sits above the topmost node) and is represented by a leading "`/`".
- The current position — in XPath, this is called the context node and is represented by "`.`".
- The node directly above the current position — in XPath, this is called a *reverse step* (specifically, the *parent*) and is represented by "`..`".
- The nodes directly below the current position — in XPath, this is a *step*, and is represented by a "`/`" (a step separator), typically followed by a condition.
- A condition — in XPath, this can be a *node test* or a *predicate list*. A node test is used to test either the name of the node or its kind (element, attribute, comment, etc.). A predicate tests either the position of the node as the *N*-th child (child nodes are numbered starting from 1) or it tests the value of the node.

Once you can express these five concepts, and you can combine them into an arbitrarily complex expression, you have a language for traversing a tree. In the case of XPath, you have a language for traversing the XML tree and therefore for querying XML. (Of course, XPath offers far more than these five concepts — we're just describing the basics here.)

Let's look at some examples using the movies tree (Figure 3-2). Since XML is hierarchical in nature, we can represent any set (or collection) of documents as a single document simply by concatenating them and wrapping them in a pair of element tags. With XML, then, the boundary between documents is often unclear (some have suggested that all the data in the universe could be represented as a single XML document, though we're not sure what the top-level element should be called).

The following examples illustrate the kinds of tree traversal you might want to do and give solutions in XPath. The explanations describe in a slightly more formal way how the XPath works.

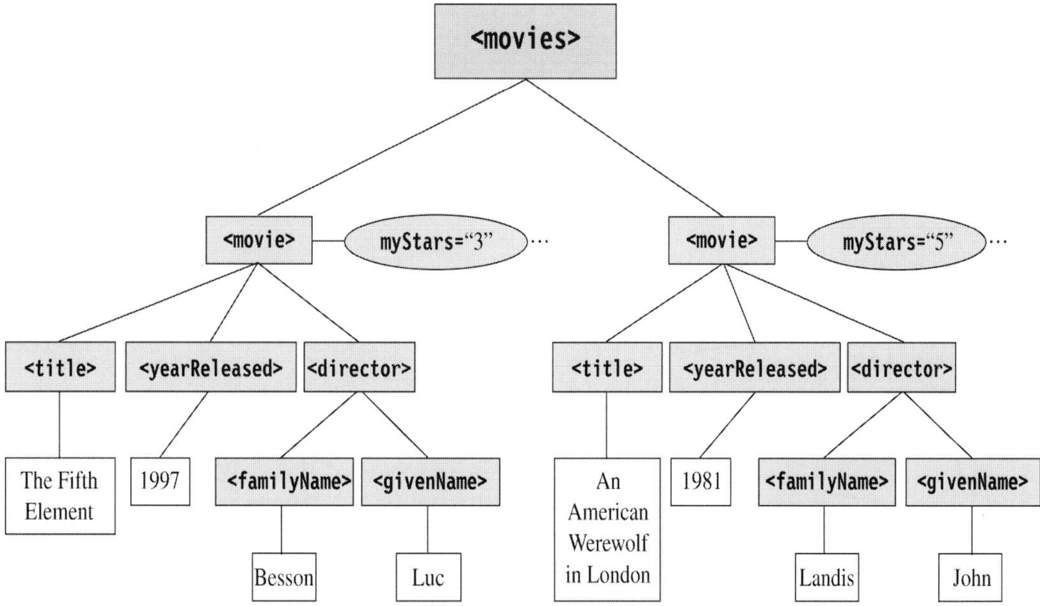

Figure 3-2 *movies Document Tree.*

A Simple Walk Down the Tree

In Example 3-1, we simply walk down the tree, starting at the top node and deciding which way to go next according to the names of the child elements – walk to the element named "movies," then down to the element named "movie," then down to the element named "title." In fact, it's not *quite* as simple as that – we walk to "movies," then there are *two* child nodes named "movie," so we walk to both at once. Another way to describe the same process is to talk about selecting and filtering a sequence of nodes,[3] which is the way the evaluation of an XPath expression is generally described. We select the "movies" node, then we select the sequence of child element nodes with the name "movie," then we select the sequence of child element nodes with the name "title." You might prefer to think of this as *pruning*, rather than *walking*, the XML tree.

3 The XPath 1.0 spec refers to a node *set*, even though document order is preserved. In this chapter, we use the term node *sequence*, which is used in the XQuery 1.0 and XPath 2.0 spec.

Example 3-1 *A Simple Walk Down the Tree*

English query	Find the titles of all movies.
XPath expression	`/movies/movie/title`
Explanation	1. `/` – select the notional top node in the tree. 2. `/movies` – select the child node(s) named "movies". 3. `/movies/` – select the child node(s) of `/movies`. 4. `/movies/movie` – select the nodes named "movie". 5. `/movies/movie/` – select the child node(s) of `/movies/movie`. 6. `/movies/movie/title` – select the nodes named "title".

Note that the result of evaluating the XPath expression in Example 3-1 is *not* a string containing the titles of all the movies in the document — it's a sequence of nodes (title element nodes). If you want to do anything with the results (other than pass them to a program that knows about sequences of nodes), you need to *serialize* the results, i.e., convert the results from the data model of your query language into something you can read or print. When you serialize a sequence of title element nodes, it's reasonable to take the *string value* of each node[4] (take the characters between the start and end tags of the node and convert them to a string), along with some representation of the element tag ("title").

If you run the XPath expression `/movies/movie/title` using your favorite XPath engine, it will probably do a good job of serializing the results in an intuitive way. XMLSpy, for example, displays a table where the first column is the name of the element and the second is the value — each row represents a member of the sequence. If you need to convert the node sequence into a sequence of strings (e.g., to pass them into a Java program), you can use `/movies/movie/title/text()` to pull out the text nodes, but even then you may need to do some more work to map those text nodes into something your host language will understand. See Chapter 14, "XQuery APIs," for a description of one way to solve that problem.

Adding a Value Predicate

If you want to *query* the XML data, as opposed to just walking its structure and pulling out values according to their positions, you need to be able to walk (or prune) the tree according to some conditions. Example 3-2 shows how XPath expresses *value predicates* —

4 For details on how XQuery 1.0 and XPath 2.0 defines serialization, see *XSLT 2.0 and XQuery 1.0 Serialization* (Cambridge, MA: World Wide Web Consortium, 2005). Available at: http://www.w3.org/TR/xslt-xquery-serialization/.

now we are walking down the tree, pruning branches that do not meet the predicate condition as we go.

***Example 3-2** Adding a Value Predicate*

English query	Find the titles of all 5-star movies.
XPath expression	`/movies/movie[@myStars=5]/title`
Explanation	1. `/` – select the notional top node in the tree. 2. `/movies` – select the child element node(s) named "movies". 3. `/movies/` – select the child node(s) of `/movies`. 4. `/movies/movie` – select the nodes named "movie". 5. `/movies/movie[@myStars=5]` – from the sequence of movie nodes, select all those nodes where the value of the attribute named "myStars" equals 5. 6. `/movies/movie[@myStars=5]/title` – from the sequence of movie nodes where "myStars" equals 5, select just the child nodes with the name "title".

This begs the question of, "What constitutes a match?" For example, if the predicate is "[@myStars=5]," does this match elements where the attribute myStars is "05"? "5.00"? That depends on the data type associated with the myStars attribute and on the assumptions you make about how the "=" operator deals with types (type promotion, casting, etc.). We'll talk a lot more about data types later in this book.[5]

Adding a Positional Predicate

Adding a positional predicate (Example 3-3) lets you choose the *N*-th node from a sequence of nodes. Of course, this implies that there is a persistent ordering to the XML document that you are querying — the XQuery Data Model spec[6] defines document order like this: "Informally, document order is the order in which nodes appear in the XML serialization[7] of a document." Document order is one of the things that sets XML data apart from, say, SQL data — in a relational database, the order of rows in a table is undefined, and a query must specify an order explicitly or the results of the query will be unor-

---

5 Especially in Chapter 6, "The XML Information Set (Infoset) and Beyond," and Chapter 10, "Introduction to XQuery 1.0."

6 *XML Path Language (XPath) Version 1.0* (Cambridge, MA: World Wide Web Consortium, 2005). Available at: http://www.w3.org/TR/xpath-datamodel/.

7 You can think of *serialization* as "the way XML is written down on paper (or displayed on a screen)," as opposed to any abstract model of the data. You'll read more about serialization in Chapter 10, "Introduction to XQuery 1.0."

dered.[8] In our movies document, order is not significant unless the author gives it some special significance. For example, you might append movies to the end of the document as you watch them so that the last movie in the document is the last movie you watched, though it would be better practice to add an element for "dateWatched" to make this explicit. In general, *data*-centric XML documents, such as movies, do not rely on document order. On the other hand, *document*-centric XML documents, such as books, articles, and papers, rely heavily on document order. Without document order, XML authors would have to number every chapter, section, paragraph, bolded term, *etc.*, and explicitly order every query.

Example 3-3 *Adding a Positional Predicate*

English query	Find the titles of the 5th movie.
XPath expression	`/movies/movie[5]/title`
Explanation	1. `/movies/movie` – select the sequence of movie element nodes under each movie's element node. 2. `/movies/movie[5]` – from the sequence of movie nodes, select the node in position 5. 3. `/movies/movie[5]/title` – from the 5th movie node, select the element child named "title".

The Context Item

Example 3-4 uses `contains`, which is an XQuery/XPath built-in function[9] that takes two string parameters and returns `true` if the string in the first parameter contains the string in the second parameter. This example illustrates the use of the context item ("`.`"). The context item indicates the current node being considered, as the predicate is applied to each title element node in turn.

8 By *unordered* we mean "in no particular order." SQL query results are not generally in *random* order; they are ordered in some implementation-specific way, but the SQL user cannot rely on that order.

9 *XQuery 1.0 and XPath 2.0 Functions and Operators* (Cambridge, MA: World Wide Web Consortium, 2005). Available at http://www.w3.org/TR/xpath-functions/.

Example 3-4 *The Context Item*

English query	Find the titles of movies that contain the string "Werewolf".
XPath expression	`/movies/movie/title[contains(.,"Werewolf")]`
Explanation	1. `/movies/movie/title` – select the sequence of nodes that represent all titles under movie under movies. 2. `/movies/movie/title[contains(.,"Werewolf")]` – filter the sequence of title nodes by the condition 'contains(., "Werewolf")', where '`contains`' is a built-in function. The first parameter to '`contains`' is the context item "`.`". Note this is equivalent to: `/movies/movie[contains(title,"Werewolf")]/title`

Up the Tree and Down Again

The XPath expression in Example 3-5 illustrates walking down to a leaf node (`runningTime`), then back up to that node's parent (`..`), and then down another branch of the tree (to `title`) to apply a condition. The equivalent XPath expression noted in the example walks down to `movie` and then walks down from `movie` to `title` to apply a condition and down from `movie` to `runningTime` to select the result.

Example 3-5 *Up the Tree and Down Again*

English query	Find the running times of movies where the title contains the string "Werewolf".
XPath expression	`/movies/movie/runningTime[contains(../title,"Werewolf")]`
Explanation	1. `/movies/movie/runningTime` – select all runningTime nodes under movie under movies. 2. `/movies/movie/runningTime(../title,"Werewolf")]` – filter the runningTime nodes by looking back up the tree ("`..`") and testing whether the parent of the runningTime node has a child called "title" that contains the string "Werewolf". Note this is equivalent to: `/movies/movie[contains(title,"Werewolf")]/runningTime` (this is also a better *style* for an XPath expression).

Comparison in Different Parts of the Tree

Example 3-6 involves walking down two different subtrees, and comparing the results.

Example 3-6 *Comparison in Different Parts of the Tree*

English query	Find the titles of all movies where the director is also the producer*.
XPath expression	`/movies/movie/title[../director/familyName=../producer/familyName]`
Explanation	1. `/movies/movie/title` – select all title nodes under movie under movies 2. `/movies/movie/title[../director/familyName=../producer/familyName]` – for each title, look up the tree and down again to find the familyName under director under movie, and again to find the familyName under producer under movie, and retrieve the titles where these two are equal. Note this is equivalent to: `/movies/movie[director/familyName=producer/familyName]/title`

* For simplicity, we assume that directors and producers can be uniquely identified by their family names.

This operation looks quite straightforward, until you consider the case where there is more than one director and/or more than one producer. Comparison of sequences might be defined in a number of ways, including:

1. The condition holds if any director's name matches any producer's name (*existential comparison*[10]).
2. The condition holds if any director's name matches all producers' names.
3. The condition holds if the sequences are identical – i.e., same number of names, same names, in the same order.
4. The condition holds if the first director's name matches the first producer's name.

XPath (1.0 and 2.0) uses the first definition of "=" when comparing sequences.

What about comparing nodes rather than values? An element node might contain just text (like `familyName`), or it might be a complex element, containing subelements (like `movie`). If you want to know whether two nodes are equal, you might choose:

---

10 *Existential comparison* means that this expression evaluates to `true` if there exists any pair of values, one taken from the sequence specified on the left side of the comparison operator and the other taken from the sequence specified on the right side, for which the comparison operator yields `true`.

1. Two nodes are equal if their string values (all the text content between the start and end tags of the element) are equal.
2. Two nodes are equal if they have the same children, in the same order, and those children are equal.
3. Two nodes are equal if they are the same node – that is, you are not comparing two different nodes that happen to have the same content, but you are comparing the exact same node with itself (i.e., the same node from the same document).

XPath (1.0 and 2.0) uses the first definition of "=" when comparing nodes, which can lead to some odd results.[11] XQuery 1.0 and XPath 2.0 introduced the `deep-equal()` function, so you can make the comparison in the second definition, and the "`is`" operator,[12] to enable the comparison in the third definition.

XQuery 1.0 and XPath 2.0 also introduced a new set of comparison operators (`eq`, `ne`, `lt`, `le`, `gt`, and `ge`) for comparing values rather than sequences. These new operators are called *value comparison operators* to distinguish them from the *general comparison operators* (=, `!=`, <, <=, >, and >=).

When querying XML, we are often dealing with *sequences* (ordered lists) rather than single items, and the items in a sequence may be values (strings, integers, dates, . . .) or nodes (elements, complex elements such as those containing child elements, attributes, . . .), or a mixture of values and nodes.[13]

---

11 For example, in the XML snippet

```
<a>
  <w>abc<y color="blue">def</y>ghi</w>
  <z flavor="chocolate">abcdefghi</z>
</a>
```

the elements w and z are equal according to this rule, since both have the string value "abcdefghi." See Bob DuCharme, *Transforming XML, Seeking Equality* (XML.com, 2005). Available at: http://www.xml.com/pub/a/2005/06/08/tr.html.

12 In some earlier drafts of the XQuery 1.0 and XQuery 2.0 Functions and Operators spec, there was a built-in function `node-id()` for this purpose.

13 This is how XQuery 1.0 defines a sequence, which is its basic unit of operation. Other languages for querying XML have less flexible data models.

3.2.2 Some Additional Wrinkles

So far in this section, we have presented issues around querying XML using very simple examples on very simple data — the movie and movies documents. Before we leave this section, we must mention a few more common issues, which require a slightly more complicated document. Figure 3-3 is a tree representation of an XML book — the rest of the examples in this section are based on the data represented in Figure 3-3.

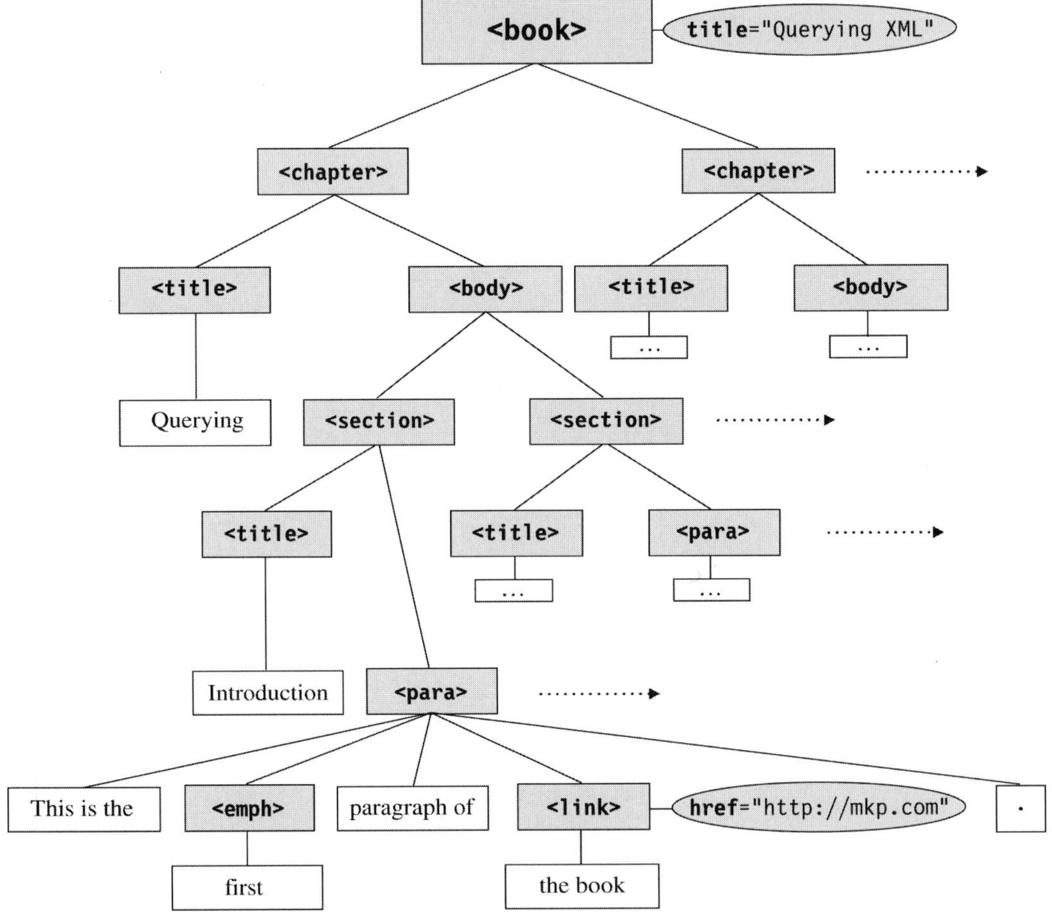

Figure 3-3 book Document Tree.

Find an Element by Name

Example 3-7 *Find an Element by Name*

English query	Find all nodes named "title."
XPath expression	//title
Explanation	1. // — select all the nodes in the document (select the root node and all its descendants). 2. //title — from those nodes, select the nodes named "title."

At the start of this section, we said you should be able to query XML by asking for an element by name. Example 3-7 shows a simple way to get all the titles from our movies sample, effectively requesting all elements named "title." But this method is considered dangerous (or at least sloppy) by some people. The method breaks down when the element name "title" is used in more than one place in the tree, as in the book document represented by the tree in Figure 3-3. Here, context is important. Do you really want to find *all* titles in *any* context? Or just chapter titles? Or section titles? In general, context is important, and a request by the element name alone doesn't include any context. If context were *not* important, we could simplify XML massively by making it a system of name–value pairs.[14]

Attributes vs. Elements

If you evaluate the XPath expression in Example 3-7 (`//title`) in the context of the data represented by Figure 3-3 (the book document), you will miss the title of the book. That's because the book title is an *attribute* of the book element (while the chapter title is an *element child* of the chapter element), and `//title` returns only *elements* named title.

There are a number of different views on attributes — some people think you should design XML documents that use elements rather than attributes, some think leaf elements and attributes should be entirely interchangeable. Of course, you may well need to query XML data whose structure was designed by someone else — i.e., you just need to query whatever is thrown at you. We'll just say here that

14 Another consideration here is efficiency. If your query engine is doing a simple tree walk (as is common with simple DOM implementations), then `//title` may involve examining every node in the document. If the document is large, this can be horribly expensive. On the other hand, more sophisticated implementations will use an index rather than actually walking the XML tree.

attributes *are* different from elements (they have different properties),[15] and XML query languages should and do treat elements and attributes differently.

Mixed-Content Models and Text Nodes

The movies tree illustrated in Figure 3-2 is very simple – it only has data at its leaf nodes, and each leaf node has exactly one piece of data. This is fairly typical for data-centric XML documents (such as purchase orders). Figure 3-3 is more typical of document-centric XML documents (such as books and reports) – if you were to look at the XML for this document, you'd see element tags sprinkled throughout the text. In XPath, this is represented as a number of child elements plus a number of text nodes (see Chapter 6, "The XML Information Set (Infoset) and Beyond," for a description of the XPath 1.0 data model and text nodes).

It's not obvious, without knowing both the structure and the semantics of the data, what a query should search, or return, when confronted with this kind of node (which the XML recommendation calls *mixed content*). XPath gives us a couple of ways of dealing with it. First, we can filter out all the text nodes. For example,

```
/book/chapter[1]/body/section[1]/paragraph[1]/text()
```

returns a sequence of the text nodes of the first paragraph in the first section of the first chapter, i.e., the sequence ("This is the "," paragraph of ", ".").[16] This result does not include child elements, so the word "first" (which is part of the child element named "`emph`"), and the phrase "the book" (which is part of the child element named "link") are missing. Sometimes you do want to collect together only the text nodes, for example, when the tags inside the text represent footnotes or annotations or reviewers' comments. But in this case the paragraph makes more sense if you take its string value, like this:

```
string(/book/chapter[1]/body/section[1]/paragraph[1])
```

---

15 For example, attributes have no implicit order, they cannot have children, and they do not have a parent-child relationship with the element they appear in. Attributes are conceptually "stuck on the side" of the XML tree.

16 We wrote this as a sequence of strings, but the careful reader will notice that it is, in fact, a sequence of text nodes.

This returns "This is the first paragraph of the book," which is all the character data between the start and end tags for this paragraph (and no attribute data).[17] You will read in Chapter 13, "What's Missing?," that it's particularly difficult to make rules about what is searched, and what is returned when you do full-text search over mixed-content XML.

Querying the Structure Only

We discussed at some length querying XML by walking the XML tree, and we discussed briefly querying by asking for an element by name. There is another way to query XML, which is to use only the structure.

In the context of the movie document in Figure 3-1, `/*/*[1]` returns the title by starting at the root node and navigating to the first child. The leading "`/`" means "start at the top of the tree." "`*`" is a wildcard, so it means "take all the element nodes at this level, no matter what their names are." And "`[1]`" is a positional condition — it means "take just the first node." So `/*/*[1]` means "starting from the top of the tree, take all the child element nodes, go down one level, take the first node, and return it."

Building Up a Result Set

The results returned by the examples in this section are somewhat limited. For example, in Example 3-6 we found the titles of all movies whose director was also a producer. It would be nice to return the title plus the full name of the director/producer and perhaps some other information about the movie (or about the director/producer). XPath is limited in this area — you need XQuery (or XSLT)[18] to build up XML result sets.

---

17 It's not obvious from the tree diagram, but all the white space in "This is the first paragraph of the book" is present in the character data between the start and end tags for this paragraph — taking the string value doesn't *add* any white space, so it doesn't always give you the result you might expect. The serialized form of this paragraph element is:

```
<paragraph>This is the <emph>first</emph> paragraph of <link
href="http://mkp.com">the book</link>.</paragraph>
```

18 XSLT (XSL transformations) is a language for transforming XML documents into other XML documents, which makes heavy use of XPath. See: *XSL Transformations (XSLT) Version 1.0* (Cambridge, MA: World Wide Web Consortium, 1999). Available at: http://www.w3.org/TR/xslt.

Documents, Collections, Elements

We said earlier in this chapter (at the start of this section) that, with XML, the distinction between individual documents and collections of documents is not as sharp as, say, the distinction between rows and tables in a SQL database — any collection of documents can be expressed as a single document. Similarly, each document can be seen as a set of subdocuments. This is the nature of tree structures. Sometimes the decision about what to call a document is somewhat arbitrary. Querying XML and returning *documents*, then, is far too coarse-grained to be generally useful. For example, if you decided to store data about your movies in a collection of movie documents (as in Figure 3-1), then returning the documents that satisfy the query would be somewhat useful.[19] On the other hand, if all the movies were in a single document (as in Figure 3-2), then every query would simply return the whole movies document (or nothing). Clearly, an XML query on documents like the movies document needs to return fine-grained results, i.e., results that are subtrees at any level (including leaves).[20]

3.2.3 Summary — Things to Consider

The examples in the previous section illustrate a number of the factors that make querying XML interesting. Let's summarize here before moving on.

- XML is hierarchical, and you can think of an XML document as a tree.
- When querying XML, you must be able at least to ask for an element by name and walk the XML tree. When walking the tree, you must be able to go up, down, and across and apply conditions. You should be able to walk the XML tree without knowing the names of any of the elements or attributes.
- When querying XML, you are likely to be working with sequences of nodes and values. You need special rules to define how to compare nodes and sequences of nodes, and you need special rules to define how to serialize (output) nodes and sequences of nodes.

---

19 In SQL terms, this would satisfy the requirement for *selection* but not *projection*.

20 That is, XML query needs to do both *selection* and *projection* of arbitrary subtrees.

- In many (but not all) XML documents, document order is important.
- When comparing values, the data types of the values is generally important.
- "//" is considered by many to be dangerous (and expensive) – it's a simple way to get to a named element, but it may give unexpected results if the structure of the data changes.
- Elements and attributes are different – if you expect to see attributes in your query result, you generally need to do something extra to get them.
- Mixed content – an element that contains a mixture of text and child elements – presents issues around what should be taken into account when querying and what should be returned.
- It is often useful to build up a result set, typically in XML. XPath is limited here, though XQuery can build arbitrarily complex XML output.

3.3 What Do You Know about Your Data?

We have often heard that one of the big advantages of XML is that it's so flexible. Compared to SQL, say, where you have to put a lot of effort into data modeling to define the properties of your data – its structure, data types, relationships to other data – XML is simple and easy to use. Just open up a text editor and start writing tags. We hope that, having read the introductory chapters to this book, you can already see the shortcomings of this worldview.

Knowing about Structure

It's very difficult to query data if you don't know how it's laid out. Just as it would be impossible to write a SQL query if you didn't know how the data was laid out in tables and columns, it's impossible to query XML unless you know something about how the XML documents you are querying are structured. For example, if you want to find the titles of all movies released in 1985, you have to know which part of the XML tree contains the title, which part contains the year released, and at least something about how they are related. You read in the section with the heading "Attributes vs. Elements" that if your query looks for a piece of data in an element but the data occurs in an attribute, then your query will miss it. To query XML in the simplest possible way (walking the XML tree, paying attention to context, and preferably using node names along the way to improve robustness) you have to know something about the structure of the document.

Knowing about Data Types

If you want to include conditions in your query, in general you'll need to know about the data types you are dealing with (though you can get a long way with the simple type system in XPath 1.0). If the XML documents you are querying are text-centric, then data typing is less important.

Knowing about the Semantics of the Data

Clearly, there is no point in searching for "titles" if you don't know what a "title" is — you need to know the semantics of the XML data in order to write sensible queries.

We have often heard that XML is "self-describing," meaning that an XML document contains *content* plus *metadata* about that content. In fact, XML documents typically contain content plus metadata plus *marked-up content*. The marked-up content may be marked up to provide additional semantic information about the data, or it may be marked up to provide presentation information about the data (though this is rightly frowned on). There is no way to distinguish between these different elements in an XML document without some outside reference.

XML element names should (but do not always!) say something about the data they enclose. But the tags do not *describe* the data in any way that can be used by a query language or any other application. In our movies example, we could just as easily have used "film" as "movie" in the tag names. Similarly, there's no way to tell how the "yearReleased" data was derived. Was it the year the movie was first shown in some theater in the United States? Or was it the year when the first DVD was released in Europe? And how do you know that all the data is about movies? There's nothing preventing us from adding plays, books, and songs and keeping the same tags. At best, tag names merely give some hints about what the data represents.

In some cases we know very little about the data we are querying. The obvious case is the web, which contains billions of documents with a loosely defined structure and almost no metadata or semantic information. We discuss this scenario in Chapter 18, "Finding Stuff."

But in most cases, you know — and need to know — all about the data you are querying. For effective, accurate, and efficient querying of XML, as with querying any data, you should know the structure of the data, the types of the data, and the semantics of the data. An XML document on its own is not self-describing, but an XML document plus a DTD or XML Schema plus an XML language definition does fully describe the data.

3.4 Some Ways to Query XML Today

We use XPath in this chapter to illustrate querying XML, but there are other ways to query XML.

The Document Object Model (DOM) defines an interface to the data and structure of an XML (or HTML) document so that a program can navigate and manipulate them. Using the DOM API (Application Programming Interface), you can write a program to return values of named elements/attributes or to walk the XML tree and return values of elements and/or attributes at specified positions in the tree. The DOM API also supports *manipulation* of the tree — inserting and deleting elements and attributes. The DOM is a popular API for accessing and manipulating XML (for example, it's used in JavaScript), but by itself it's not very useful for *querying* XML. The DOM is largely untyped — element content and attribute values are returned as strings — so you have to explicitly cast values in order to perform comparison operations that depend on type (equality, greater than, less than, and so on). We describe the DOM in Chapter 6, "The XML Information Set (Infoset) and Beyond."

The Simple API for XML (SAX) and the Streaming API for XML (StAX) are described in Chapter 14, "XQuery APIs." Like the DOM, these are both APIs rather than query languages, but they are popular ways to walk the XML tree and return results. SAX is an *event-based* API for XML, for use with Java and other languages. To write a SAX program you will need to obtain a SAX XML parser and then register an event handler to define a callback method for elements, for text, and for comments. SAX is a *serial access* API, which means you cannot go back up the tree, or rearrange nodes, as you can with DOM. But SAX has a smaller footprint and is more flexible.

StAX is a Java *pull parsing* API. That is, StAX lets you pull the next item in the document as it parses. You (the calling program) decide when to pull the next item (whereas with an event-based parser, it's the parser that decides when to cause the calling program to take some action). StAX also lets you write XML to an output stream.

Lastly, XQuery is a language defined by the W3C specifically for querying XML data. It is a strongly typed, expression-based, highly expressive language. XQuery 1.0 also includes the XPath 2.0 expressions. Manually coding programs to manipulate DOM or SAX is tedious and error-prone, and a standardized query language that eliminates the need for manual coding of parsing operations will increase productivity and improve software quality. We confidently predict that, while APIs such as DOM, SAX, and StAX (and their cousins such as JAXP and JAXB) will continue to be used for general-purpose XML access and manipulation, XQuery 1.0 and XPath 2.0 will become *the* standard way to query XML.

Many people believe that SQL/XML (the extensions to SQL first introduced as part of SQL:2003) competes with XQuery as an XML query language. As you will read in Chapter 15, "SQL/XML," that's not true! SQL/XML provides an API — a harness — for querying XML data in a SQL environment, using XPath and XQuery to query the XML structure and values.

3.5 Chapter Summary

In this chapter we discussed querying XML — the process of either retrieving element contents and attribute values by requesting them by name or walking the XML tree, possibly with some conditions, and retrieving values or subtrees from that XML data. We gave some examples of queries involving walking the XML tree, illustrated with XPath expressions, and introduced some of the challenges of querying XML. We argued that if you know more about the data you are querying — its structure and data types — then you can formulate better (more accurate, more efficient) queries. Lastly, we introduced a number of ways to query XML today and argued that XQuery 1.0 and XPath 2.0 will be *the* standard languages for querying XML.

This introductory part of the book — Chapters 1, 2, and 3 — provide a framework for understanding the rest of the book. Now that you have read these first three chapters, you are ready to dig deeper into *Querying XML*.

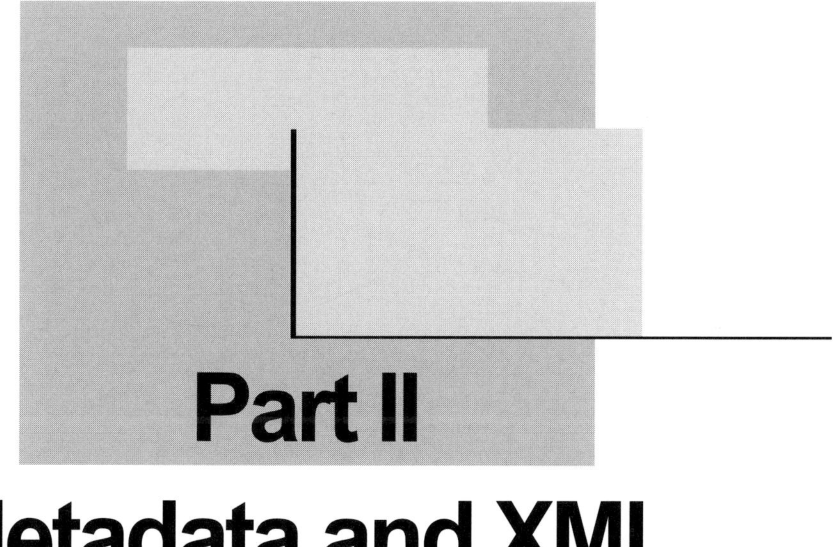

Part II

Metadata and XML

Chapter 4

Metadata — An Overview

4.1 Introduction

The word *metadata* has a number of meanings, not all obviously related to one another. Several formal definitions exist, most of them defining the word to mean "data about data." The word seems to have been coined in 1969 by Jack E. Myers, who intended to choose a term with no particular meaning in the data management community. In the ensuing years, the word has been enthusiastically adopted by the data community, but with varying meanings.

Multiple online dictionaries define the word. Wikipedia[1] says this: "***Metadata*** has come to be used to refer to data about data." Dictionary.com[2] includes this definition: "Data about data. In data processing, metadata is definitional data that provides information about or documentation of other data managed within an application or environment." Both definitions, and others, are consistent in saying that metadata is data about data. Another helpful definition that we found on the World Wide Web[3] is this: "Metadata is information about a thing, apart from the thing itself." While wholly consistent with the more terse definitions, this one calls out a

1 *Wikipedia, The Free Enclyopedia,* http://en.wikipedia.org

2 http://dictionary.reference.com

3 *Metadata Is Nothing New,* Ned Batchelder (2003). Available at: http://www.nedbatchelder.com/text/metadata-is-nothing-new.html

particularly important characteristic about metadata — it is something different than what it is describing. A paper we encountered[4] contains an interesting discussion of metadata and related concepts as they are used to find information. Although the paper concentrates on two particular kinds of metadata (semantic and catalog — see the following paragraph), its contents may be helpful to readers of this book who want a better grasp of the concepts involved.

We have found four different usages of the word *metadata* (sometimes spelled "meta-data" and sometimes given as two words: meta data) in the data management community, briefly described next. For each meaning, we provide an adjective that clarifies the intent of that meaning. (We have chosen to use the term *data field* or sometimes just *field* to mean some component of data that is an identifiable "piece" of some data structure. The use of "field" is not intended to evoke the image of some particular structure, such as a row.)

- **Structural metadata**: Information about the *structure* of the data, the *types* of data fields, and the *relationships* between data fields. Some references refer to this sort of metadata as the *schema* for the data. However, we don't find that particularly helpful, because it depends on a definition of "schema," of which there are many.
- **Semantic metadata**: Information defining the *meanings* of various data values and of the names given to data fields.
- **Catalog metadata**: Information providing high-level facts about desired data, often used to *locate* that data.
- **Integration metadata**: Information about the *correspondence* between data components, often from different sources — that is, which data fields or groups of data fields have the same meaning; for example, "firstname" together with "lastname" can be substituted for "fullname." The term *mapping metadata* is sometimes applied to this concept.

In this chapter, we introduce each of the meanings of the word, with examples. At least one example in each section is provided in an XML context.

---

4 *Metadata? Thesauri? Taxonomies? Topic Maps! Making Sense of It All*, Lars Marius Garshol (Oslo, Norway: Ontopia, 2004). Available at: http://www.ontopia.net/topicmaps/materials/tm-vs-thesauri.html.

Since metadata is "data about data," it's easy to get confused by the terminology. To avoid confusion, we use the bare word *data* to mean the data that an application needs to do its job. Similarly, we use the word *metadata,* with or without an adjective, to mean that data that somehow describes that other, application-required, data.

Although we do not discuss this further, it is worth mentioning that many environments provide still higher-level metadata that describes other metadata. This concept can be extended to as many levels as needed, as illustrated in the ISO Reference Model for Data Management.[5]

4.2 Structural Metadata

Structural metadata is metadata that describes the structure, type, and relationships of data. For example, in a SQL database, the data is described by metadata stored in the Information Schema and the Definition Schema. In the international standard for SQL, part 11[6] (called SQL/Schemata) specifies SQL views and base tables that describe a SQL database. The SQL standard provides quite a number of components that applications can define within a database: tables, columns in those tables, views, user-defined types, attributes and methods of those user-defined types, other types of user-defined routines, parameters of those methods and other routines, constraints of various sorts, triggers, and so forth. Each of those objects is described by rows that appear in one (or more) of the various views of the Information Schema and one (or more) of the tables of the Definition Schema.

The descriptions of those objects specify such information as the name of the object, the characteristics of the object, and the relationships that the object has with other objects of the same sort and/or of different sorts.

For example, the SQL standard's most fundamental object is the *table*, which roughly corresponds to the *relation* in the relational model of data. Tables are composed of one or more *columns*, each of which

5 ISO/IEC 10032:1995, *Information Technology – Reference Model of Data Management* (Geneva, Switzerland: International Organization for Standardization, 1995).

6 ISO/IEC 9075-11:2003, *Information Technology – Database Languages – SQL – Part 11: Information and Definition Schemas (SQL/Schemata)* (Geneva, Switzerland: International Organization for Standardization, 2003).

has a specified *data type*.[7] SQL/Schemata provides a TABLES view and a COLUMNS view that, together, describe each of the tables in a database as well as each column of each of those tables. In addition, each constraint that is defined for a table or for one of its columns is described in one or more of several views: TABLE_CONSTRAINTS, COLUMN_CONSTRAINTS, CHECK_CONSTRAINTS, and REFERENTIAL_CONSTRAINTS. Those views are specified in such a way that they retrieve their information from underlying "base tables" with the same name.

Consider the SQL table definition in Example 4-1.

Example 4-1 *Example SQL Table Definition*

```
CREATE TABLE book_catalog.querying_xml.movies (
  movie_ID              INTEGER
    CONSTRAINT movid_ID_not_null
      NOT NULL,
  movie_title           CHARACTER VARYING (50),
  movie_description     CLOB(1M) )
```

This definition creates a table whose fully qualified name is BOOK_CATALOG.QUERYING_XML.MOVIES (SQL automatically converts ordinary identifiers to uppercase). This table contains three columns, named MOVIE_ID, MOVIE_TITLE, and MOVIE_DESCRIPTION. Each of those columns is given a particular data type, which means that each value stored in that column must be a value of that type. One of the columns has a NOT NULL constraint defined on it, meaning that no value stored in that column can be the null value.

The *structural* metadata that describes SQL tables looks something like the table definition in Example 4-2 (for brevity, we have omitted many of the columns of these metadata tables).

Example 4-2 *Table Definition of the TABLES Table*

```
CREATE TABLE tables (
  TABLE_CATALOG          INFORMATION_SCHEMA.SQL_IDENTIFIER,
  TABLE_SCHEMA           INFORMATION_SCHEMA.SQL_IDENTIFIER,
```

---

7 When a data type is specified for some SQL storage site, such as a column, it is called the *declared type* of that site. If the declared type is a supertype of one or more other types, then the value stored at that site might have a *most specific type* that is a subtype of the declared type.

```
    TABLE_NAME            INFORMATION_SCHEMA.SQL_IDENTIFIER,
    TABLE_TYPE            INFORMATION_SCHEMA.CHARACTER_DATA
      CONSTRAINT TABLE_TYPE_NOT_NULL
        NOT NULL
      CONSTRAINT TABLE_TYPE_CHECK
      CHECK ( TABLE_TYPE IN
              ( 'BASE TABLE', 'VIEW',
                'GLOBAL TEMPORARY', 'LOCAL TEMPORARY' ) ),
    ...,
    CONSTRAINT TABLES_PRIMARY_KEY
      PRIMARY KEY ( TABLE_CATALOG, TABLE_SCHEMA, TABLE_NAME ),
    CONSTRAINT TABLES_FOREIGN_KEY_SCHEMATA
      FOREIGN KEY ( TABLE_CATALOG, TABLE_SCHEMA )
        REFERENCES SCHEMATA,
    ...
  )
```

Each row of the TABLES table specifies the fully qualified name of some table. Since TABLES is itself a table, it includes a row containing metadata about itself — that is, SQL's metadata is *self-describing*. The name of each table is provided in the form of three columns: TABLE_CATALOG, TABLE_SCHEMA, and TABLE_NAME. The metadata also specifies which of four sorts of table that table is: base table, view, or one of two types of temporary table. Several constraints are specified to govern values stored in the TABLES table. One, named TABLES_PRIMARY_KEY, specifies that the values of the combination of the three _NAME columns must be unique within the table. Another, called TABLES_FOREIGN_KEY_SCHEMATA, mandates that values of the combination of the two columns TABLE_CATALOG and TABLE_SCHEMA be found in columns of the same names in the SCHEMATA table.

Our MOVIES table would be described by a row in the TABLES table with the values in Table 4-1.

Table 4-1 *Contents of the TABLES Table*

CATALOG_NAME	SCHEMA_NAME	TABLE_NAME	TABLE_TYPE	...
BOOK_CATALOG	QUERYING_XML	MOVIES	BASE TABLE	...

The columns of our MOVIES table are defined in a different Definition Schema table, COLUMNS. The columns of each row of the COLUMNS table include the fully qualified name of some column of some table, the ordinal position of that column within its parent table, the data type of the column, and whether or not the column is nullable. The COLUMNS table also specifies several constraints, such as a primary key that requires the combination of values of the four _NAME columns to be unique within the COLUMNS table, that no two columns occupy the same ordinal position in their parent table, and so on. For example, the columns of our MOVIES table would be described by rows in the COLUMNS table with the values given in Table 4-2.

The column in Table 4-2 named DTD_IDENTIFIER deserves a brief explanation. The values of that column are foreign keys into the DATA_TYPE_DESCRIPTOR table. The corresponding rows in that latter table contain information about every variation of data type in the database. For example, if some column C1 in some table T1 has the data type INTEGER and some other column C2 in some other table T2 has the data type INTEGER, there will be two rows in the DATA_TYPE_DESCRIPTOR table, each row identifying the name of the column and the data type (INTEGER), as well as some implementation-specific value that uniquely identifies each row in the table. That unique value is the value stored in the DTD_IDENTIFIER column of a row in the COLUMNS table for the given column.

Table 4-2 *Contents of the COLUMNS Table*

CATALOG_ NAME	SCHEMA_ NAME	TABLE_ NAME	COLUMN_ NAME	ORDINAL_ POSITION	DTD_ IDENTIFIER*	...
BOOK_ CATALOG	QUERYING_ XML	MOVIES	MOVIE_ID	1	...	...
BOOK_ CATALOG	QUERYING_ XML	MOVIES	MOVIE_ TITLE	2	...	...
BOOK_ CATALOG	QUERYING_ XML	MOVIES	MOVIE_ DESCRIP- TION	3	...	...

* The values of DTD_IDENTIFIER are created by the implementation and refer to rows in the DATA_TYPE_DESCRIPTOR base table that describe each data type in the database. (Unfortunately, the name of this column includes the acronym DTD, which might mislead readers to assume that it refers to a Document Type Definition. It does not; it stands for Data Type Descriptor.)

The Definition Schema base tables fully describe every table, column, constraint, *etc.* in the database. The structure of each table is fully defined by specifying each of its columns and the order in which those columns appear in the table. The data type of each column (meaning, of course, the data type of the value of that column for every row in the table) is specified. And, of course, the relationships between various columns and between the columns and their own values are also specified.

You might wonder why so much space is spent describing SQL metadata in a book whose subject matter is XML. Simply put, the broad familiarity that SQL has in the software community makes it an obvious choice for introducing the subject of structural metadata.

The world of XML is not always quite as convenient as the SQL world, largely because of the difference in data model. SQL's data is completely *regular*, because every row in a table contains a value of every column of the table; in some rows, the value for a given column might be the null value (if the table's and a column's constraints permit null values), but there are no "cells" of a table that are simply "not there."

By contrast, as you read in Chapter 1, "XML" is inherently *semistructured*, which means that some data elements might be missing entirely from a given XML document. As a result, the nature of XML structural metadata is significantly different from that of SQL.

Metadata for XML documents must provide necessary information about the names and the "types" of each component of those documents. In the context of XML, the word *type* has a somewhat less obvious definition than it does in SQL. In particular, the type of an XML element may include information such as the attributes and children of the element. The type of an XML element might be some simple type, such as ordinary text, but it might also be a *complex type* that permits the element to have child elements and even *mixed content* (combination of child elements and text). When XML Schema[8] (or other, analogous facility) is used, an element's content or an attribute can be given a more traditional "data type," such as integer, character string, or datetime.

For example, consider an XML document that we might have chosen to represent information about actors, as seen in Example 4-3. (Not having gender-based biases, we have chosen to characterize both males and females as "actors.")

Example 4-3 *Actors and Actresses*

```
<actors>
  <actor>
    <name>Johnny Depp</name>
```

8 See Chapter 5, "Structural Metadata."

```
    <gender>Male</gender>
    <film runtime="122">
      <title>From Hell</title>
      <role>Inspector Fred Abberline</role>
    </film>
    <film>
      <title>Blow</title>
      <role>George Jung</role>
    </film>
    <film runtime="97">
      <title>Don Juan de Marco</title>
      <role>Don Juan</role>
    </film>
  </actor>
  <actor>
    <name>Iliana Douglas</name>
    <gender>Female</gender>
    <film runtime="111">
      <title>Ghost World</title>
      <role>Roberta</role>
    </film>
    <film runtime="116">
      <title>Grace of My Heart</title>
      <role>Denise Waverly</role>
      <role>Edna Buxton</role>
    </film>
    <film runtime="106">
      <title>The Thin Pink Line</title>
      <role>Julia Bullock</role>
    </film>
  </actor>
</actors>
```

We readily see that the element "actors" is made up of one or more "actor" elements. Each "actor" element contains a "name" element, a "gender" element, and one or more "film" elements. "film" elements each contain a "title" element, one or more "role" elements, and optionally an attribute named "runtime." The data type of the nonelement content of each element is obviously character string, but the data type of the "runtime" attribute seems to be integer.

The information in the immediately preceding paragraph is the *structural metadata* of the element "actors." It can also be characterized as the *type* of that element. Of course, in order for this structural metadata to be useful to computer systems, it has to be presented in some machine-readable form, perhaps in an XML form (such as XML Schema) or a non-XML form (such as Document Type Definitions or even SQL-like tabular representations).

It is important to observe that none of this structural metadata — for either SQL or XML — offers any hope of understanding the meaning of the data. Sure, we human readers can reasonably presume that an element named "title" might contain the title of a film or that an attribute named "runtime" probably contains the running time of a film (but in what units?). But, absent any other information about the *meaning* of all of those names and the content of the elements and attributes, no application program is likely to "understand" the data in any significant sense.

In summary, structural metadata serves to describe the data components, the types of those components, and their relationships to one another. However, it has nothing to do with the meaning of the data being described. Structural metadata is discussed in greater detail in Chapter 5, "Structural Metadata."

4.3 Semantic Metadata

Semantic metadata is metadata that describes the "meaning" of data. Of course, the very term "meaning of data" requires an explanation, if for no other reason than we've found that different individuals interpret it differently. We believe that there are two distinct applications of the term *semantic metadata* that are relevant here. The first applies to the meaning of data *values*, the other to the meaning of the *names* of things that can take on such values.

In any context in which data exist, there are values that represent certain concepts. Associating specific values with specific concepts is one way of assigning *meaning* to the data made up of those values. For example, when we needed to capture the gender of an actor in Example 4-3, we chose to use the values "Male" and "Female" to represent men and women, respectively. Other creators of such data might have chosen "male" and "female," "M" and "F," "0" and "1," or even "♂" and "♀" to represent the same concepts.

There is an international standard[9] that defines how to represent this particular information in a standardized way. This standard specifies that "0" represents "Not known" (which might apply to an essentially androgynous character, such as the one played by Julia Sweeney in the film *It's Pat*), "1" represents "Male," "2" represents "Female," and "9" represents "Not applicable" (which could be applied to inanimate "actors," such as robots, that lack a human gender). It also seems to recommend that the term used to describe this concept is "SEX." Thus, ISO 5218 contains semantic metadata about gender (sex). Unfortunately, that semantic metadata is not readily accessible to computer programs since it is in an ordinary text document.

Which brings us to the second application of the term *semantic metadata*: the meaning of names of things (fields, columns, elements, even variables) that can be assigned values associated with some meaning. In Example 4-3, we put the name "gender" on the element specifying the (human) sexes of our actors. Had we followed the recommendation of ISO/IEC 5218, we might have named that element "SEX" (or perhaps, to be easier on the eyes, "sex"). Had we chosen to apply ISO 5218 by naming the element according to that standard's conventions, then the standard would provide the semantic metadata to tell us what the element name "SEX" means.

But how can the names of such "things" and the values assigned to them be given a "meaning" that can be handled by computer programs? Part of the answer lies in the notion of *metadata registries*. A metadata registry, managed by some *registration authority*, provides a mechanism by which the names of "things" and the values assigned to them can be managed, making them easier to find and interpret in various data sources.

Another ISO standard, ISO/IEC 11179, is a multipart standard in which each part standardizes a separate aspect of constructing and managing metadata registries. Various parts of this standard describe "a conceptual model of a [metadata registry] and the processes of classification, naming, identification, forming definitions, and registration in order to make data understandable and shareable."[10] We emphasize that semantic metadata exists to make data

---

9 ISO/IEC 5218:2003, *Information Technology — Codes for the Representations of Human Sexes* (Geneva, Switzerland: International Organization for Standardization, 2003).

10 ISO/IEC 11179-1:1999, *Information Technology — Metadata Registries — Part 1: Framework* (Geneva, Switzerland: International Organization for Standardization, 1999).

more understandable (to programs and to humans) but also more sharable (by programs and by humans).

The framework of that standard states the following in its introduction:

> Humans are aware of things or ideas that exist through their properties. Data represents the properties of these things or ideas. A data element is the construct by which we consider the thing or idea, one of its properties, and the possible representations of the property as data. A value domain specifies how a data element is represented, *i.e.*, is the set of allowed values for that data element. Specification of data elements, value domains, and related data entities involves documenting relevant characteristics of each. Data that has been carefully specified greatly enhances its usefulness and shareability across systems and organizations. Sharing data involves the ability to locate and retrieve desired data and to exchange the data with others. When data elements and value domains are well documented according to ISO/IEC 11179 and the documentation is managed in a metadata registry (MDR), finding and retrieving them from disparate databases as well as sending and receiving them via electronic communications are made easier.

According to Clause 1, "Scope," of this framework, "[ISO/IEC 11179] applies to the formulation of data representations, concepts, meanings, and relationships between them to be shared among people and machines, independent of the organization that produces the data." Other parts of ISO/IEC 11179 address the use of metadata registries to record the meanings of the tags that make up various XML vocabularies. Other standards or additional parts of ISO/IEC 11179 could be created that address the use of XML for semantic metadata representation. (We are unaware of efforts to create such standards or parts of ISO/IEC 11179 at this time, but hope springs eternal!)

Design of a metadata registry for some particular purpose might well be driven by an *ontology,* which is defined by the Wikipedia as an "attempt to formulate an exhaustive and rigorous conceptual schema within a given domain, a typically hierarchical data structure containing all the relevant entities and their relationships and rules (theorems, regulations) within that domain." The Wikipedia also mentions that T. R. Gruber described an ontology as "an explicit specification of conceptualization." Computer programs may be written to take advantage of (machine-readable) ontologies to apply a sort of machine understanding of data described by those ontologies. The terms used by such ontologies may well be managed in some metadata registry, such as those specified according to ISO/IEC 11179.

There are several important XML-related standards under development that will allow the development and application of ontologies — and thus semantics metadata — to pages of the World Wide Web. Arguably the most important of these is OWL,[11] which provides XML-based mechanisms for defining ontologies that can be used to provide semantic metadata about XML documents on the web.

In summary, semantic metadata is the description of the meanings of values and of the names of data components, at least for human reference and possibly for programmatic use as well.

4.4 Catalog Metadata

Catalog metadata specifies information about identifying and locating data that (usually) cannot be found in the data itself. Catalog metadata includes the kind of information you might use to locate data in a repository of some sort. For example, the title, author, publisher, ISBN, and publication date of a book are pieces of catalog metadata that makes it easier to locate a particular book than searching all known books for some passages dimly remembered from the text of the book.

There are countless mechanisms in common use for *cataloging* resources of many different sorts, including books, periodicals, conferences, buildings, web pages, automobiles, words, people, theories, galaxies, molecules, cancers, tools, *etc.*

For example, until rather recently (historically speaking, of course), public and other libraries cataloged the books they held by using index cards stored in large cabinets with many file drawers just the size of the index cards — a *card catalog*. The cards themselves contained additional information about the book, such as the full title, the author, the publisher, and the publication date. Because this medium was so labor-intensive, books were almost never cataloged in multiple ways. Therefore, locating a book required having an idea

11 *OWL Web Ontology Language* (Cambridge, MA: World Wide Web Consortium, 2001). Available at: http://www.w3.org/2001/sw/WebOnt/.

of the topic of the book and using that knowledge to identify the most likely *Dewey Decimal Number* of the subject matter of the book.

Once the Dewey Decimal Number for the subject matter is known, the section of the card catalog in which books of that topic were found can be located. After that, a linear search of the cards associated with books of that subject is performed. Either the card identifying the desired book is found or the absence of such a card indicates that the book was not cataloged under that subject. All in all, this process was workable — demonstrated by the fact that it was in use for quite a few years — but tedious and time-consuming, both for catalogers and for seekers. The advent of computers and their application to libraries provided the opportunity to search for books based on a variety of knowledge about the book: complete or partial titles, complete or incomplete author information, ISBN, and so forth.

Of course, other resources used other mechanisms to catalog individual instances of the resource, such as postal addresses to identify buildings, vehicle identification numbers (VINs) to identify motor vehicles, and taxonomical names to identify species of organism. Each type of resource requires a different set of identifying data to catalog instances of the resource type. Catalog information about books is considerably different than catalog information about chemical compounds or catalog information about stars and galaxies.

Examination of many types of resources for which cataloging is necessary led to a generalization of the requirements for cataloging, which in turn led to standardized vocabularies for catalog metadata. One important standard in this field is the Dublin Core,[12] a set of metadata elements that can be used to describe any resource, that is, anything that has identity. The metadata elements specified by the Dublin Core are: Title, Creator, Subject, Description, Publisher, Contributor, Date, Type, Format, Identifier, Source, Language, Relation, Coverage, and Rights.

One possible Dublin Core representation of a movie appears in Table 4-3.

It may not be completely obvious that there could be a number of different ways to organize the Dublin Core representation of "The Scariest Sci-Fi Thriller in Years!," as *TNT Roughcut* called this film. But it's very easy to see how knowing the information shown in Table 4-3 would help locate the film in a catalog, web store, *etc.*

12 http://dublincore.org.

In the XML world, a well-known example of a catalog metadata standard is the Resource Description Framework (RDF). One of the documents in this standard, the Primer,[13] clarifies that RDF is intended "for representing information about resources on the World

***Table 4-3** A Movie Described Using the Dublin Core*

Dublin Core Element Name	Value
Title	Pitch Black
Creator	David Twohy
Subject	Science Fiction
Subject	Drama
Description	It's evil vs. evil in an electrifying showdown that *USA Today* calls ". . . best excuse to root for the bad guy since Arnold in the original *Terminator*."
Publisher	Universal Pictures
Publisher	Interscope Communications
Contributor	Vin Diesel
Contributor	Radha Mitchell
Contributor	Cole Hauser
Contributor	Keith David
Date	2000
Resource Type	Movie
Format	DVD: Region 1
Resource Identifier	ISBN 0-7832-4922-5
Language	en: US
etc.	etc.

Wide Web. It is particularly intended for representing metadata about Web resources, such as the title, author, and modification date of a web page, copyright and licensing information about a web document, or the availability schedule for some shared resource." In the RDF model, assertions about resources take the form of a *subject*, an *object*, and a *predicate* that specifies the relationship between the subject and the object. For example, the website http://sqlx.org (the sub-

13 *RDF Primer* (Cambridge, MA: World Wide Web Consortium, 2001). Available at: http://www.w3.org/TR/rdf-primer/.

ject) is maintained (the predicate) by the authors of this book (the object). Of course, most subjects, including this one, have many characteristics that can be represented in this way. That website has a title, it has a date of most recent update, it has several web pages, and so forth. Each of those characteristics can be represented in the RDF model. In fact, many (or most) of the objects themselves are subjects for other predicates. Thus, a complete RDF description of an entity often forms a tree structure – for which XML is extremely well suited. RDF is discussed more fully in Chapter 18, "Finding Stuff."

Dublin Core and RDF are not competing ways of creating and representing catalog metadata about documents. Dublin Core defines a number of metadata elements used to describe documents and represents a consensus among information retrieval specialists about the minimal information necessary to identify and locate such documents. By contrast, RDF is an architecture for representing and organizing metadata (or, indeed, data) that does not predetermine what that metadata must be.

It is not uncommon to find environments in which RDF is used to record Dublin Core metadata. For example, the following RDF-like assertion identifies the title of the movie described in Table 4-3:

```
our:movie-number-495 | dc:title | "Pitch Black"
```

(In this case, "our" is a prefix representing information about stuff we own – including movies – and "dc" is a prefix representing concepts belonging to the Dublin Core specifications. As you will see in Chapter 18, those prefixes are only illustrative.)

In summary, catalog metadata is information that makes it easier to locate desired resources among a collection of like resources. Catalog metadata is not homogenous, though. We identify three subcategories of catalog metadata:[14] *descriptive* (or *bibliographic*, supporting discovery and interpretation of data), *administrative* (addressing rights management, physical media descriptions, encoding conventions, and so on), and *preservational* (to track the lineage or provenance of data, the archival requirements, *etc*.). There are undoubtedly many other ways of subdividing the notion of catalog metadata.

---

14 Steve Ledwaba, *Standards and Quality Deployment in Digital Libraries: The Metadata Role* (Pretoria, S.A.: National Research Foundation, 2004).

4.5 Integration Metadata

Integration metadata is metadata that makes it possible to pull together data designed or created by different organizations, where the data from all sources is intended to have the same purpose.

For example, one organization might represent information about actors by using the data elements we illustrated in Example 4-3, while a different organization might choose the approach shown in Example 4-4.

Example 4-4 *Other Actors and Actresses*

```
<Actors-and-Actresses>
  <Actor>
    <name>Martin Short</name>
    <sex code="1">
    <movie>
      <title>Mars Attacks!</title>
      <length>106</length>
      <released>1996</released>
      <character>Press Secretary Jerry Ross</character>
    </movie>
    <movie>
      <title>Innerspace</title>
      <length>120</length>
      <released>1987</released>
      <character>Jack Putter</character>
    </movie>
    <movie>
      <title>La La Wood</title>
      <length>unknown</length>
      <released>2003</released>
      <character>Jiminy Glick</character>
    </movie>
  </Actor>
  <Actress>
    <name>Rikki Lake</name>
    <sex code="2">
    <movie>
      <title>Serial Mom</title>
      <length>95</length>
      <released>1994</released>
      <character>Misty Sutphin</character>
```

```
      </movie>
      <movie>
        <title>Last Exit to Brooklyn</title>
        <length>102</length>
        <released>1989</released>
        <character>Donna</character>
      </movie>
      <movie>
        <title>Hairspray</title>
        <length>92</length>
        <released>1988</released>
        <character>Tracy Turnblad</character>
      </movie>
    </Actress>
  </Actors-and-Actresses>
```

Even a casual examination of the XML in Example 4-3 and Example 4-4 reveals that the two have a great deal in common but that there are important differences as well. For example, Example 4-3 contains an element named "actors," while Example 4-4 contains one named "Actors-and-Actresses." Most of the data in each of the two examples can be found in the other, even though some of the data appears as an attribute in one and as a child element in the other, the names of the elements differ, the sequence of elements differ, and some data in one example (the element "released" in Example 4-4) has no analog in the other example.

Integration metadata could provide a mapping between the two designs, as illustrated in Table 4-4. (We hasten to observe that the problem of mapping between two XML vocabularies, however similarly they are structured, is significantly more complex in practice than we have space to explore here.)

Table 4-4 *Integrating Two XML Document Designs*

Data Purpose	Example 4-3	Example 4-4
Top-level container	<actors>	<Actors-and-Actresses>
Individual actor container	<actor>	<Actor> or <Actress>
Actor's name	<name> (content)	<name> (content)
Actor's gender	<gender> (content)	<sex> (attribute: code)

Table 4-4 Integrating Two XML Document Designs (continued)

Data Purpose	Example 4-3	Example 4-4
Filmography	<film>	<movie>
Running time of film	Attribute of <film>: runtime	<length> (content)
Name of film	<title> (content)	<title> (content)
Year film was released	(not present)	<released> (content)
Character played in film	<role> (content)	<character> (content)

Of course, several questions are left unanswered by the information captured in Table 4-4, such as the meanings of the values for the element "gender" in Example 4-3 and for the attribute "code" of the element "sex" in Example 4-4. Clearly, the table could be enhanced to add such mapping information as well. For example, it happens that the values of the element "sex" in Example 4-4 follow the practices of ISO 5218. (In fact, it is exactly this sort of problem that is addressed by the use of semantic metadata — understanding the *meanings* of data names and values.)

Given the kind of mapping illustrated in Table 4-4, application programmers — or, indeed, application generators — can readily integrate the data represented in the two XML documents given in Example 4-3 and in Example 4-4.

We are unaware of any existing standards meant specifically for integration metadata, but it's worth pointing out that the creation such facilities is enhanced through the use of semantic metadata implementations, such as an ISO 11179 metadata registry.

In summary, integration metadata is information that assists in correlating data designed by different organizations or individuals.

4.6 Chapter Summary

In this chapter we have introduced the term *metadata* and the four forms of metadata that affect life in the information technology industry: structural metadata, semantic metadata, catalog metadata, and integration metadata.

Of these four forms, we believe that it is most urgent to learn more about structural metadata and semantic metadata. Only then does catalog metadata become an important concept. Because we are not aware of standardized facilities for creating and using integration metadata, we do not further discuss that form in this book.

Chapter 5

Structural Metadata

5.1 Introduction

In Chapter 4, we provided a brief discussion of several types of metadata. In this chapter, you'll read more about structural metadata. In particular, you'll learn what Document Type Definitions (or DTDs) are and how they add value to XML documents, about XML Schema and the additional values that it provides, and about other structural metadata specification languages.

You'll recall that Chapter 4 described structural metadata thusly: *Structural metadata* is metadata that describes the structure, type, and relationships of data. In this chapter, we explore how each of those aspects of data — its structures, its types, and its relationships — can be specified for XML documents. We also discuss how that metadata can be used to ensure that a specific XML document is *valid* according to the metadata that has been provided to describe the document.

As you'll discover in Chapter 6, "The XML Information Set (Infoset) and Beyond," metadata exists — or can be constructed — even for XML documents for which no explicit metadata description has been provided. Simply by parsing a single XML document, it is possible to describe the structure of that single document and some of the relationships between various parts of the data that it contains. It is also possible to *infer* some information about the types of some of that data. But that is rarely sufficient for meaningful applications, so this chapter will focus on metadata that has been provided to (potentially) describe one or more, perhaps many, XML documents.

When multiple documents conform to a single structural metadata definition, such as those covered in this chapter, it becomes possible to express meaningful queries across all of those documents. Such queries can depend on the documents' structural characteristics as well as the data contained in the documents.

Other reasons for using structural metadata for XML documents include the ability to guarantee certain types of data integrity – for example, all purchase orders can be required to have ship-to addresses or all books can be required to have titles. Similarly, document creation tools (such as XML editors) can use structural metadata to prevent data entry errors while a document is still in the process of being created.

5.2 DTDs

The first form of explicit metadata that many people encounter is the DTD, or Document Type Definition. The syntax and usage of DTDs are defined as part of the specification for XML.[1]

In the XML specification, we find the following definition: "The XML *document type declaration* contains or points to markup declarations that provide a grammar for a class of documents." The markup declarations that a document type declaration contains or to which a document type declaration points is, in fact, a Document Type Definition. When the DTD is contained within the document type declaration, it's referred to as an *internal subset DTD* (which is illustrated in Example 5-10); when the document type declaration points to the DTD, that DTD is called an *external subset DTD* (as illustrated in Example 5-11).[2]

The definition of those markup declarations states that "A *markup declaration* is an element type declaration, an attribute list declaration, an entity declaration, or a notation declaration."

Let's dissect those definitions a little bit before getting into the details of DTDs. First, a DTD provides a *grammar* for a *class* of XML

---

1 *Extensible Markup Language (XML) 1.1* (Cambridge, MA: World Wide Web Consortium, 2004). Available at: http://www.w3.org/TR/xml11.

2 Internal subset DTDs, since they are specified within a specific XML document, are relevant only to that specific document. By contrast, external subset DTDs may be referenced by many XML documents.

documents. That means, of course, that a specific DTD might describe a very large number of documents or only a single document. Second, by providing a grammar, it describes the possible elements and attributes that those documents might contain and the relationships among them. What it does not do, though, is specify the data types of any data values that might be contained in those elements and attributes.[3]

The term *element type declaration* doesn't necessarily imply the declaration of an ordinary data type, like string or integer, for an element's content. Quite often, it implies specification of the structure of the element's content — that is, the structural type of the element.

DTDs use a non-XML syntax to provide those markup declarations. The use of a non-XML syntax has some advantages, but there are significant disadvantages as well. The most important disadvantage is that an XML parser cannot be used to extract information from a DTD; instead, a distinct DTD parser is required.

5.2.1 SGML Heritage

One reason for the non-XML syntax of DTDs is its heritage. DTDs were invented as a metadata description language for the Standard General Markup Language (SGML).[4] As we learned in Chapter 1, "XML" is defined as a subset of SGML, so it's natural that XML originally depended on DTDs for its metadata description language. Why SGML used a non-SGML syntax for DTDs is unclear, but that decision was inherited by XML.

The SGML standard, Annex B, "Basic Concepts," provides a brief DTD tutorial, but the complete specification of DTDs in SGML is found in Clause 11, "Markup Declarations: Document Type Definition." Like many standards, the SGML standard is tedious and even difficult to read, but a fairly casual perusal of SGML's DTD specification would be enough to persuade most readers that XML's DTDs are a subset of SGML's, in the same manner that XML is itself a subset of SGML.

3 Technically, as you'll read in Example 5-11, DTDs can specify a very limited set of data types for some attributes.

4 *ISO 8879:1986(E), Information Processing — Text and Office Systems — Standard Generalized Markup Language (SGML)* (Geneva, Switzerland: International Organization for Standardization, 1986).

5.2.2 Relatively Simple, Easy to Write, and Easy to Read

It is beyond the scope of this chapter (indeed, of this book) to give a complete presentation of XML DTDs. However, a review of the major components of DTDs and their syntax will be useful in understanding how they provide structural metadata for XML documents.

XML documents *may* contain a document type declaration. XML documents that do not contain such a declaration must be well formed but, using the rules of XML only, cannot be *valid* because there is no metadata information against which they can be validated. A significant fraction of XML documents found "in the wild" today fall into this category. However, there are also a great many XML documents that are also intended to be valid according to the declarations contained in DTDs.

An XML document that includes a *document type declaration* can be validated against the DTD provided by, or identified by, that declaration. A valid document is one whose structure adheres to the structure, including constraints, defined by the markup declarations contained in that DTD, as determined by a validating parser.

A document type declaration in an XML document must occur as part of the document's prolog. It has the syntax shown in Example 5-1.

Example 5-1 *Document Type Declaration Syntax*

```
<!DOCTYPE document-type-name
optional-external-reference
optional-internal-declarations>
```

Note that this may include a reference to some DTD resource (*e.g.*, a file) separate from the document itself (called, as we said earlier in this chapter, the *external subset*), or it may contain internal DTD declarations surrounded by square brackets (the *internal subset*), or it may contain both (in that order). The ability to reference an external subset from many documents makes it easy to ensure that all of those documents are consistently constructed. The ability to include an internal subset in each document makes it possible to allow the documents to differ in some way while ensuring that each of those documents remains self-consistent.

We observe that the syntax of the document type declaration doesn't follow most of the rules of what we normally consider to be "XML." For example, the document type declaration is surrounded by angle brackets (<. . .>), but there's that exclamation point (`!`) after the left angle bracket and there's neither a slash (`/`) preceding the right angle bracket nor a separate closing tag. This characteristic applies to all of the components of DTDs.

Example 5-2 illustrates what a document type declaration might look like in an actual XML document.

Example 5-2 *Example Document Type Declaration*

```
<!DOCTYPE bibliography
  SYSTEM "biblio.dtd">
```

In this example, the document type declaration specifies an external subset by means of a system file name, and no internal subset is specified. The name specified for the DOCTYPE (`bibliography`, in this case) must match the name of the root element of every document that depends on the DTD.

DTDs are defined using markup declarations (*parsed entity references*, not covered in this book, can also be used to aid in readability). Markup declarations come in several forms: element declarations, attribute list declarations, entity declarations, notation declarations, processing instruction declarations, and comments. For our purposes in this chapter, we need consider only element declarations and attribute list declarations.

The names provide clear indication of their uses: Element declarations specify the element structure within an XML document and constrain the content of the elements they declare, while attribute list declarations specify the sets of attributes that can appear with particular elements and constrain the content of those attributes.

An element declaration specifies the name of the element and the rules that its content must follow; these rules are called the *content model* of the element. The content of an element can be required to be empty or can be permitted to have any content at all (a mixture of text and element children that are declared in the DTD but not specified in the element declaration). Between those two extremes, a DTD can specify that an element may have mixed content (that is, ordinary text, possibly intermixed with specified element children) or that it may have only (specified) element children. Example 5-3 illustrates element declarations for each of these four alternatives, while Example 5-4 provides a sample usage of each of those declared elements. We note in passing that all elements must be declared in the DTD as "global" elements — that is, elements that can appear anywhere in an XML document – except for elements used purely in mixed content.

Example 5-3 *Examples of Element Declarations*

```
<!ELEMENT catalogued EMPTY>

<!ELEMENT review ANY>

<!ELEMENT title ( #PCDATA | ital | bold | under )*>

<!ELEMENT author ( salutation?, given, family, suffix? )>
```

In Example 5-3, the element named `catalogued` is required to be empty. Of course, in an instance XML document, you may specify this element either as `<catalogued/>` or as `<catalogued></catalogued>`, because there is no semantic difference between those representations. Elements declared to be `EMPTY` may nonetheless have attribute list declarations associated with them.

There are a couple of good reasons to declare an element to be `EMPTY`. The element can be optional, so its presence indicates some fact about the document and its absence indicates the opposite fact. For example, the `catalogued` element might appear as part of an XML document's `book` element to indicate that information about the book has been entered into a catalog, while the absence of that `catalogued` element could mean that the book has not been catalogued.

An element declared to be `EMPTY` that is not optional isn't very helpful unless it is declared to have one or more attributes. For example, our `catalogued` element could be defined to have an attribute named `date`, the value of which might indicate the date on which the information about the containing `book` element was catalogued. And, of course, the optionality of an element and the definition of attributes for that element can be used together.

The element named `review` is permitted to have any content at all, including an arbitrary mixture of text and child elements. The child elements have to be declared somewhere in the DTD, but they are not cited in the definition of an element declared as `ANY`.

The content of the `title` element can be a mixture of ordinary text (indicated as `#PCDATA`) and child elements taken from `ital`, `bold`, and `under` but no others. They can appear in any order and any number of times.

The author element's content is limited strictly to child elements, and they must be a salutation element, a given element, a family element, and a suffix element, in that order. The use of the comma between child element names indicates that the elements must appear one after the other; another possibility would be a vertical bar (|) to indicate a choice of two elements. Some of the child elements are optional, as indicated by the question mark (?); other possibilities for this occurrence indicator are an asterisk (*) to indicate that the child element may appear zero or more times and a plus (+) to indicate that the child must appear at least one time. The absence of this indicator requires that the child element appear exactly once.

Example 5-4 *Elements Based on Element Declaration Examples*

```
<catalogued/>

<review>This is a <ital>really</ital> interesting book, but
<pronoun>I</pronoun>, for one, didn't <under>really</under>
understand it and I doubt that <name>Roger</name> did,
either.</review>

<title>A <bold>Bold</bold> Tale of <ital>Three</ital>
Towns</title>

<author><salutation>Dr.</salutation><given>Bob</given>
<family>Smith</family></author>
```

Example 5-4 contains a number of "snippets" of XML — elements that are presumably part of some complete XML document — that illustrate the implications of the declarations in Example 5-3.

Note that, as required, the element catalogued is empty. The review element has mixed content that includes a number of child elements that were not specified as part of the review element's definition.

By contrast, the example of the title element contains mixed content, but it includes only child elements that were specified in the element's definition. It's worth pointing out that it is not possible in DTDs to restrict the order in which such child elements can appear or the number of times that they can appear.

Finally, the author example demonstrates that the content must comprise *only* child elements and that they must appear in the sequence specified. Notice that the `suffix` element does not appear; this omission is valid because it was declared to be optional.

Element declarations can (optionally) have attribute list declarations associated with them. The syntax of an attribute list declaration can be seen in Example 5-5.

Example 5-5 *Attribute List Declaration Syntax*

```
<!ATTLIST element-name
attribute-name attribute-type attribute-default
... >
```

element-name specifies the element to which the attribute list declaration applies. The syntax of DTDs does not require that the attribute list declarations appear close to their associated element declarations, though it makes for easier reading if the attribute declarations immediately follow the associated element declarations. An attribute list declaration isn't required to actually declare any attributes; we haven't seen many examples of this in the wild, but it's valid anyway.

Each attribute is given a unique (within the associated element) *attribute-name,* and each attribute has a specific *attribute-type* and an *attribute-default*. Attribute types are either the keyword CDATA,[5] one of a list of "token" types, a notation reference, or a list of specific identifiers that are permitted, as shown in Example 5-6.

Example 5-6 *Attribute Types*

```
CDATA

ID
IDREF
IDREFS
```

5 CDATA, CDATA, and #PCDATA: XML documents are allowed to contain "CDATA sections," which allow the documents to contain literal left angle brackets and ampersands (that is, without being represented as character references or entities); in a CDATA section, the appearance of "`<title>`" is treated as ordinary character data and not as markup. Attribute declarations may declare the data type of an attribute to be CDATA, or character data; perhaps surprisingly, the value of an attribute declared to be CDATA cannot contain left angle brackets or ampersands. The keyword #PCDATA derives historically from the term *parsed character data,* which means that character data is expected, but it must be parsed to determine whether it contains markup.

```
ENTITY
ENTITIES
NMTOKEN
NMTOKENS

NOTATION ( notation-name )
NOTATION ( notation-name | notation-name | ... )

( identifier )
( identifier | identifier | ... )
```

An element is allowed to have at most one attribute whose type is ID (and, in our experience, the most common name for such attributes is `id`), and the value of that attribute must be unique among the values of all attributes of type ID throughout the containing document.

Attributes whose types are IDREF or IDREFS have values that must match the ID attribute of some element in the same document. Attributes of type ENTITY or ENTITIES have values that must be the names of unparsed entities declared in the DTD (we do not cover the concept of unparsed entities in this book). Attributes declared to be of type NMTOKEN or NMTOKENS have values that are valid identifiers ("name tokens").

An attribute whose type is a list of one or more identifiers is obviously related to one whose type is NMTOKEN or NMTOKENS. However, if the explicit list is specified, then the values of that attribute must be one of the specified identifiers.

An attribute of type NOTATION has values that identify notations declared in the DTD (we do not cover notations in this book). No element can have more than a single attribute declared of type NOTATION.

The attribute declaration may declare a specific value that is the default value for the attribute whenever it is omitted from an instance of the containing element. If that specific value is preceded by "#FIXED", then the attribute must be included in all element instances and its value is never allowed to be different from the specified value.

An attribute default may place additional limits on the values that an attribute can take. If the default is specified to be "#REQUIRED", then the attribute has no default and must be specified for every use of the element in which it is declared. If the default is "#IMPLICIT", then the attribute is optional.

Example 5-7 illustrates several variations of attribute declarations.

Example 5-7 *Examples of Attribute Declarations*

```
<ATTLIST book
  ISBN          ID                    #REQUIRED
  retail-price  CDATA                 #IMPLICIT
  size          ( folio | quarto ) ( quarto )
  document-type NMTOKEN               (#FIXED book) >
```

This review of DTDs covered only those characteristics that determine the structure of XML documents that are expected to be valid with respect to their DTDs. There are other features of DTDs that are useful in defining a document type, but that don't affect the instance documents structurally.

In Section 5.2.4 is a complete example of an XML document and its associated DTD.

5.2.3 Limited Capabilities, Especially with Respect to Data Types

DTDs have a number of limitations in their descriptions of instance documents. One of these, mentioned in Section 5.2.2, makes it impossible for a DTD to govern the sequence of child elements in an element defined to have mixed content. As you saw in the discussion of Example 5-3, such an element in an instance document is allowed to have a mixture of ordinary text and any number of each of the child elements cited in its definition, in any order.

As a result, each of the occurrences of the `para` element illustrated in Example 5-8 are valid with respect to the DTD fragment in the same example.

Example 5-8 *Examples of Elements with Mixed Content*

```
<!ELEMENT para ( #PCDATA | ital | bold | under )*>

<para>This <ital>really</ital> is <bold>not</bold> helpful.</para>

<para>George should get a raise this year.</para>
```

```
<para><bold>Three</bold> years before <ital>this</ital> mast really is enough for
anybody.</para>

<para><ital>I</ital> do <ital>my</ital> work <ital>my</ital> way.</para>
```

Recall that the origin of DTDs is in SGML and that the principle purpose of SGML is to mark up *text*. When marking up, say, paragraphs of ordinary text, it's entirely appropriate that the DTD not specify the sequence in which child elements may occur, the number of times they may occur, or the interweaving of those elements and plain text. This gives the authors of that text considerable flexibility in marking up the text for the eventual readers' consumption.

However, when the text being marked up must be highly structured, such as a formal description of an automobile, one might wish to adopt some rules, such as the following:

- Start off with plain text.
- Use the `automobile` element to identify which automobile is being discussed.
- Continue with more plain text, optionally marked up for appearance (*e.g.*, italics, boldface).
- Use the `price` element to specify the cost of the automobile.
- Optionally, include more plain text.
- Use the `availability` element to state when deliveries will start.
- Continue with more plain text.
- Optionally, use any number of `feature` elements to cite features of the automobile.
- Continue with more plain text, optionally marked up for appearance.

DTDs are unable to express such sets of structural rules. One might wish for the ability to define a mixed-content `automobile` element such as the DTD fragment illustrated in Example 5-9, but it's simply not possible according to the current rules for DTDs.

Example 5-9 *Mixed Content: Wishful Thinking*

```
<!ELEMENT automobile ( #PCDATA, automobile, ( #PCDATA | emph | bold ),
    price, #PCDATA?, availability, #PCDATA, feature*,
    ( #PCDATA | emph | bold ) )>
```

Another limitation of DTDs concerns the data types that it supports. Essentially, the only data type that DTDs support is text. The content of every nonempty element is either child elements, ordinary text, or a mixture of the two. "Ordinary text" is represented as PCDATA (or "parsed character data"). Attributes are limited to contain text, either in the form of CDATA (which is ordinary character data, or text) or in the form of one of the more specialized types, such as ID, IDREF, ENTITY, or NOTATION. While each of those types have certain semantics associated with them (for example, the ID type requires that the value of the attribute be unique among all attributes of type ID in the instance document), their values are in fact nothing more than character strings, or text.

But consider the `retail-price` attribute declared in Example 5-7. Most people would expect an attribute with that name to represent some sort of monetary value, perhaps in U.S. dollars, Japanese yen, or Turkish lira. Such values are by nature *numeric,* and one might want to be able to validate them as numbers and manipulate them using numeric operations, such as addition and multiplication.

Unfortunately, DTDs provide no way to specify that the values of attributes or the content of elements are limited to numeric data, dates, or any other type beyond textual data. As a result, it is perfectly valid, if perhaps meaningless, to find a `book` element in an instance XML document that contains a `retail-price` attribute whose value is "Twenty One Dollars and Thirty Nine Cents" or even "If you have to ask, you can't afford it." Such values would clearly be rather unhelpful to applications that wish to compute the average retail price of all books referenced in a bibliography!

Writing queries to retrieve information from XML documents and to report and analyze that information depends to some degree on being able to reliably use data values in the manner in which the documents' authors intended them to be used. Without enforceable rules about the detailed structure of the XML (structural typing) and about the values of attributes and the content of elements (data typing) within that XML, the act of writing queries is necessarily more an art than a science.

5.2.4 An Example Document and DTD

It's frequently easier to understand concepts when a concrete example is available to illustrate the uses of those concepts. DTDs are no exception to that broad rule.

Let's see what a complete example — both an instance XML document and its associated DTD — would contain. The instance document (including an internal subset DTD) can be seen in Example 5-10 and the external subset DTD in Example 5-11. In this example, the internal subset DTD adds a declaration for a new global element, named `author`, that can be used in the document itself.

Example 5-10 *An XML Document with DTD*

```
<?xml version="1.0" encoding="UTF-8"?>
<!DOCTYPE bibliography SYSTEM "biblio.dtd" [
  <!ELEMENT author ( salutation?, given, family, suffix? )> ]>
<bibliography>
  <books>
    <book ISBN="ISBN-0-19-853737-9" document-type="book"
          retail-price="189.00">
      <title>The SGML Handbook</title>
      <author><salutation>Dr.</salutation><given>Charles F.</given>
              <family>Goldfarb</family>
      </author>
      <review>
        <para>This review was found on the web and seems a little
              harsh, but what can one do?
        </para>
        <para>
          This book is, regrettably, the one authoritative book on the
          SGML standard. Given how broad and confusing the SGML standard
          is, it's not surprising that this book on it is equally opaque
          -- this is, in my experience, the worst-written technical book
          I've ever seen that is not actually inaccurate.
          But if you're doing serious SGML development, you have no
          choice but to get this book and to spent forever trying to
          make sense of it.
        </para>
        <para>
          But beware: if you're doing just XML, and if you think
          <quote>well, since XML is a form of SGML, I might as well
```

```
        get the SGML standard</quote>, don't do it!
        XML is all you need to know, then just look at the
        XML standard, at ... and maybe also get a book specifically
        about XML.
        I happen to like Eckstein and Casabianca's
        <emph>XML Pocket Reference</emph>,
        partly because it's less than one-tenth the price of
        the SGML standard, and a hundred times more useful!
      </para>
    </review>
    <catalogued date="1991-03-22"/>
  </book>
  <book ISBN="1-55860-456-1" document-type="book">
    <title>SQL:1999 Understanding Relational Language Components</title>
    <author><given>Jim</given>
            <family>Melton</family>
    </author>
    <author><given>Alan R.</given>
            <family>Simon</family>
            <suffix>PhD.</suffix>
    </author>
    <catalogued/>
  </book>
  <book ISBN="1-861005-06-7" retail-price="34.99" document-type="book">
    <title>XSLT Programmer's Reference</title>
    <author><given>Michael</given><family>Kay</family></author>
    <review>Dang, this book is great!</review>
  </book>
  <book ISBN="0-864742-321-7" document-type="book">
    <title>India</title>
    <author><given>Hugh</given><family>Finlay</family></author>
    <author><given>Tony</given><family>Wheeler</family></author>
    <author><given>Bryn</given><family>Thomas</family></author>
    <author><given>Michelle</given><family>Coxall</family></author>
    <author><given>Leanne</given><family>Logan</family></author>
    <author><given>Geert</given><family>Cole</family></author>
    <author><given>Prakash A.</given><family>Raj</family></author>
    <review>
      Not yet reviewed: be the first on your block to review this book!
        </review>
        <catalogued date="2001-07-13"/>
```

```
    </book>
  </books>
  <papers/>
</bibliography>
```

Example 5-11 *An External Subset DTD (in biblio.dtd)*

```
<?xml version="1.0"?>
<!ELEMENT bibliography ( books, papers )>

<!ELEMENT books ( book* )>

<!ELEMENT papers ( paper* )>

<!ELEMENT book ( title, author+, review?, catalogued? )>
<!ATTLIST book
  ISBN          ID                  #REQUIRED
  retail-price  CDATA               #IMPLICIT
  size          ( folio | quarto )  quarto
  document-type NMTOKEN             #FIXED book >

<!ELEMENT title ( #PCDATA | ital | bold | under )*>

<!ELEMENT salutation ( #PCDATA )>

<!ELEMENT given ( #PCDATA )>

<!ELEMENT family ( #PCDATA )>

<!ELEMENT suffix ( #PCDATA )>

<!ELEMENT review ANY>

<!ELEMENT catalogued EMPTY>
<!ATTLIST catalogued
  date CDATA #IMPLIED>

<!ELEMENT ital ( #PCDATA | ital | bold | under )*>

<!ELEMENT bold ( #PCDATA | ital | bold | under )*>
```

```
<!ELEMENT under ( #PCDATA | ital | bold | under )*>
<!ELEMENT para ( #PCDATA | ital | bold | under | quote | emph )*>

<!ELEMENT quote ( #PCDATA )>

<!ELEMENT emph ( #PCDATA )>
```

5.3 XML Schema

In Section 5.2, we explored DTDs and the ways in which they specify the structural metadata for XML documents. Among other things, we learned that DTDs have some deficiencies that may prevent certain important classes of applications from accomplishing their goals. Among these are the inability to specify certain types of limitations on the content of elements and the inability to specify the data types required for both attribute values and element content.

In this section, we discuss another W3C specification that supports the definition of structural metadata for XML documents. This specification, usually called "XML Schema" or just "Schema," was published in 2001 as three documents. The first is a primer[6] and is not normative but is intended more as a tutorial to illustrate various important features of the normative parts.

The second part[7] specifies the XML document structures that XML Schema can be used to specify. As we'll see shortly, XML Schema structure definitions are considerably more powerful than those supported by DTDs. The last part[8] provides a number of data types that can be used to specify the types of attribute values and element content.

XML Schema, especially Part 1, has sometimes been criticized for its complexity. Although the documents themselves are somewhat difficult to read and grasp, the facilities that XML Schema provides have proven to be extremely valuable to applications of all sorts. Not surprisingly, more requirements have been submitted for future versions of XML Schema by enterprise-level users as well as by indi-

---

6 *XML Schema Part 0: Primer* (Cambridge, MA: World Wide Web Consortium, 2001). Available at: http://www.w3.org/TR/2001/REC-xmlschema-0-20010502/.

7 *XML Schema Part 1: Structures* (Cambridge, MA: World Wide Web Consortium, 2001). Available at: http://www.w3.org/TR/2001/REC-xmlschema-1-20010502/.

8 *XML Schema Part 2: Datatypes* (Cambridge, MA: World Wide Web Consortium, 2001). Available at: http://www.w3.org/TR/2001/REC-xmlschema-2-20010502/.

viduals. Like many standards, it seems likely that Schema's complexity is likely to increase along with corresponding improvements in its capabilities.

The development of XML Schema, which began in late 1998, came about because of increasing use of XML for purposes beyond simple document markup. DTDs, as we said in Section 5.2.3, have several shortcomings with respect to complex XML requirements. One of these is the inability to express the sorts of complex structures, and constraints on those structures, that applications were beginning to require in their XML documents. The other, of course, was the desire to express the data types of values found in XML documents, enabling much more powerful manipulation of that data. (We observe that XML Schema lacks some of the capabilities of DTDs, the most important one being the ability to specify and use entities.)[9]

We explore the capabilities of XML Schema with respect to these requirements over the next few sections. However, we think it's worth observing that most people are intimidated by the complexity of *XML Schema Part 1: Structures*, when they first start to read, understand, and use it. We agree that the document and the language are rather complex, but we also believe that diligent study and experimentation will allow most users to write meaningful XML Schemas and begin to appreciate the power that it provides.

In our discussion of XML Schema, we start off gently, illustrating — through a couple of relatively simple examples — XML Schema documents' "look and feel." Next, we cover the data type facilities provided by XML Schema, followed by some exploration of the structural capabilities it provides. We end up with a modest example that puts it all together.

5.3.1 Exploring an XML Schema

The first thing you'll notice about the XML Schema in Example 5-12 is that, unlike a DTD, an XML Schema is itself written in XML — that is, it is an XML document. This simple fact means that all of the many XML tools built to edit, process, and transform XML docu-

9 We have been told that the decision not to support entities in XML Schema was intentional: In SGML, as well as in the pre-Schema days of XML, entities were often used in the same way as macros in programming languages, thereby obfuscating DTDs to the point where they became almost useless. The intent of XML Schema was to offer more appropriate mechanisms, such as groups, attribute groups, include, import, redefine, and so forth.

ments can be employed for handling XML Schema documents. (Another important side effect of this fact is that XML Schema documents can be queried in the same manner as other XML documents.)

This example, by the way, is taken directly from XML Schema Part 0 (the primer).

Example 5-12 *Sample XML Schema Document*

```
<xs:schema xmlns:xsd="http://www.w3.org/2001/XMLSchema">

 <xs:annotation>
  <xs:documentation xml:lang="en">
   Purchase order schema for Example.com.
   Copyright 2000 Example.com. All rights reserved.
  </xs:documentation>
 </xs:annotation>

 <xs:element name="purchaseOrder" type="PurchaseOrderType"/>

 <xs:element name="comment" type="xsd:string"/>

 <xs:complexType name="PurchaseOrderType">
  <xs:sequence>
   <xs:element name="shipTo" type="USAddress"/>
   <xs:element name="billTo" type="USAddress"/>
   <xs:element ref="comment" minOccurs="0"/>
   <xs:element name="items"  type="Items"/>
  </xs:sequence>
  <xs:attribute name="orderDate" type="xsd:date"/>
 </xs:complexType>

 <xs:complexType name="USAddress">
  <xs:sequence>
   <xs:element name="name"   type="xsd:string"/>
   <xs:element name="street" type="xsd:string"/>
   <xs:element name="city"   type="xsd:string"/>
   <xs:element name="state"  type="xsd:string"/>
   <xs:element name="zip"    type="xsd:decimal"/>
  </xs:sequence>
  <xs:attribute name="country" type="xsd:NMTOKEN"
     fixed="US"/>
 </xs:complexType>
```

```
<xs:complexType name="Items">
 <xs:sequence>
  <xs:element name="item"
              minOccurs="0" maxOccurs="unbounded">
   <xs:complexType>
    <xs:sequence>
     <xs:element name="productName" type="xsd:string"/>
     <xs:element name="quantity">
      <xs:simpleType>
       <xs:restriction base="xsd:positiveInteger">
        <xs:maxExclusive value="100"/>
       </xs:restriction>
      </xs:simpleType>
     </xs:element>
     <xs:element name="USPrice"  type="xsd:decimal"/>
     <xs:element ref="comment"   minOccurs="0"/>
     <xs:element name="shipDate"
                 type="xsd:date" minOccurs="0"/>
    </xs:sequence>
    <xs:attribute name="partNum" type="SKU" use="required"/>
   </xs:complexType>
  </xs:element>
 </xs:sequence>
</xs:complexType>

<!-- Stock Keeping Unit, a code for identifying products -->
<xs:simpleType name="SKU">
 <xs:restriction base="xsd:string">
  <xs:pattern value="\d{3}-[A-Z]{2}"/>
 </xs:restriction>
</xs:simpleType>

</xs:schema>
```

There's a lot of information to absorb in this example, so we'll take it in small chunks.

The very first line, paired with the very last line, identifies this bit of XML as an XML Schema document. The portion of the line that reads

```
xmlns:xs="http://www.w3.org/2001/XMLSchema"
```

defines a *namespace* by means of a Uniform Resource Identifier (URI) and a corresponding *prefix* by which the namespace will be referenced within this particular document. Namespaces[10] are used as qualifiers for element names, attribute names, and such in XML documents. To put it another way, namespaces allow a developer to define a group of names without having to check that none of his names clashes with any other name.

As with qualifiers for identifiers in any language, this permits multiple objects with the "same name" to be differentiated based on the value of the qualifier. (For example, SQL users are familiar with the ability to create multiple columns with the name PRICE, provided those columns are in different tables. The table name is used as a qualifier for the column name to ensure that the proper column is uniquely identified. Similarly, Java programmers are able to qualify the names of classes with the name of the package that contains them, which prevents any confusion arising from the coincidence of a class contained in one package having a name that is the same as the name of a class contained in a different package.)

Throughout this XML Schema document, the namespace prefix `xs:` is used to reference the namespace identified by the URI `http://www.w3.org/2001/XMLSchema`. It's allowable for an XML document to contain multiple prefixes that reference the same namespace, but it's rather uncommon except in applications that use Schema documents that are composed of fragments with different authors.

The content of the (optional) element `<xs:annotation>` serves to document all or part of an XML Schema document as well as providing information to applications that might process the schema document. In the schema in Example 5-12, the content of the `<xs:annotation>` element is nothing more than an `<xs:documentation>` element, but XML Schema permits `<xs:appinfo>` elements as well.[11]

---

10 *Namespaces in XML 1.1* (Cambridge, MA: World Wide Web Consortium, 2004). Available at: http://www.w3.org/TR/xml-names11.

11 The `<xs:documentation>` element children of an `<xs:annotation>` element is intended for human consumption and is permitted to contain user-defined elements and attributes as needed. By contrast, the `<xs:appinfo>` element children are intended for use by software; it also may contain user-defined elements and attributes, as needed by the software that utilizes this element. The XML Schema Recommendation does not limit what user-defined elements and attributes are allowed in either the `<xs:annotation>` or `<xs:appinfo>` element.

The line

```
<xs:element name="purchaseOrder" type="PurchaseOrderType"/>
```

defines an element that documents based on this XML Schema can include. (This particular element, `purchaseOrder`, happens to be the "root" of the structure definition; as such, it has to be the first declaration in the schema.) The element's name, as you can readily ascertain, is `purchaseOrder`. The type of that element is perhaps a little less obvious.

Many people new to XML tend to think of a "type" as something like an integer, floating-point, or character string, as this Schema document uses to define the `comment` element:

```
<xs:element name="comment" type="xsd:string"/>
```

In most modern programming languages (and in XML as a markup language), the word *type* is somewhat broader than that. In the XML context, it describes the legitimate content of an element or attribute. Sometimes, that type might be a *simple type* (which, as discussed in Section 5.3.2, corresponds to ordinary data types), but it might also be a *complex type* (a structure type, as discussed in Section 5.3.3).

Complex types can be given an explicit name, or they can be *anonymous*. In this case, the type of the element `purchaseOrder` is a complex type named `PurchaseOrderType`. Another way of saying the same thing is that the complex type `PurchaseOrderType` defines the *content model* of the `purchaseOrder` element. But what does that mean? To determine that, we have to read only a little further, where we see:

```
<xs:complexType name="PurchaseOrderType">
```

which is where the `PurchaseOrderType` complex type is defined, repeated in Example 5-13.

Example 5-13 *Content of Complex Type Definition: PurchaseOrderType*

```
<xs:complexType name="PurchaseOrderType">
  <xs:sequence>
    <xs:element name="shipTo" type="USAddress"/>
```

```
      <xs:element name="billTo" type="USAddress"/>
      <xs:element ref="comment" minOccurs="0"/>
      <xs:element name="items"  type="Items"/>
    </xs:sequence>
    <xs:attribute name="orderDate" type="xsd:date"/>
  </xs:complexType>
```

This is, obviously, a named complex type. Its definition tells us that a usage of the PurchaseOrderType (such as in the definition of the purchaseOrder element) has only child element content — that is, no mixed content is allowed — and that those children must be a sequence of elements. The first element is named shipTo and the second is named billTo; both are of type USAddress. After the billTo element, there are any number of instances of the comment element (including none at all), which was defined earlier. Finally, elements defined to be of the PurchaseOrderType must contain one additional element, whose name is items and whose type is Items. Elements defined to be of PurchaseOrderType must also have an attribute named orderDate, whose type is xsd:date.

Subsequent lines in Example 5-12 define the two complex types USAddress and Items. Consider the snippet of the Items element definition that appears in Example 5-14.

Example 5-14 *Simple Type Definition*

```
<xs:element name="quantity">
  <xs:simpleType>
    <xs:restriction base="xsd:positiveInteger">
      <xs:maxExclusive value="100"/>
    </xs:restriction>
  </xs:simpleType>
</xs:element>
```

This defines the element named quantity to have a simple (not complex) type, and that simple type is based on an XML Schema built-in type named positiveInteger. However, the <xs:restriction> element within this simple type definition limits the values of the quantity element's content to the range 1 through 99.

With this relatively simple example and brief explanation under our belts, let's explore the primitive and other simple types provided by *XML Schema Part 1*.

5.3.2 Simple Types (Primitive Types and Derived Types)

XML Schema Part 2: Datatypes defines a fairly large set of data types that can be used to specify the types of attributes and of element content.

In that document, a data type is defined to be "a 3-tuple, consisting of (a) a set of distinct values, called its value space; (b) a set of lexical representations, called its lexical space; and (c) a set of facets that characterize properties of the value space, individual values, or lexical items." While some of that terminology might not be familiar, it's not particularly complex, so let's break it down.

In an abstract sense, a data type is really nothing more than a collection of values. In effect, it is the mathematical domain over which some collection of operations can act. XML Schema, quite helpfully, goes somewhat further than that abstract definition, by distinguishing between the set of values involved and the manner(s) in which those values can be represented as a sequence of characters. For example, the character sequences "1," "01," and "0000000000001" are all lexical representations of the number we commonly call "one." Some data types may allow other representations as well, such as "1.0" and "0.1E1."

In the context of XML Schema, the values belonging to a data type can be specified in several ways: *axiomatically* (that is, from fundamental notions, such as mathematical rules), by enumeration, or by restricting the values belonging to another data type. The lexical representations are character strings that represent the values.

The set of facets cited in the *XML Schema Part 2* definition of data type provides a way for XML Schema to define precisely what characteristics the value of a data type may have. For example, a character string value has a length, and the character string type uses two specific facets, minLength and maxLength, to specify the minimum allowed length and the maximum allowed length, respectively. For example, the character string represented by "Querying XML" has a length of 12 characters.

Many implementations of a character string type limit the lengths of character string values to approximately 4 billion characters (even though others might have no limit other than the size of available storage). Every character string must contain at least zero characters — that is, negative lengths are not permitted, but zero-length strings are. Therefore, the minimum value of the minLength and maximum value of the maxLength facets for the character string type for some implementations might have the values zero and 4 billion, respectively.

XML Schema provides a number of built-in primitive data types as well as a number of additional built-in types that are derived from the built-in primitives. A derived type is a type that is derived from another simple type, normally by restricting the set of values allowed; the derivation may also arise from forming a list of values of another data type or by forming the union of two or more data types (meaning the union of their value spaces and their lexical spaces). Primitive types are limited to those specified by *XML Schema Part 2*, while derived types include not only those provided by part 2 but also those that might be provided by applications.

We could derive our own type based on the character string type, applying further restrictions on the maximum and minimum lengths. For example, we might need a type to represent U.S. postal codes (ZIP codes), which must always have at least five characters and can have no more than 10 characters. The minimum- and maximum-length facets of such a derived type, possibly named `ZIPcodes`, would thus be 5 and 10, respectively.

The (built-in) primitive types defined by XML Schema are shown in the first column of Table 5-1; the built-in types that are derived from each of those primitive types are shown in the second column. Notice that some derived types have yet more types derived from them. Unless we indicate otherwise, each of these derivations is done by restricting the values of the type from which the derivation is performed. We note that the actual names of each of these types is associated with the namespace for which the `xs:` prefix is commonly used. Readers should consult *XML Schema Part 2* for the specific meaning of each of these types.

***Table 5-1** Built-in Types*

Primitive Types	Derived Types	Source of Derived Type
string	normalizedString	
	token	normalizedString
	language	token
	NMTOKEN	token
	NMTOKENS	NMTOKEN (derived by list)
	Name	token
	NCName	Name

Table 5-1 *Built-in Types (continued)*

Primitive Types	Derived Types	Source of Derived Type
	ID	NCName
	IDREF	NCName
	IDREFS	IDREF (derived by list)
	ENTITY	NCName
	ENTITIES	ENTITY (derived by list)
boolean		
decimal	integer	
	nonPositiveInteger	integer
	negativeInteger	nonPositiveInteger
	long	integer
	int	long
	short	int
	byte	short
	nonNegativeInteger	integer
	unsignedLong	nonNegativeInteger
	unsignedInt	unsignedLong
	unsignedShort	unsignedInt
	unsignedByte	unsignedShort
	positiveInteger	nonNegativeInteger
float		
double		
duration		
dateTime		
date		
time		
gYearMonth		
gYear		
gMonthDay		
gDay		
gMonth		
hexBinary		
base64Binary		

Table 5-1 *Built-in Types (continued)*

Primitive Types	Derived Types	Source of Derived Type
`anyURI`		
`QName`		
`NOTATION`		

All of the built-in data types of XML Schema belong to the XML Schema namespace, often indicated by the prefix "`xs:`." The corresponding namespace URI is: `http://www.w3.org/2001/XMLSchema`. Any namespace prefix can be used, as long as it is associated with the appropriate namespace URI. Application-defined schemas can derive additional types from any type in that list, but those application-defined derived types must belong to an application-defined namespace (that is, not the namespace indicated in this chapter by the prefix `xs:`).

In the sample schema in Example 5-12, the line that reads

```
<xs:element name="USPrice"  type="xs:decimal"/>
```

defines an element (`USPrice`) whose content is of type `xs:decimal`.

XML Schema Part 2 spends a considerable fraction of its size specifying various characteristics of data types, their facets, and their limitations. Much of that space provides an XML representation of the XML Schema definition of the types themselves. That material is beyond the scope of this book, as is describing each of the built-in types.

5.3.3 Complex Types and Structures

A detailed presentation of the XML Schema facilities defined in Part 2 would easily fill a book as large as this one. Rather than attempt to compress that amount of information into a few pages, this section discusses only the fundamental concepts that are especially relevant to querying XML documents.

As we told you in Section 5.3, XML Schema's ability to describe rules for constructing XML documents, especially the structure of element content, significantly exceeds that of DTDs in several ways. Conversely, it is possible by using combinations of XML Schema's facilities to represent any content model that can be represented by a DTD.

Example 5-12 illustrates a number of XML Schema's abilities to specify complex types and structures, so we'll use that sample Schema to describe some of the features, starting off by recapping some of what we said in Section 5.3.1. Consider the lines in Example 5-15 that we copied from Example 5-12.

Example 5-15 *Complex Type Definition: PurchaseOrderType*

```
<xs:complexType name="PurchaseOrderType">
  <xs:sequence>
    <xs:element name="shipTo" type="USAddress"/>
    <xs:element name="billTo" type="USAddress"/>
    <xs:element ref="comment" minOccurs="0"/>
    <xs:element name="items"  type="Items"/>
   </xs:sequence>
  <xs:attribute name="orderDate" type="xsd:date"/>
</xs:complexType>
```

The `<xs:complexType>` element is used in an XML Schema to define a *named* complex type that can then be used in one or more element declarations to specify the content model and attributes of those elements. For instance, in Example 5-15 we see two elements, `shipTo` and `billTo`, that are defined to be of a single type, `USAddress`. There must, of course, be a definition of a type with that name elsewhere, and a definition elsewhere (see Example 5-12) provides that (complex) type. This instance of `<xs:complexType>` defines a type named `PurchaseOrderType`, which can then serve as the type of some element declared in this schema.

The `<xs:sequence>` element specifies that the object in which it is contained (a complex type definition, in this case) contains a sequence of child elements that must appear in the specified order.

The `<xs:element>` element declares an element that is used as the content of the object in which it is contained (in this case, the sequence). In the case of the first instance of `<xs:element>`, the `shipTo` element is declared as the first element in the sequence comprising the complex type named `PurchaseOrderType`. Several features of the `<xs:element>` element are illustrated in this snippet. First, you see that both the `shipTo` and `billTo` elements are declared with the `USAddress` type, showing both that elements can be declared to have a complex type that is defined elsewhere in the schema and that multiple elements can be declared to have the same (named) complex type.

Second, note that the comment element is declared with the attribute minOccurs, which is given a value of 0. As the name implies, use of this attribute requires that the element being defined must occur a minimum number of times; the value 0 means that the comment is optional. The corresponding maxOccurs attribute could be specified but is not in this case. The default value for both attributes is 1. The absence of the maxOccurs attribute thus means that the comment element can appear a maximum of once. If the intent is to permit the element to occur any number of times, the maxOccurs attribute can be given the value "unbounded."

The <xs:attribute> element specifies that all elements declared to be based on PurchaseOrderType have this one attribute, named orderDate, whose data type is xsd:date.

In the definition of the complex type Items found in Example 5-16, you'll see that Items is a sequence, the first element of which is an element named item.

Example 5-16 *Complex Type Definition: Items*

```
<xs:complexType name="Items">
  <xs:sequence>
   <xs:element name="item"
               minOccurs="0" maxOccurs="unbounded">
    <xs:complexType>
     <xs:sequence>
      <xs:element name="productName" type="xsd:string"/>
      <xs:element name="quantity">
       <xs:simpleType>
        <xs:restriction base="xsd:positiveInteger">
         <xs:maxExclusive value="100"/>
        </xs:restriction>
       </xs:simpleType>
      </xs:element>
      <xs:element name="USPrice"  type="xsd:decimal"/>
      <xs:element ref="comment"   minOccurs="0"/>
      <xs:element name="shipDate"
                  type="xsd:date" minOccurs="0"/>
     </xs:sequence>
     <xs:attribute name="partNum" type="SKU" use="required"/>
    </xs:complexType>
   </xs:element>
  </xs:sequence>
 </xs:complexType>
```

The interesting thing about the declaration of the `item` element is its type. Let's zoom in a little closer on the initial lines of the definition of the `item` element in Example 5-17.

Example 5-17 *Anonymous Complex Type Definition*

```
<xs:element name="item"
            minOccurs="0" maxOccurs="unbounded">
  <xs:complexType>
    ...
  </xs:complexType>
  ...
</xs:element>
```

Note that the type of the `item` element is another complex type but that this type isn't given a name — it's an *anonymous* complex type, indicated by the absence of a `name` attribute on the `<xs:complexType>` element.

The anonymous type of the `item` element is a sequence, the first two components being elements named `productName` and `quantity`. Comparing the declarations of those two elements, we see that the first is declared to be of type `xs:string`, while the second is of type `xs:positiveInteger`. However, the two declarations are significantly different in construction. The type of the `productName` element is specified through use of the `type` attribute, while the type of the `quantity` element has a child element, `<xs:simpleType>`.

In the case of the `quantity` element, the use of `<xs:simpleType>` is required in order to define the element to have a restriction on its values (in this case to be no less than 1, the smallest value of a positive integer, and no greater than 99, as indicated by the `maxExclusive` attribute's value).

Table 5-2 *Features of XML Schema Part 1: Structures*

Feature	XML Schema	DTD
Syntax	XML document	Non-XML
Simple types	Part 2's xs: types	Strings and string-like attribute types
Occurrence constraints	minOccurs, maxOccurs attributes	?, *, +
Complex type definition	<xs:complexType>	*No real analog*

Table 5-2 *Features of XML Schema Part 1: Structures (continued)*

Feature	XML Schema	DTD
Mixed content	<xs:complexType mixed="true">	#PCDATA used with element names as alternatives
Sequence of child elements	<xs:sequence>	Element names separated by commas
Choice of child elements	<xs:choice>	Element names separated by vertical bar
Groups	<xs:group>	Parameter entities, parenthesized sequences, or parenthesized choices
Entities	*No analog*	<!ENTITY>
Type derivation	Yes	No
Type re-use	Yes	No

When you need to declare an element that has both a simple type (such as `xs:string`, `xsd:positiveInteger`, or `xsd:date`) and an attribute, you (counterintuitive though it may be) cannot just use the `type` attribute but must instead declare the element as an `<xs:complexType>` with `<xs:simpleContent>`. Example 5-12 contains no instance of such an element, so we've illustrated this situation in Example 5-18.

Example 5-18 *Allowing Attributes on Elements of Simple Types*

```
<xs:element name="deliveryDate">
  <xs:complexType>
    <xs:simpleContent>
      <xs:extension type="xsd:date">
        <xs:attribute name="verified" type="xsd:Boolean"/>
      </xs:extension>
    </xs:simpleContent>
  </xs:complexType>
</xs:element>
```

Table 5-2 compares and contrasts some of common features of *XML Schema Part 2* with similar features of DTDs. The table's three columns identify an item of interest, the XML Schema approach, and the DTD approach, respectively. The items in the XML Schema column and the DTD column are not identical in semantics; major differences between the two technologies make exact comparisons difficult in some cases.

5.4 Other Schema Languages for XML

XML Schema, especially the aspects defined in Part 1, is a complex language with great flexibility and power. It is somewhat intimidating when first encountered (which some products ameliorate through the use of a graphical user interface, or GUI). Many people find XML Schema instance documents difficult to read and interpret. As a consequence, other ways of expressing structural metadata for XML have been devised (though not in the context of the W3C).

5.4.1 RELAX NG

One of the best-known alternative schema languages is RELAX NG.[12] The RELAX NG tutorial[13] describes the language as "based on RELAX and TREX." RELAX[14] (regular language description for XML) is an earlier effort by Murata Mokoto to provide a schema language for XML documents, while TREX[15] (tree regular expressions for XML) is a language designed by James Clark of the Thai Open Source Software Center for the same purpose. (The "NG" in the name is widely assumed to stand for "New Generation," but that's not officially part of the name.)

Like XML Schema, RELAX NG is a language that specifies structural metadata (which it calls a "pattern") for XML documents and thus "identifies a class of XML documents consisting of those documents that match the pattern." Also like schemas defined using XML Schema, RELAX NG schemas are themselves XML documents. Unlike XML Schema, RELAX NG provides both the "formal" XML syntax and an equivalent non-XML syntax called the "compact syntax."

---

12 *RELAX NG Specification* (OASIS, 2001). Available at: http://www.relaxng.org/spec-20011203.html.

13 *RELAX NG Tutorial* (OASIS, 2001). Available at: http://www.relaxng.org/tutorial-20011203.html.

14 ISO/IEC TR 22250-1, *Document Description and Processing Languages – Regular Language Description for XML (RELAX) – Part 1: RELAX Core* (Geneva, Switzerland: International Organization for Standardization, 2001).

15 James Clark, *TREX – Tree Regular Expressions for XML Language Specification*, James Clark (Bangkok, Thailand: Thai Open Source Software Center, 2001). Available at: http://www.thaiopensource.com/trex/spec.html.

RELAX NG's XML syntax is, in some ways, reminiscent of XML Schema's syntax. For example, elements are declared with an `<element>` element, while attributes are declared with `<attribute>` elements. Instead of using the occurrence indicators (?, *, and +) used by XML Schema, RELAX NG uses elements `<optional>`, `<zeroOrMore>`, and `<oneOrMore>`. The `<mixed>` element allows arbitrary interleaving of ordinary text and (specified) child elements, analogous to XML Schema's `<complexType mixed="true">`.

RELAX NG depends on a number of W3C specifications, including Namespaces. It also allows applications to reference externally defined data types, including those defined by *XML Schema Part 2*. Specific RELAX NG schemas are allowed to use data types defined in one namespace (such as the XML Schema namespace indicated by the prefix `xs:`) for some elements in the schema and data types defined in another namespace for other elements. Implementations of RELAX NG are allowed to choose the externally defined data types that are permitted in the schemas they support.

Example 5-19 contains an illustrative RELAX NG schema expressed in the full syntax, while Example 5-20 contains the compact syntax for the same schema.

Example 5-19 *RELAX NG Schema: Full Syntax*

```
<element name="toDoList" xmlns="http://relaxng.org/ns/
structure/1.0">
  <zeroOrMore>
    <element name="actionItem">
      <element name="action">
        <text/>
      </element>
      <element name="dueDate">
        <text/>
      </element>
    </element>
  </zeroOrMore>
</element>
```

Example 5-20 *RELAX NG Schema: Compact Syntax*

```
element toDoList {
  element actionItem {
    element action { text },
    element dueDate { text }
  }*
}
```

5.4.2 Schematron

Yet another schema language, which serves a somewhat narrower purpose than RELAX NG, is Schematron.[16] Schematron is a "language for specifying assertions about arbitrary patterns in XML documents" and can be used in conjunction with (in fact, embedded within) other schema languages, including XML Schema and RELAX NG. Like XML Schema and RELAX NG, Schematron depends on several W3C specifications, including Namespaces. Unlike those other two languages, Schematron is not grammar-based but uses XPath path expressions to express the structures and constraints of the XML documents it describes.

Schematron uses `<assert>` elements to make positive assertions about an XML document; when that document is validated against a Schematron schema instance with an assertion and the test for that assertion fails, the application that invoked the validation is notified and can take whatever action it deems appropriate. Schematron `<assert>` elements may include a `test` attribute that specifies, in XPath notation, a predicate that evaluates to a Boolean value corresponding to the truth of the assertion. The `<report>` element can make negative assertions about a document.

The `<assert>` and `<report>` elements are always children of a `<rule>` element, which includes a `context` attribute that identifies the context in which the `<assert>` and `<report>` elements are evaluated. Example 5-21 shows a simple Schematron rule that could be used to validate an XML document containing the element `<car><wheel/><wheel/><wheel/><wheel/></car>`.

Example 5-21 *Schematron Rule*

```
<rule context="car">
   <assert test="count(wheel) = 4">A 'car'
    element should contain four 'wheel' elements.</assert>
   <report test="propeller">
    This car has a propeller.</report>
</rule>
```

Note that this rule specifies that the context of the rule is a `car` element, that it asserts that the `car` element must contain exactly

16 Rick Jelliffe, The Schematron Assertion Language 1.5. Available at http://xml.ascc.net/resource/schematron/Schematron2000.html.

four `wheel` elements, and that human-readable text corresponding to the formal assertion `test="count(wheel) = 4"` is included. The rule also includes the assertion that the `car` element must *not* contain a `propeller` element, along with human-readable text corresponding to that negative assertion, `test="propeller"`.

5.4.3 Decisions, Decisions, Decisions

You've just had a brief survey of each of three schema languages, and you might be a bit confused about which one to use. After all, learning a schema language can be a considerable commitment, particularly when you end up with huge collections of instance XML documents that are expected to validate against schemas in that language.

XML Schema has the advantage of being supported by the W3C and thus is likely to fit quite nicely into applications that depend on other W3C recommendations. It has the further advantage of being extremely powerful and flexible. In exchange, it is rather complex and intimidating.

RELAX NG is less powerful and flexible than XML Schema, meaning that it cannot express every possible construct that XML Schema can express. But it is arguably easier to learn and, when the compact syntax is used, usually found to be easier to read – and perhaps easier to write. It has another possible advantage in that it doesn't come "bundled" with a particular set of simple types but can use any simple type library that the application chooses.

Schematron is not really a complete schema language. Instead, it is a language in which constraints on data can be expressed. In general, the constraints that can be expressed in Schematron are somewhat more powerful than those that either XML Schema or RELAX NG can express. Consequently, some applications might choose to use both XML Schema and Schematron (or both RELAX NG and Schematron) concurrently to validate XML instance documents.

While it's not obvious to us which of the various schema languages are likely to capture the greatest mind share, we suspect that XML Schema will be used by most enterprises simply because of its W3C support and the significant number of tools and other applications that depend on it.

5.5 Deriving an Implied Schema from a DTD

As suggested by Example 5-22 and Example 5-23, it's possible to transform one structural metadata language into another. The RELAX NG specifications include a document[17] that describes the relationship between XML's DTDs and RELAX NG schemas. A number of XML tools (including products such as Altova's XMLSpy and Sonic Software's Stylus Studio, cited here only because we are personally familiar with their capabilities) provide the ability to convert from DTDs to XML Schemas. (Interestingly, Stylus Studio performs the transformation by means of a tool, Trang, licensed from the Thai Open Source Software Center, the home of TREX.)

For comparison purposes, Example 5-22 shows the internal subset DTD equivalent to the RELAX NG schema shown in Example 5-19 and Example 5-20, while Example 5-23 holds a corresponding XML Schema document. This particular XML Schema document was produced by XMLSpy, transforming the DTD into an XML Schema. Other XML Schemas could be created that have the same effect, perhaps using named types instead of anonymous types.

Example 5-22 *DTD Equivalent to RELAX NG Schema*

```
<!DOCTYPE toDoList [
<!ELEMENT toDoList (actionItem*)>
<!ELEMENT actionItem (action, dueDate)>
<!ELEMENT action (#PCDATA)>
<!ELEMENT dueDate (#PCDATA)>
]>
```

Example 5-23 *An XML Schema Equivalent to RELAX NG Schema and DTD*

```
<?xml version="1.0" encoding="UTF-8"?>
<xs:schema xmlns:xs="http://www.w3.org/2001/XMLSchema"
           elementFormDefault="qualified">
  <xs:element name="toDoList">
    <xs:complexType>
      <xs:sequence>
        <xs:element name="actionItem" ref="actionItem"
                    minOccurs="0" maxOccurs="unbounded"/>
      </xs:sequence>
```

17 *RELAX NG DTD Compatibility* (OASIS, 2001). Available at: http://relaxng.org/compatibility.html.

```
      </xs:complexType>
    </xs:element>
    <xs:element name="actionItem">
      <xs:complexType>
        <xs:sequence>
          <xs:element name="action" ref="action"/>
          <xs:element name="dueDate" ref="dueDate"/>
        </xs:sequence>
      </xs:complexType>
    </xs:element>
    <xs:element name="action" type="xs:string"/>
    <xs:element name="dueDate" type="xs:string"/>
  </xs:schema>
```

5.6 Chapter Summary

In this chapter, we have illustrated and discussed several mechanisms that allow the specification of structural and data type metadata for XML documents. Each of the methods has its adherents and its detractors. Each also has its own set of capabilities. As we saw, DTDs are in many ways less flexible and powerful than XML Schemas, but they are arguably easier to read and may suffice when more complex structures or specific data types are not required. RELAX NG may be attractive when its compact syntax is appropriate but well-defined data types are needed in element and attribute definitions.

The benefits for querying XML documents, when structural and data type metadata for those documents exists, is clear. If each of a group of XML documents is known to have the structure implied by the XML Schema shown in Example 5-12, we could retrieve information from each of those documents based on that structure. For example, we could ask for the order date of every purchase shipped to New York City but billed to an address in San Francisco. The query might be worded (in pseudo-code) thusly:

> Return the value of the `orderDate` attribute of each `purchaseOrder` element in which (a) the value of the content of the `city` element that is a child of the `shipTo` element is "New York" and the value of the content of the `state` element that is a child of the `shipTo` element is "NY" and (b) the value of the content of the `city` element that is a child of the `billTo` element is "San Francisco" and

> the value of the content of the `state` element that is a child of the `billTo` element is "CA".

Writing such a query is trivial when the documents are known to adhere to the structure required by that schema but difficult and unreliable when the documents have arbitrary structures.

Chapter

6

The XML Information Set (Infoset) and Beyond

6.1 Introduction

Look at any XML document and you will see a sequence of tags and values set out on a page or a computer screen. Zoom in (metaphorically) and it's a sequence of characters. Zoom in again and it's some ink on a page or pixels on a screen or bits in memory or on a disk. In whatever form the XML document is presented, that form *represents* some information – the cast of a movie, the line items in a purchase order, or the sections and chapters of this book. When a program performs operations on XML – query, update, extract – it does not need or want to deal with bits in memory or even with tags and values. The program wants to operate on the information itself.

To that end, the W3C has defined a more abstract representation of that information, the XML Information Set, or Infoset. In this chapter, we look at the Infoset in some detail and then describe some of the later developments. The Post-Schema-Validation Infoset (PSVI) was defined by the XML Schema Working Group to add type and validation information to the Infoset. The XPath 1.0 Data Model, though similar to the Infoset, added some important notions that influenced the data models that followed (particularly the XQuery Data Model). The Document Object Model (DOM), though strictly speaking an API, has an implicit data model closely related to the Infoset. We end the chapter with a brief introduction to the XQuery

Data Model (described in more detail in Section 10.6, "The Data Model"), the most ambitious effort yet, which has both strong typing and an API.

The descriptions in this chapter (and indeed in this book) are necessarily incomplete. The goal is to give the reader a general understanding of the concepts rather than a reference manual from which to implement a query engine. That said, we go into a fair amount of detail on the Infoset, which lays the foundations for other data models. And we go into some detail on the XQuery Data Model and type system in the next chapter, since it is so central to the XQuery language.

6.2 What Is the Infoset?

The XML Information Set, or Infoset, is an abstract representation of the core information in an XML document. That is, the Infoset encapsulates the meaning of a document, so an XML processor need not be concerned about variations in syntax. Every *well-formed* XML document that conforms to the W3C XML Namespace recommendation[1] can be represented as an Infoset. An XML document does not have to be *valid* (conform to a DTD or Schema) to be represented as an Infoset.

The W3C XML Information Set Recommendation[2] ("Infoset") defines the Infoset representation of a document as a set of information items. There are 11 information items, and each information item has a set of properties. The Infoset information items are summarized in the next section; for a complete description, see the Information Set Recommendation.

Note that not all the information contained in a document is represented in the Infoset (see Section 6.4). The goals of the Infoset Recommendation are to select the most generally useful information in a document and to define how to represent that information in a standard way using standard terminology. Interestingly, the recommendation itself says it exists only so that other specs have a standard way of talking about information in a document. Nonetheless, the Infoset has become the basis for several more sophisticated data models used by XML processors (more on data models later).

---

1 *Namespaces in XML* (Cambridge, MA: World Wide Web Consortium, 1999). Available at: http://www.w3.org/TR/REC-xml-names/.

2 *XML Information Set (Second Edition)* (Cambridge, MA: World Wide Web Consortium, 2004). Available at: http://www.w3.org/TR/xml-infoset/.

6.3 The Infoset Information Items and Their Properties

The W3C XML Information Set Recommendation defines 11 kinds of information items. Each information item (except the Namespace information item) is associated with a definition and/or some syntax given in the W3C XML recommendation.[3] Each information item has a set of properties, and a property may itself contain one or more information items – for example, the [children] property of an element might include element information items.

The Infoset information items and their properties are summarized next. The top-level bullets represent information items, and their names are **in bold**. The second-level bullets describe properties of those information items. Property names are enclosed in square brackets [ ].

1. **Document Information Item** –The document information item is the starting point for all the information items in the Infoset. Think of an Infoset as a tree in which each tree node represents either some character data or an XML marked-up construct (*e.g.*, an element, a comment, or a processing instruction) and each branch is a "parent/child" relationship. The document information item is the *root node* in that tree. It is a notional node; *i.e.*, it is not represented in the character string or printed form of the XML document. It exists only so that the Infoset is truly a tree – so that an XML processor can start at the document information item and visit any part of the Infoset using common tree-walking algorithms. Take a look at Figure 6-4 (near the end of the chapter). An Infoset representing only the nodes that are part of the XML document, those below the dashed line, would not be a tree – we need to add a notional root node (the document information item) to make it a tree. Its properties include:
   a. Information from the XML declaration ([character encoding scheme], [standalone], [version]).
   b. The **[document element]** property – contains the element information item for the document element. The document element is the single top-level

3 *Extensible Markup Language (XML) 1.0 (Third Edition)* (Cambridge, MA: World Wide Web Consortium, 2004). Available at: http://www.w3.org/TR/REC-xml/.

element in the XML document ("movie" or "movies" in most of our examples). This top-level element is sometimes referred to as the "root element," since it is the root of the tree of elements within the Infoset tree. We said the document information item (see earlier) is the root node — remember, not all *nodes* in the Infoset tree are *elements*. The root element may have sibling nodes that are *not* elements (the prolog, comments, processing instructions). In Figure 6-4, the element "A" is the root element, while "R" is the root node. Other XML abstractions have the same concepts but use different names. We will refer back to the "root element" and "root node" for consistency.

c. **[children]** — a list of information items representing the children of the document information item, in document order. This list contains exactly one *element* information item, which represents the "document element," plus information items for processing instructions and comments that are children of the root node. If there is a DTD declaration, its information item appears here, too.

d. **[all declarations processed]** — is "not strictly speaking part of the Infoset of the document" (according to the Infoset spec). This property is metadata describing the state of the Infoset build. If true, it means that all declarations in the document have been read and processed, that is, everything that can be known about the document is known. If false, some properties may be "unknown" (*e.g.*, the references property of the attribute information item).

2. **Element Information Item** — Each element information item represents an XML element. Its properties include:

   a. **[children]** — a list of child information items, in document order. The list includes an element information item for each child element as well as information items for processing instructions and comments in the XML element. [children] also includes an information item for each data character and unexpanded entity reference in the XML element.

b. **[parent]** – the information item for the parent of this XML element. This is an element information item, except where the XML element is the root element, in which case the parent is a document information item. Notice that the treelike structure of an XML document is preserved by the [parent] and [children] properties.

c. **[attributes]** – an unordered set of attribute information items. Information items in this set may come directly from the text of the document, or they may be introduced by DTD defaults.

d. **[local name]** – the (local) name of this element, *e.g.*, "movie" or "title."

e. **[namespace name]** – the namespace URI reference (if any). The namespace name and the local name together uniquely name this element.[4]

f. **[prefix]** – the namespace prefix, if any. If the prefix is present, it must be associated with a namespace name.

3. **Attribute Information Item** – The attribute information item represents an attribute. Its properties are:

   a. **[owner element]** – the element information item of the element in which this attribute appears. Note that, according the Infoset specification, the relationship between an attribute and its associated element is *not* a parent/child relationship; it's an owner element/attribute relationship.[5]

---

4 The XML 1.0 spec refers to the string between "<" and ">" in a start tag that names an element as the element's **type**, or **element-type**. Oddly, it refers to the analogous string for an attribute as an **attribute name**. These strings may consist of a namespace prefix plus a local name, separated by a colon (making up a **qualified name**). The namespace prefix, if it exists, must be associated with a namespace URI reference (also known as a **namespace name**). If the Infoset is processed by a namespace-aware processor, the processor must use the namespace name, not the prefix – the prefix is just a placeholder for the namespace name.

5 The XPath 1.0 spec refers to an attribute's owner element as its parent, but it explicitly says that an attribute is *not* a child of its owner (parent) element. The XQuery Data Model spec uses this same definition for an element/attribute relationship.

b. **[normalized value]** – the value of the XML attribute, normalized as specified by the W3C XML Recommendation. Normalization resolves character references and entity references, replaces each white-space character (#x20,[6] #xD, #xA, #x9) with a space character (#x20) and replaces all end-of-line characters with #xA. Unless the attribute type is CDATA, normalization also collapses sequences of spaces to a single space and removes leading and trailing spaces.

c. **[specified]** – a flag to show whether the attribute was specified as part of its owner element or produced by defaults in a DTD. This is one place where the Infoset preserves information that would be needed to reconstruct the XML document exactly. We will see other places where the Infoset discards such information.

d. **[local name]** – the name of this attribute.

e. **[namespace name], [prefix]** – the namespace name and namespace prefix, if any, of the name of this attribute (see also the earlier discussion of the element information item).

f. **[attribute type]** – the type, if any, of this attribute. Possible values are ID, IDREF, IDREFS, ENTITY, ENTITIES, NMTOKEN, NMTOKENS, NOTATION, CDATA, and ENUMERATION. The Infoset specification first became a recommendation in the same year as XML Schema (2001), and it deals with only DTD types, not the much richer set of types available in XML Schema.

g. **[references]** – if the attribute type is IDREF, IDREFS, ENTITY, ENTITIES, or NOTATION, then the [references] property is an ordered list of the element, unparsed entity, or notation information items referenced in the attribute value. Otherwise, this property has no value.[7]

---

6 The convention here for character codepoints is used in many XML specifications. "#xN" denotes the codepoint with the hexadecimal value N.

4. **Processing Instruction (PI) Information Item** – The PI information item represents a processing instruction. Its properties include:
   a. **[target]** – the target of the PI.
   b. **[content]** – the content of the PI.
   c. **[parent]** – the document, element, or document type declaration information item for the parent of this PI.
5. **Unexpanded Entity Reference Information Item** – The unexpanded entity reference information item provides a mechanism for a nonvalidating XML parser to indicate that an entity reference has been read but not expanded. The motivation for this information item is that some applications, such as browsers, may not want to immediately expand every entity reference. Unexpanded entity reference properties include:
   a. **[name]** – the name of the entity.
   b. **[system identifier]** – the system identifier of the entity, as it appears in the entity declaration.

---

7 Actually, this is a simplification. The Infoset spec describes three other cases that result in the [references] property of an attribute having no value. The attribute value might be syntactically invalid. The attribute type might denote that the attribute value can only legally reference a unique thing, whereas the attribute value actually references something that is *not* unique within the document (*e.g.*, the attribute might be an IDREF that references an ID that occurs more than once in the document). Or the attribute type might denote that the attribute value references some (not necessarily unique) thing, whereas the attribute value actually references something that does not exist within the document (*e.g.*, the attribute might be an IDREF that references an ID that does not occur in any ID attribute in the document). In this latter case, there is an exception when the [all declarations processed] property of the document information item is false. This means the thing we are trying to reference *might* exist somewhere, and we just haven't read it yet, so the [references property] is "unknown."

How did this description get so complicated? Most of the complexity arises when we need to account for the cases where the document is not valid (*e.g.*, there are multiple attributes of type ID with the same value) or where the processor has not yet attempted to find out whether or not the document is valid (*i.e.*, where not all declarations have been processed). If the tiny amount of type information taken into account when building the Infoset (the 10 attribute types available in the DTD) can introduce this much complexity, imagine how complicated it is to build the XQuery Data Model based on the broad range of data types, structure types, and validation/validity states allowed in the PSVI. Or just read on.

   c. **[public identifier]** – the normalized public identifier of the entity.
   d. **[parent]** – the element information item that contains this information item in its [children] property.

6. **Character Information Item** – The Infoset contains a character information item for each data character in the XML document. Information about where this character came from – whether it appeared literally in the document, as a character reference or in a CDATA section – is discarded. Only the contents of elements (and not, for example, attribute values) are counted as "data characters."[8] Character information item properties are:
   a. **[character code]** – the ISO 10646 (UCS) character code (equivalently, the Unicode code point).
   b. **[element content white space]** – a flag to indicate whether this character is "white space in element content." This property enables an XML processor to *preserve* white space in element content when it sees the xml:space [**preserve**] attribute.
   c. **[parent]** – the element information item of the element containing this character data.
7. **Comment Information Item** – The comment information item represents a comment. Its properties are:
   a. **[content]** – a string, the content of the comment.
   b. **[parent]** – the element information item for this comment's parent.
8. **Document Type Declaration Information Item** – The Infoset contains at most one Document Type Declaration information item, containing information about processing instructions from the DTD. Information about entities and notations from the DTD appears in the document information item, not here. PIs from the internal DTD subset appear before those in the external subset, but there is no way to distinguish between the two sources. Much of the content of the DTD, including the definition of element and attribute

8 This is consistent with the XPath 1.0 Data Model notion of a "text node" as a collection of data characters that does not include attribute values and with the idea that attribute values are somehow not quite data.

structures, is discarded. The Document Type Declaration information item properties are:

a. **[system identifier]** – the system identifier of the external DTD subset, as it appears in the DOCTYPE declaration.

b. **[public identifier]** – the normalized public identifier of the external DTD subset.

c. **[children]** – an ordered list of processing instruction information items, representing processing instructions appearing in the DTD.

d. **[parent]** – the document information item.

9. **Unparsed Entity Information Item** – There is an unparsed entity information item for each unparsed general entity declared in the DTD. An unparsed entity references non-XML data – data that the XML processor is not expected to parse – such as a gif image. Unparsed entity properties include:

    a. **[name]** – the name of the entity.

    b. **[system identifier]** – the system identifier of the unparsed entity, as it appears in the DOCTYPE declaration.

    c. **[public identifier]** – the normalized[9] public identifier of the unparsed entity.

    d. **[notation name]** – the notation name associated with the unparsed entity.

    e. **[notation]** – the information item for the notation named in [notation name].[10]

10. **Notation Information Item** – There is a notation information item for each notation declared in the DTD. Notation properties include:

    a. **[name]** – the name of the notation.

---

9 To **normalize** an identifier, replace each string of white space with a single space character (#x20), and remove leading and trailing white space.

10 The [notation] property of an unparsed entity may have no value (if there are zero or many notations with the name in [notation name]), or it may be "unknown" (if there are no notations with that name and not all declarations have been processed). See also the footnote discussion of the [references] property of an attribute.

   b. **[system identifier]** – the system identifier of the external DTD subset, as it appears in the DOCTYPE declaration.
   c. **[public identifier]** – the normalized public identifier of the notation.
11. **Namespace Information Item** – For every element, there is a namespace information item for each of its in-scope namespaces. Namespace properties are:
   a. **[prefix]** – the namespace prefix.
   b. **[namespace name]** – the namespace name (URI) to which the prefix is bound.

From this description of the information items that go to make up an Infoset, it is clear that the Infoset represents both the data and the structure of an XML document. The data is represented in the information items and their properties, and the treelike structure is preserved by the [parent] and [children] properties. The Infoset also preserves some, but not all, of the information needed to reconstruct the original XML document, so parts of the Infoset can be serialized – put back into an XML document – in only one way, while other parts could map to an XML document in several ways.

Consider a sample `movie` document, Example 6-1.

***Example 6-1** A Sample `movie` Document*

```
<?xml version="1.0" encoding="UTF-8"?>
<!-- movie – a simple XML example -->
<movie myStars="5">
     <title>An American Werewolf in London</title>
     <yearReleased>1981</yearReleased>
     <director>
        <familyName>Landis</familyName>
        <givenName>John</givenName>
     </director>
     <producer>
        <familyName>Folsey</familyName>
        <givenName>George, Jr.</givenName>
        <otherNames/>
     </producer>
     <producer>
        <familyName>Guber</familyName>
```

```
            <givenName>Peter</givenName>
            <otherNames/>
        </producer>
        <producer>
            <familyName>Peters</familyName>
            <givenName>Jon</givenName>
            <otherNames/>
        </producer>
        <runningTime>98</runningTime>
        <cast>
            <familyName>Agutter</familyName>
            <givenName>Jenny</givenName>
            <maleOrFemale>female</maleOrFemale>
            <character>Alex Price</character>
        </cast>
    </movie>
```

Figure 6-1 shows a tree representation of (part of) the Infoset for Example 6-1.

6.4 The Infoset vs. the Document

We started this chapter by saying that the Infoset is "an abstract representation of the core information in an XML document." Before we go any further, let's dissect this definition to clarify the relationship between Infoset and document.

The Infoset is *not* the document. The Infoset takes some of the information conveyed by the XML document and represents it in an abstract way. This abstract representation may in turn be represented in a number of ways — as a tree diagram, as a table, or even as another XML document. The most common representation of an Infoset is an in-memory structure as part of an application. Unfortunately, the Infoset Recommendation does not specify an API to such a structure. Both the representation of the Infoset and the provision of an API to get at information items are left up to the implementation.

As we just said, the Infoset does not represent *all* the information in an XML document. So what information is included and what is left out? Let's take another look at the sample movie document in Example 6-1. Assume for now that when we say "the document," we actually mean the ink on the page. (Of course, the ink on the page is itself an abstraction. You may even be reading a different abstraction — say,

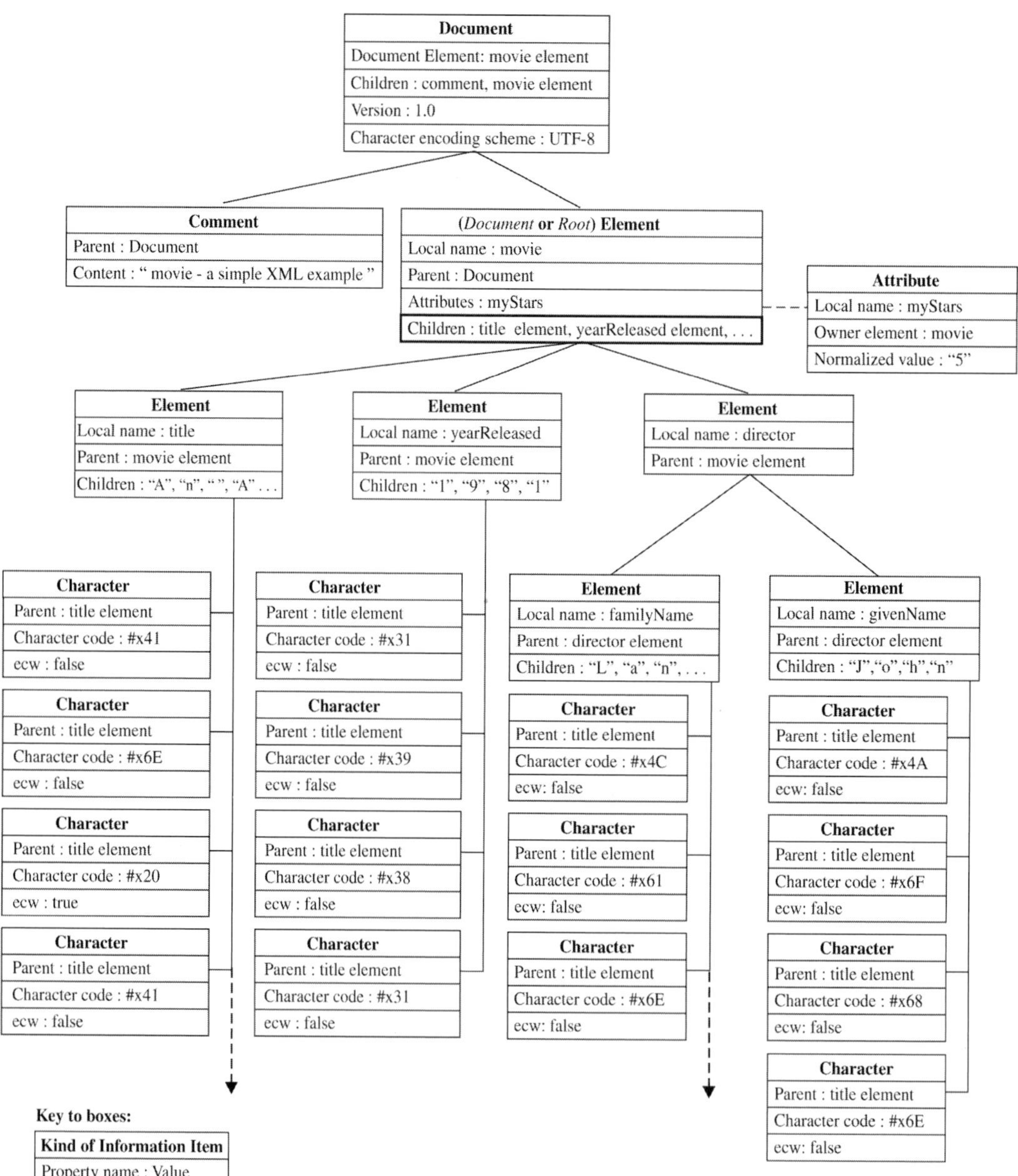

Figure 6-1 *Infoset Tree for a Sample movie Document.*

pixels on a screen. But for now we'll assume that the ink on the page is the ultimate reality.) There is some information conveyed by the ink on the page that is obviously *not* relevant to an XML processor — the size of the font, the color of the ink, the kinds of quotes around attribute values. And most of the information in the Infoset clearly *is* relevant — such as the data itself and the parent–child structure. But some information is borderline — information that is in the document, but not in the Infoset, that might be considered relevant. For example:

- **The source of characters** — Character information is represented in the Infoset as character information items. The only properties of a character information item are [character code], [element content white space], and [parent]. In other words, the Infoset tells us what characters are in the data but not how they got there. CDATA sections, general parsed entities, and character references, if present in the XML document, cannot be reconstructed just by looking at the Infoset.
- **Order of attributes** — Attributes appear in a document in a particular order, but the [attributes] property of the element information item in the Infoset is an unordered set — *i.e.*, the Infoset Recommendation says that attribute order is unimportant, and so it is not preserved. In addition, attribute values are white-space-normalized (*e.g.*, multiple white-space characters are collapsed to a single white space, and leading and trailing white space is removed).
- **Empty elements** — An empty element may appear in a document either in the form "`<movie/>`" or in the form "`<movie></movie>`." The Infoset does not distinguish between the two.

See Appendix D of the Infoset Recommendation for a nonexhaustive list of information not represented in the Infoset.

Interestingly, an early working draft of the Infoset[11] defined six more information items (for a total of 17). The extra information items — internal entity, external entity, entity start and end markers, and CDATA start and end markers — would have made it easier to reconstruct a document from its Infoset. The decision to drop these information items was a good one — this information is syntactic rather than semantic and does not belong in the Infoset.

11 *XML Information Set, W3C Working Draft 2* (Cambridge, MA: World Wide Web Consortium, 2001). Available at: http://www.w3.org/TR/2001/WD-xml-infoset-20010202/.

Some of the Infoset information may come from a DTD. DTDs have a small amount of information about types — for example, an attribute may have a type, one of ID, IDREF, IDREFS, ENTITY, ENTITIES, NMTOKEN, NMTOKENS, NOTATION, CDATA, or ENUMERATION. But the Infoset does not include type information from an XML Schema. This is the biggest shortcoming of the Infoset, and it's addressed by an extension to the Infoset known as the Post-Schema-Validation Infoset, or PSVI (see Section 6.6).

An Infoset may[12] be created from a document, usually via an XML parser. The resulting Infoset is an abstract representation of the essence of that document. If the Infoset is then serialized, the resulting document will contain the same information as the document we started with, but the two documents will probably not be identical.[13]

Now we have a good picture of what the Infoset is, what's in it, and how it relates to a document. But what is the Infoset good for? The main benefit of the Infoset is that it offers an XML processor an abstraction of what's important in the document. Operations on documents can be defined in terms of the Infoset, and the XML processor can ignore details like character entity evaluation.

6.5 The XPath 1.0 Data Model

The XPath 1.0 Data Model, though similar to the Infoset, added some important notions that influenced the data models that followed (particularly the XQuery Data Model). The XPath 1.0[14] Data Model is a tree representation of an XML document. The tree is defined in terms of seven types of nodes — root, element, text, attribute, namespace, processing instruction, and comment nodes. Four of the Infoset information items are not represented in the XPath Data Model — unexpanded entity references, unparsed entities, DTD, and notation items. Six of the others map one-to-one to XPath data model nodes. And one — the Infoset's character item — is represented as a collection of character items in the XPath Data Model's text node. See

12 An application may create an Infoset that does *not* represent any document — *e.g.*, an Infoset that represents an intermediate result of some processing.

13 For some tips on creating XML in a canonical form, see *Canonical XML* (Cambridge, MA: World Wide Web Consortium, 2001). Available at: http://www.w3.org/TR/xml-c14n.

14 *XML Path Language (XPath) Version 1.0* (Cambridge, MA: World Wide Web Consortium, 1999). Available at: http://www.w3.org/TR/1999/REC-xpath-19991116.

the XPath 1.0 Recommendation for a mapping from the XPath Data Model to the Infoset.[15]

The XPath 1.0 Data Model introduces several important notions:

- The Infoset describes the information in an XML document as information items. Though these items are hierarchic in nature and have a single top-level item, the Infoset spec purposely avoids using the terms *tree* and *nodes*.[16] The XPath 1.0 Data Model, on the other hand, talks about the data model as a *tree*, made up of *nodes*.
- The XPath 1.0 Data Model introduces the notion of a *text node*, made up of "a sequence of one or more consecutive character information items."
- In the XPath 1.0 Data Model, every node has an associated string value. The string value may represent a single value (as in the string value of a text node or an attribute node), or it may be the concatenation of the string values of all the descendant text nodes.
- Since XPath 1.0's purpose is to query (*address* is the XPath term) documents, it includes the notion of a *node set*, the precursor to XQuery's sequences. Interestingly, the node set is not a part of the XPath 1.0 Data Model, which models only input to XPath expressions, not output.

Figure 6-2 shows an XPath 1.0 Data Model tree for the sample `movie` document, Example 6-1. The figure is smaller than Figure 6-1 because the individual character items are now collected together into text nodes. It is also simpler because a lot of the information in the Infoset (such as anything to do with entities or DTDs) is not represented.

---

15 *XML Path Language (XPath) Version 1.0, Appendix B* (Cambridge, MA: World Wide Web Consortium, 1999). Available at: http://www.w3.org/TR/1999/REC-xpath-19991116#infoset.

16 The Infoset spec says: The terms *information set* and *information item* are similar in meaning to the generic terms *tree* and *node*, as they are used in computing. However, the former terms are used in this specification to reduce possible confusion with other specific data models. Information items do *not* map one-to-one with the nodes of the DOM or the "tree" and "nodes" of the XPath data model.

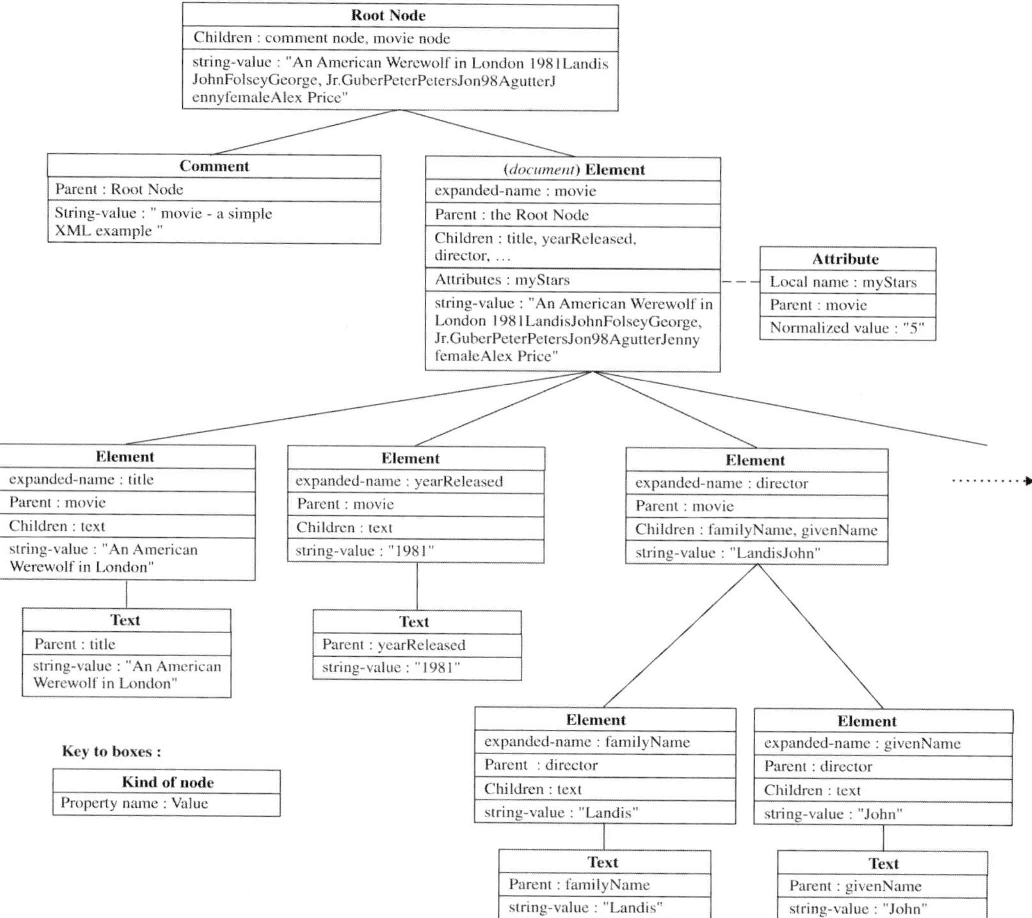

Figure 6-2 *XPath 1.0 Data Model Tree for a Sample movie Document.*

6.6 The Post-Schema-Validation Infoset (PSVI)

The Infoset provides an abstraction of the data and structure in a document, so a processor can deal with information items and their properties. The only type information in the Infoset is the attribute type information available in a DTD. However, if the document can be associated with an XML Schema, then there is a lot of valuable information available — type information — that cannot be represented in the Infoset as it is defined by the Infoset Recommendation. To address this, the XML Schema Recommendation Part 1[17] ("Schema 1") defines extensions ("augmentations") to the Infoset, to form a Post-Schema-Validation Infoset, or PSVI. The PSVI is an abstraction, just as the Infoset is — it's an abstraction of the information represented in the document *augmented by* the information in the XML Schema.

6.6.1 Infoset + Additional Properties and Information Items

When you validate an XML document against an XML Schema, the Schema processor augments the Infoset of that document by adding properties to attribute and element information items. Validation also adds some new information items not defined in the Infoset.

"Schema 1" defines about two dozen additional properties of element information items. For example:

- **[validity]** — validity of the element: valid, invalid, or notKnown.
- **[validation attempted]** — what kind of validation was attempted: full, none, or partial.
- **[validation context]** — a reference to the nearest ancestor with a [schema information] property, *i.e.*, a pointer to the schema against which the document was validated.
- **[schema normalized value]** — generally, the white-space-normalized content of a leaf node. Similar to the string value in the XPath Data Model, but here white-space-normalization rules are derived from the element's schema definition.
- **[type definition type]** — simple type or complex type.
- **[type definition anonymous]** — true (anonymous type) or false (named type).
- **[type definition name]** — if not anonymous, the name of the type. If anonymous, may contain a processor-supplied unique name.

---

17 *XML Schema Part 1: Structures Second Edition* (Cambridge, MA: World Wide Web Consortium, 2004). Available at: http://www.w3.org/TR/xmlschema-1/.

- **[identity constraint table]** – contains an identity-constraint binding information item for each unique or key constraint in the schema.

As well as these additional properties, the PSVI introduces several other information items, such as:

- **Identity-constraint binding information item** – contains information on unique and key constraints.
- **Namespace schema information item** – Properties include [schema documents], a set of schema document information items.
- **Schema document information item** – Properties are [document location], a URI, and [document], a document information item.

Many of these additional properties can be associated with attributes as well as elements.

6.6.2 Additional Information in the PSVI

So what information can we get from a PSVI that we cannot get from an Infoset? The PSVI gives us lots of information about the schema validity of the document as well as information about types.

Schema Validity

Schema validity, as "Schema 1" tells us, is "not a binary predicate"! First, you can choose to validate in a number of ways – strict (everything must be valid), lax (if it's defined in the schema it must be valid, else ignore it), or skip (don't try to validate anything against the schema). Second, you can mix and match these validation modes within a document – *i.e.*, you can do strict validation on some parts of the document, skip on some others, and lax on the rest. The PSVI tracks which kind of validation was done where as well as the result (valid, invalid, notKnown) for each element and attribute.

Types

An XML Schema may contain a lot of information about types. In the Schema world, type information covers structure type information as well as data type information.

Complex types define the structure of an element — the valid attributes, children and content of an element.

Simple types define the data type of the (simple)[18] content of an element or of the value of an attribute.

XML Schema data types are defined in *XML Schema Part 2: Data Types*[19] [Schema 2]. XML Schema has the following built-in data types:

- Primitive types — familiar data types such as string, Boolean, decimal, float.
- Derived types — built-in types derived from the primitive types, such as normalizedString, integer, positiveInteger.

In addition, users can define:

- Complex types (named or anonymous) — Complex type, as opposed to a simple type, describes an element that has one or more attributes or child elements. Think of a complex type as describing a subtree rather than a leaf node.
- Derived types — defined by restricting or extending built-in types or user-defined types.

See Chapter 5, "Structural Metadata," for a more detailed discussion of XML Schema types.

6.6.3 Limitations of the PSVI

We have seen that the PSVI adds structure type and data type information to the Infoset. This information is useful when querying XML. But the PSVI does not go far enough.

---

18 *Simple content* is the content of an attribute or of an element that does not have any child elements.

19 *XML Schema Part 2: Datatypes Second Edition* (Cambridge, MA: World Wide Web Consortium, 2004). Available at: http://www.w3.org/TR/xmlschema-2/.

- The PSVI type system is not quite extensive enough for query purposes (we see in Chapter 10, "Introduction to XQuery 1.0," that the XQuery Data Model adds some more types).
- There is no API for the PSVI – the DOM, probably the most widely used API, only knows about the Infoset (see Section 6.7).
- The PSVI only deals with documents – when querying XML, we need to consider arbitrary *sequences* of documents, nodes, and/or values. (Some would argue that "sequences" should also be on that list, but at the time of writing even the XQuery Data Model cannot model sequences of sequences.)

6.6.4 Visualizing the PSVI

There is an enormous amount of information in the PSVI for even a simple document – Figure 6-3 shows just a small part of the PSVI information for one element (the title) of the sample `movie` document, Example 6-1.

6.7 The Document Object Model (DOM) — An API

The Document Object Model (DOM) is fundamentally different from the Infoset and the PSVI. While the Infoset and PSVI are data models – they define an abstract representation of the data in an XML document – the DOM is an API. It defines an interface to the data and structure of an XML (or HTML) document so that a program can navigate and manipulate them. The DOM is language- and platform-independent: The specification defines bindings for Java and ECMAScript (a scripting language very close to JavaScript). If you have written any dynamic web pages using JavaScript, you have probably used the DOM without realizing it.[20]

The DOM is defined in a suite of W3C Recommendations.[21] The DOM Level 1 Specification[22] defines a set of objects – in the sense of

20 For a simple description of how the DOM plays in DHTML (Dynamic HTML), see Fabian Guisset, *The DOM and JavaScript*. Available at: http://www.mozilla.org/docs/dom/reference/javascript.html.

21 *Document Object Model Activity Statement* (Cambridge, MA: World Wide Web Consortium, 2005). Available at: http://www.w3.org/DOM/Activity.

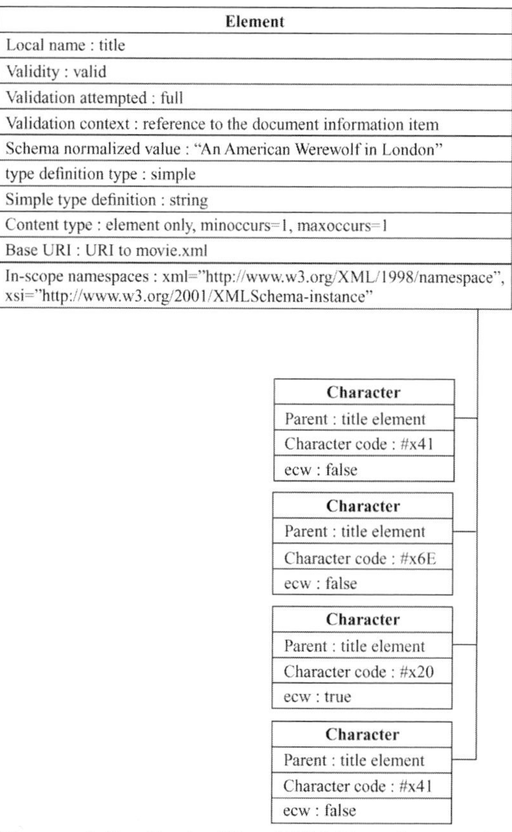

Figure 6-3 *Part of the PSVI Tree for movie.xml.*

"object-oriented programming" – that can represent any structured document, including an XML document. Later specs build on Level 1. DOM Level 2[23] adds a DOMTimeStamp data type, support for namespaces, plus several extra specifications, including views and events. DOM Level 3[24] adds load and save, and validation. There are also some notes associated with Level 3, including a note on DOM and XPath.[25]

The DOM is a *tree*-based (as opposed to *event*-based)[26] API. DOM Level 1 defines a hierarchy of node objects. The spec refers to this

22 *Document Object Model Level 1 (Second Edition)* (Cambridge, MA: World Wide Web Consortium, 2004). Available at: http://www.w3.org/DOM/DOMTR#dom1.

23 *Document Object Model Level 2* (Cambridge, MA: World Wide Web Consortium, 2004). Available at: http://www.w3.org/DOM/DOMTR#dom2.

24 *Document Object Model Level 3* (Cambridge, MA: World Wide Web Consortium, 2004). Available at: http://www.w3.org/DOM/DOMTR#dom3.

hierarchy as "The DOM Structure Model" — an appropriate name, since it looks a lot like a data model without the data type information. In DOM Level 1, all element and attribute content is treated as character data (as in the Infoset), and all values are returned as strings of type DOMString. Though DOM Level 2 did introduce one more data type — DOMTimeStamp — the DOM data model is still essentially untyped, except for some vendor extensions. Notably, Microsoft has introduced a number of proprietary extensions to the DOM, including the nodeTypedValue property of a node. nodeTypedValue returns the value of a node, with the type specified in an associated XML Schema, if present.

For an XML document, the hierarchy of node objects is a tree, with a single (notional) document node. Remember that the DOM provides an API to *manipulate* a document, not just to navigate around a static document. When editing a document, it is often useful to deal with a fragment — a part of the tree that may have more than one top node. To handle fragments, the DOM introduces the DocumentFragment node type, which adds a notional root element to a fragment.

There are 12 DOM node types, which are similar to the information items in the Infoset. Table 6-1 compares the DOM node types with the Infoset items.

Table 6-1 *DOM Node Types and Infoset Items*

DOM Structure Model Node Type	Corresponding Infoset Information Item	Differences
Document	Document	—
DocumentFragment	—	A part of a document, possibly with multiple top-nodes — not defined in the Infoset.
Element	Element	—
Attr	Attribute	—

25 *Document Object Model (DOM) Level 3 XPath Specification* (Cambridge, MA: World Wide Web Consortium, 2004). Available at: http://www.w3.org/TR/2004/NOTE-DOM-Level-3-XPath-20040226/.

26 For an example of *event*-based parsing, see *Java API for XML Parsing (JAXP)* at http://jcp.org/en/jsr/detail?id=5, or the SAX (Simple API for XML) home page at http://www.saxproject.org.

Table 6-1 DOM Node Types and Infoset Items (continued)

DOM Structure Model Node Type	Corresponding Infoset Information Item	Differences
DocumentType	Document type declaration	DOM DocumentType includes entities and notations. In the Infoset these are properties of Document.
ProcessingInstruction	Processing Instruction	–
Comment	Comment	–
Text	Character	DOM groups character Infoset items together into text nodes, like XPath.
CDATASection	–	The Infoset does not model CDATA sections.
Entity	–	The Infoset does not model entities.
EntityReference	Unexpanded entity reference	
Notation	Notation	–
–	Namespace	Although DOM Level 2 supports namespaces via several of its interfaces, it does not represent namespaces in its structure model.

A DOM parser builds instances of these node types. The DOM also introduces some objects to represent results:

- **NodeList** – an ordered list (sequence) of Nodes.
- **NamedNodeMap** – an unordered list of nodes, *e.g.*, all the attributes of an element.

NodeLists and NamedNodeMaps contain references to parts of the actual document, not copies, so DOM methods manipulate the "live" document.

The important part of the DOM spec is the interfaces and methods it defines on this underlying data model – the DOM is, after all, an API. We will not describe these interfaces and methods in detail. We will just observe that the DOM, by itself, is not very useful for querying.

- The DOM defines only two ways to access the values in elements and attributes. Neither allows for accurate, simple, efficient queries over XML.
  - You can access values of elements and their attributes by name. This is useful only if you know the name of the element (or attribute) for which you are looking. The DOM method getElementsByTagName returns all elements with the given name that are descendants of the current node, so this access method does not take account of where the element occurs.
  - You can access values of elements and their attributes by "walking the DOM tree" — *i.e.*, get the top-level node and look at its children, then look at their children, and so on.
- The DOM is not type-aware (though there are proprietary extensions to the DOM that *are* type-aware) — all values are returned as strings. That means that, if you want to perform any operations that depend on type (equality, greater than, less than, *etc.*), you have to explicitly cast the returned value to some appropriate host-language type.

That said, the DOM is a very popular way to access and manipulate XML, and many query implementations use the DOM at some level.

6.8 Introducing the XQuery Data Model

For the rest of this book we focus on the XQuery 1.0 and XPath 2.0 Data Model and its relationship to the SQL data model.

We said early in this chapter that the Infoset is an abstract representation of the information in an XML document, invented so that XML processors could perform operations on XML without having to deal with the details of how that information is represented in the original source input. The XQuery Data Model could be described as "the (extended) Infoset for XQuery" — that is, it is an abstract representation of the information in an XML document, defined for the purpose of an XQuery engine.

The XQuery language is defined in terms of the XQuery Data Model — that is, it is assumed that every query takes an XQuery Data Model instance as input and returns an XQuery Data Model instance as output. How one or more input documents get converted into an XQuery Data Model instance and how the resulting XQuery Data Model instance is presented to the user are left up to the implementation.

Why doesn't XQuery just use the Infoset? The Infoset is insufficient, for a couple of reasons. First, the Infoset has no data type information, and any reasonable query language needs to know about the types of the data values with which it's dealing in order to do comparisons, ordering, and so on. So why not use the PSVI? After all, that is the Infoset extended with type information. The PSVI was defined as part of XML Schema, which is concerned about *validating* documents, not *querying* them. That said, the XQuery Data Model is based largely on the PSVI, with some additional types.

Second, the Infoset represents only well-formed XML documents. XQuery needs to be able to represent a result (and, by extension, an intermediate result or input) that is an XML document, a subtree, a value, or a sequence of (a mixture of) any of these. The XQuery Data Model introduces the notion of a *sequence* — in XQuery, everything is a sequence of 0, 1, or more items, where an item is indistinguishable from a sequence of items of length 1. An item may be a value or a node. A node may be a document, element, attribute, text, namespace, processing instruction, or comment node.

We describe the XQuery Data Model and its relationship to the Infoset and XML Schema in more detail in Section 10.6, "The Data Model."

6.9 A Note Regarding Data Model Terminology

More than one W3C specification defines terms related to a data model for XML. Unfortunately, there is no universal agreement on the concepts involved, much less the terminology used for those concepts. In particular, several of these specifications are, in our opinion, unnecessarily confusing in the terms they use to reference the topmost elements of XML documents.

We struggled more than once with the problems caused by this lack of uniformity of concept and terminology. To aid our readers, we offer the following information to better their understanding.

Consider the trivial XML document illustrated in Example 6-2. That document corresponds to the tree structure shown in Figure 6-4.

Example 6-2 *Trivial XML Document*

```
<?xml version="1.0"?>
<!-- A simple, well-formed XML document -->
<a>
  This is a text node.
  <b>A child of a.</b>
  <c><!-- Comments can occur (almost) anywhere -->
      Another child of a, a sibling of b.</c>
</a>
```

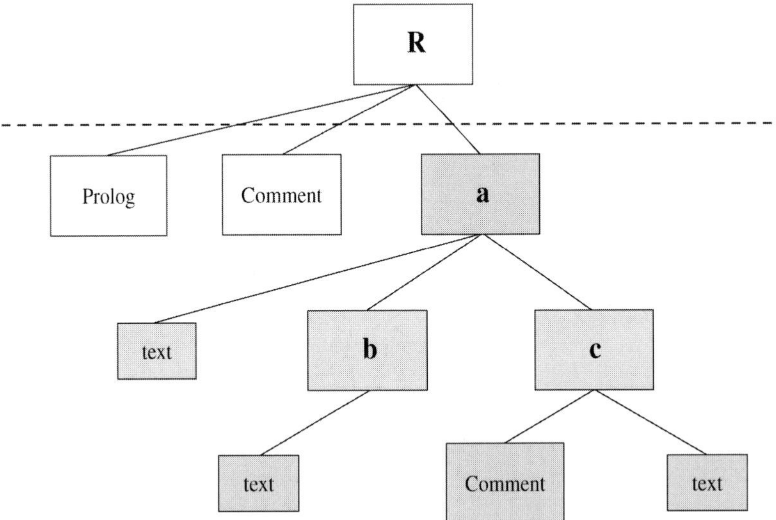

Figure 6-4 *Tree Structure Corresponding to a Trivial XML Document.*

The mere fact that some specifications have multiple names for the same concept (see, for example, the XML column's cell corresponding to tree node A in Table 6-2) is problem enough. But the fact that different specifications use certain words (*root* is a good example) for different purposes — or not at all — just makes things difficult for no good reason.

Table 6-2 *Tree-Related Terminology*

Tree node	XML	Infoset and PSVI	XPath 1.0	XPath 2.0 and XQuery 1.0 Data Model
R	No corresponding concept, but "document" comes closest	Document information item	Root node	Root node or document node
A (<a>)	Document element, document entity, root element, or root (varies within spec)	Document element (or document element information item)	Element node for document element	Element node
B (<b>)	Element	Element information item	Element node	Element node

6.10 Chapter Summary and Further Reading

We started this chapter by looking at the Infoset – an abstract representation of the information in an XML document. The Infoset is extended with type information in the Post-Schema-Validation Infoset, defined by XML Schema. XQuery defined its own data model – the XQuery Data Model – based on the Infoset, with additional type information and sequences. We also mentioned the DOM, an API for accessing and manipulating XML, which has its own underlying data model (the DOM Structure Model), which is similar to the Infoset.

For further reading, there are a number of mappings between data models – see especially the mapping from DOM to XPath 1.0 Data Model in the DOM Level 3 Note,[25] and the mapping from XPath 1.0 Data Model to Infoset that we saw earlier in this chapter.[15] If you want to see the details of the PSVI, take a look at the XSV (XML Schema Validator)[27] tool. XSV takes as input an XML document and an XML Schema document and outputs its PSVI as an

27 Henry S. Thompson and Richard Tobin, *Current Status of XSV: Coverage, Known Bugs, etc.* (Edinburgh, England: University of Edinburgh, 2005). Available at: http://www.ltg.ed.ac.uk/~ht/xsv-status.html.

XML document according to the PSVI Schema.[28] There's also a stylesheet[29] to display validity information from the PSVI as a color-coded HTML page.

Related readings include the W3C Recommendation on Canonical XML[30] (interestingly, this is defined on the XPath Data Model) and Erik Wilde's proposal to make the Infoset extensible in a standard way.[31]

---

28 Richard Tobin and Henry Thompson, *A Schema for Serialized Infosets* (Edinburgh, England: University of Edinburgh, 2005). Available at: http://www.w3.org/2001/05/serialized-infoset-schema.html.

29 C. M. Sperberg-McQueen, *Document List* (Cambridge, MA: World Wide Web Consortium, 2005). Available at: http://www.w3.org/People/cmsmcq/doclist.html#xslt.

30 *Canonical XML* (Cambridge, MA: World Wide Web Consortium, 2001). Available at: http://www.w3.org/TR/xml-c14n.

31 Erik Wilde, *Making the Infoset Extensible* (Zurich, Switzerland: Swiss Federal Institute of Technology, 2002). Available at: http://www.idealliance.org/papers/xml02/dx_xml02/papers/05-01-06/05-01-06.html.

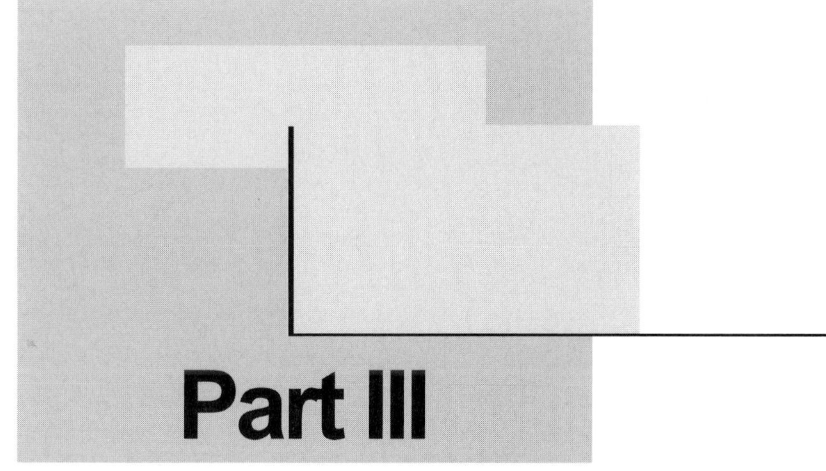

Part III

Managing and Storing XML for Querying

Chapter

7

Managing XML: Transforming and Connecting

7.1 Introduction

XML documents rarely exist in a vacuum. As you read in Section 6.6, "The Post-Schema-Validation Infoset (PSVI)," and as you will see in Chapter 10, "Introduction to XQuery 1.0," XML documents being queried often conform to (that is, are validated against) an XML Schema and they may be transformed into an instance of the XQuery Data Model.

XML documents interact in many ways with their environment. For instance, they can be transformed from one structure to a different structure, or they can be transformed into some user-friendly format such as HTML[1] or PDF.[2] They are frequently modularized to place some information into one physical resource (*e.g.*, a file) and other information into a different resource. They reference one another in various ways, both simple and complex.

In this chapter, we explore several of the more important ways in which XML documents interact with their environments and how those interactions are related to querying XML. To select but one

1 *HTML 4.01 Specification* (Cambridge, MA: World Wide Web Consortium, 2003). Available at: http://www.w3.org/TR/html401.

2 PDF, or Portable Document Format, is a specification created by Adobe Systems, Inc., http://www.adobe.com.

example, any system for querying XML must decide whether or not to include in the data being queried those resources that might be related in some modular way or resources that are referenced from one document into another.

7.2 Transforming, Formatting, and Displaying XML

XML documents, as a glance at any example in this book will convince you, are not especially pretty to look at. All those angle brackets — and even the presence of the elements and attributes themselves — make the document more difficult to read and understand.

It is for this reason that the W3C has created two languages for "reshaping" documents in various ways. One of these, which we cover in Section 7.2.1, is a language for transforming the content and structure of XML documents into any of several other forms, including HTML or plain text, as well as new XML documents. The other, briefly discussed in Section 7.2.2, provides a mechanism by which XML documents can be converted into formats suitable for printing or viewing, such as PostScript and PDF (or even Microsoft's Rich Text Format, RTF).

What does this have to do with querying XML? Well, in order to transform an XML document into some other form, you have to be able to find the elements, text, and so forth in the original document that you want to be represented in the result. Finding those things requires querying the input document, as you'll see in, for instance, Example 7-2.

In addition, when you're querying XML documents — or collections of documents — it's quite likely that you'll sometimes want to represent the result in a different form than your query language produces directly. As you'll see in Chapter 11, "XQuery 1.0 Definition," XQuery is capable of producing whatever XML structure you might need as a result of its query operations. But XQuery can produce only XML as its output, while your application might require query results to be displayed in HTML or even plain text — or in PDF. In such situations, the results of XQuery operations can be further transformed into those other formats using technologies described in this section.

7.2.1 Extensible Stylesheet Language Transformations (XSLT)

XSLT 1.0[3] is a language (developed by the W3C's XSL Working Group, where "XSL" means "Extensible Stylesheet Language") designed for transforming XML documents into another form. The name "XSLT" stands for "XSL Transformations." The specification for XSLT 1.0 contains provisions — called *output methods* — for producing (new) XML documents from such transformations, for producing HTML documents, or for producing plain text. It also allows implementations to provide additional output methods that produce formats other than these three.

XSLT 1.0 depends on XPath 1.0 as the language in which search and matching criteria are expressed — that is, as its query language. XSLT 1.0 was one of the driving forces behind the development of XPath 1.0 and was arguably its most important "customer." When the W3C began development of an XML querying language (the language that became XPath 1.0), it recognized that there was significant overlap between the requirements of XPath and of the planned XML query language. As a result the charter to develop XQuery included responsibility for developing a new version of XPath at the same time.

At the same time that XPath 2.0 and XQuery 1.0 were being developed, a new version of XSLT (known, naturally, as XSLT 2.0)[4] was being specified. The details of XSLT 2.0 differ in significant ways from those of XSLT 1.0, but the overall goals and mechanisms remain the same. XSLT 2.0 adds XHTML[5] to the choices of output methods.

XSLT is a *functional language* without side effects (which, as you'll see in Chapter 11, "XQuery 1.0 Definition," is a characteristic of XQuery, too), in which you can write *stylesheets* that are based on *templates* used to process various components of the input XML documents. This design leads to a number of characteristics, most of them specifically intended to make your stylesheets very robust, and makes it possible for your stylesheets to be executed efficiently (which, of course, doesn't guarantee that all XSLT engines are efficient). An important characteristic of XSLT, one that is probably the

---

3 *XSL Transformations (XSLT) Version 1.0* (Cambridge, MA: World Wide Web Consortium, 1999). Available at: http://www.w3.org/TR/xslt.

4 *XSL Transformations (XSLT) Version 2.0* (Cambridge, MA: World Wide Web Consortium, 2004). Available at: http://www.w3.org/TR/xslt20/.

5 *XHTML 1.0 The Extensible Hypertext Markup Language (Second Edition) A Reformulation of HTML 4 in XML 1.0* (Cambridge, MA: World Wide Web Consortium, 2002). Available at: http://www.w3.org/TR/xhtml1.

greatest source of confusion to programmers used to more conventional languages like Java and C, is that the concept of iteration is applied in only a very limited sense; instead, capabilities that would employ iteration in a Java program must normally[6] be written using recursion in XSLT. (A further artifact of this design principle is that variables, once created and given a value, *never* change their values! That is the nature of functional languages. While this might sound insane to some readers, it makes great sense in a language built on principles of recursion.)

XSLT is a language expressed in XML, which makes it possible to manipulate XSLT stylesheets with ordinary XML tools, including XSLT (it's possible to transform stylesheets into other stylesheets!), and XQuery (perhaps to determine what stylesheets dealing with particular situations are available in a repository). Since XSLT is expressed in XML, all of its features and functionality are expressed as XML elements and attributes. These elements are defined to be in a namespace that is often identified by the namespace prefix "xsl:". In this book, wherever we use XSLT, we'll apply that prefix.

To get a sense of XSLT's use, let's consider the reduced movie example in Example 7-1; this example omits most of the data in our "real" movie document (see Appendix A: The Example).

Example 7-1 *Reduced movie Example*

```
<?xml version="1.0" encoding="UTF-8"?>
<!-- movie - a simple XML example -->
<movies xmlns:xsi="http://www.w3.org/2001/XMLSchema-instance">
  <movie myStars="5">
    <title>An American Werewolf in London</title>
    <yearReleased>1981</yearReleased>
    <director>
      <familyName>Landis</familyName>
      <givenName>John</givenName>
    </director>
```

6 XSLT 1.0 provides the element `<xsl:for-each>`, which applies a specified transformation to each node in a selected node set; this is often viewed as a type of iteration. Similarly, XSLT 2.0 provides `<xsl:for-each>`, in this version applying the specified transformation to each item in a selected sequence, as well as a new `<xsl:for-each-group>` element that allocates items in a sequence into groups (based on some common criteria) and then evaluates a "sequence constructor" once for each group. The behavior of those XSLT 2.0 elements is also often viewed as a type of iteration.

```
  </movie>
  <movie myStars="4">
    <title>The Thing</title>
    <yearReleased>1982</yearReleased>
    <director>
      <familyName>Carpenter</familyName>
      <givenName>John</givenName>
    </director>
  </movie>
  <movie myStars="3">
    <title>National Lampoon's Animal House</title>
    <yearReleased>1978</yearReleased>
    <director>
      <familyName>Landis</familyName>
      <givenName>John</givenName>
    </director>
  </movie>
</movies>
```

In this example, our three movies are represented only by their titles, the years in which they were released, and the names of their directors. An XSLT stylesheet might be written to transform this data into a new document based on directors' names instead; that new document could be an XML document, an HTML (or, in XSLT 2.0, XHTML) document, or just plain text. Such a stylesheet appears in Example 7-2, which transforms the XML from Example 7-1 into an XML document that contains only directors.

Example 7-2 *XSLT 1.0 Stylesheet to Produce XML Output*

```
<?xml version='1.0'?>
<xsl:stylesheet version="1.0"
                xmlns:xsl="http://www.w3.org/1999/XSL/Transform">
<xsl:output method="xml"/>

  <xsl:template match="/">
    <xsl:apply-templates/>
  </xsl:template>

  <xsl:template match="movies">
    <movie-directors>
      <xsl:apply-templates/>
    </movie-directors>
```

```
    </xsl:template>

    <xsl:template match="movie">
      <director movie="{title}">
        <name>
          <xsl:value-of select="director/givenName"/>
          <xsl:text> </xsl:text>
          <xsl:value-of select="director/familyName"/>
        </name>
      </director>
    </xsl:template>

  </xsl:stylesheet>
```

It's beyond the scope of this book to explain that stylesheet in detail, but a brief summary will be useful. The line that reads "`<xsl:output method="xml"`" instructs the stylesheet to produce XML as a result of the transformation. The lines containing "`<xsl:template match=`" each start a template that is invoked whenever templates are being applied and the "`match=`" expression is satisfied. Inside the double quotes (`"..."`) following the "`match=`" is an XPath expression that identifies the criteria determining whether or not the template is to be applied. As you'll discover in Chapter 9, "XPath 1.0 and XPath 2.0," the notation "/" specifies the root node (you learned in Chapter 6, "The XML Information Set (Infoset) and Beyond," that the root node is not the same as the element node for the document element, `<movies>`). This template is invoked as soon as the stylesheet is executed, and it is invoked exactly once since there is always exactly one root node in a well-formed XML document. Notice that this template contains nothing other than "`<apply-templates/>`." That instruction says "Using the current context (in this case, the root node), invoke every template whose match expression identifies some child node."

In this case, there is only one template whose match expression matches a child of the root node: the template whose match expression contains "`movies`." That template is invoked once for each element whose name is "`movies`" that occurs within the current context. And, of course, since the `<movies>` element is the document element, there is only one of them, so the template is invoked exactly once. The content of this template is a single element: `<movie-directors>`. This element is not in the `xsl:` namespace, so it is not an instruction to XSLT, but it is intended to be part of the result of the transformation. Therefore, that element is put into the result tree and its content, `<xsl:apply-templates/>`, is evaluated. Since this element *is* in the `xsl:` namespace, it is executed. As before, the `<apply-templates>` element instructs the XSLT processor to start applying templates whose match expression matches some child of "this" element – in this case, children of the `<movies>` element. In this document, these are the three `<movie>` elements.

The third template's "`match=`" attribute instructs the XSLT processor to invoke this template whenever a `<movie>` element is encountered in the current context while templates are being applied. Since the `<movies>` element is the context in which templates are now being applied and there are three `<movie>` elements, this template will be invoked three times. The elements in that template instruct the processor to create a new "`<director>`" element *within* the `<movie-directors>` element that the "`movies`" template generated. It also creates an attribute, `title`, for that element and assigns it a value that is computed from the value (that's what the curly braces mean) of the `<title>` element that is a child of the `<movie>` element being processed. Next, this template creates a `<name>` element within the `<director>` element, inserting the value of the `<givenName>` element contained in the `<director>` element that is, in turn, contained in the `<movie>` element being processed. The template then inserts a single space and finally inserts the value of the `<familyName>` element contained in the `<director>` element.

Whew!

The result of this transformation is seen in Result 7-1.

Result 7-1 *Result of Reduced Movie Transformation to XML*

```
<?xml version="1.0" encoding="utf-8"?>
<movie-directors>
  <director movie="An American Werewolf in London">
    <name>John Landis</name>
  </director>
  <director movie="The Thing">
    <name>John Carpenter</name>
  </director>
  <director movie="National Lampoon's Animal House">
    <name>John Landis</name>
  </director>
</movie-directors>
```

If the output method of the stylesheet had instead been "text," the output would be that seen in Result 7-2.

Result 7-2 *Result of Reduced Movie Transformation to Text*

```
John Landis
John Carpenter
John Landis
```

Note that the movie titles are not represented in the text output, because plain text has no analog to attributes.

A common use of stylesheets is to transform XML data for display in a web browser, which normally involves HTML instead of XML or plain text. A somewhat different stylesheet, seen in Example 7-3, might produce HTML for a web page, as illustrated in Result 7-3 and Figure 7-1.

Example 7-3 *XSLT 1.0 Stylesheet to Produce HTML Output*

```
<?xml version='1.0'?>
<xsl:stylesheet version="1.0"
                xmlns:xsl="http://www.w3.org/1999/XSL/Transform">
<xsl:output method="html"/>

<xsl:template match="/">
  <xsl:apply-templates/>
</xsl:template>

<xsl:template match="movies">
  <H1>My favorite movies</H1>
    <table border="2">
      <xsl:apply-templates/>
  </table>
</xsl:template>

<xsl:template match="movie">
  <tr>
    <td><xsl:value-of select="director/givenName"/><xsl:text> </xsl:text>
<xsl:value-of select="director/familyName"/></td>
    <td><xsl:value-of select="title"/></td>
  </tr>
</xsl:template>

</xsl:stylesheet>
```

Result 7-3 *HTML Created by XSLT Transformation*

```
<H1>My favorite movies</H1>
<table border="2">
   <tr>
      <td>John Landis</td>
      <td>An American Werewolf in London</td>
   </tr>
   <tr>
      <td>John Carpenter</td>
      <td>The Thing</td>
   </tr>
   <tr>
      <td>Landis John</td>
      <td>National Lampoon's Animal House</td>
   </tr>
</table>
```

It's obvious that XSLT offers significant power in transforming XML documents to various other forms, including new XML documents (as in Result 7-1). Normally, you would write queries to retrieve information directly from the original XML documents. However, there may sometimes be a reason to transform those original documents into some new XML form before querying them. For example, your existing queries might require the XML to be in some format other than that in which the XML already exists. Your queries might assume that the XML data is in the form of a SOAP[7] (SOAP once stood for "Simple Object Access Protocol") message or that it

My favorite movies

John Landis	An American Werewolf in London
John Carpenter	The Thing
Landis John	National Lampoon's Animal House

Figure 7-1 *Web Page Created by XSLT Transformation.*

7 *SOAP Version 1.2 Part 0: Primer* (Cambridge, MA: World Wide Web Consortium, 2003). Available at: http://www.w3.org/TR/soap12-part0/. *SOAP Version 1.2 Part 1: Messaging Framework* (Cambridge, MA: World Wide Web Consortium, 2003). Available at: http://www.w3.org/TR/soap12-part1/. *SOAP Version 1.2 Part 2: Adjuncts* (Cambridge, MA: World Wide Web Consortium, 2003). Available at: http://www.w3.org/TR/soap12-part2/.

can be validated against a particular XML Schema, and so forth. XSLT is a tool to be considered in such circumstances.

Because of the ability of XSLT to perform sophisticated data location and structural transformation of XML documents, it is sometimes viewed as a way of querying XML. We don't categorize XSLT as an XML querying facility, although it can serve that purpose in limited situations – especially when your intent is to retrieve and reorganize data from within a single XML document.

We find it far more likely that you might wish to query your XML documents in another language, such as XQuery, and then perhaps transform the results into HTML, plain text, or some other form (perhaps the one discussed in Section 7.2.2).

At the time of writing, we were aware of very few XSLT 2.0 implementations, so this section has concentrated on the more widely implemented (and used) first version of XSLT. We believe that, when XQuery 1.0 and XPath 2.0 are finally released and we start seeing implementations of them, more and more implementations of XSLT 2.0 will begin to appear.

7.2.2 Extensible Stylesheet Language: Formatting Objects (XSL FO)

The *original* mission of the W3C's XSL Working Group was to define a true stylesheet language for XML that would serve approximately the same purpose that CSS (Cascading Style Sheets)[8] serves for HTML and that DSSSL[9] serves for SGML[10] – to determine the visual display characteristics of documents on a computer display and/or on paper. As you read in Section 7.2.1, the XSL Working Group is also responsible for the XSLT specification.

The XSL specification (which many people, including us, call "XSL FO" to clearly distinguish it from XSLT) defines, like XSLT, a number of XML elements and attributes that allow an application to control

---

8 *Cascading Style Sheets, Level 2*, http://www.w3.org/TR/REC-CSS1 (Cambridge, MA: World Wide Web Consortium, 1998) and *Cascading Style Sheets, Level 2 CSS2 Specification*, http://www.w3.org/TR/REC-CSS2 (Cambridge, MA: World Wide Web Consortium, 1996).

9 ISO/IEC 10179:1996, *Information Technology – Processing Languages – Document Style Semantics and Specification Language (DSSSL)*, (Geneva, Switzerland: International Organization for Standardization, 1996).

10 ISO 8879:1986, *Information Processing – Text and Office Systems – Standard Generalized Markup Language (SGML)*, (Geneva, Switzerland: International Organization for Standardization, 1986).

such formatting characteristics as page structure, font and size of text, list element numbering, and image placement as well as structural characteristics such as tables, blocks of text (*e.g.*, paragraphs), and footnotes. The elements defined by XSL FO are placed into a specific namespace, often indicated by the namespace prefix "fo:".

XSL FO is not intended to be, nor is it utilized as, a language for querying XML documents. Its purpose is strictly to give instructions to a formatting engine on how to apply formatting to an XML document for display, so it is not discussed further in this book. However, it can be a valuable tool in an application that must publish, in a reader-friendly format, XML documents (which may be the results of XML queries). A typical workflow for such an application is seen in Figure 7-2.

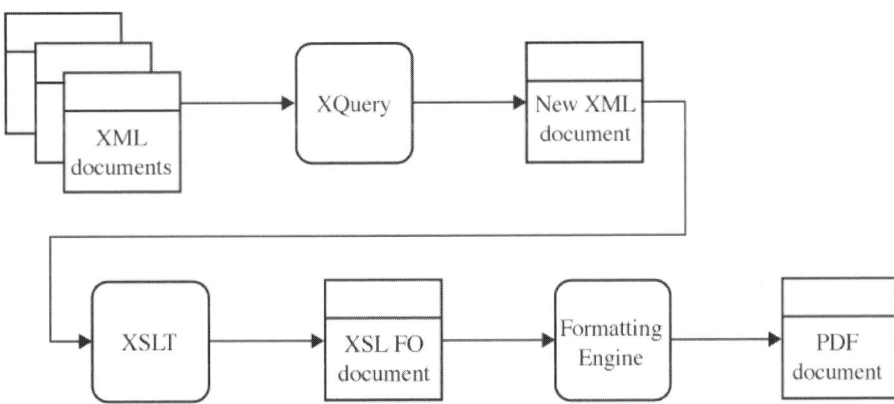

Figure 7-2 *Query-and-Publish Workflow.*

7.3 The Relationships between XML Documents

This section, as its title suggests, deals with technology intended to help define and strengthen the relationships between two or more XML documents. While we believe that the material in this section is interesting, useful, and relevant, you should take note of this *caveat lector*: The technologies described in this section have not been widely implemented and are not in common use, and at least some of them have not yet reached the final recommendation stage in the W3C.

If these factors make the section of little interest to you, then you might want to skip ahead to Section 7.4.

7.3.1 XML Inclusions (XInclude)

Virtually all programmers are familiar with the ability to *modularize* program code. Modularization is a process in which an entity is broken into several parts that can then be reassembled into the desired whole. In the context of programming, programs are frequently written as a set of modules, each containing code that performs specific, usually closely related tasks. The code in those modules is then invoked by code in other modules, only one of which is the "main" module that is invoked to initiate execution of the program as a whole. One of the advantages of this approach is that modules providing widely needed functionality can be reused by many different applications simply by making them available to those other applications. One effect of this advantage is that, if a module must be changed, the programmer needs to make the change in one place only. Programs that uses that module will behave consistently, since they all use the same code.

Documents can be, and frequently are, modularized in the same manner. For example, a book typically has multiple components, such as chapters, appendices, tables, and figures. Those components may be written and updated by different people, at different times, using different tools. They are all brought together to form the final book. When a document, such as a book, is represented in some source form on a computer, each of the components might be stored in separate files.

XML documents are no different in this respect. It's quite common to create certain XML resources (such as computer files) that each contain some frequently used XML and to cause those resources to be incorporated into some ultimate document. In an application requiring many documents, all of which tend to use the same set of terms, an XML resource might be created that contains a glossary of those terms. Instead of the glossary's being written for each of the documents that need it, it can be written once and incorporated into all of those documents.

The W3C has published a specification (not yet a final recommendation) for including XML resources into other XML resources. This spec, known as XML Inclusions (XInclude),[11] "introduces a generic mechanism for merging XML documents." In fact, this specification actually defines the mechanism for merging the *Infosets* of XML doc-

11 *XML Inclusions (XInclude) Version 1.0* (Cambridge, MA: World Wide Web Consortium, 2004). Available at: http://www.w3.org/TR/xinclude/.

uments into a single Infoset; you should not expect this facility to merge two serialized XML documents into a single character string.

The XML language itself provides a facility known as *external entities*, by which information contained in various resources can be incorporated into an XML document while that document is being parsed. External entities can be used only by XML documents that declare them as part of a DTD (including an internal DTD subset), and the material contained in them need not be XML. That material can, of course, be XML, but it can also be ordinary text or even binary data, such as graphics (which are, not parsed). External entities — both parsed and unparsed — provide one way of modularizing XML documents. The capability is very widely employed by many XML documents.

XInclude, by contrast, provides a way of merging (the Infosets of) XML documents into a single XML document (that is, a single Infoset). This merger is unrelated to parsing an XML source into an Infoset, because it occurs only *after* all of the related documents have been parsed. It also has nothing to do with validation, using either a DTD or an XML Schema; such validation is not defined in the XInclude spec, although, of course, it can be applied before or after the merger takes place.

XInclude is expressed in XML and defines only two elements, both included in a namespace that is frequently indicated with the namespace prefix "xi:". The first of the elements, `xi:include`, is permitted to have at most one child, `xi:fallback`. `xi:include` has a number of attributes. One attribute, `parse`, indicates whether the included material is to be parsed as XML (that is, with an Infoset to be merged) or as ordinary text; if "text" is specified, then the `encoding` attribute might be used to specify the character set encoding of the text. Another pair of attributes, `href` and `xpointer`, are used to identify the material to be included. When the `parse` attribute indicates that the included material is text, the `xpointer` attribute is prohibited and only the `href` attribute is used; when XML is indicated, either or both of the `href` and `xpointer` attributes can be used. It's interesting to note that the source text of XML documents can be included as ordinary text simply by specifying "text" as the value of the `parse` attribute. Such inclusions cause the included material to be represented in the including document's Infoset as a series of character information items (which, in the XQuery Data Model, are transformed into a text node).

That last paragraph is, to say the least, a bit of a mouthful. A few examples might help make it somewhat clearer. Table 7-1 illustrates some of the more meaningful combinations of attributes.

Table 7-1 *`xi:include` Attributes*

Example `xi:include` Element	Interpretation
`<xi:include parse="xml" .../>`	The material to be included is well-formed XML (the `encoding` attribute is not needed since the encoding of XML can be determined automatically; if it is present, it's ignored).
`<xi:include parse="text" encoding="UTF-8" .../>`	The material to be included is plain text, encoded in UTF-8.
`<xi:include parse="text" encoding="UTF-8" xpointer="..." .../>`	Error: The `xpointer` attribute is prohibited with `parse="text"`.
`<xi:include parse="text" encoding="UTF-8" href="..."/>`	The text located by the value of the `href` attribute is included in the XML document at the point where the `<xi:include>` element appears.
`<xi:include parse="xml" xpointer="..." .../>`	The XML document located by the value of the `xpointer` attribute is included in the XML document at the point where the `<xi:include>` element appears.

The value of the `href` attribute is an ordinary URI (Uniform Resource Identifier) reference or IRI (Internationalized Resource Identifier) reference that specifies the location of the resource to be included. When the material being included is XML, the value of the `xpointer` attribute is an XPointer (see Section 7.3.2) that identifies the portion of the resource to be included; if the `xpointer` attribute is absent, then the entire resource is included.

The `xi:fallback` element, which can appear only as a child of the `xi:include` element, allows the including document to specify content to be used when the resource indicated by the `href` or `xpointer` attributes of the `xi:include` element cannot be retrieved (*e.g.*, because it does not exist, is temporarily unreachable, or is protected in some way).

In our collection of movies, we have discovered that we have a large number of films starring Teri Garr. We could avoid constantly recoding the fragment shown in Example 7-4 if we use XInclude, as shown in Example 7-5, to incorporate her data.

Example 7-4 *XML Fragment Representing Teri Garr*

```
<actress>
  <givenName>Teri</givenName>
  <familyName>Garr</familyName>
</actress>
```

Example 7-5 *Using XInclude for Teri Garr*

```
<?xml version="1.1"?>
<movies xmlns:xi="http://www.w3.org/2001/XInclude">
  <movie>
    <movie-title>One From the Heart</movie-title>
    <year-made>1982</year-made>
    <xi:include href="http://example.com/movie-information/terigarr.xml"
              parse="xml">
    ...
  </movie>
  <movie>
    <movie-title>Young Frankenstein</movie-title>
    <year-made>1974</year-made>
    <xi:include href="http://example.com/movie-information/terigarr.xml"
              parse="xml">
    ...
  </movie>
  ...
</movies>
```

Of course, that `<xi:include>` element required at least as many keystrokes as Teri's `<actress>` element, but it illustrates the mechanism. It provides one additional advantage: Should we ever discover that we've misspelled Teri's name, we can change it in exactly one place (terigarr.xml) and that change will be automatically incorporated everywhere we used that XInclude element.

This particular example could have just as easily used an external parsed entity. However, XInclude offers features that external parsed entities don't provide. For example, external parsed entities require that the external entity be declared and named (in a DTD, typically the internal DTD subset) and then invoked separately; XInclude provides inclusions with all of the information specified in exactly one place. Furthermore, it's normally a fatal error if an external entity cannot be retrieved (*e.g.*, because a URI is unreachable), but XInclude allows specification of a fallback value in the event that the referenced material cannot be retrieved.

XInclude allows references to the document in which the <xi:include> element appears, as long as those references are not to the <xi:include> element itself or to one of its parents (thus avoiding "inclusion loops"). This might serve, for example, to cause a complex element that appears at one place in a document to be included ("copied") in many other places in that same document.

The question we have not yet addressed is how this facility interacts with various querying mechanisms, such as XPath and XQuery. Remember that XInclude operates on Infosets, not on any other representation of the XML documents involved. As you'll learn in Chapter 10, "Introduction to XQuery 1.0," XQuery 1.0 and XPath 2.0 both operate on XML documents that are represented in the XQuery Data Model — which can be constructed from an Infoset representation of a document or from a PSVI representation. Although neither the XPath 2.0 spec nor the XQuery spec explicitly recognizes XInclude, it is clear to us that XInclude processing precedes any querying of the (now-merged) documents, simply because the XInclude processing operates on the Infoset from which the data model instance is derived. We would be quite surprised if the answer were different if XPath 1.0 were used for querying.

7.3.2 XML Pointer Language (XPointer)

If you're familiar with Uniform Resource Identifiers (URIs),[12] then you will recognize that URI references are allowed to include a *fragment identifier.* A fragment identifier in a URI reference comprises the characters following the number sign (#) and consists of "additional reference information to be interpreted by the user agent," such interpretation being dependent on the nature of the data being retrieved.

For example, in HTML documents, one might find a link like this one:

12 *Uniform Resource Identifiers (URI): Generic Syntax* (Internet Engineering Task Force, 1998). Available at: http://ietf.org/rfc/rfc2396.txt.

```
<a href="http://www.w3.org/TR/2004/REC-xml-names11/
#IRIComparison">Comparing IRI References</a>
```

This link includes a URI reference containing a fragment identifier ("`IRIComparison`"). When that link is followed, the HTML document found at the location indicated by the URI ("`www.w3.org/TR/2004/REC-xml-names11`") is retrieved and the "user agent" (a browser, usually) looks for an HTML element with an attribute named "id" whose value is identical to the value of the fragment identifier. Once that element is found, the user agent (browser) positions the document so that the portion starting with that identified element is displayed in the viewing window.

URI references containing this sort of fragment identifier work well in HTML, but they are not sufficiently powerful for all meaningful fragment identification in the larger XML world. The XPointer specifications define an extensible system for XML addressing. There are currently four specifications covering the XPointer language: XPointer Framework,[13] XPointer element() Scheme,[14] XPointer xmlns() Scheme,[15] and XPointer xpointer() Scheme.[16]

The XPointer Framework defines an extensible system for XML addressing, which is then used by various "schemes" to define fragment identifier languages. XPointer defines two sorts of pointers: *shorthand pointers* and *scheme-based pointers*.

Shorthand Pointers

A shorthand pointer is merely an identifier (in XML terminology, an NCName)[17] and identifies at most one element in the target resource's Infoset — the first element that has a matching NCName as an identifier (such as one defined by either an XML Schema or a

---

13 *XPointer Framework* (Cambridge, MA: World Wide Web Consortium, 2003). Available at: http://www.w3.org/TR/2003/REC-xptr-framework/.

14 *XPointer element() Scheme* (Cambridge, MA: World Wide Web Consortium, 2003). Available at: http://www.w3.org/TR/2003/REC-xptr-element/.

15 *XPointer xmlns() Scheme* (Cambridge, MA: World Wide Web Consortium, 2003). Available at: http://www.w3.org/TR/2003/REC-xptr-xmlns/.

16 *XPointer xpointer() Scheme* (Cambridge, MA: World Wide Web Consortium, 2002). Available at: http://www.w3.org/TR/2002/WD-xptr-xpointer/.

17 An NCName is a "noncolonized" name — that is, a name without any colons embedded in it. By contrast, a QName is a "qualified" name that is qualified by a namespace prefix. The namespace prefix and the "local part" of the QName are each NCNames.

DTD against which the document has been validated). Shorthand pointers provide a rough analog of HTML fragment behavior.

Scheme-Based Pointers

A scheme-based pointer contains one or more *pointer parts;* a pointer part is a portion of a pointer that contains a scheme name and some pointer data conforming to the definition of the scheme identified by that name. A software component that handles an XPointer scheme is called an *XPointer processor;* such components need not be distinct software applications or modules, but they might be an integral component of some other application — possibly including a query facility. Although the XPointer specifications define only three schemes at present, the W3C may in the future add more schemes, and the creation of application-specific schemes is explicitly accommodated in the XPointer Framework. In fact, the Internet Engineering Task Force (IETF) once published an Internet Draft describing an xpath1() scheme[18] (we have not, however, been able to find any evidence that this draft was ever accepted as an IETF RFC).

Each pointer part has a scheme name and (within parentheses) data conforming to the named scheme. When a pointer contains multiple parts, the XPointer processor must evaluate them from left to right. If a processor doesn't support a particular scheme, then it skips that pointer part. If a pointer part doesn't identify any part of an XML resource (that is, a *subresource*), then it is skipped and evaluation continues with the next pointer part (if any). As soon as one pointer part identifies a subresource, evaluation of the pointer stops and the identified subresource is the result of the pointer as a whole — meaning that the identified subresource is the thing to which the pointer points.

XPointer (like XInclude) operates on Infosets and not on the serialized form of XML documents. However, the way in which the XPointer Framework is specified, an XPointer processor might operate on a PSVI representation of an XML document or even on an XQuery Data Model representation.

Conveniently, XPointers have been designed so that they can serve as fragment identifiers in URI references. For example, the following URI reference using a shorthand pointer identifies the XML element corresponding to arguably the worst film ever made, *Plan 9 from Outer Space*, in an XML document representing movies:

---

18 S. St. Laurent, *The XPointer xpath1() Scheme* (2002). Available at: http://www.simonstl.com/ietf/draft-stlaurent-xpath-frag-00.html.

```
http://example.com/movie_information/movies.xml#Plan9fromOuterSpace-1959
```

The three XPointer schemes defined by the W3C correspond to the three references cited earlier in this section.

The xmlns() Scheme

One of these, the xmlns() scheme, has the sole purpose of adding a prefix/namespace binding to the namespace binding context that is used by other schemes; it never identifies a subresource. Since pointer parts are processed left to right, the binding added by a scheme-based pointer using the xmlns() scheme is available only to subsequence scheme-based pointer parts.

The element() Scheme

The element() scheme allows basic addressing of elements in target XML resources. This scheme does not permit the identification of any other component of an XML resource, such as attributes, comments, or processing instructions. If the data within the parentheses following the scheme name ("element") is solely an NCName, then it serves to identify the first element in the document that has an identifier identical to that NCName. If the data within the parentheses comprises a sequence of slash/integer pairs (such as "/2/15/3," called a *child sequence*), the XPointer processor must identify the top-level element indicated by the first integer (the *second* top-level element, in this case), then the child element indicated by the next integer (the 15th one), and so forth. If the data comprises an NCName followed by a child sequence, then the step-by-step location of elements is performed starting at the element located by the NCName.

The xpointer() Scheme

The xpointer() scheme is the most powerful and the most complex of the three schemes defined by the W3C. This scheme is based on XPath 1.0 (see Chapter 9, "XPath 1.0 and XPath 2.0") but adds the ability to address character strings, specific points in an XML resource, and ranges of components in a resource. It gives access to all nodes of XML documents (and external parsed entities) except for the XML declaration and any associated DTDs, which are omitted because they are not explicitly represented in a document's Infoset or PSVI.

A *point* is a location in an Infoset that has no content or children — for example, the location between two adjacent nodes or after a particular character within a text node. A *range* is an identification of all of the Infoset components lying between two points.

Like XPath 1.0, the xpointer() scheme uses iterative selection, in which each component of a given xpointer() operates on the result of the previous component. Components in XPath 1.0 return *node sets* (unordered collections of nodes), while the components in an xpointer() operate on *location sets* (unordered collections of locations). A *location* is either a node, a point, or a range. Selection of portions of the Infoset in both XPath and in the xpointer() scheme is done through three main constructs: axes, predicates, and functions. An axis is an operator that identifies a sequence of candidate components that might be located, while a predicate tests those candidate components according to specified criteria. Functions might generate new candidate components or perform some other task.

Consider the XML fragment illustrated in Example 7-4. The xpointer() scheme would allow us to identify the portion of the fragment shown in Figure 7-3 but not the portion shown in Figure 7-4.

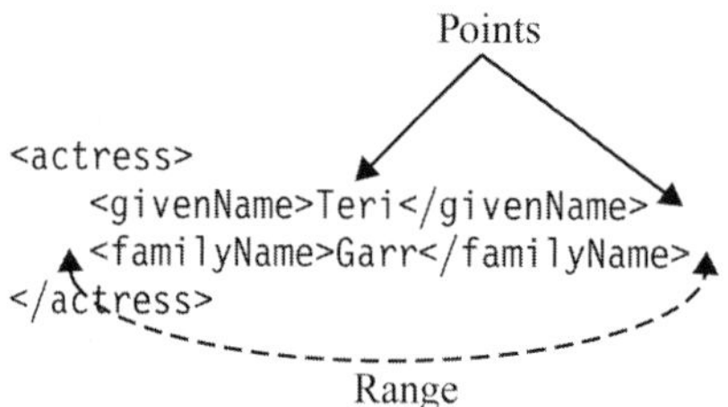

Figure 7-3 *Valid xpointer() Usage.*

An XPointer that identifies the first of the points in Figure 7-3 appears in Example 7-6.

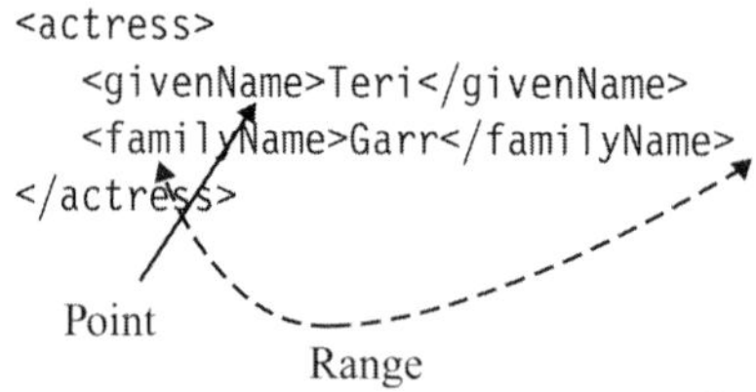

Figure 7-4 *Invalid xpointer() Usage.*

Example 7-6 *XPointer Identifying a Point*

```
xpointer(/actress/givenName/point()[2])
```

The point in Figure 7-4 is invalid because a point cannot occur *within* an element name — a meaningless concept in an Infoset. The range in that figure is invalid for a similar reason.

The fact that XPointer's xpointer() scheme is based on XPath 1.0 (with a few extensions) should make it evident that, if XPath is (as we believe it to be) a tool for querying XML, then the xpointer() scheme is also a tool for querying XML — and perhaps a slightly more powerful tool, at that! The element() scheme could also be considered a querying tool, since it allows identification (that is, location) of an element by its identity. According to the W3C's website, several implementations of XPointer existed in late 2002 and several more were planned.

7.3.3 XML Linking Language (XLink)

XPointer, as you read in Section 7.3.2, provides the ability to "point into" an XML resource (*i.e.*, an XML document or an external parsed entity), identifying specific elements and other locations of interest, such as points and ranges. Many of us, based on our experience with HTML and the links that it provides through its <a> tag, might think that an XPointer is all the linking capability that we need. For many purposes — such as HTML web pages — that's probably true.

However, for many applications, a more general definition of *link* is needed. For example, an indexing facility that correlates documents based on their content might not have the authority to make modifications to those documents; therefore, links among them must be stored external to the documents themselves. Another application where more complex links are useful is in document reviewing; a review of a particular part of a document might include several different parts, such as a comment on the paragraph, the identification of the paragraph itself, and perhaps a suggested resolution of the comment.

The XML Linking Language, also known as XLink,[19] defines an XML syntax for the creation of both basic unidirectional links and more complex links among resources, not all of them necessarily XML resources. A *link* is an explicit relationship between resources or portions of resources, expressed in the form of a *linking element*. Resources and portions of resources are addressed by URI references, and all of the resources associated by a link are said to *participate* in the link.

---

19 *XML Linking Language (Xlink) Version 1.0* (Cambridge, MA: World Wide Web Consortium, 2001). Available at: http://www.w3.org/TR/xlink/.

The XPointer specification discussed in Section 7.3.2 could be considered a little unusual because it doesn't actually define any XML syntax, instead specifying a syntax that can be used (for example) as part of a URI reference. Similarly, XLink is unusual in that it defines no XML elements but instead defines XML attributes (in a namespace that is often indicated by the namespace prefix "xlink:") that can be applied to ordinary elements of XML documents.

According to the XLink specification, an element "conforms to XLink" if it contains an attribute whose name is "xlink:type" and whose value is chosen from a short list of alternatives (*e.g.*, "simple," "extended," "locator") and if it also adheres to a number of constraints associated with the specified xlink:type value. The XLink rules for those constraints are a little complex and aren't critical to the subject of this book, so we'll look at only a few of them, to illustrate how XLink works and how it relates to querying XML.

Simple links (defined by elements having an attribute `xlink:type="simple"`) provide an outbound-only link (that is, from "here" to some other indicated location) with exactly two participating resources; they correspond to the link capabilities supported by HTML's <a> and <img> tags. An example of an element that creates a simple link is shown in Example 7-7. The XML fragment in that example uses a <SeeAlso> element that has two attributes, both from the xlink: namespace. The `xlink:type` attribute indicates a simple link, and the `xlink:href` attribute contains a relative URI reference containing only a fragment identifier (implying that the reference is to the same document containing this fragment).

Example 7-7 *An XLink Simple Link*

```
<movie xmlns:xlink="http://www/w3/org/1999/xlink">
  <title id="TheThing1982">The Thing</title>
  ...
  <plotSummary>
  This remake of the 1951 thriller
    <SeeAlso xlink:type="simple"
             xlink:href="#TheThing1951">The Thing</SeeAlso>
    almost seems to pick up where the original left off.
   ...
  </plotSummary>
</movie>
```

Extended links are more complex. They include inbound links (from somewhere else to "here"), third-party links (from "there" to "yonder"), and multiresource links. They may require definition (in a DTD, for example) of new elements specifically to provide link-specific information, such as the rules for traversing from one participant in a link to another. Extended links are often stored in places other than the resources that they associate, particularly when those resources are read-only or are expensive to update and when those resources are not in an XML format.

The film world (as any look at the Internet Movie Database, or IMDB,[20] will demonstrate) can be quite complex. Films have directors, cast members, crew members, scripts, locations, and so forth. But the director of a given film is very often the director of one or more other films. And most actors and actresses appear in several films. Some directors appear in the cast of films they (or others) direct. Some cast members are also producers, or editors, or script writers. In short, the world of movies is not a neat hierarchy that fits cleanly into an XML tree — in spite of the fact that we've chosen movies for our sample application.

Instead, the relationships between movies, the people involved in them, and so forth are complex and have a great many linkages. XLink's extended links provides a useful way to specify those linkages.

Let's consider an example that involves some movies, directors, and cast members we enjoy.

- Dustin Hoffman appears in the cast of many films; among them (in no particular order) are *Tootsie, Little Big Man, The Graduate,* and *Midnight Cowboy.*
- Sydney Pollack has directed a number of films; they include *Jeremiah Johnson, Out of Africa, Tootsie,* and *This Property Is Condemned.* He also appeared in *Tootsie.*
- *Midnight Cowboy* starred both Dustin Hoffman and Jon Voight.
- *Tootsie* starred Hoffman, Bill Murray, Teri Garr, and Jessica Lange.
- *The Graduate* starred Hoffman, Anne Bancroft, and Katherine Ross.
- *Little Big Man* starred Hoffman, Faye Dunaway, and Chief Dan George.

20 Internet Movie Database, http://imdb.com.

- *Jeremiah Johnson* starred Robert Redford and Will Geer.
- *Out of Africa* starred Meryl Streep, Klaus Maria Brandauer, and Robert Redford.
- *This Property Is Condemned* starred Natalie Wood, Robert Redford, and Charles Bronson.

Starting with just Dustin Hoffman and only four of his films plus Sydney Pollack and four of his films, we've now got eight films and 15 people. If we were to include all of the credited cast members, the crew, the producers, *etc.*, undoubtedly 200 people or more would be involved. And merely linking to one other movie for each of those people would cause our data collection to grow very quickly indeed!

Let's see how XLink might address this problem. Assuming that we were sufficiently imaginative when designing the XML documents for capturing our movie data, we would probably have one document for movies and another for people. Therefore, we might have created documents containing fragments like those shown in Example 7-8.

Example 7-8 *movies.xml and people.xml*

```
<?xml version="1.0"?>
<movies xmlns:xlink="http://www/w3/org/1999/xlink">
  <movie id="Tootsie1982">
    <title>Tootsie</title>
    <MPAArating>PG</MPAArating>
    <plotSummary>An unemployed actor with a reputation for being
difficult disguises himself as a woman to get a role in a soap
opera.</plotSummary>
  </movie>
  <movie id="LittleBigMan1970">
    <title>Little Big Man</title>
    <MPAArating>PG-13</MPAArating>
    <plotSummary>Jack Crabb, looking back from extreme old age, tells
of his life being raised by Indians and fighting with General Custer.
</plotSummary>
  </movie>
  <movie id="TheGraduate1967">
    <title>The Graduate</title>
    <MPAArating>PG</MPAArating>
```

```
    <plotSummary>A young man just out of college doesn't know what to
do with his life. But being involved with a young woman AND her mother
probably wasn't it. </plotSummary>
  </movie>
  <movie id="MidnightCowboy1969">
    <title>Midnight Cowboy</title>
    <MPAArating>R</MPAArating>
    <plotSummary>A naive male prostitute and his sickly friend
struggle to survive on the streets of New York City. </plotSummary>
  </movie>
  <movie id="JeremiahJohnson1972">
    <title>Jeremiah Johnson</title>
    <MPAArating>PG</MPAArating>
    <plotSummary>A mountain man who wishes to live the life of a
hermit becomes the unwilling object of a long vendetta. </plotSummary>
  </movie>
  <movie id="OutOfAfrica1985">
    <title>Out of Africa</title>
    <MPAArating>PG</MPAArating>
    <plotSummary>Follows the life of Karen Blixen, who establishes a
plantation in Africa. Her life is complicated by a husband of
convenience. </plotSummary>
  </movie>
  <movie id="ThisPropertyIsCondemned1966">
    <title>This Property Is Condemned</title>
    <MPAArating>Unrated</MPAArating>
    <plotSummary>A railroad official, Owen Legate, comes to Dodson,
Mississippi to shut down much of the town's railway (town's main
income). </plotSummary>
  </movie>
</movies>

<?xml version="1.0"?>
<people xmlns:xlink="http://www/w3/org/1999/xlink">
  <person id="DustinHoffman1">
    <name>
      <personalName>Dustin</personalName>
      <familyName>Hoffman</familyName>
    </name>
    <birthdate>1937-08-08</birthdate>
    <deathDate></deathDate>
  </person>
  <person id="NatalieWood1">
```

```
  <name>
    <personalName>Natalie</personalName>
    <familyName>Wood</familyName>
  </name>
  <birthdate>1938-07-20</birthdate>
  <deathDate>1981-11-29</deathDate>
</person>
<person id="RobertRedford1">
  <name>
    <personalName>Robert</personalName>
    <familyName>Redford</familyName>
  </name>
  <birthdate>1937-08-18</birthdate>
  <deathDate></deathDate>
</person>
<person id="CharlesBronson1">
  <name>
    <personalName>Charles</personalName>
    <familyName>Bronson</familyName>
  </name>
  <birthdate>1921-11-03</birthdate>
  <deathDate>2003-08-30</deathDate>
</person>
<person id="WillGeer1">
  <name>
    <personalName>Will</personalName>
    <familyName>Geer</familyName>
  </name>
  <birthdate>1902-03-09</birthdate>
  <deathDate>1987-04-22</deathDate>
</person>
<person id="MerylStreep1">
  <name>
    <personalName>Meryl</personalName>
    <familyName>Streep</familyName>
  </name>
  <birthdate>1949-06-22</birthdate>
  <deathDate></deathDate>
</person>
<person id="KlausMariaBrandauer1">
  <name>
```

```
      <personalName>Klaus</personalName>
      <familyName>Brandauer</familyName>
    </name>
    <birthdate>1943-06-22</birthdate>
    <deathDate></deathDate>
  </person>
  <person id="FayeDunaway1">
    <name>
      <personalName>Faye</personalName>
      <familyName>Dunaway</familyName>
    </name>
    <birthdate>1941-01-14</birthdate>
    <deathDate></deathDate>
  </person>
  <person id="CheifDanGeorge1">
    <name>
      <personalName>Dan</personalName>
      <familyName>George</familyName>
    </name>
    <birthdate>1899-07-24</birthdate>
    <deathDate>1981-09-23</deathDate>
  </person>
  <person id="BillMurray1">
    <name>
      <personalName>Bill</personalName>
      <familyName>Murray</familyName>
    </name>
    <birthdate>1950-09-21</birthdate>
    <deathDate></deathDate>
  </person>
  <person id="TeriGarr1">
    <name>
      <personalName>Teri</personalName>
      <familyName>Garr</familyName>
    </name>
    <birthdate>1949-12-11</birthdate>
    <deathDate></deathDate>
  </person>
  <person id="JessicaLange1">
    <name>
      <personalName>Jessica</personalName>
```

```
      <familyName>Lange</familyName>
    </name>
    <birthdate>1949-04-20</birthdate>
    <deathDate></deathDate>
  </person>
  <person id="SydneyPollack1">
    <name>
      <personalName>Sydney</personalName>
      <familyName>Pollack</familyName>
    </name>
    <birthdate>1934-07-01</birthdate>
    <deathDate></deathDate>
  </person>
</people>
```

Notice that the `<movie>` elements in Example 7-8 have no child elements (or attributes) that identify who directed them, who produced them, or who starred in them. Similarly, the `<person>` elements don't indicate what roles they played in what films. By using the facilities of XLink, we can establish all of those relationships *without changing the documents themselves*. We could create a separate document that contains nothing but the links between people and films, indicating what relationships they have.

To do this, we need to define the elements that appear in that separate linkage document; those elements will use the various `xlink:` attributes defined by XLink. For the purposes of this example, let's limit ourselves to tracking only two sorts of relationships between movies and people and the corresponding inverse relationships: the director or directors of a movie, the movies directed by a person, the principal players in a movie, and the movies in which a person played.

Using DTD notation (see Chapter 5, "Structural Metadata"), we could define elements to track these relationships as illustrated in Example 7-9.

Example 7-9 *DTD Definitions for Movie Relationships Elements*

```
<!ELEMENT relationships ((director | player)*)>
<!ATTLIST relationships
```

```
  xmlns:xlink       CDATA       #FIXED "http://www.w3.org/1999/xlink">

<!ELEMENT director ((who | what)*)>
<!ATTLIST director
  xlink:type        (extended)  #FIXED "extended">

<!ELEMENT player ((who | what)*)>
<!ATTLIST what
  xlink:type        (extended)  #FIXED "extended">

<!ELEMENT who EMPTY>
<!ATTLIST who
  xlink:type        (locator)   #FIXED "locator"
  xlink:href        CDATA       #REQUIRED
  xlink:title       CDATA       #IMPLIED
  xlink:label       NMTOKEN     #REQUIRED>

<!ELEMENT what EMPTY>
<!ATTLIST what
  xlink:type        (locator)   #FIXED "locator"
  xlink:href        CDATA       #REQUIRED
  xlink:title       CDATA       #IMPLIED
  xlink:label       NMTOKEN     #REQUIRED>
```

That doesn't look terribly complicated, but this is meant to be a simple example. In this example, a locator (`xlink:type="locator"`) is a type of link that simply identifies a resource that participates in an XLink. Elements with that particular attribute definition can appear only as a child of an element with an `xlink:type="extended"` attribute. The document in Example 7-10 shows how we might use these elements to capture the information we want about our movies and people.

Example 7-10 *Relationships Between Movies and People*

```
<?xml version="1.0"?>
<relationships>
  <director>
    <who href="http://example.com/movie_info/people#SydneyPollack1"
         title="Sydney Pollack"
         label="SydneyPollack-director"/>
    <what href="http://example.com/movie_info/movies#Tootsie1982"
```

```
          title="Tootsie (1982)"
          label="Tootsie-movie"/>
    <what href="http://example.com/movie_info/movies#JeremiahJohnson1972"
          title="Jeremiah Johnson (1972)"
          label="JeremiahJohnson-movie"/>
    <what href="http://example.com/movie_info/movies#OutOfAfrica1985"
          title="Out of Africa (1985)"
          label="OutOfAfrica-movie"/>
    <what href="http://example.com/movie_info/movies#ThisPropertyIsCondemned1966"
          title="This Property Is Condemned (1966)"
          label="ThisPropertyIsCondemned-movie"/>
  </director>
  <player>
    <who href="DustinHoffman1"
         title="Dustin Hoffman"
         label="DustinHoffman-actor">
    <what href="http://example.com/movie_info/movies#Tootsie1982"
          title="Tootsie (1982)"
          label="Tootsie-movie"/>
    <what href="LittleBigMan1970"
          title="Little Big Man (1970)"
          label="LittleBigMan-movie">
    <what href="TheGraduate1967"
          title="The Graduate (1967)"
          label="TheGraduate-movie">
    <what href="MidnightCowboy1969"
          title="Midnight Cowboy (1969)"
          label="MidnightCowboy-movie">
  </player>
  <player>
    <who href="RobertRedford1"
         title="Robert Redford"
         label="RobertRedford-actor">
    <what href="OutOfAfrica1985"
          title="Out of Africa (1985)"
          label="OutOfAfrica-movie">
    <what href="JeremiahJohnson1972"
          title="Jeremiah Johnson (1972)"
          label="JeremiahJohnson-movie">
    <what href="ThisPropertyIsCondemned1966"
          title="This Property Is Condemned (1966)"
```

```
          label="ThisPropertyIsCondemned-movie">
  </player>
  ...
  <player>
    <who href="NatalieWood1"
         title="Natalie Wood"
         label="NatalieWood-actress">
    <what href="ThisPropertyIsCondemned1966"
          title="This Property Is Condemned (1966)"
          label="ThisPropertyIsCondemned-movie">
  </player>
</relationships>
```

To relieve the tedium of including all of the players in our (very small) sample, we've omitted most of them, as indicated by the ellipsis.

Our design captures relationships between people and movies, but it doesn't indicate anything that a program can or should do with those relationships. In the most simplistic view of things, an application willing to process these Xlinks (that is, an XLink processor) would probably interrogate the relationships document, searching for a person or movie of interest and then allowing traversals to the movies and/or people of interest.

We could make those traversals somewhat more explicit by adding elements that define *arcs* between various components. An arc is an optional type of link (`xlink:type="arc"`) that makes relationships between resources (`xlink:type="resource"`) explicit along with the rules governing the traversals between those resources. We illustrate a possible design for a new element that defines arcs between our movies and people, as shown in Example 7-11.

Example 7-11 *Extending the DTD with Arcs*

```
<!ELEMENT relationships ((director | player)*)>
...
<!ELEMENT director ((who | what | visit)*)>
...
<!ELEMENT player ((who | what | visit)*)>
...
<!ELEMENT visit EMPTY>
<!ATTLIST visit
  xlink:type        (arc)        #FIXED "arc"
  xlink:from        NMTOKEN      #REQUIRED
```

```
xlink:to          NMTOKEN      #REQUIRED
xlink:show        ( new
                  | replace ) #IMPLIED>
```

The `visit` element defines an arc from one resource to another; the `xlink:show` attribute specifies what the XLink processor should do when the arc is followed. The values (*new* and *replace*) might function in a display application to open a new window to display the target resource or to replace the display in the current window with the target resource. Example 7-12 illustrates the use of the `visit` element.

Example 7-12 *Using Arcs*

```
<?xml version="1.0"?>
<relationships>
  <director>
    <who href="http://example.com/movie_info/people#SydneyPollack1"
         title="Sydney Pollack"
         label="SydneyPollack-director"/>
    <what href="http://example.com/movie_info/movies#Tootsie1982"
          title="Tootsie (1982)"
          label="Tootsie-movie"/>
    <what href="http://example.com/movie_info/movies#JeremiahJohnson1972"
          title="Jeremiah Johnson (1972)"
          label="JeremiahJohnson-movie"/>
    <what href="http://example.com/movie_info/movies#OutOfAfrica1985"
          title="Out of Africa (1985)"
          label="OutOfAfrica-movie"/>
    <what href="http://example.com/movie_info/movies#ThisPropertyIsCondemned1966"
          title="This Property Is Condemned (1966)"
          label="ThisPropertyIsCondemned-movie"/>
    <visit from="SydneyPollack-director"
           to="Tootsie-movie"
           show="new"/>
    <visit from="Tootsie-movie"
           to="SydneyPollack-director"
           show="new"/>
    ...
  </director>
  ...
</relationships>
```

Notice that there are two instances of the `visit` element in Example 7-12. The first allows a traversal from Sydney's information to the information about *Tootsie*, while the second defines the reverse traversal.

The document in Example 7-10 shows the relationships based on directors and on players, but it doesn't adequately capture the fact that Sydney Pollack was both a director of several of our movies and a player in at least one of them. A different design of these linkages would have done a better job of capturing that information. Similarly, we don't indicate what role (or, as happens sometimes, roles) a single actor or actress might play in a film. And we haven't planned very well for queries to discover all of the people involved in a single movie. The reader is invited to explore alternate linkage designs that capture those relationships between movies and people.

Unlike XPointers, which could be described as XPath++, while serving a similar function for querying XML, XLink is not itself any sort of querying capability. However, XLink allows the description of complex relationships between resources, and applications that query XML documents may need the ability to traverse such relationships in order to find the data they seek. There are, of course, other ways of achieving similar goals by using application-defined relationships, much as relational databases allow applications to include SQL statements that join information from multiple tables. Any given XML querying facility might use a join-like approach, an approach of exploring XLinks, or both. We are not aware of any widely used language for querying XML that navigates Xlinks, but they may arise in the future.

7.4 Relationship Constraints: Enforcing Consistency

SQL provides a type of constraint, called a *primary key*, that allows the database system itself to enforce uniqueness of the values stored in a particular column of a table; it also provides a second sort of constraint, a *foreign key*, that allows the database management system (DBMS) to ensure that a reference from a row in one table to a row of another (usually different but possibly the same) table identifies a row that has the same value in the target table's primary key. These constraints, together referred to as *referential integrity constraints*, provide a very powerful mechanism for enforcing consistency between the rows in one table and the rows in another.

The XML specification itself provides a mechanism[21] that allows XML document authors to ensure that selected elements are uniquely identified (and identifiable) within a document. As you read in Section 5.2.2, "Relatively Simple, Easy to Write, and Easy to Read," elements can be declared to have an attribute whose type has attribute type ID. The value of such an attribute must be unique among the values of all such attributes in a given XML document. Correspondingly, elements may also be defined to have one or more attributes whose attribute type is IDREF or IDREFS. The values of such attributes must be identical to the value of some attribute of attribute type ID in the same XML document.

In the relational database world, the functionality corresponding to attributes of type ID is provided by primary keys and unique constraints. The functionality corresponding to attributes of types IDREF and IDREFS is provided by foreign keys. Thus, basic XML (without support from any additional specification) provides functionality analogous to SQL's PRIMARY KEY and FOREIGN KEY constraints. Of course, this is a good thing, but notice that we said "analogous to" and not "the same as" — that's because SQL's foreign keys are allowed to reference rows in tables other than the table in which the foreign key is defined. By contrast, XML's IDREF values can (and must) reference other elements only in the same document.

Adding XML Schema to the equation raises the bar considerably. XML Schema (as you read in Section 5.3.2, "Simple Types [Primitive Types and Derived Types]"), supports the derived types ID, IDREF, and IDREFS. Although we didn't discuss the semantics of those types explicitly in Chapter 5, "Structural Metadata," XML Schema provides roughly the same behavior for values of those types that the XML specification and its DTDs do. One significant difference is that XML Schema allows elements as well as attributes to be given a type of ID, IDREF, or IDREFS. However, XML Schema still does not support the notion that an element of type ID can be referenced by an element or attribute of type IDREF in a separate document.

Instead, XML Schema provides three new constructs that support referential integrity constraints. These constructs, which are included as part of the definition of an element, provide simple uniqueness constraints (similar to those provided by attributes and elements with the type ID), key constraints (similar to a uniqueness constraint but with the specified values mandatory), and referencing con-

21 http://www.w3.org/TR/REC-xml#NT-TokenizedType.

straints (which mandate that specified values correspond to matching key or unique constraints).

Let's explore an example. In our database of movies, we have observed that there are never any movies with both the same title and same year of release. (In the real world, that situation might arise, of course. But not in *our* database!) That immediately suggests that the combination of title and yearReleased would satisfy a unique constraint.

In an XML Schema for describing our data, we could provide a simple unique constraint by using declarations like those seen in Example 7-13. Note the <xs:unique> component at the bottom of the movie element declaration.

Example 7-13 *Declaring a Unique Constraint for an Element*

```
<xs:element name="movies">
  <xs:complexType>
    <xs:sequence>
      <xs:element name="movie">
        <xs:complexType>
          <xs:sequence>
            <xs:element name="title" type="xs:string"/>
            <xs:element name="yearReleased">
              <xs:simpleType>
                <xs:restriction base="xs:integer">
                  <xs:minInclusive value="1900"/>
                  <xs:maxInclusive value="2100"/>
                </xs:restriction>
              </xs:simpleType>
            </xs:element>
            <xs:element name="director">
              <xs:complexType>
                <xs:sequence>
                  <xs:element ref="familyName"/>
                  <xs:element ref="givenName"/>
                </xs:sequence>
              </xs:complexType>
            </xs:element>
          </xs:sequence>
        </xs:complexType>
      </xs:element>
    </xs:sequence>
```

```
  </xs:complexType>

  <xs:unique name="uniqueMovie">
    <xs:selector xpath="./movie"/>
    <xs:field xpath="title"/>
    <xs:field xpath="yearReleased"/>
  </xs:unique>
</xs:element>
```

In that `<xs:unique>` element (for which the `name` attribute is mandatory, the value of which must itself be unique), the child `<xs:selector>` element identifies a node set — the set of `<movie>` nodes that are children of the "current" node (the `<movies>` node). The `<xs:field>` element identifies the descendants and/or attributes of the nodes that are in that node set, forming a second node set for each node in the `<movie>` node set; in this case, we've declared that there are two nodes in that second node set — the `<title>` child element and the `<yearReleased>` child element. The way to read the `<xs:unique>` declaration is "for each child element named `movie`, the combination of that element's children named `title` and `yearReleased` must be unique within the containing `<movies>` element."

The declarations in Example 7-13 have one characteristic that may or may not be desirable: while the `<xs:unique>` element prohibits the existence in any single XML document of two `<movie>` elements whose combined `<title>` and `<yearReleased>` child elements have equal content, it makes no requirement that the declarations of those child elements be nonnillable (this means that the elements must not be declared with an attribute named `xsi:nillable` whose value is "`true`"). It also allows the possibility that one or more `<movie>` elements might be missing a `<title>` child element and/ or a `<yearReleased>` child element.

If we wanted to require that both fields be nonnillable *and* that every member of the node set chosen by the `<xs:selector>` have exactly one `<title>` child element and exactly one `<yearReleased>` element, we would replace the `<xs:unique>` element with the `<xs:key>` element that you see in Example 7-14. When you use an `<xs:key>` constraint, you should not declare any of the `<xs:field>` elements to refer to descendant elements or attributes that are optional.

Example 7-14 *Declaring a Key Constraint for an Element*

```
<xs:key name="reallyUniqueMovie">
  <xs:selector xpath="./movie"/>
  <xs:field xpath="title"/>
  <xs:field xpath="yearReleased"/>
</xs:key>
```

Now that we know how to create both a unique constraint and a key constraint for an element, we can consider how to use such constraints to ensure that other elements that claim to reference a <movie> element actually reference a movie that exists. In the SQL world, this role is played by a type of referential constraint called a *foreign key constraint.*

In XML Schema, that role is played by the <xs:keyref> element. That element has two required attributes: name and refer. Like the eponymous attribute of the <xs:unique> and <xs:key> elements, the name attribute of the <xs:keyref> element is required, as is the refer attribute. The value of the refer attribute must be equal to the value of the name attribute of an <xs:unique> or <xs:key> element declared in the same XML Schema. The content of the <xs:keyref> element comprises the usual <xs:selector> element and one or more <xs:field> elements. In this element, the number of <xs:field> children must be the same as the number of <xs:field> elements in the <xs:unique> or <xs:key> constraint identified by the name attribute.

In our movies database, we have the requirements that every review in the database be a review of exactly one movie and that that movie also be in the database. We could express this constraint via code like that in Example 7-15.

Example 7-15 *Declaring a Referencing Constraint for an Element*

```
<xs:element name="movies">
  <xs:complexType>
    <xs:choice minOccurs="1" maxOccurs="unbounded">
      <xs:element name="movie">
        ...
        <xs:key name="reallyUniqueMovie">
          <xs:selector xpath="./movie"/>
          <xs:field xpath="title"/>
          <xs:field xpath="yearReleased"/>
        </xs:key>
```

```
      </xs:element>

      <xs:element name="review">
        <xs:complexType>
          <xs:sequence>
            <xs:element name="reviewer" type="xs:string"/>
            <xs:element name="title" type="xs:string"/>
          </xs:sequence>
        </xs:complexType
        <xs:attribute name="yearMovieReleased"
                      type="xs:integer"/>
      </xs:element>
    </xs:complexType>

    <xs:keyref name="mustBeAMovie" refer="reallyUniqueMovie">
      <xs:selector xpath="./review"/>
      <xs:field xpath="title"/>
      <xs:field xpath="@yearMovieReleased"/>
    </xs:keyref>
  </xs:element>
```

Note that the <xs:keyref> element contains one <xs:field> whose xpath attribute specifies the name of a child element (title), while the other specifies the name of an attribute (@yearMovieReleased). The <xs:field> elements can identify any descendant or attribute (including attributes of descendants), as long as the number of <xs:field> child elements in the <xs:unique> or <xs:key> element is equal to the number in the <xs:keyref> element.

In this chapter, the discussion of XPointer describes the behavior of shorthand pointers, which behave somewhat like HTML's <a> tag: They match the (first) element with an ID-typed attribute whose value is identical to the NCName in the shorthand pointer. Unlike XML's IDREF semantics, the shorthand pointer can identify a point in an XML document other than the one in which the pointer itself is located. This improves the analogy with SQL's foreign keys, even to the error that occurs if the referenced point doesn't exist. Similarly, XPointer's element() scheme, when only an NCName is used, offers that same functionality.

SQL provides syntax for joining information from multiple tables based on the foreign key relationships, thus allowing query authors to create queries with greater chances of correct behavior. Unfortunately, we are unaware of widely accepted XML querying facilities that take advantage of ID/IDREF relationships by supporting joins of information in XML documents based on those relationships.[22] Perhaps some future version of XQuery will consider this possibility, but it's far too soon to say.

7.5 Chapter Summary

In this chapter, we've examined several W3C specifications that deal with managing XML in ways that interact (more or less — but mostly less) with querying XML. XSLT arguably provides a type of XML querying capability, but it is specialized for transforming XML documents rather than specifically searching within documents or identifying documents within collections. XSL FO, as we saw, is a formatting language and has nothing to do with querying XML, but it is very useful for publishing the results of queries in reader-friendly formats.

XInclude allows the modularization of XML documents and does so in a way that makes it possible to query the result of the merger of the various modules. XPointer can provide an IDREF-like capability through its shorthand pointers and its element() scheme; its xpointer() scheme is an extension of XPath and is thus powerful enough to easily be considered a tool for querying XML. XLink provides the ability to define sophisticated linkages between and among XML resources, but it offers very little in the form of querying XML documents. Until popular XML querying languages such as XPath and XQuery support the sort of relationships created through ID/IDREF-typed attributes and elements, through XPointer utilization, or through XLink capabilities, none of these will offer the same promise that SQL's referential constraint-based joins provide.

22 In SQL, foreign keys are permitted to reference tables that are in other databases, while XML's ID/IDREF capabilities are relevant only within a single XML document. This inherently limits the ability of XML querying languages to use ID/IDREF as a mechanism to join information from multiple separate documents.

Chapter

8

Storing: XML and Databases

8.1 Introduction

The act of querying XML obviously requires that there is XML to be queried. What most standards related to querying XML do not address is the question of where that XML is found.

In this chapter, we discuss several ways in which XML documents can be made available for querying. Among these are ordinary computer file systems, websites, relational database systems, XML database systems, and other persistent storage systems. Such persistence facilities may present a single XML document at a time, or they might provide the ability to query a collection of documents at once. Another source of XML, however, does not require persistent storage but involves XML that is presented to a client (such as a querying facility) as it is generated. The capability of generating XML (usually dynamically) and transmitting it to one or more clients in "real time" is often called *streaming*. Querying XML that is persistently stored offers several advantages and challenges, while querying streaming XML presents other advantages and challenges.

As you read this chapter, you'll learn about the differences in ways that XML can be stored (persistent XML) along with the advantages and challenges involved in querying that persistent XML. The mechanisms for storing persistent XML data range up to enterprise-level database systems, with all of the robustness, scalability, transaction control, and security that such systems offer.

You'll also learn about the advantages and challenges associated with queries evaluated against XML streams. Such data might be broadcast for consumption by many clients (stock ticker data, for example) or might be streamed to a single client (real-time communication systems, such as instant messaging). The common thread is that data, once transmitted, cannot be retrieved a second time.

There is also a middle ground in which XML is often used: message queuing systems. Such systems often require that data be stored in some temporary location until it can be transmitted to its consumer, but they rarely involve long-term persistence of the data. Such data is sometimes queried while it resides in its temporary storage locations and sometimes when it has been released from storage and is being transmitted to a receiving agent — and thus behaves more like streamed data.

8.2 The Need for Persistence

A great deal of the XML data most people encounter today is stored somewhere — that is, it is *persistent*. Storing XML data persistently makes a great deal of sense for data that may be used many times, especially when that data has a high value and may have been expensive, even difficult, to create.

Examples of such XML abound: Our movie collection is documented in an XML document; corporations are increasingly likely to store business data like purchase orders in an XML form; many technical books are being produced from XML sources; the W3C's specifications themselves are all coded in XML; even computer applications' initialization and scripting information is increasingly represented in XML. Of course, different types of information present different requirements for persistent storage. Some sorts — such as the books owned by a publisher — probably need to be retained for lengthy periods of time, while others — messaging data, for example — might have a lifetime measured in seconds or minutes. The various mechanisms discussed in the remainder of this section easily support the wide variety of requirements for storing XML.

8.2.1 Databases

A database, according to the Wikipedia,[1] is "an information set with a regular structure." A database system, or database management system (DBMS), is thus (for our purposes, at least) a computer system that manages a computerized database. While it's not unknown for some people to apply the term *database management system* to extremely primitive data management products, the term is most often used to describe systems that provide a number of important characteristics for data integrity. Among these characteristics are:

- Query tools, such as a query language like SQL or XQuery
- Transaction capabilities that include the so-called ACID properties: atomicity of operations, consistency of the database as a whole, isolation from other concurrent users' operations, and durability of operations even across system crashes
- Scalability and robustness
- Management of security and performance, including registration and management of users and their privileges, creation of indices on the data, and provision hints for the optimization of operations

Several types of database management systems are in wide use by enterprises of all sorts, but we believe that only three are commonly employed to store and manage XML data: relational, object-oriented, and "pure XML." All of these types of database inherently provide the ability not only to store and retrieve XML documents but also to search that data through the use of query languages of some sort. Querying XML data in a DBMS is probably more effective than querying XML data stored in other media, if for no other reason than the existence of various performance-enhancing features of a DBMS, such as indices.

It is worth noting one important consideration when storing XML in a database system: XML, by definition, is based on the Unicode character set.[2] Not all database systems support Unicode, and some

---

1 *Wikipedia, The Free Enclyopedia*, http://en.wikipedia.org.

2 *The Unicode Standard, Version 4.1.0* (Mountain View, CA: The Unicode Consortium, 2005). Available at: http://www.unicode.org/versions/Unicode4.1.0/.

support Unicode only when that character set was chosen when the database system was installed or when the specific database was created. Increasingly, however, we see that all of the major relational database systems are being updated to employ Unicode internally — implying that this may no longer be a serious issue in a few years. We have not investigated the status of Unicode in object-oriented DBMSs, but the fact that many of them have Java interfaces suggests that they may use Unicode internally. Naturally, pure XML databases will always use Unicode internally.

Relational Databases

You won't be surprised to hear that a very large fraction of persistent XML is found in relational databases, right along with other data vital to an enterprise's business. Most large businesses today — and an increasing percentage of smaller businesses — depend on relational databases to store and protect their data.

Relational database management systems (RDBMSs) have been on the scene since the early 1980s and have arguably become the most widely used form of DBMS. The billions of dollars that have been invested into commercial relational database systems (such as Oracle's Oracle database, IBM's DB2, and Microsoft's SQL Server) have given them formidable strengths in the data management environment. Such systems are tremendously scalable, often able to handle thousands of concurrent users accessing many terabytes — even petabytes — of data.

Some say that the relational database systems — because of the two decades and billions of dollars invested in their infrastructure and code, their proven ability to adapt to new types of data, and their entrenchment in so many organizations — might never be superseded in the marketplace by other, more specialized database products. Whether this is mere hubris or a realistic view of the world, we see that the vendors of RDBMS products are adapting very quickly to a world in which XML support is a major requirement.

Starting in roughly 2001, most commercial relational database vendors began adding support for XML data into their products. Initially, the focus was on merely storing XML documents and retrieving them in whole, without the ability to perform any significant operations on the content of those documents. Some systems merely stored serialized XML data in character string columns or CLOB (character large object) columns, while others explored ways of breaking the XML data down into component elements, attributes, and other nodes for storage into columns in various tables. (This latter mechanism, commonly called *shredding* the XML, is discussed further in Section 8.2.3.)

As the vendors' experience with — and customers' requirements for — XML grew, the products gained more direct support for XML as a true data type of its own. A native XML type (see Section 8.3) was defined for the use of database designers and application authors. New built-in functions (see Chapter 15, "SQL/XML") were developed to transform ordinary relational data into XML structures of the users' choice. And a variety of ways were invented to query within XML stored in that native XML type, including the ability to invoke XPath and XQuery (see Chapter 9, "XPath 1.0 and XPath 2.0," Chapter 10, "Introduction to XQuery 1.0," Chapter 11, "XQuery 1.0 Definition," and Chapter 15, "SQL/XML") on that XML. In addition, these products have been given the ability to support XML metadata, largely in the form of XML Schema (see Chapter 5, "Structural Metadata").

Of course, we may be biased by our years of participation in the relational database world, but we believe that RDBMS products are rapidly becoming as fully capable of managing XML data as they are of managing ordinary business data.

Object-Oriented Databases

In the late 1980s and early 1990s, a new form of DBMS was introduced to the data management marketplace, the object-oriented database management system (OODBMS). Unlike the RDBMS products, OODBMS products suffered from not having a formal data model on which their design was based. As a result, the meaning of the term OODBMS varied widely between implementations. What they all had in common, of course, was that they managed *objects* instead of *tuples* of *attributes* or *rows* of *columns*.

Arguably, the real world is better represented as a collection of objects, each having a state (data about the individual object) and behaviors (functions that implement common semantics of classes of objects). Object-oriented programming languages (OOPLs) were coming into prominence (and have since tended to dominate some application domains), and it was natural to want to persistently store the objects being manipulated in OOPL programs. Some OODBMSs took the approach of allowing individual objects (or classes of objects) handled by a particular OOPL program to be "marked" with a flag that indicated whether or not the object (or members of the class) were to be automatically placed into persistent storage — without any specific action (*e.g.*, a "store" command) taken by the program. Others made the OODBMS an integral part of the OOPL so that storing and retrieving objects was done completely seamlessly without any application code involved. Still others required that the OOPL programs explicitly store and retrieve objects when the program made the decision to do so.

What was generally missing from all of these OODBMS products was a common query language that allowed applications to locate objects based on their states and to retrieve information about specific objects. The RDBMS world had standardized on the database language SQL, so the OODBMS community[3] decided to adapt SQL for use as a query language in their world; the result of that adaptation is a language called OQL, which is a search-and-retrieval-only language without built-in update capabilities.

A significant portion of the XML community views XML as naturally object-oriented (for example, every node in an XML document has unique identity, as do objects in all object-oriented systems). Consequently, when XML became a significant market force, we expected that Object Data Management Group (ODMG) would quickly move to incorporate this new type of data, if only by adapting an XML data model like the DOM (Document Object Model)[4] for use in the context of ODMG. While the owners of the ODMG standard have not yet published a new version with explicit XML support, a group of academics did just that in a system they called Ozone.[5] Subsequently, an open-source effort providing an Ozone database system[6] was established. The documentation of this effort states that "ozone [sic] includes a fully W3C-compliant DOM implementation that allows you to store XML data."

We are unaware of any significant presence in the marketplace of OODBMS products that incorporate explicit support of XML as a data type (in the sense that the Ozone system does, at least). This may be due to the fact that OODBMSs in general have found secure niches in the data management community and that those niches have little need for XML except as a data interchange format. It may

---

3 R. G. G. Cattell (ed.), et al., *The Object Data Standard (ODBM 3.0)* (San Francisco: Morgan Kaufmann Publishers, 2000) .

4 *Document Object Model (DOM) Level 3 Core Specification Version 1.0* (Cambridge, MA: World Wide Web Consortium, 2004). Available at: http://www.w3.org/TR/DOM-Level-3-Core.

5 Serge Abiteboul, Jennifer Widom, and Tirthankar Lahiri, *A Unified Approach for Querying Structured Data and XML* (1998). Available at: http://www.w3.org/TandS/QL/QL98/pp/serge.html.

6 *The Ozone Database Project*, http://www.ozone-db.org.

also be due to the fact that many (but not all) relational database systems have embraced object technology and are popularly known as object-relational database management systems (ORDBMSs). In any case, we do not perceive a near-term movement toward the use of OODBMS products for large-scale management of XML data.

Native XML Databases

We were not surprised that a number of start-up companies as well as some established data management companies determined that XML data would best be managed by a DBMS that was designed specifically to deal with semistructured data – that is, a native XML database.

But what, exactly, is a native XML database? One resource we found [7] defines it in terms of three principle characteristics:

- Defines a (logical) model for an XML document
- Has an XML document as its fundamental unit of (logical) storage
- Is not required to have any particular underlying physical storage model

Undoubtedly, the most important of those three criteria is the first one, the definition of a model for XML documents. As you've seen elsewhere in this book (*e.g.*, Chapter 5, "Structural Metadata," and Chapter 6, "The XML Information Set (Infoset) and Beyond"), a number of data models for XML are in current use. The specific model chosen for a native XML database system is less important than the requirement that it support arbitrarily deep levels of nesting and complexity, document order, unique identity of nodes, mixed content, semistructured data, *etc.*

Unfortunately for companies that invested heavily in the development of what we call "pure XML" database systems, the widely accepted definition of "native XML" database systems doesn't exclude other existing technologies. The definition cited earlier makes it clear that relational database systems can provide all of the required characteristics of a native XML database. This can be done either by building an XML-centric layer atop a relational system or

7 Kimbro Staken, *Introduction to Native XML Databases* (2001). Available at: http://www.xml.com/pub/a/2001/10/31/nativexmldb.html.

by incorporating new XML-specific facilities directly into relational engines. Of course, that doesn't mean that there is no marketplace for pure XML DBMSs. However, we suspect that, like OODBMSs before them, pure XML DBMSs will find small but secure niches for themselves where they satisfy very specific needs that are not targeted by RDBMS (or ORDBMS) products.

8.2.2 Other Persistent Media

While a great proportion of enterprise XML data is managed by explicit database management systems, we believe that a large majority of XML in the world today does not get stored in DBMSs at all. Instead, XML documents are found in ordinary operating system files and on web pages. A quick search of just one of our computers found several thousand XML documents — most of which we didn't even realize were there, since they were created as part of the installation of several software products.

The advantage of storing XML documents in ordinary files on your own computer is, of course, that everybody with a computer has a file system — while most of us don't (yet) have formal DBMSs installed on our computers or even unrestricted access to our organizations' DBMSs. Better yet, those files are completely under your control and not governed by some database administrator somewhere in your organization. Of course, there are disadvantages as well: You're usually responsible for backing up your own files, lack of transactional control makes data loss more likely, and the problems of keeping track of perhaps thousands of XML files are quite tedious. Perhaps more importantly, there is usually no way to enforce any consistent relationships among those thousands of XML files — those documents that specify configuration information for software products might define the same operating system environment variable in multiple, incompatible ways.

Some people argue that a single XML document can be a sort of "database-in-a-file." If you take this sort of approach, you would just mark up your data on the fly, making up tag names as you go. Unfortunately, unless you write a good XML Schema to validate that document, it's awfully difficult to keep that data internally consistent, because you might use different "spellings" of tags to represent the same conceptual entity (<SerialNumber> one time, <SerNum> another time, <Serial-num> a third, all to represent the serial numbers of products you own). We recommend strongly against such an approach to storing your data, although the concept might be very useful for transporting your data from one environment to another — that is, as a data exchange representation.

XML documents that are found across the World Wide Web probably don't outnumber those found in ordinary file systems, but you are personally likely to find more web-available XML documents than there are XML documents on your personal file system. The problem with those web documents is that a given website may or may not be "reachable" at any given time, making access to those documents somewhat less dependable at any moment than access to your own documents.

That, of course, has implications on querying those XML documents. A query facility that accesses files stored in your local file system always has access to those files (subject only to the availability of your file system), whereas a query facility that searches data on the web may sometimes find a given document and other times not find it because of websites going offline temporarily (or permanently).

Nonetheless, we believe there is a market for XML querying tools that don't depend on the existence of a DBMS but that search XML documents in local file systems and across the web. Many of these tools will implement XQuery, while others may provide some other query language.

8.2.3 Shredding Your Data

In Section 8.2.1, under the subheading "Relational Databases," we mentioned that some relational database vendors provided a way for XML documents to be broken down into their component elements, attributes, and other nodes for storage into columns in one or more tables. It can be argued that such *shredding* of XML documents does not preserve the integrity — the "XML-ness" — of those documents. While that argument is probably valid for some shredding implementations, other implementations manage to preserve the XML-ness of the documents. In fact, such implementations usually provide options that allow the user to control what level of XML-ness must be preserved. Vendors of those products typically provide a variety of ways of reconstructing the XML documents from the shredded fragments. What many of the shredding implementations do not do particularly well is to allow queries to be written that depend heavily on complex structures in some XML documents or that search for data located at arbitrarily deep levels of nesting.

The purpose of shredding is to improve (relative to character string or CLOB – character large object – representations, that is) the efficiency of access to the data found in XML documents. When XML serves the same purposes as its ancestor SGML – that is, representation of *documents*, such as books and technical reports – the data represented in the XML is semistructured by nature. However, XML is also used to represent much more regular, or structured, data, such as purchase orders and personnel records. Most people would not consider shredding an appropriate way of handling books or magazine articles marked up in XML. Instead, it is much more likely to be used for dealing with data-oriented XML.

Shredding can be done in a very naïve manner, such as defining a SQL table for each element type (at least those allowed to have mixed content) in a document, with columns for each attribute, the nonelement content of those elements, and the content of child elements that are not allowed to have element content themselves. For simple documents like most of the movie examples you've already seen in this book, that naïve approach might not be completely inappropriate, as illustrated in Example 8-1 and Table 8-1. (You may recall that a similar example appeared in Chapter 1, "XML," in our introduction to the various ways in which XML data can be stored.)

Example 8-1 *Shredding an XML Document into a Relational Database*

First, the XML to be shredded:

```
<movies>
  <movie runtime="99">
    <title>What About Bob?</title>
    <MPAArating>PG</MPAArating>
    <yearReleased>1991</yearReleased>
    <director>
      <givenName>Frank</givenName>
      <familyName>Oz</familyName>
    </director>
  </movie>
  <movie runtime="108">
    <title>A Fish Called Wanda</title>
    <MPAArating>R</MPAArating>
    <yearReleased>1988</yearReleased>
    <director>
      <givenName>Charles</givenName>
```

```
      <familyName>Chrichton</familyName>
    </director>
  </movie>
  <movie runtime="90">
    <title>Best in Show</title>
    <MPAArating>PG-13</MPAArating>
    <yearReleased>2000</yearReleased>
    <director>
      <givenName>Christopher</givenName>
      <familyName>Guest</familyName>
    </director>
  </movie>
</movies>
```

Now, the definitions of (reasonable) SQL tables into which the shredded XML data will be placed:

```
CREATE TABLE movies_table (
  movie_id       INTEGER PRIMARY KEY,
  FOREIGN KEY(movie_id) REFERENCES movie_table(movie_id) )

CREATE TABLE movie_table (
  movie_id       INTEGER PRIMARY KEY,
  runtime        INTEGER,
  title          CHARACTER VARYING(100),
  MPAArating     CHARACTER VARYING(10),
  yearReleased   INTEGER,
  director_id    INTEGER )

CREATE TABLE director_table (
  director_id    INTEGER PRIMARY KEY,
  givenName      CHARACTER VARYING(50),
  familyName     CHARACTER VARYING(50) )
```

Table 8-1 Result of Shredding Movies Document

movies_table
movie_id
124
391
227P

movie_table					
movie_id	**runtime**	**title**	**MPAA-rating**	**year-released**	**director_id**
124	99	What About Bob?	PG	1991	12
227	90	Best in Show	PG-13	2000	418
391	108	A Fish Called Wanda	R	1988	693

director_table		
director_id	**givenName**	**familyName**
693	Charles	Chrichton
12	Frank	Oz
418	Christopher	Guest

The data shown in Table 8-1 contains something that the input document did not contain: an id code for each movie and each director. Since the input didn't contain those id codes, from where did they come? Well, the application that performed the shredding simply had to make them up.

Now that the data has been shredded, applications are dealing with purely relational data and can write ordinary SQL statements to query and otherwise manipulate that data. At this point, it's trivially easy to write SQL queries to find out the longest movie in our collection:

```
SELECT MAX(runtime) FROM movie_table;
```

Similarly, to know the name of the director of the longest movie, we could join data from two tables:

```
SELECT givenName || ' ' || familyName
FROM movie_table AS m, director_table as d
WHERE m.director_id = d.director_id
  AND m.runtime = ( SELECT MAX(runtime) FROM movie_table )
```

What's a bit harder to do is to reconstruct the original structure of the input. In order to restore the original XML document from that shredded data, a somewhat complicated SQL query would have to be written to discover the names of the tables and columns (using the standardized SQL schema views such as the TABLES view and the COLUMNS view, unless the table names are known *a priori* by the application), then join the various tables together on their respective PRIMARY KEY and FOREIGN KEY relationships, and finally construct the resulting XML document. We leave the writing of such a sequence of SQL statements as an exercise for the reader; after all, most vendors of shredding-capable relational systems provide tools that reproduce the original XML document automatically.[8] We note, however, that such relational systems normally aim to preserve a data model representation of the XML documents and not the actual sequence of characters that may have been provided in the serialized XML input. The ordering of XML elements (remember that elements in an XML document have a defined and stable order) is preserved in those systems by a variety of techniques — "magic" — that may involve the assignment of some sort of sequence numbering scheme to sibling elements of a given parent.

More complex XML documents, like those you'll undoubtedly find throughout your organization's business documents, don't lend themselves to naïve shredding techniques. The tools doing the shredding often permit users knowledgeable about the data to give clues about how the shredding should be performed (sometimes using a graphical interface) or to "tweak" the table and column definitions before the XML-to-relational mapping is finished.

There will always be a use for shredding, particularly in applications that merely receive structured data in an XML format and

8 In fact, such tools often do not produce a new XML document that is identical in every respect to the initial document. Differences often include changes in non-significant white space and the exact representation of literals (canonical form for such literals may be used instead).

always need to store it as ordinary relational data.[9] However, with the increased emphasis in all major relational database implementations on true native XML support, we believe that shredding is going to diminish in popularity for most applications. It's only fair to note, however, that implementers continue to come up with more and more sophisticated shredding techniques targeted at a variety of usage scenarios.

8.3 SQL/XML's XML Type

In Chapter 15, "SQL/XML," you'll read about a relatively new part of the SQL standard[10] designed to allow applications to integrate their XML data and their ordinary business data in their SQL statements.

The centerpiece of SQL/XML is the creation of a new built-in SQL type: the XML type. Logically enough, the name of the type is "XML," just as the type intended for storing integers is named "INTEGER."

The design of SQL/XML's XML type makes it a true native-XML database type. Therefore, if you were to create a SQL table with a column of type XML, the values stored in that type must be XML values, and those values retain all of their "XML-ness." In SQL/XML:2003, the XML type was based on the XML Information Set, about which you read in Chapter 6, "The XML Information Set (Infoset) and Beyond." The next edition of SQL/XML[11] replaces its use of the Infoset with the adoption of the XQuery 1.0 and XPath 2.0 Data Model (discussed in Chapter 10, "Introduction to XQuery 1.0"). Along with the adoption of the XQuery Data Model, the basic definition of the XML type will be updated accordingly.

Of course, that does not mean that SQL/XML implementations are required to store values of the XML type in a collection of data

---

9 For those who need to do shredding (or, in a more generalized sense, mapping of XML to relational data), a number of XML mapping products make that task easier. Some with which we are familiar are Altova's MapForce (http://www.altova.com), Oracle's XDB schema processor and the Schema annotations it supports (http://www.oracle.com), and IBM's DAD (Document Access Definition) component of DB2's XML Extender (http://www.ibm.com).

10 ISO/IEC 9075-14:2003(E), *Information Technology – Database Languages – SQL – Part 14: XML-Related Specifications (SQL/XML)* (Geneva, Switzerland: International Organization for Standardization, 2003).

11 FDIS (Final Draft International Standard) 9075-14:2005, *Information technology – Database Languages – SQL – Part 14: XML-Related Specifications (SQL/XML)* (Geneva, Switzerland: International Organization for Standardization, 2005).

structures that are isomorphic to the XQuery Data Model descriptions. Implementations might choose to store serialized XML documents and dynamically parse them into data model instances whenever they are referenced, or they might store some other already-parsed representation that can be mapped onto the data model definitions when required. In fact, implementations could even choose to shred (fully or partially) those XML values, as long as the process is transparent to applications. The internal storage details of XML type values are left up to the implementation, in the same way as the corresponding details of DATE and FLOAT values are the concern of only the implementation.

With the advent of the XML type in SQL, concerns such as "CLOB vs. shredding" will, for the most part, become even less visible to the application developer. XML will be stored in XML columns, and native SQL facilities (augmented, when desired, by XQuery) will be used to manipulate those XML values.

8.4 Accessing Persistent XML Data

Neither XQuery nor SQL (nor, for that matter, any query language) exists in a vacuum – in spite of the fact that they are generally specified as though nothing else existed. Instead, applications are typically written in one or more other programming languages, such as C/C++, Java, and even COBOL. When those applications require access to a query language, they must use some sort of API to cause their queries to be executed and the results to be materialized in the host language environment.

Most of the more conventional programming languages (such as C and COBOL) access SQL database systems by invoking a call-level interface such as SQL/CLI[12] or one of the various proprietary APIs that correspond to SQL/CLI. SQL/XML:2003 did not provide SQL/CLI extensions to deal with the XML type, but that was a deliberate choice. Because languages like C and COBOL do not have built-in data types for XML, all results of SQL statements that return a value of the XML type are implicitly cast to character string (that is, serialized) before the result is given to the invoking program.

---

12 ISO/IEC 9075-3:2003(E), *Information Technology – Database Languages – SQL – Part 3: Call-Level Interface (SQL/CLI)* (Geneva, Switzerland: International Organization for Standardization, 2003).

Java programs typically access SQL database systems through the JDBC API.[13] The current version of JDBC, 3.0, contains no provisions for exchanging XML values between a Java program and a SQL DBMS. The spec does say that it "does not preclude interacting with other technologies, including XML, CORBA, or nonrelational data," but it offers no additional information about how such interaction should be done (other Java-related specifications provide those capabilities). It's not inconceivable that the next version of JDBC, 4.0, will offer more direct support for access to XML data handled by SQL database systems, but no details of any such capability are available at the date of publication.

There are, however, proprietary JDBC API extensions offered by a number of vendors of SQL database engines and by vendors of middle-tier ("middleware") facilities. Nonetheless, the "most standard" way for Java programs to access the XML data stored in SQL databases is for them to retrieve XML data using JDBC's getObject() method and then to cast the retrieved object to an XML class defined in another Java-related specification, such as JAXP.[14] At that point, the interfaces defined in that other specification can be employed to handle the XML data.

On the horizon is another API that will assist Java programs in accessing persistent XML data, whether it's stored in a relational database system, an object-oriented database system, a pure native-XML database system, or flat files. This API, called XQJ,[15] "will define a set of interfaces and classes that enable an application to submit XQuery queries to an XML data source and process the results of these queries." In other words, it will provide a direct interface from Java programs to XML data sources without those programs having to intermix multiple APIs, such as JDBC and JAXP.

At the time of writing, an Early Draft Review version of the XQJ specification is available at the URI referenced in footnote 15. While that document is decidedly incomplete, it allows interested parties to gain an idea of what the final API will provide. We encourage our readers to become familiar with XQJ, because we believe that it will

---

13 *JDBC 3.0 API* (Santa Clara, CA: Sun Microsystems, Inc., 2002). Available at: http://java.sun.com/products/jdbc/download.html#corespec30.

14 *Java API for XML Processing (JAXP) 1.3* (Santa Clara, CA: Sun Microsystems, Inc., 2002). Available at: http://jcp.org/aboutJava/communityprocess/pfd/jsr206/index2.html.

15 *XQuery API for Java™*. Available at: http://jcp.org/en/jsr/detail?id=225 (currently in development).

be one of the dominant APIs for querying and updating XML data from Java applications.

8.5 XML on the Fly: Nonpersistent XML Data

Throughout this chapter so far, we have focused on XML data that is persistently stored on various media. In fact, the rest of this book tends to discuss querying XML from the viewpoint of persistent storage. There are significant advantages to be had when the XML data to be queried is persistently stored. For example, query processors might be able to access specialized data structures (such as indices) to improve a query's performance.

But not all applications find it suitable to store XML data persistently before querying it. For example, XML data containing stock market quotations might be broadcast to WAP-enabled cell phones that are programmed to alert their owners whenever particular stocks achieve a particular price. Not only are the phones generally incapable of storing very large quantities of data, but the nature of the data stream is unsuitable for storage before querying.

In particular, such data streams are literally never-ending — they may continue uninterrupted for months on end, perhaps with each stock quotation represented as a separate XML document. In addition, the queries are supposed to detect the specified conditions immediately and not after periodic store-and-query episodes.

Consequently, XML querying systems must be able to process XML documents that never exist on any persistent medium but that are only temporarily stored (perhaps in RAM) while the query is evaluated against them. There are several reasons why querying streaming XML is problematic. Consider the XML document shown in Example 8-2, in which we've incorporated a large number of stock ticker elements into a single document for illustrative purposes.

Example 8-2 *Streamed XML Document*

```
<?xml version="1.0"?>
<stockTrades>
  <stockTicker symbol="XMPL">
    <tradeTime>2005-06-02T14:53:13.055</tradeTime>
    <tradeUnits>2000</tradeUnits>
    <tradePrice>193.21</tradePrice>
  </stockTicker>
  ...
```

```
  <stockTicker symbol="XDOCS">
    <tradeTime>2005-06-02T14:56:41.683</tradeTime>
    <tradeUnits>100</tradeUnits>
    <tradePrice>12.45</tradePrice>
  </stockTicker>
  ...
  <stockTicker symbol="XMPL">
    <tradeTime>2005-06-02T14:58:34.002</tradeTime>
    <tradeUnits>400</tradeUnits>
    <tradePrice>194.65</tradePrice>
  </stockTicker>
</stockTrades>
```

Now imagine a query that must retrieve the current price of XMPL if and only if the preceding 10 trades all increased in price. Further, imagine that there are hundreds, even thousands, of `stockTicker` elements represented by the ellipses (. . .). A query that examines this XML document — as it streams past — is forced to evaluate information without having access to all of the information in the document. In this case, the query would retrieve information from "this `stockTicker` element's `tradePrice` child element," if and only if "this `stockTicker` element's preceding sibling `stockTicker` element's `tradePrice` child element" had a lesser value, and that `stockTicker` element's preceding sibling `stockTicker` element's `tradePrice` child element had a lesser value than *that*, and so on until the 10th preceding sibling `stockTicker` element's `tradePrice` child element matched the required criterion.

In general, access to an element's ancestors and preceding siblings (and other "reverse axis" nodes) requires the ability to traverse "backwards" in the document. But how can that be done when the document is too large for available storage? In general, it cannot. Because the stream relentlessly flows past, there's no way to go back "upstream" to capture data that has already gone by. And there lies the principal difficulty in querying streaming XML. There are (again, in general) only two ways to resolve this problem:

1. Queries can be prohibited (syntactically or by means of execution-time checks) from accessing nodes reachable only through the use of one of those reverse axes.

2. Queries are permitted to access such nodes only in documents (or document fragments) sufficiently small to be handled using limited resources.

Most streaming XML query processors choose one of these two alternatives.

Queries against streaming XML are best suited for small XML documents and relatively simple queries, perhaps involving a transformation of source XML into a more desirable form of XML or directly into HTML or even plain text. Another form of query eminently suitable for streaming applications is the sort that depends solely on "very local" data. For example, if we wanted to know the trade price of XMPL every time a trade was recorded, it's quite easy to detect those elements as they stream past and to supply the value of the `tradePrice` child element whenever a `stockTicker` element whose `symbol` attribute having the value "XMPL" is seen.

8.6 Chapter Summary

In this chapter we have explored the various facilities through which XML data can be stored persistently and the implications on querying such persistent XML. We've explored the pros and cons of using database technology vs. ordinary file systems for storing and querying XML documents, and we've looked at shredding as a mechanism for storing XML documents into ordinary relational (or, indeed, other sorts of) databases. We've also examined the SQL standard's new built-in XML type, its relationship to shredding, and the implications on the APIs that application programs use to access SQL database management systems. Finally, we reviewed the nature of streaming XML, its uses, and the difficulties raised when querying such nonpersistent XML data.

Our conclusion, which we hope is clear from the text, is that we believe that most applications are better served by storing XML in some persistent medium and then querying that persistent XML data. Only when the XML data is inherently unsuitable for storing, we believe, are queries against streaming XML desirable.

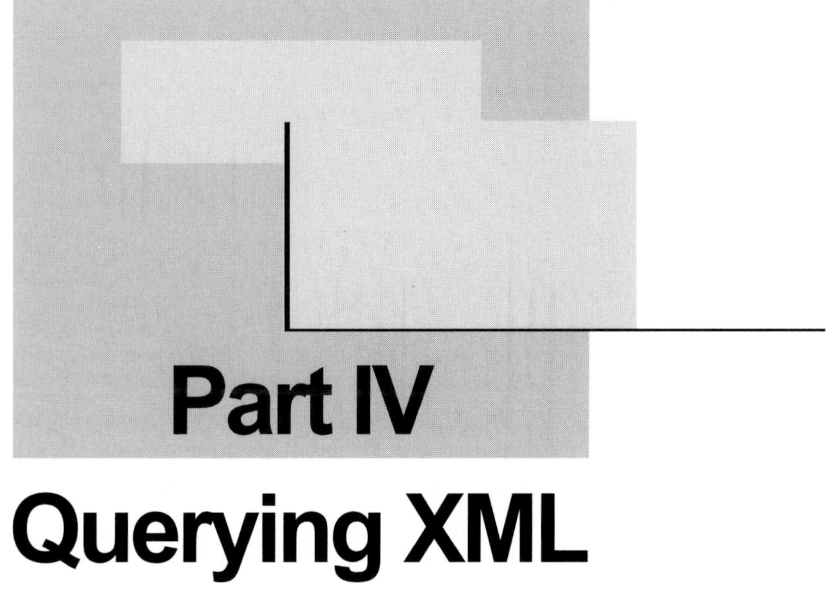

Part IV

Querying XML

Chapter

9

XPath 1.0 and XPath 2.0

9.1 Introduction

The XML Path Language — XPath, as it is more commonly known — was first published as a recommendation[1] by the W3C in 1999. According to its specification, XPath was created "to provide a common syntax for functionality shared between XSL Transformations [XSLT] and XPointer" (see Chapter 7, "Managing XML: Transforming and Connecting"), and its purpose is "to address parts of an XML document." Like nearly all of the W3C specifications, XPath "operates on the abstract, logical structure of an XML document, rather than its surface syntax."

What does it mean to say that XPath is used to "address parts of an XML document"? If we simply replace *address* with *locate* or *identify* or even *point to*, the meaning would be the same. Because querying facilities in general function to locate or identify certain information, it's easy to see that XPath is itself a sort of query language.

The first part of this chapter deals with XPath 1.0 and the second part handles XPath 2.0.[2] Even though XPath 2.0 is poised for approval as a recommendation in early 2006, we expect that many

---

1 *XML Path Language (XPath) Version 1.0* (Cambridge, MA: World Wide Web Consortium, 1999). Available at: http://www.w3.org/TR/xpath.

2 W3C Candidate Recommendation of *XML Path Language (XPath) Version 2.0* (Cambridge, MA: World Wide Web Consortium, 2005). Available at: http://www.w3.org/TR/xpath20.

people will continue to use XPath 1.0 for some time to come. (This expectation is due in large part to the existence of only a few XPath 2.0 engines.) In addition, we find that a good understanding of the concepts in XPath 1.0 leads to faster understanding of both XPath 2.0 and XQuery 1.0.

XPath, as you just read, was designed to be a language for addressing parts of XML documents, providing functionality for other specifications, particularly XSLT. The dependence of XSLT on XPath led to the XSL Working Group (WG) having the responsibility for specifying XPath (in consultation with other WGs). As we demonstrate in Section 9.2, XPath can quite reasonably be viewed as a language for querying XML documents. As you'll see in this chapter, XPath is used to query only one document at a time — that is, it's suitable not for finding documents of interest but to find desired information within a known document.

In 1999, the W3C established the XML Query Working Group, with the charter to develop a language designed specifically for querying XML documents — the XML query language now known as XQuery. The requirements for this new language implied significant capabilities beyond those available in XPath 1.0, and the XSL WG recognized that many of those new capabilities would be quite useful for the planned new version of XSLT. As a result, the two WGs agreed to accept joint responsibility for designing and specifying a new version of XPath, XPath 2.0.

As development proceeded, it became obvious that the requirements for XPath 2.0 were for the most part a subset of those for XQuery and that the two languages should be designed — and specified — together. In fact, because one language is very nearly a subset of the other, both specifications are generated from the same source files, via a variety of techniques that allow the production of one specification or the other as needed.

In addition to the significant commonality in the syntax of the two languages, they share a number of other specifications, including the data model, formal semantics, and functions and operators (all discussed in Chapter 10, "Introduction to XQuery 1.0"). Consequently, our coverage of XPath 2.0 in this chapter is relatively brief, since most of the aspects of the language are covered in that other chapter.

9.2 XPath 1.0

As you read in Section 9.1 above, XPath is a language for addressing parts of XML documents. Throughout Section 9.2, you'll learn the details of how that addressing is performed in XPath 1.0. But we think it's a good idea to introduce you to the appearance of XPath expressions before delving into the details. In fact, because XPath 1.0 is the foundation on which XPath 2.0 is built and because XQuery is so closely related to XPath 2.0, the concepts and syntax discussed in this section apply to XQuery as well.

The notation chosen for XPath deliberately bears a resemblance to the notation used by some computer operating systems for referencing files and directories (or, if you prefer, folders) in a file system. A typical XPath expression looks something like this:

```
/company/employee[@id="123"]/salary
```

In a file system's path notation, that might identify the file named "employee" in the "employee" subdirectory of the "company" directory, ignoring for the moment the notation "`employee[@id="123"]`." Analogously, XPath interprets that expression to mean the "salary" element that is a child of an "employee" element having an "id" attribute whose value is "123" that is itself a child of an element named "company."

The notation also resembles that used for URLs (Uniform Resource Locators) on the web. In this case, the first component identifies a primary resource, often the identification of a server somewhere. Subsequent components identify resources and subresources available at that server (or other primary resource).

In the file system notation, the URL notation, and the XPath notation, the context — directory structure, resource structure, or XML document — in which the expression is evaluated is strictly hierarchical, so each step in the path "drills down" deeper into the hierarchy.

Like any other query language, XPath[3] comprises a number of different facets that are used together to locate some specific piece of data. Among the most interesting of these components are the context in which an XPath expression is evaluated, the steps within an XPath expression that navigate among a document's structure, a

3 Throughout Section 9.2, the unqualified word "XPath" must be interpreted as "XPath 1.0."

number of axes that direct the navigation, predicates that filter out unwanted parts of the document, and expressions that express various sorts of operations in the language. We'll discuss each of these and more in the next few sections.

Before digging into the components of XPath and their syntax and semantics, you need to know that XPath, like most W3C specifications, does not operate on the serialized, character string, form of an XML document. Instead, XPath 1.0 operates on the Infoset (see Chapter 6, "The XML Information Set [Infoset] and Beyond") corresponding to a serialized document. Furthermore, the results of an XPath expression are not serialized XML but Infoset fragments. (More precisely, XPath 1.0 operates on instances of the XPath 1.0 Data Model, which is derived from the Infoset. Appendix B of the XPath 1.0 specification defines how an Infoset is mapped onto the XPath 1.0 Data Model.) In this chapter, to illustrate the behavior of various XPath expressions, we represent the source data as a serialized document and represent the result as though it had been serialized; we also employ a convention of indentation that highlights the relationships of child elements to their parents.

Section 9.2.8, "Putting the Pieces Together," may help you gain a better overall picture of how XPath 1.0 does its job.

9.2.1 Expressions

The principal concept in XPath is the *expression*. An expression is always evaluated in a context (see Section 9.2.2), and it evaluates to a value (the recommendation calls this "an object") that has one of four possible types: node set (an ordered collection of nodes), a Boolean value, a number, or a string.

There are a number of different kinds of expressions. Perhaps the most important is the *path expression*, which we cover in Section 9.2.3.

A second kind, which we might loosely call the *value expression*, includes:

- String and numeric literals
- Variable references
- Function invocations
- Logical expressions ("`and`" and "`or`")

- Comparison expressions[4] (=, <, >, <=, >=, and `!=`)
- Arithmetic expressions (`+`, `-`, `*`, `div` [because / is used for other purposes in path expressions], and `mod`)

The third kind of expression in XPath is the *node set expression*:

- Node set expressions (|, pronounced "union" — combines two node sets into one)

String literals are any sequence of characters enclosed with quotation marks, either double quotation marks ("...") or single quotation marks ('...'). Literals that are enclosed in double quotation marks cannot *contain* double quotation marks (which would be interpreted as ending the literal). Similarly, literals enclosed in single quotation marks cannot contain single quotation marks. In some contexts (such as XPath expressions that appear in an XML attribute), literals cannot contain certain other characters, most prominently < and &. When you need to use a less-than sign, an ampersand, or a quotation mark (double-quote or apostrophe) of the same sort that encloses your literal, you can represent them by means of a *character entity reference* notation, such as <, &, or "e; and ', respectively. You can also use a *character reference* notation (don't blame us for the confusingly similar phrases — that's the way the XML recommendation defines them), such as <, &, or " and ', respectively. Here are some examples:

- `"My favorite film is rarely shown on television."`
- `'The films shown on television are often bowdlerized.'`
- `"Do you like the music in 'The Rose'?"`

---

4 In XPath 1.0, these comparison operators have "existential" semantics. That characteristic means that, for operands that are not singletons, if there exists any value in the first operand that satisfies the comparison with respect to any value in the second operand, then the comparison is true. Thus, if a set of values (1, 2, 3) is compared to another set of values (2, 4, 6) for equality, the answer is true because the value 2 in the first set is equal to the value 2 in the second set. Surprisingly, if the two sets are compared for inequality, the answer is also true, because there is at least one value in the first set that is unequal to at least one value in the second set (1 is not equal to 4, for example).

- `'What movie had the tag line "Be afraid. Be very afraid."?'`
- `'Is the title "Bonnie and Clyde" or "Bonnie & Clyde"?'`

Numbers in XPath are always treated as double-precision floating-point values. Numeric literals are either: a sequence of digits; a sequence of digits followed by a decimal point; a decimal point followed by a sequence of digits; or a sequence of digits, followed by a decimal point, followed by another sequence of digits. (In XPath, the decimal point is always a period, also called a *full stop,* rather than the comma used in many countries. Furthermore, XPath does not employ commas or periods to separate groups of digits, such as the three-digit groups – thousands, millions, etc. – common in many Western societies.) Some examples:

- `42`
- `451.`
- `3.14159`
- `.33333`

Variable references are, syntactically, a dollar sign (`$`) followed by a QName[5] that names a variable provided by the external context from which XPath is invoked. An obvious example is:

- `$var1`

The value of a variable can be of any type supported by XPath: string, double-precision floating point, Boolean, or node set. It can also be of any type supported by the invoking environment.

A function invocation is, syntactically, a function name followed by a matching pair of parentheses. Here are the principle characteristics of a function invocation:

- The parentheses may or may not enclose an argument or a comma-separated list of arguments.

5 *Namespaces in XML 1.0* (Cambridge, MA: World Wide Web Consortium, 1999). Available at: http://www.w3.org/TR/ REC-xml-names.

- Every argument is an expression.
- The value of each argument of a function can be of any type supported by XPath (string, double-precision floating point, Boolean, or node set).
- The value returned by a function is also permitted to be any one of those data types.
- Those values may sometimes have other types, depending on the environment in which XPath is being invoked.
- Function names are QNames, but they cannot be equivalent to the name of any of these node types: `comment`, `text`, `processing-instruction`, or `node`. (You'll read more about XPath functions in Section 9.2.7.)

Some examples of function invocations:

- `fn:upper-case($name-variable)`
- ```
  myfns:longest-movie
  (fn:doc("http://example.com/movies"))
  ```
- `true()`

Logical, comparison, and arithmetic expressions are familiar to most programmers, as in the following example, which returns true if the value of `$cost` is less than 19.95 *or* if the value of `$length` is greater than 30 minutes less than the length of the longest movie (otherwise, it returns false):

- ```
  $cost &lt; 19.95 or
  ( $length >
    myfns:length(myfns:longest-movie(fn:doc("...")))
    - 30 )
  ```

The values of logical and comparison expressions are always of type Boolean, while the value of an arithmetic expression is always double-precision floating point.

Arguably, node set expressions are the most important type of expression, largely because they are returned by path expressions; we discuss these along with paths and steps in Section 9.2.3.

9.2.2 Contexts

If you're searching a document containing information about movies, then the most fundamental context of your searches is that document. However, once you've located information in a document that narrows your search a bit — such as a particular movie, or the cast of a particular movie — the additional parts of your search will typically use other nodes — perhaps the `<movie>` node or the `<actors>` node — as the context for those further search operations.

The XPath specification states that the context comprises five items:

1. A (single) node, which may be any of the seven node types (root nodes, element nodes, text nodes, attribute nodes, namespace nodes, processing instruction nodes, and comment nodes).
2. A pair of integers, one of which identifies the *context position* (that is, the position of the context node within its parent node, if any) and the *context size* (the number of child nodes within the parent of the context node).
3. A set of variable bindings that define a mapping from variable names to variable values. Variables are never created in an XPath expression, but are supplied by the external environment (such as XSLT).
4. A function library. The XPath recommendation defines a core library of 27 functions, but invoking environments are allowed to add more functions.
5. The set of namespace declarations that are in scope for the expression. Each namespace declaration provides a mapping between a namespace prefix and a namespace URI.

Example 9-1 helps to illustrate the concepts of context position and size. Let's consider the `<actor>` element representing the actor whose name is Tommy Lee Jones. Assuming we have somehow located that node, then:

- That node is the context node.
- The context size is 6 (the number of nodes that are children of the `<actors>` element).

- The context position is 3 (the `<actor>` element representing Jones is the third of those 6 children of the `<actors>` element).

Example 9-1 *Determining Context Position and Context Size*

```
<actors>
  <actor>...</actor>
  <actor>...</actor>
  <actor>
    <familyName>Jones></familyName>
    <personalName>Tommy Lee</personalName>
    ...
  </actor>
  <actor>...</actor>
  <actor>...</actor>
  <actor>...</actor>
</actors>
```

Consider some expression that identifies one or more `<actor>` elements found in Example 9-1. If that expression contains a second expression, then the first expression is called the *containing expression* and the second is often called a *subexpression*. At the time when a subexpression is evaluated, there are several items in its evaluation context:

- The variable bindings
- The function library
- The set of namespace declarations

These items are always the same as the corresponding items in the context in which the containing expression is evaluated. They are (effectively) inherited from the containing expression's content.

By contrast, the context node, the context position, and the context size of the subexpression's context may be the same as or different from those values in the containing expression's context (depending on the nature of the subexpression).

Evaluation of every XPath expression occurs within a context. The "outermost" expression (that is, the expression that is not contained within any other expression) must be given a node from the external environment that caused the expression to be evaluated. Subexpressions get their context node from the containing expression in which they are contained.

Several kinds of expressions, particularly steps of path expressions, may cause a different node to become the context node. For example, an expression that is given the `<actors>` element in Example 9-1 as its context node might begin with a step expression that causes an `<actor>` element to become the context node. When a different node becomes the context node, the context position and context size are recomputed based on the new context. It is also possible for the context position and context size to be changed when the context node does not change. Only one kind of expression causes this to happen — predicates, which are covered in Section 9.2.6.

9.2.3 Paths and Steps

Given the name of the language being discussed in this chapter — XPath, or XML Path Language — it's not surprising that the most important kind of expression in the language is the path expression, also known as the *location path*. There are two sorts of location paths: relative location paths and absolute location paths.

Relative location paths (the full term is tedious to say over and over, so we'll call them *relative paths* from here on) are a sequence of steps separated by a slash, or solidus, character: "`/`." Relative paths are evaluated relative to the "current" context node. An identifying characteristic of relative paths is that they do not start with a slash.

Absolute paths comprise a leading slash, optionally followed by a relative path. The leading slash means "start the evaluation of this path expression using the root node of the document being queried as the context node."

The notion of *path* is the very essence of XPath. The "elevator speech" about path expressions goes something like this:

- Start with some context, possibly the root of a document, possibly some element within a document.
- Find out what its children are, either by name or by position.
- Filter out some or all of those children based on one or more criteria.
- Repeat as necessary.

To explore this concept, let's consider the XML document illustrated in Example 9-2.

Example 9-2 *Reduced movie Example*

```
<?xml version="1.0" encoding="UTF-8"?>
<!-- movies - a simple XML example -->
<movies xmlns:xsi="http://www.w3.org/2001/XMLSchema-instance">
  <movie myStars="5">
    <title>An American Werewolf in London</title>
    <yearReleased>1981</yearReleased>
    <director>
      <familyName>Landis</familyName>
      <givenName>John</givenName>
    </director>
  </movie>
  <movie myStars="4">
    <title>The Thing</title>
    <yearReleased>1982</yearReleased>
    <director>
      <familyName>Carpenter</familyName>
      <givenName>John</givenName>
    </director>
  </movie>
  <movie myStars="3">
    <title>The Shining</title>
    <yearReleased>1980</yearReleased>
    <director>
      <familyName>Kubrick</familyName>
      <givenName>Stanley</givenName>
    </director>
  </movie>
</movies>
```

The absolute path expression "`/`" means "address/locate/identify the root of the document." Therefore, the path expression "`/movies`" will find the `<movies>` node that is immediately beneath the root of the document. However, "`/movie`" or "`/yearReleased`" will never find anything, because the root has no element children of those names.

If the current context node happens to be the `<director>` node associated with the movie *An American Werewolf in London*, then the relative path expression "`familyName`" means "address the element node or nodes that are children of the current context node and that are named '`familyName`'."

Each step expression has three parts:

- An *axis*, which we cover in Section 9.2.4, that determines the navigation within the abstract tree that represents the XML document.
- A *node test*, discussed in Section 9.2.5, that specifies the name or the type (or both) of the nodes that are to be identified by the step.
- Zero or more *predicates* that provide further criteria by which the step identifies the nodes of interest.

Each step in a location path can be envisioned as navigating from some current context node to one or more other nodes (that is, nodes in a node set). There are a significant number of ways in which the steps can navigate to the new node or nodes. Each axis specifies how the path expression determines the next node or nodes from the current context node.

The complete syntax of a step expression is:

- An axis name and a node test, separated by a double colon (`::`)
- Zero or more predicates, each of which is enclosed in square brackets (`[...]`)

For example, the step expression `child::familyName[2]` uses the `child` axis, a node test that will identify element nodes named `familyName`, and a predicate that causes selection of the second node that satisfies the node test, if it exists.

When a step expression is evaluated, the axis, combined with the node test, is applied to the current context node, producing a node set. In our example, the `child` axis creates a node set containing all, and only, those nodes that are children of the current context node. The node test `familyName` causes all nodes without that name to be removed from the node set.

If the step contains predicates, then that node set is filtered by applying the first predicate to each node in the node set, eliminating nodes that do not satisfy the predicate. That filtering operation produces a new node set. The next predicate, if any, serves to filter that new node set, producing yet another new node set. This continues until all predicates have been applied. In our example, the predicate `[2]` is merely an abbreviated notation equivalent to "`position() = 2`" (the `position()` function returns the context position of each node, in turn, in the node set). In other words, if there are two or more predicates, they must all evaluate to true in order to retain the nodes identified by the axis/node test combination.

The result of the step expression is the set of all nodes along the specified axis for which the node test is satisfied and all of the predicates are true. If no nodes are identified after application of the axis and evaluation of the node test and predicates, then the result of the step expression is an empty node set. In our example, if only one child node of the current context node is named `familyName` (or if there are no such nodes), then application of the predicate `[2]` would cause the result of the step expression to be an empty node set.

If the resulting node set is not empty, then each node in that node set is used in turn as the current context node for the next step in the path expression, if any. The results of that next step, after it has been applied to each node in the previous step's node set, is a node set that is the union of each node resulting from the application of the step to each of that previous step's node set's nodes.

Let's follow a specific example. Suppose we want to determine the family name of the director of *An American Werewolf in London*. Starting with the first bullet in the earlier algorithm, the absolute path expression "`/movies`" will find the `<movies>` node that is immediately beneath the root of the document. The context node, after evaluating that path expression, is that `<movies>` node. But we're clearly not done; we need more steps in our path.

Steps in a path are separated by slashes, as we learned earlier in this section, so we can update our path expression to "`/movies/`," after which we must place a relative path expression. Since the children of the `movies` node all seem to be named `movie`, our path can be updated to "`/movies/movie`." But we don't want all of the `movie` nodes — only the one dealing with a specific film.

A predicate is just the thing to handle this requirement. We must add a predicate that filters out all `movie` nodes whose `title` child node does not have the value representing the film we want. The predicate looks like this: `[title="..."]`. Our updated path expression is now "`/movies/movie[title="An American Werewolf in`

`London"]`." At this point, the context node is the specific `movie` node for that film.

But we're interested in information about the director of that film, so we navigate to the `director` node: "`/movies/movie[title="An American Werewolf in London"]/director`."

And, finally, we can navigate to and retrieve the director's family name: "`/movies/movie[title="An American Werewolf in London"]/director/familyName`."

9.2.4 Axes and Shorthand Notations

XPath defines a modestly large, perhaps intimidating, number of axes along which step expressions determine how to identify a node set from the current context node; many of the axes depend on the document order[6] of the XML tree. Let's list them, along with a very brief statement of what they do, before examining some of them in more detail:

- `child` – identifies every child node of the context node; attribute nodes and namespace nodes are not children of any node.
- `descendant` – identifies every descendant node of the context node (this includes child nodes, the nodes that are child nodes of those child nodes, and so forth until all offspring are identified); naturally, attribute nodes and namespace nodes are not included.
- `parent` – identifies the parent node, if any, of the context node; both attribute nodes and namespace nodes have a parent (even though they are not children of their parent!).
- `ancestor` – identifies the parent node, as well as that node's parent, and so forth until the root of the tree has been identified.

6 The term *document order* is defined in the XPath 1.0 specification to be "the order in which the first character of the XML representation of each node occurs in the XML representation of the document after expansion of general entities." The root node is the first node; element nodes precede their children; attribute and namespace nodes precede the children of the element node; and namespace nodes precede attribute nodes. The relative positions of attribute nodes and of namespace nodes is not defined. Reverse document order is, quite logically, the reverse of document order.

- `following-sibling` – identifies all nodes that are siblings of the context node (that is, they have the same parent node) that appear, in document order, *after* the context node; if the context node is an attribute node or a namespace node, then the `following-sibling` axis produces an empty node set.
- `preceding-sibling` – identifies all nodes that are siblings of the context node that appear, in document order, *before* the context node; if the context node is an attribute node or a namespace node, then the `preceding-sibling` axis produces an empty node set.
- `following` – identifies every node in the document that appears, in document order, *after* the context node, excluding all descendant nodes, attribute nodes, and namespace nodes of the context node.
- `preceding` – identifies every node in the document that appears, in document order, *before* the context node, excluding all ancestor nodes, attribute nodes, and namespace nodes of the context node.
- `attribute` – identifies every attribute node belonging to the context node; the attribute axis produces an empty node set unless the context node is an element node.
- `namespace` – identifies every namespace node belonging to the context node; the namespace axis produces an empty node set unless the context node is an element node.
- `self` – identifies only the context node.
- `descendant-or-self` – identifies the context node *and* all of its descendants.
- `ancestor-or-self` – identifies the context node *and* all of its ancestors.

Using the XML document in Example 9-2 and the corresponding XML tree illustrated in Figure 9-1, let's explore these axes. Some of the terminology we employ in this exploration might be unfamiliar. We urge you to keep a bookmark in Chapter 6, "The XML Information Set (Infoset) and Beyond," particularly at Table 6-2 – Tree-Related Terminology.

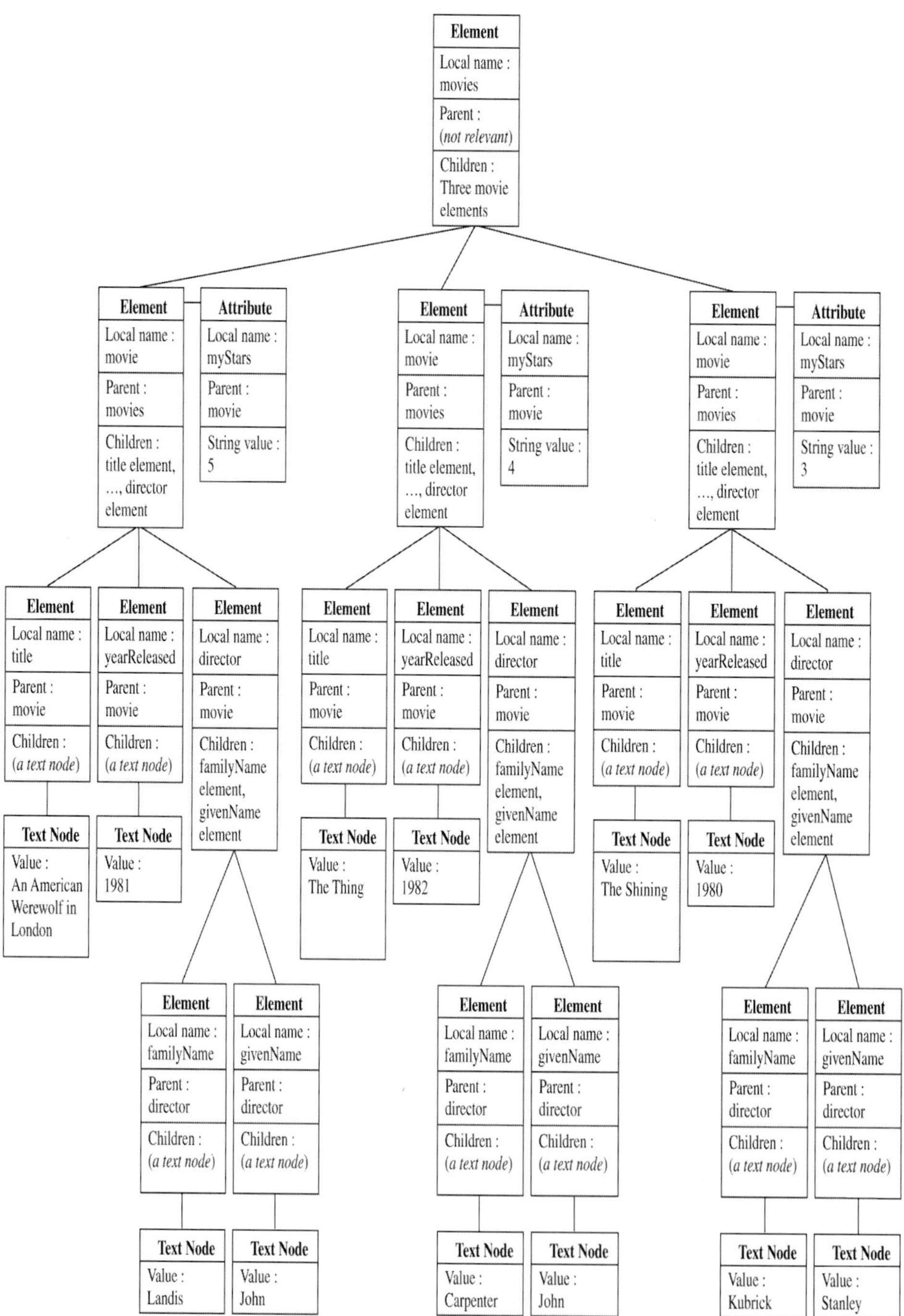

Figure 9-1 *XML Tree Representing <movies> Example.*

- `child` — The <movies> element has three children, each of them a <movie> element. Each of the <givenName> elements has one child, which is a text node. (Note that all of these axes identify nodes *by reference;* the nodes they identify include not only the nodes themselves, but also their entire subtree of descendants. That is why we can apply additional steps.)
- `descendant` — The first <movie> element has nine descendants: (1) the <title> element, (2) its child text node ("An American Werewolf in London"), (3) the <yearReleased> element node, (4) its child text node ("1981"), (5) the <director> element node, (6) its <familyName> child element node, (7) its child text node ("Landis"), (8) the <director> node's <givenName> child element node, and (9) its child text node ("John").
- `parent` — Each <director> element has a parent that is a <movie> element node.
- `ancestor` — Each <director> element has three ancestors: a <movie> element node, the <movies> element node, and the root node.
- `following-sibling` — The <director> element nodes do not have any following siblings. But the <yearReleased> elements each have a following sibling that is a <director> element node.
- `preceding-sibling` — The <title> element nodes do not have any preceding siblings. But the <yearReleased> elements each have a preceding sibling that is a <title> element node. Among the <movie> element nodes, two have a preceding sibling and two have a following sibling (and one has one of each).
- `following` — The <yearReleased> element node whose text node child contains "1981" has 25 following nodes: the <director> element node that is the <yearReleased> element node's following sibling, the <familyName> and <givenName> element nodes that are children of that <director> node, the text node children of those two element nodes, the <movie> element nodes having descendant <familyName> nodes whose child text nodes contains "Carpenter" and "Kubrick," and all of their descendants.
- `preceding` — The <yearReleased> element node whose text node child contains "1981" has two preceding nodes: its

preceding sibling element node `<title>` and that element node's child text node. Note that neither that `<yearReleased>` element nodes parent `<movie>` element node or its ancestor `<movies>` element node are preceding nodes.

- `attribute` — Each of the `<movie>` nodes in this example has one attribute, so the `attribute` axis of each of those nodes contains one attribute node, named `myStars`.
- `namespace` — None of the nodes in this example have namespaces, so the `namespace` axis of each element node is empty.
- `self` — The `self` axis for the `<yearReleased>` element node whose text node child contains "1981" contains exactly one node: the `<yearReleased>` node itself.
- `descendant-or-self` — The `descendant-or-self` axis for the `<yearReleased>` element node whose text node child contains "1981" contains two nodes: the `<year-Released>` element node whose text node child contains "1981" and that same text node child.
- `ancestor-or-self` — The `ancestor-or-self` axis for the `<yearReleased>` element node whose text node child contains "1981" contains four nodes: the `<yearReleased>` element node whose text node child contains "1981," its parent `<movie>` element node, its grandparent `<movies>` element node, and the root node.

Now let's put the knowledge we've gained so far into practice. Let's ask the question "In what years were all of these movies released?" The answer, framed as an XPath expression in the notation we've seen so far, is shown in Example 9-3.

Example 9-3 *Path Expression to Find `yearReleased` Nodes*

```
/child::movies/child::movie/child::yearReleased
```

Remember that the leading slash (`/`) means "start with the root of the document" and that the syntax of a step expression is an axis name (`child`, in this example) followed by a double colon (`::`) followed by a node test. (In this example, the node test is the name of the element, but you'll learn in Section 9.2.5 about other kinds of node tests.) Also, recall that step expressions are separated by slashes.

Our example path expression has a leading slash followed by two step expressions. Therefore, its interpretation is:

- Starting with the root of the document, first create a node set containing every child element node whose name is `movies` (there is only one such node).
- Next, using each node in the first node set in turn as a new context node, create a node set containing every child element node whose name is `movie` (there are three such nodes).
- Finally, using each node in the second node set as a new context node, create a third node set containing every child element node whose name is `yearReleased` (there are three such nodes, one per `movie` node).

The answer to our query is that third node set, which we might envision as suggested in Result 9-1.

Result 9-1 *Result of Path Expression to Find yearReleased Nodes*

```
<yearReleased>1981</yearReleased>
<yearReleased>1982</yearReleased>
<yearReleased>1980</yearReleased>
```

What about asking about all of the ancestors of the `familyName` element node whose child text node contains "Carpenter"? From looking at Figure 9-1, we see that the first ancestor encountered is the parent element node `director`. The next ancestor is that `director` node's parent element node `movie`. The next is that `movie` node's parent element node `movies`. And the final ancestor is the `movies` node's parent node, the document root.

Assuming that the context node is that `familyName` element node, this query is expressed as the relative path expression in Example 9-4. As you'll learn in Section 9.2.5, the function-like notation "`node()`" is a node test that means "any node is acceptable, regardless of its name or type."

Example 9-4 *Path Expression to Find Ancestor Nodes*

```
ancestor::node()
```

Now, the result of that simple query is not necessarily what you might expect. You might expect to envision the results as shown in Result 9-2.

Result 9-2 *Possible Result of Path Expression to Find Ancestor Nodes*

```
(root node)
<movies>
<movie>
<director>
```

Reality is slightly more complex, though. The result shown in Result 9-2 is correct, but its implications are not obvious. The result, as seen in detail in Result 9-3, is actually:

- The root node and all of its children (and all of their descendants), followed by
- The `<movies>` node and all of its children (and all of their descendants), followed by
- The appropriate `<movie>` node and all of its children (and all of their descendants), finally followed by
- The appropriate `<director>` node and all of its children (and all of their descendants)

Observe the way that we've indented the results to illustrate the four different kinds of ancestor — the root node, the `<movies>` node, the `<movie>` node, and the `<director>` node. (The indentation is not part of the result; it is merely our presentation style to help demonstrate the various results and their relationships to one another. In addition, our comments in italics within parentheses are not part of the result; they are our way of showing you where the value of the root node begins and ends. Similarly, the XML comments are not part of the result.)

Result 9-3 *Actual Result of Path Expression to Find Ancestor Nodes*

```
<!-- First, we get the root node and all of its descendants -->
(root node)
  <!-- movie - a simple XML example -->
  <movies xmlns:xsi="http://www.w3.org/2001/XMLSchema-instance">
    <movie myStars="5">
```

```
      <title>An American Werewolf in London</title>
      <yearReleased>1981</yearReleased>
      <director>
        <familyName>Landis</familyName>
        <givenName>John</givenName>
      </director>
    </movie>
    <movie myStars="4">
      <title>The Thing</title>
      <yearReleased>1982</yearReleased>
      <director>
        <familyName>Carpenter</familyName>
        <givenName>John</givenName>
      </director>
    </movie>
    <movie myStars="3">
      <title>The Shining</title>
      <yearReleased>1980</yearReleased>
      <director>
        <familyName>Kubrick</familyName>
        <givenName>Stanley</givenName>
      </director>
    </movie>
  </movies>
(end of the root node)
<!-- Next, we get the <movies> node and all of its descendants -->
<movies xmlns:xsi="http://www.w3.org/2001/XMLSchema-instance">
  <movie myStars="5">
    <title>An American Werewolf in London</title>
    <yearReleased>1981</yearReleased>
    <director>
      <familyName>Landis</familyName>
      <givenName>John</givenName>
    </director>
  </movie>
  <movie myStars="4">
    <title>The Thing</title>
    <yearReleased>1982</yearReleased>
    <director>
      <familyName>Carpenter</familyName>
      <givenName>John</givenName>
```

```
    </director>
  </movie>
  <movie myStars="3">
    <title>The Shining</title>
    <yearReleased>1980</yearReleased>
    <director>
      <familyName>Kubrick</familyName>
      <givenName>Stanley</givenName>
    </director>
  </movie>
</movies>
<!-- Now we get a specific <movie> node, plus its descendants -->
<movie myStars="4">
  <title>The Thing</title>
  <yearReleased>1982</yearReleased>
  <director>
    <familyName>Carpenter</familyName>
    <givenName>John</givenName>
  </director>
</movie>
<!-- Finally, we get our parent <director> node, plus its descendants -->
<director>
  <familyName>Carpenter</familyName>
  <givenName>John</givenName>
</director>
```

The reason that it's important for you to understand the complexity of this answer is because you may frequently want to "drill down" from some ancestor node into one of its descendants. Again, assuming that the context node is that same `familyName` element node (the one whose child text node contains "Carpenter"), we can discover the names of the movies represented by the following siblings of "this movie," as illustrated in Example 9-5.

Example 9-5 *Taking Advantage of the Actual Results*

```
ancestor::movie/following-sibling::movie/child::title/text()
```

The result of the query in Example 9-5 is seen in Result 9-4.

Result 9-4 *Result of "Drill Down" Path Expression*

```
The Shining
```

If you examine the path expression in Example 9-5, you'll see that it first finds the context node's ancestor named "movie," then finds all of the following siblings of that node (there happens to be only one), then finds the children elements of that new `movie` node that are named "title," and finally extracts the value of that `title` node — that's what the node test "`text()`" does, as you'll read in Section 9.2.5.

If the result of that `ancestor` axis did not include all of the found nodes' descendants, then this query would have been impossible to evaluate. Frankly, it would be much more surprising if XPath did not behave this way, because "returning" the ancestor `<movie>` node requires that the entire node, meaning it and all of its descendants (which are simply part of that node), be returned.

Axes can be *forward* axes or *reverse* axes. Axes that contain only the context node and/or nodes that follow the context node in document order are forward axes; axes that contain only the context node and/ or nodes that precede the context node in document order are reverse axes. Thus, the `child`, `descendant`, `descendant-or-self`, `following`, `following-sibling`, `attribute`, and `namespace` axes are all forward axes, while the `parent`, `ancestor`, `ancestor-or-self`, `preceding`, and `preceding-sibling` axes are all reverse axes. The `self` axis could be considered either a forward axis or a reverse axis — the concept is irrelevant, since that axis can never contain more than one node.

When traversing a forward axis such as the `child` axis, the first node encountered in document order along that axis is in position 1, the second is in position 2, and so forth. When traversing a reverse axis such as the `preceding-sibling` axis, the first node encountered in *reverse* document order along that axis (which would be the last node encountered in document order were the nodes being traversed along a forward axis) is in position 1, the next is in position 2, and so forth. In spite of the convention of counting nodes along a reverse axis in reverse document order, the nodes returned by a step along a reverse axis are still returned in (forward) document order.

The syntax for using axes is often lengthy and cumbersome, so XPath provides some shorthand notations[7] to make the job of writing path expressions a little less tedious. Not all axes have shorthand notations, but the most common ones do. The effect of one of these

7 In fact, the discussions and examples in this chapter that precede Section 9.2.4 are all done with shorthand notations.

shorthand notations is identical to the corresponding full notation. The shorthand notations are:

- *nodename* — A step expression may contain a node name without an axis name (and without the double colons that separate axis names from node names). This is a shorthand for `child::`*nodename*, so `/movies` means "start at the root node and locate every element node child named `movies` of the root node." (As we saw earlier, when a slash appears as the first character in a path expression, it has the meaning "start at the root node." When it appears elsewhere in a path expression, it serves to separate two step expressions from one another.)
- /*nodename* — A step expression that contains a slash followed by a node name (without an axis name or the double colons) is equivalent to specification of the `descendant-or-self` axis, so `/movies//familyName` means "start at the root node, find all element node children named `movies` of the root node, and then find every element node descendant (including, if relevant, the context node) named `familyName`." Similarly, `//givenName` means "start at the root node and find every element descendant named `familyName`." (Recall that the first slash between two step expressions is just the separator, so it is the second slash that really means "`descendant-or-self`.")
- @*nodename* — A step expression that contains an "at" sign — which is called by different names in various countries — followed by a node name (without an axis name or the double colons) is equivalent to specification of the attribute axis. Therefore, `movie/@myStars` means "start at the context node, find every element node child named `movie`, and then find every attribute child node named `myStars`." (Arguably, the "`@`" notation was chosen because Americans call it the "at" sign and that syllable is the first syllable of the word "attribute.")
- `.` — For the sake of readability, it is sometimes convenient to make explicit the fact that you want the path expression to start operating at the context node. If you wish to do this, the period, or full stop, (`.`) serves the purpose. This notation is equivalent to specification of `self::node()`. Therefore, the path expression `./director` means "starting with the

context node, find all element child nodes named `director`." Readers familiar with some computer file systems will recognize the inspiration for this notation, which indicates "this directory" in those file systems.

- `..` — A step expression that contains two consecutive periods, or full stops, is equivalent to the use of the `parent` axis. The path expression `../movie/yearReleased` means exactly the same thing as the path expression `parent::node()/child::movie/child::yearReleased`, and it returns the siblings of the context node's `yearReleased` children. (That raises this question: Are those the nieces and nephews of the context node?) This notation was also inspired by analogous usage in some computer file systems.

9.2.5 Node Tests

Every axis has a *principal node type*. The principal node type for axes that can contain elements is element. The principal node type for axes that cannot contain elements is the type of the nodes that the axis *can* contain — the only two axes with this property are the attribute axis, which can contain only attribute nodes, and the namespace axis, which can contain only namespace nodes. A node test is a way of testing the result of traversing an axis to determine whether the nodes in which you're interested have been returned.

There are two sorts of node tests:

- Name tests
- Node type tests

A name test provides a way for you to instruct a step expression that you're only interested in nodes with a particular name. A name test is, syntactically, a QName. It is true if and only if the type of the node is the principal node type of the axis specified in the step expression *and* the expanded name of the node is equivalent to the expanded name of the supplied QName. (An expanded name is a tuple comprising the URI associated with the QName's prefix part, if any, and the QName's local part.) For example, the step expression `child::director` selects the `director` element children of the context node. If the context node is one of the `<movie>` nodes, the step expression `attribute::myStars` identifies the attribute children named `myStars`.

Name tests come in a couple of other flavors as well. The name test "*" is true for any node of the principle node type, no matter what its QName happens to be. For example, if the context node is a <movie> node, the step expression `child::*` selects all element children, including the <title> node, the <yearReleased> node, and the <director> node.

Since name tests usually involve QNames, let's explore the implications associated with that kind of name. Recall that a QName is, syntactically, a namespace prefix followed by a colon followed by a "local" name. The namespace prefix and local name are both instances of NCName (no-colon name – a name without a colon). For example, `example:movies` might be the namespace-qualified name of a document of movies defined by somebody other than ourselves.

But that namespace prefix has to be associated with a "namespace name," which is always some sort of URI. If `example` is a namespace prefix, it might be associated with the URI `http://entertainment.example.com/multimedia/`. Note that (as Gertrude Stein famously said about Oakland, California) there is no "there" there. That is, the URI is not required to resolve to an actual page on the web; it's nothing more than an identifier. (Many people consider it good web etiquette to place an actual web page at the address indicated by a namespace URI, if only to inform a human reader of the intent of that address. Such pages are often referred to as *namespace documents*.)

The name test `example:*` selects all nodes of the principle node type whose namespace name (the URI) is the namespace URI associated with the namespace prefix `example`. Note that those nodes might have prefixes other than `example`; that matters not at all, because it's only the associated namespace URI that is used for the name test. Similarly, the name test `*:familyName` selects all nodes of the principle node type whose local name is `familyName`, regardless of their namespaces.

Node type tests allow you to instruct step expressions to select only nodes of a specified type. For example, the node type test `comment()` is true for all comment nodes, the node type test `text()` is true for all text nodes, and the node type test `processing-instruction()` is true for all processing instruction nodes, while the node type test `node()` is true for nodes of any type. Recall that the step expression "/*", because it is merely a shorthand for `child::*`, identifies only element children – never attribute nodes.

But `/node()`, as well as `child::node()`, identifies *all* node children, including attributes.

A processing instruction node type test can include a string literal within the parentheses; if it does, then it matches only those processing instructions whose name (also known as its *target*) is equal to the literal. Thus the node type test `processing-instruction("xml-stylesheet")` matches all processing instruction nodes whose name, or target, is `xml-stylesheet`.

The way that you write a path expression can sometimes give slightly surprising results, especially when parentheses come into play. Consider the following two path expressions:

- `//director[3]`
- `(//director)[3]`

The first of those expressions can be read like this: Select all `director` element nodes anywhere in the document that are the third `director` child of their parent, including all of their descendants. The result in this case is an empty node set, because our sample data contains no movie that has three directors.

By contrast, the second expression is read: Select all `director` element nodes anywhere in the document, and then identify the third (in document order) of those director nodes, including all of its descendants. With the data in Example 9-2, that result is:

```
<director>
  <familyName>Kubrick</familyName>
  <givenName>Stanley</givenName>
</director>
```

9.2.6 Predicates

In XPath, as in all computer languages, a predicate is an expression that evaluates to true or false. (In some languages, there may be a third possible result to indicate that the result cannot be determined from the information provided; in SQL, for example, some predicates evaluate to *unknown* if the expression being evaluated includes null values.) It is appropriate to think of predicates as *filters*, because they exclude objects (nodes, for instance) for which the predicate evaluates to any value other than *true*.

Predicates are applied to node sets that are returned by evaluating the node test with respect to the specified axis and the context node. They may reduce the number of nodes in the node set by eliminating nodes for which the predicate does not return *true*, but they can never add to the nodes in a node set. When a predicate is applied to each node in a node set in turn, that node is treated as the context node for the purpose of evaluating the predicate, while the context size is the number of nodes in the node set and the context position is the position of the node within that node set with respect to the specified axis.

Syntactically, a predicate is represented as an ordinary XPath expression surrounded by square brackets, as you saw in Section 9.2.3. Of course, ordinary XPath expressions may have types other than Boolean – string, number, and node set, to be precise. XPath includes rules for determining a Boolean value from the result of any XPath expression.

- If the type of the expression's result is number, then the predicate is *true* if and only if the value of that number is equal to the context position. Therefore, the predicate `[3]` is equivalent to the predicate `[position() = 3]`, where `position()` is an XPath function that returns the context position. Please note that the first position is always position 1 (not position 0, as in some languages).
- If the type of the expression's result is string, then the predicate is *true* if and only if the length of the string is greater than zero (that is, there is at least one character in the string). For example, considering the XML document from Example 9-2, if the predicate `[title/text()]` were applied to the expression `/movies/child::movie`, it would be true for all of the movies, since they all have `title` element children whose value is not the zero-length string.
- If the type of the expression's result is node set, then the predicate is *true* if and only if the node set contains at least one node. The implication of this rule is that you can easily test whether the current context node has at least one of a given type of node as a child, as an attribute node, or as a namespace node. Again considering the XML document from Example 9-2: If the predicate `[descendant::familyName]` were applied to the expression `/movies/child::movie`, it would be true because `movie` elements do have a descendant

element called `familyName`; however, the predicate `[descendant::dogName]` applied to the same expression would return false because those `movie` elements do not have a descendant element called `dogName`.

9.2.7 XPath Functions

XPath supplies us with a number of built-in functions. Implementations, as well as the host environment from which XPath is invoked, are free to supply additional functions.

First, let's expand a bit on the description of function invocations that you read in Section 9.2.1. Functions are invoked in XPath as part of a step expression, and the notation is entirely familiar to programmers: *`function-name`*`(`*`argument`*`, `*`argument`*`, ...)`. The *`function-name`*, of course, serves to identify the function to be invoked. Each *`argument`* is evaluated and, if necessary, converted to the data type required by the corresponding parameter of the function. (If the number of arguments is not the same as the number of function parameters or if any of the arguments cannot be converted to the proper data type, that's an error.)

Since function invocations are just another sort of XPath expression, they must return a value of a particular type. The result of a function expression is the value returned by the function itself.

The XPath 1.0 specification categorizes functions according to the sorts of objects on which they operate, so we'll do the same here.

Some XPath functions are focused on node sets:

- `last()` – returns a number equal to the current context size.
- `position()` – returns a number equal to the current context position.
- `count(`*`nodeset`*`)` – returns a number equal to the number of nodes in the node set specified by the argument.
- `id(`*`object`*`)` – If the argument identifies a node set, then this function first takes the string value of each node in that node set and (recursively) applies the `id()` function to the resulting string value; the result is the union of the sets of nodes that are returned from those applications of the `id()` function. If the argument has any other type, it is first converted to a string that is split along white-space boundaries

(if any) into a list of tokens; the result is a node set containing every node in the same document as the context node that has an attribute of type ID whose value is equal to any of those tokens.

- `namespace-uri(`*`nodeset?`*`)` — returns a string equal to the URI component of the expanded name of the first node (in document order) in the node set identified by the argument. If the optional *nodeset* argument is empty or if the first node in the node set identified by that argument does not have an expanded name or if the namespace URI of that first node is null, then the function returns a zero-length string. If the argument is not provided, then the context node is the node set used by the function.
- `local-name(`*`nodeset?`*`)` — returns a string equal to the local name component of the expanded name of the first node (in document order) in the node set identified by the argument. If the optional *nodeset* argument is empty or if the first node in the node set identified by that argument does not have an expanded name, then the function returns a zero-length string. If the argument is not provided, then the context node is the node set used by the function.
- `name(`*`nodeset?`*`)` — returns a string containing a QName that represents the expanded name of the first node (in document order) in the node set identified by the argument, with respect to the namespace declarations in effect for that node. In most cases, the QName will contain the namespace prefix that was used in the original XML document; however, if the namespace represented by that prefix was declared for multiple prefixes, then the function might use any of those prefixes in the QName. If the optional *nodeset* argument is not provided or if the first node in the node set identified by that argument does not have an expanded name, then the function returns a zero-length string. If the argument is not provided, then the context node is the node set used by the function.

Another group of functions concerns itself with string values:

- `string(`*`object?`*`)` — returns the object (that is, some value, node, or node set) converted to a string. If the object is a node set (a single node is a node set with only one member), then the function returns the string value of the first node (in document order) of the node set. If the object is a Boolean, then the value *false* is converted to the string "`false`" and the value *true* is converted to the string "`true`." If the object is a string, then its value is returned. If the object is a number, then it is converted to that number's string representation, corresponding approximately to the notation defined in IEEE 854.[8] For the details, we suggest that you consult the XPath 1.0 specification.

For example, using the XML document in Example 9-2, `string(//director[2])` would return `CarpenterJohn`.

- `concat(`*`string`*`, `*`string`*`, ...)` — returns the string that results from concatenating all of the arguments together (in the order supplied).

  For example, `concat('Director: ', //director[2]/familyName)` would return `Director: Carpenter`.

- `starts-with(`*`string`*`, `*`string`*`)` — returns *true* if the value of the first argument contains as its leading characters the value of the second argument; otherwise, it returns *false*.

  Invoking `starts-with(string(//director[2]), "John")` returns false, but invoking `starts-with(string(//director[2]), "Car")` returns true.

- `contains(`*`string`*`, `*`string`*`)` — returns *true* if the value of the first argument contains anywhere within it the value of the second argument; otherwise, it returns *false*.

  The expression `contains(string(//director[2]), "rJ")` returns true.

- `substring-before(`*`string`*`, `*`string`*`)` — returns the portion of the value of the first argument that occurs before the first occurrence of the value of the second argument; if the value of the second argument doesn't appear as part of the value of the first argument, the function returns *false*.

  If you invoke `substring-before(string(//director[2]), "John")`, you'll get the string `Carpenter`.

- `substring-after(`*`string`*`, `*`string`*`)` — returns the portion of the value of the first argument that occurs after the

8 ANSI/IEEE Std. 854:1987, *IEEE Standard for Radix-Independent Floating-Point Arithmetic* (New York: American National Standards Institute, 1987).

first occurrence of the value of the second argument; if the value of the second argument doesn't appear as part of the value of the first argument, the function returns *false*.

Evaluation of `substring-after(string(//director[2]), "John")` returns the zero-length string.

- `substring(`*`string, number, number?`*`)` – returns the portion of the value of the first argument starting with the position indicated by the value of the second argument (the first character is at position 1) – if the third argument is not supplied, then the returned value includes all characters in the value of the first argument following that starting position; if the third argument is provided, then its value determines the maximum number of characters returned. If the value of the second argument is not an integer, then it is rounded up to the next higher number. If the third argument is specified and is not an integer, then the position of the last character returned is less than or equal to the rounded value of the second argument plus the rounded value of the third argument.

  `substring(string(//director[2]), 4, 7)` yields the string `penterJ`.

- `string-length(`*`string?`*`)` – returns the length, in characters, of the value of the argument; if no argument is supplied, the length of the string value of the context node is returned.

  `string-length(string(//director[2]))` is 12.

- `normalize-space(`*`string?`*`)` – returns the value of the argument with white space normalized (meaning that all leading and trailing white space is removed, and each sequence of white space within the value is replaced by a single space character); if no argument is supplied, then the function operates on the string value of the context node.

  `normalize-space("My favorite film is not on DVD!  ")` yields the string "`My favorite film is not on DVD!`".

- `translate(`*`string, string, string`*`)` – returns the value of the first argument after replacing each occurrence of a character that appears in the value of the second argument with the character at the corresponding position in the value of the third argument; if the value of the third argument is shorter than the value of the second argument, then characters in the value of the first argument that appear in the "excess" portion of the value of the second argument are simply deleted from the returned value.

Use of `translate(string(//director[2]), "Jh", "R")` results in `CarpenterRon`. Note that the `J` in `John` has been translated to an `R` and that the `h` in `John` has been eliminated entirely.

Yet another group of functions deals with Boolean values:

- `Boolean(`*`object`*`)` — returns a Boolean value computed from the value of the argument. If the type of the argument is a node set, then the function returns *true* if and only if the node set has at least one node. If the type of the argument is string, then the function returns *true* if and only if the string contains at least one character. If the type of the argument is Boolean — well, the function returns that value. If the type of the argument is number, then the function returns *true* if and only if the value of the argument is neither positive zero, negative zero, nor NaN (not a number).
- `not(`*`object`*`)` — returns the Boolean value *true* if the value of the argument is *false* and returns *false* if the value of the argument is *true*.
- `true()` — returns the Boolean value *true*.
- `false()` — returns the Boolean value *false*.
- `lang(`*`string`*`)` — returns *true* if and only if the language of the context node, as expressed by an `xml:lang` attribute on the context node (or if the context node has no such attribute, the nearest ancestor node with such an attribute), is the same as or is a sublanguage of the language indicated by the value of the argument (ignoring case). If there is no applicable `xml:lang` attribute, then the function returns *false*.

The final group of functions return numeric values:

- `number(`*`object?`*`)` — returns the value of the argument, converted to a number. If the argument is a number, then its value is returned. If the argument is a string whose value corresponds to a valid representation of a number in XPath, then the function returns the corresponding number; other strings are converted to NaN. If the argument is a Boolean, the *true* is converted to 1 (one) and *false* is converted to 0 (zero). If the argument is a node set, then the string value of the first node, in document order, of the node set is used as the effective value of the argument. If no argument is supplied, then the function operates on the node set containing only the context node.

- `sum(`*`nodeset`*`)` — returns the sum of the numbers that result from converting the string value of each node in the node set to a number.
- `floor(`*`number`*`)` — returns the largest integer number (that is, the number closest to positive infinity) that is not greater than the value of the argument.
- `ceiling(`*`number`*`)` — returns the smallest integer number (that is, the number closest to negative infinity) that is not less than the value of the argument.
- `round(`*`number`*`)` — returns the integer number that is closest to the value of the argument. If there are two possible values, then the one closest to positive infinity is returned.

9.2.8 Putting the Pieces Together

Before leaving the subject of XPath 1.0, let's consider a few examples that illustrate the various concepts we've discussed in this part of the chapter. These examples are all based on the XML document contained in Example 9-2.

In this section, each example contains the XPath expression being illustrated and its results (using our indentation convention — with a reminder that the actual results are not serialized into character strings at all but remain in the more abstract form of an instance of the Xpath 1.0 data model).

Example 9-6 *Average Rating of Movies Directed by "John"*

```
sum(/movies/movie[director/givenName="John"]/@myStars) div
count(/movies/movie[director/givenName="John"]/@myStars)
```

Result:

```
4.5
```

Let's look in detail at the expression in Example 9-6. To compute an average, we apply the time-honored mechanism of adding up a collection of values and then dividing that sum by the number of values in that collection; notice that the arguments given to the `sum()` function and the `count()` function are identical. In both cases, the argument should be read thusly:

- Starting at the root of the document, create a node set containing all child element nodes named `movies`.
- Create a second node set containing, for every node in the first node set (there will never be more than one, because the root node never has more than one child element node), every child element node named `movie` (the second node set contains three element nodes).
- Create a third node set containing every node in the second node set that satisfies the predicate. The predicate should be understood to say that, for each node in the second node set:
    - Create a fourth node set containing every child element node named `director` (there are three such nodes).
    - For all nodes in the fourth node set, create a fifth node set containing every child element node named `givenName` (again, there are three such nodes)
    - For all nodes in the fifth node set whose string value is equal to "John" (there are two such nodes), node being considered in the second node set is satisfied (and thus included in the third node set).
- Create a sixth node set containing every node in the third node set that has an attribute named `myStars` (there are two such nodes).

The `sum()` function, as described earlier, "returns the sum of the numbers that result from converting the string value of each node in the node set to a number." The string values of the two nodes in the sixth node set are "5" and "4," respectively, and the result of converting those string values to numbers are 5 and 4, respectively. The `count()` function counts the number of nodes in the node set; that count is, of course, 2. Therefore, the expression finally divides (5 + 4) by 2 and returns 4.5.

Example 9-7 *Titles of Movies with High Ratings*

```
string(movie/title[../@myStars>3])
```

```
Result:
An American Werewolf in London
```

In Example 9-7, assuming that the context node is the `<movies>` node, the expression:

- Builds a nodeset containing every child element named `movie`.
- Creates a second node set containing, for every node in the first node set, the child element nodes named `title`.
- Creates a third node set containing every node in the second node set that satisfies the predicate. The predicate, for each node in the second node set:
  - Creates a fourth node set containing the parent of the node (from the second node set) being considered. There is one such node (every node has no more than one parent).
  - Creates a fifth node set containing, for all of the nodes in the fourth node set, the attribute named `myStars`. (There is one such node.)
  - If the value of any node in the fifth node set is greater than 3, then the predicate is satisfied for the node being considered from the second node set and that node is included into the third node set.

The `string()` function returns the string value of *the first* node in the third node set, which is an element node named `title`. Intuitively, one might expect for the string function to return the string value of all nodes (there are two of them) in the third node set, strung together: "`An American Werewolf in LondonThe Thing`." However, the `string()` function was described earlier this way: "If the object is a node set, then the function returns the string value of the first node (in document order) of the node set." Consequently, only the first node that satisfies the predicate is used to produce the result.

Example 9-8 *Titles of Movies with High Ratings and Low Ratings*

```
concat(string(movie/title[../@myStars>3]), " ",
       string(movie/title[../@myStars<4]))
```

```
Result:
An American Werewolf in London The Shining
```

In Example 9-8, the two instances of the `string()` function are evaluated very much according to the process described for Example 9-7, and the results are concatenated together with a single space between them. Don't forget that the first `string()` function returns the string value of the *first* node in the resulting node set.

Example 9-9 *Manipulating the Titles of Movies with High Ratings and Low Ratings*

```
substring(
  substring-after(
    translate(
      concat(string(movie/title[../@myStars>3][starts-with(., "The")]),
             " ",
             string(movie/title[../@myStars<4])),
      "eTh",
      "yM"),
    "My "),
  1,
  11)
```

```
Result:
Ming My Sin
```

By now, you should be able to work through the expression in Example 9-9. Consult the descriptions of the `substring()`, `substring-after()`, and `translate()` functions in Section 9.2.7 as you work out this example.

Example 9-10 *Is There a Movie with a Rating of Fewer Than Four Stars?*

```
Boolean(//@myStars<4)
```

```
Result:
true
```

In Example 9-10, the expression first forms a node set containing all nodes that have an attribute whose name is `myStars` and whose value is less than 4. The `Boolean()` function returns `true` because the constructed node set is not empty.

Interestingly, the `Boolean()` function is not necessary in this case. The expression "`//@myStars<4`" also returns `true`. We leave it as an exercise for our readers to determine why this shorter expression behaves like the first.

9.3 XPath 2.0 Components

XPath 2.0 is a significant improvement over XPath 1.0. In adding the major enhancements, a small number of incompatibilities were introduced, most of which can be avoided if the environment that invokes XPath[9] simply sets a "backwards compatibility" flag.

XPath shares a great deal of syntax and semantics with XQuery, allowing most of XPath to be described in Chapter 11, "XQuery 1.0 Definition." Our relatively brief discussion of XPath 2.0 in this chapter focuses on those aspects of XPath that are distinct from XQuery — particularly identifying the language features that are absent in XPath but present in XQuery.

The most significant driving factor involved in the differences between XPath 1.0 and XPath 2.0 is probably the change in data model. XPath 1.0, as you read in Section 9.2, based its data model on the Infoset (however, you'll recall that the XPath 1.0 is not exactly the same as the Infoset). By contrast, XPath 2.0 is defined with respect to the XPath 2.0 and XQuery 1.0 Data Model (for the remainder of this chapter, we'll simply call it the "Data Model"), about which you will read in Chapter 10, "Introduction to XQuery 1.0."

9.3.1 Expressions

One consequence of having a much richer data model is that the number of types of expressions grew. In XPath 1.0 (see Section 9.2.1), there are three kinds of expressions: node set expressions that allow formation of a union of two node sets; value expressions that operate on string, numeric, and Boolean values; and path expressions.

9 Throughout Section 9.3, the unqualified word *XPath* must be interpreted as *XPath 2.0*.

In XPath 2.0, node sets have been replaced with *sequences*, which are among the most important concepts of the Data Model. A node set contains zero or more nodes, no node can appear in the node set more than once (that is, no duplicates are possible), and the nodes are not in any particular order. A sequence, by contrast, allows a node to appear more than once (duplicates are permitted), and the nodes in the sequence are in a particular order; in addition, sequences can contains nodes, atomic values, or any mixture of the two. The so-called *set expressions* that operate on sequences of nodes includes the union operator; XPath still allows this operator to be represented by the vertical bar "|" but also allows it to be spelled out: `union`. Two new operators have been added: intersection (spelled `intersect`), which returns a sequence containing only those nodes that appear in *both* of the source sequences, and difference (spelled `except`), which returns a sequence containing only those nodes that occur in the first source sequence but not in the second.

Value expressions have been enhanced significantly in XPath 2.0. The most fundamental changes are driven by the adoption of the Data Model. The Data Model, as you'll learn in Chapter 10, provides a much larger collection of data types, which are based on the types supported by XML Schema Part 2;[10] additional types are defined by the Data Model itself. To support the new set of data types, a number of new operators have been provided. A much larger collection of "built-in" functions has been provided, many of them to support the new data types. Additional functions, called *external functions*, can be supplied by XPath implementations and even by users.

Path expressions in XPath 2.0 serve the same purpose as in XPath 1.0. Path expressions are still composed of a sequence of steps, and steps (which we prefer to call *step expressions*) still comprise the same three components: an axis, a node test, and zero or more predicates. However, XPath 2.0 extends this by allowing a step to be any expression that evaluates to a sequence of nodes, without an axis being involved at all.

In addition, the slash "/" that was described in Section 9.2.3 as a separator between step expressions now behaves more like a true operator. Recall that XPath 1.0's steps produced node sets and that sets have no particular order; XPath 1.0 generally processed the nodes in document order, but that was not an attribute of the node sets themselves. In XPath 2.0, sequences are inherently ordered, and

10 *XML Schema Part 2: Datatypes* (Cambridge, MA: World Wide Web Consortium, 2001). Available at: http://www.w3.org/TR/2001/REC-xmlschema-2-20010502/.

the slash operator causes duplicate elimination to be performed and for the nodes in the sequence to be rearranged into document order.

Node tests are still name tests or kind tests. In XPath 1.0, name tests could be specified in three forms: a QName, `*`, `NCName:*`. XPath 2.0 adds one more: `*:NCName` (all nodes with a specified local name, regardless of the namespace in which they are defined).

XPath 2.0 adds three new kinds of expression: sequence expressions, the conditional expression, and type expressions. A sequence expression is one that manipulates sequences. The XQuery Data Model, which introduces the concept of sequences, is discussed in detail in Chapter 10. A sequence is an ordered collection of items, which may be atomic values, nodes, or even mixtures of both; unlike a node set, the order of items in a sequence is not necessarily document order.

Sequence Expressions

There are several varieties of sequence expression:

- `,` (a comma) – Sequence concatenation, construction of a sequence from other sequences
- `to` – Numeric range, producing a sequence of consecutive values starting with the value of the first argument and ending with the value of the second argument
- `some` and `every` – Quantified expressions, evaluating whether at least one item, or all items, respectively, in a sequence satisfies a specified condition

Arguably the most powerful sort of sequence expression is:

- `for` and `return` – Application of an expression to every item in a sequence, returning the results of each such application in a sequence that contains all of the results in the order in which they were generated

The `for` expression, accompanied by the `return` expression, is closely related to the FLWOR expression in XQuery (which we discuss in detail in Chapter 11, "XQuery 1.0 Definition"), but it is significantly limited by comparison. This pair of expressions as defined for XPath are important enough to justify their own section, Section 9.3.2.

The Conditional Expression

The conditional expression is better known as the `if` expression:

```
if (expr1) then expr2 else expr3
```

Unlike in many languages, the `else` clause is mandatory. The semantics are exactly what you expect: The first expression, `expr1`, is evaluated. If it evaluates to `true`, then the second expression, `expr2`, is evaluated and is the value of the `if` expression; if the first expression evaluates to `false`, then the third expression, `expr3`, is evaluated and is the value of the `if` expression.

XPath determines the (Boolean) value of the first expression using the semantics of the *effective Boolean value* of that expression. In general, all values of that expression evaluate to `true`, except: the empty sequence, a single zero-length string (`xs:string` and `xdt:untypedAtomic`), a single number (`xs:decimal`, `xs:float`, and `xs:double`) whose value is 0, a single floating-point number (`xs:float` and `xs:double`) whose value is NaN (not a number), and a single Boolean whose value is `false`. An error is raised if the expression produces more than one atomic value.

Type Expressions

Type expressions deal with the data types defined for XPath, including the types that are built into the Data Model and other types that are defined in XML Schemas associated with the context in which an XPath expression is evaluated. Every value in the Data Model is an instance of some type and is inherently a member of a sequence (an individual item is actually a sequence of length 1). XPath uses the term *sequence type* to talk about *items*. An item is either a node or an atomic value. The Data Model provides two generalized item types: `item()`, which allows any sort of item at all, and `empty()`, which prohibits every kind of item.

The type expressions used in XPath include:

- Expressions related to converting values to a new data type
- Expressions dealing with determining the data type of a value

In XPath, as in XQuery and SQL, the expression that converts an atomic value of one atomic data type into a corresponding value of another atomic type is called a *cast*. Neither XPath nor XQuery support any form of error recovery, so any attempt to cast a value into an inappropriate type results in an error that causes evaluation of the "outermost" expression to terminate. Run-time failures are generally a bad idea, and many languages — especially query languages — strive to minimize the possibility of such failures. XPath and XQuery provide a *castable* expression that allows a query to determine whether a cast will succeed before actually performing the cast:

```
if ($var castable as xs:integer)
then cast $var as xs:integer
else 0
```

There are a number of limitations on permissible casts. Some limitations are absolute — it is a type error to attempt to cast a value whose type is `xs:dateTime` into the `xs:NCName` type, because no value of `xs:dateTime` could ever be a valid `xs:NCName` value. Other limitations depend on actual values — casting a value of `xs:string` into `xs:decimal` will fail unless the `xs:string` value has the same lexical form as a valid literal for `xs:decimal` values.

The other components of XPath are philosophically the same as they were in XPath 1.0, meaning that they serve the same purpose with essentially the same syntax. The differences in them are caused by factors we mentioned earlier, such as the adoption of the Data Model. For example, in XPath 1.0, determination of effective Boolean values did not have to contend with decimal numbers or single-precision floating-point values, while XPath 2.0's use of the Data Model brings those data types into consideration.

9.3.2 The `for` and `return` Expressions

The `for` expression and the sequence data type defined in the Data Model are closely related. The `for` expression always returns a sequence of zero or more items, and the sequence data type is most powerful when a mechanism is provided to iterate through the items in a sequence. When coupled with the `return` expression (which, in XPath, it always is), the `for` expression produces a sequence of items — not necessarily nodes — in much the same way that step expressions and the other sequence expressions do.

Consider the `for` expression in Example 9-11, which uses the XML document given in Example 9-2.

Example 9-11 *Using the `for` Expression*

```
for $m in //movies[yearReleased > "1980"]
return $m/title/text()
```

The variable `$m` is the *range variable* of the expression, while the value of the path expression `//movies[yearReleased="1984"]` is the *binding sequence,* and the expression following `return` is the *return expression.* The result of this `for` expression is the result of evaluating the return expression once for every item in the binding sequence. In this case, the result is shown in Result 9-5.

Result 9-5 *Result of Simple `for` Expression*

```
An American Werewolf in London
The Thing
```

A note about Result 9-5: The `for` expression in Example 9-11 returns a sequence of items. In this case, each of the items is a string value. The expression does not insert a new line or even a space between the two string values. However, to ensure that the result of the expression is clear, we have illustrated the result on two lines.

It's worth observing that the `for` expression in Example 9-11 is both a valid XPath 2.0 expression and a valid XQuery 1.0 expression. If shown without any context in which to evaluate it, we could not tell you whether it was XPath 2.0 or XQuery 1.0 — because it is both. This characteristic is true of virtually all XPath 2.0 expressions. The only exception is that XPath 2.0 supports, in backwards-compatibility mode only, a `namespace::` axis, while XQuery does not.

XPath allows `for` expressions to be nested, in which the result is produced by evaluating the "inner" `for` expression once for each item in the result of the "outer" `for` expression, and the inner `return` clause produces one item for each item in the result of all those evaluations of the inner `for` expression. XPath provides a syntactic shorthand for nesting for expressions: The sequence "`$var in expression`" can be repeated, with multiple instances of that sequence separated by commas.

XPath 2.0 offers considerable more power than XPath 1.0. Here are some of the more obvious new capabilities introduced by XPath 2.0.

- There is a dependence on the Data Model, implying sequences and new data types.

- Node tests can now test the type of a node and not merely its name.
- Function calls can be used in place of step expressions.
- It introduces several new operators (such as operators that test the positional relationship between two nodes, the `idiv` operator, and the new set operators).
- It includes new expression types (the `for` expression explored earlier, the `if` expression also discussed earlier, and existential expressions using `some` and `every`).
- The library of built-in functions available for use is much enlarged, and user-defined functions are possible.

In Chapter 11, "XQuery 1.0 Definition," you'll read much more about the XPath expressions discussed in this section.

9.4 XPath 2.0 and XQuery 1.0

In Section 9.1, we told you that "one language is a subset of the other." To be very clear about that relationship, XPath 2.0 is a subset of XQuery 1.0. Both languages are free of side effects (except for possibly side effects caused by invocation of external functions). Because they are both functional languages, expressions written in them can be arbitrarily nested. That is, XQuery expressions can be used within other XQuery expressions, and XPath expressions can appear within XQuery expressions. Because XPath is a subset of XQuery, the second part of that previous statement is redundant – (virtually) every XPath expression *is* an XQuery expression.

The converse is not true, since XQuery has significantly more features than XPath 2.0 (and even more differences from XPath 1.0). XQuery, as you'll read in Chapter 11, "XQuery 1.0 Definition," provides many more expressions. For example, XPath 2.0 supports the `for` expression with the following syntax (using the extended BNF notation that the XPath 2.0 specification uses):

```
for $VarName in ExprSingle ( , $VarName in ExprSingle )*
return ExprSingle
```

where "`ExprSingle`" is a BNF nonterminal symbol that corresponds to a single expression (as opposed to a comma-separated list of expressions).

By comparison, XQuery 1.0 provides a similar but extended variant called a FLWOR (For, Let, Where, Order by, Return) expression. Using the same EBNF notation, it looks like this:

```
( ForClause | LetClause )+
WhereClause?
OrderByClause?
Return ExprSingle
```

The definitions of `ForClause`, `LetClause`, `WhereClause`, and `OrderByClause` are, respectively:

```
for $VarName TypeDeclaration? PositionalVar? in ExprSingle
    ( , $VarName TypeDeclaration?
        PositionalVar? in ExprSingle )*
    return ExprSingle

let $VarName TypeDeclaration? := ExprSingle
    ( , $VarName TypeDeclaration? := ExprSingle )*

where ExprSingle

stable? order by ExprSingle OrderModifier
    ( , ExprSingle OrderModifier )*
```

By contrast with XPath 2.0's `for` expression, XQuery's FLWOR expression provides the abilities to define variables without creating a loop over a node set, to filter the results with a predicate, and to specify an ordering of the results.

9.5 Chapter Summary

In this chapter, we've described both versions of XPath. XPath 1.0 was covered in some detail, while XPath 2.0 was discussed somewhat less thoroughly. In Chapter 11, "XQuery 1.0 Definition," we discuss XQuery in detail and consequently discuss XPath 2.0 in more detail than in this chapter.

XPath is, as we've seen, a language for addressing parts of XML documents. The nature of that "addressing" makes XPath a query language. While the ability to express complex queries has improved significantly between XPath 1.0 and XPath 2.0, it remains somewhat limited when compared to more powerful languages, such as XQuery.

Chapter

10

Introduction to XQuery 1.0

10.1 Introduction

In Chapter 9, "XPath 1.0 and XPath 2.0," we presented one language for querying XML documents, XPath. In this chapter, you'll be introduced to a much more powerful language for querying XML called XQuery.

We start with a brief history of the language. We think it's useful to know the background of a language's development, because it gives some insight into how and why things are as they are, but feel free to skip this section if it doesn't interest you.

Next, we look at the specs that laid the foundation for the design of the language – the Requirements and the Use Cases. These two specs tell us what the language is for (what problems the language is meant to solve) and give us some examples of its expected use. Then we give an overview of the XQuery suite of specifications (there are nine of them, as well as three related XML specs) and say how they are related.

With this background, we are ready to dive into the XQuery Data Model and the XQuery type system. The XQuery Data Model is one of the features that sets XQuery apart from XPath 1.0 and XSLT 1.0. Every XQuery operates over an instance of the XQuery Data Model, and its result is an instance of the XQuery Data Model.

We leave a detailed description of the syntax and semantics of XQuery for the next chapter (Chapter 11, "XQuery 1.0 Definition"). In this chapter we describe the functions and operators of the language, and the formal description of the semantics of the language.

We said that the output of an XQuery is an instance of the XQuery Data Model — clearly, we need some way to communicate those data to the outside world. One way is to serialize the output Data Model (*i.e.*, create an XML representation of it). We describe serialization in the last section of this chapter.

After reading this chapter, you should know a good deal about the XQuery language — certainly enough to start using it.

10.2 A Brief History

Like its relational database predecessor, SQL, XQuery was designed from the start to be a nonprocedural language in which query authors express the sources of the data they wish to query and the rules they wish to have applied to those data in order to achieve the answers they need. In neither language does the query author specify *how* the system produces those answers. XQuery goes beyond XPath — even XPath 2.0 — in its ability to bring together information from multiple documents simultaneously, correlating the data in those documents based on common characteristics, and producing answers that cannot be determined from one document alone.

Also like SQL, XQuery was not created out of whole cloth. Instead, it is the offspring of a number of earlier languages that explored how to query XML without every quite achieving widespread acceptance in the XML or data management communities. Some of the ancestors of XQuery were designed with the needs of the document community in mind, while others were oriented more toward the data community (and XQuery addresses both communities with equal vigor).

One of the philosophical ancestors of XQuery is a language called XQL.[1] The first draft of a specification for XQL was written in February 1998 by Jonathan Robie, then with Software AG. The XQL FAQ says that "XQL is a query language that uses XML as a data model, and it is very similar to XSL Patterns," and that it has a number of implementations. Design of XQL apparently ceased in mid-1999,

1 *XQL FAQ*, Jonathan Robie (1999). Available at: http://www.ibiblio.org/xql/.

after the language was submitted as a candidate for consideration at the W3C's QL 98 Workshop.[2]

Another language named XQL was also submitted by three researchers from Fujitsu Labs to that same Workshop.[3] The two languages appear to be unrelated, in spite of the choice of name. It seems unlikely that there were any implementations of this second XQL other than the initial research implementation.

A language named XML-QL[4] was submitted to the W3C as a Note by a number of researchers (Alin Deutsch, Mary Fernandez, Daniela Florescu, Alon Levy, and Dan Suciu) from industry and academia. XML-QL, like the Fujitsu XQL, explicitly drew aspects of its design from SQL, as well as from other research query languages for semistructured data. The W3C Note states that "XML-QL can express *queries,* which extract pieces of data from XML documents, as well as *transformations,* which, for example, can map XML data between DTDs and can integrate XML data from different sources."

A project named Lore[5] (Lightweight Object REpository) at Stanford University that ran from about 1996 through 2000, headed by Jennifer Widom, provided a database system for semistructured data. A principle component of Lore was a declarative query language for XML, known as Lorel (Lore Language). Lore and Lorel took an object-oriented approach to managing semistructured data, minimizing dependencies on predetermined schema information about the data being queried.

Another research language, YATL,[6] was developed by Sophie Cluet and Jérôme Siméon at INRIA to "query, convert and integrate XML data." (By "integrate," the authors meant the ability to bring together information from multiple data sources in one query.) YATL was not intended to be computationally complete, but to capture a large and useful class of data transformations. The language is "able

---

2 *QL '98 – Query Languages 1998* (Cambridge, MA: World Wide Web Consortium, 1998) Available at: http://www.w3.org/TandS/QL/QL98/.

3 *XQL: A Query Language for XML Data,* Hiroshi Ishikawa, Kazumi Kubota, Yasuhiko Kanemasa. Available at: http://www.w3.org/TandS/QL/QL98/pp/flab.txt.

4 *XML-QL: A Query Language for XML,* (Cambridge, MA: World Wide Web Consortium, 1998). Available at: http://www.w3.org/TR/NOTE-xml-ql/.

5 See http://www-db.stanford.edu/lore/.

6 Sophie Cluet and Jérôme Siméon, *YATL: A Functional and Declarative Language for XML* (2000). Available at: http://www-db.research.bell-labs.com/user/simeon/icfp.ps.

to resolve structural conflicts between sources and features high-level primitives for the manipulation of collections and references."

The language that contributed most directly to the creation of XQuery was named Quilt,[7] designed by Don Chamberlin, Jonathan Robie, and Daniela Florescu. The last two of these designers appear earlier as participants in the creation of other XML querying languages. Don Chamberlin may be best known as one of the inventors of the premiere relational data management language: SQL. Quilt was presented to the W3C's XML Query Working Group as a proposed starting point for the language that has become known as XQuery. Quilt originated "when the authors attempted to apply XML query languages such as XML-QL, XPath, XQL, YATL, and XSQL to a variety of use cases," finding that each language had distinct advantages and disadvantages. By selecting the strongest notions from each, as well as from SQL and OQL,[8] they created a language that met the requirements of the XML Query Working Group, was implementable, and retained a deep reliance on the structure of XML itself.

XQuery is manifestly *not* Quilt, but its relationship with that language is easily discerned. Just as the world owes a great deal to Don Chamberlin and Ray Boyce for the creation of SQL as a language to access relational databases, Quilt's inventors are to be recognized for giving their talents to the immediate parent of XQuery 1.0.

In this chapter, you'll read about the data model underlying XQuery 1.0 (and XPath 2.0) and its relationship to XML Schema and to the Infoset (see Chapters 5, "Structural Metadata" and 6, "The XML Information Set (Infoset) and Beyond," respectively). In Chapter 11, "XQuery 1.0 Definition," you'll learn more details about XQuery syntax and semantics, the function library defined for the language, and how results can be transformed into character strings of XML markup.

10.3 Requirements

Like any well-run software project, the XQuery effort started with a set of requirements. The XQuery Requirements[9] specification

7 Don Chamberlin, Jonathan Robie, and Daniela Florescu, *Quilt* (2000). See http://www.almaden.ibm.com/cs/people/chamberlin/quilt.html.

8 Rick Cattell et al., *The Object Database Standard: ODMG-93, Release 1.2* (San Francisco: Morgan Kaufmann, 1996).

9 *XML Query (XQuery) Requirements*, (Cambridge, MA: World Wide Web Consortium, 2005). Available at: http://www.w3.org/TR/xquery-requirements/.

describes what the XQuery language sets out to achieve. The latest version is annotated with colored bullets to show which requirements have been met, so you can track progress against requirements. The XQuery Requirements specification provides an overview of the guiding principles of the language, so it is an appropriate place to start this overview of the XQuery 1.0 language. Today's XQuery Requirements document owes much to the pioneering 1998 paper by David Maier, "Database Desiderata for an XML Query Language."[10]

As an aside, the XQuery Requirements specification raises an interesting question on naming. Its full title is "XML Query (XQuery) Requirements." If you look at the full titles of the other specifications in the XQuery suite, there is no consistent convention for using "XML Query" vs. "XQuery." The Use Cases specification has "XML Query" in its title, the Data Model specification has "XQuery," and the Requirements specification has "XML Query (XQuery)." Some of the specification titles include "XPath" or its alter ego, "XML Path." "XQuery" seems to have become the term applied to "XQuery 1.0 and XPath 2.0" in common parlance. Throughout this book we use "XQuery" to mean exactly that – the language described by "XQuery 1.0: An XML Query Language,"[11] which includes most of[12] the language described by "XML Path Language (XPath) 2.0."[13,14] We overload the word "XQuery" – it might also mean "XQuery query expression," as in "writing an XQuery" or "running XQueries." Overloading the word is unfortunate, but the alternative is to talk about "running XQuery query expressions." We use the term "XPath" when talking about that part of XQuery explicitly, for example when we talk about XPath requirements. And we use "Querying XML" when talking about the more general problem of doing queries against XML data.

One more general comment before we look at the XQuery requirements. The XQuery specifications use the terms "must," "may," and

10 David Maier, *Database Desiderata for an XML Query Language* (1998). Available at: http://www.w3.org/TandS/QL/QL98/pp/maier.html.

11 *XQuery 1.0: An XML Query Language*, (Cambridge, MA: World Wide Web Consortium, 2005). Available at: http://www.w3.org/TR/xquery/.

12 XPath 2.0 is very nearly a true subset of XQuery 1.0. One exception is that some of the XPath axes are optional in XQuery.

13 *XML Path Language (XPath) 2.0*, (Cambridge, MA: World Wide Web Consortium, 2005). Available at: http://www.w3.org/TR/xpath20/.

14 In fact both documents are created from the same source, so the description of, *e.g.*, path expressions is identical in the XQuery and the XPath language specifications.

"should" in a special way. Some link to RFC 2119;[15] others include an abbreviated RFC 2119–like definition in the body of the specification. Below we quote the definitions from the "XQuery Requirements," and we use **boldface** in the text of this book when those terms are meant to have their special meaning.

- **must** — This word means that the item is an absolute requirement.
- **should** — This word means that there may exist valid reasons not to treat this item as a requirement, but the full implications should be understood and the case carefully weighed before discarding this item.
- **may** — This word means that an item deserves attention, but further study is needed to determine whether the item should be treated as a requirement.

10.3.1 General Requirements for XQuery

XQuery is a declarative language, which **must** not mandate any evaluation strategy, such as the order of evaluation of parts of a query. A declarative language describes what the processor should do rather than how to do it. This makes for relatively simple, readable queries that can be optimized by the XQuery processor. It is independent of any particular protocol, so that XQueries[16] can run in any environment.

XQuery **may** have more than one syntax, but it **must** have one syntax that is human-readable and one syntax that is XML. The XML syntax **must** "reflect the underlying structure of the query." This pair of requirements led to XQueryX,[17] a language for describing an XQuery in XML. One can safely assume that any XML representation that "reflects the underlying structure of the query" will not be "convenient for humans to read and write," hence the need for two syntaxes. With XQueryX, a query can be created, modified, and even

15 S. Bradner, *Key Words for Use in RFCs to Indicate Requirement Levels* (Cambridge, MA: Harvard University Press, 1997). Available at: http://www.ietf.org/rfc/rfc2119.txt.

16 In this book, we use the word "XQueries" as the plural of "XQuery" when we mean "more than one XQuery expression."

17 *XML Syntax for XQuery 1.0 (XQueryX)*, (Cambridge, MA: World Wide Web Consortium, 2005). Available at: http://www.w3.org/TR/xqueryx/.

queried using standard XML tools. You'll read more about XQueryX later (Chapter 12, "XQueryX").

XQuery 1.0 does not include any update functionality, which many consider a serious shortcoming. It is clear that, from the start of the XQuery effort, update capability was considered to be important for inclusion in *some* version of XQuery, but not necessarily the *first* version. The first XQuery Requirements specification[18] (January 2000) said only that XQuery must leave the door open for update to be included in XQuery in a future version. The latest XQuery Requirements says the same.

10.3.2 Data Model Requirements

The XQuery Requirements document describes requirements for the Data Model separately — an indication of the importance of the Data Model in XQuery. We describe the XQuery Data Model in detail in Section 10.6. In this section, we review the requirements for that Data Model.

The XQuery language is defined as an operation over an instance of the XQuery Data Model. The XQuery Language takes an instance of the Data Model as input, and returns an instance of the Data Model as output (*i.e.*, the XQuery language is closed with respect to the XQuery Data Model). The XQuery Requirements document says that only information that can be found in the Infoset and the PSVI (see Chapter 6, "The XML Information Set (Infoset) and Beyond") can be used to construct an instance of the XQuery Data Model. This is not the same as saying that an instance of the Data Model can only be *constructed* from an instance of the Infoset or from a PSVI — on the contrary, it can be constructed directly by a program, or as the result of an XQuery. But no information that does not exist in either the Infoset or the PSVI specifications can ever find its way into an instance of the XQuery Data Model. (Some readers might claim that the fact that the XQuery Data Model can represent heterogeneous sequences is an exception to that rule, but we disagree — the *information* in those sequences is still limited to the information that can exist in an Infoset or PSVI instance.)

The XQuery Requirements document also says that the XQuery Data Model **must** provide a mapping from any instance of the Infoset or PSVI to an instance of the XQuery Data Model. The Data

18 *XML Query Requirements*, (Cambridge, MA: World Wide Web Consortium, 2000). Available at: http://www.w3.org/TR/2000/WD-xmlquery-req-20000131.

Model **must** represent the character data available in the Infoset and data types and structure types defined in XML Schema. Interestingly, there are no requirements for mapping *from* the XQuery Data Model *to* any other data model. The Serialization specification does define an output mapping from the XQuery Data Model to HTML, XML, XHTML or text, but not (directly) to an Infoset or a PSVI.

The XQuery Data Model **must** represent "collections." Collections can be collections of documents – returned by the `fn:collection()` function – or ordered collections (sequences) of documents, nodes, and/or values. There is, as you read in Chapter 6, no notion of a collection or a sequence in the Infoset.

Queries **must** run whether or not a (complete) Schema is available. This leads to a quagmire of how to deal with data that are untyped (when there is no Schema available) or only partially typed (when there is a Schema available, but it only validates some of the data).

10.3.3 XQuery Functionality Requirements

The XQuery Requirements document includes some basic functionality requirements – XQuery **must** be able to aggregate and sort results, **must** include support for universal and existential quantifiers, and **must** support composition of expressions. The XQuery Requirements document (unsurprisingly) says a lot about the ability to deal with structure. XQuery **must** support operations on hierarchy and sequence; combine information from different parts of a document (or parts of different documents); and preserve, transform, and/or create structures in results, including intermediate results.

There is a requirement that XQuery **must** support null values. This has led to some interesting debates among members of the SQL community (where "null" is a well-understood, well-defined term) and the XML community (who have mapped "null" to its closest relative in the XQuery Data Model, the empty sequence). Of course, the XML community prevailed. Similarly, the requirement that "queries **must** be able to express simple conditions on text, including conditions on text that spans element boundaries" has been punted on, with a reference to the `fn:string()` function (which returns the string value of a node or value, as defined by the PSVI). We'll just have to wait for some future XQuery Full-Text specification to get true full-text query capability from XQuery.

One requirement that has not been met in XQuery 1.0 is to support both interdocument and intradocument references. Support for

XPointer was discussed, but the XPointer Recommendation[19] was published too late (March 2003) to be considered. Another is the requirement to provide access to a document's Schema (if it has one) – this was felt to be too complex for the first version of the language.

10.3.4 XPath 2.0 Requirements

The XPath 2.0 requirements are laid out in "XPath Requirements Version 2.0."[20] XQuery 1.0 includes XPath 2.0 as a subset of the language, so the XPath 2.0 requirements had a big influence on XQuery 1.0 requirements.

While XQuery 1.0 is a brand new language, XPath 1.0 has been around since 1999 and has many users. So XPath 2.0 **must** be backward-compatible with XPath 1.0. One common use of XPath 1.0 is in XSLT, so XPath 2.0 needs to satisfy XSLT users as well as XQuery users, by providing a common "core" expression language for both XSLT 2.0 and XQuery 1.0. Naturally, it is extremely desirable for the syntax and semantics of XPath-in-XSLT and XPath-in-XQuery to be the same.

XPath 2.0 extends the type system of XPath 1.0 considerably. XPath 1.0 has a simple type system in which every expression evaluates to one of four available types – node-set, Boolean, number, or string. By contrast, XPath 2.0 must support the data types and structure types defined by XML Schema.

Finally, the XPath 2.0 Requirements include lots of detailed requirements for functionality that had been requested by real-world users. This is one of the advantages of a 2.0 specification – there is a wealth of user experience to call upon when gathering requirements.

10.4 Use Cases

The XQuery Requirements document briefly describes a set of "usage scenarios" for XQuery, showing that XQuery is meant to apply in a very broad range of situations. The "XML Query Use Cases"[21] describes use cases across that range. The Use Cases specifi-

---

19 *XPointer Framework* (Cambridge, MA: World Wide Web Consortium, 2003). Available at: http://www.w3.org/TR/xptr-framework/.

20 *XPath Requirements Version 2.0* (Cambridge, MA: World Wide Web Consortium, 2005). Available at: http://www.w3.org/TR/xpath20req/.

21 *XML Query Use Cases* (Cambridge, MA: World Wide Web Consortium, 2005). Available at: http://www.w3.org/TR/xquery-use-cases/.

cation is a good starting point for the XQuery beginner, particularly for someone who likes to see concrete examples (as opposed to the more formal descriptions in, say, the Data Model or Formal Semantics specifications).

Note that the purpose of the Use Cases specification is very different from that of a test suite. The use cases illustrate some of the functionality of XQuery, but there is no attempt to exercise every operation or permutation. The Use Cases specification includes some 77 queries, while a test suite could be expected to include many thousands. Anyone starting to test an implementation, or to test her own understanding, would do well to start with the use cases and the examples in the XQuery Language specification (thoughtfully supplied as script files).[22]

Each use case includes:

- One or more DTDs describing the input data. Only one of the use cases comes with an XML Schema — Use Case "STRONG," "queries that exploit strongly typed data," needs an XML Schema to represent the data types.
- One or more pieces of sample data. The data are represented in the queries as an XML document at the end of a URL, introduced using the doc function — *e.g.*, "for $b in doc("http://bstore1.example.com/bib.xml")/bib/book."
- For each query in the Use Case, there are:
  - An English language description of the query.
  - The query in XQuery.
  - The result of the query.

Let's take a look at one of the use cases, to give a feel for what an actual XQuery does and looks like. The very first query in the Use Cases specification is fairly simple — it is reproduced in Example 10–1.

22 See http://www.w3.org/XML/Query for a pointer to the "grammar test pages," which includes an XQuery parser applet and query scripts derived from the examples in the Use Cases and Language specs.

Example 10-1 *Use Case XMP, Q1*

DTD:

```
<!ELEMENT bib  (book* )>
<!ELEMENT book  (title,  (author+ | editor+ ), publisher, price )>
<!ATTLIST book  year CDATA  #REQUIRED >
<!ELEMENT author  (last, first )>
<!ELEMENT editor  (last, first, affiliation )>
<!ELEMENT title  (#PCDATA )>
<!ELEMENT last  (#PCDATA )>
<!ELEMENT first  (#PCDATA )>
<!ELEMENT affiliation  (#PCDATA )>
<!ELEMENT publisher  (#PCDATA )>
<!ELEMENT price  (#PCDATA )>
```

Sample Data:

```
<bib>
    <book year="1994">
        <title>TCP/IP Illustrated</title>
        <author><last>Stevens</last><first>W.</first></author>
        <publisher>Addison-Wesley</publisher>
        <price> 65.95</price>
    </book>

    <book year="1992">
        <title>Advanced Programming in the Unix environment</title>
        <author><last>Stevens</last><first>W.</first></author>
        <publisher>Addison-Wesley</publisher>
        <price>65.95</price>
    </book>

    <book year="2000">
        <title>Data on the Web</title>
        <author><last>Abiteboul</last><first>Serge</first></author>
        <author><last>Buneman</last><first>Peter</first></author>
        <author><last>Suciu</last><first>Dan</first></author>
        <publisher>Morgan Kaufmann Publishers</publisher>
        <price>39.95</price>
    </book>
```

```
    <book year="1999">
        <title>The Economics of Technology and Content for Digital TV</title>
        <editor>
               <last>Gerbarg</last><first>Darcy</first>
               <affiliation>CITI</affiliation>
        </editor>
        <publisher>Kluwer Academic Publishers</publisher>
        <price>129.95</price>
    </book>

</bib>
```

Description of the query:

"List books published by Addison-Wesley after 1991, including their year and title."

The query in XQuery:

```
<bib>
 {
  for $b in doc("http://bstore1.example.com/bib.xml")/bib/book
  where $b/publisher = "Addison-Wesley" and $b/@year > 1991
  return
    <book year="{ $b/@year }">
     { $b/title }
    </book>
 }
</bib>
```

The expected result:

```
<bib>
    <book year="1994">
        <title>TCP/IP Illustrated</title>
    </book>
    <book year="1992">
        <title>Advanced Programming in the Unix environment</title>
    </book>
</bib>
```

This simple example illustrates:

- The F, W, and R of the FLWOR expression.
- XPath integration – the query includes several path expressions.
- Data input via the `doc()` function, and output using element construction.

Since this is a fairly representative example of an XQuery, let's describe what the query does informally, to give you the general flavor of the XQuery language.

```
<bib>
 {
   . . .
 }
</bib>
```

This is a constructed element. One of the strengths of XQuery (over, say, XPath 1.0) is that XQuery lets you construct XML on the fly like this, so you can output sensible XML as the result of a query. The result of the query is a `bib` element, and the content of `bib` is the result of evaluating the XQuery expression enclosed in curly braces.

```
for $b in doc("http://bstore1.example.com/bib.xml")/bib/book
```

This is the `for` clause (the "F" in "FLWOR"). It says we should iterate over the sequence produced by evaluating the expression after the keyword `in`. That is, consider each member of the sequence in turn, assigning the value of each member of that sequence to the variable `$b`. The expression after the keyword `in` is an XPath expression, beginning with an invocation of the built-in function `doc()`. The XPath expression says we should take the document represented by the URI "http://bstore1.example.com/bib.xml," select its children elements named `bib`, and select their children elements named `book`.

```
where $b/publisher = "Addison-Wesley" and $b/@year > 1991
```

This is the `where` clause (the "W" in "FLWOR"). The `where` clause says we should not consider *all* the members of the sequence indicated by the `for` clause (all books), but we should only consider those books where the condition is true – in this case, where the publisher is "Addison-Wesley" and the year is 1991.

```
return
  <book year="{ $b/@year }">
   { $b/title }
  </book>
```

This is the return clause (the "R" in "FLWOR"). For each book that satisfies the `where` clause, construct an element called `book` with an attribute `year`. The value of the `year` attribute and the content of the `book` element are both XQuery expressions (delineated by curly braces, since they are inside an element constructor). Note that the result is a single `bib` element containing multiple `book` elements – one for each `book` in the for-clause sequence that satisfies the where-clause condition.

The careful reader will have noticed that the "L" and "O" in "FLWOR" are missing from this particular use case. The `let` clause assigns values to variables inside the `for` iteration. It's a convenience, but a very important one. The `order by` clause lets you define an ordering of the result sequence.

The use cases are grouped into the following scenarios:

- XMP – Experiences and Exemplars. Simple queries about books, chapters, and reviews to get you started.
- TREE – Queries that preserve hierarchy. These queries operate over a flexible "book" structure, to produce highly structured, ordered output such as a table of contents.
- SEQ – Queries based on Sequence. Queries across a medical report that illustrate the importance of order (such as "what Instruments were used in the first two Actions after the second Incision?").
- R – Access to Relational Data. Queries across an XML View of three relational tables that might be part of an auction system – USERS, ITEMS, and BIDS.

- SGML – Standard Generalized Markup Language. Some example queries taken from a conference on SGML (the ancestor of XML).
- STRING – String Search. Some examples use the "contains" function, which looks for a string inside a node. These use cases simultaneously illustrate the need for a full-text search capability in XQuery, and the limitations of the contains function (which does substring, as opposed to token-based, search).
- NS – Queries Using Namespaces. Illustrates XQuery across data from different sources, disambiguated by using different namespaces.
- PARTS – Recursive Parts Explosion. Recursive queries to create a "parts explosion" (bill of materials, or BOM) from data stored in a relational database.
- STRONG – Queries that exploit strongly typed data. These queries make use of the type information in an XML Schema. The example data and Schema are for purchase orders.

10.5 The XQuery 1.0 Suite of Specifications

XQuery 1.0 is defined by the W3C in a collection of several specifications, some of which are shared with the specification of XPath 2.0. The sheer size of that collection is intimidating to many readers, but we believe that it seems much more reasonable when we look at what each specification does and how it accomplishes its goals.

Figure 10-1 illustrates how each of the XQuery specifications, and other related specifications, fit into the overall scheme of things.

Specifications developed in whole or in part by the W3C's XML Query Working Group are shaded in Figure 10-1, while other specifications are left unshaded. Specifications represented by boxes to which the arrows point are dependent on documents represented by boxes from which those arrows originate. For example, the XQuery 1.0 Language spec is dependent on the XPath 2.0 and XQuery 1.0 Data Model spec, the XPath 2.0 and XQuery 1.0 Functions & Operators spec, and the XPath 2.0 and XQuery 1.0 Formal Semantics spec. In addition, it is *indirectly* dependent on the XML specs, the Namespaces specs, and the XML Schema specs. It is not, however, dependent on the XPath 2.0 Language spec.

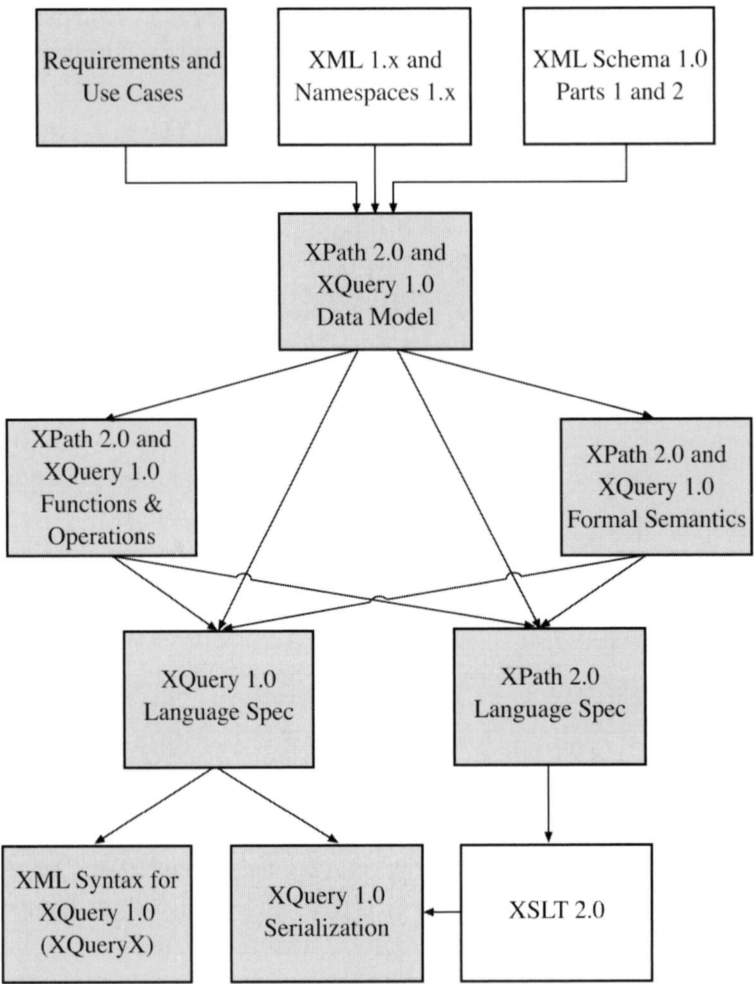

Figure 10-1 *Relationship of specifications.*

The group of documents that include the Data Model, the Functions & Operators, the Formal Semantics, XQuery 1.0, and XPath 2.0 seem to have complex relationships among themselves. In fact, the relationships are not as complex as they may appear, as you'll see in this section.

10.5.1 XQuery 1.0 Language Specification

The syntax and much of the *dynamic semantics* of XQuery (that is, the behavior of the language and its component parts at run time) are defined in a rather lengthy and detailed specification[23] of the XQuery 1.0 language. That document specifies a *human-readable* syntax for XQuery. (A separate document[24] specifies an XML syntax for XQuery, about which you'll read in Chapter 12, "XQueryX.") What is XQuery, though? The XQuery specification says this:

> XQuery is designed to meet the requirements identified by the W3C XML Query Working Group and the use cases that demonstrate the validity of the requirements. It is designed to be a language in which queries are concise and easily understood. It is also flexible enough to query a broad spectrum of XML information sources, including both databases and documents.

We agree with most of that statement, although we occasionally find ourselves wondering about the "easily understood" aspect.

The XQuery specification, as indicated in Figure 10-1, depends on several other specifications. Because XQuery operates on, and constructs, instances of the Data Model, its most important dependency is on the Data Model specification,[25] about which you read in this chapter. The design of XQuery and the details of its operation are heavily influenced by the Data Model. (Of course, the converse is also true, which isn't surprising since the two specifications were written concurrently by the same Working Group.)

The other two documents on which the XQuery specification depends are the Formal Semantics spec[26] and the Functions & Operators (sometimes called "F&O") spec.[27]

---

23 *XQuery 1.0: An XML Query Language, W3C Last Call Working Draft* (Cambridge, MA: World Wide Web Consortium, 2005). Available at: http://www.w3.org/TR/xquery/.

24 *XML Syntax for XQuery 1.0 (XQueryX), W3C Last Call Working Draft* (Cambridge, MA: World Wide Web Consortium, 2005). Available at: http://www.w3.org/TR/xqueryx/.

25 *XQuery 1.0 and XPath 2.0 Data Model, W3C Last Call Working Draft* (Cambridge, MA: World Wide Web Consortium, 2005). Available at: http://www.w3.org/TR/xpath-datamodel/.

26 *XQuery 1.0 and XPath 2.0 Formal Semantics, W3C Last Call Working Draft* (Cambridge, MA: World Wide Web Consortium, 2005). Available at: http://www.w3.org/TR/xquery-semantics/.

27 *XQuery 1.0 and XPath 2.0 Functions and Operators, W3C Last Call Working Draft* (Cambridge, MA: World Wide Web Consortium, 2005). Available at: http://www.w3.org/TR/xpath-functions/.

10.5.2 XPath 2.0 and XQuery 1.0 Formal Semantics

The word *formal,* as used by the XQuery specifications, means "a strict, mathematical definition" and the word *semantics* means "meanings." Therefore, the Formal Semantics spec defines the meaning of expressions in a strict mathematical manner. The part of the Formal Semantics spec that defines the *meanings* of expressions is not normative — that is, a definition in the XQuery language spec takes precedence over the formal definition, if they disagree. However, the *static typing* feature is defined only here, so its definition is normative. Sometimes, we refer to static typing as the *static semantics* of XQuery and the determination of the meanings of expressions as the *dynamic semantics.*

Static typing is a way of determining the data types of XQuery expressions without considering any specific data *values.* It is static typing that allows XQuery implementations to support XQuery as a strongly typed query language more efficiently — for example, to assist the query optimizer in producing an effective query evaluation plan. It also allows many errors to be detected earlier than they otherwise would be. Without the use of the static typing feature, XQuery is still a strongly typed language, but the type determination is done at query evaluation time, and errors are often detected later than they would have been under a static typing implementation. When operating on untyped data, XQuery is a weakly-typed language (perhaps "untyped" would be more appropriate).

The Formal Semantics spec defines static typing pessimistically. That is, the rules derive the types of all expressions in a manner that guarantees that no type errors can occur at query evaluation time. One of the side effects of this approach is that queries that might run without type errors — when used with a particular set of data — are prohibited from being evaluated because of the very possibility of a type error with *some* set of data. Consequently, we believe that the marketplace will demand both XQuery implementations that support static typing and implementations that do not.

10.5.3 XPath 2.0 and XQuery 1.0 Functions & Operators

The Functions and Operators (F&O) specification, covered in detail in Section 10.9, defines a large collection of functions that users can invoke in their XQuery expressions, as well as a number of "hidden" functions that the XQuery spec uses to define the semantics of its operators. In general, any operator in a programming language can be represented by a function with one or two arguments. Each of the operators in XQuery is defined in the XQuery 1.0 language spec by referencing the equivalent function in the F&O spec. These so-called "backup" functions cannot be invoked directly from XQuery expression — they exist only for definitional purposes and are not necessarily implemented as functions by any specific XQuery implementation.

The F&O spec contributes to both the strong typing of XQuery and to the definition of the language's semantics. It is an extension of the XQuery spec that is published separately for convenience — and to avoid creating an (even more) intimidatingly large combined spec.

10.5.4 XQuery 1.0 Serialization

The Serialization specification[28] was not mentioned in Section 10.5.1 because XQuery does not depend on it. Instead, the Serialization spec depends on XQuery (as well as on XSLT 2.0, which is discussed in Chapter 7, "Managing XML: Transforming and Connecting"). Serialization is covered in greater detail in Section 10.10.

Serialization is the process by which Data Model instances are transformed into character strings that represent those values in a form convenient to transport over the web, to print, to be read by a human, or to be parsed by an XML parser. Some Data Model instances represent XML documents; serializing such instances results in the so-called "angle bracket," character string form of XML documents — the form you see printed throughout this book, for example. Other Data Model instances represent atomic values, and serializing them results in character strings that form literals in the lexical space of their data types.

The Serialization specification provides facilities for producing XML strings that are suitable for treatment as XML documents or well-formed XML external parsed entities. It also provides the ability to produce XHTML, provided the value being serialized conforms to the requirements of the XHTML specification,[29] and the ability to produce

28 *XSLT 2.0 and XQuery 1.0 Serialization, W3C Last Call Working Draft* (Cambridge, MA: World Wide Web Consortium, 2005). Available at: http://www.w3.org/TR/xslt-xquery-serialization/.

HTML.[30] Finally, it provides the ability to generate ordinary text corresponding to the string value of the XML value being serialized. (Incidentally, serialization doesn't have to mean "conversion to a character string" – one might serialize a Data Model instance to some compact binary representation for exchange between processes – even though the XQuery and XPath Serialization spec only provides for serialization to a sequence of characters.)

10.5.5 XQueryX

The XQueryX specification defines an XML syntax in which XQuery expressions can be coded. It does so by defining an XML Schema to specify an XML vocabulary that XQueryX documents must use. In order to avoid the necessity of redefining all of the semantics of XQuery merely for the sake of having a second syntax, the spec also defines an XSLT 1.0 stylesheet that (literally or metaphorically) serves to transform XQueryX documents into XQuery's "human-readable" syntax, after which the semantics are well-defined.

We discuss XQueryX in more detail in Chapter 12.

10.6 The Data Model

The "XQuery 1.0 and XPath 2.0 Data Model" specification[31] is central to the definition of XQuery. The type system represented in the Data Model (and defined formally in the Formal Semantics specification)[32] has fueled more discussion in the Working Groups than the rest of the XQuery specifications put together. The XQuery Data Model (XDM) is the most comprehensive in the XML world, encompassing the Infoset and the PSVI and more.

---

29 *XHTML™ 1.0 The Extensible HyperText Markup Language, A Reformulation of HTML 4 in XML 1.0, W3C Recommendation* (Cambridge, MA: World Wide Web Consortium, 2005). Available at: http://www.w3.org/TR/xhtml/; a corresponding specification for XHTML 1.1 is Available at: http://www.w3.org/TR/xhtml1/.

30 *HTML 4.01 Specification, W3C Recommendation* (Cambridge, MA: World Wide Web Consortium, 2005). Available at: http://www.w3.org/TR/html401/.

31 *XQuery 1.0 and XPath 2.0 Data Model*, (Cambridge, MA: World Wide Web Consortium, 2005). Available at: http://www.w3.org/TR/xpath-datamodel/.

32 *XQuery 1.0 and XPath 2.0 Formal Semantics*, (Cambridge, MA: World Wide Web Consortium, 2005). Available at: http://www.w3.org/TR/xquery-semantics/.

We said in Chapter 6, "The XML Information Set (Infoset) and Beyond," that the Infoset is an abstract representation of the core information in an XML document, and that the PSVI (Post-Schema-Validation Infoset) is an Infoset with additional information about validity and data and structure types, produced by validating the document against an XML Schema. The XQuery Data Model is, at its simplest, a tree representation of the PSVI. However, the PSVI cannot model everything that the XQuery Data Model needs to deal with. The PSVI, like the Infoset, can only model well-formed XML documents, while the XQuery Data Model needs to represent an XML document, a node, a value, or a sequence of (a mixture of) any of these. That is, the XQuery Data Model needs to be able to represent anything that can be the output of a query, or the intermediate results of a query, as well as anything that can be the input to a query. The XQuery Data Model also needs to represent the value of any expression that can be part of a query. We will talk about the Data Model tree in the rest of this section, but bear in mind that this may not be a true tree at all — *i.e.*, it may not have a single root.

There are seven kinds of nodes in the XQuery Data Model tree, corresponding almost exactly to the seven kinds defined in the XPath 1.0 Data Model. Document Element, text, attribute, namespace, processing instruction, and comment nodes are common to both. The XQuery Data Model's document node, which is the root of the tree, is more permissive than its XPath 1.0 cousin. In an XQuery Data Model instance, there is at most one document node that, if it exists, sits at the top of the tree. There are no data corresponding to this node — it is a notional node, created so that the tree has a single root. It must not have an attribute, namespace, or document node as a child, but, unlike its XPath 1.0 cousin the root node, it may be empty, and it may have more than one element child node.

For intermediate (by which we mean "not serialized") query results, the tree might not have a document node at all. In such cases, the Serialization specification[33] insists that a document node must be added as part of the serialization process.

XQuery Data Model instances can be constructed in a number of ways. The XQuery Data Model specification describes how to construct an XDM instance from an Infoset or a PSVI, but instances can also be created directly, either as the output of an XQuery or via direct construction by an application.

33 *XSLT 2.0 and XQuery 1.0 Serialization*, World Wide Web Consortium (Cambridge, MA: 2005). Available at: http://www.w3.org/TR/xslt-xquery-serialization/.

The XQuery Data Model specification defines an XQuery Data Model instance as a sequence of items, where each item is either a node or a value. Nodes in the XQuery Data Model map roughly to Information Items in the Infoset, with properties and accessor functions. Every value has an associated type name.

10.6.1 Data Model Instances

The term *Data Model instance* is equivalent to the phrase "value in the context of the Data Model." The following are examples of valid Data Model instances:

- Parsed XML documents
- Atomic values of an atomic type defined by *XML Schema Part 2*[34]
- Sequences of nodes intermixed with atomic values
- Sequences of attribute nodes

In short, a Data Model instance is any value that satisfies the requirements of the Data Model specification.

Every specification in the XQuery collection depends entirely on the Data Model, operates on Data Model instances, and/or produces Data Model instances. The only spec that violates that rule is Serialization, which operates on Data Model instances and produces sequences of characters that represent those Data Model instances.

XQuery is *an* XML transformation language in the same sense that XSLT is. XSLT, you'll recall from Chapter 7, "Managing XML: Transforming and Connecting," is the W3C's XML Transformation language. But what does XSLT really do? It uses XPath to identify nodes in a document that is being processed and produces *new* nodes in a *new* document that the XSLT process creates. Similarly, XQuery allows you to process one or more input documents and to create any of several types of XML values as a result of that processing.

XQuery defines two mechanisms for the construction of new Data Model instances. As you will see in detail in Chapter 11, "XQuery 1.0 Definition," XQuery allows you to construct a Data Model instance

34 *XML Schema Part 2: Datatypes Second Edition* (Cambridge, MA: World Wide Web Consortium, 2004). Available at: http://www.w3.org/TR/xmlschema-1/.

using *constructors* (XQuery expressions that evaluate to XML in one form or another). *Direct* constructors use an XML-like notation to specify the Data Model values you wish to construct, and *computed* constructors use a notation based on computed expressions. A direct element constructor, for instance, is one in which the name of the element is known *a priori* — that is, it's a constant, literal sequence of characters. A computed element constructor is, by contrast, one in which the name of the element is not known in advance, but is specified by means of an expression.

Both sorts of constructors can be used to construct element nodes (including their attributes, namespace declarations, and content), processing instruction nodes, comment nodes, and text nodes. Document nodes cannot be created using direct constructors, but they can be created with computed constructors.

10.6.2 What Is an XQuery Data Model Instance?

To understand what makes up an XQuery Data Model instance, we start with the set of cascading definitions in the XQuery Data Model specification:

- Every **instance of the data model** is a **sequence**.
- A **sequence** is an ordered collection of zero or more **items**.
- An **item** is either a **node** or an **atomic value.**
- Every **node** is one of the seven kinds of nodes defined in [the Data Model specification]. Nodes form a tree that consists of a root node plus all the nodes that are reachable directly or indirectly from the root node via the dm:children, dm:attributes, and dm:namespaces accessors. Every node belongs to exactly one tree, and every tree has exactly one root node.
- An **atomic value** is a value in the value space of an **atomic type.**
- An **atomic type** is a **primitive simple type** or a type derived by restriction from another atomic type.
- There are 24 **primitive simple types**: the 19 defined in [Schema Part 2] and `xdt:anyAtomicType`, `xdt:untyped`, `xdt:untypedAtomic`, `xdt:dayTimeDuration`, and `xdt:yearMonthDuration`, defined in [the XQuery Data Model specification].

These definitions completely describe what constitutes an XQuery Data Model instance, if you understand "the seven kinds of nodes," the accessor functions dm:children, dm:attributes, and dm:namespaces, and the XQuery type system. The seven kinds of nodes are defined partly in terms of the Data Model accessor functions — abstract functions in the "dm:" namespace.

10.6.3 The Seven Kinds of Nodes

Before we discuss the seven kinds of nodes represented in the XQuery Data Model and their properties, we need to make it clear that the term *node* is not necessarily being used in its most common meaning — XQuery Data Model nodes do not necessarily form part of a tree. XQuery's seven kinds of nodes strongly resemble the seven kinds of nodes in the XPath 1.0 Data Model (see Section 6.5, "The XPath 1.0 Data Model"), where, with the exception of attributes, they really are nodes of a tree.

The seven kinds of nodes in the XQuery Data Model are: document, element, attribute, namespace, processing instruction (PI), comment, and text nodes. (*Note:* These are the seven kinds of nodes at the time of writing — namespace nodes are somewhat redundant, and may be dropped before XQuery reaches Recommendation). Each node kind has a number of **properties**. There is a set of accessor functions defined on nodes — abstract functions in the "dm:" namespace, which are not exposed in XQuery (though some of the XQuery accessor functions, such as `string()` and `data()`, are defined in terms of these abstract functions).

Properties

In Section 6.3, "The Infoset Information Items and Their Properties," we looked at the properties of each Infoset Information Item in detail. The XQuery Data Model specification does not directly define properties of nodes; it only talks about how to construct each property from an Infoset or a PSVI, and gives some general rules. While this is not the most convenient way to read about the XQuery Data Model definitions, we know that it is complete, since the XQuery Data Model cannot contain any information that cannot be derived from an Infoset or a PSVI. Of course, programs are free to construct Data Model instances directly; *i.e.*, a Data Model instance might not *really* be derived from either an Infoset or a PSVI, but it must be identical to a Data Model instance that might have been derived from an Infoset or a PSVI for the same data.

In the following lists we take one node kind – the element node – and examine each property. We continue to employ the convention of referring to property names in square brackets [ ]. The following XQuery Data Model properties of the Element Node map closely to the Infoset properties:

- **[children]** – derived from the **[children]** property of the Element Information Item in the Infoset (or PSVI), except that character information items are collected together to form text nodes (as in the PSVI).
- **[parent]** – derived from the **[parent]** property of the Element Information Item in the Infoset (or PSVI), except that an attribute's owner element is included as the attribute's parent.
- **[base-uri]** – derived from the **[base uri]** property of the Element Information Item in the Infoset (or PSVI).
- **[node-name]** – derived from the **[local name]** and **[namespace name]** Infoset properties.
- **[attributes]** – derived from the **[attributes]** property of the Element Information Item in the Infoset (or PSVI).
- **[namespaces]** – derived from the **[in-scope namespaces]** Infoset (or PSVI) property.

The XQuery Data Model also includes information from the Schema contributions to the Infoset (the PSVI) if they are available. The following XQuery Data Model properties of the Element Information Item map closely to PSVI properties:

- **[nilled]** – true if the PSVI properties **[validity]** and **[nil]** are "valid" and "true," respectively, and otherwise false; also false if the Data Model instance is constructed from an Infoset.
- **[type-name]** – derived from the **[validity]**, **[validation attempted]**, **[type definition]**, and **[type definition namespace]** of the PSVI. xdt:untyped if the Data Model instance is constructed from an Infoset. If the element node has an anonymous type definition, then the processor building the Data Model instance must invent a name for that anonymous type.

- **[is-id], [is-idref]** – If the Data Model instance is constructed from a PSVI, then **[is-id]** and **[is-idref]** are derived from the **[type name]** Data Model property. If the **[type name]** is `xs:ID`, then **[is-id]** is true; otherwise, **[is-id]** is false. If the **[type name]** is `xs:IDREF` or `xs:IDREFS`, then **[is-idref]** is true; otherwise, **[is-idref]** is false.

  If the Data Model instance is constructed from an Infoset, then **[type name]** is always xdt:untyped, so we cannot derive **[is-id]** or **[is-idref]** from that – in that case, **[is-id]** and **[is-idref]** are always false for an element node, and are derived from the **[attribute type]** Infoset property for an attribute node.

Finally, there are two properties of an Element Node that do not map directly to any Infoset or PSVI property (though the values of these two properties *can* be derived from either an Infoset or a PSVI):

- **[string-value]** – the **[string-value]** property of an Element Information Item, sometimes referred to as the *string value* of an element, is the concatenation of all the **descendant** (not just the **child**) text nodes. The string value of a text node is the value of its **[content]** property, which in turn is either a string containing all the **[character code]** properties of the character information items in the Element Information Item (if constructed from an Infoset), or the **[schema normalized value]**[35] of the Element Information Item (if constructed from a PSVI).
- **[typed-value]** – if the Data Model instance is derived from an Infoset (*i.e.*, there is no XML Schema involved), then the typed value of an element is its string value, represented as a typed value, with the type `xdt:untypedAtomic`. If the Data Model instance is derived from a PSVI (*i.e.*, there *is* a Schema), then there is a set of rules for determining the

---

35 The **[schema normalized value]** is a property in the PSVI, added during Schema validation. The **[schema normalized value]** of a text node is a string containing all the **[character code]** properties of the character information items in the Element Information Item, with some whitespace normalization applied (according to the value of the element's whiteSpace facet).

More generally, the **[schema normalized value]** in the PSVI is similar to the string value of an element, except that it takes into account only direct child text nodes (the string value includes all descendant text nodes).

typed value based on the type of the element (see the subsection entitled "More on [typed-value]"). In the simplest case, where the element is of complex type (*i.e.*, the element has one or more attributes and/or child elements) with element-only content (*i.e.*, the element has child elements but no text nodes), the typed-value is undefined.

Both string value and typed value are new in the XQuery Data Model; *i.e.*, they don't exist in the Infoset or PSVI. They mean what you would expect from their names. Let's look at Example 10–2 to be completely clear.

Example 10-2 *Typed movie (Cut-Down Version)*

```
<?xml version="1.0" encoding="UTF-8"?>
<!-- movie - a simple XML example -->
<movie xmlns:xs="http://www.w3.org/2001/XMLSchema-instance"
       xs:noNamespaceSchemaLocation="movie-cutdown.xsd">
  <title>An American Werewolf in London</title>
  <yearReleased>1981</yearReleased>
  <director>
    <familyName>Landis</familyName>
    <givenName>John</givenName>
  </director>
</movie>
```

Example 10-3 *movie-cutdown.xsd: An XML Schema for Typed Movie (Cut-Down Version)*

```
<?xml version="1.0" encoding="UTF-8"?>
<xs:schema xmlns:xs="http://www.w3.org/2001/XMLSchema">
  <xs:element name="familyName" type="xs:string"/>
  <xs:element name="givenName" type="xs:string"/>
  <xs:element name="movie">
    <xs:complexType>
      <xs:sequence>
        <xs:element name="title" type="xs:string"/>
        <xs:element name="yearReleased">
          <xs:simpleType>
            <xs:restriction base="xs:integer">
              <xs:minInclusive value="1900"/>
              <xs:maxInclusive value="2100"/>
```

```
            </xs:restriction>
          </xs:simpleType>
        </xs:element>
        <xs:element name="director">
          <xs:complexType>
            <xs:sequence>
              <xs:element ref="familyName"/>
              <xs:element ref="givenName"/>
            </xs:sequence>
          </xs:complexType>
        </xs:element>
      </xs:sequence>
    </xs:complexType>
  </xs:element>
</xs:schema>
```

Example 10-2 shows a cut-down version of our movie example, with just `title`, `yearReleased`, and `director`. Example 10-3 shows a possible XML Schema that might be used to validate the cut-down movie example. Once the movie example has been validated against the schema, the element `yearReleased` has a string value of "the string '1981'" but a typed value of "the integer 1981". Both look the same on paper (*i.e.*, after serialization). You can do arithmetic with "the integer 1981" – *e.g.*, add "the integer 10" to it. You can do string manipulation with "the string '1981'" – *e.g.*, find the first character (string of length 1). But you cannot do arithmetic on "the string '1981'" or string manipulation on "the integer 1981". Note that the string value of `movie` is "the string 'An American Werewolf in London1981LandisJohn'", and the typed value of `movie` is undefined.

More on [typed-value]

The [typed-value] property of an element node deserves some more explanation. In the previous section, we said that the XQuery Data Model introduces two properties that don't exist in either the Infoset or the PSVI – [string-value] and [typed-value]. These are clearly useful, yielding a string and an item (or sequence of items) with an atomic type (date, integer, *etc.*), respectively. The idea is that if you want to do operations that are specific to certain data types (such as arithmetic), then you should use the typed value of an element. While it's easy to see what the string value of any element should be, it's not always obvious what the typed value of an element should be. For example, in the previous section we said that the typed value of the element `movie` in Example 10-2 is undefined, and it's difficult to imagine what the typed value could possibly be.[36] The rules for deriving the typed value are a little complicated — we think it's worth summarizing them here.

If the Data Model instance is derived from an Infoset (*i.e.*, there is no XML Schema involved), then the typed value of an element is its string value, represented as a typed value, with the type `xdt:untypedAtomic`.

If the Data Model instance is derived from a PSVI (*i.e.*, there *is* a Schema), then the way the typed value is derived depends on the Schema type of the element. If the element has only simple content (the element may have attributes, but no children), then:

- If the Schema type of the element is `xs:anySimpleType` — the typed value is the [schema normalized value], represented as type `xdt:untypedAtomic`.
- If the Schema type of the element is some atomic type — the typed value is derived from the [schema normalized value] in some obvious way (*e.g.*, if the element has a Schema type of `xs:integer`, then the typed value will be an `xs:integer`).
- If the Schema type of the element is a union or list type, then special rules apply (we leave it as an exercise for the reader to find these rules in the XQuery Data Model spec, Section 3.3.1.2).

If the Data Model instance is derived from a PSVI and the element has *anything other than* simple content, then:

- If the Schema type of the element is `xdt:untyped`, or if the element has mixed content (text and child elements) — the typed value is the string value represented as `xdt:untypedAtomic`.
- If the element is empty — the typed value is the empty sequence.

---

36 The Data Model spec does say, "Regardless of how an instance of the data model is constructed, every node and atomic value in the data model must have a typed-value that is consistent with its type." We can only speculate that, in the case of an element like the `movie` element, a typed value is said to exist but is undefined. This seems odd.

- If the element has a complex type with element-only content — the typed value is undefined, and the typed-value accessor will raise an error.

These rules are not at all obvious — for example, the typed value of the `parent` element in

```
<parent>some text <child>42</child></parent>
```

is "some text 42" as `xdt:untypedAtomic`, since `parent` has mixed content. But take away `"some text"` to give

```
<parent><child>42</child></parent>
```

and the typed value of parent is undefined, since it has element-only content. This is somewhat surprising, but it does follow the spirit of the typed value as something on which you can do data type–dependent operations such as arithmetic and string manipulation.

Before we leave [typed-value], we should point out another wrinkle that may lead to surprising results. The XQuery Data Model spec explicitly says that a conforming implementation may store *either* the string value *or* the typed value of an element, and that, whichever one it stores, it may derive the other from it. At first glance, that seems reasonable — if the string value of an element is "the string '1981'", the type is `xs:integer`, and the typed value is "the integer 1981", then you can store only the string value and the type. You can derive the typed value "the integer 1981" whenever you want to access it — you don't need to store it. But what if the string value is "the string '0001981'" and the type is `xs:integer` — can you get away with storing only the typed value and the type? If the XQuery Data Model instance only contains the typed value "the integer 1981", then it will derive the string value "the string '1981'" and not the original string value, "the string '0001981'". The spec says that's OK — specifically, it says that "some variations in the string value of a node are defined as insignificant. . . . Any string that is a valid lexical representation of the typed value is acceptable."

Accessors — Toward an API

The XQuery Data Model is different from its predecessors (the XML Infoset and the XPath 1.0 Data Model) in two important ways — it has a sophisticated type system, and it (arguably) has an API. The type system is described in Section 10.7. The API consists of a set of accessors — functions in the "dm:" namespace that are defined for each kind of node — that are not exposed to the end user. These accessors define what information is available from the Data Model. They are used in the definition of some of the functions described in the Functions and Operators specification (see Section 10.9.1).

The most important accessors are dm:string-value and dm:typed-value. These are defined for each of the seven kinds of nodes, and they return the contents of the [string-value] and [typed-value] properties, respectively. Table 10-1 shows the result of applying the XQuery Data Model accessors to the XQuery Data Model node kinds. The table is incomplete — some of the accessors have been left out for brevity, and the Namespace node kind has not been included. At the time of writing, the Namespace node kind is in doubt and may be removed from the XQuery Data Model. This would be a good move, as it seems the Namespace node kind is an exception to almost every Data Model rule (*e.g.*, dm:node-name returns the **[prefix]** property of a Namespace node rather than the name of a node).

Table 10-2 shows another way of looking at accessor/property mapping. This table shows how to retrieve the value of each of the XQuery Data Model properties using an accessor or an XQuery (user-accessible) function. Under Function, we have put a " — " where there is no function available. For some properties, there is no need for a function because an XPath axis is available — you don't need a special function to get the value of the parent, children, or attributes of an element. The absence of functions for type-name, on the other hand, requires some explanation.

Table 10-1 *XQuery Data Model Accessors*

	Document	**Element**	**Attribute**	**Processing Instruction**	**Comment**	**Text**
dm:document-uri	[document-uri]	()	()	()	()	()
dm:base-uri	[base-uri]	[base-uri]	parent [base-uri]	[base-uri]	parent [base-uri]	parent [base-uri]
dm:node-name	()	[node-name]	[node-name]	[target]	()	()
dm:parent	()	[parent]	[parent]	[parent]	[parent]	[parent]
dm:string-value	[string-value]	[string-value]	[string-value]	[content]	[content]	[content]

Table 10-1 XQuery Data Model Accessors (continued)

	Document	Element	Attribute	Processing Instruction	Comment	Text
dm:typed-value	[typed-value]	[typed-value]	[typed-value]	[content] as xs:string	[content] as xs:string	[content] as xs:string
dm:type-name	()	[type-name]	[type-name]	()	()	xdt:untyped-Atomic
dm:children	[children]	[children]	()	()	()	()
dm:attributes	()	[attributes]	()	()	()	()
dm:namespaces	()	[namespaces]	()	()	()	()
dm:nilled	()	[nilled]	()	()	()	()

The user-accessible function for type-name has been intentionally left out of the XQuery specifications. In most cases, you need to know the type-name of a node only so that you can check that type-name against a known type-name. For example, you might want to check to see if a variable named `$a` is an `xs:integer`. If there were a function `fn:type-name()`, you might say something like "`if fn:type-name($a) eq 'xs:integer'`". This would only succeed if the type of `$a` were `xs:integer`, and it would fail if the type of `$a` were any type *derived from* `xs:integer`. A better way to test for type is to say, "`if $a instance of xs:integer`". The `instance of` expression will evaluate to true if `$a` is an `xs:integer`, or if `$a` is of any type *derived from* `xs:integer`. This principle – subtype substitutability – is considered fundamental to XQuery, so you must use `instance of` for type-checking instead of explicitly checking the [type-name] property against a known type name. Access to the [type-name] property and other XML Schema-related metadata (such as base-type, facets, *etc.*) may be added in a future version of the XQuery Data Model.

Finally, there is no function to directly access the [namespaces] property. There is a namespace XPath axis, but it is deprecated in XPath 2.0. And you can use a combination of `fn:in-scope-prefixes()` (which returns the *prefixes* for the in-scope namespaces) and `fn:namespace-uri-for-prefix()` (which returns the namespace URI for a given prefix) to find all the namespace information in the [namespaces] property.

Table 10-2 Accessing XQuery Data Model Properties

	Document	Element	Attribute	Processing Instruction	Comment	Text	Function
[document-uri]	dm:document-uri	–	–	–	–	–	fn:document-uri( )
[base-uri]	dm:base-uri	dm:base-uri	dm:base-uri*	dm:base-uri	dm: base-uri†	dm: base-uri†	fn: base-uri( )
[node-name]	–	dm:node-name	dm:node-name	–	–	–	fn:node-name( )
[parent]	–	dm:parent	dm:parent	dm:parent	dm:parent	dm:parent	–
[string-value]	dm:string-value	dm:string-value	dm:string-value	–	–	–	fn:string( )
[content]	–	–	–	dm:string-value	dm:string-value	dm:string-value	fn:string( )
[typed-value]	dm:typed-value	dm:typed-value	dm:typed-value	–	–	–	fn:data( )
[content]	–	–	-	dm:typed-value	dm:typed-value	dm:typed-value	fn:data( )
[type-name]	–	dm:type-name	dm:type-name	–	–	–‡	–
[children]	dm:children	dm:children	–	–	–	–	–
[attributes]	–	dm: attributes	–	–	–	–	–
[namespaces]	–	dm: namespaces	–	–	–	–	–
[nilled]	–	dm:nilled	–	–	–	–	fn:nilled( )

* returns the [base-uri] of the parent (owner) element.

† returns the [base-uri] of the parent.

‡ always xdt:untypedAtomic.

10.6.4 The Data Model as Tree — Representing a Well-Formed Document

Let's look at our movie example again and see what a Data Model tree might look like.

Figure 10-2 shows a representation of a Data Model instance for the movie example in Example 10-2, validated according to the XML Schema in Example 10-3. The figure is not complete – it does not show every property for every node. The tree is similar to the XPath 1.0 Data Model Tree (in Section 6.5, "The XPath 1.0 Data Model"). Some of the terminology has changed – the Root Node is now the Document Node; the [expanded-name] property is now called the [node-name]; the comment [string-value] property is now called

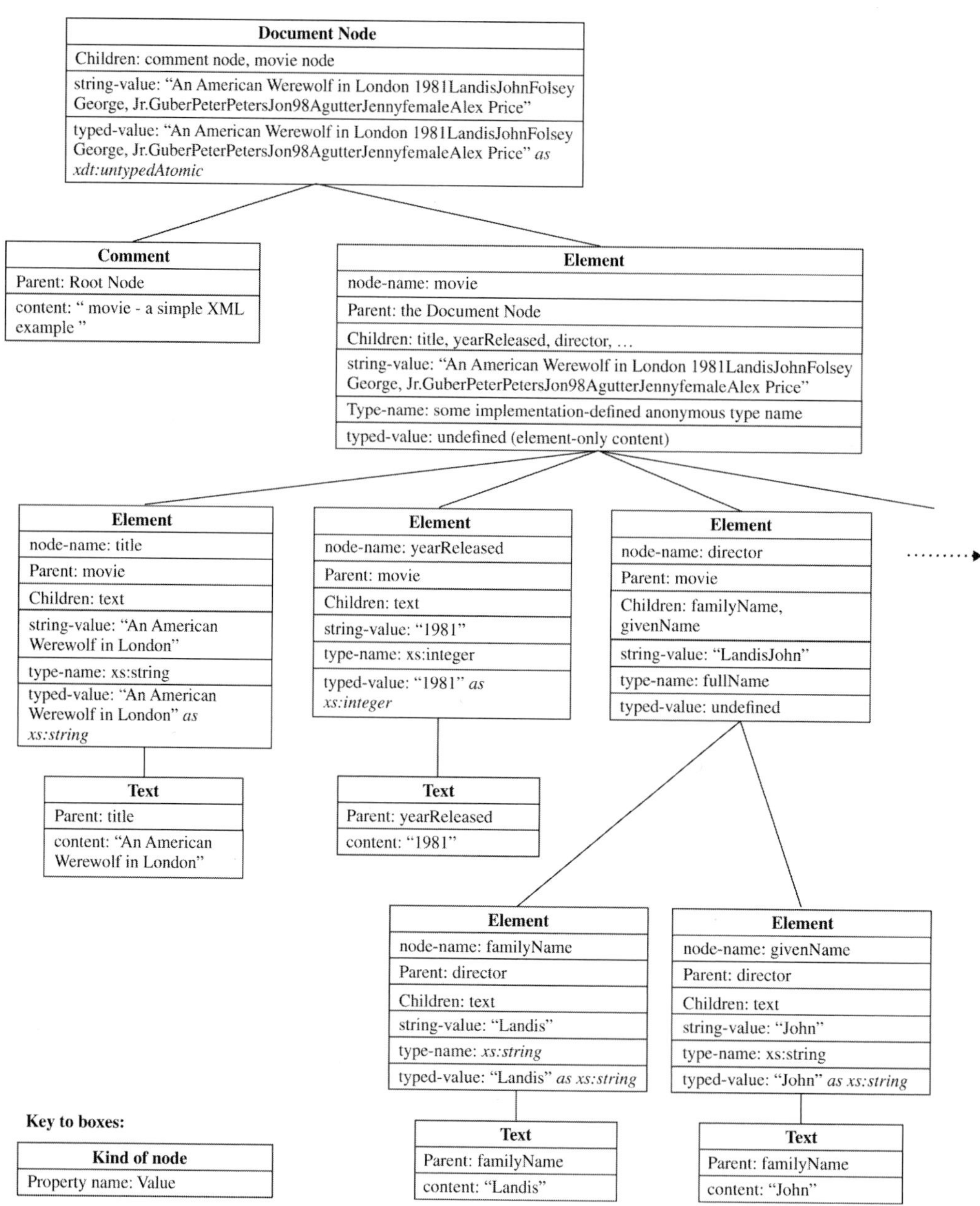

***Figure 10-2** movie Data Model Instance.*

[content], and so on. The main difference is that every node now has type information, either explicitly – in the [type-name] and [typed-value] properties – or implicitly, via the definition of the dm:type-name and dm:typed-value accessors.

Figure 10-2 shows that the XQuery Data Model definition is not as clean or as symmetrical as one might like it to be. For example, it would be nice to say that every node has a string value ([string-value]) and a typed value ([typed-value]). While the "leaf" element nodes title, yearReleased, familyName, and givenName each have a string value and a typed value with the expected contents, some of the contents are surprising:

- The document node has a typed value of:

  `"An American Werewolf in London1981LandisJohn-FolseyGeorge,Jr.GuberPeterPetersJon98Agutter-JennyfemaleAlex Price"`

  as xdt:untypedAtomic (one might have expected xs:string).
- The typed value of the `movie` element is undefined (one might have expected the string value *as xs:string*).
- The comment node has neither a [string-value] nor a [typed-value] property, but the string value of the comment is the value of its [content] property, and the typed value of the comment is its string value *as xs:string*.
- Similarly, the text nodes have neither a [string-value] nor a [typed-value] property. Like the comment node, the text node's string value is the value of its [content] property, but its typed value is its string value *as xdt:untypedAtomic* (not *as xs:string*).

10.6.5 The Data Model as Sequence — Representing an Arbitrary Sequence

One of the challenges the XQuery Data Model addresses is that of typed XML – the other is that of arbitrary sequences. The XML Infoset models only well-formed XML documents, while the XQuery Data Model must model an arbitrary sequence of documents, nodes, and/or atomic values. That's because the XML Infoset only needs to provide an abstract representation of the information in an XML document, for consumption by an XML processor (*e.g.*, a stylesheet processor), while the XQuery Data Model must represent any input to, and any output from, a query.

To emphasize this difference between a model of an XML document and a model of arbitrary sequences, Figure 10-3 is a diagram of an XQuery Data Model instance of the result of a query. Suppose we want to find the title and director of every movie released before 1985. The movies document and XML Schema are included in Appendix A: The Example — they look like many instances of Example 7-1 wrapped in a <movies> tag. A possible XQuery is shown in Example 10-4, with the serialized result in Example 10-5.

Example 10-4 *A Simple XQuery*

```
for $b in doc("movies-we-own.xml")/movies/movie
  where $b/yearReleased < 1985
  return (data($b/title), $b/director)
```

Example 10-5 *Simple XQuery Result*

```
An American Werewolf in London
<director>
  <familyName>Landis</familyName>
  <givenName>John</givenName>
</director>
American Graffiti
<director>
  <familyName>Lucas</familyName>
  <givenName>George</givenName>
</director>
Alien
<director>
  <familyName>Scott</familyName>
  <givenName>Ridley</givenName>
</director>
Animal House
<director>
  <familyName>Landis</familyName>
  <givenName>John</givenName>
</director>

... etc.
```

Note that the result shown in Example 10-5 is not a well-formed XML document, since it does not have a single top-level element.[37] This result is a sequence of (title-string, director) sequences, where "title-string" is the string that makes up the title (the atomic value

37 See the XSLT 2.0 and XQuery 1.0 Serialization spec at http://www.w3.org/TR/xslt-xquery-serialization/ for a way to serialize the XQuery Data Model as XML or HTML.

'An American Werewolf in London', as opposed to the element node '<title>An American Werewolf in London</title>'). Since the XQuery Data Model cannot represent sequences of sequences, this got flattened to a single sequence of (title-string, director, title-string, director, . . .). If this were a final result that we wanted to use as, say, input to a printed report, we would probably use element constructors to format the result (see Chapter 11). Let's assume that this is an intermediate result where it is important to have a typed (atomic) value as well as some XML. Figure 10-3 shows (part of) the XQuery Data Model for the result in Example 10-5.

Figure 10-3 illustrates the power of the XQuery Data Model to represent arbitrary sequences. Again, this arbitrary sequence might include any atomic value (a string, integer, or date), an element with no parent, an attribute with no parent, a well-formed XML document including a document node, or any combination of these.

10.7 The XQuery Type System

In Section 10.6, we saw how the XQuery Data Model represents the values, structure, and type information in an XML document, an XML fragment, a node, a value, or a sequence of any of these. Each item in the XQuery Data Model has at least a value and a type name. In this section, we look at the XQuery type system in a bit more detail — why it's there, what it consists of, and how it affects queries.

10.7.1 What Is a Type System Anyway?

A type system is a system of splitting entities up into named sets. In general programming, an entity may be a value ("Hello", 5, 24th October 1956, . . .), or a variable ($a, Inum, . . .), or it may be something more abstract like the input and output parameters of a function or the result of evaluating an expression. In XML-land it may also be a piece of structure — an XML element with some attributes and some children.

As we saw in Section 10.6.3, the type of an entity is useful because we can define the operations that are allowed on each type — you cannot do arithmetic on strings, and you cannot find the first character of a date. It is not clear what the result of "Hello" + 5 or substring(42, 1) should be. Weakly-typed languages such as Perl are easy to use because you don't have to think about data types too much — you don't have to declare variables, and values are cast at run time to

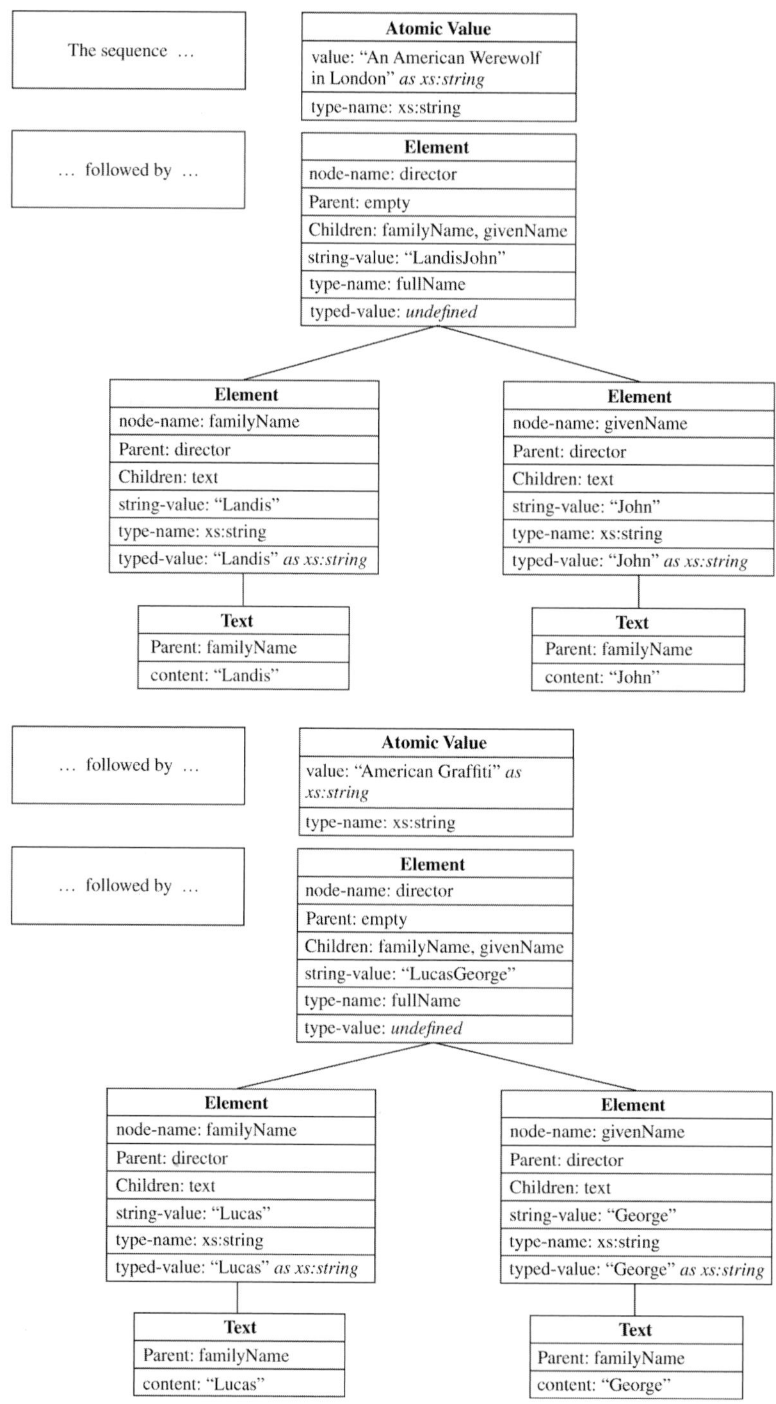

Figure 10-3 *Data Model Instance of a Sequence.*

whatever type makes most sense. In Perl, the result of "Hello" + 5 is "Hello5", and the result of substring(42, 1) is "4". Many programmers argue that this is undesirable behavior. If the processor sees "Hello" + 5, then something has probably gone wrong, and it is "more correct" to return an error than to return a best-guess answer that is likely to be wrong. A strongly typed language such as Java or SQL will return an error for "Hello" + 5 or substring(42, 1). People who write in a strongly typed language have to do a little more work, but the result is a more robust application

A strongly typed language such as Java or SQL may do type checking at compile time (static typing) or at run time (dynamic typing). Static typing is more efficient than dynamic typing, because it identifies type errors earlier. That is, in a static typing environment, a type error will be returned very quickly during the compile phase, while in a dynamic typing environment, a program or query may run almost to completion before detecting and returning a type error. On the other hand, the processor may not have complete information at compile time. With *pessimistic* static typing, the processor returns a type error whenever there *may* be a type error at run time, but if this pessimistic static type check succeeds, then the processor can confidently proceed with the rest of the program or query without bothering with any further type checking. So pessimistic static type checking gains efficiency at the expense of some false type errors.

XQuery is a strongly typed language — every entity (every element, attribute, atomic value, *etc.*) has both a value and a type name, and functions and operators are defined to work only on some (combinations of) types. XQuery has an optional static typing feature, which uses pessimistic static typing. If an XQuery engine implements the XQuery static typing feature, it must do pessimistic static typing — *i.e.*, it may sometimes throw false type errors, but it must never return a dynamic type error. If an XQuery engine does *not* implement the XQuery static typing feature, it must report dynamic type errors, and it may report some static type errors.

Dynamic *vs.* static typing has been the subject of many hours of discussions in the XQuery Working Group. We expect the debate to be resolved in the marketplace as XQuery vendors produce dynamic-only, static-only, and hybrid implementations.

10.7.2 XML Schema Types

The XQuery type system is based on the types defined in *XML Schema Part 2: Datatypes*[38] and the structure types defined in *XML Schema Part 1: Structures*.[39]

Datatypes (simple types)

Every item (document, node, or atomic value) in the XQuery Data Model has both a value and a named type. If the item is an atomic value, an attribute node, or an element node with simple content (that is, an element node with no children), then it has a data type in the straightforward sense that "Hello" has the data type "string" and 5 has the data type "integer".

XML Schema defines 19 built-in, atomic, primitive data types.

- *built-in* — defined as part of XML Schema, as opposed to *user-derived* (user-defined) data types.
- *atomic* — a single, indivisible data type definition, as opposed to *list* (a data type defined as a list of atomic data types) or *union* (a data type defined as the union of one or more data types).
- *primitive* — a data type that is not defined in terms of other data types. For example, `xs:decimal`[40] is a primitive data type, while `xs:integer` is a *derived* data type, defined as a special case of `xs:decimal` where *fractionDigits* is 0.

In addition to those 19 built-in, atomic, primitive data types, XML Schema defines 25 built-in, atomic, *derived* data types. These 44 built-in data types are defined in terms of a *value space* — the set of values that "belong" to the data type — and a *lexical space* — the set of valid literals for a data type. It follows that each value in the value space of a data type can be serialized (written down) as one or more literals in the lexical space of that data type. Each data type also has some *fun-*

38 *XML Schema Part 2: Datatypes Second Edition*, (Cambridge, MA: World Wide Web Consortium, 2004). Available at: http://w3.org/TR/xmlschema-2/.

39 *XML Schema Part 1: Structures Second Edition*, (Cambridge, MA: World Wide Web Consortium, 2004). Available at: http://w3.org/TR/xmlschema-1.

40 Throughout this book, we adopt the common practice of using the namespace prefix "`xs:`" to denote the XML Schema built-in Datatypes. Later, we use "`xdt:`" to denote XQuery-only built-in Datatypes.

damental facets — properties of the data type such as whether the values in the value space have a defined order, whether the value space is bounded, whether the cardinality of the value space is finite or infinite, and so forth.

In addition to these 44 built-in data types, XML Schema allows for *user-derived* (user-defined) data types based on the built-in data types. These user-derived data types may combine the built-in data types using list or union, or they may restrict the value space (and hence the lexical space) of a built-in via some *constraining facets* — properties that restrict the value space, such as length, or an enumeration of allowable values.

Finally, XML Schema defines one *top-level* data type, `xs:anySimpleType`. A top-level data type (sometimes called an *ur*[41] data type) is a type from which all other types of a certain category are derived. In XML Schema, `xs:anySimpleType` is defined as the *base type* of all the primitive types. (Note this is *not* the universe of all possible types, as we will see later in this chapter.)

Confused? OK, let's look at a few examples. We start by looking at a couple of data types that everyone is familiar with.

`xs:decimal` is a built-in, atomic, primitive data type in XML Schema. Its value space is "the set of the values $i \times 10^{-n}$, where i and n are integers such that n >= 0" (the word *integer* here is used to represent the standard mathematical concept of an integer, which XML Schema does not attempt to define). The lexical space of `xs:decimal` is "a finite-length sequence of decimal digits (#x30-#x39) separated by a period as a decimal indicator. . . . An optional leading sign is allowed. . . . Leading and trailing zeroes are optional. If the fractional part is zero, the period and following zero(es) can be omitted." So 42, 1234.5678, and +888888.00000 are all valid representations of `xs:decimal`, but Hello, --42, 1234,5678 and 1,234.5678 are not. `xs:decimal` has a defined ordering relation (a fundamental facet) — "x < y if y - x is positive". And `xs:decimal` has nine constraining facets — totalDigits, fractionDigits, pattern, whiteSpace, enumeration, maxInclusive, maxExclusive, minInclusive, and minExclusive. That means that, for example, you can define a data type based on `xs:decimal` that is restricted to four total digits and two fraction digits (+1.34, 4256, or 98.50, but not 4256.1 or 98.504).

---

41 The prefix *ur* comes from German and means "proto" or "first" or "original." The ur type is the type from which all other types are derived and is thus a prototype for other types.

`xs:integer` is a built-in, atomic, derived data type in XML Schema. It is derived from `xs:decimal` by defining the fractionDigits facet to be 0. Its value space is "the infinite set {. . .,-2,-1,0,1,2,. . .}." The lexical space of `xs:integer` is "a finite-length sequence of decimal digits (#x30-#x39) with an optional leading sign." So 42, 1234, and +888888 are all valid representations of xs:integer, but Hello, --42, 1234,5678, and 95.80 are not. `xs:integer` has the same ordering as `xs:decimal` and the same constraining facets (though fractionDigits must be 0). That means you can define a data type based on `xs:integer` that is restricted by setting maxInclusive to 42 (+12, 42, or 9 but not 43 or 1.5).

The 44 primitive and derived built-in data types in XML Schema cover all the string, numeric, and binary types commonly used in programming and query languages — integer, decimal, float, double, string, positive integer, byte, hexadecimal, *etc.* — plus 9 data types for dealing with dates and times — date, time, dateTime, duration, gYearMonth, gYear, gMonthDay, gDay, and gMonth.[42]

Structure Types (Complex Types)

Earlier in this section we said that Datatypes are useful because, when you define an operation, you can specify which Datatypes make sense with that operation. So if you write a program to reserve seats on an airplane, you want to be sure that it assigns a passenger name to a flight. If someone reversed the passenger name and flight number when making a reservation, you want the program to notice that mistake and throw an error, rather than assigning passenger "UA42" to flight "John Doe." XML contains structure as well as values, and we want to run checks on the structure of XML for the same reasons we want to check the values — to ensure robustness of programs when the input is incorrect.

XML Schema defines a type system for XML structures (*complex types*) as well as values (*simple types*). A complex type definition constrains elements in the following ways:

- Defines the presence and content of attributes allowed in the element. The complex type defines the name, simple type, occurrence information, and optionally the default value of each attribute that may be associated with this element.

42 The date/time types beginning with "g" are sometimes referred to as "the Australian Datatypes" — a pun on the common Australian greeting "g'day (gDay)."

- Defines the elements that may be children of this element, and their order and type.
- Defines whether the element has *mixed content* — child elements plus text nodes — or child elements only.

Note that the type of an element with simple content is a simple type. For example, the title element — `<title>American Werewolf in London</title>` — is of type `xs:string`. There is no structure type (complex type) associated with this element — if you know that it is an element whose content is of type `xs:string`, you know everything there is to know about its Datatype and structure.

To complete the XML Schema type hierarchy, XML Schema adds one more abstract type, `xs:anyType`, to sit at the top (root) of the hierarchy. `xs:anySimpleType` is a subtype of `xs:anyType`. Every complex type is a subtype of `xs:anyType`.[43] See *XML Schema Part 2* for a diagram of the XML Schema type hierarchy.[44]

There are no built-in complex types as such, though there is a Schema Type Library[45] covering some common structures. Example 10-6 shows a simple example, the text structure type.

Example 10-6 *text, Part of the XML Schema Type Library*

```
<xs:complexType name="text">
   <xs:annotation>
   <xs:documentation xmlns="http://www.w3.org/1999/xhtml">
    <p>Use this for elements with text-for-reading content.
       It's mixed so that things like bidi markup can be added,
       either on an ad-hoc basis in instances, or in types
       derived from this one.
    </p>
   </xs:documentation>
  </xs:annotation>

  <xs:complexContent mixed="true">
   <xs:restriction base="xs:anyType">
```

43 The type hierarchy diagram would be more symmetrical if there were an abstract type xs:anyComplexType, but there isn't.

44 See http://w3.org/TR/xmlschema-2/#built-in-datatypes.

45 *The Complete XML Schema Type Library* (Cambridge, MA: World Wide Web Consortium, 2001). Available at: http://www.w3.org/2001/03/XMLSchema/TypeLibrary.xsd.

```
      <xs:sequence>
       <xs:any processContents="lax" minOccurs="0" maxOccurs="unbounded"
                                     namespace="##any"/>
      </xs:sequence>
      <xs:attribute ref="xml:lang">
       <xs:annotation>
        <xs:documentation xmlns="http://www.w3.org/1999/xhtml">
         <p>Not required, since according to XML 1.0 its semantics
            is inherited, so we don't need it when text is nested
            inside text, or other elements which already give
            xml:lang a value.</p>
        </xs:documentation>
       </xs:annotation>
      </xs:attribute>
     </xs:restriction>
    </xs:complexContent>
  </xs:complexType>
```

10.7.3 From XML Schema to the XQuery Type System

The XML Schema type system gives us a solid basis for a query type system, but it does not go quite far enough. An XML Schema processor performs validation on an XML document, given an XML Schema document, and produces a Post Schema-Validation Infoset (PSVI), containing validation status and type information for each element and attribute. This is not enough for an XQuery Data Model.

- XML Schema validation provides a normalized string value and a type name for each element and attribute. It's left to the XQuery Data Model builder to create a typed value based on the string value and type name.
- XML Schema only deals with well-formed XML documents. The XQuery Data Model must be able to represent documents, nodes, atomic values, and arbitrary sequences of any of these.
- XQuery does not require XML Schema validation. Although an XQuery Data Model might be built from a PSVI, it might also be built directly by an application.

- XQuery adds two atomic types that are subtypes of xs:duration (xdt:yearMonthDuration[46] and xdt:dayTimeDuration).
- Every item in XQuery has a type. The XQuery Type System adds types for items for which an explicit type cannot be found.

This last point deserves a bit more explanation. The XQuery Type System adds the following abstract types:

- `xdt:untyped` – is a special type, meaning that no type information is available. For example, an element or attribute in an XML document that has not been validated against an XML Schema is of type `xdt:untyped`. `xdt:untyped` is a subtype of `xs:anyType`, and it cannot be a base type for user-derived types.
- `xdt:anyAtomicType` – is a subtype of `xs:anySimpleType`. It is a little more restrictive than `xs:anySimpleType`, encompassing all the subtypes of `xs:anySimpleType` except `xs:IDREFS`, `xs:NMTOKENS`, `xs:ENTITIES`, and user-defined list and union types. `xdt:untypedAtomic` is useful for defining function signatures, where arguments may belong to any of the primitive atomic types (or `xdt:untypedAtomic`).
- `xdt:untypedAtomic` – if an item has this type, we know that it is an atomic value, but it has not been validated against an XML Schema.

10.7.4 Types and Queries

The XQuery Data Model is at the core of the XQuery language, since every XQuery has an instance of the Data Model as input and output. And the XQuery type system is at the core of the Data Model. Both are somewhat complex (and in places controversial). But they provide useful extensions to existing data model and type systems from XML, XPath 1.0, and XML Schema. The Data Model defines exactly what an XQuery processes and what it is expected to return as a

46 As mentioned in a previous footnote, we adopt the common convention of using the "`xdt:`" (XQuery data type) namespace prefix with types defined by XQuery.

result. The type system determines which queries are legal and which are not. And the matter of static typing *vs.* dynamic typing determines the efficiency and robustness of XQueries.

We expect the XQuery Data Model and type system to be the foundation of *all* XML processing, not just XQuery, over time.

10.8 XQuery 1.0 Formal Semantics and Static Typing

The Formal Semantics specification defines the static semantics of XQuery, particularly the rules for determining the static types of expressions.

These static semantics are defined in a formal, mathematical manner, making XQuery one of relatively few languages to be defined so formally. In this section, we show you how to read the formal specifications. The Formal Semantics spec also defines most of the dynamic semantics of XQuery using the same sort of formal notation. However, the normative ("official") specification of the dynamic semantics is given in the XQuery 1.0 spec itself. We do not (definitely not!) include all of the formal definitions from the spec, but we do illustrate the technique through a sampling of the notations in use.

Before we get into the thick of Formal Semantics, let's explore what it means to determine the *static type* of an expression. The static type of an expression is a data type that is determinable without seeing any instance data on which the expression might be evaluated. In some languages, it is called the *compiled type* or the *declared type* of an expression. This is in contrast to the *dynamic type*, also known as the *run-time type* or the *most-specific type*.

Consider the XQuery expression in Example 10-7.

Example 10-7 *An XQuery Expression*

```
let $i xs:integer := 3 return $i + 5
```

As you will learn in Chapter 11, this expression includes the following components: declare a variable, $i, whose data type is `xs:integer`; assign the value 3 to that variable; compute the value resulting from adding 5 to the value of the variable; return the result of that computation. The question we will answer is this: What is the static type of that XQuery expression?

The first step is to determine the type of the variable $i. That part is easy, because the variable declaration makes it explicit: `xs:integer`. Next, we need to determine the type of the literal being assigned to the variable as its initial value. The literal is "3," which is apparently an integer — that is, a value of type `xs:integer` (while it is also a value of type `xs:decimal`, the XQuery specs treat a number without any decimal point — such as 3.0 — as a value of type `xs:integer`). Assigning a value of type `xs:integer` to a variable of type `xs:integer` does nothing to the type of the variable. (For that matter, assigning a value of type `xs:decimal` to the same variable would not change the type of the variable, but it would require a data conversion of the initial value to the type of the variable.)

The third step requires determining the type of the literal "5"; again, its type is `xs:integer`. Fourth, the type of the arithmetic expression "$i + 5" must be determined. Since the expression represents the sum of two values of type `xs:integer`, the type of the expression itself is `xs:integer`. Returning the result of evaluating that arithmetic expression does nothing to the type of the expression, so the type of the value returned is `xs:integer` — and that is the type of the entire XQuery expression in Example 10-7.

10.8.1 Notations

The Formal Semantics spec is intimidating to readers who are not versed in the formal notation used in the document. Once we got used to the notation, it became much less intimidating and we were able to follow the rules without too much difficulty. But we warn you: Undertake the reading of the Formal Semantics spec (and, for that matter, this section) only if you're prepared to deal with the difficulties associated with the notations used.

Let's look at the notation using a few examples, some of which are taken directly from the Formal Semantics spec itself. This notation depends on the concepts of *judgments*, *inference rules*, and *mapping rules*. A judgment is a statement about whether some property holds ("is a fact") or not. An inference rule states that some judgment holds if and only if other specified judgments also hold. A mapping rule describes how an ordinary XQuery expression is mapped onto a "core XQuery expression."

In Example 10-8, the symbol "=>" means "evaluates to," a colon ("`:`") separates an expression from a type name, and the "turnstile" symbol (which should be "$\vdash$" but is simulated in the Formal Semantics spec by "`|-`" because of HTML and font limitations) separates the name of an *environment* from a judgment regarding something in that environment. In the Formal Semantics, an environment is a context in which objects can exist; XQuery's static context and dynamic context are the environments used in the spec.

Judgments don't always use the symbols "=>" and "`:`". They are sometimes written using ordinary English words ("is" or "raises," for example).

In each example contained in Example 10-8, we provide an English summary of what the example shows, followed by the actual text of the judgment. We have used *italics* to indicate symbolic values to distinguish them from literal values.

Example 10-8 *Sample Formal Semantics Judgments*

The following judgment always holds, because 3 always evaluates to 3.

```
3 => 3
```

The following judgment holds if, and only if, *Film* is depressing

```
Film is depressing
```

The following judgment holds when *Expr* evaluates to *Value*

```
Expr => Value
```

For example, this judgment holds for many older movies

```
movies/movie/releaseDate = 1989
```

The following judgment holds if *Expr* has the type *Type*

```
Expr : Type
```

For example, in our sample data, this judgment holds

```
NetMovieStore[title=movies/movie/title]/price : xs:decimal
```

The following judgment holds when *Expr* raises the error *Error*

```
Expr raises Error
```

For example, this judgment always holds

```
15 div 0 raises err:FOAR0001
```

The following judgment holds when, in the static environment `statEnv` (that is, in the static context), an expression ***`Expr`*** has type ***`Type`***

```
statEnv |- Expr : Type
```

For example, in our sample data, the following judgment always holds

```
statEnv |- $DVDCost : xs:decimal
```

In Example 10-9, we illustrate a couple of inference rules. The notation for inference rules can be read like this: If all of the judgments above the horizontal line (called *premises*) hold, then the judgments below the horizontal line (called *conclusions*) also hold.

Example 10-9 *Sample Formal Semantics Inference Rules*

Without any premises, the conclusion always holds

```
          ____________
             3 => 3
```

Given these two premises, the conclusion holds

```
$x => 0   3 => 3
________________
$x + 3 => 3
```

The preceding inference rule can be generalized

```
Variable => Integer
____________________
Variable +0 => Integer
```

If two expressions $Expr_1$ and $Expr_2$ are known to have the static types $Type_1$ and $Type_2$ (the two premises above the line), then it is the case that the expression below the line, "$Expr_1$, $Expr_2$" (the sequence of the two expressions $Expr_1$ and $Expr_2$), must have the static type "$Type_1$, $Type_2$," which is the sequence of types $Type_1$ and $Type_2$.

```
statEnv |- Expr1 : Type1  staticEnv |- Expr2 : Type2
-----------------------------------------------------
statEnv |- Expr1 , Expr2 : Type1 , Type2
```

Simplifying things a bit, the Formal Semantics only has to define the semantics for *core* XQuery expressions — all other XQuery expressions are rewritten (for the purposes of the Formal Semantics) into core XQuery expressions. (An XQuery core expression is one of a small set of expression types that are the basis for the full set of expression types.) This rewriting is accomplished by the introduction of one more notation, called a *mapping rule* or a *normalization judgment*. Mapping rules specify precisely how XQuery expressions are rewritten into XQuery core expressions. In Example 10-10, the mapping rules use double-equals ("==") to separate the original object from the rewritten object, while the subscripts indicate the *kind* of object being mapped. The mapping is always performed in the static context, the use of "`staticEnv |-`" would be redundant and is omitted.

Example 10-10 *Sample Formal Semantics Mappings*

Map an object of a specified type to a rewritten object

```
[ Object ] subscript
==
Mapped Object
```

Map an arbitrary expression into a core expression

```
[ Expr ] Expr
==
Core Expression
```

Map an actual XQuery expression into the corresponding core expression

```
[ for $i in (1,2), $j in (3,4) return element pair{ ($i,$j) } ] Expr
==
for $i in (1,2) return for $j in (3,4) return element pair{ ($i,$j) }
```

After you've absorbed the notation, you have the tools necessary to read the Formal Semantics — the judgments, inference rules, and mapping rules — and understand how the spec defines the precise semantics of XQuery expressions. The spec is little more than a rather large collection of judgments and rules, with explanatory text to help interpret many of them. Unfortunately, it is difficult to prove that the spec is complete — that is, that it has specified the semantics of every nook and cranny of the XQuery language. Obviously, the Working Group believes that it has accomplished that goal, but omissions are still occasionally found.

10.8.2 Static Typing

In Example 10-8, you saw a judgment involving the type of an expression: `Expr => Type`. Let's modify it very slightly to account for the static environment: `statEnv |- Expr => Type`. As you know, that judgment is interpreted like this: The judgment holds when, in the static environment (called statEnv), expression *Expr* has type *Type*. That judgment is the basis for XQuery's static typing rules. Judgments of this kind are used in inference rules, called *type inference rules* because they tell us (and the XQuery system) how to infer the type of an expression based on the types of subexpressions.

Consider another simple XQuery expression: `let $i := 10, $j := 20 return $i + $j`. Because the input literal "10" is easily determined to be an integer, as is the literal "20" (see Example 10-11 for an example of the inference rule that lets us know this fact), and because the associated type inference rules tell us that both variables $i and $j are integers (because they are not given an explicit type, but are instead assigned values that are integers), and that the sum of two integer variables is also an integer, type inferencing tells us that the result of the entire XQuery is an integer.

Example 10-11 *Inference Rule Determining the Static Type of an Integer Literal*

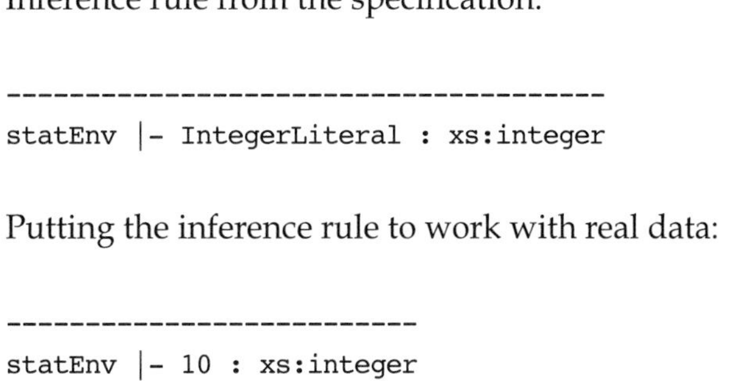

Inference rule from the specification:

```
--------------------------------------
statEnv |- IntegerLiteral : xs:integer
```

Putting the inference rule to work with real data:

```
--------------------------
statEnv |- 10 : xs:integer
```

We're not going to mince words: reading the Formal Semantics to prove all of the statements in the preceding paragraph is not trivial. In fact, it's rather difficult and requires close attention to a lot of detail. We urge you to take a look at the Formal Semantics specification and, if you are interested in really learning what it has to say, reading it from the beginning in order to be sure that you have all of the concepts before starting on the details.

In spite of the difficulties associated with reading the specification, implementers of XQuery should seriously consider inclusion of static typing in their implementation. We are told repeatedly about the significant improvements in code optimization for XQuery expressions when static typing is implemented and enabled. There are, of course, situations in which static typing is less relevant, or even completely meaningless. For example, XQueries written to query XML documents that are not associated with an XML Schema do not often benefit from static typing.

One more thing: Static typing as specified in the Formal Semantics spec is *pessimistic*. It might have been possible, using *optimistic* typing, to refine the algorithms to calculate a more specific static type for an expression, but the dynamic type of the expression's result might in some cases fail to be an instance of the predicted type. The use of pessimistic typing guarantees that no result will ever fail to be an instance of the predicted type.

10.8.3 Dynamic Semantics

The dynamic semantics of XQuery are, as we said earlier, defined normatively in the XQuery 1.0 specification. However, the Formal Semantics specifies the dynamic semantics in the same formal way that the static typing is specified, using judgments, inference rules, and mappings. Consider again the simple XQuery expression from Section 10.8.2: `let $i := 10, $j := 20 return $i + $j`.

The dynamic semantics tell us that the value of an integer literal is determined solely by the literal (see Example 10-12 for the inference rule that covers this, noting the use of dynEnv, the dynamic environment), that the value of a variable to which that value is assigned is that same value, that the value of adding two integers together is the sum of those two integers, and that the value of an expression that returns an integer value is that value.

Example 10-12 *Inference Rule Determining the Value of an Integer Literal*

An inference rule taken from the spec:

```
-----------------------------------------------------
dynEnv |- IntegerLiteral => xs:integer(IntegerLiteral)
```

Putting the inference rule to work with real data:

```
------------------------------

dynEnv |- 10 => xs:integer(10)
```

Again, we urge interested readers to sit down with a copy of the Formal Semantics specification and work through a few examples.

10.9 Functions and Operators

Many modern programming languages define relatively small core languages, providing the great majority of their functionalities through a collection of subprograms, often called a *function library.* XQuery has followed this model and, as a result, the XQuery suite of specifications includes one dedicated to functions and operators, Functions and Operators, or F&O.

The very name of the F&O specification requires some explanation. The document includes the specification for a large number of functions that can be invoked from your XQuery expressions. F&O also defines the operators of the XQuery language, but it defines them in terms of functions. These "backup" functions are not available to users to invoke in XQuery expressions.

The Functions and Operators spec is divided into several major sections, each of which is devoted to specific data types; for example, the title of F&O's Section 6 is "Functions and Operators on Numerics." Many of those sections are divided into subsections addressing classes of operations and other activities on values of the section's type; for example, Section 6.2 deals with operators on numeric values, Section 6.3 covers comparison of numeric values, and Section 6.4 addresses functions on numeric values.

10.9.1 Functions

The F&O spec fills many pages with definitions of functions that can be invoked from XQuery code. Each user-invocable function is defined in its own subsection of the F&O spec. That subsection has the same name as the function it defines. The syntax of the function — called its *signature* — is given in a shaded box, followed by a summary of the function's actions. The function signature includes the name of the function, the name and data types of each of its parameters (if any), and the data type of the value that it returns.

As the first example below illustrates, some functions defined in F&O are *overloaded*, meaning that there are two or more functions with the same name. XQuery 1.0 does not support overloading of user-defined functions, but it does allow for the "built-in" functions defined in F&O to be overloaded by the *number* of parameters (not by the data types of those parameters). Therefore, function `fn:substring-before()` has two signatures: one with two parameters and one with three. However, no F&O function of any given name has two or more signatures that each have the same number of parameters with the intent of choosing the specific function based on the specific data type of the arguments to the function invocation.

In cases where the semantics are complex, the summary is typically followed by a list of steps that, taken in order, define the function's semantics precisely. Many such subsections also include one or more examples.

Here are some examples:

7.5.4 fn:substring-before

```
fn:substring-before($arg1 as xs:string?,
                    $arg2 as xs:string?) as xs:string
fn:substring-before($arg1      as xs:string?,
                    $arg2      as xs:string?,
                    $collation as xs:string) as xs:string
```

Summary: Returns the substring of the value of $arg1 that precedes in the value of $arg1 the first occurrence of a sequence of collation units that provides a minimal match to the collation units of $arg2 according to the collation that is used.

Note:

"Minimal match" is defined in [Unicode Collation Algorithm].

If the value of `$arg1` or `$arg2` is the empty sequence, it is interpreted as the zero-length string.

If the value of `$arg2` is the zero-length string, then the function returns the zero-length string.

If the value of `$arg1` does not contain a string that is equal to the value of `$arg2`, then the function returns the zero-length string.

The collation used by the invocation of this function is determined according to the rules in 7.3.1 Collations. If the specified collation does not support collation units, an error ·may· be raised [err:FOCH0004].

7.5.4.1 Examples

CollationA used in these examples is a collation in which both `"-"` and `"*"` are ignorable collation units.

> **Note:**
>
> "Ignorable collation unit" is equivalent to "ignorable collation element" in [Unicode Collation Algorithm].

- `fn:substring-before ( "tattoo", "attoo") returns "t".`
- `fn:substring-before ( "tattoo", "tatto") returns "".`
- `fn:substring-before ((), ()) returns "".`
- `fn:substring-before ( "abcdefghi", "--d-e-", "CollationA") returns "abc".`
- `fn:substring-before ( "abc--d-e-fghi", "--d-e-", "CollationA") returns "abc--".`
- `fn:substring-before ( "a*b*c*d*e*f*g*h*i*", "***cde", "CollationA") returns "a*b*".`
- `fn:substring-before ( "Eureka!", "--***-*---", "CollationA") returns "".` The second argument contains only ignorable collation units and is equivalent to the zero-length string.

9.3.1 fn:not

```
fn:not($arg as item()*) as xs:boolean
```

Summary: `$arg` is first reduced to an effective Boolean value by applying the `fn:boolean()` function. Returns `true` if the effective Boolean value is `false`, and `false` if the effective Boolean value is `true`.

9.3.1.1 Examples

- `fn:not(fn:true())` returns `false`.
- `fn:not("false")` returns `false`.

15.1.9 fn:reverse

```
fn:reverse($arg as item()*) as item()*
```

Summary: Reverses the order of items in a sequence. If `$arg` is the empty sequence, the empty sequence is returned.

For detailed type semantics, see Section 7.2.9 The fn:reverse function[FS]

15.1.9.1 Examples

```
let $x := ("a", "b", "c")
```

- `fn:reverse($x)` returns `("c", "b", "a")`
- `fn:reverse(("hello"))` returns `("hello")`
- `fn:reverse(())` returns `()`

10.9.2 Operators

In XQuery, numeric addition is represented by the plus sign ("+"). However, the semantics of that operator are not defined in the XQuery 1.0 specification, nor are they fully defined in the Formal Semantics. Instead, they are defined in an operator function specified in F&O: `op:numeric-add()`. Similarly, determining whether two numeric values are equal in XQuery uses the syntax element "`eq`"; the semantics of that operator are defined in F&O's `op:numeric-equal()`. We say that these functions are used to "back up" the operators themselves.

In this section, we'll introduce you to the way in which F&O defines its operator functions and illustrate a small number of these functions. As you need to learn the semantics of various XQuery operators, you should consult the Functions and Operators specification for those details.

The operator-backing functions, like the user-invocable functions, are each given a complete subsection of the F&O spec. The subsection has the same name as the operator-backing function that it defines. The syntax (signature) of the function is given in a shaded box, followed by a summary of the function's actions.

In cases where the semantics are complex, the summary may be followed by a list of steps that, taken in order, define the function's semantics precisely. The operator-backing functions usually (but, we regret to say, not always) contain a statement of the operators for which they provide the semantics. Finally, many such subsections include one or more examples.

As you read the specifications of the operator functions in the F&O spec, you'll notice that none of them have optional parameters (that is, parameters whose data types have the question mark indicating optionality – which, in this context, would mean that the argument can be the empty sequence). That's because the XQuery and XPath language specs deal with operator arguments that are the empty sequence before the operator function is even invoked. This contrasts with the parameters of the nonoperator functions (the "`fn:` functions"), which are often optional.

Here is a copy of the subsection dealing with `op:numeric-equal()`.

6.3.1 op:numeric-equal

```
op:numeric-equal($arg1 as numeric,
                 $arg2 as numeric) as xs:Boolean
```

Summary: Returns true if and only if the value of `$arg1` is equal to the value of `$arg2`. For `xs:float` and `xs:double` values, positive zero and negative zero compare equal. `INF` equals `INF` and `-INF` equals `-INF`. `NaN` does not equal itself.

This function backs up the "eq" and "ne" operators on numeric values.

Here's another example:

6.2.6 op:numeric-mod

```
op:numeric-mod($arg1 as numeric, $arg2 as numeric) as numeric
```

Summary: Backs up the "mod" operator. Informally, this function returns the remainder resulting from dividing `$arg1`, the dividend, by `$arg2`, the divisor. The operation `a mod b` for operands that are `xs:integer` or `xs:decimal`, or types derived from them, produces a result such that `(a idiv b)*b+(a mod b)` is equal to `a` and the magnitude of the result is always less than the magnitude of `b`. This identity holds even in the special case that the dividend is the negative integer of largest possible magnitude for its type and the divisor is –1 (the remainder is 0). It follows from this rule that the sign of the result is the sign of the dividend.

For `xs:integer` and `xs:decimal` operands, if `$arg2` is zero, then an error is raised [err:FOAR0001].

For `xs:float` and `xs:double` operands, the following rules apply:

- If either operand is `NaN`, the result is `NaN`.
- If the dividend is positive or negative infinity, or the divisor is positive or negative zero (0), or both, the result is `NaN`.
- If the dividend is finite and the divisor is an infinity, the result equals the dividend.
- If the dividend is positive or negative zero and the divisor is finite, the result is the same as the dividend.
- In the remaining cases, where neither positive or negative infinity, nor positive or negative zero, nor `NaN` is involved, the result obeys `(a idiv b)*b+(a mod b) = a`. Division is truncating division, analogous to integer division, not [IEEE 754-1985] rounding division; *i.e.*, additional digits are truncated, not rounded to the required precision.

6.2.6.1 Examples

- `op:numeric-mod(10,3)` returns `1`.
- `op:numeric-mod(6,-2)` returns `0`.
- `op:numeric-mod(4.5,1.2)` returns `0.9`.
- `op:numeric-mod(1.23E2, 0.6E1)` returns `3.0E0`.

Not only does this function's definition include some examples, but note that there is a list of some detailed semantics when the operands are of particular types.

10.10 XQuery 1.0 and XSLT 2.0 Serialization

Just as the FLWOR expression needs a `return` clause to say exactly what gets returned, XQuery needs a way to transform its results (which are, remember, Data Model instances) into a serialized form (that is, output in some readable – and parsable – way). Of course, not every XQuery result has to be serialized. In many case, the results are used by other XQuery expressions or passed through some API to another process that can use Data Model instances directly.

Serialization, according to the XSLT 2.0 and XQuery 1.0 Serialization spec, is "the process of converting an instance of the Data Model into a sequence of octets." We normally prefer to say that the result is a sequence of characters, but a Data Model instance may include data whose type is base64Binary or hexBinary, which is truly serialized as "octets." Serialization is a well-defined operation for most, but not all, "legal" Data Model instances; for example, it is not possible to serialize a sequence of attributes that do not belong to an element. In addition, some Data Model instances cannot be serialized given a particular set of serialization parameters. It's also worth noting that there are many *possible* serializations of many Data Model instances, but the Serialization spec narrows the selection down to just one.

Every Data Model instance is a sequence of items. Before that sequence can be serialized, it must first be normalized in order to ensure that the result of serialization is a well-formed XML document or external general parsed entity. Normalization involves the following steps (adapted from the Serialization spec), performed in the order given here, with the result of each step used as input to the next step.

1. Create a new empty sequence, S1. If the sequence submitted for serialization is not the empty sequence, each item in the sequence submitted for serialization is copied in order into S1.
2. Create a new empty sequence, S2. For each item in S1, if the item is atomic, the lexical representation of the item is obtained by casting it to an `xs:string` (using the rules for casting to `xs:string` that are defined in Functions and Operators) and that string representation is copied to S2. Otherwise, the item (which, not being atomic, is a node) is copied to S2.
3. Create a new empty sequence, S3. For each subsequence of adjacent strings in S2, a single string, equal to the values of the strings in the subsequence concatenated in order, each separated by a single space, is copied to S3. All other items are simply copied to S3.
4. Create a new empty sequence, S4. For each item in S3, if the item is a string, create a text node in S4 whose string value is equal to the string. All other items are simply copied to S4.
5. Create a new empty sequence, S5. For each item in S4, if the item is a document node, copy its children to S5. All other items are simply copied to S5.
6. It is a serialization error if an item in S5 is an attribute node or a namespace node. Otherwise, construct a new sequence, S6, that comprises a single document node, and copy all the items in S5 (which are all nodes) as children of that document node in S6.
7. S6 is the normalized sequence.

The result tree rooted at the document node that is created by the final step of this sequence normalization process is the data model instance to which the rules of the appropriate output method (see the following subsections) are applied.

There are a number of serialization parameters that affect the precise behavior of serialization. These are summarized in Table 10-3, taken directly from the Serialization spec.

There are four defined output methods: XML, XHTML, HTML, and text. In the next sections, we discuss each of them briefly, but we refer you to the Serialization spec for details.

Table 10-3 *Serialization Parameters*

Parameter	Permitted Values
`byte-order-mark`	One of the enumerated values yes or no. This parameter indicates whether the serialized sequence of octets is to be preceded by a Byte Order Mark. (See Section 5.1 of [Unicode Encoding].) The actual octet order used is implementation-dependent. If the concept of a Byte Order Mark is not meaningful in connection with the value of the encoding parameter, the byte-order-mark parameter is ignored.
`cdata-section-elements`	A list of expanded QNames, possibly empty.
`doctype-public`	A string of Unicode characters. This parameter may be absent.
`doctype-system`	A string of Unicode characters. This parameter may be absent.
`encoding`	A string of Unicode characters in the range #x21 to #x7E (that is, printable ASCII characters); the value SHOULD be a charset registered with the Internet Assigned Numbers Authority [IANA], [RFC2278] or begin with the characters x- or X- (in which case, any sequence of characters in that range is permitted).
`escape-uri-attributes`	One of the enumerated values yes or no.
`include-content-type`	One of the enumerated values yes or no.
`indent`	One of the enumerated values yes or no.
`media-type`	A string of Unicode characters specifying the media type (MIME content type) [RFC2046]; the charset parameter of the media type MUST NOT be specified explicitly in the value of the media-type parameter. If the destination of the serialized output is annotated with a media type, this parameter MAY be used to provide such an annotation. For example, it MAY be used to set the media type in an HTTP header.

Table 10-3 Serialization Parameters (continued)

Parameter	Permitted Values
`method`	An expanded QName with a empty namespace URI, and the local part of the name equal to one of xml, xhtml, html or text, or having a nonempty namespace URI. If the namespace URI is nonnull, the parameter specifies an implementation-defined output method.
`normalization-form`	One of the enumerated values NFC, NFD, NFKC, NFKD, fully normalized, or none, or an implementation-defined value.
`omit-xml-declaration`	One of the enumerated values yes or no.
`standalone`	One of the enumerated values yes or no.
`undeclare-namespaces`	One of the enumerated values yes or no.
`use-character-maps`	A list of pairs, possibly empty, with each pair consisting of a single Unicode character and a string of Unicode characters.
`version`	A string of Unicode characters.

10.10.1 XML Output Method

As its name suggests, the XML output method is used to serialize a Data Model instance into XML.

Once the Data Model instance — a sequence of items — has been normalized, if the document node has a single element node child and no text node children, then the Data Model instance is serialized as a well-formed XML document entity that is required to conform to the Namespaces recommendation.[47] If the document node does not satisfy that condition (single element node child and no text node children), then the serialized result is a well-formed XML external general parsed entity. That entity must satisfy a specific condition. Let's let *URI* be some URI that identifies the entity and `version` be the relevant version of XML (either 1.0 or 1.1). If the entity is referenced within a trivial XML document element like this:

47 *Namespaces in XML, W3C Recommendation* (Cambridge, MA: World Wide Web Consortium, 1999). Available at: http://www.w3.org/TR/REC-xml-names. *Namespaces in XML 1.1, W3C Recommendation* (Cambridge, MA: World Wide Web Consortium, 2004). Available at: http://www.w3.org/TR/xml-names11.

```
<?xml version="version"?>
<!DOCTYPE wxd [
<!ENTITY wfe SYSTEM "URI">
]>
<wxd>&wfe;</wxd>
```

then the document that results from incorporation of the entity must be a well-formed XML document conforming to the Namespaces Recommendation.

The document that is produced, either directly (when the specified condition is satisfied) or indirectly (the trivial document), could, if desired, be parsed to produce a *reconstructed tree*. That hypothetical reconstructed tree must be highly similar to the original result tree (that is, the tree corresponding to the Data Model instance being serialized) because it is supposed to faithfully represent the original Data Model instance. The following differences are permitted in order to take into account various properties (of various node types) that are considered unimportant for this comparison.

- If the document was produced by adding a document wrapper as described earlier, then it will contain an extra top-level element (`wxd`, in our example) as the document element.
- The orders of attribute and namespace nodes in the two trees are allowed to be different.
- The following properties of corresponding nodes in the two trees are allowed to be different:
  - The `base-uri` property of document nodes and element nodes.
  - The `document-uri` and `unparsed-entities` properties of document nodes.
  - The `type-name` and `typed-value` properties of element and attribute nodes.
  - The `nilled` property of element nodes.
  - The `content` property of text nodes, due to the effect of the indent and use-character-maps parameters.
- The reconstructed tree is also permitted to contain additional attributes and text nodes resulting from the expansion of default and fixed values in its DTD or schema.

- The type annotations of the nodes in the two trees are allowed to be different. (Type annotations in a result tree are discarded when the tree is serialized. Any new type annotations obtained by parsing the document will depend on whether the serialized XML document is assessed against a schema, and this could result in type annotations that are different from those in the original result tree.)
- The reconstructed tree may contain additional namespace nodes if the serialization process did not undeclare one or more namespaces and the initial instance of the data model contained an element node with a namespace node that declared some prefix, but a child element of that node did not have any namespace node that declared the same prefix.
- The reconstructed tree might not have every namespace node that the original result tree has, because the process of creating an instance of the data model ignores namespace declarations in some circumstances.
- If the `indent` parameter has the value `yes`:
  - Additional text nodes consisting of whitespace characters might be present in the reconstructed tree.
  - Text nodes in the original result tree that contained only whitespace characters might correspond to text nodes in the reconstructed tree that contain additional whitespace characters that were not present in the original result tree.
- The reconstructed tree might contain additional nodes due to the effect of character mapping in the character expansion phase, and the values of attribute nodes and text nodes in the reconstructed tree might be different from those in the result tree, due to the effects of URI expansion, character mapping, and Unicode Normalization in the character expansion phase of serialization.

One issue raised by that last bulleted point is that serialization of the original result tree will preserve certain characters — CR (carriage return), NEL (new line), and LINE SEPARATOR — when they appear in text nodes only by serializing them as either entity references or character references (*e.g.*, "`
`," "`…`," and "` `," or equivalents). Similarly, several characters — CR (carriage return), TAB, LF (Line Feed), NEL (new line), and LINE SEPARATOR — are properly preserved when they appear in

attribute nodes only by serializing them as either entity references or character references (*e.g.*, "`
`," "`	`," "`
`," "`…`," and "` `," or equivalents).

Various serialization parameters affect the precise behavior of the XML output method. If serialization is a topic that interests you, we encourage you to read more about the effects of these parameters in the Serialization specification.

10.10.2 XHTML Output Method

The XHTML output method causes the Data Model instance to be serialized as XML, using the HTML compatibility guidelines contained in the XHTML Recommendation. The author of the XQuery (or XSLT 2.0 stylesheet) must make sure that the Data Model instance conforms to the requirements of the XHTML Recommendation (and whether it conforms to XHTML Strict, XHTML Transitional, XHTML Frameset, or XHTML Basic), because the serialization process will not raise an error if the Data Model instance does not conform.

In general, serialization using this output method follows the same rules as the XML output method. There are a few exceptions, based on the HTML compatibility guidelines in the XHTML Recommendation, that are intended to ensure that the output can be rendered by HTML rendering agents such as browsers. These exceptions are:

- Serializers are not allowed to use the minimized form of an empty XHTML element whose content model is not EMPTY (such as a title or paragraph without content). That is, a serializer is required to output (for example) `<p></p>` and not `<p/>`.
- By contrast, serializers are required to use the minimized form of an empty XHTML element whose content model *is* EMPTY (for example, `<br />`), because the alternative syntax (such as, `<br></br>`) that XML allows gives unpredictable results in much existing software. Furthermore, the serializer must include a space before the trailing `/>` for such minimized forms.
- Serializers cannot use the entity reference `'` which, although valid in XML and thus in XHTML, is *not* defined in HTML — it may not be recognized by all HTML user agents, such as older browsers.

- Serializers are encouraged, whenever possible, to output namespace declarations so that they are consistent with the requirements of the XHTML DTD. That DTD requires the namespace declaration `xmlns="http://www.w3.org/1999/xhtml"` to appear on — but *only* on — the `html` element. Serializers are required to output namespace declarations that are consistent with the namespace nodes present in the result tree, but they are prohibited from outputting *redundant* namespace declarations on elements where the DTD would make them invalid.
- If the Data Model instance includes a `head` element in the XHTML namespace and the `include-content-type` serialization parameter has the value `yes`, serializers are required to add a `meta` element as the first child element of the `head` element, specifying the character encoding actually used. In addition, the content type must be set to the value given for the `media-type` parameter (if any). If a `meta` element has been added to the `head` element as described earlier, then the serializer is required to discard any `meta` element child having an `http-equiv` attribute with the value `"Content-Type"` that was originally specified as a child of the `head` element.
- Serializers must apply URI escaping to URI attribute values if the `escape-uri-attributes` parameter has the value `yes`, except that relative URIs cannot be turned into absolute URIs.
- If the `indent` parameter has the value `yes`, serializers are allowed to add or remove whitespace as they serialize the result tree, but only as long as they do not change the way that a conforming HTML user agent would render the output.

10.10.3 HTML Output Method

As one would expect, the HTML output method is used to serialize Data Model instances as HTML. The `xsl:output` element's `version` attribute specifies the version of the HTML Recommendation to be generated. If the serializer does not support the version of HTML specified by this attribute, it will signal an error.

In addition, there are special rules for HTML markup of elements, especially related to the presence or absence of namespaces and namespace nodes. Other special rules govern the serialization of parameter values.

As with the XML and XHTML output methods, the precise behavior of the HTML output method is affected by various serialization parameters. If serialization is a topic of interest, the Serialization specification should be consulted for details of the effects of those parameters.

10.10.4 Text Output Method

The text output method is used to serialize Data Model instances into their string values, without any escaping. Serializers are allowed to serialize newline characters as any character used on the chosen platform as conventional line endings.

Serializers are required to use the `encoding` parameter to identify the mechanism to be used in converting the characters of a Data Model instance string value into a sequence of octets. The UTF-8 and UTF-16 encodings are mandated for all serializers, and serializers may support any other encodings their markets require. Similarly, serializers are required to use the `normalization-form` parameter to determine what Unicode normalization is performed during serialization. Values of `NFC` (Normalization Form C) and `none` must be supported, but other forms may be supported in addition.

We recommend that you consult the Serialization spec to learn the effects of other serialization parameters.

10.11 Chapter Summary

In this chapter we gave some background to the XQuery language, then described the features of the language in some detail.

In the introduction, we gave some of the historical context and motivation for an XML query language. Then we described the requirements and use cases specifications, both essential for framing what the XQuery language is meant to achieve, and gave an overview of the XQuery suite of specifications.

Armed with this background information, you read about the XQuery Data Model and type system, which, though based on XPath 1.0 and the XML Schema, extend both to provide a firm foundation for XML processing. Then you saw how the Formal Semantics spec formally defines the semantics of the XQuery language.

You also read about the Functions and Operators defined in XQuery, and, finally, you saw how XQuery can serialize its output to XML.

Now that you have a broad overview of XQuery, you are ready for the next chapter, in which we describe the gory details of the XQuery syntax and semantics.

Chapter 11

XQuery 1.0 Definition

11.1 Introduction

After introducing you to XQuery in Chapter 10, and mentioning different aspects of the language in various places throughout this book so far, we're ready to get into the details of the W3C's XML Query Language, XQuery 1.0.

You already read something about the history of XQuery's development in the W3C (in Chapter 10, for example) and the requirements that led to the language currently progressing through the W3C's Recommendation process.[1] In addition, you've seen in Chapter 10 the "big picture" view of the suite of documents that have been developed under the umbrella of XQuery.

Chapter 6, "The XML Information Set (Infoset) and Beyond," introduced you to the XQuery 1.0 and XPath 2.0 Data Model ("XQuery Data Model," or just "XDM" for brevity), and Chapter 10 provided more detail. Consequently, the Data Model is not addressed in any depth in this chapter.

The bulk of the chapter is spent on the details of the XQuery syntax and semantics, including the contexts in which XQuery exists

1 *XML Query (XQuery) Requirements, W3C Working Draft* (Cambridge, MA: World Wide Web Consortium, 2003). Available at: http://www.w3.org/TR/xquery-requirements/.

and is executed; the formal semantics of the language, including the static typing facility; the rather large collection of functions and operators available to the language; and the mechanisms for transferring the results of an XQuery expression evaluation to the outside world (serialization).

We don't expect that, when you finish this chapter, you'll be an instant XQuery expert, but we do believe that you'll be equipped to start experimenting with XQuery implementations and prototyping applications based on XQuery. In Appendix A: The Example, we have provided an extended example to show how XQuery and its companion specifications would be used in realistic situations.

11.2 Overview of XQuery

XQuery is, according to some observers, a large language. We do not completely agree with that observation, being very familiar with much larger languages (including Ada, COBOL, and SQL). Of course, we must acknowledge that there is a lot to absorb from the entire suite of XQuery-related documents. But we have found that, by taking in one document at a time, understanding the basic concepts specified in that document, it's not difficult to get a good feel for the language as a whole.

To understand how XQuery works, you first need to understand the environment in which it works – its context and how it is processed. In the remainder of this section, we describe some important concepts, the contexts (both static and dynamic) of a query, and the processing model used to evaluate an XQuery expression.

11.2.1 Concepts

Every language has concepts that are necessary to an understanding of the language and how to use it. XQuery is no exception. Here are a few terms we consider especially important to know.

- Document order – This term is defined in the XQuery Data Model, but it is used in specifications as basic as the Infoset[2] (about which you read in Chapter 6, "The XML Information

2 *XML Information Set (Second Edition), W3C Recommendation* (Cambridge, MA: World Wide Web Consortium, 2004). Available at: http://www.w3.org/TR/xml-infoset/.

Set (Infoset) and Beyond"). The term is in sufficiently wide use that we do not repeat its definition here.

- Sequence — The sequence is the most fundamental kind of value in the data model. A sequence is an ordered collection of zero or more items. A sequence that contains no items is called an *empty sequence*. A sequence containing one item is completely indistinguishable from that item by itself; it is called a *singleton sequence*. A consequence of this last provision is that every atomic value and every complex value is indistinguishable from a singleton sequence containing that value. Another consequence is that the Data Model does not support sequences of sequences.

  To illustrate these concepts, we use parentheses to enclose each sequence. Thus, ("Be afraid — be very afraid") is a singleton sequence that is indistinguishable from the character string that it contains. Similarly, ( ) is an empty sequence, and (3.14159, 2.71828, 0.5772) is a sequence of three decimal numbers. A sequence like (1, 2, (3, 4), 5) cannot be in the Data Model, because the Data Model does not support sequences that contain other sequences; that sequence is "flattened" into the sequence (1, 2, 3, 4, 5).

- Atomization — Atomization is applied to a sequence when the sequence is used in a context in which a sequence of atomic values is required. The result of atomization is either a sequence of atomic values or a type error. Formally, atomization is the result of invoking the `fn:data()` function on the sequence. That result is the sequence of atomic values produced by applying the following rules to each item in the input sequence:

  — If the item is an atomic value, it is returned.
  — If the item is a node, its typed value is returned (an error is raised if the node has no typed value).

  When atomization is applied to the sequence (3) — which, you read just above, is identical to the number 3 — the result is (3). Atomization applied to the sequence (87, "Four score and seven years ago") results in the exact same sequence. Atomizing the sequence (<address>Gettysburg</address>, 42, <a>Today <b>is a day</b> which will live in infamy</a>) results in the sequence ("Gettysburg", 42, "Today is a day which will live in infamy").

- Effective Boolean value (EBV) – Formally, the effective Boolean value of an expression is the result of invoking the `fn:boolean()` function on the value of the expression. That result is a Boolean value produced by applying the following rules, in this order:
  - If its operand is an empty sequence, `fn:boolean()` returns false.
  - If its operand is a sequence whose first item is a node, `fn:boolean()` returns true.
  - If its operand is a singleton value of type `xs:Boolean` or derived from `xs:boolean`, `fn:boolean()` returns the value of its operand unchanged.
  - If its operand is a singleton value of type `xs:string`, `xdt:untypedAtomic`, or a type derived from one of these, `fn:boolean()` returns false if the operand value has zero length and true otherwise.
  - If its operand is a singleton value of any numeric type or derived from a numeric type, `fn:boolean()` returns false if the operand value is NaN or is numerically equal to zero and true otherwise.
  - In all other cases, `fn:boolean()` raises a type error.
- String value – Every node has a string value. The string value of a node is a string and, formally, is the result of applying `fn:string()` to the node. Less formally, the string value of a node is the concatenation of the string values of all of its child nodes, in document order (this includes both child element nodes and child text nodes). The string value of a node that doesn't have any child nodes – a text node, for example – is simply the string representation of the value of that node.
- Typed value – Every node has a typed value. The typed value of a node is a sequence of atomic values and, formally, is the result of applying `fn:data()` to the node. Less formally, the typed value of a node is the result of converting the string value of the node into a value of the node's type. For some node types (such as nodes whose type is `xs:string`, as well as comment or processing instruction nodes), the typed value is the same as the string value. For other node types (such as a node that has a type annotation indicating that its value is of type `xs:decimal`), the typed value is the result of converting the string value to that type

(`xs:decimal`, in this case); if the conversion fails, then an error is raised by the `fn:data()` function.

11.3 The XQuery Processing Model

The XQuery Processing Model is a description of how an XQuery processor interacts with its environment and what steps it must take in order to evaluate a query. The XQuery 1.0 specification contains a very nice diagram to describe the Processing Model, which we have adapted in Figure 11-1.

This Processing Model has several aspects worth noting.

- The Data Model instances can be created by parsing, and perhaps validating, XML documents, thereby creating Infosets or PSVIs. The Data Model spec describes how to derive a Data Model instance from an Infoset or a PSVI. They can also be created by other means, such as by programs that directly generate Data Model instances for XQuery engines to evaluate.
- Similarly, the In-Scope Schema Definitions can be created by parsing XML Schema documents, thereby generating XML Schemas. Alternatively, they can be created by other means, analogous to direct Data Model instance generation.
- The static context is initialized from the environment (*e.g.*, by the XQuery implementation), as is the dynamic context. Both are affected by other parts of the Processing Model, such as the inclusion of in-scope schema definitions.
- The execution engine (perhaps "evaluation engine" would be more appropriate) acts on the Data Model instances provided to the XQuery expression being evaluated and (normally) generates other Data Model instances. Those instances may be serialized when query evaluation has completed, but the Processing Model does not require that. Data Model instances so generated can be passed directly to other processes, perhaps another XQuery expression evaluation.
- The execution engine depends on the dynamic context and, by implication, on the static context, while the process of parsing an XQuery expression, and converting it into whatever internal execution constructs that the execution engine uses, depends only on the static context.

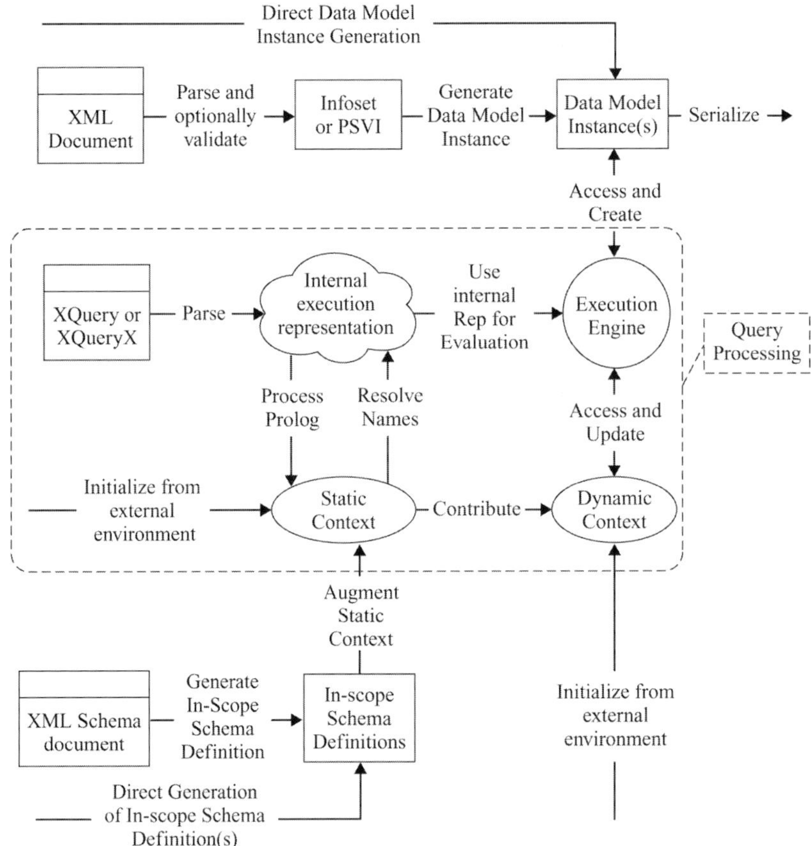

Figure 11-1 *XQuery Processing Model.*

Actual XQuery implementations will undoubtedly use variations of this Processing Model – for example, some implementations might not support direct generation of Data Model instances – but they will all provide the same essential capabilities indicated by this Model.

11.3.1 The Static Context

Whenever an XQuery expression is processed, the set of initial conditions governing its behavior is called the *static context*. The static context is a set of components, with values that are set globally by the XQuery implementation before any expression is evaluated. The values of a few of those components can be modified by the query prolog (see Section 11.7), and the values of a very few can be modified by the actions of the query itself. Figure 11-1 illustrates just where in the XQuery processing model the static context is used.

Table 11-1, adapted from the XQuery 1.0 specification, summarizes the components of the XQuery static context and how their values can be changed. For an explanation of the meaning of each component identified in the first column of the table, please refer to the XQuery 1.0 specification.

In the headers of the rightmost three columns, "Implementation" means "the XQuery implementation," "Prolog" means "the XQuery prolog," and "Expression" means "the expression itself." Within the rows of those columns, an "s" means that the corresponding object can set the value of the component, an "a" means that the object can augment[3] the value of the component, and a dash ("—") means that the object cannot change the value of the component.

Table 11-1 *XQuery Static Context Components*

		Change By		
Component	**Initial Value**	**Implementation**	**Prolog**	**Expression**
XPath 1.0 compatibility mode	"false"	—	—	—
Statically-known namespaces	"fn," "xml," "xs," "xsi," "xdt," "local"	s (except xml), a	s, a	s, a
Default element namespace	*No namespace*	s	s	s
Default function namespace	"fn"	s (not recommended)	s	—
In-scope schema types	*All types in* xs *and* xdt *namespaces*	s, a	a (schema imports)	—
In-scope element declarations	*None*	s, a	a (schema imports)	—
In-scope attribute declarations	*None*	s, a	a (schema imports)	—

3 In this context, "augment" means to add to the value; for example, an implementation is permitted to add more function signatures to the collection already defined in the fn namespace and by the constructors for all built-in types.

Table 11-1 *XQuery Static Context Components (continued)*

		Change By		
Component	**Initial Value**	**Implementation**	**Prolog**	**Expression**
In-scope variables	*None*	s, a	a	a (variable binding expressions)
Static type of context item	"none"	s	—	s (implicitly)
Function signatures	*Functions in* fn *namespace, constructors for all built-in types*	a	a (module import, function declaration)	—
Statically-known collations	*Only the default collation*	a	—	—
Default collation	*Unicode codepoint collation*	s	s	—
Construction mode	"preserve"	s	s	—
Ordering mode	"ordered"	s	s	s
Default ordering for empty sequences	*Implementation-defined*	s	s	—
Boundary-space policy	"strip"	s	s	—
Copy-namespaces mode	"inherit" and "preserve"	s	s	—
Base URI	*None*	S	s	—
Statically-known documents	*None*	s, a	—	—
Statically-known collections	*None*	s, a	—	—
Statically-known collection default type	"node()*"	s	—	—

When a component's value can be changed by the implementation or by the prolog, the initial value can be overwritten and/or it can be augmented. Some components can be overwritten, while others cannot. Other components can be augmented, while others cannot. For such fine detail, we recommend that you consult the XQuery 1.0 specification.

11.3.2 The Dynamic Context

The dynamic context represents aspects of the environment that may change during the evaluation of an XQuery or that might be changed by environmental factors other than the XQuery implementation itself. Some people, us included, view the static context as part of the dynamic context; others don't.

Table 11-2, also adapted from the XQuery 1.0 specification, summarizes the components of the XQuery dynamic context and how their values are set. For an explanation of the meaning of each component identified in the first column of the table, please refer to the XQuery 1.0 specification. In this table, "y" means that the corresponding object can change the value of the component and "—" means that it cannot.

Table 11-2 *XQuery Dynamic Context Components*

		Change By		
Component	**Initial Value**	**Implementation**	**Prolog**	**Other**
Context item	*None*	y	—	Evaluation of path expressions and predicates
Context position	*None*	y	—	Evaluation of path expressions and predicates
Context size	*None*	y		Evaluation of path expressions and predicates
Variable values	*None*	y	y	Variable-binding expressions
Function implementations	*Functions in the* fn *namespace and constructors for all built-in types*	y	y (module import and function declaration)	—
Current dateTime	*None*	y (mandatory)	—	—

Table 11-2 *XQuery Dynamic Context Components (continued)*

Component	Initial Value	Change By		
		Implementation	**Prolog**	**Other**
Implicit time zone	*None*	y (mandatory)	—	—
Available documents	*None*	y (mandatory)	—	—
Available collections	*None*	y (mandatory)	—	—
Default collection	*None*	y	—	—

For additional details, we recommend that you consult the XQuery 1.0 specification.

11.4 The XQuery Grammar

Appendix C: XQuery 1.0 Grammar contains the complete XQuery 1.0 grammar in EBNF (Extended Backus-Nauer Form). In the following sections, we refer to a number of nonterminal symbols defined in that grammar without elaborating on them in the text of this chapter. Please reference that appendix to see the definitions of those symbols in context. In addition, the EBNF conventions used to define the XQuery grammar are given in that appendix.

Before we get started with our discussion on XQuery expressions, there's one subject to address that doesn't obviously fit anywhere else: XQuery comments. Like all good (and most bad) programming languages, XQuery allows its users to embed comments into XQuery expressions. XQuery's chosen comment syntax is often called "smiley comments" because of the delimiting characters chosen to start and end those comments. A comment is started with the sequence "`(:`" and terminated with the sequence "`:)`", which bear a striking resemblance to those well-known *emoticons* used in ordinary text messages.

XQuery comments can be used anywhere that *ignorable whitespace* is acceptable. An XQuery comment can contain any string of characters, except that it must not contain "`:)`", which would cause the text following that sequence to be interpreted as part of the query itself. Comments can be nested to any level, which means that "`(:`" within a comment will be interpreted as the beginning of a nested comment.

11.5 XQuery Expressions

XQuery is, as you've read elsewhere in this book, a *functional language*. The XQuery 1.0 specification says in Section 2 Basics: "XQuery is a functional language, which means that expressions can be nested with full generality." It continues: "(However, unlike a pure functional language, it does not allow variable substitutability if the variable declaration contains construction of new nodes.)"

More generally, a functional (programming) language[4] is one that encourages a style of programming that emphasizes the *value of expressions* instead of the algorithms by which those values are computed. (Languages that focus on procedural mechanisms for computing values are sometimes called *imperative* programming languages; languages that encourage the statement of the problem in a nonprocedural way, allowing the system to determine the best way to solve the problem, are often called *declarative* languages.) Expressions in a functional language are formed by building them up from smaller expressions (in some languages, those smaller expressions are literally functions – subprograms, if you will). For example, the expression "2*(3+4)" computes the product of 2 and a number that is itself computed as the sum of 3 and 4 – that's a very functional way of expressing such a computation. In an imperative programming language, you might instruct the computer system to do something like this by a sequence of instructions (shown here in pseudo-code rather than in any particular language):

```
Set the value of variable I to the sum of 3 and 4
Set the value of variable J to the product of 2 and the value
of variable I
```

(Of course, virtually all modern programming languages allow expressions such as "2*(3+4)" to be written directly, but our point is made.)

One characteristic of many functional languages is that the "functions" (including all expressions in the language) are free of *side effects*. A side effect in this context is a computational effect that persists even after the computation has completed. A common example of a side effect in data management systems is updating persistent

4 A good discussion of functional programming can be found in the Wikipedia, at http://en.wikipedia.org/wiki/Functional_programming.

data on a mass storage device. Arguably, another kind of side effect is printing or displaying results onto some output device.

Most useful programs involve side effects, at least of this last kind. Even languages, such as SQL, that have side effects such as changing the values of persistent data can behave as a functional language when they are evaluating expressions (dividing their operation into the functional aspect of computing a value in a nonprocedural manner, followed by a phase of causing side effects). Many languages that appear to be functional in nature are not always so, if they support the use of functions written in some other programming language and that other language permits side effects to take place.

XQuery is a functional language because its expressions are made of other, "smaller" expressions, down to the irreducible level of literal values, references to variables and parameters, and function invocations. It is, for now, a side effect–free language — as long as no external functions are used that generate side effects. We say "for now" because it is inevitable (as you'll read in Chapter 13, "What's Missing?") that the XQuery language will be extended to support updating of XML, possibly in persistent stores — and that, by almost any definition, is a side effect.

In Appendix C: XQuery 1.0 Grammar, we show you the syntax of XQuery's modules. In that grammar, the rather important BNF nonterminal symbol `QueryBody` is not resolved. As you might expect, knowing that XQuery is a functional language, a `QueryBody` is simply an expression, as shown in Grammar 11-1. (See Appendix C: XQuery 1.0 Grammar for an explanation of how to read these EBNF productions.)

Grammar 11-1 *Syntax of a Query Body*

```
QueryBody ::= Expr
```

Grammar 11-4 illustrates the syntax of expressions, but the basic primitive expressions in XQuery are called *primary expressions*, the syntax of which is found in Grammar 11-2. These expressions are used to build up more complex expressions in an XQuery.

Grammar 11-2 *Primary Expression Syntax*

```
PrimaryExpr ::=
    Literal
  | VarRef
```

```
| ParenthesizedExpr
| ContextItemExpr
| FunctionCall
| Constructor
| OrderedExpr
| UnorderedExpr
```

In the following subsections, we discuss each of these primary expressions as well as some of the other expressions that make up the XQuery language. We have not rigidly ordered these subsections according to the sequence of alternatives in various grammar productions; instead we have organized the discussion by starting with simpler kinds of expressions before dealing with more complex ones.

11.5.1 Literal Expressions

The most primitive kind of expression in XQuery is a literal. A literal is a character string that lies in the *lexical space*[5] of one or more data types (the lexical space of a data type is the collection of character strings that can be used to express any possible value of that data type). For example, the character string `1.1E1` is a literal lying in the lexical space of the XML Schema data types `xs:float` and `xs:double`, while `'Mars Attacks!'` is a literal lying in the lexical space of `xs:string`, and `3.14159` is a literal in the lexical space of `xs:decimal`, `xs:float`, and `xs:double`.

Broadly speaking, a literal is an expression whose value is itself. Therefore, the value of `3.14159` is, well, 3.14159 and the value of `1.1E1` is 11. As you see in Grammar 11-3, numeric literals come in three "flavors": integer literals, decimal literals, and double literals. String literals can be enclosed in double quotes (`""`) or in apostrophes (`''`, sometimes called "single quotes"). The characters permitted in a string literal include all Unicode characters other than ampersands (`&`). To include a double quote in a literal enclosed in double quotes, you simply, well, double it. Similarly, to include an apostrophe in a literal enclosed in apostrophes, you simply use two consecutive apostrophes. You can also use character references of the form `&#xnnnn;` (where "`nnnn`" is one to six hex digits specifying the Unicode code point for the desired character). This comes in handy

5 The term *lexical space* is defined in *XML Schema Part 2: Datatypes, W3C Recommendation* (Cambridge, MA: World Wide Web Consortium, 2001). Available at: http://www.w3.org/TR/xmlschema-2/, to be "the set of valid literals for a datatype."

when you need to use characters that might not appear on your keyboard, such as ∭ for the character *triple integral*: ∭. Finally, you can use one of the five predefined entity references defined by XML itself (<, >, &, ", and ').

Grammar 11-3 *Syntax of Literals*

```
Literal ::=
    NumericLiteral
  | StringLiteral

NumericLiteral ::=
    IntegerLiteral
  | DecimalLiteral
  | DoubleLiteral

IntegerLiteral ::= Digits

DecimalLiteral ::=
    ("." Digits)
  | (Digits "." [0-9]*)

DoubleLiteral ::=
    (("." Digits) | (Digits ("." [0-9]*)?)) [eE] [+-]? Digits

StringLiteral ::=
    ('"' (PredefinedEntityRef | CharRef | ('"' '"') | [^"&])* '"')
  | ("'" (PredefinedEntityRef | CharRef | ("'" "'") | [^'&])* "'")

PredefinedEntityRef ::= "&" ("lt" | "gt" | "amp" | "quot" | "apos") ";"

Digits ::= [0-9]+
```

11.5.2 Constructor Functions

An expression that is almost as primitive as a literal is a constructor function invocation. As you saw earlier, the value 3.14159 is a valid literal in the lexical space of three data types: xs:decimal, xs:float, and xs:double. Because XQuery is a strongly typed language, it's sometimes necessary to specify more precisely the data type you want a literal to be.

XQuery provides constructor functions for this purpose. Constructor functions are defined in the Functions and Operators specification (about which you learned in Chapter 10), but they are sufficiently central to XQuery itself that we briefly mention them here. For the purposes of the XQuery grammar, constructor functions are invoked exactly like ordinary functions.

To ensure that your literal `3.14159` is a value of `xs:double`, you can write the constructor function invocation `xs:double(3.14159)` or the equivalent constructor function invocation `xs:double("3.14159")`. If your query requires a decimal value instead, you could simply write `xs:decimal(3.14159)`. However, XQuery is clever enough to infer that the literal `3.14159` by itself is intended to be of type `xs:decimal` and not of type `xs:double` or of type `xs:float`.

By contrast, values of some data types can be constructed only with an explicit constructor function invocation or an explicit cast from string to the desired data type. For example, to express the date commonly known as American Independence Day, it is not sufficient to write `1776-07-04`. XQuery would interpret that to mean "the integer value 1765" (the result of subtracting 7 from 1776 and then subtracting 4 from that result). Instead, one must write `xs:date("1776-07-04")` or `"1776-07-04" cast as xs:date`.

XQuery automatically provides a constructor function for every built-in data type defined in *XML Schema Part 2*, as well as for every data type derived from them in any schemas that you might import (see Section 11.7) in your query.

11.5.3 Sequence Constructors

Another simple kind of XQuery expression is the sequence constructor. There are many ways in XQuery of generating a sequence – after all, the fundamental building block in the Data Model is the sequence (and every XQuery value is a sequence of zero, one, or more items). As a result, it is technically accurate to say that *every* expression evaluates to a sequence.

In fact, the XQuery grammar fragment in Grammar 11-4 defines XQuery expressions in general to be a sequence of `ExprSingles`. Note that this is *not* a type of primary expression.

Grammar 11-4 *Syntax of Sequence Construction*

```
Expr ::= ExprSingle ( "," ExprSingle )*
```

```
RangeExpr ::= AdditiveExpr ( "to" AdditiveExpr )?
```

There are only two types of sequence constructor in XQuery. One of these uses commas (`,`) as the operator that constructs a sequence from two items, as illustrated in Example 11-1. In general, this first form of sequence constructor can be used in any context where a general `Expr` is appropriate; however, in a context where a *single value* (`ExprSingle` in XQuery terms) is required, a sequence constructed using the comma operator can be used only when enclosed in parentheses. (This is because a sequence of values separated by commas without surrounding parentheses is not recognized in the XQuery grammar as a single value. It requires the parentheses to group the values into a single value that is a sequence.) By convention in this book, we enclose all such sequences in parentheses.

Example 11-1 *Construction of a Sequence Using the Comma Operator*

```
( 'This reviewer gives ', 3, 'stars ', 'to ', 'this film' )
```

Don't be fooled: the result of the sequence constructor in Example 11-1 is entirely different from the character string `'This reviewer gives 3 stars to this film'`. Example 11-1 results in a sequence of five items:[6] an `xs:string` value, an `xs:integer` value, and three more `xs:string` values. By contrast, the character string is a sequence of only one item: a single `xs:string` value.

Sequences constructed with comma operators are not limited to containing items of atomic types. They can contain any sort of item, including elements, XML comments, and so forth (but, as you read earlier in this chapter, not other sequences).

The other kind of sequence constructor is called the *range expression*, written `RangeExpr` in Grammar 11-4. (The BNF nonterminal symbol `AdditiveExpr` is addressed in the next subsection, Arithmetic Expressions. For our purposes here, it's just an expression that evaluates to a value of type `xs:integer`.)

A range expression constructs a monotonically increasing sequence of consecutive integers beginning with the value of the first (or only) `AdditiveExpr` in the `RangeExpr` and ending with the value of the last (or only) `AdditiveExpr` in the `RangeExpr`, as illus-

---

6 An *item* is either a *node* or an *atomic value*.

trated in Example 11-2, which constructs the sequence `(5, 6, 7, 8, 9, 10)`.

Example 11-2 *Construction of a Sequence Using the Range Expression*

```
5 to 10
```

If the second `AdditiveExpr` is specified and its value is less than the value of the first `AdditiveExpr`, then the `RangeExpr` evaluates to an empty sequence, represented in XQuery as an empty pair of parentheses: `()`. (If you need to generate a sequence of consecutive integers in descending order, you can apply the F&O function `fn:reverse()` to a range expression.)

11.5.4 Variable References

Variable references are another kind of primitive expression in XQuery. As you can see in Appendix C: XQuery 1.0 Grammar, XQuery allows the declaration of variables in query prologs. In addition, variables are declared as part of certain other expressions, particularly the `for` and `let` clauses of FLWOR expressions. Of course, those variables are of little use unless they can be referenced in XQuery expressions. The name of a variable is a QName and is always preceded by a dollar sign (`$`) when the variable is being defined and when it is being referenced. Grammar 11-5 provides the syntax of variable references. Recall that a QName is made up of two parts: an optional namespace URI, lexically represented by a namespace prefix, and a local name. Two variable references reference the same variable if their local names are the same and the namespace URIs bound to their namespace prefixes are the same.

Grammar 11-5 *Syntax of Variable Reference*

```
VarRef ::= "$" VarName

VarName ::= QName
```

A variable reference is syntactically invalid if there is not a variable of the same QName in the in-scope variables (see Table 11-1). If there exists a variable named "studio," then that variable is referenced using "`$studio`."

11.5.5 Parenthesized Expressions

A parenthesized expression is exactly what its name implies — an expression surrounded by parentheses, as expressed in Grammar 11-6. Note that the contained expression is, in fact, optional, allowing a bare pair of parentheses — `()` — to be used as the representation of an empty sequence.

Grammar 11-6 *Syntax of Parenthesized Expressions*

```
ParenthesizedExpr ::= "(" Expr? ")"
```

In an XQuery expression, parentheses can be used to force a desired precedence of operators that is different from the default precedence. For example, the expression "2*3+4" has a different result — 10 — than the expression "2*(3+4)" — 14. Parentheses can also be used where they don't change the semantics of an expression, perhaps to make the precedence in an expression explicit, or for aesthetic purposes.

11.5.6 Context Item Expression

In Chapter 9, "XPath 1.0 and XPath 2.0," as well as in Section 11.2, you learned that XPath and XQuery nearly always have a context item (as well as a context position and context size) that is used as the context in which many expressions are evaluated.

In XQuery, the context item is referenced using the syntax shown in Grammar 11-7. This is commonly referred to as "dot."

Grammar 11-7 *Syntax of Context Item Expression*

```
ContextExpr ::= "."
```

A context item expression evaluates to the context item (which may be either a node or an atomic value). Evaluation of a context item expression when the context item is undefined results in an error.

11.5.7 Function Calls

A function call, like almost everything else in XQuery, is an expression. In Appendix C: "XQuery 1.0 Grammar," we see that functions are declared using syntax that includes the name of the function (a QName) and a pair of parentheses that optionally includes a comma-separated list of parameter declarations. Once declared, a function can be invoked as part of an XQuery expression, returning a value of the type specified when the function was declared. The Functions and Operators specification defines a number of functions that are always available to use in XQuery expressions. Other functions can be made available for use in an XQuery expression in three ways: They can be declared in the XQuery prolog, they can be imported from a library module, and they can be provided by the external environment as part of the static context.

A function call (or function invocation), shown in Grammar 11-8, bears some resemblance to the function declaration syntax mentioned in the previous paragraph. The important difference, of course, is that a function call specifies arguments that provide the values for the function's parameters.

Grammar 11-8 *Function Call Syntax*

```
FunctionCall ::= QName "(" ( ExprSingle ( "," ExprSingle )* )? ")"
```

When a function call is evaluated, the name of the function has to be equal to the name of a function in the static context, and the number of arguments in the function must be equal to the number of parameters in the function's declaration.

Function calls are evaluated in several steps.

1. Each argument is evaluated. Multiple arguments can be evaluated in any order — and might not be evaluated at all, if the implementation can determine the result of the function without knowing the value of any particular argument.
2. Each argument value is converted to its expected type using these rules:
    a. If the type of the argument matches the type of the corresponding parameter, then no conversion is performed.
    b. The argument value is atomized, which results in a sequence of atomic values.
    c. Each item in that sequence whose type is `xdt:untypedAtomic` is converted to the expected type of the corresponding parameter. When the function being invoked is one of the built-in functions defined by the Functions and Operators spec (see Section 10.9, "Functions and Operators"), if the

expected type is *numeric*, then argument values whose types are `xdt:untypedAtomic` are converted to `xs:double`. (This last provision applies only to built-in functions because user-defined functions cannot declare parameters with an expected type of *numeric*.)

d. Each numeric item in the sequence that can be promoted to the expected atomic type using the type promotion rules (detailed in the XQuery language spec) is promoted.

e. Each item whose type is `xs:anyURI` that can be promoted to the expected atomic type using the type promotion rules is promoted.

f. Each item whose type is neither `xdt:untypedAtomic`, a numeric type, or `xs:anyURI` is converted to its expected type as though the XQuery `cast` operator had been used.

3. If the function being invoked is one of the built-in functions, it is evaluated using the converted argument values, and the result of the evaluation is either a value of the function's declared type or an error. If the function is a user-defined function, then the function body is evaluated, with each argument value bound to the corresponding parameter, and the value returned by the function body is converted to the function's declared type using the argument conversion rules described earlier (an error is raised only if the conversion fails).

An example of a function declaration and a corresponding function call is given in Example 11-3.

Example 11-3 *Function Call Example*

```
declare function my:stars ( $film as movie, $mood as xs:integer )
  as xs:string

my:stars(doc("movie.example.com/movies/movie[title='Ronin']", 3)
```

Result:

```
****1/2
```

11.5.8 Filter Expressions

A filter expression is merely any primary expression followed by zero or more predicates, as specified in Grammar 11-9. The result of a filter expression comprises each item returned by the primary expression for which *all* of the predicates are true. If there are no predicates, then the value of the filter expression is exactly the same as the value of the primary expression.

Grammar 11-9 *Syntax of Filter Expressions*

```
FilterExpr ::= PrimaryExpr PredicateList

PredicateList ::= Predicate*
```

The order of items in the result of the filter expression is the same as the order in which those items appeared in the primary expression.

You were exposed to predicates in Chapter 9, "XPath 1.0 and XPath 2.0," so they are not addressed in detail in this chapter. Recall that a predicate is an expression whose value is a Boolean value, such as a comparison expression. Below, Section 11.5.11 discusses Boolean-valued expressions that are used in predicates.

11.5.9 Node Sequence-Combining Expressions

Now that we've covered the simpler kinds of expressions, let's look at expressions that combine node sequences – `union`, `intersect`, and `except`. The syntax used for these sequence-combining expressions is seen in Grammar 11-10. The operands of these three operators are *node sequences*, not values (as they are in SQL, for example). Consequently, it is not possible to evaluate an expression such as `(1, 2) union (2, 1)` – the contents of the two sequences are values and not nodes.

One of these, using the `union` operator (equivalently, the vertical bar operator, |), returns a sequence containing all nodes that appear in *either* of its node sequence operands. Another, using the `intersect` operator, returns a sequence containing only those nodes that appear in *both* of its node sequence operands. The third, using the `except` operator, returns a sequence containing all nodes that appear in its first node sequence operand but not in the second.

Grammar 11-10 *Syntax of Node Sequence-Combining Expressions*

```
UnionExpr ::=
  IntersectExceptExpr ( ( "union" | "|" ) IntersectExceptExpr )*

IntersectExceptExpr ::=
  InstanceOfExpr ( ( "intersect" | "except" ) IntersectExceptExpr )*
```

All three of these expressions eliminate duplicate nodes (based, of course, on node identity) and, unless the ordering mode is *unordered*, return the result node sequence in document order. Example 11-4 illustrates some of these expressions. For the purposes of these examples, assume that "A" represents the movie node corresponding to the movie *Absolute Power*, "B" represents the movie node for the film *Below*, and "C" represents the movie node of the film *Corruption*, and also assume that the document containing these three nodes happens to contain them in that sequence: A followed by B followed by C. The XQuery comments preceding each example indicates the value computed by the expression.

Example 11-4 *Node Sequence-Combining Examples*

```
( A, B ) union ( A, B )

result:

( A, B )


( A, B ) union ( B, A )

result:

( A, B )


( A, B ) union ( A, C )

result:

( A, B, C )
```

```
( A, B ) intersect ( A, B )
```

result:

```
( A, B )
```

```
( A, B ) intersect ( B, C )
```

result:

```
( B )
```

```
( A, B ) except ( A, B )
```

result:

```
( )
( A, B ) except ( B, C )
```

result:

```
( A )
```

11.5.10 Arithmetic Expressions

Let's get back to basics. XQuery supports the basic kinds of arithmetic operations that most programming languages provide: addition, subtraction, multiplication, and division; it also provides a modulus operator. In addition (pun noted, but not intended), XQuery provides unary plus and minus operators.

Because XQuery is not primarily intended as a mathematical computation language, it does not provide built-in operators for operations such as exponentiation, extraction of roots, or logarithmic computations. (However, we do anticipate that each community will develop libraries of user-defined functions to support the operations on which their work depends.)

The syntax of XQuery's arithmetic operators is shown in Grammar 11-11, and a few examples are seen in Example 11-5.

Grammar 11-11 *Grammar of Arithmetic Expressions*

```
AdditiveExpr ::= MultiplicativeExpr ( ( "+" | "-" ) MultiplicativeExpr )*

MultiplicativeExpr ::=
  UnionExpr ( ( "*" | "div" | "idiv" | "mod"  ) UnionExpr )*

UnaryExpr ::= ( "+" | "-" )* ValueExpr
```

Because the hyphen (-) is used as the subtraction operator, as the negation operator ("unary minus"), and as a valid character in XML names, XQuery requires that the subtraction operator be preceded by white space if it could possibly be mistaken as part of the preceding token. For example, "`MyStars-1`" is a valid XML name; if your intent is to subtract 1 from the rating of a film (number of stars) given by a reviewer, then XQuery requires that to be expressed something like this: "`MyStars -1`" or "`MyStars - 1`."

In an `AdditiveExpr`, the plus sign (+) indicates addition of the values of the two operands, and the hyphen, also called a minus sign (-), specifies the subtraction of the value of the second operand from the value of the first.

In a `MultiplicativeExpr`, the asterisk (*) means multiplication of the values of the two operands. In many programming languages, a slash (/) is used to indicate division. However, XQuery uses the slash as a path expression operator, so the keyword "`div`" was chosen to indicate division and a second keyword, "`idiv`," indicates integer division – specifically, division of the value of the first operand by the value of the second. The keyword "`mod`" indicates the modulus operation (which, simplified, means to return the remainder of a division operation instead of returning the quotient).

In Example 11-5, we use XQuery comments to state the result of the example.

Example 11-5 *Examples of Arithmetic Expressions*

```
1+3              (: the xs:integer value 4 :)
14 idiv 3        (: 4, by truncating the fractional part of the division :)
12 mod 5         (: 2, which is the remainder of 12 idiv 5 :)
12.5 mod 5.1     (: 2.3: 12.5 idiv 5.1 = 2; 12.5 - (5.1*2) = 12.5 – 10.2 :)
$ProdBudget * 2 – 1000000  (: Twice the budget less one million :)
-5               (: negative 5 :)
++-+---+-+++10   (: negative 10 :)
```

```
3              (: positive 3 :)
3.14 * 1.0E5   (: the xs:float value 0.314E6, or 314000 :)
```

In XQuery, numbers are handled using rules that are needed when mixing integers, decimal numbers, and floating-point numbers. These rules say that any arithmetic operation that involves numbers of two different data types requires one number to be "upcast," or "promoted," to the type of the other. XQuery deals with only four of the many XML Schema numeric types – `xs:integer`, `xs:decimal`, `xs:float`, and `xs:double`. Even though, in XML Schema, there is no type derivation relationship between `xs:decimal`, `xs:float`, and `xs:double` (but `xs:integer` is derived from `xs:decimal`), XQuery treats them as though there were such a relationship. Example 11-6 illustrates the numeric type hierarchy and provides a couple of examples.

Example 11-6 *Numeric Type Promotion*

Type promotion hierarchy:

`xs:integer` ➔[7] `xs:decimal` ➔ `xs:float` ➔ `xs:double`

Double required, integer provided:

`12 ➔ xs:double(12) = 1.2E1`

Decimal required, integer provided:

`31 ➔ xs:decimal(31) = 31.0`

Float required, decimal provided:

`3.14159 ➔ xs:float(3.14159) = 3.14159E0`

Decimal required, double provided:

`2.71E3` ➔ *`error`*

("demotion" is not supported)

If an operation requires promotion of one value to the type of the other value, then `xs:integer` values can be promoted to any of the other three types, `xs:decimal` values can be promoted to `xs:float`

7 Because XML Schema defines xs:integer as a subtype of xs:decimal, every value of type xs:integer *is* a value of type xs:decimal; therefore, this relationship is not technically a type promotion.

or `xs:double`, and `xs:float` values can be promoted to `xs:double`. If the variable `$i` is of type `xs:integer` and the variable `$j` is of type `xs:float`, then the expression `$i - $j` requires that the value of `$i` be promoted to `xs:float` before the operation is performed; it also requires the result of the operation to be of type `xs:float`.

Each operand of an arithmetic operator is evaluated in four steps:

1. The operand is atomized as described earlier in this chapter. (Because the operand is atomized, it is possible to provide a node — instead of an atomic value — as an operand. This allows the use of, say, element nodes directly as operands of an operator.)
2. If the atomized operand is the empty sequence, then the result of the operation is the empty sequence. Note that implementations are not required to evaluate the other operand, but they are permitted to do so if (for example) they want to exhaustively discover errors.
3. If the atomized operand is a sequence of length greater than 1, a type error is raised.
4. If the atomized operand is of type `xdt:untypedAtomic`, it is converted to `xs:double`; if that conversion fails (*e.g.*, the value is the string "`Midnight Cowboy`"), then an error is raised.

If, after these steps have been applied to both operands, one or both operands are not of a type suitable for the operation — such as an effort to subtract a value of type `xs:decimal` from a value of type `xs:IDREF` — an error is raised. Even when the operands are both of suitable types, errors can be raised by the operation itself, such as an attempt to divide by zero.

As we have seen, XQuery has a rich set of arithmetic operators, but that set will be complemented by function libraries that provide even more functionality.

11.5.11 Boolean Expressions: Comparisons and Logical Operators

There are two kinds of expressions in XQuery that produce Boolean results. One kind, comparison expressions, provides the ability to compare two values. The other, logical expressions, allow the combination of Boolean values, such as those produced by comparisons.

Comparison expressions can be divided into three categories: value comparison, general comparison, and node comparison. Value comparisons are used to compare two single values, general comparisons are (for all practical purposes) quantified comparisons – also called existential comparisons – that can be used to compare sequences of any length, and node comparisons are used to compare two nodes.

The grammar of comparison expressions is presented in Grammar 11-12 (slightly modified for clarity from the grammar as published in the XQuery specification). Note that the three types of comparison use different sets of operators. It's tempting to conclude that the ordinary comparison operators (=, >, *etc.*) could have been used for all three types; however, if XQuery had done so, it would be impossible in many instances to determine whether any given comparison was intended to be a value comparison, a general comparison, or a node comparison.

Grammar 11-12 *Comparison Expression Grammar*

```
ComparisonExpr ::= RangeExpr ( ComparisonOp RangeExpr )?

ComparisonOp ::= ValueComp | GeneralComp | NodeComp

ValueComp ::= "eq" | "ne" | "lt" | "le" | "gt" | "ge"

GeneralComp ::= "=" | "!=" | "<" | "<=" | ">" | ">="

NodeComp ::= "is" | "<<" | ">>"
```

Value comparisons require that the value of each operand be determined. The steps are very similar to those involved in determining the values of the operands of arithmetic expressions, except for the fourth step:

1. The operand is atomized as described earlier in this section.
2. If the atomized operand is the empty sequence, then the result of the operation is the empty sequence. Note that implementations are not required to evaluate the other

operand, but they are permitted to do so if (for example) they want to exhaustively discover errors.

3. If the atomized operand is a sequence of length greater than 1, a type error is raised.
4. If the atomized operand is of type `xdt:untypedAtomic`, it is converted to `xs:string`. While operand type conversion for arithmetic operators naturally falls back to a numeric type (`xs:double`), comparisons are more often based on comparing string values than strictly numeric values.

If the values of the two operands have types that are compatible for the purposes of comparison, then they are compared. If the value of the first operand is *equal to, not equal to, less than, less than or equal to, greater than*, or *greater than or equal to* the value of the second operand, then the comparison using the "`eq`," "`ne`," "`lt`," "`le`," "`gt`," or "`ge`" operator, respectively, is true; otherwise, the comparison is false. Some value comparisons are illustrated in Example 11-7.

Example 11-7 *Value Comparison Examples*

```
1 gt 3                        (: false :)
"abc" ne 5                    (: error (incompatible operands) :)
<a>Shogun</a> lt "Titanic"    (: true :)
( 1, 2 ) eq ( 1, 2 )          (: error (sequence longer than one) :)
```

General comparisons, as we said earlier, act as *existential comparisons*. By "existential comparison" we mean this: If there exists at least one value in the sequence that is the value of the first operand that has the proper comparison relationship (using the value comparison rules!) with at least one value in the sequence that is the value of the second operand, then the general comparison is true; otherwise, it is false.

In principle, every value belonging to each of the two sequences is compared to *every* value in the other sequence. In practice, implementations are very often able to determine the result without actually doing so many comparisons, so the rules of XQuery allow implementations to return the result without compulsively comparing every combination of values. One consequence of this permissive rule is that there may be errors that would result from comparing some particular value in the first sequence with some other specific value in the second sequence, but the implementation might return a true/false result and not raise the error. The second example in Example 11-8 illustrates such a situation.

Of course there are a few rules to cover the relationships between the types of the operands:

- If one operand is of type `xdt:untypedAtomic` and the other is of any numeric type, then they are both converted to `xs:double`.
- If one operand is of type `xdt:untypedAtomic` and the other is of either type `xdt:untypedAtomic` or type `xdt:string`, then they are converted to `xs:string` as required.
- If one operand is of type `xdt:untypedAtomic` and the other is of neither `xdt:untypedAtomic`, `xdt:string`, nor any of the numeric types, then the `xdt:untypedAtomic` operand is converted to the runtime type of the other operand.

Example 11-8 provides a few sample general comparison expressions.

Example 11-8 *General Comparison Examples*

```
( 1, 2, 3 ) = 2.0           (: true :)

(: The following comparison is either true because 3 gt 2, or raises an
   error because a string cannot be compared with an integer,
         nor can strings or integers be compared with dates :)
( 1, 2, 'The Magnificent Seven', 3) > ( 2, 12, xs:date('2005-02-27') )

(: The following comparison is true if there is at least one director
   whose given name compares greater than 'Xavier'; it returns false
   only if there are no directors who have a given name that compares
   greater than "Xavier" :)
//movie/director/givenName > "Xavier"

(: The following comparison is true if we have any movie whose title
   is equal to the given name of any producer of any movie we have :)
//movie/title = //movie/director/givenName

fn:currentDate() > xs:date("2003-06-30")  (: Already true! :)
```

The final example is a valid general comparison, even though the operands are single values — remember that a single value is a singleton sequence containing that value.

General comparisons do not behave like comparisons that use the same operators in most other languages (it's value comparisons that behave like comparisons in those other languages, albeit with different operators). The differences are caused by the existential semantics of general comparison. Therefore, even though "`(1, 2) = (2, 3)`" is true and "`(2, 3) = (3, 4)`" is true, "`(1, 2) = (3, 4)`" is false! That is, general comparisons are not transitive. Similarly, both "`(1, 2) = (2, 3)`" and "`(1, 2) != (2, 3)`" are true — inverted operators do not imply inverted results.

Node comparisons are different from both value comparisons and general comparisons, in that they do not compare values at all, but compare nodes based on their *identities*. In a node comparison, if either operator evaluates to a sequence of more than one node, then an error is raised. If either operand evaluates to an empty sequence, then the result of the comparison is also the empty sequence (node comparisons can have three values: true, false, and the empty sequence).

If the two operands have the same identity — that is, they are the same node — then the "`is`" comparison is true; otherwise, that comparison is false. If the first operand is a node that appears earlier in document order than the node identified by the second operand, then the "<<" comparison is true and the ">>" is false. There is an exception to this rule: If the ordering mode is unordered (see Section 11.4.7, "Function Calls"), then the results are nondeterministic, because document order is not maintained. Example 11-9 demonstrates these principles.

Example 11-9 *Node Comparison Examples*

```
(: false, because two newly-constructed nodes are not the same node :)
<a>42</a> is <a>42</a>


(: This example uses the let clause described in Section 11.5 :)
let $a := <a>42</a>
let $b := <a>42</a>
$a is $b                (: false, for the same reason :)


(: This example also uses the let clause described in Section 11.5 :)
let $a := <a>42</a>
let $b := $a
```

```
$a is $b              (: true: both variables "contain" the same node :)

(: true, unless there is more than one movie with that title :)
//movie[title="The Sting"] is //movie[title="The Sting"]

(: true, because givenName comes before familyName and
   The Matrix has only one director :)
//movie[title="The Matrix"]/director/givenName <<
    //movie[title="The Matrix"]/director/familyName
```

As you have seen in this discussion of comparison expressions, the result of such an expression is either a Boolean value (true or false) or the empty sequence. A frequent requirement in applications is to combine the results of multiple comparisons: "I want to find the MPAA rating of all movies whose titles contain the word 'Outlaw' that were released after 1965." In this example, two comparisons are combined: "titles contain the word 'Outlaw'" and "released after 1965" — both must be true for the movies I want to find. The ability to combine multiple comparison expressions is provided in XQuery with *logical expressions*.

A *logical expression* is an expression that permits the combination of Boolean values to achieve an aggregated Boolean result. Logical expressions in XQuery operate on the effective Boolean value of their operands and, naturally, follow the rules of Boolean algebra. XQuery defines only two Boolean operators: `and` and `or`. (Many languages include a third Boolean operator: `not`. In XQuery, the functionality of that operator is provided by a function, `fn:not`.)

Grammar 11-13 *Grammar of Logical Expressions*

```
OrExpr ::= AndExpr ( "or" AndExpr )*

AndExpr ::= ComparisonExpr ( "and" ComparisonExpr )*
```

The behaviors of these two operators are defined in Table 11-3 and Table 11-4. The cells that contain "true or error" or "false or error" imply that an implementation may choose to determine the value of the expression from the value of the one operand that does not generate an error, or it may choose to raise an error instead. It's worth pointing out that XQuery, like SQL and many other programming languages, but unlike a few popular languages such as C, does not require evaluation of the operands of logical expressions in any particular order. Instead, implementations are free to reorder the evaluation of the operands for such reasons as query optimization.

Table 11-3 *Semantics of* `or`

or	$oper_1$ true	$oper_1$ false	$oper_1$ error
$oper_2$ true	true	true	true or error
$oper_2$ false	true	false	error
$oper_2$ error	true or error	error	error

Table 11-4 *Semantics of* `and`

and	$oper_1$ true	$oper_1$ false	$oper_1$ error
$oper_2$ true	true	false	error
$oper_2$ false	false	false	false or error
$oper_2$ error	error	false or error	error

Example 11-10 *Examples of Logical Expressions*

```
1 eq 1 and 2 eq 2      (: true, because both comparisons are true :)
1 eq 1 or 2 eq 3       (: true, because at least one comparison is true :)
1 eq 2 and 3 div 0     (: either false or division by zero error :)
(1,2,3,4) = 3 to 6 and (1,2,3,4) = 1    (: true, because both are true :)
```

Comparison expressions and logical expressions can be combined in powerful ways, making up arbitrarily complex predicates that are used in the FLWOR expression's `where` clause and in the predicates of path expressions. But users new to XQuery must be careful to use the correct operator when comparing two items. Remember that most languages use the symbol "=" to mean "this value is equal to that value," while XQuery uses it in an existential sense to mean "any item in this sequence is equal to any item in that sequence." In order to get the semantics that "=" provides in other languages (including gaining protection from situations where it is possible for one or both operands to be a sequence of length greater than 1), XQuery expressions use the "`eq`" operator instead.

11.5.12 Constructors — Direct and Computed

One of the strengths of XQuery (over, say, XPath) is its ability to construct XML nodes and thus to build up brand new XML fragments or complete documents in the result of a query. In addition to the constructor functions and sequence constructors that we discussed earlier in this section, XQuery provides two different classes of constructors for nodes. Document nodes can be constructed using only one class of constructors, while five of the other six node types can be constructed by both classes. XQuery does not represent namespace bindings as nodes, so there is no way in XQuery to construct namespace nodes (the seventh node type).

The two classes of node constructor are *direct constructors* and *computed constructors*. Direct constructors use an XML-like syntax, while computed constructors use a syntax based on *enclosed expressions*. (An enclosed expression is an expression enclosed within curly braces: `{ ... }`.)

Direct Constructors

Direct constructors are, in most ways, nothing more than well-formed XML that appears in an XQuery. We say "in most ways" because — as you'll read later — it is possible to supply the *content* of elements and the *values* of attributes (but not element or attribute names) using enclosed expressions. A very simple example of a direct element constructor is:

```
<title>A Bridge Too Far</title>
```

The syntax for direct constructors appears in Grammar 11-14. Throughout this grammar, we have omitted specific indication of where white space is required or permitted — such indications merely clutter up the grammar and can be obtained from the published XQuery specification.

Grammar 11-14 *Grammar of Direct Constructors*

```
DirectConstructor ::=
    DirElemConstructor
  | DirCommentConstructor
  | DirPIConstructor
```

```
DirElemConstructor ::=
    ("<" QName DirAttributeList "/>")
  | ("<" QName DirAttributeList ">" DirElemContent* "</" QName ">")

DirElemContent ::=
    DirectConstructor
  | ElementContentChar
  | CDataSection
  | CommonContent

ElementContentChar ::= Char - [{}<&]

CommonContent ::=
  PredefinedEntityRef | CharRef | "{{" | "}}" | EnclosedExpr

CDataSection ::= "<![CDATA[" CDataSectionContents "]]>"

CDataSectionContents ::= (Char* - (Char* ']]>' Char*))

DirAttributeList ::= ( (QName "=" DirAttributeValue)?)*

DirAttributeValue ::=
    ('"' (EscapeQuot | QuotAttrValueContent)* '"')
  | ("'" (EscapeApos | AposAttrValueContent)* "'")

QuotAttrValueContent ::=
    QuotAttrContentChar
  | CommonContent

AposAttrValueContent ::=
    AposAttrContentChar
  | CommonContent

QuotAttrContentChar ::= Char - ["{}<&]

AposAttrContentChar ::= Char - ['{}<&]

EscapeQuot ::= '""'

EscapeApos ::= "''"
```

```
EnclosedExpr ::= "{" Expr "}"

DirCommentConstructor ::= "<!--" DirCommentContents "-->"

DirCommentContents ::= ((Char - '-') | ('-' (Char - '-')))*

DirPIConstructor ::= "<?" PITarget DirPIContents? "?>"

DirPIContents ::= (Char* - (Char* '?>' Char*))
```

There's a lot of detail in that grammar that we don't need to examine, but we encourage our readers to ensure that they understand most of it.

Document nodes cannot be created using direct constructors, so Grammar 11-14 does not define any syntax related to document node construction. Neither does it include syntax for direct construction of text nodes — that's done simply by the inclusion of text as the content of a directly-constructed element.

Let's examine the various direct constructors one at a time. The constructors included in this discussion are: direct element constructors (and the direct attribute constructors they might contain), direct comment constructors, and direct processing instruction constructors. (Remember that there is no way to construct document nodes using direct constructors, and no way at all to construct namespace nodes in XQuery.) The direct comment constructors and direct processing instruction constructors are simple, so let's get them out of the way before we explore direct element constructors.

An XML comment looks like this:

```
<?-- comment-text -->
```

The text of the comment (`comment-text`) is restricted because of the XML rule that prohibits two consecutive hyphens (`--`) in a comment. The syntax of the `DirCommentConstructor`, found near the end of Grammar 11-14, is an exact copy of the corresponding grammar production for comments in the XML Recommendation.[8]

8 *Extensible Markup Language (XML) 1.0, Third Edition, W3C Recommendation* (Cambridge, MA: World Wide Web Consortium, 2004). Available at: http://www.w3.org/TR/REC-xml.

Therefore, in XQuery, a direct comment constructor is nothing more than an XML comment.

An XML processing instruction (frequently abbreviated "PI," which is not to be confused with pi, π) is superficially similar in appearance to an XML comment. A PI looks like this:

```
<? PI-target PI-content ?>
```

The content of the PI (`PI-content`) — which is optional — is also restricted because of an XML rule, this one prohibiting a question mark followed by a right angle bracket (`?>`) in the content. In addition, following rules imposed by the XML Recommendation, a PI's target (`PI-target`) must not be spelled with a leading "X" or "x" followed by an "M" or "m" followed by an "L" or "l." The syntax of the `DirPIConstructor`, found at the end of Grammar 11-14, is an exact copy of the corresponding grammar production for comments in the XML Recommendation. Consequently, in XQuery, a direct PI constructor is exactly the same as an XML PI.

Direct element constructors are a bit more involved, but they still closely follow the syntax of elements in XML. That is, like ordinary elements in XML, empty elements can be written thusly:

```
<tag-name/>
```

while nonempty elements are written like this:

```
<tag-name>element-content</tag-name>
```

The `element-content` is optional, which makes it possible to write an empty element using the start tag/end tag notation used by nonempty elements.

Both empty elements written using the short notation and nonempty elements can have an attribute list immediately following the `tag-name` in the start tag. In fact, the XML Recommendation considers the attribute list to be part of the start tag itself; XQuery calls it out separately for expositional purposes.

An attribute list is, naturally, a list of attributes. In this case, it is a list of direct attribute constructors. A direct attribute constructor is, as you see in Grammar 11-14, an attribute name followed by an equal sign, and a quoted attribute value. It's important to note that the quoted attribute value is permitted to contain enclosed expressions by which part or all of the attribute value is computed at query evaluation time! This computation of the attribute's value does not change the constructed nature of the attribute constructor.

The content of a nonempty element can include several different objects. It can contain other direct constructors, including direct element constructors, direct comment constructors, and direct PI constructors. It can contain CDATA constructors that are identical to the CDATA sections defined in the XML Recommendation (recall that the Data Model does not support CDATA sections directly, but represents them as ordinary text nodes), as well as arbitrary character sequences (excluding left and right braces, ampersands, and left angle brackets: `{}&<`) and enclosed expressions. The inclusion of an enclosed expression makes it possible for part or all of an element's content to be computed at query evaluation time, which does not change the constructed nature of the element constructor. In Example 11-11, we've illustrated some direct element constructors – be sure to note the strong similarity to ordinary elements in XML documents. It's also important to say that the XQuery comments have absolutely no effect on the constructed XML – they simply disappear from the results of the construction.

Example 11-11 *Direct Constructor Examples*

```
(: Two direct element constructors of empty elements :)
<MovieGenre/>
<MovieEdition></MovieEdition>

(: Direct element constructor of a movie element with a comment :)
<!-- This element was copied from Chapter 6, "The XML Information Set
            (Infoset) and Beyond" -->
<movie>
  <title>An American Werewolf in London</title>
  <yearReleased>1981</yearReleased>
  <director>
    <familyName>Landis</familyName>
    <givenName>John</givenName>
  </director>
  <producer>
    <familyName>Folsey</familyName>
    <givenName>George, Jr.</givenName>
    <otherNames/>
  </producer>
```

```
    <producer>
      <familyName>Guber</familyName>
      <givenName>Peter</givenName>
      <otherNames/>
    </producer>
    <producer>
      <familyName>Peters</familyName>
      <givenName>Jon</givenName>
      <otherNames/>
    </producer>
    <runningTime>98</runningTime>
    <cast>
      <familyName>Agutter</familyName>
      <givenName>Jenny</givenName>
      <maleOrFemale>female</maleOrFemale>
      <character>Alex Price</character>
    </cast>
</movie>

(: Direct element constructor of element with attribute :)
<character age="{$var1}">Alex Price</character>

(: A direct processing instruction constructor :)
<?xml-stylesheet type="text/xsl" href="publish-movies.xsl"?>
```

Computed Constructors

Computed constructors make it possible for XQuery expressions to generate XML even when certain key information – such as the name of an element or of an attribute – is unknown when the XQuery expression was coded. Computed constructors have a completely different look than direct constructors. There is no effort to make the syntax look XML-like, because the focus is on ease of specifying the information that must be computed in order to create the node, especially the names of element and attribute nodes.

The grammar of computed constructors is presented in Grammar 11-15.

Grammar 11-15 *Grammar of Computed Constructors*

```
ComputedConstructor ::=
    CompDocConstructor
  | CompElemConstructor
```

```
  | CompAttrConstructor
  | CompTextConstructor
  | CompCommentConstructor
  | CompPIConstructor

CompDocConstructor ::= "document" "{" Expr "}"

CompElemConstructor ::=
    ("element" QName "{" ContentExpr? "}")
  | ("element" "{" Expr "}" "{" ContentExpr? "}")

ContentExpr ::= Expr

CompAttrConstructor ::=
    ("attribute" QName "{" Expr? "}")
  | ("attribute" "{" Expr "}" "{" Expr? "}")

CompTextConstructor ::= "text" "{" Expr "}"

CompCommentConstructor ::= "comment" "{" Expr "}"

CompPIConstructor ::=
    ("processing-instruction" NCName "{" Expr? "}")
  | ("processing-instruction" "{" Expr "}" "{" Expr? "}")
```

The most obvious difference between the syntax in Grammar 11-14 and that in Grammar 11-15 is the absence of all those angle brackets used by direct constructors. Instead of using the syntax of XML to create the various node types, computed constructors require an explicit keyword to specify the kind of node being created. That keyword is followed in some cases either by the name of the node or by an expression whose value is to be used as the name of the node. The node-type keyword is also followed by an expression supplying additional information needed to construct a node. Let's look at each in turn.

A computed comment constructor is very straightforward:

```
comment { "Computed constructors are vital in XQuery" }
```

The result of that constructor is this XML comment:

```
<!-- Computed constructors are vital in XQuery -->
```

Note that the enclosed expression is a character string literal in this case. It would have been incorrect to have used the enclosed expression `{ Computed constructors are vital in XQuery }` (that is, omitting the quotes) because the content of the enclosing braces would not correspond to any valid XQuery expression. Another computed comment constructor is:

```
comment { fn:concat($typeVar, " constructors are vital in XQuery") }
```

in which the computed comment's expression is an invocation of the built-in function `fn:concat()` to concatenate the value of the variable `$typeVar` with a character string literal. If the value of `$typeVar` happened to be "`Direct`," then the comment constructed by this computed comment constructor would be:

```
<!-- Direct constructors are vital in XQuery -->
```

Computed text constructors are just as straightforward as computed comment constructors. The differences are the name of the constructor and the precise result. The computed text constructor:

```
text { "starring two members of the famous “Brat Pack”" }
```

results in a text node whose value is:

```
starring two members of the famous “Brat Pack”
```

Note that the keyword `text` is followed by an enclosed expression, which means that the material between the braces must be an expression, which in this example is a string literal. As with computed comment constructors, the enclosed expressions of computed text constructors can contain subexpressions whose values must be computed at query evaluation time. It is possible to construct a text node whose value is a zero-length string; such nodes, when used as the content of a constructed element or document node, will simply disappear. Incidentally, two adjacent text nodes in the content of a constructed element are merged into a single text node.

Computed PI constructors are only slightly more complex, the added complexity arising entirely from the fact that processing instructions have targets. If the value of the variable `$tgtVar` is "`xml-stylesheet`", then the following two computed PI constructors are equivalent in their effects:

```
processing-instruction xml-stylesheet
  { 'type="text/xsl" href="publish-movies.xsl"' }

processing-instruction { $tgtVar }
  { 'type="text/xsl" href="publish-movies.xsl"' }
```

Both of those computed constructors produce the following XML PI:

```
<?xml-stylesheet type="text/xsl" href="publish-movies.xsl"?>
```

Perhaps obviously, the first of those computed PI constructors could have just as easily been written as a direct PI constructor. The choice of which to use in situations like this is largely a matter of personal style.

Looking at Grammar 11-15, you'll notice that computed attribute constructors are not contained within computed element constructors, but are true peers to computed element constructors. Contrast this with Grammar 11-14, in which attributes could be constructed only as part of a directly constructed element. An implication of this fact is that you are able to create stand-alone attributes — part of the XQuery Data Model, but not allowed in XML or in the Infoset.

To construct an attribute, you'd write something like:

```
attribute age { "24" }
```

or:

```
attribute { $attrName } { $attrVal }
```

A computed attribute constructor that creates an attribute of an element being created with a computed element constructor is expressed as part of the computed element's content. (Again, contrast this with the treatment of attributes in Grammar 11-14.) A computed element constructor looks like this:

```
element character {
```

```
attribute age { $characterAge },
text "Alex Price" }
```

When the value of the variable `$characterAge` is 24, that computed element constructor produces the following element:

```
<character age="24">Alex Price</character>
```

The final kind of computed constructor is the computed document constructor. Its syntax is exactly the same – except for the name of the constructor – as the computed text and comment constructors, but its content would naturally be a bit more complex. And, of course, the result is a complete document. A useful exercise for the reader is to write a computed document constructor for any of the XML documents found in this book.

11.5.13 Ordered and Unordered Expressions

XML, used as a markup language, creates documents that are inherently ordered. Think about a book that is marked up in XML – the second chapter must always follow the first chapter, and the paragraphs in each chapter must always be in the sequence in which the author wrote them. As a result, XQuery treats the XML that it queries as ordered (and, in particular, it handles that XML in document order) unless instructed to do otherwise. One way in which an XQuery can be instructed to "do otherwise" is through the `order by` clause (see Section 11.6.3), through which the author of an XQuery forces the results of an expression to be ordered according to specified criteria.

However, because XQuery is sometimes applied to information that doesn't represent books or other traditional "documents" – such as relational data, as you'll see in Chapter 15, "SQL/XML" – the notion of "document order" is not always a meaningful one. Instead, any ordering to be applied to query evaluation is imposed as part of the query (such as the `order by` clause just mentioned) or is an artifact of the optimizations that the query processing engine applies to the evaluation of that particular query, often based on factors such as indexes or other physical storage facets.

In order to provide applications with the ability to write queries that selectively bypass considerations of inherent ordering, XQuery provides, as primary expressions, both *ordered* expressions and *unor-*

dered expressions. The syntax of these two expressions appears in Grammar 11-16.

Grammar 11-16 *Syntax of* `ordered` *and* `unordered` *Expressions*

```
OrderedExpr ::= "ordered" "{" Expr }"

UnorderedExpr ::= "unordered" "{" Expr "}"
```

In Section 11.2.3, our description of XQuery's static context included a component named "ordering mode." When either an ordered expression or an unordered expression appears as a part of an XQuery expression, the ordering mode in the static context is set to *ordered* or *unordered*, respectively, for the lexical scope of the `Expr` that appears between the curly braces (`{}`). Of course, that `Expr` can be any XQuery expression and thus can have arbitrarily deep nesting of other expressions, including other ordered and unordered expressions.

The ordering mode affects the behavior of most step expressions (as discussed in Chapter 9, "XPath 1.0 and XPath 2.0"), the set operators (`union`, `intersect`, and `except`), and FLWOR expressions that don't have an `order by` clause. If the ordering mode of those expressions is "ordered," then the node sequences that they return are in document order; if the ordering mode is "unordered," then the node sequences are in an implementation-dependent order. (Note, however, that the ordering mode has no effect on elimination of duplicate nodes from those node sequences.) Because the order of nodes in those node sequences is implementation-dependent, the behavior of certain functions, such as `fn:position()`, as well as numeric predicates in path expressions, is nondeterministic.

In addition to ordered and unordered expressions, XQuery provides the `fn:unordered()` function that takes any sequence (not necessarily of nodes) and returns it in a nondeterministic order. This function is *not* a "randomizing" function – that is, it might well return the sequence in its original order. It merely gives permission to the XQuery evaluation engine to reorder the sequence if necessary for reasons such as performance optimization.

11.5.14 Conditional Expression

Generally speaking, a conditional expression is one that returns one of two values based on the evaluation of a predicate. (This is not the "if statement" used by imperative languages that causes execution to take one of two branches.) In most languages offering conditional expressions, as in XQuery, those expressions are defined using the keyword `if`. In fact, XQuery's grammar uses the BNF nonterminal symbol "`IfExpr`" to define such expressions, as seen in Grammar 11–17.

Grammar 11-17 *Conditional Expression Grammar*

```
IfExpr ::= "if" "(" IfTestExpr ")" "then" IfTrueExpr "else" IfFalseExpr

IfTestExpr ::= Expr

IfTrueExpr ::= ExprSingle

IfFalseExpr ::= ExprSingle
```

When an `IfExpr` is evaluated, the `IfTestExpr` is first evaluated to find its effective Boolean value, as described in Section 11.2. If the effective Boolean value is `true`, then the result of the `IfExpr` is the result of evaluating the `IfTrueExpr`. Otherwise, the result of the `IfExpr` is the result of evaluating the `IfFalseExpr`. Example 11-12 illustrates how we might decide which of two movies to watch tonight based on which of two other movies was released first.

Example 11-12 *Conditional Expression Example*

```
if ( /movies/movie[title="Caddyshack"]/yearReleased >
     /movies/movie[title="Spies Like Us"]/yearReleased )
  then "The Magnificent 7"
  else "Ocean's 11"
```

11.5.15 Quantified Expressions

In XQuery, quantified expressions provide the ability to do existential quantification ("Does at least one of these values meet this criterion?") and universal quantification ("Do all of these values meet this criterion?"). Let's examine the syntax of quantified expressions in Grammar 11-18.

Grammar 11-18 *Quantified Expression Grammar*

```
QuantifiedExpr ::=
    Quantifier QuantifiedInClause ( "," QuantifiedInClause )*
```

```
    "satisfies" QuantifiedTestExpression

Quantifier ::= "some" | "every"

QuantifiedInClause ::=
    "$" VarName TypeDeclaration? "in" QuantifiedBindingSequence

QuantifiedBindingSequence ::= ExprSingle

QuantifiedTestExpression ::= ExprSingle
```

The `Quantifier` keyword `some` causes existential quantification to be evaluated, while the keyword `every` causes universal quantification. Each `QuantifiedInClause` declares a variable, whose type may optionally be specified, and binds it to the sequence of items resulting from the evaluation of the `QuantifiedBindingSequence` expression.

A variable declared in one `QuantifiedInClause` can be used in the `QuantifiedTestExpression`, and even in the `QuantifiedBindingSequence` of the `QuantifiedInClauses` that follow its own `QuantifiedBindingSequence`. (Wow! What a mouthful.)

The result of a `QuantifiedExpr` that specifies `some` is true if at least one evaluation of the `QuantifiedTestExpression` results in a value of `true`, while the result of a `QuantifiedExpr` that specifies `every` is true only if every evaluation of the `QuantifiedTestExpression` results in `true`. When `some` is specified and the result of the `QuantifiedBindingSequence` is the empty sequence, the result is `false`. Why? Because there are no values for which the `QuantifiedTestExpression` can evaluate to `true`. By contrast, when `every` is specified and the result of the `QuantifiedBindingSequence` is the empty sequence, the result is `true`, because there are no values for which the `QuantifiedTestExpression` can evaluate to `false`.

Example 11-13 illustrates the use of quantified expressions.

Example 11-13 *Quantified Expression Examples*

```
(: true because 3 is greater than 2 :)
some $x in (1, 2, 3) satisfies $x > 2

(: false because neither 1 nor 2 are greater than 2 :)
```

```
every $x in (1, 2, 3) satisfies $x > 2

(: true because $x value 1 equals value 2 divided by 2 :)
(: and because $x value 3 is equal to $y value 5 integer-divided by 2 :)
some $x in (1, 2, 3), $y in (2, 3, 5) satisfies $x = $y idiv 2

(: true if at least one movie in our collection was released
           before 1950 :)
some $m in /movies/movie/releaseYear < 1950
```

11.5.16 Expressions on XQuery Types

When you read Appendix C: XQuery 1.0 Grammar, you will see that a *sequence type* is the (data) type of something that can appear in a Data Model sequence – which is pretty much anything recognized by the Data Model. Sequence types can be specified (using the sequence type syntax) in variable declarations, as well as in function parameter declarations and results.

There are several other places in XQuery where sequence types are specified. In a couple of these, the sequence type itself is tested. The syntax of the five additional expressions in which sequence types are used – `instance of`, `typeswitch`, `cast`, `castable`, and `treat` – is shown in Grammar 11-19.

Grammar 11-19 *Grammar of Expressions on Sequence Types*

```
InstanceOfExpr ::= TreatExpr ( "instance" "of" SequenceType )?

TypeSwitchExpr ::=
  "typeswitch" "(" Expr ")"
    CaseClause+
    "default" ( "$" VarName )? "return" ExprSingle

CaseClause ::= "case" ( "$" VarName "as" ) SequenceType "return" ExprSingle

CastExpr ::= UnaryExpr ( "cast" "as" SingleType )?

CastableExpr ::= CastExpr ( "castable" "as" SingleType )?

SingleType ::= AtomicType "?"?

TreatExpr ::= CastableExpr ( "treat" "as" SequenceType )?
```

Let's examine them one at a time.

An `InstanceOfExpr` is used to determine whether a given expression has a particular sequence type or not. Example 11-14 provides examples of using this expression and one example illustrating how it might be put to use in the context of a larger expression.

Example 11-14 *Examples Using `instance of`*

```
(: true because a sequence of integers is an instance of xs:integer* :)
( 1, 2, 3 ) instance of xs:integer*

(: false; it is an instance of movie, not of director :)
/movies/movie[title="Jeremiah Johnson"] instance of director

(: Using 'instance of' productively :)
(: Note that the type of $x must be very general, such as xs:anyType :)
if $x instance of movie
  then $x/director/givenName
  else if $x instance of director
         then $x/givenName
         else "(not a clue)"
```

A query uses a `TypeSwitchExpr` to choose one of several expressions based on the dynamic (run-time) type of a test expression. In Example 11-15, you see an example of a type switch expression and an example of using it in context.

Example 11-15 *Examples Using `typeswitch`*

```
(: Determine whether $x is of a known numeric type or something else :)
typeswitch ( $x )
  case xs:integer return "We've got an integer value"
  case xs:decimal return "We've got a decimal value"
  case xs:float return "We've got a float value"
  case xs:double return "We've got a double value"
  default return "We have something else"

(: Using 'typeswitch' in an expression computing the average running
   time of all of our movies :)
(: Assume that runningTime is sometimes an xs:integer (representing
   seconds) and sometimes an xdt:dayTimeDuration :)
fn:avg ( typeswitch ( //movie/runningTime )
```

```
    case $rt as xs:integer return $rt
    case $rt as xdt:dayTimeDuration
      return ( ( ( fn:hours-from-duration($rt) * 60 ) +
                   fn:minutes-from-duration($rt) ) * 60 +
                 fn:seconds-from-duration($rt) )
)
```

It is often necessary to convert values of one data type to another data type, depending on the specific needs of a query. For example, your query might retrieve a string from some element, knowing that the string is a sequence of digits, convert the string to an integer, and then use that integer value in a computation. The `cast` expression provides that capability for XQuery, as illustrated in Example 11-16.

Example 11-16 *Examples Using `cast`*

```
(: Results in an xs:double value equivalent to 100, or 1.0E2 :)
100 cast as xs:double

(: Results in an xs:time value equivalent to a quarter past noon :)
'12:15:00' cast as xs:time
```

There are several reasons why a cast might fail. The value being cast is first atomized. If atomization results in a sequence longer than 1, a run-time error is raised. If atomization results in an empty sequence and the sequence type was specified without the "`?`" (indicating that an empty sequence is permitted), a run-time error is raised. If the static type of the value being cast is not one that can be converted to the target type as indicated in the Functions and Operators specification, a run-time error is raised. Finally, if the actual value being cast cannot be converted to the target type, a run-time error is raised.

Which brings us to the next expression, the `castable` expression. Sometimes, in the context of a query, a cast is required under conditions where the query cannot guarantee that the values being cast are always appropriate for the target type. If such a cast is attempted, a run-time error is raised. But run-time errors are generally Not A Good Thing, especially when queries may be very complex and long-running – nobody wants her query to simply report "Error" after running for 15 minutes. (Unfortunately, XQuery 1.0 doesn't have a way for a query to detect and handle errors – such as the try/catch blocks used in some languages.)

The `castable` expression allows you to write your queries in a self-protective manner, so casts that would fail at run time can be avoided.

Example 11-17 *Examples Using* `castable`

```
(: Will always return zero :)
if ( 'Twenty' castable as xs:integer )
  then 'Twenty' cast as xs:integer
  else 0

(: Returns a string resulting from casting runningTime values
   either to xs:integer (preferred) or to xs:decimal; if
   neither is possible, then raise an error :)
if ( //movie[title="The Abyss"]/runningTime castable as xs:integer )
  then //movie[title="The Abyss"]/runningTime cast as xs:integer
  else if ( //movie[title="The Abyss"]/runningTime castable as xs:decimal )
         then //movie[title="The Abyss"]/runningTime cast as xs:decimal
         else fn:error() ) cast as xs:string
```

Frequently, your query knows that a value being used is always of a specific known type or of a type derived from that known type. For example, your query might have to deal with data off the web that has not been carefully constructed with attention paid to certain details. One element, let's call it `RegionCode`, in the data might be instances of either `xs:integer` or `my:DVDRegionCode`, which is derived from `xs:integer`. But the query author wants to ensure that only values representing region codes (that is, whose type is `my:DVDRegionCode` but not `xs:integer`) are actually processed and is willing to endure a run-time error if any other sort of data is encountered. The first `treat` expression, illustrated in Example 11-18, is used to provide this capability. A more relaxed query author might decide that values of either `xs:integer` or `my:DVDRegionCode` are acceptable, but not values of `xs:double` or `xs:float`. The second `treat` expression in the example illustrates this usage.

Example 11-18 *Examples Using* `treat`

```
(: Raises a run-time error if the RegionCode is merely an xs:integer :)
//movie[title contains "Terminator"]/RegionCode treat as my:DVDRegionCode

(: Raises a run-time error if the RegionCode is an xs:double or xs:float,
   but returns the RegionCode value if it's either an xs:integer or
```

```
   my:DVDRegionCode :)
//movie[title contains "Terminator"]/RegionCode treat as xs:integer
```

The purpose of the `treat` expression is to allow a query author to provide a guarantee that instance data being queried have appropriate data types. It has particular value when the static typing features is implemented and in use, because it provides information that the static type evaluation algorithms can use to determine and enforce the type correctness of expressions that use `treat`.

11.5.17 Validation Expression

Every XQuery expression that does not raise an error evaluates to some result, which is a sequence of items. As discussed both earlier in this chapter and in Chapter 10, that sequence might contain no items (the empty sequence), one item (singleton), or more than one item. The items in the sequence might be atomic values or complex values (such as XML documents or elements). When the result of an XQuery expression — whether it's the "top-level" expression (that is, the `QueryBody` of an XQuery `Module`) or some expression nested deep within a `QueryBody` — is an XML document or an element, it's very useful to know whether the result is *valid* or not (and even just how valid it is!) according to the associated XML Schemas.

In order to validate the result of an XQuery expression, the XML Schema or Schemas against which that result is to be validated either must be implicitly included in the environment in which the XQuery expression is evaluated, or it must have been *imported* via the use of the `import schema` clause in the XQuery prolog.

The result of successfully validating some node is a *copy* of that node (with a different identity!) in which it and all of its descendent nodes have been annotated with a validity assessment and a Data Model type. If validation fails, an error is raised.

XQuery supports validation of the results of expressions through the `validate` expression, whose syntax is given in Grammar 11-20.

Grammar 11-20 *Syntax of `validate` expression*

```
ValidateExpr ::= "validate" ValidationMode? "{" Expr "}"

ValidationMode ::= "lax" | "strict"
```

The syntax of the `validate` expression is deceptively simple. Why? Because it depends on the rules of *XML Schema Part 1*[9] to provide the detailed semantics of validation. The actual process of validation is discussed in Chapter 10 of this book.

The validated node either corresponds directly to the node being validated or, for a validated document node, to the only element child of the document node.

Example 11-19 provides a few examples of successful validation and validation efforts that will raise errors.

Example 11-19 *Validation Expression Examples*

```
(: Successful validation of typed element :)
validate lax { <givenName xsi:type="xs:string">George</givenName> }

(: Assume that the in-scope schemas contain a top-level element
   declaration for an element named "directorName" that contains
   two element children, "givenName" and "familyName," in that order,
   each of which is an xs:string :)

(: Under that assumption, the following validate expression succeeds :)
validate strict {
  element directorName { element givenName { "George" }
                         element familyName { "Romero" } }

(: Under the same assumption, the following validate expression fails :)
validate strict {
  element directorName { element familyName { "Romero" }
                         element givenName { "George" } }

(: Assume that the in-scope schemas do not contain a top-level element
   declaration for an element named "birthDate" :)

(: Under that assumption, the following validate expression fails :)
validate strict { <birthdate style="American">11/23/2003</birthdate> }

(: Under the same assumption, the following validate expression succeeds :)
validate lax { <birthdate style="American">11/23/2003</birthdate> }
```

9 *XML Schema Part 1: Structures, Second Edition* (Cambridge, MA: World Wide Web Consortium, 2004). Available at: http://www.w3.org/TR/xmlschema-2/.

11.6 FLWOR Expressions

The FLWOR expression is arguably the very heart of XQuery. If you've programmed in SQL, it might be helpful if we told you that the FLWOR expression serves approximately the same purpose in XQuery that the SELECT expression serves in the SQL language. Section 11.10 contains some discussion of the relationship between the two languages and the two expressions.

In this rather lengthy section, we first describe the process of producing a *tuple stream* from the `for` and `let` clauses. Then we look at cutting down (or filtering) that tuple stream using a `where` clause, followed by seeing how to order the results using the `order by` clause. Finally, we cover the `return` clause, which defines what actually gets returned by the FLWOR expression — that is, what the expression evaluates to.

In the introductory parts of Appendix C: XQuery 1.0 Grammar, we see the syntax of XQuery's FLWOR expressions. As you can infer from the syntax, the term FLWOR is derived from the first letter of the names of each immediate subexpression: `for`, `let`, `where`, `order by`, and `return`.

The XQuery 1.0 specification says that the FLWOR expression "supports iteration and binding of variables to intermediate results" and that "[this] kind of expression is often useful for computing joins between two or more documents and for restructuring data."

With that in mind, let's look at the purposes and behaviors of each of the subexpressions of FLWOR.

11.6.1 The `for` Clause and the `let` Clause

The XQuery spec introduces the `for` and `let` expressions with the unfortunate sentence "The purpose of the `for` and `let` clauses in a FLWOR expression is to produce a tuple stream in which each tuple consists of one or more bound variables." Those of you familiar with relational theory will certainly recognize the word *tuple*, as will many others.

In this context, a tuple is a binding of a variable to a sequence of (zero or more) values or, by extension, pairs (or triples, *etc.*) of such bindings, depending on the number of variables used in the combination of `for` clauses and `let` clauses. A tuple stream is a sequence of such tuples that can be considered in turn.

Consider the `for` clause illustrated in Example 11-21, which calls on the `movies` document in Example 11-20 (seen in earlier chapters as well). Of course, as we can tell from the syntax of FLWOR expressions, a `for` clause cannot appear alone — at a minimum, it must be followed by a `return` clause.

Example 11-20 *Reduced `movie` Example and Trivial `studio` Example*

```
<?xml version="1.0" encoding="UTF-8"?>
<!-- movie - a simple XML example -->
<movies xmlns:xsi="http://www.w3.org/2001/XMLSchema-instance">
  <movie myStars="5">
    <title>An American Werewolf in London</title>
    <yearReleased>1981</yearReleased>
    <director>
      <familyName>Landis</familyName>
      <givenName>John</givenName>
    </director>
  </movie>
  <movie myStars="4">
    <title>The Thing</title>
    <yearReleased>1982</yearReleased>
    <director>
      <familyName>Carpenter</familyName>
      <givenName>John</givenName>
    </director>
  </movie>
  <movie myStars="3">
    <title>The Shining</title>
    <yearReleased>1980</yearReleased>
    <director>
      <familyName>Kubrick</familyName>
      <givenName>Stanley</givenName>
    </director>
  </movie>
</movies>

<?xml version="1.0" encoding="UTF-8"?>
<!-- studios - a second XML example -->
<studios xmlns:xsi="http://www.w3.org/2001/XMLSchema-instance">
  <studio>Paramount</studio>
  <studio>Disney</studio>
  <studio>Searchlight</studio>
</studios>
```

Example 11-21 *Trivial `for` Clause and Corresponding Tuple Stream*

```
for $m in movies/movie
```

result:

```
$m:   <movie myStars="5">
        <title>An American Werewolf in London</title>
        <yearReleased>1981</yearReleased>
        <director>
          <familyName>Landis</familyName>
          <givenName>John</givenName>
        </director>
      </movie>
$m:   <movie myStars="4">
        <title>The Thing</title>
        <yearReleased>1982</yearReleased>
        <director>
          <familyName>Carpenter</familyName>
          <givenName>John</givenName>
        </director>
      </movie>
$m:   <movie myStars="3">
        <title>The Shining</title>
        <yearReleased>1980</yearReleased>
        <director>
          <familyName>Kubrick</familyName>
          <givenName>Stanley</givenName>
        </director>
      </movie>
```

Note that the result contains three instances of the variable `$m`, each instance being *bound* to a separate `movie` element from the original document. That result is a *tuple stream* comprising three tuples, each of which is an instance of the variable and the value (called its *binding sequence*) to which that instance is bound.

The `for` clause iterates over the items in the binding sequence, binding the variable to each of those items in turn. When the ordering mode applied to the FLWOR expression is `ordered`, the tuple stream is also ordered (in the same order as the binding sequence);

when the ordering mode is `unordered`, the tuple stream's order is implementation-dependent.

A `for` clause can have multiple variable bindings, as shown in Example 11-22, which depends on the two documents seen in Example 11-20. In this case, the two variables, `$m` and `$s`, are each associated with a binding clause, but they are not independent of one another. Instead, each binding of `$m` is associated with every binding of `$s`. The XQuery 1.0 spec says, "The resulting tuple stream contains one tuple for each combination of values in the respective binding sequences." Those of you familiar with the relational model — or with vector operations from your math classes — will recognize this as a *cross product*.

This concept can be extended arbitrarily to cover as many variables as the `for` clause supplies.

Example 11-22 *`for` Clause with Multiple Variables and Corresponding Tuple Stream*

```
for $m in doc("movies")/movies/movie,
    $s in doc("studios")studios/studio
```

result:

```
$m:  <movie myStars="5">                        $s:  Paramount
       <title>An American Werewolf in
         London</title>
       <yearReleased>1981</yearReleased>
       <director>
         <familyName>Landis</familyName>
         <givenName>John</givenName>
       </director>
     </movie>
$m:  <movie myStars="5">                        $s:  Disney
       <title>An American Werewolf in
         London</title>
       <yearReleased>1981</yearReleased>
       <director>
         <familyName>Landis</familyName>
         <givenName>John</givenName>
       </director>
     </movie>
```

```
$m:  <movie myStars="5">                              $s:  Searchlight
       <title>An American Werewolf in
         London</title>
       <yearReleased>1981</yearReleased>
       <director>
         <familyName>Landis</familyName>
         <givenName>John</givenName>
       </director>
     </movie>
$m:  <movie myStars="4">                              $s:  Paramount
       <title>The Thing</title>
       <yearReleased>1982</yearReleased>
       <director>
         <familyName>Carpenter</familyName>
         <givenName>John</givenName>
       </director>
     </movie>
$m:  <movie myStars="4">                              $s:  Disney
       <title>The Thing</title>
       <yearReleased>1982</yearReleased>
       <director>
         <familyName>Carpenter</familyName>
         <givenName>John</givenName>
       </director>
     </movie>
$m:  <movie myStars="4">                              $s:  Searchlight
       <title>The Thing</title>
       <yearReleased>1982</yearReleased>
       <director>
         <familyName>Carpenter</familyName>
         <givenName>John</givenName>
       </director>
     </movie>
```

```
$m:  <movie myStars="3">                          $s:  Paramount
       <title>The Shining</title>
       <yearReleased>1980</yearReleased>
       <director>
         <familyName>Kubrick</familyName>
         <givenName>Stanley</givenName>
       </director>
     </movie>
$m:  <movie myStars="3">                          $s:  Disney
       <title>The Shining</title>
       <yearReleased>1980</yearReleased>
       <director>
         <familyName>Kubrick</familyName>
         <givenName>Stanley</givenName>
       </director>
     </movie>
$m:  <movie myStars="3">                          $s:  Searchlight
       <title>The Shining</title>
       <yearReleased>1980</yearReleased>
       <director>
         <familyName>Kubrick</familyName>
         <givenName>Stanley</givenName>
       </director>
     </movie>
```

If the ordering mode in effect for a FLWOR expression whose `for` clause defines multiple variables is `ordered`, then the first variable provides the primary sort order, the second provides the secondary sort order, and so forth.

The `let` clause also binds variables with the values returned by expressions, but without iteration. Instead, the `let` clause binds its variables with the entire value of their respective expressions – the entire sequence, not one item of the sequence at a time. A `let` clause that binds two or more variables generates a single tuple containing all of the variable bindings, as illustrated in Example 11-23.

Example 11-23 *The `let` clause and Resulting Tuple*

```
let $m := /movies/movie, $s := /studios/studio
```

result:

```
$m:  <movie myStars="5">                              $s:  Paramount
       <title>An American Werewolf in                      Disney
         London</title>                                    Searchlight
       <yearReleased>1981</yearReleased>
       <director>
         <familyName>Landis</familyName>
         <givenName>John</givenName>
       </director>
     </movie>
     <movie myStars="4">
       <title>The Thing</title>
       <yearReleased>1982</yearReleased>
       <director>
         <familyName>Carpenter</familyName>
         <givenName>John</givenName>
       </director>
     </movie>
     <movie myStars="3">
       <title>The Shining</title>
       <yearReleased>1980</yearReleased>
       <director>
         <familyName>Kubrick</familyName>
         <givenName>Stanley</givenName>
       </director>
     </movie>
```

The scope of the variables bound in a `for` clause or a `let` clause is every subexpression in the same FLWOR expression that *follows* the individual `for` clause or a `let` clause in which the variable is bound (but not, of course, the expression to which the variable is bound). Consequently, an expression such as that in Example 11-24 is possible (if not necessarily useful in this case).

Example 11-24 *Binding a Variable and Then Using It*

```
for $m in movies/movie, $d in data($m/director/familyName)
```

```
Resulting tuples:

$m:  <movie myStars="5">                          $d:  Landis
       <title>An American Werewolf in
         London</title>
       <yearReleased>1981</yearReleased>
       <director>
         <familyName>Landis</familyName>
         <givenName>John</givenName>
       </director>
     </movie>
$m:  <movie myStars="4">                          $d:  Carpenter
       <title>The Thing</title>
       <yearReleased>1982</yearReleased>
       <director>
         <familyName>Carpenter</familyName>
         <givenName>John</givenName>
       </director>
     </movie>
$m:  <movie myStars="3">                          $d:  Kubrick
       <title>The Shining</title>
       <yearReleased>1980</yearReleased>
       <director>
         <familyName>Kubrick</familyName>
         <givenName>Stanley</givenName>
       </director>
     </movie>
```

One often misunderstood implication of the rule that the "scope of the variables bound . . . is every subexpression . . . that *follows*" is that a variable declared in one clause (a `for` clause, for example) can be apparently redeclared in a subsequent clause (a `let` clause, perhaps) in the same FLWOR expression, as illustrated in Example 11-25. However, that apparent redeclaration does no such thing. Instead, the second declaration is actually a declaration of a *new* variable of the same name, whose declaration *obscures* the previously declared variable of that name. As a result, expressions in clauses following the `let` clause (in this example) can never access the value of the variable `$i` declared in the `for` clause; all such efforts will see only the *other* variable `$i` declared in the `let` clause.

Example 11-25 *Redeclaring Variables*

```
for $i in ...
let $i := ...
```

In both `for` clauses and `let` clauses, each variable being bound may be specified to have an explicit type. If the value bound to a variable with an explicitly declared type does not match that type, using the rules of sequence type matching, then a type error is raised.

In a `for` clause, a bound variable can be accompanied by a *positional variable,* whose value is an integer that represents the position of each value in the bound variable's binding sequence in turn. Repeating Example 11-21 with a positional variable, we get the same results, as shown in Example 11-26.

Example 11-26 *Trivial `for` Clause with Positional Variable*

```
for $m at $i in movies/movie

Resulting tuples:
$m:  <movie myStars="5">                                 $i   1
       <title>An American Werewolf in London</title>
       <yearReleased>1981</yearReleased>
       <director>
         <familyName>Landis</familyName>
         <givenName>John</givenName>
       </director>
     </movie>
$m:  <movie myStars="4">                                 $i   2
       <title>The Thing</title>
       <yearReleased>1982</yearReleased>
       <director>
         <familyName>Carpenter</familyName>
         <givenName>John</givenName>
       </director>
     </movie>
```

```
$m:  <movie myStars="3">                              $i   3
       <title>The Shining</title>
       <yearReleased>1980</yearReleased>
       <director>
         <familyName>Kubrick</familyName>
         <givenName>Stanley</givenName>
       </director>
     </movie>
```

11.6.2 The `where` Clause

As the grammar in Appendix C: XQuery 1.0 Grammar shows, FLWOR expressions can optionally include a `where` clause, the purpose of which is to filter the tuples generated by the preceding `for` and/or `let` clauses. The `ExprSingle` contained in the `where` clause, called the `where` *expression*, is evaluated once for each of those tuples, and only those tuples for which the effective Boolean value of the `where` expression is `true` are retained.

In Example 11-27, we have coded a FLWOR expression fragment in which a `where` clause is applied to a positional variable generated in a `for` clause that is otherwise identical to Example 11-26.

Example 11-27 *Trivial `for` Clause and `where` Clause Using Positional Variable*

```
for $m at $i in movies/movie
where $i != $m/@myStars
```

Resulting tuples:

```
$m:  <movie myStars="5">                              $i   1
       <title>An American Werewolf in London</title>
       <yearReleased>1981</yearReleased>
       <director>
         <familyName>Landis</familyName>
         <givenName>John</givenName>
       </director>
     </movie>
```

```
$m:  <movie myStars="4">                              $i   2
       <title>The Thing</title>
       <yearReleased>1982</yearReleased>
       <director>
         <familyName>Carpenter</familyName>
         <givenName>John</givenName>
       </director>
     </movie>
```

Note that the result in Example 11-27 is identical to the result in Example 11-26, except that one tuple — the tuple in which the value of `$i` and the value of the `myStars` attribute are both 3 — is absent.

And, yes, the `where` clause really is that simple. We leave as an exercise for the reader to determine the result of the FLWOR fragment in Example 11-28.

Example 11-28 *Another `where` Clause*

```
for $m at $i in movies/movie
where $m/director/givenName != "John"
```

11.6.3 The `order by` Clause

The `order by` clause is used to reorder the tuples in the tuple stream generated by the `for` and/or `let` clauses, possibly filtered by a `where` clause. If a FLWOR expression does not contain an `order by` clause, then the order of tuples is determined by the `for` and/or `let` clauses and by the ordering mode (`ordered` or `unordered`, as discussed earlier in Section 11.4.13). If an `order by` clause is present, then it determines the order of those tuples based on *values* present in the tuples themselves. (Note that the ordering done by the `order by` clause is done by values and not by nodes or by node identity.)

An `order by` clause has one or more ordering specifications (`OrderSpec`), each of which contains an `ExprSingle` and an optional ordering modifier (`OrderModifier`). The `ExprSingle` is evaluated using the variable bindings in each tuple. The relative ordering of two tuples is determined by evaluating each `OrderSpec`, in left-to-right sequence, until an `OrderSpec` is encountered for which the two tuples do not compare equal. When evaluating an `OrderSpec`:

- The result of the `ExprSingle` is atomized; if the result of atomization is neither a single atomic value nor an empty sequence, then an error is raised.
- Values of type `xdt:untypedAtomic` are cast to `xs:string`.
- The values of the `ExprSingle` in every row in the tuple stream must be able to be cast into a single data type that has the `gt` (value greater than) operator defined; if there is no such type, then an error is raised.

The optional `OrderModifier` can specify that the ordering is to be `ascending` or `descending` (that is, whether the tuples are delivered with the lowest values appearing first or last). It can also specify whether empty sequences and, for values of type `xs:float` and `xs:double`, the special value `NaN` (Not a Number), are sorted as greater than all other values (`empty greatest`) or less than all other values (`empty least`). The `OrderModifier` can also specify a collation that governs how `xs:string` (and, because of the cast cited earlier, `xsd:untypedAtomic`) values are compared.

If the `order by` clause specifies `stable`, then for any two tuples that compare equal for every `OrderSpec`, the relative order of those tuples is the same as in the original tuple stream. If `stable` is not specified, then the relative order of two such tuples is implementation-dependent.

Example 11-29 illustrates a FLWOR expression fragment that uses an `order by` clause.

Example 11-29 *Trivial `for` Clause, `where` Clause, and `order by` Clause*

```
for $m at $i in movies/movie
where $i > 1
order by $m/yearReleased ascending
```

```
Resulting tuples:

$m:  <movie myStars="3">                                    $i   3
       <title>The Shining</title>
       <yearReleased>1980</yearReleased>
       <director>
         <familyName>Kubrick</familyName>
         <givenName>Stanley</givenName>
       </director>
     </movie>
$m:  <movie myStars="4">                                    $i   2
       <title>The Thing</title>
       <yearReleased>1982</yearReleased>
       <director>
         <familyName>Carpenter</familyName>
         <givenName>John</givenName>
       </director>
     </movie>
```

11.6.4 The `return` Clause

Every FLWOR expression contains a `return` clause (which is why previous examples in this section are characterized as FLWOR *fragments*). The `ExprSingle` contained in a return clause is evaluated once for each tuple that is produced by the `for` clauses and/or `let` clauses and/or `where` clause and/or `order by` clause. The results of these evaluations are concatenated (as if they were assembled using the comma operator) into a sequence; the resulting sequence is the value of the FLWOR clause.

Example 11-29 can be completed by adding a return clause, as shown in Example 11-30.

Example 11-30 *A Complete FLWOR Expression*

```
for $m at $i in movies/movie
where $i > 1
order by $m/yearReleased ascending
return data($m/@myStars)

result:

3 4
```

The result in Example 11-30 is a sequence of two values, each the value of the attribute `myStars` of the element `movie` contained in a tuple in the tuple stream produced by the `for` clause, filtered by the `where` clause, and sorted by the `order by` clause.

In Appendix A: The Example, you will see other examples of FLWOR expressions.

11.7 Error Handling

XQuery provides three categories of errors that can be raised: static errors that can be raised only during the static analysis phase (such as a syntax error), dynamic errors that can be raised during either the static analysis phrase or the dynamic analysis phrase (such as division by zero), and type errors that can also be raised during either the static analysis phrase (such as the static type of an expression being compatible with the type required by the context) or the dynamic analysis phrase (such as the dynamic type of a value being incompatible with the static type of the expression producing that value).

In the XQuery 1.0 specification and all of its accompanying specifications, errors are indicated by the convention `err:XXYYnnnn`, where "`err`" is used in these documents as a namespace prefix for the namespace "`http://www.w3.org/date/xqt-errors`" (the final value for "`date`" will be determined by the publication date of the final Recommendation for XQuery); "`XX`" is a two-letter code identifying the particular document in which the error is defined (*e.g.*, "`XQ`" for the XQuery specification or "`FO`" for the Functions and Operators spec); "`YY`" is another two-letter code indicating the category of error (*e.g.*, "`ST`" for an XQuery static error or "`AR`" for a Functions and Operators arithmetic error); and "`nnnn`" is a unique numeric code for the specific error. For example, "`err:XQST0032`" identifies the static error that results from a query prolog containing more than one base URI declaration. (By the way, "`err`" is not a predefined prefix and must be declared explicitly if you wish to use it.)

If the XQuery implementation reports errors to the external environment from which XQuery modules are invoked, it does so in the form of a URI reference that is derived from the QName of the error. The error mentioned in the previous paragraph, "`err:XQST0032`", would be reported as the URI reference "`http://www.w3.org/date/xqt-errors#XQST0032`". Implementations may also return a descriptive string along with the URI reference of an error, as well as any values that the external environment might use to attempt to recover from the error or to diagnose a problem.

The Functions and Operators specification provides a special function, `fn:error()`, that returns no value at all (in fact, its return type is explicitly "none"). Its sole purpose is to permit a query expression to raise an error under user-defined circumstances. If your XQuery needs to raise the error mentioned twice in this section, you could do so by invoking `fn:error("err:XQST0032")`. As you will find in the F&O specification, this function allows argument values of other types than the QNames of error conditions, including strings that might contain a human-readable message.

11.8 Modules and Query Prologs

In Appendix C: XQuery 1.0 Grammar, we see the syntax for XQuery modules, including module prologs. In this section, we take a closer look at the reasoning behind modules, the components of modules and prologs, and how they are used.

What *is* a module? Why does the concept exist in XQuery? According to the XQuery 1.0 spec, a module is "a fragment of XQuery code that conforms to the `Module` grammar and can independently undergo the static analysis phase." The first part of that definition is almost a tautology, but the second part gives a pretty good clue: An XQuery module is a bit of XQuery code that can be compiled separately. (The XQuery 1.0 spec doesn't mention compilation, but that intent is easy to discern.)

As anybody who has developed complex software systems knows, breaking applications into modules that can be written, compiled, and even debugged separately, and then allowing those modules to interact with one another, has many advantages, not the least of which is the potential for code reuse. That lesson was not lost on XQuery's definers.

In XQuery, there are two kinds of modules: *main modules* and *library modules*. A main module is one that contains both a *prolog* and a *query body* (an expression that can be evaluated), while a library module is one that includes only a *module namespace declaration* and a prolog. It's easy to figure out the purpose of a main module: It's the "thing" that can be executed, or evaluated. By contrast, a library module is one that cannot be evaluated directly, but that provides declarations for functions and variables that can be imported into other modules (ultimately into a main module).

Every user of XQuery uses main modules, even if it's not obvious that they are doing so. The reason is obvious from the grammar: The version declaration and everything in the query prolog are optional! Consequently, this is a perfectly valid XQuery main module: `42`. By contrast, because library modules require explicit syntax, they are likely to be used in more complex applications.

Before delving into the details of prologs, main modules, library modules, and module namespace declarations, let's consider the first bit of syntax in a `Module`, the optional `VersionDecl`.

Knowing that the future is difficult to predict, the definers of XML realized that requirements not yet known might lead to new versions of the language; as a result, authors of XML documents are free — even encouraged — to indicate the version of XML used by those documents; they are also able to indicate the character coding (*e.g.*, UTF-8 or UTF-16) used to encode those documents. Similarly, there may well be future versions of XQuery, so it is desirable to allow authors of XQueries the freedom to indicate the version of XQuery being used, as well as the freedom to specify an encoding declaration — the name of the character coding in which they are encoded. Currently, the only version number allowed in an XQuery is "1.0." The encodings permitted are defined by each XQuery implementation, but we expect that all implementations will support at least one of UTF-8 or UTF-16 (which is precisely what XML requires). Example 11-31 provides a few examples of valid `VersionDecl`s.

Example 11-31 *Examples of* `VersionDecl`

```
xquery version "1.0" ;

xquery version '1.0';

xquery version "1.0" encoding "UTF-8" ;
```

11.8.1 Prologs

A `MainModule` is a `Prolog` followed by a `QueryBody`. We have seen examples of `QueryBody`s, and we have referred to the contents of the `Prolog`. Now it's time to see exactly what the `Prolog` is.

The `Prolog` (frequently called the *query prolog* to distinguish it from the XML document prolog) provides syntax that allows authors of XQuery modules to declare several things that affect the behaviors of XQuery expressions. Some of the items that can be specified in a query prolog — such as boundary space policy, ordering mode, and default collation — override the implementation defaults for those items. Others — such as variable and namespace declarations — may *augment* implementation defaults, but do not override them. Information about each of these items is available in Table 11-1, and you can find the details of which can be overridden and that can be augmented in the XQuery 1.0 specification in its section entitled "The Static Context."

- `declare boundary-space` — Overrides the implementation-defined boundary space policy that determines whether boundary whitespace is preserved by element constructors during evaluation of the query; `preserve` means that boundary whitespace is preserved, and `strip` means that it is deleted.
- `declare default collation` — Overrides the implementation-defined default collation used for character string comparisons in the module that do not specify an explicit collation. The specified collation must be among the statically known collations or an error is raised.
- `declare base-uri` — Overrides the implementation-defined default base URI that is used to resolve relative URIs within the module.
- `declare construction` — Overrides the implementation-defined default that determines whether attribute and element nodes being copied into a constructed element or document node retain (`preserve`) or lose (`strip`) existing type information.
- `declare ordering` — Overrides the implementation-defined default ordering mode (`ordered` or `unordered`) applied to all expressions in the module that do not have an explicit ordering mode.
- `declare default order` — Overrides the implementation-defined default that determines whether empty sequences sort less than (`empty least`) or greater than (`empty greatest`) other values.
- `declare copy-namespaces` — Controls the namespace bindings that are assigned when existing element nodes are copied by element constructors (`preserve` or `no-preserve`, as well as `inherit` or `no-inherit`).

It is a syntax error if any of these declarations are specified more than once in a query prolog. Some other declarations are permitted to appear more than once:

- `import schema` – Imports the element and attribute declarations and the type definitions from a schema into the in-scope namespaces, possibly binding a namespace prefix to the target namespace of the schema. Multiple schemas can be imported, but the definitions they contain must not conflict or an error is raised. Location hints may be provided, but their meaning is completely determined by the XQuery implementation.
- `import module` – Imports the function and variable declarations from one or more library modules into the function signatures and in-scope variables of the importing module. Modules are identified by their target namespaces, and all modules with a given target namespace are imported when that target namespace is specified. Importing a module that in turn imports another module does not make the function and variable declarations of that last module available to the original importing module. Location hints may be provided, but their meaning is completely determined by the XQuery implementation.
- `declare namespace` – Augments the implementation-defined predefined (statically known) namespaces and prefixes, making an additional namespace available to the query.
- `declare default element namespace` and `declare default function namespace` – Specifies the namespace URI that is associated with unprefixed element (and type) names and function names, respectively, within a module.
- `declare variable` – Declares one or more variables, optionally with a type. Variables can be declared to be `external` or can be given an initial value. External variables can be given a value only by the external environment from which the module is invoked.
- `declare function` – Declares one or more functions (along with their parameters) that can be invoked from expressions contained in the module. Functions can be declared to be `external` or can be declared with an

(XQuery) expression that comprises the function body. External functions are implemented outside of the query environment. An external function is one written in a language other than XQuery. We expect that many XQuery implementations will support external functions written in Java, C#, and other common programming languages.

- `declare option` – Declares an implementation-defined option, the meaning of which is completely defined by the XQuery implementation.

11.8.2 Main Modules

A main module is one that contains, in addition to a (possibly empty) query prolog, a query body — an expression that is evaluated when the module is invoked. A *query* has exactly one main module. Evaluating the expression that is the query body of a main module is the same as executing, or running, the query.

How a main module is invoked is very much left to the XQuery implementation. Some implementations may provide a command-line interface or a graphical user interface (GUI) that allows a query to be typed directly by a user. Other implementations may provide ways to embed XQueries into some other programming language, such as Java, C, or Python. Still others might allow applications to invoke methods in some application programming interface (API) and pass the text of XQueries and main modules for evaluation (see Chapter 14, "XQuery APIs," for more information). Still others might provide for a GUI facility that builds queries without having to enter the character strings conforming to XQuery syntax. We expect that all implementations will provide at least one of these methods, and that some will provide more than one.

However, the sequence of events once a main module is invoked is well defined. In fact, it is generally described in Section 11.2.2, "The XQuery Processing Model." That description does not cover every detail, so here is a more precise list of the steps involved in the invocation of a main module. Of course, before these steps can be performed, the invoking environment has to provide input data in the form of a Query Data Model instance, possibly by parsing a serialized XML document into an Infoset, perhaps performing Schema validation on that Infoset to produce a PSVI, and then transforming the result into a Data Model instance. (Note that several of these steps depend on the implementation's providing optional features: schema import, modules, and static typing are all optional.)

- The in-scope schema definitions in the static context are initialized, possibly by extracting them from actual XML schemas, as well as through implementation-defined means.
- The `MainModule` undergoes static analysis. This involves several steps of its own.
  - The module is transformed into an *operation tree* that represents the query (the transformation to an operation tree is a definitional technique — implementations are free to handle this in any way they wish).
  - The static context is initialized by the implementation and then modified according to information in the `Prolog`, which is done in a couple of steps:
    - The in-scope schema definitions are augmented by the schema imports in the `Prolog`.
    - The static context is augmented with function and variable declarations from modules that are imported.
  - The augmented static context is used to resolve names (schema type names, function names, namespace prefixes, and variable names) appearing in the module.
  - The operation tree is *normalized* by transforming various implicit operations (such as atomization, type promotion, and determination of Effective Boolean Values) into explicit operations.
  - Every expression in the query is assigned a static type.
- The `MainModule` undergoes dynamic analysis. Several actions are involved in dynamic analysis.
  - The operation tree is traversed, evaluating subexpressions at the leaves of the tree, and then combining their results when evaluating the subexpressions at the appropriate branches of the tree.
  - The dynamic context is augmented or changed by creation of new Data Model instances, by binding values to variables, *etc.*
  - The *dynamic type* of each expression is determined as the expression is evaluated. If the dynamic type of an expression is incompatible with the static type of the expression, an error is raised.

- The result of dynamic analysis is often (but not necessarily) serialized into a character string; if the result of the dynamic analysis is an XML document, then the result of the XQuery is an XML document in character string form.

Complete examples of main modules can be found in Appendix A: The Example.

11.8.3 Library Modules

Library modules support the notion of modularizing applications, which is done for reasons of design, maintenance, and code reuse. A library module comprises only a `ModuleDecl` and a `Prolog`. The `ModuleDecl` defines the target namespace of the library module, while the `Prolog` contains declarations for functions and variables that are *exported* (made available) for *importation* (inclusion) by other library modules and by main modules. Example 11-32 contains a scenario of importing library modules.

Example 11-32 *Importing Library Modules*

```
(: Main module -- only the module imports are shown here :)
xquery version "1.0" encoding "UTF-8";
import module namespace myLibs = "http://lib.example.com/libraries/filmlib"
   at "http://lib.example.com/libraries/filmlib/movie-functions.xq";
...

(: Library module: movie-functions.xq :)
module namespace myLibs = "http://lib.example.com/libraries/filmlib";
declare default function namespace
   "http://lib.example.com/libraries/filmlib";
(: Note that a module can import its own namespace :)
import module namespace myLibs = "http://lib.example.com/libraries/filmlib"
   at "http://lib.example.com/libraries/filmlib/rating-functions.xq";
import module namespace rev = "http://lib.example.com/libraries/reviews"
   at "http://lib.example.com/libraries/filmlib/reviewing-functions.xq";
(: No default namespace prefix for variables :)
declare variable $myLibs:stars as xs:integer;
declare variable $myLibs:one as xs:decimal := 10.0;
declare variable $myLibs:movies external;
(: No explicit namespace prefix, use default :)
declare function getDirector( $movie as movie ) as xs:string
```

```
  {
    return fn:concat( $movie/director/givenName, ' ',
                      $movie/director/familyName )
  };
(: External function :)
declare function averagePrice ( $name as xs:string, $year as xs:integer )
  as xs:decimal external;

(: Library module: rating-functions.xq :)
(: Note that the namespace URI must be the same as on the import, but
   the prefix can be anything, but used consistently in this module :)
module namespace films = "http://lib.example.com/libraries/filmlib";
...


(: Library module: reviewing-functions.xq :)
module namespace revs = "http://lib.example.com/libraries/reviews";
...
```

Some of the components of Example 11-32 deserve a few additional words of discussion.

- `import module namespace myLibs...at...`: The way in which a module is imported into another module (main or library) is to import the module's namespace. All of the functions defined in a library module are named with QNames whose namespace is typically the module's namespace. The `at` clause allows the query author to provide the XQuery implementation with a hint about where the code for a library module might be found.
- `module namespace myLibs`: Every module other than a main module is declared by specifying its module namespace.
- `import module namespace myLibs`: A library module is allowed to import its own namespace. Doing so does not cause an infinite loop of a module including itself forever. Instead, it allows modularization of a single namespace into multiple "physical" modules that can be "merged" into one module for query evaluation purposes.

- `import module namespace rev`: No surprise — one module is allowed to import different module namespaces to use the functions declared in those other modules.

11.9 A Longer Example with Data

You will find more examples of XQuery expressions, along with the source data on which they operate to give the specified results, in Appendix A: The Example.

11.10 XQuery for SQL Programmers

Before we complete our discussion of XQuery 1.0, we think it's worth responding to requests from any number of SQL programmers who, while learning XQuery 1.0, have asked us to explain XQuery concepts in terms of more familiar SQL concepts. Not at all incidentally, the similarities of some of the two languages' concepts is due in part to the fact that they share a lot of the same concepts — and at least one of the same creators (our friend and colleague, Don Chamberlin of IBM)!

Arguably, the most important syntax element of XQuery is the FLWOR expression, while the best analogy in SQL is the query expression, better known as the SELECT expression. (Many programmers refer to this as the SELECT *statement*, but that statement is used only in interactive SQL and is not used in SQL programs.)

Figure 11-2 graphically illustrates the relationships between the clauses, or subexpressions, of FLWOR and the analogous syntax elements of SQL's SELECT.

Note that XQuery's `let` clause has no analog in SQL's SELECT expression,[10] while SQL's GROUP BY and HAVING clauses have no analog in XQuery (strictly speaking, SQL's HAVING clause is merely another WHERE clause that uses a different keyword and that is applied to the result of the GROUP BY clause). Finally, note that SQL's ORDER BY clause is not actually part of the SELECT expression, but is used only in cursor declarations and a very limited number of additional places.

Of course, in SQL, the FROM clause identifies tables from which rows are chosen, joining them with rows from other tables if speci-

10 However, it's not irrational to suggest that the `let` clause is similar to SQL's `SELECT expression FROM some_single_row_table`.

fied, while the `for` expression in XQuery identifies XML nodes. There are other important differences as well, but it's not our purpose in this book to detail the similarities and differences between these two popular query languages. We won't belabor the analogy further, except to mention that XQuery's `for` clause supports *joins* in which nodes from one document are combined with nodes from another document, just as the joins specified in SQL's FROM clause combines rows from one table with rows from another table.

There are other concepts that the two languages share but for which there are important differences. For example, SQL's collection of data types is not the same as XQuery's. Many of the data types in the two languages are similar in purpose, but the details vary, often considerably.

In Table 11-5, we have provided a correspondence between SQL's set of data types and the XQuery Data Model's set of data types. Note that most of the XQuery Data Model's types are shown with the namespace prefix "`xs:`", indicating that those types are defined in XML Schema. Other types are shown with the namespace prefix "`xdt:`" to indicate that they are defined by the Data Model itself. Some of SQL's data types have no analogy in XQuery, and some types used in XQuery have no analogy in SQL; we use a dash ("—") to indicate that situation. Chapter 15, "SQL/XML," has more discussion of type correspondences between the two languages.

Many of SQL's expressions have analogs in XQuery (the reverse is true as well). Both languages have arithmetic expressions, string expressions, comparison expressions (and predicates), datetime expressions, and so forth. The details naturally vary, because the languages' needs are different, as are their data types' details.

With this modest discussion, we believe that most SQL programmers will be able to use this chapter to begin learning XQuery and applying it in their own applications.

11.11 Chapter Summary

In this rather lengthy chapter, we've taken a fairly close look at XQuery proper, after introducing several basic concepts. We discussed every important type of expression in some detail, most of them accompanied by illustrative examples. We spent considerable space on the FLWOR expression, examining each of its clauses in turn, because of its key role in XQuery. We also gave you an overview of XQuery modules, their contents, and how they are used.

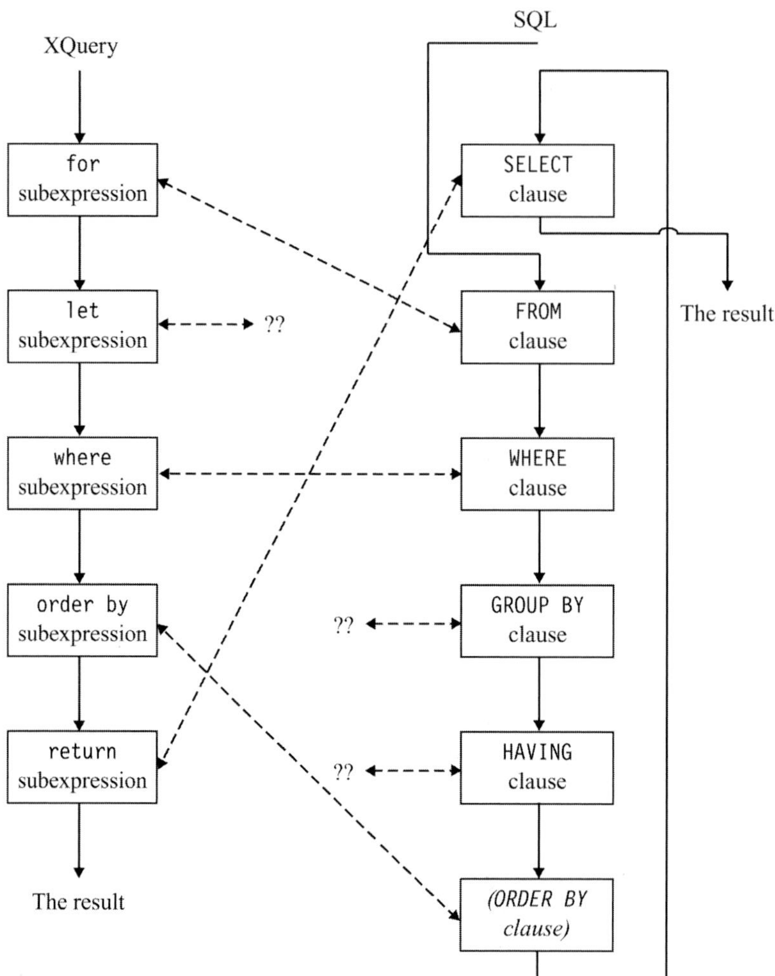

Solid lines indicate the flow of control between clauses.
Dotted lines show the correspondences between the two languages' clauses.
Lines terminating in "??" indicate that there is no corresponding clause in the other language.

Figure 11-2 *Relationship between FLWOR and SELECT.*

After studying this chapter, you are qualified to take that shiny new XQuery engine (already available from major vendors, minor organizations, and open source efforts) for a serious test drive. No single chapter (or book, for that matter) can possibly cover every possible

Table 11-5 *SQL Data Types vs. XQuery 1.0 types*

SQL data types	XQuery 1.0 types
CHARACTER, CHARACTER VARYING, CHARACTER LARGE OBJECT, NATIONAL CHARACTER, NATIONAL CHARACTER VARYING, NATIONAL CHARACTER LARGE OBJECT	xs:string
–	xs:normalizedString
–	xs:token
–	xs:language
–	xs:NMTOKEN
–	xs:NMTOKENS
–	xs:Name
–	xs:NCName
–	xs:ID
–	xs:IDREF
–	xs:IDREFS
–	xs:ENTITY
–	xs:ENTITIES
BOOLEAN	xs:Boolean
NUMERIC, DECIMAL	xs:decimal
INTEGER	xs:integer
–	xs:nonPositiveInteger
–	xs:negativeInteger
BIGINT	xs:long
INTEGER	xs:int
SMALLINT	xs:short
–	xs:byte
–	xs:nonNegativeInteger
–	xs:unsignedLong
–	xs:unsignedInt
–	xs:unsignedShort
–	xs:unsignedByte
–	xs:positiveInteger
FLOAT, REAL	xs:float

Table 11-5 *SQL Data Types vs. XQuery 1.0 types (continued)*

SQL data types	XQuery 1.0 types
FLOAT, DOUBLE	xs:double
–	xs:duration
TIMESTAMP WITH TIME ZONE, TIMESTAMP WITHOUT TIME ZONE	xs:dateTime
DATE WITH TIME ZONE, DATE WITHOUT TIME ZONE	xs:date
TIME WITH TIME ZONE, TIME WITHOUT TIME ZONE	xs:time
–	xs:gYearMonth
–	xs:gYear
–	xs:gMonthDay
–	xs:gDay
–	xs:gMonth
BINARY LARGE OBJECT	xs:hexBinary
BINARY LARGE OBJECT	xs:base64Binary
–	xs:anyURI
–	xs:QName
–	xs:NOTATION
INTERVAL *(day-time interval)*	xdt:dayTimeDuration
INTERVAL *(year-month interval)*	xdt:yearMonthDuration
XML	xs:anyType
–	xs:anySimpleType
–	xdt:untyped
(*Structured types?*)	Node types
(*Structured types?*)	*User-defined complex types*
ROW	–
REF	–
ARRAY	(*List types, sequences*)
MULTISET	(*List types, sequences*)
DATALINK	–

twist and turn of a language as complete – and as complex – as XQuery, but we think this chapter has provided a good introduction.

Chapter 12

XQueryX

12.1 Introduction

XQueryX is an alternative syntax for the XQuery language, where a query is represented as a well-formed XML document (as opposed to just a string of characters). There is a mindset in the XML world that says, "XML is a good way of representing stuff, and therefore all stuff should be represented as XML." For example, one of the advantages of XML Schema over DTDs is that an XML Schema is an XML document, while a DTD is not. This turns out to be a very practical way to go about things – it really *is* useful to be able to treat an XML Schema, or an XQuery, as an XML document. It means you can:

- Validate it against an XML Schema (an XML Schema can be validated against the Schema for Schemas,[1] and an XQueryX can be validated against the XQueryX Schema).[2]
- Create it with an XML editing tool.

---

1 *XML Schema Part 1: Structures, Second Edition, Appendix A: Schema for Schemas (normative)* (Cambridge, MA: World Wide Web Consortium, 2004). Available at http://w3.org/TR/xmlschema-1/#normative-schemaSchema.

2 *XML Syntax for XQuery 1.0 (XQueryX), Section 4: An XML Schema for the XQuery XML Syntax* (Cambridge, MA: World Wide Web Consortium, 2005). Available at http://www.w3.org/TR/xqueryx/#Schema.

- Store it the same way you store other XML documents.
- Pass it around as an XML document, *e.g.*, as a SOAP message.
- Query it, using XPath or XQuery — or XQueryX.
- Embed it in another XML document.

The XQueryX spec[3] notes a couple of other benefits of an XML representation of an XQuery — parser reuse and automatic query generation. In fact, many people believe that XQueryX is the only XML query syntax we need — after all (the argument goes), nobody actually writes queries by hand; they write *applications* that write queries. So what if XQueryX is verbose and difficult to read and write, only *applications* will read and write XQueries, so it's more important to make the language machine-readable/writable than human-readable/writable. That argument does have supporters, but the bulk of the XQuery Working Group's efforts have gone into creating the human-readable/writable syntax for XQuery. XQueryX, though recognized as a requirement early on, has been defined as an adjunct to the non-XML syntax.

Given the XQuery language, there are a number of ways you *could* define an XML syntax (that is, a way to represent any possible XQuery in XML). In Section 12.2 we describe two possible extremes — a trivial embedding and a fully parsed XQuery — and we describe some of the design features of XQueryX. In Section 12.3 we describe how the XQueryX spec defines XQueryX. In Section 12.4 we look closely at some example XQueries and their XQueryX representations. And in Section 12.5 we discuss how and why you might query XQueryX documents.

12.2 How Far to Go?

There is a non-XML, human-readable/writable syntax for the XQuery language, and we want to define an XML syntax based on that language. The XML syntax must be able to express exactly what the non-XML syntax expresses, no more and no less. And it probably should be recognizable as an XML representation of the non-XML

3 *XML Syntax for XQuery 1.0 (XQueryX)* (Cambridge, MA: World Wide Web Consortium, 2005). Available at: http://www.w3.org/TR/xqueryx/.

syntax, reusing the same keywords and clauses.[4] But how far should XQueryX go in the direction of XML? Let's look at the two possible extremes – a trivial embedding of XQuery into XML, and an XML representation of a parsed XQuery – before discussing what XQueryX actually does.

12.2.1 Trivial Embedding

The simplest way to represent the XQuery syntax as XML is just to wrap each query in a start tag and an end tag, as in Example 12-1.

Example 12-1 *Trivial Embedding (1)*

```
<xquery>
for $b in doc("movies-we-own.xml")/movies/movie
where $b/yearReleased = 1981
return ($b/title, $b/director)
</xquery>
```

This trivial embedding works for some queries, but what if the query includes, *e.g.*, a less-than sign? The resulting XML would not be well-formed, unless you escaped the less-than sign somehow. You could wrap the whole query in a CDATA section, effectively escaping any special characters that might occur in the query (Example 12-2).

Example 12-2 *Trivial Embedding (2)*

```
<xquery>
<![CDATA[
for $b in doc("movies-we-own.xml")/movies/movie
where $b/yearReleased < 1981
return ($b/title, $b/director)
]]>
</xquery>
```

But you can't apply that strategy blindly either – if there is already a CDATA section as part of the query, wrapping it in another CDATA section again creates something that is not well-formed XML

4 This is not, of course, necessary. The XQuery Working Group could have defined an abstract notion of the XQuery language and then defined two (or more!) ways to serialize instances of that language independently.

(CDATA sections cannot be nested in well-formed XML). So the most trivial embedding that will work for all queries is one that involves either wrapping each special character in the query in a CDATA section, or replacing each special character with a character entity reference (Example 12-3).

Example 12-3 *Trivial Embedding (3)*

```
<xquery>
for $b in doc("movies-we-own.xml")/movies/movie
where $b/yearReleased &lt; 1981
return ($b/title, $b/director)
</xquery>
```

So the "trivial embedding" approach is not entirely trivial. And it only achieves *some of* the goals for an XML syntax. A query like the one in Example 12-3 is certainly well-formed XML, but it has no real structure to it – it's just a single element that contains the full text of the query. You could pass this in a SOAP message or embed it in an XML document, but you could not perform meaningful queries against it, nor could you store it as XML. And this syntax does not help with parser reuse or automatic query generation – the text of the query needs to be parsed (or generated) in exactly the same way as the non-XML query, but with two more tags and some CDATA sections and/or character entity references to consider. However, the "trivial embedding" approach is considered useful, and the XQueryX Schema and stylesheet both support it – *i.e.*, Example 12-3 is a valid XQueryX instance.

12.2.2 Fully-Parsed XQuery

The opposite extreme to trivial embedding would be to represent the fully-parsed form of an XQuery as XML, where each language construct, down to individual characters, is a separate element or attribute. By adopting this approach, you achieve all the benefits of XQueryX – a query needs to be parsed only once (when you first create the XQueryX), and this form is easy to generate automatically (as a natural by-product of parsing the query). The downside to this approach is its verbosity – you'll see in Example 12-5 just how long the simplest XQueryX would be if it mapped every XQuery grammar production. And, as you'll see in Section 12.2.3, it is possible to define XQueryX so that XQueryX queries are even more amenable to being queried than this fully-parsed representation.

12.2.3 The XQueryX Approach

The approach taken in the XQueryX spec is fairly close to the "Fully-Parsed XQuery." That is, an XQueryX looks *quite* like an XML representation of the parsed form of an XQuery. There are two broad areas where XQueryX deviates from a straightforward parsed query mapping.

First, XQueryX does not reflect every production, and it does not represent "empty" parts of a production (parts of a production that are optional, and that don't exist in the XQuery being represented). If XQueryX *did* faithfully represent every part of every grammar production, then XQueryX queries would be even more verbose than they are under the current spec — see Example 12-5 for an example.

Second, XQueryX represents constructs such as expressions, operators, and literals so that their representation (in an XQueryX instance document) is concise, yet you can create broad or narrow queries (to search for nodes higher or lower in the parse tree). We look at each of these in turn, illustrating them with fragments of the XQueryX Schema and fragments of an XQueryX instance document. In the XQueryX instance fragments, we use the namespace prefix "`xqx`."

Expressions

There are many different kinds of expressions in XQuery — the FLWOR expression, the path expression, *etc.* In XQueryX, each kind of expression is represented by an element with a name describing that kind of expression. For example, a path expression is represented by an element called "`pathExpr`." An element representing a kind of expression has a Schema type with the same name as the element name, based on the "`expr`" type. For example, the type "`pathExpr`" is defined in the XQueryX Schema as an extension of the "`expr`" type, like this:

```
<xs:complexType name="pathExpr">
  <xs:complexContent>
    <xs:extension base="expr">
      <xs:sequence>
        <xs:sequence minOccurs="0">
          <xs:element name="argExpr" type="exprWrapper"/>
          <xs:element name="predicates" type="exprList" minOccurs="0"/>
        </xs:sequence>
        <xs:element ref="stepExpr" minOccurs="0" maxOccurs="unbounded"/>
```

```
      </xs:sequence>
    </xs:extension>
  </xs:complexContent>
</xs:complexType>
```

The *element* "`pathExpr`" has the *type* "`pathExpr`" (an extension of the *type* "`expr`"), and is a member of the *substitution group* "`expr`":

```
<xs:element name="pathExpr" type="pathExpr" substitutionGroup="expr"/>
```

The *type* "`expr`" is defined in the XQueryX Schema, along with an "`expr`" element, like this:

```
<xs:complexType name="expr"/>
<xs:element name="expr" type="expr" abstract="true"/>
```

Notice that the "`expr`" element is marked as *abstract*. That means you can't have an element of that name in a valid XQueryX instance document, but you can define a *substitution group* with the element "`expr`" as its *head element*.[5] In general, we can say that "`expr`" represents a *base class* for all expressions in XQueryX, and each kind of expression is a sub*class* of "`expr`."

A path expression in an XQuery is represented in an XQueryX instance as:

```
<xqx:pathExpr>
    ....
</xqx:pathExpr>
```

It is easy for the human reader to see that this is a path expression (an element with both name and type of "`xqx:pathExpr`"). Perhaps more importantly, it is easy to run an XQuery over one or more XQueryX instance documents to find all path expressions. You can also do a broader search, for all expressions. There are (at least) two ways to achieve such a search. First, `schema-element(expr)` matches any element in the substitution group headed by "`expr`"

5 For information about substitution groups and abstract types, see Sections 4.6 and 4.7 of: *XML Schema Part 0: Primer, Second Edition* (Cambridge, MA: World Wide Web Consortium, 2004). Available at: http://www.w3.org/TR/xmlschema-0/#SubsGroups.

whose type matches, or is derived from, the type of the "`expr`" element (*i.e.*, matches any expression). Second, `element(*, expr)` matches any element with any name ("`*`") with a type that matches, or is derived from, the type "`expr`" (again, matches any expression). See Example 12-10 and Example 12-11.

Operators

Let's look closely at the "less than" comparison operator ("<") as an example of an operator. The relevant XQuery grammar production is:

```
[48] ComparisonExpr        ::= RangeExpr ( (ValueComp
                                | GeneralComp
                                | NodeComp) RangeExpr )?
```

XQueryX does not map this production exactly. Instead, XQueryX represents "less than" as an element called "`lessThanOp`", of type "`binaryOperatorExpr`", belonging to the substitution group headed by "`generalComparisonOp`". The type "`binaryOperatorExpr`" is based on the type "`operatorExpr`", which in turn is based on the type "`expr`". The Schema definition of the type "`binaryOperatorExpr`" dictates that an element of this type must have two child elements, "`firstOperand`" and "`secondOperand`", each of type "`exprWrapper`". Here's how all that looks in the XQueryX Schema document:

```
<xs:element name="lessThanOp" type="binaryOperatorExpr"
      substitutionGroup="generalComparisonOp"/>

<xs:complexType name="binaryOperatorExpr">
  <xs:complexContent>
    <xs:extension base="operatorExpr">
      <xs:sequence>
        <xs:element name="firstOperand" type="exprWrapper"/>
        <xs:element name="secondOperand" type="exprWrapper"/>
      </xs:sequence>
    </xs:extension>
  </xs:complexContent>
</xs:complexType>

<xs:complexType name="operatorExpr">
  <xs:complexContent>
```

```
      <xs:extension base="expr"/>
    </xs:complexContent>
  </xs:complexType>
```

The "less than" comparison operator is represented in an XQueryX instance document like this:

```
<xqx:lessThanOp>
  <xqx:firstOperand>
    <xqx:varRef>
      <xqx:name>b</xqx:name>
    </xqx:varRef>
  </xqx:firstOperand>
  <xqx:secondOperand>
    <xqx:integerConstantExpr>
      <xqx:value>1985</xqx:value>
    </xqx:integerConstantExpr>
  </xqx:secondOperand>
</xqx:lessThanOp>
```

See Example 12-11 for a complete example.

Given this structure — a type hierarchy plus a substitution group — you can write XQueries to find all "less than" comparisons in one or more XQueryX instances, and you can broaden the search in two ways. First, `schema-element(generalComparisonOp)` matches any element in the substitution group headed by "`generalComparisonOp`" whose type matches, or is derived from, the type of the "`generalComparisonOp`" element (*i.e.*, matches any general comparison operator — "=", "!=", "<", "<=", ">", ">="). Second, `element(*, binaryOperatorExpr)` matches any element with any name ("`*`") with a type that matches, or is derived from, the type "`binaryOperatorExpr`" (*i.e.*, matches any binary operator expression — general comparisons, value comparisons, or node comparisons).

Literals

The XQuery grammar defines two kinds of literals (constants) — string and numeric — and then breaks down numeric literals into integer, decimal, and double, like this:

```
[85] Literal            ::= NumericLiteral | StringLiteral
[86] NumericLiteral     ::= IntegerLiteral
                              | DecimalLiteral
                              | DoubleLiteral
```

The XQueryX Schema, on the other hand, defines a type "`constantExpr`" based on "`expr`", and four subtypes of "`constantExpr`", one each for integers, decimals, doubles, and strings. The XQueryX Schema for "`constantExpr`" and "`integerConstantExpr`" looks like this:

```
<xs:complexType name="constantExpr">
  <xs:complexContent>
    <xs:extension base="expr">
      <xs:sequence>
        <xs:element name="value" type="xs:anyType"/>
      </xs:sequence>
    </xs:extension>
  </xs:complexContent>
</xs:complexType>

<xs:element name="constantExpr" type="constantExpr" abstract="true"
      substitutionGroup="expr"/>

<xs:complexType name="integerConstantExpr">
  <xs:complexContent>
    <xs:restriction base="constantExpr">
      <xs:sequence>
        <xs:element name="value" type="xs:integer"/>
      </xs:sequence>
    </xs:restriction>
  </xs:complexContent>
</xs:complexType>

<xs:element name="integerConstantExpr" type="integerConstantExpr"
      substitutionGroup="constantExpr"/>
```

An XQueryX representation of the integer 42 looks like this:

```
<xqx:integerConstantExpr>
  <xqx:value>42</xqx:value>
</xqx:integerConstantExpr>
```

Once again, you can write an XQuery to do broad or narrow searches across one or more XQueryX instances — find all constants (literals), or all integer constants, or all expressions.

Summary

In summary, XQueryX *nearly* represents the parsed form of an XQuery, representing tokens and atomic values, but not individual characters, as elements. XQueryX represents all the *structure* of the XQuery grammar, including, for example, each step in an XPath expression. This means you can query a collection of queries to find out, *e.g.*, how many queries include some string literal, or which queries include a particular XPath axis (see Section 12.5). XQueryX does *not* include a one-to-one representation of every XQuery grammar production — instead, it uses subtyping and substitution groups to enable broad or narrow queries over (fairly) concise XQueryX instances.

12.3 The XQueryX Specification

Now that you have the general flavor of the XQueryX approach to representing XQueries in XML, let's look at the XQueryX specification before stepping through some complete examples.

The XQueryX specification defines XQueryX by providing an XML Schema, which defines the syntax of XQueryX, and a stylesheet, which defines the semantics. The spec also includes some worked examples and a definition of a *trivial embedding*.

The XQueryX Schema defines what an XQueryX query can look like. The Schema follows the XQuery grammar quite closely. The size of an XQueryX query is kept manageable by skipping some productions, and by not forcing empty productions to be represented. In Section 12.4, we take some example XQueries and look at the XQuery grammar rules, the XQueryX Schema, and the XQueryX representation of the query together.

The semantics of XQueryX are defined by the XQueryX stylesheet — *i.e.*, the meaning of any XQueryX instance is the meaning of the XQuery produced by applying the XQueryX stylesheet to it. The XQueryX spec does not explain how to get from XQuery to XQueryX, but the stylesheet ensures that we always know when we get there.

12.4 XQueryX By Example

The XQueryX specification does not give any guidelines on how to produce an XQueryX instance (query), given an XQuery. But if you study the XQuery grammar productions, the XQueryX Schema, and the examples in the XQueryX specification, it's not too difficult to produce XQueryX queries. If you are not too sure how your XQuery should parse, you can get (some of) the parse tree for an XQuery from the XQuery grammar test applet.[6] And of course you can check the resulting XQueryX query by running it past the XQueryX stylesheet and checking the result against your original XQuery.

12.4.1 The Simplest XQueryX Example — 42

Let's start with a simple example — the number 42. 42 is a valid XQuery, so we can produce an XQueryX query that represents it. In the XQueryX query examples in this section, we show first the XQuery, then the XQueryX query, and then the result of applying the XQueryX stylesheet to the XQuery. The latter is semantically equivalent to the original XQuery.

Example 12-4 *XQueryX (1)*

XQuery:

```
 42
```

XQueryX query:

```
<?xml version="1.0" encoding="UTF-8"?>
<!-- XQueryX syntax for:
      42
-->
<xqx:module
      xmlns:xsi="http://www.w3.org/2001/XMLSchema-instance"
      xmlns:xqx="http://www.w3.org/2005/07/XQueryX"
      xsi:schemaLocation="http://www.w3.org/2005/07/XQueryX xqueryx.xsd">
  <xqx:mainModule>
    <xqx:queryBody>
```

6 At the time of writing, the latest XQuery grammar test applet is at http://www.w3.org/2005/04/qt-applets/xqueryApplet.html — you can find a link to it on the main W3C XQuery page, http://www.w3.org/XML/Query.

```
        <xqx:integerConstantExpr>
          <xqx:value>42</xqx:value>
        </xqx:integerConstantExpr>
      </xqx:queryBody>
    </xqx:mainModule>
</xqx:module>
```

XQuery, XQueryX query + stylesheet:

```
42
```

To see how we got from the XQuery 42 to Example 12-4, take a look at the XQuery grammar EBNF. The first production is:

```
[1]  Module        ::=  VersionDecl? (MainModule | LibraryModule)
```

This says that an XQuery is a `Module`, which is an optional `VersionDecl` followed by either a `MainModule` or a `LibraryModule`. We don't need a version declaration, and we don't have any library modules, so our XQueryX query is just a module element with one child, `mainModule`. So, what constitutes a `MainModule`?

```
[3]  MainModule    ::=  Prolog QueryBody
[6]  Prolog        ::=  (Setter Separator)* ((Import | NamespaceDecl |
                        DefaultNamespaceDecl) Separator)* ((VarDecl |
                        FunctionDecl) Separator)*| VarDecl | FunctionDecl)
                        Separator)*
```

A `MainModule` is a Prolog followed by a `QueryBody`, and all the parts of the Prolog are optional. One *could* argue that the XQueryX should contain an empty `prolog` element — after all, the prolog is not optional, it's mandatory, though it may be empty. The XQueryX spec misses this subtlety, so we can leave out the prolog altogether and look at what makes up a `QueryBody`.

```
[30] QueryBody     ::=  Expr
[31] Expr          ::=  ExprSingle ("," ExprSingle)*
```

A `QueryBody` is an `Expr`, and an `Expr` is one or more `ExprSingles` separated by commas. At this point we have to take a long walk through several grammar productions to find that an `ExprSingle` can be just a `PathExpr`. This may look a little convoluted, but it works for XQuery — the grammar is (mostly) LL(1) (meaning you can parse any statement by looking at each token from left to right, never having to look ahead more than one token), and the precedence of the operators such as "and" and "or" is implicitly defined by the grammar productions — operator precedence doesn't have to be defined separately. Scott Boag, XQuery grammar guru, calls this *cascading precedence*. You'll read more about the XQuery grammar in Appendix C: XQuery 1.0 Grammar. For now, it's enough to read through the next few grammar productions, ignoring anything that is optional.

```
[32]  ExprSingle     ::=  FLWORExpr
                          | QuantifiedExpr
                          | TypeswitchExpr
                          | IfExpr
                          | OrExpr
[46]  OrExpr         ::=  AndExpr ( "or" AndExpr )*
[47]  AndExpr        ::=  ComparisonExpr ( "and" ComparisonExpr )*
[48]  ComparisonExpr      ::=  RangeExpr ( (ValueComp
                               | GeneralComp
                               | NodeComp) RangeExpr )?
[49]  RangeExpr      ::=  AdditiveExpr ( "to" AdditiveExpr )?
[50]  AdditiveExpr   ::=  MultiplicativeExpr ( ("+" | "-")
                            MultiplicativeExpr )*
[51]  MultiplicativeExpr   ::=  UnionExpr ( ("*" | "div" | "idiv" | "mod")
                                   UnionExpr )*
[52]  UnionExpr      ::=  IntersectExceptExpr ( ("union" | "|")
                             IntersectExceptExpr )*
[53]  IntersectExceptExpr ::=  InstanceofExpr ( ("intersect" |
                                  "except") InstanceofExpr )*
[54]  InstanceofExpr      ::=  TreatExpr ( <"instance" "of">
                                  SequenceType )?
[55]  TreatExpr      ::=  CastableExpr ( <"treat" "as"> SequenceType )?
[56]  CastableExpr   ::=  CastExpr ( <"castable" "as"> SingleType )?
[57]  CastExpr       ::=  UnaryExpr ( <"cast" "as"> SingleType )?
[58]  UnaryExpr      ::=  ("-" | "+")* ValueExpr
[59]  ValueExpr      ::=  ValidateExpr | PathExpr
```

So an `ExprSingle` can be a `PathExpr`. In the same way, a `PathExpr` can be simply an `IntegerLiteral` (`PathExpr` = `RelativePathExpr` = `StepExpr` = `FilterExpr` = `PrimaryExpr` = `Literal` = `NumericLiteral` = `IntegerLiteral`).

```
[68]  PathExpr        ::=  ("/" RelativePathExpr?)
                           | ("//" RelativePathExpr)
                           | RelativePathExpr
[69]  RelativePathExpr   ::=  StepExpr (("/" | "//") StepExpr)*
[70]  StepExpr        ::=  AxisStep | FilterExpr
[81]  FilterExpr      ::=  PrimaryExpr PredicateList
[84]  PrimaryExpr     ::=  Literal | VarRef | ParenthesizedExpr |
                           ContextItemExpr | FunctionCall | Constructor |
                           OrderedExpr | UnorderedExpr
[85]  Literal         ::=  NumericLiteral | StringLiteral
[86] NumericLiteral     ::= IntegerLiteral | DecimalLiteral |
                             DoubleLiteral
```

Finally, an `IntegerLiteral` is a `Digits`, which is a sequence of one or more characters in the range 0 through 9.

```
[141] IntegerLiteral       ::=  Digits
[158] Digits          ::=  [0-9]+
```

The simplest way to represent the XQuery 42 as XML, mapping each grammar rule in turn into a new element, would yield the XQueryX-like syntax in Example 12-5.

Example 12-5 Not *an XQueryX*

```
<?xml version="1.0" encoding="UTF-8"?>
<!-- notXQueryX syntax for: 42 -->
<notxqx:module
      xmlns:xsi="http://www.w3.org/2001/XMLSchema-instance"
      xmlns:notxqx="http://example.com/notXQueryX"
      xsi:schemaLocation="http://example.com/notXQueryX notxqueryx.xsd">
            <notxqx:mainModule>
  <notxqx:queryBody>
   <notxqx:expr>
    <notxqx:exprSingle>
     <notxqx:orExpr>
      <notxqx:andExpr>
```

```
<notxqx:comparisonExpr>
 <notxqx:rangeExpr>
  <notxqx:additiveExpr>
   <notxqx:multiplicativeExpr>
    <notxqx:unionExpr>
     <notxqx:intersectExceptExpr>
      <notxqx:instanceofExpr>
       <notxqx:treatExpr>
        <notxqx:castableExpr>
         <notxqx:castExpr>
          <notxqx:unaryExpr>
           <notxqx:valueExpr>
            <notxqx:pathExpr>
             <notxqx:relativePathExpr>
              <notxqx:stepExpr>
               <notxqx:filterExpr>
                <notxqx:primaryExpr>
                 <notxqx:literal>
                  <notxqx:numericLiteral>
                   <notxqx:digits>42</notxqx:digits>
                  </notxqx:numericLiteral>
                 </notxqx:literal>
                </notxqx:primaryExpr>
               </notxqx:filterExpr>
               <notxqx:elementTest/>
              </notxqx:stepExpr>
             </notxqx:relativePathExpr>
            </notxqx:pathExpr>
           </notxqx:valueExpr>
          </notxqx:unaryExpr>
         </notxqx:castExpr>
        </notxqx:castableExpr>
       </notxqx:treatExpr>
      </notxqx:instanceofExpr>
     </notxqx:intersectExceptExpr>
    </notxqx:unionExpr>
   </notxqx:multiplicativeExpr>
  </notxqx:additiveExpr>
 </notxqx:rangeExpr>
</notxqx:comparisonExpr>
</notxqx:andExpr>
```

```
      </notxqx:orExpr>
     </notxqx:exprSingle>
    </notxqx:expr>
   </notxqx:queryBody>
  </notxqx:mainModule>
</notxqx:module>
```

Example 12-5 is quite a mouthful for a simple query, and it's not terribly useful for searching. To improve this situation, XQueryX represents only the meaningful steps in parsing this query. The definition of "meaningful" here is somewhat subjective – in general, XQueryX includes elements that have some content and/or are useful for searching. In Example 12-4, the XQueryX query contains an element for each of the `module`, `mainModule`, and `queryBody` productions, and then it skips to an `integerConstantExpr` element. `module`, `mainModule`, and `queryBody` are defined in the XQueryX Schema in an obvious way, like this:

```
<xs:element name="module">
  <xs:complexType>
    <xs:sequence>
      <xs:element ref="versionDecl" minOccurs="0"/>
      <xs:choice>
        <xs:element ref="mainModule"/>
        <xs:element ref="libraryModule"/>
      </xs:choice>
    </xs:sequence>
  </xs:complexType>
</xs:element>

<xs:element name="mainModule">
  <xs:complexType>
    <xs:sequence>
      <xs:element ref="prolog" minOccurs="0"/>
      <xs:element name="queryBody" type="exprWrapper"/>
    </xs:sequence>
  </xs:complexType>
</xs:element>
```

This gives us the pattern for our example XQueryX query, minus the contents of the `queryBody`:

```
<xqx:module
      xmlns:xsi="http://www.w3.org/2001/XMLSchema-instance"
      xmlns:xqx="http://www.w3.org/2005/07/XQueryX"
      xsi:schemaLocation="http://www.w3.org/2005/07/XQueryX xqueryx.xsd">
  <xqx:mainModule>
    <xqx:queryBody>
     ...
    </xqx:queryBody>
  </xqx:mainModule>
</xqx:module>
```

We have already met the `integerConstantExpr` element, in Section 12.2.3 – it has a single child element, `value`, of type `xs:integer`, which yields the XQueryX query in Example 12-4 – a relatively compact, easy-to-search XML representation of the XQuery 42.

Before we look at a slightly less simple example, we should point out that embedded expressions – expressions that occur "inside" other expressions – are defined as type `xqx:exprWrapper` in the XQueryX Schema, not as `xqx:expr`. `xqx:exprWrapper` is, as its name implies, a wrapper around the `expr` type:

```
<!-- Simple wrapper class -->
<xs:complexType name="exprWrapper">
  <xs:sequence>
    <xs:element ref="expr"/>
  </xs:sequence>
</xs:complexType>
<xs:element name="exprWrapper" type="exprWrapper"/>
```

The purpose of `exprWrapper` is to provide an additional level of abstraction on `expr`, which may be used in a later version of the spec. At the time of writing, it serves no useful purpose.

12.4.2 Simple XQueryX Example

Now let's look at an XQuery that is a bit less simple than Example 12-4. Example 12-6 is still not a terribly useful query, but it has a few more constructs for us to look at.

Example 12-6 *Simple XQuery Example*

```
xquery version "1.0";
let $b := 42
return $b
```

We start, as before, with a Module. This time there is a VersionDecl as well as a MainModule. The VersionDecl is

```
[1]   Module        ::= VersionDecl? (MainModule | LibraryModule)
[2]   VersionDecl   ::= <"xquery" "version"> StringLiteral ("encoding"
                        StringLiteral)? Separator
[9]   Separator     ::= ";"
[144] StringLiteral ::= ('"' (PredefinedEntityRef | CharRef | EscapeQuot |
                        [^"&])* '"') |
                        ("'" (PredefinedEntityRef | CharRef | EscapeApos |
                        [^'&])* "'")
```

But the only nonkeyword information in VersionDecl is the string containing the xquery version, so the XQueryX Schema defines the version declaration like this:

```
<xs:element name="versionDecl">
  <xs:complexType>
    <xs:sequence>
      <xs:element name="version" type="xs:string"/>
    </xs:sequence>
  </xs:complexType>
</xs:element>
```

So we represent the module (this time with a version declaration), mainModule, and queryBody in our XQueryX query like this:

```
<xqx:module
     xmlns:xsi="http://www.w3.org/2001/XMLSchema-instance"
     xmlns:xqx="http://www.w3.org/2005/07/XQueryX"
     xsi:schemaLocation="http://www.w3.org/2005/07/XQueryX xqueryx.xsd">
  <xqx:versionDecl>
    <xqx:version>1.0</xqx:version>
  </xqx:versionDecl>
  <xqx:mainModule>
```

```
    <xqx:queryBody>
      ...
    </xqx:queryBody>
  </xqx:mainModule>
</xqx:module>
```

Inside the `mainModule` we have a `queryBody`, as before. This time the expression inside the `queryBody` is a FLWOR expression. The XQuery grammar defines a FLWOR expression like this:

```
[30]  FLWORExpr    ::=  (ForClause | LetClause)+ WhereClause?
                         OrderByClause? "return" ExprSingle
```

The XQueryX Schema represents a FLWOR expression like this:

```
<xs:complexType name="flworExpr">
  <xs:complexContent>
    <xs:extension base="expr">
      <xs:sequence>
        <xs:choice maxOccurs="unbounded">
          <xs:element ref="forClause"/>
          <xs:element ref="letClause"/>
        </xs:choice>
        <xs:element ref="whereClause" minOccurs="0"/>
        <xs:element ref="orderByClause" minOccurs="0"/>
        <xs:element ref="returnClause"/>
      </xs:sequence>
    </xs:extension>
  </xs:complexContent>
</xs:complexType>

<xs:element name="flworExpr" type="flworExpr" substitutionGroup="expr"/>
```

So the XQueryX looks like this:

```
<xqx:module
      xmlns:xsi="http://www.w3.org/2001/XMLSchema-instance"
      xmlns:xqx="http://www.w3.org/2005/07/XQueryX"
      xsi:schemaLocation="http://www.w3.org/2005/07/XQueryX xqueryx.xsd">
```

```
    <xqx:versionDecl>
      <xqx:version>1.0</xqx:version>
    </xqx:versionDecl>
    <xqx:mainModule>
      <xqx:queryBody>
        <xqx:flworExpr>
          <xqx:letClause>
                ...
          </xqx:letClause>
          <xqx:returnClause>
                ...
          </xqx:returnClause>
        </xqx:flworExpr>
      </xqx:queryBody>
    </xqx:mainModule>
  </xqx:module>
```

Inside the `letClause`, the XQueryX maps less closely to the XQuery grammar productions, because XQueryX represents the structure of the query as an XML tree instead of with keywords. The XQuery grammar defines the `LetClause` as:

```
[36]  LetClause    ::=  <"let" "$"> VarName TypeDeclaration? ":="
                        ExprSingle ("," "$" VarName TypeDeclaration? ":="
                        ExprSingle)*
[88]  VarName      ::=  QName
[154] QName        ::=  [http://www.w3.org/TR/REC-xml-names/#NT-QName]
```

This becomes the XQueryX Schema definitions:

```
<xs:element name="letClauseItem">
  <xs:complexType>
    <xs:sequence>
      <xs:element ref="typedVariableBinding"/>
      <xs:element name="letExpr" type="exprWrapper"/>
    </xs:sequence>
  </xs:complexType>
</xs:element>

<xs:element name="letClause">
  <xs:complexType>
```

```
    <xs:sequence>
      <xs:element ref="letClauseItem" maxOccurs="unbounded"/>
    </xs:sequence>
  </xs:complexType>
</xs:element>

<xs:element name="typedVariableBinding">
  <xs:complexType>
    <xs:sequence>
      <xs:element name="varName" type="QName"/>
      <xs:element ref="typeDeclaration" minOccurs="0"/>
    </xs:sequence>
  </xs:complexType>
</xs:element>
```

Adding the content of the `LetClause` to our XQueryX, we get:

```
<xqx:module
      xmlns:xsi="http://www.w3.org/2001/XMLSchema-instance"
      xmlns:xqx="http://www.w3.org/2005/07/XQueryX"
      xsi:schemaLocation="http://www.w3.org/2005/07/XQueryX
xqueryx.xsd">
  <xqx:versionDecl>
    <xqx:version>1.0</xqx:version>
  </xqx:versionDecl>
  <xqx:mainModule>
    <xqx:queryBody>
      <xqx:flworExpr>
        <xqx:letClause>
          <xqx:letClauseItem>
            <xqx:typedVariableBinding>
              <xqx:varName>b</xqx:varName>
            </xqx:typedVariableBinding>
            <xqx:letExpr>
              <xqx:integerConstantExpr>
                <xqx:value>42</xqx:value>
              </xqx:integerConstantExpr>
            </xqx:letExpr>
          </xqx:letClauseItem>
        </xqx:letClause>
        <xqx:returnClause>
          ...
```

```
        </xqx:returnClause>
      </xqx:flworExpr>
    </xqx:queryBody>
  </xqx:mainModule>
</xqx:module>
```

Finally, we need to add the contents of the `returnClause`. We follow the same steps as for the `LetClause` — that is, look at the XQuery grammar definition:

```
[33] FLWORExpr     ::=  (ForClause | LetClause)+ WhereClause?
                        OrderByClause? "return" ExprSingle
```

Here, the XQuery grammar designers have decided not to split out return as a separate clause. This rule could have been (but was not) written as two rules:

```
[33] FLWORExpr     ::=  (ForClause | LetClause)+ WhereClause?
                        OrderByClause? returnClause
[NN] returnClause  ::=  "return" ExprSingle
```

The XQueryX Schema is written as though the `returnClause` were a separate grammar rule:

```
<xs:element name="returnClause" type="exprWrapper"/>
```

Here's how the `returnClause` looks in XQueryX:

```
<xqx:returnClause>
  <xqx:varRef>
    <xqx:name>b</xqx:name>
  </xqx:varRef>
</xqx:returnClause>
```

Putting it all together, the XQuery in Example 12-6 can be written in XQueryX as in Example 12-7.

Example 12-7 *XQueryX (2)*

```
XQuery:

xquery version "1.0";
let $b := 42
return $b

XQueryX query:

<?xml version="1.0" encoding="UTF-8"?>
<!-- XQueryX syntax for:
      xquery version "1.0";
      let $b := 42
      return $b
-->
<xqx:module
      xmlns:xsi="http://www.w3.org/2001/XMLSchema-instance"
      xmlns:xqx="http://www.w3.org/2005/07/XQueryX"
      xsi:schemaLocation="http://www.w3.org/2005/07/XQueryX
xqueryx.xsd">
  <xqx:versionDecl>
    <xqx:version>1.0</xqx:version>
  </xqx:versionDecl>
  <xqx:mainModule>
    <xqx:queryBody>
      <xqx:flworExpr>
        <xqx:letClause>
          <xqx:letClauseItem>
            <xqx:typedVariableBinding>
              <xqx:varName>b</xqx:varName>
            </xqx:typedVariableBinding>
            <xqx:letExpr>
              <xqx:integerConstantExpr>
                <xqx:value>42</xqx:value>
              </xqx:integerConstantExpr>
            </xqx:letExpr>
          </xqx:letClauseItem>
        </xqx:letClause>
        <xqx:returnClause>
          <xqx:varRef>
            <xqx:name>b</xqx:name>
```

```
                    </xqx:varRef>
                  </xqx:returnClause>
                </xqx:flworExpr>
              </xqx:queryBody>
            </xqx:mainModule>
          </xqx:module>
```

```
XQuery, XQueryX query + stylesheet:
 xquery version "1.0";

 let $b:=42
 return $b
```

12.4.3 Useful XQuery Example

These first two example queries are too simple to be useful. We'll close this section with Example 12-8, a query taken from Chapter 10, "Introduction to XQuery 1.0."

Example 12-8 *A Simple but Useful XQuery Written in XQueryX (3)*

```
XQuery:

for $b in doc("movies-we-own.xml")/movies/movie
where $b/yearReleased < 1985
return (data($b/title), $b/director)
```

```
XQueryX:
```

```
<?xml version="1.0" encoding="UTF-8"?>
<!-- XQueryX syntax for:
  for $b in doc("movies-we-own.xml")/movies/movie
  where $b/yearReleased < 1985
  return (data($b/title), $b/director)
-->
<xqx:module
      xmlns:xsi="http://www.w3.org/2001/XMLSchema-instance"
      xmlns:xqx="http://www.w3.org/2005/07/XQueryX"
      xsi:schemaLocation="http://www.w3.org/2005/07/XQueryX xqueryx.xsd">
  <xqx:mainModule>
    <xqx:queryBody>
      <xqx:flworExpr>
```

```
<xqx:forClause>
  <xqx:forClauseItem>
    <xqx:typedVariableBinding>
      <xqx:varName>b</xqx:varName>
    </xqx:typedVariableBinding>
    <xqx:forExpr>
      <xqx:pathExpr>
        <xqx:argExpr>
          <xqx:functionCallExpr>
            <xqx:functionName>doc</xqx:functionName>
            <xqx:arguments>
              <xqx:stringConstantExpr>
                <xqx:value>movies-we-own.xml</xqx:value>
              </xqx:stringConstantExpr>
            </xqx:arguments>
          </xqx:functionCallExpr>
        </xqx:argExpr>
        <xqx:stepExpr>
          <xqx:xpathAxis>child</xqx:xpathAxis>
          <xqx:elementTest>
            <xqx:elementName>
              <xqx:QName>movies</xqx:QName>
            </xqx:elementName>
          </xqx:elementTest>
        </xqx:stepExpr>
        <xqx:stepExpr>
          <xqx:xpathAxis>child</xqx:xpathAxis>
          <xqx:elementTest>
            <xqx:elementName>
              <xqx:QName>movie</xqx:QName>
            </xqx:elementName>
          </xqx:elementTest>
        </xqx:stepExpr>
      </xqx:pathExpr>
    </xqx:forExpr>
  </xqx:forClauseItem>
</xqx:forClause>
<xqx:whereClause>
  <xqx:lessThanOp>
    <xqx:firstOperand>
      <xqx:pathExpr>
```

```
            <xqx:argExpr>
              <xqx:varRef>
                <xqx:name>b</xqx:name>
              </xqx:varRef>
            </xqx:argExpr>
            <xqx:stepExpr>
              <xqx:xpathAxis>child</xqx:xpathAxis>
              <xqx:elementTest>
                <xqx:elementName>
                  <xqx:QName>yearReleased</xqx:QName>
                </xqx:elementName>
              </xqx:elementTest>
            </xqx:stepExpr>
          </xqx:pathExpr>
        </xqx:firstOperand>
        <xqx:secondOperand>
          <xqx:integerConstantExpr>
            <xqx:value>1985</xqx:value>
          </xqx:integerConstantExpr>
        </xqx:secondOperand>
      </xqx:lessThanOp>
    </xqx:whereClause>
    <xqx:returnClause>
      <xqx:sequenceExpr>
        <xqx:functionCallExpr>
          <xqx:functionName>data</xqx:functionName>
          <xqx:arguments>
            <xqx:pathExpr>
              <xqx:argExpr>
                <xqx:varRef>
                  <xqx:name>b</xqx:name>
                </xqx:varRef>
              </xqx:argExpr>
              <xqx:stepExpr>
                <xqx:xpathAxis>child</xqx:xpathAxis>
                <xqx:elementTest>
                  <xqx:elementName>
                    <xqx:QName>title</xqx:QName>
                  </xqx:elementName>
                </xqx:elementTest>
              </xqx:stepExpr>
```

```
                </xqx:pathExpr>
              </xqx:arguments>
            </xqx:functionCallExpr>
            <xqx:pathExpr>
              <xqx:argExpr>
                <xqx:varRef>
                  <xqx:name>b</xqx:name>
                </xqx:varRef>
              </xqx:argExpr>
              <xqx:stepExpr>
                <xqx:xpathAxis>child</xqx:xpathAxis>
                <xqx:elementTest>
                  <xqx:elementName>
                    <xqx:QName>director</xqx:QName>
                  </xqx:elementName>
                </xqx:elementTest>
              </xqx:stepExpr>
            </xqx:pathExpr>
          </xqx:sequenceExpr>
        </xqx:returnClause>
      </xqx:flworExpr>
    </xqx:queryBody>
  </xqx:mainModule>
</xqx:module>
```

XQuery, XQueryX + stylesheet:

```
for $b in
    doc(movies-we-own.xml)/child::element(movies)/child::element(movie)
 where ($b/child::element(yearReleased) < 1985)
 return (data($b/child::element(title)),
    $b/child::element(director))
```

12.5 Querying XQueryX

As we said in Section 12.1, one of the reasons for having an XML syntax for XQuery is so that you can do queries over queries. In this section, we look at two kinds of queries you might want to do over a collection of XQueries — queries that will help you tune your XQuery engine, and queries that will help you improve your application or service. In the examples in the rest of this section we use a new document, "xqueryxs.xml," made up of the XQueryX queries in Example

12-6, Example 12-7, and Example 12-8, with a new root element <queries>. Of course, you could use stylesheets and XSLT transformations to produce reports on XQueryXs instead of using XQueries.

12.5.1 Querying XQueryX for XQuery Tuning

Let's suppose you have built an XQuery engine, and that engine is running all the queries against your movies database. Unfortunately, the queries are not running as fast as you'd like them to. You could look into the XQuery engine code and try to speed up every subroutine, but it would be much more efficient if you knew what kinds of queries people were doing in your application, so that you could focus on that area of the code. (Most readers of this book will not build their own XQuery engine; they will buy one or download one for free. But the creator of that engine needs to know which parts of the engine are being exercised, so that he can improve the engine on your behalf.)

Example 12-9 is a simple XQuery to count how many queries we are dealing with.

Example 12-9 *How Many Queries?*

```
declare namespace xqx = "http://www.w3.org/2005/07/XQueryX";
let $b := doc("xqueryxs.xml")/queries
return count($b/xqx:module)
```

Result:

```
3
```

Example 12-10 is an XQuery that returns an XML document containing a count of all expressions and a count of path expressions. This query makes use of the fact that each expression element has a type based on the "`expr`" type, with the kind of expression denoted by its element name (in this case, "`xqx:pathExpr`"). You can count occurrences of *expressions* (without enumerating them) as well as counting a particular *kind of* expression.

Example 12-10 *Count Expressions and Path Expressions*

```
declare namespace xqx = "http://www.w3.org/2005/07/XQueryX";
let $b := doc("xqueryxs.xml")/queries
return
```

```
  <result>
    <expressions>{count($b/xqx:module//element(*, xqx:expr)}</expressions>
    <pathExpressions>
      {count($b/xqx:module//xqx:pathExpr)}
    </pathExpressions>
  </result>
```

Result:

```
<result>
  <expressions>18</expressions>
  <pathExpressions>4</pathExpressions>
</result>
```

Finally, Example 12-11 produces a report showing all general comparison operators and their parameters. Example 12-11 makes use of the fact that all the general comparison operators are part of the substitution group headed by "`generalComparisonExpr`."

Example 12-11 *Show All General Comparison Operators and Their Parameters*

```
declare namespace xqx = "http://www.w3.org/2005/07/XQueryX";
<result>
  {for $b in
    doc("xqueryxs.xml")/queries//schema-element(generalComparisonExpr)
  return
    <comparison>
      <operator>{ name($b) }</operator>
      <parameter1>{ $b/firstOperand }</parameter1>
      <parameter2>{ $b/secondOperand }</parameter2>
    </comparison>
  }
</result>
```

Result:

```
<result>
  <comparison>
    <operator>lessThanOp</operator>
    <parameter1>
      <xqx:pathExpr>
        <xqx:argExpr>
          <xqx:varRef>
            <xqx:name>b</xqx:name>
```

```
          </xqx:varRef>
        </xqx:argExpr>
        <xqx:stepExpr>
          <xqx:xpathAxis>child</xqx:xpathAxis>
          <xqx:elementTest>
            <xqx:elementName>
              <xqx:QName>yearReleased</xqx:QName>
            </xqx:elementName>
          </xqx:elementTest>
        </xqx:stepExpr>
      </xqx:pathExpr>
    </parameter1>
    <parameter2>
      <xqx:integerConstantExpr>
        <xqx:value>1985</xqx:value>
      </xqx:integerConstantExpr>
    </parameter2>
  </comparison>
</result>
```

12.5.2 Querying XQueryX for Application Improvement

Even if you are not building your own XQuery engine, you probably want to know what kinds of queries your users are doing. You may want to know what kinds of things they are searching for, so that you can make them more readily available.

Suppose you created a public web page so that anyone can search your movies archive. You know lots of people come to the site and do searches, but you want to improve the user experience by offering pull-down lists for some fields and by showing some movies on the home page without the need for a search. Example 12-12 shows a query that would tell you which fields were being used as filters. If you found that "yearReleased" was a popular filter, you might add a pull-down list to your search page to filter on the year that movies were released. Further queries would tell you which ranges were appropriate (5 years? 20 years?). If most of the queries restricted the search to a particular 5-year period, you might display those movies on the first page of your browsable movie archive.

Example 12-12 *Show Which Filters Are Being Used*

```
declare namespace xqx = "http://www.w3.org/2005/07/XQueryX";
  doc("xqueryxs.xml")/queries//xqx:whereClause//xqx:QName
```

12.6 Chapter Summary

In this chapter we looked at XQueryX, an XML syntax for XQueries. There are many ways that an XQuery could be represented as XML — we described two extremes, trivial embedding and completely mapping the parsed query, and then we described the XQueryX approach. The XQueryX approach is to represent the parsed query, leaving out BNF steps that are not useful and treating expressions, operators, and literals in a special way. This leads to a relatively compact XML representation of an XQuery that is particularly useful for searching.

Chapter

13

What's Missing?

13.1 Introduction

In Chapters 9, "XPath 1.0 and XPath 2.0," 10, "Introduction to XQuery 1.0," and 11, "XQuery 1.0 Definition," you've read about the capabilities of XPath and XQuery. XQuery is a rich, expressive language for querying XML representations of data. You will also see in Chapter 15, "SQL/XML," how SQL has been extended to use the expressive capabilities of XQuery in the context of a database, providing an ideal harness for XQuery in enterprise applications. While all of these are powerful languages for querying XML, they're obviously not powerful enough to satisfy all needs.

Whether you are querying *documents* (in the sense of books, articles, papers, *etc.*) or more structured data with small snippets of text (the title and author of a book, or the name and description of a product in a purchase order), the matching expressions that you saw in Chapter 11 miss an entire class of searches – full-text searches. In Section 13.2, we explain what we mean by full-text searches and why (and how) they are different from queries with predicates over structured data. Then we discuss the W3C's efforts to add some full-text capabilities to XPath and XQuery, and we compare the W3C's current XQuery Full-Text drafts with some existing offerings in XML full-text search.

Another serious deficiency of XQuery 1.0 is the inability to *alter* the XML documents and other values that the language is designed to find. Updating data is a natural part of querying those data. Sure, pure search-and-retrieve languages are important tools, but real-world applications quite frequently require the ability to make changes to the XML that has been found and retrieved. While the Requirements for XQuery[1] state that "Version 1.0 of the XML Query Language MUST not preclude the ability to add update capabilities in future versions," there is no requirement that XQuery 1.0 provide those update capabilities.

As you'll learn in this chapter, while vendors are filling the gaps with their own proprietary extensions to XQuery, both of these missing features are already under development in the W3C's XML Query and XSL Working Groups.

13.2 Full-Text

13.2.1 What Is a Full-Text Query?

XQuery today lets you write queries that select data according to some criteria. For example, you can select movies where the running time is exactly 142 minutes, or where the year of release is between 1985 and 1990. But XQuery does *not* (yet) let you write Full-Text queries.

Most people have a general idea of what a Full-Text query does — it searches text-based information, given some words or phrases and some special operators. In this section, we give an informal description of what a Full-Text query is, and what makes it different from other (*i.e.*, structured) queries. Note that in this section we are describing generic Full-Text concepts (and not specifically the W3C work on XQuery Full-Text), and we are using pseudo-syntax in our examples. We'll look at the current W3C approach to XQuery Full-Text later in this chapter.

Words (Tokens)

A Full-Text query allows you to search for *words* inside text data. For example, with a Full-Text query you can search for the word "were-

---

1 *XML Query (XQuery) Requirements, W3C Working Draft* (Cambridge, MA: World Wide Web Consortium, 2003). Available at: http://www.w3.org/TR/2003/WD-xquery-requirements-20031112.

wolf" in the title of any of our movies. The basic unit of Full-Text search is often referred to as a *token* rather than a *word*. *Token* is a more precise term – in Western languages, tokens generally map to words, though some search engines count some phrases, parts of words, and possibly punctuation, as tokens. In many non-Western languages (especially those where whitespace is not used to separate meaningful strings), there is no clear concept of a *word*, and a Full-Text engine has to make some tough decisions on where to draw *token* boundaries (or how to otherwise derive *tokens* from a piece of text). For the rest of this chapter we use the term *word* for convenience.

A common question from non-Full-Text users is, "If Full-Text search is about looking for words inside text, then XQuery already does that with the `contains` function. So what's missing?" The `contains` function does *not* do a Full-Text search – it does a *substring* search. The main difference is that a Full-Text search will generally match only a complete word, and not just part of a string. For example, a Full-Text search for "dent" will not match a piece of text that contains the word "students," but a substring search will.

Also, when running a Full-Text search, there is generally an assumption that the match will be case-insensitive,[2] so that "dent" will match "DENT" as well as "dent" (and "Dent" and "dEnt" and "DEnt" and so on). With substring queries, matching is usually case-sensitive (depending on the collation used), so that the text being searched has to match the case of the search term.

Special Operations

A Full-Text query should be able to support some special operations that are not applicable to *structured search* (non-Full-Text search over dates, numbers, and short strings). These operations fall into four classes.

---

2 Sometimes you do need case-sensitive Full-Text search. For example, you may want to distinguish between an occurrence of a word in general use and an occurrence of the same word used as somebody's name – you may want to search for the word "melt", but not find the person's name "Melt." This is tricky, because a case-sensitive search for "melt" will miss any occurrence of "melt" at the beginning of a sentence. Perhaps more useful is a search that is case-insensitive unless all letters in the word are uppercase – with that rule, you can distinguish between the word "dare" and the acronym "DARE" in your query.

1. *Word expansions.* Often, when you query for a particular word (a query term), you actually want to find things that contain words that are related to the query term, as well as things that contain the query term exactly. For example, when you query for the word "mouse," you might expect to find "mice." This is the *stem* operation – find me all pieces of text which contain some word with the same linguistic root as the query term.[3] You might also expect to find words that are close to "mouse" in a thesaurus – broader terms (mammal, animal), narrower terms (dormouse, field mouse), or related terms (rat, shrew). You might also want to correct for errors in the query term and/or in the text being searched. Spelling errors in the search term are common (how many CD buyers know how to spell "Kajagoogoo"?), but you may also want to forgive common typing errors (letters that are close to each other on a keyboard) or, in the case of OCRed[4] text, common OCR errors (mistaking "i" for "l").
2. *Matching options.* What factors are taken into account when deciding whether a query term matches a word in the text being searched? We have already looked at one kind of matching option, *case.* The answer to the question "does 'DENT' match 'dent'?" depends on the case matching options for the query. Other common matching options are *diacritics* (consider or ignore diacritic marks) and *wildcards* (treat the query term as a string, possibly containing wildcards to be expanded, or as a literal string).
3. *Positional (or "proximity") operations.* You may want to find things that contain both "Oracle" and "CEO," but only when those words are discussed together. Of course, in order to know whether the words were actually related to each other in the text, the search engine would need to

3 The word "mouse" is interesting in a couple of respects. First, it's one of those words whose plural form is *not* just the singular form with an "s" on the end. Any simple substring search for "dog" will match things that contain "dogs," but will not match "mice" if your query term is "mouse." Second, "mouse" arguably has two plural forms – Steven Pinker argues that the plural of "computer mouse" is "computer mouses" (Steven Pinker, *The Language Instinct : How the Mind Creates Language* [New York: Morrow Publishing, 1994]).

4 OCR (optical character recognition) is technology for converting a hard copy of a document into a soft copy – typically the document is scanned into an image, and then a software program "looks" at the image to convert it into characters.

understand the meaning of the text – instead, we can approximate understanding by searching for occurrences of the two words near each other. A Full-Text search might allow you to specify "Oracle near CEO," so something containing "the CEO of Oracle" will appear higher in the results list than "Oracle introduced a new product today. Their CEO . . . ." A Full-Text query might also allow you to specify the exact distance between the words, a distance range, and/or the order of the terms to match, as well as *window* notions such as "within the same sentence" and "within the same paragraph."

4. *Combining operations*. Most structured query languages allow you to combine predicates with *and*, *or*, and *not*. A Full-Text query language should also provide those logical combinations, with a few extra wrinkles. For example, *or* might be complemented by an *accumulate* operation – while "`dog or cat or mouse`" returns anything that contains at least one of the terms *dog*, *cat*, or *mouse*, "`accumulate (dog, cat, mouse)`" ensures, in addition, that anything that contains all three terms ranks higher than anything that contains any two terms, which in turn ranks higher than anything that contains any one term, regardless of the number of occurrences of each individual term.

The *not* combiner is also a little different in Full-Text queries. First, the unary not ("`not dog`") is famously difficult to execute efficiently with most Full-Text indexes. Many Full-Text languages disallow the unary *not* altogether – *i.e.*, they only allow *not* as a combiner ("cat not dog"). Also, there is a strong case for a *mild not* in Full-Text query. The *mild not* says, "Don't match this phrase, but don't exclude text that contains it either." For example, suppose you are researching government policy on housing, and you want to search for government bills that contain the word "house." You don't want the phrase "house of representatives" to trigger a match, because that's not the sense of "house" you are looking for. At the same time, you don't want to exclude everything that contains "house of representatives," because then you would miss a lot of things that should match. So a search for "house" will bring back too many results, while a search for "house not (house of representatives)" will bring back too few. Only "house mild not (house of representatives)" will return everything that contains the word "house," while ignoring any occurrence of "house" as a part of "house of representatives."

Higher-Level Operations

If a Full-Text language implements a set of special operations such as those just discussed, then an expert searcher can get good, predictable results by combining words, phrases, and operators in intelligent ways. However, these operations are completely mechanical on the part of the search engine — they do not imply any real understanding of the content or of the user's intent, and they put the burden of formulating just the right query on the user. This may work well if the user is an expert in both the subject domain and the capabilities of the Full-Text tool, but a Full-Text query engine should be able to do better than that. We discuss search more broadly in Chapter 18, "Finding Stuff" — for now, let's briefly look at two ways to make Full-Text search smarter and easier.

Concept search allows you to search for a *concept* rather than a word or phrase. If you are a wine connoisseur, you might want to find everything that is about wine (the concept). You could start by searching for wine (the word), then apply stemming to find anything that contains the word "wine" or the word "wines," then apply the thesaurus operation to find anything that contains narrow terms for wine ("merlot," "chianti," "zinfandel," and so on). But it would be much better to be able to express directly in the Full-Text query language that you want to search for the concept of wine, *e.g.*, by querying for "about(wine)." Some Full-Text query engines already offer a concept search — as computers get smarter and faster, we expect concept search to become more widespread and more accurate.

Suppose that your Full-Text query engine is not capable of concept search, or that you are particularly knowledgeable about your domain and the needs of your users. It is common for a search application to do *progressive relaxation* — that is, to progressively relax the query that the user typed in until some reasonable set of results (say, enough to fill a computer screen) is returned. In our example of a concept search for wine, we assumed that the wine researcher wanted to find everything that was about wine. In many situations, such as e-commerce, you want the first 20 or so results that most closely match the criteria the user typed in, and you want them very quickly — the complete set of possible results is not important. So a Full-Text query engine might provide support for query templates, which allow you to describe the relaxation steps. For an online bookstore search, the steps might be:

1. Search for all the words the user typed in, treated as a phrase, in the book title.
2. Search for each word the user typed in, in the author's last name.
3. Search for each word the user typed in, with some spell-check expansion, in the author's last name.
4. Search for each word the user typed in, anded together, in the title.
5. Search for each word the user typed in, ored together, in the title.

Note that both *concept search* and *progressive relaxation* could be considered as parts of an application rather than parts of a Full-Text query language. The language designer might say, "I'm giving you the basic building blocks to express any query – if you want concept search or progressive relaxation, go build it using these blocks." Or she might say, "These higher-level operations are important and useful – I'll put some constructs into the language so you can express them directly, without a lot of coding." See also Section 13.2.5 for some discussion topics around what should go into a Full-Text query language.

Inexact Answers and Relevance (Score)

When you execute a regular structured query, you generally expect an exact answer. For example, if you search for all movies that were released in 1985, there is a single correct answer – there is no room for debate as to whether a particular movie was, or was not, released in 1985. When you run a Full-Text query, the result set *can* be subjective – the *ordering* of the results set *always* is.

Let's take a simple example first – search for "Sheltie rescue." We used Google (which is a search *application*) and found 118,000 pages on the Internet that contain the phrase "Sheltie rescue." This is an exact answer – every page in the results set contains the phrase "Sheltie rescue" at least once, and every Full-Text engine that searches the same corpus (set of documents) should return the same results set. As we make the query more complex, as long as the operations are well-defined, the results set is predictable. However, some operations will bring in the engine's "secret sauce" – *e.g.*, thesaurus operations may use different thesauri – and this make the results set inexact.

The ordering of the results set, on the other hand, is always subjective. The Salton algorithm[5] calculates a *relevance score* for a particular result by counting the number of times the query term occurs in the document. The algorithm takes account of how common the term is in the corpus overall, and some variations also take account of the length of the document. Most Full-Text engines use something based on this algorithm, plus (for web searches) some variation on the PageRank algorithm made famous by Google (see Chapter 18, "Finding Stuff") to allocate a relevance score to each result. Results can be ordered according the *relevance ranking* (the size of the relevance score). But most, if not all, Full-Text engines then add some unpublished smarts — some "secret sauce" — to make their relevance ranking more effective.

In the early days of Full-Text development at Oracle, the Full-Text team devised some simple tests to measure the accuracy of the relevance scoring (and consequently the relevance ranking) of Full-Text query results. They took a fairly small corpus and had humans rank the results of some queries, and then they had their nascent Full-Text engine rank the results of those queries. They found that the Full-Text engine agreed with a human's ranking only about 60% of the time. But they also found that humans agreed with other humans only about 40% of the time! Even when there is little ambiguity in the query term, such as a query for "dog," people disagree wildly about how "doggy" a particular item is, and whether one item is more or less "doggy" than another.

In summary, relevance scoring by humans is highly subjective, and relevance scoring by computers is generally proprietary, used by Full-Text vendors to differentiate their engines. This makes the semantics of relevance ranking impossible to standardize.

Performance

A Full-Text query is also different from a substring query in the area of performance (or at least expectations of performance). When you run a Full-Text query, you expect it to run much faster than a full scan through all the text being searched. This superior performance comes, of course, from the existence of a Full-Text index. The most common form of Full-Text index is an inverted list. This consists of a

5 Gerard Salton, *Automatic Text Processing* (Reading, MA: Addison-Wesley, 1989). A simple overview of the Salton algorithm is available on the web at: http://www.oracle.com/oramag/oracle/01-mar/o21int.html#SCORE (Douglas Scherer and Carol Brennan, Exploring Oracle Text Basics, *Oracle Magazine* [March 2001]).

list of all the words that occur anywhere in the corpus (the set of documents that is the universe of search). Associated with each word is a list of the items in which that word occurs. When you search for "dog," the Full-Text engine looks up the word "dog" in the list and finds all the items where that word occurs.

There are some common variations on the inverted list structure. Many Full-Text indexes index *n-grams* rather than words. Here's how n-grams work: If the item to be indexed is "Mary had a little lamb," a word index would split this into "Mary," "had," "a," "little," and "lamb," and track all items that contain each of those words. An n-gram index might split the same phrase into "M," "Ma," Mar," "ary," "ry," "y," "h," "ha," "had," "ad," "a," *etc.* This example is based on a 3-gram or tri-gram index, though the "n" may have other values. An n-gram index is particularly useful when many queries have wildcards at the beginning and/or end of a word, for languages such as Chinese and Japanese where the exact "word" structure is difficult to determine, and for text that is inaccurate (because it was typed or OCRed poorly).

The structure of an inverted index dictates some characteristics of Full-Text engines:

- The inverted list structure makes it very expensive to add a new item. Whenever a new item is added to the corpus, the inverted list entry for each word in the item must be updated (extended). Most Full-Text indexes get around this by adding to the index asynchronously, so that they can add many new items at once, and by adding the index information for new items at the end of the list rather than in-place. This in turn may lead to fragmentation, which leads to the need for periodic index reorganization.
- The inverted list structure makes it even more expensive to *delete* an item. When you delete a single 10,000-word item, you must update 10,000 list entries. Most Full-Text indexes get around this by performing *lazy deletes* – marking items as deleted, but not actually deleting the index entries. Each query must then check whether a potential result has been deleted before returning it. This also leads to the need to optimize the index periodically (to perform the actual deletes), and it may lead to inaccurate result counts (that's part of the reason for the "1-10 of **about** . . ." that you see on search pages).

- The inverted list may be optimized for a particular set of match options. For example, if most searches are case-insensitive, it doesn't make sense to create a case-sensitive index, and then do a case-insensitive match of the index items at query time. Instead, the index is often built as case-insensitive — all the words are converted to the same case while they are indexed. This makes queries faster for the most common (case-insensitive) searches, but it makes case-sensitive searches impossible (or very slow — it's possible to retrieve all the results of a case-insensitive search, and then to scan each one to see of it matches the case-sensitive search).

In summary, a Full-Text index increases the performance of Full-Text queries. It is generally built as an inverted list. This means that changes to the data are not (generally) reflected immediately in the index; that the index must be periodically optimized (manually or under the covers); and that some query options must be chosen at index build time.

13.2.2 Full-Text and XML

In Section 13.2.1, we were careful to talk about searching a collection of "things" or "items," and returning "things" or "items" as results. In classical Full-Text search we talk about searching for documents, and returning documents as results — *i.e.*, the document is the basic unit of search. As you read in Chapter 3, "Querying XML," XML changes all that — in XML, we still have the notion of a document, but we generally *search in* parts of the document and *return* parts of the document (not necessarily the *same* parts).

For Full-Text search, this represents both a challenge and an opportunity. The challenge is to provide a language in which you can express which parts of a document you want to search, which parts you want to take into account when calculating relevance score, and which parts you want to return. The opportunity is that Full-Text search can be much faster and more accurate when searching/returning only parts of a document.

For example, suppose you have a set of journal articles that consist of title, author, date, and a set of headings, subheadings, paragraphs, and footnotes. A Full-Text search application that searches over XML, where each of those items is a separate element, can easily search across titles first, then headings, then subheadings, and then paragraphs and never search across footnotes. Assuming each kind of element is separately indexed, most searches will be very fast, since some results will be found in a very small *title* index. Results will be highly relevant, since a document with "dog" in the title is much more likely to be relevant to a search for "dog" than one with "dog" just anywhere in the document, including footnotes. And the results will be much more useful than the typical Full-Text result, which is (a pointer to) a whole document – with XML, you can return the actual paragraph that contains the words you are looking for, or the title of the journal + the interesting paragraph + the paragraph on either side.

In short, XML and Full-Text were made for each other. Given XML's beginnings (in SGML) as a way of adding structure to unstructured text, we find it incredible that XQuery does not yet have (indeed, did not *start with*) a Full-Text capability.

13.2.3 Defining XQuery Full-Text

The W3C XQuery and XPath Working Groups have set up a Task Force – a subgroup, if you will, of the Working Groups – to come up with a proposal for an extension to XQuery, to be called XQuery Full-Text.[6] This Task Force has published three documents – the XQuery and XPath Full-Text Requirements,[7] first published in May 2003; XQuery 1.0 and XPath 2.0 Full-Text Use Cases;[8] and XQuery 1.0 and XPath 2.0 Full-Text[9] (language and semantics). The first of these documents (requirements) is now quite stable. The last two (use cases and language and semantics) are published at regular intervals as the work of the Task Force progresses – at the time of writing, the latest publication is dated November 2005.

---

6 One of the authors is the chairman of the W3C XQuery Full-Text Task Force, the other is a founder/member of the Task Force and editor of some of the specs.

7 *XQuery and XPath Full-Text Requirements, W3C Working Draft* (Cambridge, MA: World Wide Web Consortium, 2003). Latest version available at: http://www.w3.org/TR/xquery-full-text-requirements/.

8 *XQuery 1.0 and XPath 2.0 Full-Text Use Cases, W3C Working Draft* (Cambridge, MA: World Wide Web Consortium, 2005). Latest version available at: httpavailable at: http://www.w3.org/TR/xmlquery-full-text-use-cases/.

9 *XQuery 1.0 and XPath 2.0 Full-Text, W3C Working Draft* (Cambridge, MA: World Wide Web Consortium, 2005). Latest version available at: http://www.w3.org/TR/xquery-full-text/.

The requirements document says that XQuery Full-Text must be properly integrated with the XQuery/XPath language, following the same universality rules, and must be composable with XQuery. It also lists the minimum set of Full-Text functionality that must be in the first release of XQuery Full-Text. The list is:

1. single-word search
2. phrase search
3. support for stop words
4. single character suffix
5. 0 or more character suffix
6. 0 or more character prefix
7. 0 or more character infix
8. proximity searching (unit: words)
9. specification of order in proximity searching
10. combination using AND
11. combination using OR
12. combination using NOT
13. word normalization, diacritics
14. ranking, relevance

This Requirements spec balances concerns over XQuery Full-Text being created as a hastily designed bolt-on to XQuery that would have to be fully integrated in following versions against concerns that the first XQuery Full-Text version might be either too simplistic to be useful or too full-featured to be released in a reasonable time frame.

The use cases are *very* complete — they provide examples of every corner of the XQuery Full-Text language. They serve not only as a motivation for each of the features, but also as a tutorial for the new user, and even as a basic test bed for implementations.

Before describing the current state of the XQuery Full-Text language spec, let's look at some approaches that were *not* adopted by the Task Force — objects, functions, and many-functions.

Approaches — Objects

One obvious way to implement XQuery Full-Text would be to follow SQL's lead. After all, ANSI and ISO had been down this path already – they defined SQL/MM (SQL Multimedia and Application Packages) Part 2[10] to extend the SQL language to incorporate Full-Text search (Part 1 defines the framework, and other parts define SQL support for Spatial and Image data). SQL/MM takes an objects-based approach. It defines a new UDT (user-defined type) called `FullText`, to represent any data that is Full-Text-searchable. It then defines methods on the `FullText` object, including a `CONTAINS` method to test whether a document matches a text query, and a `RANK` method to return the relevance score of a text query. Example 13-1[11] shows a table created with a column of type `FullText` and a query against that table. The query returns the `docno` for each row in the table where the document contains "standard" or "standards" in the same paragraph as a word that sounds like "sequel" (*e.g.*, "SQL"). The results are ordered by the relevance score of the same text query.

Example 13-1 *SQL/MM Full-Text*

```
CREATE TABLE information (
    docno       INTEGER,
    document    FULLTEXT
 )

SELECT docno
    FROM information
    WHERE document.CONTAINS(
        'STEMMED FORM OF "standard"
        IN SAME PARAGRAPH AS
        SOUNDS LIKE "sequel"') = 1
    ORDER BY
        document.RANK(
            'STEMMED FORM OF "standard"
            IN SAME PARAGRAPH AS
            SOUNDS LIKE "sequel"')
        DESC
```

10 *ISO/IEC 13249-2:2000, Information Technology – Database Languages – SQL Multimedia and Application Packages – Part 2: Full-Text* (Geneva, Switzerland: International Organization for Standardization, 2000).

11 This example was adapted from an example in Jim Melton and Andrew Eisenberg, SQL multimedia and application packages (SQL/MM), *SIGMOD Record,* Vol. 30, Issue 4: 97–102 (New York: Association for Computing Machinery, 2001). Available at: http://portal.acm.org/citation.cfm?id=604264.604280.

Approaches — Functions

The idea of reusing the definitions generated by another standards body might seem appealing. But XQuery is an expression-based language with functions — it does not have objects. The obvious way to graft the SQL/MM approach onto XQuery would be to define two functions, say, `mmcontains` and `mmscore` (the function name `contains` is already taken by a substring function). An XQuery based on these functions might look like Example 13-2.

Example 13-2 *XQuery Full-Text, Functions*

```
for $d in doc(mydocs)/documents/document
    where mmcontains($d/body,
        'STEMMED FORM OF "standard"
        IN SAME PARAGRAPH AS
        SOUNDS LIKE "sequel"')
    order by
        mmscore($d/body,
            'STEMMED FORM OF "standard"
            IN SAME PARAGRAPH AS
            SOUNDS LIKE "sequel"')
        descending
    return
        $d/title
```

The advantages of this approach are:

- All the work is already done — the SQL/MM Full-Text definitions could be grafted onto XQuery with very little effort.
- Some database vendors have already implemented some form of SQL/MM Full-Text. It would be relatively easy for them to implement XQuery Full-Text using existing technology.

So the standard could be defined quickly, and at least some vendors could implement it quickly and easily. The disadvantages of this approach, though, are:

- The queries are verbose.
- More importantly, this approach does not address the requirement of composability.

That is, the string that makes up the second parameter is not a part of the outer language – it's a string with its own "sublanguage." Suppose you wanted to use such a query in your application but that you wanted the words "standard" and "sequel" to be replaced with variables (instead of being literals) – perhaps a user types them into some web page, perhaps they are derived somehow. You can't express that easily in the XQuery – *i.e.*, the string cannot contain variables (or expressions) where the search terms in the example are hard-coded. There are ways around this – you could allow some kind of string substitution in the parameter string, just as the Perl language does. Or you could just build up the string in a separate step, before calling the function.

Note that some of the verbosity comes from having to type in the sublanguage string twice, once for `mmcontains` and once for `mmscore`. If you want to be able to *score* (and therefore rank) results only on the same criteria you use to *select* items, you can avoid this. The filter function (`mmcontains`) could have a side effect – *e.g.*, calling `mmcontains` might set a local variable to a score value. Several existing Full-Text implementations use a side effect to filter and produce a score in one step.

Approaches — Many-Functions

In the previous sections, we explored extending XQuery and XPath to handle Full-Text search by following the ANSI/ISO approach of introducing a special object and some methods, and then we looked at the possibility of introducing those methods into XQuery and XPath as two functions, which we (arbitrarily) called `mmcontains` and `mmscore`. A major objection to this approach is that it involves a sublanguage – the string containing the text query expression is, from XQuery's point of view, just any old string (and not an expression). That means it's clumsy to construct, and users must learn and use new operators that have similar, but not identical, semantics to operators they already use in XQuery (and, or, not, *etc.*). While there are clearly workarounds to these issues, many feel that this approach makes Full-Text a second-class citizen in the world of XQuery, that Full-Text is not quite (and, more importantly, never can be) a fully integrated part of XQuery under this scheme.

An alternative approach is to make every Full-Text operation a true, first-class XQuery function, doing away with the sublanguage string altogether. So, instead of the XPath expression

```
//document/section[ mmcontains(., "dog and cat") ]
```

you would write

```
//document/section[ mfand-contains(., "dog", "cat") ]
```

We have (arbitrarily) used a prefix "mf" (for "many-functions"). This could be part of a function-naming convention, or it could (with the right syntax) be a namespace prefix that identifies the mf set of functions, or it could be dropped altogether as long as the function names didn't clash with existing XQuery function names. In this example, `mfand-contains` is a first-class XQuery function, and its arguments — `"dog"`, `"cat"` — are just regular XQuery strings. The drawback of this approach is obvious — instead of two functions with many operators (inside a sublanguage), this approach yields many functions. The maximum number of functions needed is twice the number of operators in the sublanguage, i.e., one function for each operator for contains, plus one function for each operator for ranking. However, on closer inspection it becomes clear that only *combining operations* and *proximity operations* (as described earlier in this section) need a function each, while *matching options* and *word expansions* need far fewer functions. Let's rewrite Example 13-2 to see how this might work in practice.

Example 13-3 *XQuery Full-Text, Many-Functions*

```
for $i in doc(mydocs)/information
    where mf-sameParagraph-contains($i/document,
        mf-expand-words("standard", "stemmed"),
        mf-expand-words("sequel", "soundex")
    order by
        mf-sameParagraph-rank($i/document,
            mf-expand-words("standard", "stemmed"),
            mf-expand-words("sequel", "soundex")
        descending
```

In Example 13-3, we needed to introduce two functions, `mf-sameParagraph-contains` and `mf-sameParagraph-rank`, to express "match these words in the same paragraph," but we only needed to introduce one function, `mf-expand-words`, to express stemming and soundex.[12]

Approaches — Summary

In this section, we described three alternative approaches to extending XQuery and XPath to do Full-Text search – objects, functions, and many-functions. The ability to do Full-Text queries is extremely important to XQuery – some might even say that XQuery without Full-Text is not a viable language. Some of the database and query vendors clearly appreciate this importance, and they have not waited for the W3C spec to become a Recommendation before implementing XQuery Full-Text in some form. As you will read in Section 13.2.6, the functions and many-functions approaches have already been implemented by at least one vendor.

In the next section, we look at the approach currently being pursued by the Full-Text Task Force of the W3C XQuery Working Group. We expect this will be part of some (near-)future XQuery spec.

13.2.4 W3C XQuery Full-Text — Grammar Extension

In this section, we describe the current W3C Working Draft specification of XQuery 1.0 and XPath 2.0 Full-Text. Now that we have a clear idea of what a Full-Text query is and have seen some approaches to XQuery Full-Text that were *not* adopted by the W3C XQuery Full-Text Task Force, let's look at the approach that is, at the time of writing, expected to yield the W3C XQuery Full-Text language.

The approach the W3C Task Force is pursuing is an extension to the grammar of XQuery and XPath. This is the most ambitious approach – rather than using the existing extensibility mechanisms available in XQuery (*i.e.*, functions), W3C XQuery Full-Text extends the XQuery grammar with additional grammar rules and keywords. The advantage of this approach is that W3C XQuery Full-Text is an integral part of the XQuery language – and it's first-class in every way, fully composable, and it introduces some notions (such as rank-

---

12 There is an issue here. We presented mf-expand-words as a real, ordinary XQuery function. In the case of stemming (with some means of identifying the language), this could be implemented as a real function returning a finite list of words. However, in the case of some of the match options, it would be impractical to implement the function naïvely. For example, the result of mf-expand-words ("a*b," "wildcards") is, in theory, an infinitely long list of words. In practice, it is usually finite (bounded by the set of words in the text index). Even when there is no convenient bounding mechanism, it is possible to execute such a function in the context of some particular query, even if it's not possible to return a result for the function when it is used stand-alone. That said, some people are uncomfortable defining a language that depends on such special functions.

ing) that might carry over into non-Full-Text XQuery. The downside is that the XQuery Full-Text language syntax and semantics is brand new. That means it will take (has already taken) a long time to define, and we expect it will take vendors a long time to implement (longer, anyway, than an approach based on existing standards). That said, we are excited about the prospect of a standard, rich language for doing Full-Text queries over XML.

The XQuery Full-Text Requirements laid out a minimum set of operations that had to be defined in XQuery Full-Text for it to be generally useful. These operations (and more) are described as extensions to the XQuery and XPath grammar, so it's appropriate at this point to look at the XQuery Full-Text EBNF rules. If you followed along with the discussion of the XQuery grammar in Chapter 11, you are already familiar with the style of the XQuery grammar rules. XQuery Full-Text "breaks in" to the XQuery grammar at rule 50 (48 in XQuery),[13] where `FTContainsExpr` is defined as a variation on the comparison expression `ComparisonExpr`. The XQuery grammar says:

```
[48] ComparisonExpr ::= RangeExpr ( (ValueComp
                                    | GeneralComp
                                    | NodeComp) RangeExpr )?
[49] RangeExpr      ::= AdditiveExpr ( "to" AdditiveExpr )?
```

while the XQuery Full-Text grammar says:

```
[50] ComparisonExpr ::= FTContainsExpr ( (ValueComp
                                         | GeneralComp
                                         | NodeComp) FTContainsExpr )?
[51] FTContainsExpr ::= RangeExpr
                        ( "ftcontains" FTSelection FTIgnoreOption? )?
[52] RangeExpr      ::= AdditiveExpr ( "to" AdditiveExpr )?
```

The XQuery grammar rules employ a "cascading precedence" style, so the precedence of an operator is clearly fixed by its placement in the EBNF. A `RangeExpr` – on the left-hand side of the `ftcontains` keyword – can be an instance of an `AdditiveExpr`,

13 Grammar rules are quoted from the XQuery Full-Text Working Draft and the XQuery 1.0 Working Draft, both of November 3, 2005, available at: http://www.w3.org/TR/2005/WD-xquery-full-text-20051103/ and http://www.w3.org/TR/2005/WD-xquery-20051103/, respectively. When you read this, the numbering of the rules (and of course the rules themselves) might be different.

which can be an instance of a `MultiplicativeExpr`, and so on all the way down the precedence tree, through `PathExpr` to `PrimaryExpr` and `ParenthesizedExpr`. That means that almost any expression, including a parenthesized expression, may appear on the left-hand side of `ftcontains`. If you have doubts about the precedence of any of the operators in the expression to the left of `ftcontains`, just put parentheses around that expression.

Above `ftcontains` in the precedence tree are `or` and `and`, so `ftcontains` binds more tightly than `or` and `and`.

```
[33] ExprSingle      ::= FLWORExpr
                         | QuantifiedExpr
                         | TypeswitchExpr
                         | IfExpr
                         | OrExpr

[48] OrExpr          ::= AndExpr ( "or" AndExpr )*
[49] AndExpr         ::= ComparisonExpr ( "and" ComparisonExpr )*
```

This places the XQuery Full-Text extensions within the XQuery grammar. From the productions we have looked at so far, we can expect to see XQuery Full-Text with a `where` clause something like this: ... `where $i/title ftcontains` ... . On the right-hand side of the `ftcontains` keyword, we must see an `FTSelection` optionally followed by an `FTIgnoreOption`.

Let's look at the `FTIgnoreOption` first, because it's simpler. Note that you can only have one `FTIgnoreOption` per `ftcontains`, and if it appears at all it must appear at the very end of the expression. This is for simplicity — allowing `FTIgnoreOption` in other places in the expression would make queries very difficult to parse (for humans as well as computers).

```
[172] FTIgnoreOption        ::= "without" "content" UnionExpr
```

`FTIgnoreOption` lets you say that you want to ignore some parts of the node sequence that you are searching. For example, you might want to search chapters of a book for the word "dog" but ignore footnotes. " ... `without content //footnote` ..." might achieve that objective. You could achieve the same thing with some clever XQuery coding, of course, but this kind of query is important enough in Full-Text search to have a special, more concise syntax.

The meat of the `FTContainsExpr` expression is in the rest of the right-hand side, the `FTSelection` grammar rule.

```
[144] FTSelection    ::= FTOr (FTMatchOption | FTProximity)*
                         ("weight" DecimalLiteral)?
```

The `FTSelection` describes what some Full-Text languages call the *text query expression* — just to remind you of the context, the `FTSelection` is likely to appear in the `where` clause of a `FLWOR` (or in the predicate of an XPath), *e.g.*, " `... where <some node sequence> ftcontains <some FTSelection>` ... ." The right-hand side of `FTContainsExpr` consists of the words and phrases that you want to search for, the ways those words and phrases are combined (and, or, any, all), the parameters that affect what constitutes a match (*e.g.*, the case-sensitivity option determines whether "dog" matches "Dog"), and some positional operators (within three to five words).

The `FTSelection` also allows a *weight* — the weight has no effect when doing a Boolean search (using the `ftcontains` keyword); but when this same expression is used in the description of score, a higher weight lets you say that some word is more important than some other word. So, if you search for "`(dog weight 1.0) || (cat weight 0.1)` ", you can expect a *doggy* document to appear higher in the results list than an equally *catty* document.

Let's drill down to the details of the `FTSelection` by walking down the tree of each of its components, starting with `FTOr`.

```
[145] FTOr           ::= FTAnd ( "||" FTAnd )*
[146] FTAnd          ::= FTMildnot ( "&&" FTMildnot )*
[147] FTMildnot      ::= FTUnaryNot ( "mild" "not" FTUnaryNot )*
[148] FTUnaryNot     ::= ("!")? FTWordsSelection
[149] FTWordsSelection    ::= FTWords | ("(" FTSelection ")")
[150] FTWords        ::= (Literal
                         | VarRef
                         | ContextItemExpr
                         | FunctionCall
                         | ("{" Expr "}")) FTAnyallOption?
```

This is another example of *cascading precedence*, typical of the style in which the XQuery grammar rules are written. An `FTOr` is an `FTAnd`, optionally followed by "`||`" (the Full-Text symbol that can be pronounced "or") and another `FTAnd`, any number of times. Similarly, an `FTAnd` is an `FTMildnot`, optionally followed by "`&&`" (the Full-Text symbol that can be pronounced "and") and an `FTMildNot`, any number of times. These two rules could, of course, be combined into a single rule, but this style of grammar makes it crystal clear that "`&&`" binds more tightly than "`||`." What does that mean? It means that the snippet "`cat && dog || mouse`" is an `FTOr`, where the `FTAnd`s are "`cat && dog`" and "`mouse`." That means that a node that contains both cat and dog will match this snippet, and so will a document that contains only mouse. Another way of saying that "`&&`" *binds more tightly than* "`||`" is that "`&&`" *has higher precedence than* "`||`."

It may surprise some readers that the not operator is unary in XQuery Full-Text — that is, it's possible to say "`! dog`"; you don't have to have a word or phrase on the left-hand side of the not operator. The unary not is famously difficult to implement with an index. An index typically stores information about which words a document or node contains, and it lacks any information about which words a document or node does *not* contain. So if you want to find out which items do not contain the word "dog," it's very difficult to find that out from an index — you have to assume some universe of discourse (every possible item) and subtract from that every item in the index that *does* contain the word *dog*. That said, some Full-Text users feel that this is important functionality. Of course, you can express a binary not by combining the unary not and the and, *e.g.*, "`dog && !cat`" (dog and not cat).

W3C XQuery Full-Text also supports a mild not operation (see Section 13.2.1, under the subheading "Special Operations"). A mild not lets you specify that the occurrence of a phrase should not eliminate an item from the results set, so you can say "mexico mild not new mexico" to find items that contain "mexico." Items that contain "new mexico" will not be excluded from the results, but neither will they be included, unless they also contain "mexico" on its own.

The last grammar rule in this snippet — `FTWords` — tells us what constitutes a word (or phrase). From this rule, the following can represent what you are searching for:

1. A string literal — "dog"
2. A string literal with more than one word — "Mother Mary comes to me"

3. A sequence of strings – `("Mother Mary comes to me", "Speaking words of wisdom", "Let it be")`
4. A variable – `$myVariable`
5. The context item – . ("dot")
6. A built-in function – `string-value(./title[1])`
7. A user-defined function – `myFunctions:getUserInput()`
8. An expression enclosed in `{}` – `{ for $i in collection( myRules/rule ) return rule/searchTerms }`

This list is not meant to be read as a definition, rather as a set of examples – (1) is a special case of (2), which is a special case of (3), since (2) is a sequence with only one member. The W3C XQuery Full-Text spec says that the `FTWords` "must evaluate to a sequence of string values or nodes of type "xs:string". The result . . . is then atomized into a sequence of strings which then is being [sic] tokenized into a sequence of phrases. ... If the atomized sequence is not a subtype of xs:string*, a type error ... is raised." So wherever you see `FTWords` in the grammar, you are guaranteed to get something that evaluates to a sequence of strings (which may have only one member). How does this sequence of strings get interpreted – for example, will the query try to match *all* the strings in the sequence, or *any* string in the sequence? This is dictated by the `FTAnyallOption`.

```
[165] FTAnyallOption        ::= "any" | "all" | "phrase"
                               | <"any" "word"> | <"all" "words">
```

There are five possible values for `FTAnyAllOption`.

- "any" – each member of the sequence is interpreted as a phrase, and the `FTContains` expression evaluates to true if there is a match for *any* (that is, at least one) of those phrases in the text being searched.
- "all" – each member of the sequence is interpreted (again) as a phrase, and the `FTContains` expression evaluates to true if there is a match for *all* (that is, every one) of those phrases in the text being searched.
- "phrase" – the sequence is flattened into a single string (the strings are concatenated, with whitespace in between).

The `FTContains` expression evaluates to true if there is a match for that new string, treated as a phrase, in the text being searched.

- "any word" — the sequence is flattened into a single string, and `FTContains` evaluates to true if any word in that new string matches a word in the text being searched.
- "all words" — the sequence is flattened into a single string, and `FTContains` evaluates to true if each word in that new string matches at least one word in the text being searched.

This deserves some examples! Example 13-4 shows the effect of each of these options on a string and on a sequence of strings. In the examples, the "Query snippet" is part of a W3C XQuery Full-Text query, for example:

```
... where $x ftcontains "Mother Mary comes to me" any ...
```

The "Interpretation" is alternative W3C XQuery Full-Text syntax giving the same semantics.

Example 13-4 *FTAnyAllOption*

Query Snippet	**Interpretation**
"Mother Mary comes to me" any	"Mother Mary comes to me"
"Mother Mary comes to me" all	"Mother Mary comes to me"
"Mother Mary comes to me" phrase	"Mother Mary comes to me"
"Mother Mary comes to me" any word	"Mother" || "Mary" || "comes" || "to" || "me"
"Mother Mary comes to me" all words	"Mother" && "Mary" && "comes" && "to" && "me"
("Mother Mary comes to me", "Speaking words of wisdom", "Let it be") any	"Mother Mary comes to me" || "Speaking words of wisdom" || " Let it be"

Example 13-4 *FTAnyAllOption (continued)*

Query Snippet	Interpretation
("Mother Mary comes to me", "Speaking words of wisdom", "Let it be") all	"Mother Mary comes to me" && "Speaking words of wisdom" && " Let it be"
("Mother Mary comes to me", "Speaking words of wisdom", "Let it be") phrase	"Mother Mary comes to me Speaking words of wisdom Let it be"
("Mother Mary comes to me", "Speaking words of wisdom", "Let it be") any word	"Mother" || "Mary" || "comes" || "to" || "me" || "Speaking" || "words" || "of" || "wisdom" || "Let" || "it" || "be"
("Mother Mary comes to me", "Speaking words of wisdom", "Let it be") all words	"Mother" && "Mary" && "comes" && "to" && "me" && "Speaking" && "words" && "of" && "wisdom" && "Let" && "it" && "be"

If no option is specified, the default behavior is the same as "any."

By now, you should have some sense of how the Full-Text operations fit into XQuery. Let's look briefly at the rest of the XQuery Full-Text grammar before describing some examples.

```
[151] FTProximity    ::= FTOrderedIndicator
                       | FTWindow
                       | FTDistance
                       | FTTimes
                       | FTScope
                       | FTContent
```

`FTProximity` lets you specify how close two words or phrases must be, as a number or range of words, sentences, or paragraphs.[14] You can also specify whether or not the order of the words in `FTWords` must match the order in which they appear in the text. The `FTProximity` production also includes a way to specify how many times a word must occur (though `FTTimes` doesn't fit with the name

14 All of these units (words, sentences, paragraphs) are implementation-defined.

of the production — it's not a proximity operation). `FTProximity` expands to one of the following:

- `FTOrderedIndicator` — "... 'dog' && 'cat' ordered ..." matches text that contains both "dog" and "cat," where "dog" comes before "cat." If this option is "unordered" (the default), the order of the words in the text does not affect the match.
- `FTWindow` — "... 'dog' && 'cat' window exactly 5 words ..." matches text that contains both "dog" and "cat" within a window of 5 words. The unit can be "words," "sentences," or "paragraphs." All three units are implementation-dependent (they are part of the tokenization process). The window option is a shorthand for a common form of distance (see next item) — *i.e.*, any expression using window could be rewritten using distance.
- `FTDistance` — "... 'dog' && 'cat' distance exactly 5 words ..." matches text that contains both "dog" and "cat" exactly 5 words apart (*i.e.*, with exactly 5 intervening words). The unit of distance can be "words," "sentences," or "paragraphs." The distance can be specified "exactly," as a minimum distance ("at least 3 words"), a maximum distance ("at most 7 words"), or as a range ("from 3 to 7 words").
- `FTTimes` — "... 'dog' occurs at least 3 times ..." matches text that contains the word "dog" at least 3 times. You can also specify an exact number of occurrences ("occurs exactly 5 times"), a maximum number of occurrences ("occurs at most 7 times"), or a range ("occurs from 3 to 7 times").
- `FTScope` — "... 'dog' && 'cat' same sentence ..." matches text that contains both "dog" and "cat" in the same sentence. The possible units for FTScope are "sentence" and "paragraph."
- `FTContent` — "... 'dog' at start ..." matches text that contains "dog" at the beginning (*i.e.*, "dog" is the first word in the text). You can also specify that the word must be the last word in the text ("at end"), or that the word (or phrase) must match the entire content of the text being searched ("entire content").

```
[153] FTMatchOption          ::= FTCaseOption
                                  | FTDiacriticsOption
                                  | FTStemOption
                                  | FTThesaurusOption
                                  | FTStopwordOption
                                  | FTLanguageOption
                                  | FTWildCardOption
```

`FTMatchOption` dictates how words are to be matched – *e.g.*, you might want to match words ignoring case or diacritics. This rule mixes what we previously described as *matching options* and *word expansions* – you could think of "expand this query term into all the words with the same linguistic root" as "match this query term, but consider stemming as a matching option." `FTMatchOption` expands to one of the following:

- `FTCaseOption` – "... 'Dog' case sensitive ..." matches text that contains the word "Dog" with an uppercase "D" and lowercase "og." Other options are "lowercase" or "uppercase" (convert the query term to lowercase/uppercase before attempting to match it) and "case insensitive" (do not take case into account when attempting to match the query term).
- `FTDiacriticsOption` – "... 'résumé' diacritics insensitive ..." matches text that contains "résumé without taking diacritics into account (*e.g.*, "resume" will match). As well as the diacritics options "sensitive" and "insensitive," you can specify "with diacritics" or "without diacritics."[15]

15 There is a subtle difference between "diacritics insensitive" and "without diacritics." "diacritics insensitive" tells the query processor to ignore diacritics when computing a match, so the occurrence of the query term in the text, with or without any diacritics, will result in a match. "'resumé' diacritics insensitive" matches "résumé," "resume," "résume," "resme," *etc.* On the other hand, "without diacritics" says that a term only matches text that does not contain diacritics, whether or not the query term contains diacritics. "'résumé' without diacritics" matches only "resume." Similarly, "with diacritics" only matches text that does contain some diacritics, even though the query term may not contain diacritics. So "'resume' with diacritics" matches "résumé," "resumé," and "resme," but does not match "resume" (in case the user knows there are diacritics in the text to be matched, but doesn't have a diacritic-capable input screen).

- `FTStemOption` — "... 'dog' with stemming ..." matches text that contains any word with the same linguistic root as "dog" ("dog" or "dogs").
- `FTThesaurusOption` — "... 'dog' with thesaurus at 'http://example.com/myThesaurus.xml' relationship 'BROADER TERM' at most 2 levels ... " matches text that contains "dog" or "canine" or "mammal." Possible relationships include at least those defined in the ISO 2788 Thesaurus standard,[16] but there may be additional (implementation-defined) relationships. For hierarchical relationships, you can also specify an exact/minimum/maximum/range of levels to be considered.
- `FTStopwordOption` — "... $q with stop words ..." matches text that contains any word in $q, ignoring any stop words (words that have been defined by your implementation to be "noise words").
- `FTLanguageOption` — "... 'dog' with language 'Russian' ..." tells the query processor that the query language is "Russian." This may affect the way case, diacritics, thesaurus, and stemming options are processed.
- `FTWildCardOption` — "... d.*g with wildcards ..." matches text that contains any word that starts with a "d," ends with a "g," and has zero or more characters in between. If the option is "without wildcards" (the default) then "d.*g" is interpreted literally. Other possible wildcard designators are ".?" (zero or 1 characters), ".+" (one or more characters), or, *e.g.*, "{3,7}" (from 3 to 7 characters).

Note that most of the match options can be turned on or off ("with wildcards"/ "without wildcards," "with stop words"/ "without stop words"). Remember that queries can be built up using parentheses, from the grammar production for FTWordsSelection. See, for example, the use of parentheses in Example 13-6.

```
[149] FTWordsSelection     ::= FTWords | ("(" FTSelection ")")
```

16 *ISO 2788:1986, Documentation Guidelines for the Establishment and Development of Monolingual Thesauri* (Geneva, Switzerland: International Organization for Standardization, 1986).

The remaining XQuery Full-Text grammar productions are reproduced here for completeness. At least some of these productions will almost certainly have changed in the spec by the time you read this, so we want to give you a complete snapshot of the grammar we are discussing in this chapter.

```
[154] FTCaseOption          ::= "lowercase"
                                | "uppercase"
                                | ("case" "sensitive")
                                | ("case" "insensitive")

[155] FTDiacriticsOption    ::= ("with" "diacritics")
                                | ("without" "diacritics")
                                | ("diacritics" "sensitive")
                                | ("diacritics" "insensitive")

[156] FTStemOption          ::= ("with" "stemming")
                                | ("without" "stemming")

[157] FTThesaurusOption     ::= ("with" "thesaurus" (FTThesaurusID
                                | "default"))
                                | ("with" "thesaurus" "(" (FTThesaurusID |
                                  "default") ("," FTThesaurusID)* ")")
                                | ("without" "thesaurus")

[158] FTThesaurusID         ::= "at" StringLiteral ("relationship" StringLiteral)?
                                (FTRange "levels")?

[159] FTStopwordOption      ::= ("with" "stop" "words" FTRefOrList
                                FTInclExclStringLiteral*)
                                | ("without" "stop" "words")
                                | ("with" "default" "stop" "words")
                                FTInclExclStringLiteral*)

[160] FTRefOrList           ::= "at" StringLiteral
                                | ("(" StringLiteral ("," StringLiteral)* ")")

[161] FTInclExclStringLiteral  ::= ("union" | "except") FTRefOrList

[162] FTLanguageOption      ::= "language" UnionExpr
[163] FTWildCardOption      ::= ("with" "wildcards")
```

```
                               | ("without" "wildcards")
[164] FTContent       ::= ("at" "start")
                        | ("at" "end")
                        | ("entire" "content")

[165] FTAnyallOption    ::= "any" | "all" | "phrase"
                          | ("any" "word") | ("all" "words")

[166] FTRange         ::= ("exactly" UnionExpr)
                        | ("at" "least" UnionExpr)
                        | ("at" "most" UnionExpr)
                        | ("from" UnionExpr "to" UnionExpr)

[167] FTDistance      ::= "distance" FTRange FTUnit

[168] FTWindow        ::= "window" FTRange FTUnit

[169] FTTimes         ::= "occurs" FTRange "times"

[170] FTScope         ::= ("same" | "different") FTBigUnit

[171] FTUnit          ::= "words" | "sentences" | "paragraphs"

[172] FTBigUnit       ::= "sentence" | "paragraph"

[173] FTIgnoreOption    ::= "without" "content" UnionExpr

[152] FTOrderedIndicator   ::= "ordered"
```

We urge you to browse the (most excellent) XQuery Full-Text Use Cases spec for examples of all the XQuery Full-Text operators. We have created a couple of examples later, with explanations, to illustrate just how expressive XQuery Full-Text is.

Score

We will not give a full description of score here, as the definition of score is likely to change significantly. The current draft spec shows score as a (second-order) function, taking as its argument a Boolean combination of `FTContains` expressions. Another possible approach is to make score a clause in the `FLWOR` expression (a bit like a `let` clause), binding a variable to the (second-order) evaluation of some

`FTContains` expressions combined with the XQuery `and` or `or`. The relative importance of terms in the query is set by the weight operator in the right-hand side of the `FTContains` expression(s). The grammar for a score clause might look like this:

```
FLWORExpr      ::= (ForClause | LetClause)+
                      FTScoreClause?
                      WhereClause?
                      OrderByClause?
                      "return" ExprSingle

FTScoreClause  ::= <"score" "$"> VarName "as" Expr
```

Some XQuery Full-Text Examples

Example 13-5 is a very simple XQuery Full-Text query that returns the year of every movie with "werewolf" in the title. Note that the query does not include any match options, so, *e.g.*, case sensitivity, stemming, and stop words are all defaulted.

Example 13-5 *Simple XQuery Full-Text*

```
for $m in doc("movies.xml")/movie
    let $t := $m/title
    score $s as ($t ftcontains "werewolf")
    where $t ftcontains "werewolf"
    order by $s descending
    return
      $m/yearReleased
```

Example 13-6 is a less simple example. In this example we assume an additional element in the movies data sample, a description, and we assume that a variable `$myInput` exists, representing some input typed by a user.

Example 13-6 *Less Simple XQuery Full-Text*

```
declare variable $x as xs:string external;
for $m in doc("movies.xml")/movie
    let $t := $m/title
    let $d := $m/description
    score $s as
        ($t ftcontains ("werewolf" weight 1.0) || ("american" weight 0.8))
            or ($d ftcontains "werewolf" || "american" weight 0.2)
```

```
where
    $t ftcontains ((("American" case sensitive) &&
        ("werewolf" with stemming)) distance at most 2 words ordered)
    || $x all words
    || { for $p in $myInput/phrase
           return $p/text() }
         with stop words at "http://example.com/stoplist-001"
           except ("in", "about", "around")
order by $s descending
return
  $t
```

The query in Example 13-6 returns the titles of all movies that are about American werewolves, according to some additional criteria, ordered by their American werewolf-ness. Let's start with the `where` clause — there are three criteria here, and if a movie meets any of those criteria it will get into the results set.

- The title contains "American," with an uppercase "A" and lowercase "merican," and it contains any word with the same stem as "werewolf" ("werewolf," "werewolves"). The "werewolf" words may be in any mix of cases. The word "American" and the "werewolf" word must occur within a distance of two words or less, and "American" must occur first.
- `$x` is a variable provided by the context of the query — perhaps it's a list of words that we want to match for every query, perhaps it's a list of words that get computed somewhere. Any movie where the title contains all the words in `$x` will get into the results set.
- The third criterion is a FLWOR expression, enclosed in "`{}`". Let's say this expression somehow calculates words that have been typed in by a user. Since the words have been typed in (*i.e.*, we don't know when we are writing the query what those words will be), we want to ignore some "noise words." We don't want to specify a list of (possibly hundreds of) stop words in the query, so we reference some known stop word list via a URL (the language says this only has to be a string literal, but a URL makes sense here). Then again, we don't want to ignore *all* the stop words on that reference list — if the user types in "in" or "about" or "around," then we do *not* want to ignore any of those.

So much for defining what goes into the results set. Now, in what order should we deliver the results? We use the `score` clause to calculate a relevance score, and then we order the results using the `order by` clause. Note that we could just repeat the whole query as part of the `score` clause, but we have decided we want to rank the results based on different criteria than the ones used to decide which movies appear in the results set. We want movies with "werewolf" in the title to appear *very* high in the results, and we want movies with "american" in the title to appear *somewhat* high in the results. We also want movies with either of those words in the description to get a slight boost. That's all we can say about this query – we cannot predict the score for any particular movie, for the scoring algorithm and the effect of weights are implementation-defined. Note that the two `FTContains` expressions in the `score` clause are `or`ed together, using the XQuery `or` and not the Full-Text `||`. That's because the `score` clause binds a variable to some set of (second-order) `FTContains` expressions, combined with the XQuery Boolean `and` or `or`.

Our last example is an XPath example. The Full-Text extensions are designed to be useful as part of XPath 2.0 as well as XQuery 1.0. Example 13-7 produces a sequence of titles of movies whose description contains either "American" at the start of the description or "werewolf" at least 3 times in the description.

Example 13-7 *XPath Full-Text*

```
/movies/movie[description ftcontains ("American" at start) ||
   ("werewolf" occurs at least 3 times)]/title
```

If you want to try out some examples for yourself, we recommend going to the W3C's XQuery home page and following the link to the XQuery Full-Text Test page.[17] Here, you can type in an XQuery Full-Text expression and see its parse tree (though not its results). This is an excellent way to check the syntax of any XQuery and to get a feel for how XQueries are parsed.

Semantics

We cannot leave this section without mentioning the semantics part of the XQuery Full-Text Language and Semantics spec. A great deal

17 The W3C XQuery home page is at http://www.w3.org/XML/Query. At the time of writing, the latest XQuery Full-Text test page is at http://www.w3.org/2005/04/qt-applets/xquery-fulltextApplet.html.

of care and effort have gone into formally defining the semantics of those parts of the XQuery Full-Text language that *can* be formally defined – *i.e.*, those parts that are not implementation-defined. This formal definition is an important part of the spec, but we prefer to use these formal semantics as a safety net, to help us figure out what behavior is expected when the descriptive sections are incomplete or unclear.[18] We urge the interested reader to browse the semantics section of the spec, especially if she intends to build an XQuery Full-Text engine. (The XQuery Full-Text semantics section is rather dense. As an introduction to the concepts used in describing the XQuery Full-Text semantics, you might want first to read the TexQuery paper[19] on which it's based.)

13.2.5 W3C XQuery Full-Text — Some Discussion Topics

At the time of writing, the W3C XQuery Full-Text Working Draft is still fairly fresh – for example, `score` has only recently been converted from a function to a grammar extension. Since the spec is likely to change over the next few drafts, we don't intend to describe the language in any more detail here – the interested reader now has a good idea of where to look, and what to look for, and has some context in which to read the latest specs. Instead, we introduce some discussion topics around XQuery Full-Text. This gives some insight into what kinds of issues may be on the table when you read this book, and what parts of the spec may still change. Then we describe some of the XQuery Full-Text implementations that are already commercially available, way ahead of any W3C spec that might be called a "standard."

Definition of `score`

XQuery Full-Text has two major parts. `FTContains` is a Boolean expression with a precise definition.[20] `score` is a way of measuring

18 The XQuery Full-Text Language and Semantics spec does not say which description is normative, but we suspect that the formal semantics description is intended to be the normative definition for operations that are formally defined there, rather than the description of behavior in the language sections.

19 S. Amer-Yahia, C. Botev, J. Shanmugasundaram. *TeXQuery: A Full-Text Search Extension to XQuery* (2004). Available at: http://www.cs.cornell.edu/database/TeXQuery/.

20 The definition of `FTContains` is precise where it can be, but many parts of `FTContains` are left implementation-defined or implementation-dependent (see the next subsection, "How Standard?").

the relevance of each result to the query — for each match, just how good a match is it? The XQuery Full-Text Language spec gives a lot of detailed semantic definition to say exactly what should be the result of the evaluation of any particular `FTContains` expression. But what can we say about `score`?

Certainly we must define the data type that results from the evaluation of `score` — XQuery is a strongly typed language, and we need to know whether `score` results in an integer or a float. It's fairly clear that we should also define the range of possible values for `score`; otherwise, scores from different implementations cannot be compared. But what does the value of the score actually mean? At the time of writing, the score clause binds a value to a variable, and that value must be of data type `xs:float`, in the range [0,1]. So far, so good, but with this definition I could build an XQuery Full-Text engine that always returns 0 (or 1, or 0.5, or . . .) for `score` and claim compliance with the spec.

The spec also says that for "score values greater than 0, a higher score must imply a higher degree of relevance." Yet relevance is implementation-defined, and it is in any case highly subjective. We believe this is a good rule to have, but it can only be followed in spirit (and not to the letter).

Then there is the question of the relationship between the value of score and the Boolean value of `FTContains` for the same query over the same data. Should a score of 0 imply that `FTContains` is false? Conversely, should an `FTContains` value of false imply that the score is 0? This is currently noted as an issue — we believe that, for now, the value of score and `ftcontains` should not be bound together.

Finally, there is the notion of score using second-order functions. Informally, a *second-order* function is one that has to be processed as a string, not one that can be evaluated immediately. In the current XQuery Full-Text spec, the `score` clause binds a variable to an expression. But this is no ordinary expression — a query processor cannot evaluate that expression on its own and then substitute the result in the query. The expression is always an `FTContains` (or a series of `FTContains` expressions combined using `and` or `or`), which would always evaluate to a Boolean. Rather, the processor has to consume this special expression as if it were a string — "what would the score be for a query that consisted of just these `FTContains` expressions?" XQuery has so far avoided second-order functions, so the current score clause is something "special."

How Standard?

The questions around score (earlier) bring up the question of just how "standard" XQuery Full-Text can possibly be. The basic algorithms for calculating score, and hence ranking results by relevance, are well known — we have described Salton's algorithm and PageRank elsewhere in this book (see Chapter 18, "Finding Stuff"). But search engine vendors generally add their own "secret sauce" to these algorithms, each claiming that its engine gives better ranking than any other. That means that we cannot standardize the semantics for score[21] — it has to be implementation-dependent.

Similarly, tokenization — the exact method for breaking Full-Text down into *tokens* (usually *words*) — is implementation-dependent. So an XQuery Full-Text engine can choose to tokenize text, for example, so that the tokenized output contains the stemmed values for each word in the text (all words with the same linguistic root as each word in the text). Such a tokenizer would result in every XQuery Full-Text search being a stemmed search, even though the spec says that stemming is optional and that the default is *not stemmed*.

Add to this list thesaural search (the contents of thesauri are not standardized) and stemming (the semantics of stemming is not defined), and it's clear that two compliant W3C XQuery Full-Text engines could give a wide range of results for the same query.

We believe that it *is* worthwhile to standardize the *syntax* of Full-Text search. While some would argue that we should stop there, we also believe that it is worthwhile to standardize the *semantics* of Full-Text search as much as possible, though we must also recognize the limitations of this approach.

Delineating Embedded XQuery Expressions

One of the goals of the W3C XQuery Full-Text language is that Full-Text operations should be a first-class part of the XQuery language. That means we need to be able to mix Full-Text and other kinds of expressions freely in a query. It's difficult to do that unless you know where the Full-Text productions apply and where the XQuery productions apply. The easiest way out of this dilemma is *either* to introduce a new kind of parentheses that enclose a Full-Text expression (actually an `FTSelection`, the right-hand side of a Full-Text expres-

21 Comparing scores from Full-Text searches across different data sources — even if the searches are done by the same engine using the same scoring algorithm — is famously difficult.

sion), or to introduce a new kind of parentheses that enclose an XQuery expression when it occurs inside an `FTSelection`. At the time of writing, XQuery Full-Text uses "`{}`" to enclose an XQuery expression inside an `FTSelection`, but this may change.

Defining Query Options Indirectly

It should be clear to the reader by now that a Full-Text query has a lot of options — the language, thesaurus (or thesauri), stopword list(s), *etc.*, that provide the context of a matching operation. Some of these options can be fully described as part of the query — *e.g.*, the language — but others cannot — it's not practical to reproduce a 300-word stopword list or a 10,000-term thesaurus as part of each query. That means we need a mechanism to describe some options indirectly — "I want to use the English maritime stopword list and the English pharmaceuticals thesaurus for this query." Possibly, we also need a mechanism for defining those pointers ("When I say *English maritime stopword list,* I mean the following words . . ."). Probably, we need some mechanism for setting defaults, *e.g.*, the default thesaurus to use, in the query prolog.

API vs. Solution

When looking at the progress of XQuery Full-Text, we should draw a clear distinction between a Full-Text *API* and a Full-Text *solution*. It is the API that should be standardized — a set of low-level functions and/or expressions that can be used as building blocks for real-world solutions. Any suggestions that higher-level functionality (such as the best way to search across enterprise documents) should be standardized are to be resisted.

13.2.6 XQuery Full-Text — Some Implementations

Let's switch back to talking about XQuery Full-Text in general — the W3C XQuery Full-Text spec is still quite new and incomplete, and none of the major vendors (to our knowledge) has implemented this draft spec. There are some experimental implementations of W3C XQuery Full-Text, such as Galax — go to http://www.galaxquery.com/ for details. Some of the major software vendors have found other ways to include Full-Text search with their XQuery implementations.

IBM, Microsoft

Neither IBM nor Microsoft has, at the time of writing, announced plans to support W3C XQuery Full-Text. Both have been active on the task force (as can be seen from the list of editors' affiliations), so they may well implement XQuery Full-Text when it becomes part of the standard.

Microsoft currently recommends using SQL Server's Full-Text indexing capabilities to create a Full-Text index on XML documents, and doing Full-Text search to prefilter documents before applying XQuery.[22] This approach is better than nothing, but it's a long way from XQuery Full-Text — it only allows you to search across whole XML documents (minus element tags and attributes).

We haven't managed to find any information on IBM's plans in this area. IBM does offer Full-Text search in a number of its products, and they are active on both the XQuery Working Group and the XQuery Full-Text Task Force, so we look forward to hearing about their XQuery Full-Text product plans.

Oracle

Like Microsoft, Oracle also provides Full-Text search as part of its database. But the Oracle Text index, and its operators `CONTAINS` and `SCORE`, are XML-aware — it's possible to search for a text query expression (words and phrases combined with Booleans, stemming, thesauri, fuzzy match, *etc.*) either `WITHIN` a specified element or attribute or in an XPath (`INPATH`). Oracle's `CONTAINS` follows the spirit of the SQL/MM spec — that is, it's a function that takes two arguments, a column name and a string containing a text query expression (describing what you are searching for). The text query expression language does not follow SQL/MM exactly, but it does provide an equally rich set of features.

Oracle's XQuery implementation also includes a vendor-defined extension function, `ora:contains`, that provides Full-Text search as part of XQuery or XPath. The `ora:contains` function follows the "functions" approach described earlier in this chapter — that is, it's a single function that takes in a node or item (what to search over) and a string representing the text query (what to search for) and returns a Boolean (matched or not matched).

---

22 S. Pal, M. Fussell, and I. Dolobowsky, *XML Support in SQL Server 2005* (Redmond, WA: Microsoft Press, 2004). Available at: http://msdn.microsoft.com/library/default.asp?url=/library/en-us/dnsql90/html/sql2k5xml.asp.

These two approaches represent the classic "Who's on top?" dilemma for Full-Text search over XML in a mixed environment.[23] Is it better to express the query as "`dog and cat within /movies/movie/title`" — making Full-Text "on top" and restricting the results with an XPath? Or is it better to express the query as "`/movies/movie/title[. ora:contains "dog and cat"]`" — making the XPath "on top" and describing the Full-Text search on individual elements? With Oracle's `CONTAINS` and `ora:contains`, you can do either. In fact, you can do both — and combining `CONTAINS` and `ora:contains` in the same query gives you a lot of the benefits of XQuery Full-Text without having to wait for a W3C XQuery Full-Text Recommendation. `ora:contains` can be used in any of Oracle's SQL/XML or extension functions that use XPath, so, for example, you can locate a document using `CONTAINS` and then pull out the interesting *parts* of that document using `extractNode()` with an XPath argument that uses `ora:contains`.[24]

In the latest version of Oracle's database, Oracle has implemented a pre-Recommendation version of XQuery, callable via the SQL/XML extension functions `XMLQUERY` and `XMLTABLE`. The `ora:contains` XPath function can be used as part of an XQuery in either of those functions to provide XQuery Full-Text in a SQL context — see Example 13-8.[25]

Example 13-8 *XQuery Full-Text, Oracle*

```
SELECT XMLQUERY(
  'for $r in
    $res/resolution/official-title[
```

23 By "mixed environment" we mean one where there is a set of capabilities for structured search and a separate set of capabilities (*e.g.*, a set of functions) for Full-Text search. In the W3C XQuery Full-Text grammar, the two sets of capabilities are integrated enough that you can mix'n'match them however you want — they are *fully composable.*

24 For an example, see *Searching for Content and Structure in XML Documents*, Oracle9*i* Database Daily Feature. Available at: http://www.oracle.com/technology/products/oracle9i/daily/nov30.html. See also *Oracle XML DB Developer's Guide 10g Release 1 (10.1), Chapter 9: Full Text Search Over XML*. Available at: http://download-west.oracle.com/docs/cd/B14117_01/appdev.101/b10790/xdb09sea.htm#sthref885.

25 Stephen Buxton, *Querying XML, XML 2004 Proceedings* (IDEAlliance, 2004). Available at: http://www.idealliance.org/proceedings/xml04/abstracts/paper218.html. This example was taken from Stephen Buxton, Muralidhar Krishnaprasad, and Zhen Hua Liu, *Querying XML* (Oracle Openworld 2004). Available at: http://download-west.oracle.com/oowsf2004/1136_wp.pdf.

```
      ora:contains(., "bulgaria NEAR slovenia")>0]
    return
      $r' passing resolution as "res" returning content)
  AS result FROM resolutions_xml
```

Mark Logic

Mark Logic[26] has implemented a variation on the "many-functions" approach described earlier in this chapter. The MarkLogic Content Server includes an XQuery implementation extended with a set of functions for Full-Text search. The MarkLogic Server supports a function `cts:search($searchable-expression, $search-query)`. `cts:search` is similar to Oracle's `ora:contains`, except that the second argument can be made up of other `cts` functions. There is one function to perform a simple word or phrase search (`cts:word-query`); one function for each of the *combining operations* (`cts:and-query`, `cts:or-query`, `cts:and-not-query`, `cts:not-query`); plus one function to describe *proximity operations* (`cts:near-query`). An optional argument to these functions allows you to specify *matching options* and *word expansions* (case sensitivity, punctuation sensitivity, stemming, wildcards, and language).

With this compromise – using arguments rather than functions to represent *matching options* and *word expansions* – the number of functions is kept manageable, but the language is fully integrated with XQuery. There is no string argument that represents an opaque sublanguage, so any of the query terms can be derived from XQuery expressions. One could argue that this is *more* composable than the grammar extension approach – in this many-functions approach, the *matching options* and *word expansions* are strings, which could presumably be derived from XQuery expressions, while in the grammar extension approach they are language keywords, which cannot.

Mark Logic claims their XQuery Full-Text functions map closely to the functionality in the W3C XQuery Full-Text working drafts, providing a lower-level API that can be used to implement the W3C XQuery Full-Text functionality when it becomes a Recommendation. See Example 13-9 for examples of W3C XQuery Full-Text queries and their equivalents using the Mark Logic language.

26 See http://www.marklogic.com.

Example 13-9 *XQuery Full-Text, W3C vs. Mark Logic*

```
W3C XPath:
    /books/book[title ftcontains ("dog" with stemming) && "cat"]/author

Mark Logic:
    /books/book[cts:contains(title,
        cts:and-query((cts:word-query("dog","stemmed"), "cat")))]/author

W3C XQuery:
    for $b in //book
    score $s as $b/title ftcontains "dog" && "cat"
    where $s > 0
    order by $s descending
    return $b/author

Mark Logic:
    for $b in cts:search(//book,
        cts:element-query(QName("title"), cts:and-query(("dog","cat"))))
    return $b/author
```

The Mark Logic language does have some differences in approach (as opposed to merely differences in surface syntax) from the W3C working draft. Most important, in the Mark Logic language, score is implicit – *i.e.,* the `cts:search` function returns results implicitly ordered by score. This makes the queries shorter, at the cost of some control. And there are some detailed differences, representing short-cuts – *e.g.,* if a query term is in all-lowercase, it has case-insensitive matching options by default; if it is in mixed-case or uppercase, it has case-sensitive matching options by default. These differences aside, Mark Logic's language is an important step in the direction of XQuery Full-Text.

13.3 Update

The second major piece of functionality missing from XQuery 1.0 is the ability to *update* XML documents, collections, repositories, messages, *etc.* In this section, we discuss the reasons why updating XML is necessary and how it differs from updating records in ordinary flat files, rows in tables of relational databases, or objects in object-oriented databases.

We then review the requirements that the W3C's XML Query Working Group has published for the planned XQuery Update Facility, examining each of the requirements in turn. Following that review, you will learn about some current proposals for XQuery Update Facility syntax and semantics and how they respond to those Requirements, after which we take a look at how a few XQuery vendors already deal with the problem of updating XML documents.

Finally, we speculate a bit on the future of the XQuery Update Facility, including a bit of "reading the tea leaves" to guess when a real standard will emerge.

13.3.1 Motivation: Where/Why We Need Update

For as long as computer systems have been used to store data (as opposed to merely manipulating them), it has been necessary to change stored data in many ways. As data have become more complex, more integral to our businesses and our day-to-day lives, the necessity to effect change to the data has only grown.

In the beginning (well, not the *very* beginning — only after the advent of magnetic media), data were usually stored directly on some storage medium, such as a tape, a drum, or a disk. Those media had different organizational mechanisms, which made the paradigms for accessing them very different — and the paradigms for changing their contents even more radically different. Of necessity, file systems were born; they provided a way of shielding almost all programs from the tedious details of the physical media on which data were stored while (normally) providing a kind of catalog to correlate a mnemonic name with a specific set of data.

But it didn't take long for users of computer systems to realize that their needs for data organization were not always satisfied by these "flat" files (that is, files without inherent structure). The concept of *databases* caught on very quickly because of the tremendous additional power they gave applications for protection of, organization of, and access to data stored in them. Databases gave more structure to data, whether the model on which the database was designed was hierarchical, network, relational, object-oriented, or what have you. The presence of such structure makes it possible to identify, retrieve, and manipulate data at a more granular level than feasible with less structured data. And that granularity has everything to do with how all those data can be modified.

If the data in question comprise a long string of bits without clearly determinable internal boundaries (such as an executable image) and you want to make a change, it may be necessary to replace the entire string of bits — because it's so difficult, if not impossible, to clearly identify the piece of the bit string that needs to be changed — instead of altering smaller parts of the string. Replacement of very large chunks of data is generally rather expensive, especially if only a tiny fraction of the data they contain is actually being altered.

When the data do have clearly identifiable boundaries, either because of some sort of "marker" carried in the data themselves (*e.g.*, field marks and record marks) or because of an external description of the boundaries' locations (structural metadata), then it becomes much easier to modify smaller pieces of those data. Consequently, the application changing the data becomes a bit more robust in the face of changes to the details of the data's structure, maintenance requirements for that application are reduced, and the data modifications themselves are more easily verified.

XML is all about structure. The tree-structured nature of XML generally provides for a highly granular mechanism for representing data, whether those data are the semistructured data representing literature marked up for publication or the highly structured purchase orders for DVDs being sold at a video store. In fact, one of the primary values of XML is exactly that: expressing the structure needed to make data more useful.

It is thus quite tempting to view XML data oversimplistically, imagining that the task of modifying a portion of an XML document to be no more than a trivial replacement of that portion, perhaps just replacing the value of an attribute or inserting a new element and its children or deleting part of a tree. Unfortunately, the world isn't quite that simple, in part because XML is used in enormously varied ways. XML documents might be stored in flat files, in rows of relational databases, or in native tree structures of so-called pure XML databases. But XML is also used to mark up highly transient information, such as weather or stock data being broadcast to subscribers' cell phones.

What, then, does it mean to "update" XML data? It can mean many things: replacement of an entire XML document with a new one, deletion of an XML document, creation of a new XML document, modification of some part of an XML document by replacing one or more elements with new elements, insertion of new elements or attributes, removal of PI nodes, and so forth. Clearly, any truly useful update capability must be able to accommodate this wide variety of actions.

In the next section, as we explore the requirements that the W3C has published for an update facility to augment XQuery, the varied nature of updating will emerge.

13.3.2 Requirements

In early 2005, the W3C published a first public Working Draft of the Requirements for an XQuery Update Facility.[27] These requirements are analogous to the Requirements[28] published several years earlier for an XML Query Language. They specify, at a high level, the fundamental requirements for an update facility for XQuery without saying anything at all about how such a facility might be designed to satisfy those requirements. In this section, we'll look at each of the requirements in turn, elaborating on those that are not obvious.

Usage Scenarios

The first thing found in the Requirements is a statement of the XML update usage scenarios that the Working Group believes it is necessary to address. ("Usage scenarios" are not the same thing as "use cases," the latter being more detailed. No use cases have been published for the XQuery update facility at the time of this writing.) The scenarios are:

- Updating persistent XML stores — This involves modification of XML stored on a persistent medium, such as in a file or a database.
- Modifying XML messages — In this scenario, messages could be altered either to add information generated as they are being processed or to update their statuses.
- Add to existing XML document — New data can be added to XML documents, such as appending new entries to a data log.

27 *XQuery Update Facility Requirements, W3C Working Draft* (Cambridge, MA: World Wide Web Consortium, 2005). Available at: http://www.w3.org/TR/xquery-update-requirements/.

28 *XML Query Requirements, W3C Working Draft* (Cambridge, MA: World Wide Web Consortium, 1999). Available at: http://www.w3.org/XML/Group/1999/11/xmlqueryreq-19991104/. (The most recent version is available at: http://www.w3.org/TR/xquery-update-requirements/.)

- Updating XML registries — Configuration files, user profiles, administrative logs, *etc.* can require updates.
- Creating edited copies — A new copy of an existing XML document or subtree in a document, such as a modified web page, can be created.
- Modifying XML views — It is possible to create an XML view of non-XML data,[29] leading to the desirability of updating those non-XML data through the XML view of it.

General Requirements

The Requirements include a number of items that don't fit neatly into any of the other categories discussed in this section, but that are seen as overall requirements for the XQuery Update Facility. They are:

- Query Update Syntax — Just as XQuery is defined using a human-readable syntax and an XML syntax (XQueryX), the Update Facility should have both kinds of syntax. Among other things, this will ease the process of integrating the Update Facility into XQuery.
- Declarativity — XQuery is a declarative language, and its Update Facility should also be declarative in nature. One of the advantages of this is that many optimization strategies will be possible.
- Protocol Independence — XQuery was designed to have no dependency on any sort of networking protocol, and the Update Facility will have the same characteristic.
- Error Conditions — When errors occur during the process of performing an update, the error that is reported will ordinarily be one of the standard errors defined by the Update Facility, using the same conventions that XQuery uses.
- Static Type Checking — XQuery has an optional static typing feature, and the Update Facility will provide a parallel feature.

---

29 *ISO/IEC 9075-14:2003, Information Technology — Database Languages — SQL — Part 14: XML-Related Facilities (SQL/XML)* (Geneva, Switzerland: International Organization for Standardization, 2003).

Relationship to XQuery 1.0

The XQuery Update Facility's relationship to XQuery itself has implications on the design of the Update Facility.

- Based on the Data Model – XQuery operates not on the serialized representation of XML documents, but on the Data Model representation. The Update Facility must use the same paradigm in order to integrate with XQuery.
- Based on XQuery – The Update Facility must identify items to be updated or deleted and to be used as reference points for insertions. It will use XQuery to identify those items as well as to construct new values for updates and insertions.

XML Query Update Functionality

This set of requirements identifies the specific capabilities that the XQuery Update Facility must have in order to be useful.

- Locus of Modifications – The Update Facility will be capable of altering properties of existing nodes in a Data Model instance without changing the identity of those nodes, as well as of making copies (with new identities) of nodes.
- Delete – The Update Facility will be able to delete nodes from Data Model instances.
- Insert – The Update Facility will be able to insert new nodes at specified positions in Data Model instances.
- Replace – It will be possible to replace nodes in Data Model instances.
- Changing Values – It will also be possible to alter the values of nodes (that is, the value that the typed-value accessor defined by the Data Model would return) in Data Model instances.
- Modifying Properties – It may be possible to modify a number of properties of nodes in Data Model instances, such as the name of the node, the type of the node, the nilability of the node, and so forth. The specific properties that can be changed will vary between kinds of nodes (*e.g.*, changing the name of a comment node is not a meaningful concept).

- Moving Nodes — The Update Facility might provide a way to move a node from one place in a Data Model instance to another place. Problems such as node identity may make it infeasible to implement this functionality.
- Conditional Updates — The Update Facility will provide a way to specify that certain operations are performed only when certain conditions are met. This might be done, for example, through the use of some sort of "`if`" expression or statement, or a "`case`" expression or statement.
- Iterative Updates — It will be possible to specify operations that are invoked on all nodes in a sequence of nodes generated by some sort of iterative expression (one example of such an expression in XQuery is the `for` expression in a FLWOR expression).
- Validation — XQuery allows for the results of expressions to be validated against the schema definitions that apply to them; such validation makes a copy of those results and thus changes the identities of the items within the results. The Update Facility might provide a way to validate the results of one or more changes without changing the identity of the nodes involved.
- Compositionality — It will be possible to compose the Update Facility operations with one another, and it might be possible to compose such operations with XQuery expressions (for example, allowing an update operation to be specified everywhere that XQuery expressions are permitted).
- Parameterization — The Update Facility might provide a way to parameterize the various update operations that it defines.

Transaction Characteristics

Whenever multiple changes are made to data, there is a need to ensure that the end result is consistent with the intent of those changes. Most data management systems provide some sort of transaction capability to provide that consistency. A popular and widely respected book[30] uses the term ACID to describe the properties of transactions.

30 Jim Gray and Andreas Reuter, *Transaction Processing Concepts and Techniques* (San Mateo: Morgan-Kaufmann, 1994).

- Atomicity — The Update Facility will specify some number of atomic (indivisible) operations and provide a way to group operations together so that the entire group is treated as atomic.
- Consistency — After an update has been performed, the Data Model instance that was modified will be consistent with respect to the Data Model constraints, and all type annotations will be consistent with the types of the items that they annotate. The Update Facility might also provide a way to force this level of consistency at a finer granularity, such as an individual insertion.
- Isolation — The Update Facility might define a way by which the operations that it defines can be executed in isolation from any changes made to the data from any other activity.
- Durability — The Update Facility will specify the manner in which the changes made to Data Model instances are caused to be durable. "Durable" is not the same as "persistent" — that is, changes to a Data Model instance are durable if the Data Model retains the changes until their effects are altered by additional update operations or until the Data Model instance ceases to exist for any reason.

13.3.3 Alternatives: Syntax and Semantics

There are any number of decisions that have to be made when defining an update capability for any query language. When the query language in question is a functional language without side effects, there are additional decisions to be made. XQuery is such a functional language and has been carefully designed to have no side effects (other than those that might be caused by the invocation of external functions).

But the very nature of an update capability is that side effects are intended to occur. This apparent conflict can be approached in several ways. One way is simply to abandon the notion of XQuery as a side-effect free language — we think it is extremely unlikely that the XML Query WG in the W3C would entertain such a notion.

Another way is to define a second language — let's call it the XQuery Update Language — that invokes XQuery expressions or even incorporates XQuery as a proper subset. The disadvantage of following this path is that implementers and users alike are faced with having to deal with two (apparent) languages. We doubt that the XML Query WG would choose this approach because of the possible confusion it might cause.

A third approach is to isolate the components that can cause side effects (such as insertion, deletion, and replacement) into something entirely new in XQuery: statements. As you read in Chapter 11, "XQuery 1.0 Definition," XQuery comprises only *expressions* that are contained in *modules*. If the concept of XQuery *statements* were added to the mix, then it might be acceptable to partition the language into statements that are permitted to cause side effects and expressions that are not.

A fourth alternative is to define two kinds of expression: those that are free of side effects and those that may cause side effects. The two kinds would be clearly delineated by, for example, using a particular keyword (*e.g.*, `update`) to introduce every expression that might cause a side effect.

We believe that the real choice is between those last two alternatives. In the short term (XQuery 1.0 time frame), it's almost certain that the Update Facility will be published as a separate W3C Recommendation. Why? Because the XML querying community urgently needs the Update Facility and is unlikely to wait for the next edition of XQuery to be published before adopting a solution, and XQuery 1.0 is highly unlikely to be delayed until the Update Facility definition can be completed. However, we think it's probable that the Update Facility will be more properly integrated into some future edition of XQuery itself.

The choice of statement *vs.* expression will have significant impacts on the syntax that the Update Facility will define; it will also have implications on the semantics of the language. For example, if the approach of defining update statements is taken, it seems quite unlikely that the semantics of a particular update statement will impact the semantics of any expressions used by the statement. But if updates are defined as kinds of expressions, the ability to compose all kinds of expressions together makes it likely that the semantics of update expressions will impact the semantics of expressions with which they are composed.

Questions that must be answered include the following:

- Should there be a concept of an XQuery "program," analogous to XQuery modules, in which update statements are allowed?

- Should XQuery functions be allowed to contain update statements or expressions? If so, should there be explicit syntax to mark, in XQuery library modules, the signatures of such functions as having side effects?
- Should there be explicit syntax for starting and terminating a sequence of update operations that are intended to function as an atomic unit (such as a SQL's START TRANSACTION and COMMIT/ROLLBACK statements that start and terminate transactions), or should that be done by some other facility (such as a transaction manager external to the XQuery implementation)?
- What implications are caused by update expressions or statements on the declarative nature of XQuery as a whole? What kinds of rules might be required to limit the ability of implementations to "reorder" the evaluation of expressions based on the presence of update operations?

The nature and extent of the questions that must be addressed when designing an update capability are sufficiently difficult that the design is not trivial and will be very time-consuming.

Proposals that we have seen for the XQuery Update Facility have included both the "update statement" and "update expression" approaches. They generally propose statements or expressions to insert new XML values both as children of existing elements (as first sibling or as last sibling of existing children) and as the preceding or following sibling of existing nodes. In addition, they propose facilities to delete existing XML nodes and subtrees, to rename existing nodes without changing their identities, to alter the contents of existing nodes (again, without changing their identities), and so forth.

None of the proposals we've seen have addressed the issue of transactions. That may be wise at this stage, because the subject is known to be controversial, with some participants believing that explicit syntax should be provided for terminating (as well as, perhaps, initiating) transactions, while others believe that such matters are better left to the environment in which XQuery and the Update Facility exist.

We believe that the XQuery Update Facility was delayed relative to XQuery 1.0 itself in order to allow the Working Group to focus on the base expression language without the additional distractions and workload that concurrent work on an update capability would have caused. Now that XQuery is closing in on the final Recommendation stage, we expect that the XQuery Update Facility will receive more attention.

Unfortunately, many XQuery applications don't have the luxury of waiting until the W3C publishes a final Recommendation for an XQuery Update Facility and then for implementations of the Facility to be delivered. Instead, those applications have little choice other than electing to use the proprietary features of current XQuery implementations and adopting the eventual Recommendation when it has been delivered and implemented.

13.3.4 How Products Handle Update Today

In the absence of even a public Working Draft for an XQuery Update Facility provided by the W3C and the existence of marketplace requirements for the ability to update XML documents, collections, messages, *etc.*, suppliers of several XQuery implementations have provided update solutions using several strategies.

In this section, we briefly explore the approaches taken by a few of the more prominent implementers of XQuery processors as well as an approach being proposed by a group that develops specifications related to XML databases.

Oracle

Oracle, like the other implementers discussed in this chapter, does not support an XQuery syntax-based approach to updating XML documents. Instead, Oracle provides three mechanisms for responding to users' needs in this area. Applications must choose between the three strategies and cannot, for example, locate and retrieve data using one technique and update it using another.

One approach is a DOM-based API (part of Oracle's XMLDB), which requires programs to invoke methods on a DOM object representing an XML document. That API is based on the W3C's Document Object Model,[31] which provides methods for traversing the DOM representation of an XML document, retrieving values from desired nodes, and updating the document by inserting nodes, deleting nodes, modifying the values of nodes, and so forth.

---

31 *Document Object Model (DOM) Level 3 Core Specification, W3C Recommendation* (Cambridge, MA: World Wide Web Consortium, 2004). Available at: http://www.w3.org/TR/DOM-Level3-Core/.

A second approach is a Java API that defines a class to represent the XML type, along with methods such as `deleteXML()`, `insertXML()`, and `updateXML()`. The Java API is heavily used by Oracle's customer base, and it is likely to be augmented by the emerging XQJ (XQuery API for Java™) API[32] under development in the Java Community Process. You'll read more about XQJ in Chapter 14, "XQuery APIs."

The other approach, more directly related to XQuery, is based on SQL/XML (about which you will read in Chapter 15, "SQL/XML"). In SQL/XML, applications use ordinary SQL statements to access XML data stored as values of the XML type in columns of database tables. A SQL function, `XMLQuery()`, allows applications to evaluate XQuery expressions against those XML values. Oracle extensions[33] to SQL/XML provide the ability to update those XQuery expressions. The extension functions are:

- `UpdateXML()` — Replaces an existing node (or node sequence) in an XML value (cannot be used to insert or remove nodes).
- `InsertChildXML()` — Inserts a node as a child of an existing node in an XML value, using an associated XML Schema to determine the correct insertion location among the new child node's siblings.
- `InsertXMLBefore()` — Inserts a node as the immediately preceding sibling of an existing node of an XML value.
- `AppendChildXML()` — Inserts a node as a child of an existing node in an XML value as the very last sibling of the existing node's current children.
- `DeleteXML()` — Deletes an existing node from an XML value.

Unfortunately, Oracle's extension functions are not true update functions, in that they do not update an XML value "in place." Instead, they are really transformation functions that return an

32 Information about JSR 225: XQuery API for Java™ (XQJ) can be found at http://www.jcp.org/en/jsr/detail?id=225.

33 *Oracle XML Java API Reference 10g Release 1 (10.1), XDK Java Classes* (Redwood Shores, CA: Oracle Corporation, 2004). Available at: http://download-west.oracle.com/docs/cd/B14117_01/appdev.101/b12024/toc.htm.

updated *copy* of the value on which they operate. Therefore, they are side effect–free functions. When used in a context (such as a SQL UPDATE statement) where values are being replaced, then these functions have the semantics of update functions.

Similar functions are provided by Oracle in their XML SQL Utility (SMU), which is part of their PL/SQL language.

We would anticipate that, once an XQuery Update Facility has been defined in the W3C, Oracle would update their XQuery implementation to support the Update Facility, in addition to the other strategies they already provide for updating XML.

IBM

At the time of writing, IBM had not yet released an XQuery implementation. Naturally, they have not released an XQuery update capability either.

IBM has, however, offered a tool that "provides an XML view of relational tables and a query of those views as if they were XML documents." This tool, named *XML for Tables*, is available[34] on IBM's alphaWorks site. The tool, which implements a subset of XQuery, translates XQuery expressions into SQL expressions that are executed by DB2. The tool does not, however, appear to have any ability to update the data behind those XML views.

IBM has frequently indicated that a future version of DB2 will support XQuery directly. Presumably that support will include XQuery updating capabilities at the same time. We presume that IBM will add support for the XQuery Update Facility when that spec has been finalized.

Microsoft

Microsoft's SQL Server 2005 provides an implementation of (a subset of) XQuery. As part of that implementation, they have built some extensions that support XML updates. Unlike Oracle, these extensions do not depend on SQL/XML capabilities, but are provided through a method operating on instances of their XML type.

That method, `modify()`, is invoked as part of the SET clause of a SQL UPDATE statement. The parameter of the method is a character string that expresses one of several types of updates, including insert, replace value of, delete, *etc.*, as well as an XQuery expression

34 http://www.alphaworks.ibm.com/tech/xtable.

that identifies the nodes to be modified and the values to be used for the modifications.

Microsoft provides a set of .NET classes used with XML. Some of these classes provide a wide variety of methods that support setting the values of nodes, inserting nodes into specified locations, deleting nodes, and replacing nodes. These classes and their methods are unrelated to XQuery, but they serve roughly the same function as the classes and methods of Oracle's DOM-based API.

Microsoft offers yet another approach to updating XML, based on a facility they call *updategrams*. An updategram "represent[s] changes to an XML instance that, when combined with an annotated schema, persist these changes back to relational changes."[35] Updategrams are defined to be XML documents using a specific vocabulary that captures updates to the (relational) data that underlies an XML view.

The vocabulary uses elements `<before>` and `<after>` as children of a `<sync>` element. Each `<sync>` element represents a single update to the XML view, with the `<before>` and `<after>` elements providing the values of the "existing" state of the data being updated and the new value resulting from the update, respectively. If a particular `<sync>` element contains a `<before>` element and not an `<after>` element, it represents a deletion of data; the presence of an `<after>` and not a `<before>` element indicates an insertion, and the presence of both corresponds to a modification of existing data. (Some observers suggest that an updategram is, in effect, isomorphic to a change log that records actions taken to update such data.)

As the XQuery Update Facility reaches its final development stages, we expect that Microsoft will enhance SQL Server's XQuery support to align with the Update Facility specification.

Mark Logic

The MarkLogic Content Server includes an XQuery implementation extended with a set of functions for update. The functions are:

- document-insert($uri, $root-node)
- document-delete($uri)
- node-replace($old-node, $new-node)

35 S. Pal, M. Fussell, and I. Dolobowsky, *XML Support in SQL Server 2005* (Redmond, WA: Microsoft Press, 2004). Available at: http://msdn.microsoft.com/library/default.asp?url=/library/en-us/dnsql90/html/sql2k5xml.asp.

- node-delete($old-node)
- node-insert-before($node, $new-sibling-node)
- node-insert-after($node, $new-sibling-node)
- node-insert-child($parent-node, $new-child-node)

The MarkLogic Server evaluates an XQuery module by spawning an evaluation thread that operates on a snapshot of the database. All the updates appearing in the module are collected, and a change vector (*i.e.*, a time-ordered list of changes) is computed and journaled. The XQuery module has an implied commit that guarantees that either all the changes or none of the changes become persistent.

Mark Logic update evaluation guarantees atomicity, isolation, and durability. Consistency is satisfied, but only in a relatively weak sense, since integrity constraints are not explicitly part of the Mark Logic architecture. Integrity is expressed via denormalized documents: All the elements collected in one document are maintained as a consistent collection. Isolation is maintained in the strongest sense: Each query evaluation thread operates on a static snapshot, and all the updates refer to the original values, even if an update subexpression modifies one of the values appearing elsewhere in the XQuery module

In addition, the MarkLogic Server implements the WebDAV protocol and therefore a complete document properties infrastructure. Updates to document properties are expressed using the following functions:

- document-set-properties($uri, $prop-list)
- document-add-properties($uri, $prop-list)
- document-remove-properties($uri, $prop-name-list)
- document-set-property($uri, $prop)

XUpdate

We've seen how four data management vendors are dealing with XML update requirements today. It's also worth mentioning another sort of standards activity in the open source community: XML:DB is "an industry initiative . . . [that] provides a community for collaborative development of specifications for XML databases and data manipulation technologies." It also provides open source reference implementations of their specifications.

Among the specifications being developed by XML:DB is one named "XUpdate." (Perhaps "has been developed" would be more appropriate, as the latest draft's date would suggest.) The most recent draft of the XUpdate specification[36] is dated 2000-09-14, but there continues to be a certain amount of industry buzz about XUpdate and its applicability to the strong requirement for a language to update XML documents.

XUpdate instructions are in the form of an XML document that contains elements in the xupdate namespace (http://www.xmldb.org/xupdate). XUpdate uses XPath 1.0 as the expression language used to select XML nodes for further processing by the instructions embedded in those elements. Each update must be enclosed in an <xupdate:modifications> element. The update elements themselves are:

- <xupdate:insert-before>
- <xupdate:insert-after>
- <xupdate:append>
- <xupdate:update>
- <xupdate:remove>
- <xupdate:rename>
- <xupdate:variable>
- <xupdate:value-of>
- <xupdate:if>

Most of these update elements correspond very closely to the kinds of updates supported by Oracle's and Microsoft's approaches and to the W3C's requirements for an XQuery Update Facility. In fact, one might argue that XUpdate's syntax is reasonably analogous to Microsoft's updategrams.

<xupdate:append>, <xupdate:insert-after>, and <xupdate:insert-before> may have child elements: <xupdate:element>, <xupdate:attribute>, <xupdate:text>, <xupdate:comment>, and <xupdate:processing-instruction>.

36 A. Laux and L. Martin, *XUpdate WD* (2000). Available at: http://xmldb-org.sourceforge.net/xupdate/xupdate-wd.html.

<xupdate:update> has a select attribute containing an XPath expression that identifies the node set to be updated. The content of the <xupdate:update> element supplies the new content of the elements in the identified node set.

<xupdate:remove> has a select attribute containing an XPath expression that identifies the nodes to be removed.

<xupdate:rename> has a select attribute containing an XPath expression that identifies a set of element or attribute nodes (the other node types are not allowed). The content of the <xupdate:rename> element provides the new name of the identified nodes.

<xupdate:variable> has two attributes: name (which specifies the name of the variable being created) and select (which specifies the value assigned to that variable). The value of a variable is obtained through the use of the <xupdate:value-of> element, whose select attribute provides the name of the variable whose value is wanted. <xupdate:value-of> can be used in other situations as a child element, where it provides a value to be used in evaluating that child element. The syntax and semantics of these elements are similar to those of the analogous variable declaration facility in XSLT (<xsl:variable> and <xupdate:value-of>). <xupdate:variable> and <xupdate:value-of> have no obvious correlation to anything in the update facilities of the vendors we've surveyed in this section.

The XUpdate specification has a heading for Conditional Processing, but there is no content under that heading. However, the XUpdate DTD indicates that the <xupdate:if> element has an attribute named test, whose content must be a Boolean expression, that determines whether or not the contents of the <xupdate:if> are evaluated. The contents of the element can be any mixture of text and child elements <xupdate:element>, <xupdate:attribute>, <xupdate:text>, <xupdate:processing-instruction>, and <xupdate:comment>.

A Google search for XUpdate turns up over 30,000 references, many of which describe implementations of the incomplete five-year-old specification. While XUpdate contains some very useful ideas and has received some industry attention, we don't believe that it is a long-term solution to the problem of integrating XML updating facilities into XQuery. The primary difficulty is that XUpdate uses an XML syntax instead of XQuery's more user-friendly syntax. Another, less critical, reason is that the specification is incomplete in several ways: The syntax and semantics of some elements are not specified at all, and the descriptions of the other elements are imprecise and can be interpreted by different implementers in different ways.

13.3.5 What Lies Ahead?

We've dusted off the old crystal ball and found that it's got too many cracks to be easily read. But we'll go out on a limb to suggest that the XQuery Update Facility will be fully specified not too long (six months or so) after this book goes to press and that it will be embraced fairly quickly by a good cross section of XQuery implementations. It's too soon to tell whether the specification will provide update statements or update expressions — but it will surely not contain both! Our personal experience leads us to prefer the approach of using update expressions, because we think it will be more flexible and powerful in the long run and can be specified more elegantly (perhaps more simply) than the update statement approach. Time — and the XML Query Working Group — will tell.

13.4 Chapter Summary

In this chapter, we've discussed two of the most important features of an XML query language that are missing from XQuery 1.0: a Full-Text search capability and an Update Facility.

We've given you a summary of the issues involved in the two facilities and laid out the current state of their development in the XML Query and XSL Working Groups. We've also shown how some implementations are already providing these capabilities to their users.

Both of these are already under consideration in the W3C and may be expected to hit the streets some time in 2006.

Chapter 14

XQuery APIs

14.1 Introduction

In the last few chapters, you read about XQuery 1.0 and XPath 2.0, languages for querying XML documents, collections, and fragments. But a query language cannot stand alone — it must run in some context. You will read in Chapter 15, "SQL/XML," that the SQL/XML extensions provide an ideal harness for running XQueries in the context of a SQL database. In this chapter, we focus on a more generic XQuery context, the Java context, and describe the proposed JCP standard XQJ.[1] The architecture of XQJ follows that of JDBC® (XQJ has been called "JDBC for XQuery"), which in turn follows ODBC. (See Section 14.2.1 for a description of ODBC and JDBC.)

After describing XQJ, we compare it to SQL/XML as an XQuery API. Though most of this chapter is about XQJ in particular, we urge you to consider XQJ (and, to a lesser extent, SQL/XML) as a general template for any future XQuery APIs.

---

1 Information about JSR 225: XQuery API for Java™ (XQJ) can be found at http://www.jcp.org/en/jsr/detail?id=225. JSR 225 (XQJ) is still under construction and may change radically before it becomes a standard.

Why an API?

The XQuery language lets you specify a query over an instance of the XQuery Data Model, which produces an instance of the XQuery Data Model. The definition of the XQuery language describes the environment[2] in which a query is run — such things as the available documents and collections, the default collection, in-scope variables, and in-scope schema definitions. This context needs to be set up — created and possibly updated — in some way that's external to XQuery. The input to, and output from, an XQuery need to be defined and processed — in most cases, you want to do something interesting with the result of a query, such as feed it into a report or into some other program. And you want to be able to do all this in some programming language (say, Java). An API (Application Programming Interface) is the interface between a programming language's statements, expressions, and data types, and some other data model and/or language — in this case, XQuery. An XQuery API is necessary to formulate and execute XQueries from inside a program.

Where?

As an aside, it's interesting to note that, while XQuery is defined inside the W3C, the XQuery APIs are not. One could argue that a Java API for XQuery should be defined by the W3C (because it's XQuery), or by the JCP (Java Community Process) community (because it's Java), or jointly by both standards bodies (because it's both XQuery and Java). XQJ is actually defined wholly in the JCP community — XQuery is assumed to be a given, untouchable standard around which a Java API is defined.

However, if you look at the names of the people most deeply involved with the W3C's XQuery and the JCP's XQJ, you will find there is a great deal of overlap. At the time of writing, Andrew Eisenberg of IBM and Jim Melton of Oracle are the joint spec leads on JSR 225, and they are both also cochairs of the W3C XQuery Working Group. This is not a coincidence.

14.2 Alphabet-Soup Review

Before we look at XQJ in detail, let's review some of the closely related standards.

---

2 As you will read in Section 14.3.4, this environment is split into the *static context* and the *dynamic context*.

14.2.1 ODBC and JDBC

Let's imagine you have a SQL database, and you want to run a SQL query. You know exactly the query you want to run, and you have typed, say, `SELECT title FROM movies WHERE yearReleased = 1985` into a text editor such as Notepad. Now what? To execute the query, you must run some sort of program – perhaps your database vendor supplies one. In Oracle's case, the simplest program for running queries is SQL*Plus, so you might run the SQL*Plus program, entering a username, password, and connect string (which describes how to connect to a particular database instance, possibly over some network connection) when SQL*Plus asks for them. Then you paste in the query, and you see the results – a list of titles, nicely formatted with column headings, pagination, a row count, *etc.*

SQL*Plus is fine for running simple queries and eyeballing the results, but in general you want to be able to write your own program that does all the things SQL*Plus does (simplistically) for you.[3] You want to specify your own connection details, execute a query, and then process results in whatever programming language you choose. It is possible to call SQL*Plus from your program and interpret its results,[4] but in general you want to be able to access the database directly from your program. Most vendors supply an API so that you can do just that – in Oracle's case, this is OCI,[5] the Oracle Call Interface. OCI is a set of database access and retrieval functions, supplied as a dynamic runtime library, that can be linked into your C or C++ program. Your application can call these functions to connect to an Oracle database, manipulate data, and run queries, returning results that can be understood and processed by the calling program. That's a proprietary Oracle database API.

Now let's imagine that you want to access data in several databases, and not all of them are Oracle databases. Or perhaps you are writing an application that is database-independent, leaving the choice of underlying storage to your customer. Now you need to

---

3 SQL*Plus is of course a program, and it uses the Oracle Call Interface (OCI) mentioned below to communicate with the Oracle database.

4 One of the authors once wrote a Perl (cgi) program that spawned a process called SQL*Plus, then used a pipe to send queries to, and get results to/from, that process. The Perl caller then parsed the results into an array and processed them further. This can be fun, but is not recommended for enterprise programming projects.

5 See http://www.oracle.com/technology/tech/oci/index.html.

write data access routines that can be understood by any SQL database. Enter ODBC, Open DataBase Connectivity, produced by Microsoft (in partnership with Simba) in 1992 to address the SQL Access Group's requirements for a common Call-Level Interface (CLI). ODBC is based on the CLI specs from X/Open[6] and ISO/IEC.[7] Think of ODBC as OCI made generic — ODBC today is supported in many programming languages, against almost every SQL database. ODBC works by providing a generic SQL call interface, which is then translated into the API of the target database by an *ODBC driver*. Thus, you can write a program that includes ODBC calls, plug in an Oracle ODBC driver and the program will run against an Oracle database — plug in a SQL Server ODBC driver and it will run, *unchanged*, against a SQL Server database, and so on.

Of course, the challenge in defining ODBC was in deciding which features to surface. Should ODBC include only those features that were supported by every SQL database, making available just the "lowest common denominator" of functionality? Or should it include every feature available in every SQL database, guaranteeing that programs could not, after all, be ported to other databases without breaking? ODBC represents a compromise between those two extremes (as will XQJ, we predict).

Today, ODBC[8] is extremely widely-used across SQL databases. While the goal of ODBC is to be programming language- (as well as database-) independent, ODBC does use C syntax and semantics, so it is unsuitable for languages such as Java. Enter JDBC . . .

JDBC[9] (which some people believe is an acronym for Java DataBase Connectivity — it isn't!) is a datasource-independent API to SQL data sources, just like ODBC, but it's a Java (rather than C or C++) API. JDBC lets you write standard Java code to access data sources, then supply a data source-specific JDBC *driver* for each data source. It's also possible to use JDBC with the JDBC-ODBC *Bridge*, which acts like an ODBC driver for JDBC. The bridge is useful if, for

---

6 *Structured Query Language (SQL), C201* (X/Open CAE Specification) (Reading, U.K.: X/Open Company Ltd., 1992).

7 The original SQL/CLI spec is *ISO/IEC 9075-3:1995 (E) Call-Level Interface (SQL/CLI)*. Available at: http://www.nist.fss.ru/hr/doc/mstd/iso/9075-3-95.htm.

8 For more on ODBC, see MSDN, http://msdn.microsoft.com/library/default.asp?url=/library/en-us/odbc/htm/dasdkodbcoverview.asp. For more on ODBC drivers, see DataDirect, http://www.datadirect.com/products/odbc/index.ssp.

9 See Sun's JDBC page at http://java.sun.com/products/jdbc/.

example, there is an ODBC driver, but no JDBC driver, available for some data source that you want to access.

14.2.2 DOM, SAX, StAX, JAXP, JAXB

In Chapter 6, "The XML Information Set (Infoset) and Beyond," we described the Document Object Model (DOM), and said it was really an API to XML data rather than a data model. The DOM API to XML documents is very popular — for example, it's used in JavaScript — and the DOM specification defines a language binding for Java (*i.e.*, you can use DOM to access and manipulate XML data, and pass data from XML to Java and back). In the same chapter, we briefly mentioned that DOM is a *tree*-based (as opposed to an *event*-based) API. A tree-based API parses an entire XML document and creates a tree structure from it. The API then lets you navigate around the tree. An event-based API parses an XML document, and reports each event (*e.g.*, the start and end of each element) by way of callbacks to the calling program. Obviously, an event-based parser has some footprint advantages — you don't have to build a complete parse tree to use it. An event-based parser is in some sense a "lower-level" API than a tree-based parser, since you can process the events in any way you want (including building an in-memory tree).[10]

SAX — the Simple API for XML — is an *event*-based API for XML, for use with Java and other languages. The SAX specification is in the public domain, but to write a SAX program you will need to obtain a SAX XML parser. The official website for the SAX project[11] lists a number of such parsers, including free downloads from Oracle, IBM, and others. To use SAX, you register an event handler to define a callback method for elements, for text, and for comments. SAX is a *serial access* API, which means you cannot go back up the tree, or rearrange nodes, as you can with DOM. But SAX has a smaller footprint, and is more flexible.

StAX[12] — the Streaming API for XML — is a Java *pull parsing* API. That is, StAX lets you pull the next item in the document as it parses. You (the calling program) decide when to pull the next item (whereas

10 For a concise comparison of tree-based and event-based APIs, see http://www.saxproject.org/event.html.

11 http://www.saxproject.org/.

12 http://www.jcp.org/en/jsr/detail?id=173. Note that, at the time of writing, DOM, SAX, and JAXP are all published standard APIs, while StAX is still under development.

with an event-based parser, it's the parser that decides when to cause the calling program to take some action). The StAX parser is ideally suited to state-dependent processing, where you want to treat something differently depending on what comes directly before it. StAX also lets you *write* XML to an output stream, via the cursor-based `XMLStreamWriter` or the event-based `XMLEventWriter`.

JAXP[13] – the Java API for XML Processing – is a Java API that lets you parse XML with either SAX or DOM, then process the data in Java, and display it in a variety of formats using XSLT. JAXP includes a pluggability layer so you can plug in any SAX or DOM parser, and/or an XSLT processor.

JAXB[14] – the Java API for XML Binding – provides a way to bind an XML schema-compliant document into Java objects (a package of classes and interfaces). Once a binding is defined, you can *unmarshall* an XML document into a Java content tree (a tree of Java objects), and *marshall* the Java objects back into XML.

14.2.3 Alphabet-Soup Summary

Confused? OK, before we introduce XQJ, let's summarize these existing standards for accessing and processing data within a programming language.

- Access data from any SQL database (or other table-oriented data source). The data access language is SQL, and the programming language is C or C++ – ODBC, with an ODBC driver for each data source.
- Access data from any SQL database (or other table-oriented data source). The data access language is SQL, and the programming language is Java – JDBC, with a JDBC driver for each data source (or an ODBC driver for the data source + a JDBC-ODBC bridge).
- Parse XML into a tree structure, then navigate and modify that tree – DOM.
- Parse XML, with a callback method at each event you encounter as you parse – SAX.

---

13 http://java.sun.com/xml/jaxp/.

14 http://java.sun.com/xml/jaxb/. See especially: Scott Fordin, *Java Architecture for XML Binding: Executive Summary* (July 2003). Available at: http://www.sun.com/software/xml/developers/jaxb/index.xml.

- Parse XML, where each item is parsed in response to a request from the calling program (pulled) — StAX.
- Parse XML using either DOM or SAX, process the data in Java, output the data using XSLT — JAXP.

Now, suppose you want to write a Java program that can access any database, and access and manipulate XML data. You could use JDBC to access any SQL database and then retrieve an XML document from a row in a SQL table, then cast the object to an XML class defined in JAXP, then use SAX or DOM to parse it, and manipulate the result with JAXP methods. A little clunky, but doable. But how can you query the XML data? Remember, JDBC uses SQL to query the data source. If the data source is a SQL database that understands the SQL/XML extensions (see Chapter 15, "SQL/XML"), you might be able to query the XML data using XQuery that way. Or perhaps you have a mid-tier XQuery engine that will take JAXP classes and query them. Again, doable but clunky. What we have is a set of useful *data model APIs* for manipulating XML in Java, but there is currently no *language API* to call XQuery from Java, in the way that JDBC is a *language API* to call SQL from Java.

What is needed is a Java API that talks XQuery to any XML data source, returning XML data that can be processed in Java. Think of it as JDBC, where the data access language is XQuery rather than SQL, with JAXP/JAXB-like data mappings from the XQuery Data Model into Java classes. The current proposal for such an API is JSR 225, or XQJ. XQJ is sometimes called "JDBC for XQuery" (just as JDBC is sometimes called "ODBC for Java").

14.3 XQJ — XQuery for Java

XQJ — XQuery for Java[15] — was first mentioned in Chapter 8, "Storing: XML and Databases." The XQJ spec is under construction as JSR 225, part of the Java Community Process.[16] The position of *spec lead* is shared by Oracle and IBM,[17] and there is an Expert Group working with the spec leads. At the time of writing, the latest available spec is

15 For an excellent tutorial on XQJ, see: Jonathan Robie, Jonathan Bruce, *An XQJ Tutorial: Introduction to the XQuery API for Java*. Available at: http://www.datadirect.com/developer/xquery/topics/xqj_tutorial/index.ssp.

16 For more on the Java Community Process, see Appendix C: The Standardization Processes.

17 The Oracle spec lead is an author of this book.

an Early Draft Review published in May 2004. In our "Alphabet-Soup Review" above, we looked at two kinds of APIs – *language APIs* such as ODBC and JDBC that serve as a harness for some query language (SQL), and *data model APIs* such as DOM and SAX that define ways to construct, access, and manipulate some data structure (such as a DOM tree). XQJ has elements of both, providing a Java harness for the XQuery language, and also methods to manipulate XML objects. In addition, XQJ is designed to run anywhere (client, server, or mid-tier).

In the rest of this section we describe what XQJ does, with examples,[18] and in the following section we go back to talking about APIs in general. The examples in this section have been tested against an early version of the RI (Reference Implementation) supplied by Oracle as part of the JCP (Java Community Process). Where an import statement is shown, `javax.xml.xquery` represents the XQJ classes, while `oracle.xquery.xqj` represents Oracle's XQJ driver classes. Most examples are code fragments rather than complete examples.

14.3.1 Connecting to a Data Source

The first thing we need to do is connect to a data source, so we have some data to query over. Just like ODBC and JDBC, XQJ has the following concepts.

- A *data source* – anything that has data in it, and for which you have an XQJ driver. The data source might be a SQL database, an XML database, or a collection of files. By abstracting out the data source, your XQJ Java program will run against any XML data source (with a suitable XQJ driver).
- A *connection* – the result of connecting to a data source, usually with some username, password, network protocol, *etc.*
- A *session* – an instance of a connection, providing some context for variables and for transactions.

18 At the time of writing, there is no reference implementation (RI) publicly available. Oracle is working on the RI, and the authors were fortunate to have access to an early version of that RI to test some of the examples.

Data Source

The XQJ Early Draft Review describes several ways to support a vendor-specific data source connection (via, *e.g.*, an Oracle driver) available to the Java programmer in a general way. The idea is that a vendor supplies a class that implements the `XQDataSource` interface (an XQJ driver). For example, Oracle's XQJ driver class might be called `OXQDataSource`.

- You could write an application that instantiated `OXQDataSource` every time you want a data source (see Example 14-1). That is the simplest method, but also the least portable – it introduces a dependency on the Oracle XQJ driver into your code wherever you need to define a data source.
- Use Class.forName to map the class name "XQDataSource" to the XQJ driver class name (see Example 14-2). This allows you to set the driver class name to any string, rather than having to hard-code it in your program.
- Use the system

  property `javax.xml.xquery.XQDataSource`

  and pass in the name of the XQJ driver class on the command line using the `–D` option.[19]
- Use the service provider API.[20] Specify the fully-qualified class name of the XQJ driver class in a file `META-INF/services/javax.xmlquery.XQDataSource`.

Example 14-1 *Instantiate a Vendor-Specific Data Source, Simplest Method*

```
import javax.xml.xquery.*;
import oracle.xquery.xqj.*;
. . .
XQDataSource myDatasource = new OXQDataSource();
```

19 If you're using a command line, that is.

20 See the JAR specification at http://java.sun.com/j2se/1.3/docs/guide/jar/jar.html.

Example 14-2 *Instantiate a Vendor-Specific Data Source, Using class.forName*

```
import javax.xml.xquery.* ;
import oracle.xquery.xqj.* ;
. . .
String XQJImplClassName = "oracle.xquery.xqj.OXQDataSource" ;
XQDataSource myDatasource = (XQDataSource)
    Class.forName(XQJImplClassName).newInstance() ;
```

For maximum portability, you should use JNDI (Java Naming and Directory Interface)[21] to map a logical name to your `XQDataSource` object. This additional level of naming indirection improves portability, and it improves maintainability — you can make changes to the underlying `XQDataSource` object without changing any application code.

XQJ currently defines `Username`, `Password`, and `MaxConnections` as properties of an `XQDataSource`. Additional standard properties may be defined in the future, and vendors are free to add their own properties with the appropriate setter and getter methods. For example, DataDirect takes the approach of defining all data source properties (and apparently connection properties too) in a configuration file, specified by a proprietary data source property `setConfigFile`.

We understand that the data source definition (and, in particular, ways to specify an XQJ driver in a portable, generic way) is still under discussion in the JSR 225 Expert Group so, now that you have a flavor of what the data source looks like and what it's for, we'll move on to the connection.

Connection

Once you have instantiated a data source object, you can create a connection using the `XQConnection` class. Example 14-3 creates the connection `myConnection`, given the data source `myDatasource` created in Example 14-1.

Example 14-3 *Create an XQJ Connection*

```
XQConnection myConnection = myDataSource.getConnection() ;
```

21 http://java.sun.com/products/jndi/.

Example 14-3 shows the simplest possible connection, just as Example 14-1 shows the simplest possible Oracle data source. This default setup allows you to access files in the local directory. The XQJ driver class and `getConnection` might have parameters, *e.g.* username and password. XQJ also allows you to "reuse" a JDBC connection, supplying the JDBC connection as a parameter to `getConnection`. Example 14-4 creates an XQJ connection `myConnection`, given the data source `myDatasource` created in Example 14-1 and some JDBC connection `myJdbcConnection`. Some of the properties defined in a JDBC connection are data source properties – the JDBC values will override any values defined when you set up the XQJ data source.

Example 14-4 *Create an XQJ Connection from a JDBC Connection*

```
XQConnection myConnection =
   myDatasource.getConnection(myJdbcConnection) ;
```

Session

A *session* is an instance of a connection object. A session has some corresponding *session state*, which includes the user ID, a set of XQuery expressions and results, and one or more transactions.

14.3.2 Executing a Query

We have created a data source object, and from that data source (or from a JDBC connection) we have created a connection. Now we can start executing queries.

To execute a query in XQJ, you first need to create an *expression object* from your connection. In Example 14-5, we create an expression object `Expr` in the context of connection `myConnection`, using the `createExpression` method. For convenience, we then set up a string variable `xqueryDirectorLandis` that contains the XQuery we want to run. `xqueryDirectorLandis` is a simple XQuery that evaluates to a sequence of string literals. Note this could be any XQuery expression or an XQueryX document. Finally, we call the `executeQuery` method of the expression object to run the query and return the results in the variable `ResultSeq`, of type `XQResultSequence`.

Example 14-5 *Execute an XQuery*

```
String xqueryDirectorLandis =
    "for $m in doc('movies-we-own.xml')/movies/movie " +
    "where $m/director/familyName = 'Landis' " +
    "return string($m/title)";

XQExpression Expr = myConnection.createExpression() ;
XQResultSequence ResultSeq =
    Expr.executeQuery(xqueryDirectorLandis) ;
```

Prepared Expressions

In general, any query (SQL or XQuery) is evaluated in two phases – static evaluation and dynamic evaluation.

The static evaluation phase involves all the processing that can be done with knowledge of only the syntax of the query and the values of literals (that is, without any knowledge of the values of any variables in the query). Static evaluation typically involves building an internal tree structure representing the parsed query, some optimization of the query, and possibly a computation of an execution plan (which indexes to use, in which order). This is sometimes called *compiling* a query.

Dynamic evaluation typically means plugging the values of variables into a compiled query, and computing the result.

Static evaluation can consume a significant amount of computing resource – if you want to run the same query many times with different values for its variables, it is more efficient to compile the query once and run the compiled version many times, to save the cost of recompiling each time.

JDBC and ODBC both have the notion of a *prepared (precompiled) statement*. In XQJ, the analogous notion is a *prepared (precompiled) expression*, since XQuery is an expression-based language. In the next example (Example 14-6), we run the same query as in Example 14-5, but we run it in two stages – first we *prepare* it, then *execute* it. Example 14-6 also introduces the notion of *variable binding*. Instead of preparing a query that returns the title of each movie directed by Landis, we prepare a query that returns the title of each movie directed by the name in the external variable $name, and bind the value "Landis" to $name at run-time. This is a fairly natural use of a prepared expression – you might want to query for movies directed by Landis many times, but it's much more likely that you want to run the same query with different values for some bind variable, *i.e.*, query for movies by various directors.

Example 14-6 *Execute an XQuery Using a Prepared Expression*

```
String xqueryDirectors =
    "declare variable $name as xs:string external; " +
    "for $m in doc('movies-we-own.xml')/movies/movie " +
    "where $m/director/familyName = $name " +
    "return string($m/title)" ;

XQPreparedExpression PreparedExpr =
    myConnection.prepareExpression(xqueryDirectors) ;
PreparedExpr.bindString(new QName("name"), "Landis") ;

XQResultSequence ResultSeq = PreparedExpr.executeQuery() ;
```

14.3.3 Manipulating XML Data

Now we know how to make a connection to some data source, and execute an XQuery to retrieve some result. Now, what can we do with that result? Remember that one of the challenges of a language API is to map results data from the query language (XQuery) to the host language (Java).

XQJ has four data types for storing XML results (`XQResultSequence`, `XQResultItem`, `XQCachedSequence`, `XQCachedItem`). The result of an XQuery is always an instance of the XQuery Data Model (see Chapter 10, "Introduction to XQuery 1.0"), and the XQuery Data Model is defined in terms of sequences and items. So XQJ includes an `XQItem` and an `XQSequence` interface to reflect items and sequences, respectively. `XQItem` and `XQSequence` are abstractions — they have subinterfaces `XQResult`*`xxx`*[22] and `XQCachedxxx`[23] that can be instantiated. `XQResult`*`xxx`* objects are valid only for the lifetime of a session (connection object), while `XQCached`*`xxx`* objects can persist across connections.

Before we discuss ways of manipulating this XML data and mapping it into types that Java understands, let's look at the item and sequence interfaces.

---

22 XQResultItem, XQResultSequence.
23 XQCachedItem, XQCachedSequence.

XQItem, XQResultItem, XQCachedItem

In the XQJ Early Draft Review, `XQItem` is not yet fully defined, but it is expected to have methods for the following.

- Retrieve the (XML Schema) type of the item.
- Check the type of the item against some type.
- If the item is an atomic value, retrieve the value of the item (as a java atomic value).
- If the item is a node, retrieve the node.

`XQItem` has two subinterfaces, `XQResultItem` and `XQCachedItem`. `XQResultItem` has the same methods as `XQItem`, and is created by calling the `getItem()` method of an `XQResultSequence` object. `XQCachedItem` has the same methods as `XQItem`, and is created either by calling the `getItem()` method of an `XQCachedSequence`, or by calling the `createItem()` method of a data source or connection.

XQSequence, XQResultSequence, XQCachedSequence

An `XQSequence` is a sequence of zero or more `XQItems`, with a *current position* that points to the *current item*. An `XQSequence` is either *scrollable* or *forward-only*. In the XQJ Early Draft Review, `XQSequence` is not yet fully defined, but it is expected to have methods to move the current position to the next item, to get the current item, to close the sequence, and to test whether the sequence is closed. In addition, if the `XQSequence` is scrollable, it will have methods to navigate around its items (move the current position to the first item, last item, previous item, an absolute or relative position, or before the first / after the last item).

`XQSequence` has two subinterfaces, `XQResultSequence` and `XQCachedSequence`. `XQResultSequence` has the same methods as `XQSequence` (plus methods for retrieving a reference to its connection object, and to retrieve and clear warnings). An `XQResultSequence` is created by calling one of the query execution methods, `XQExpression` or `XQPreparedExpression`.

`XQCachedSequence` inherits all the methods of `XQSequence`, and is created by calling the `createCachedSequence()` method of a data source or connection. An `XQCachedSequence` persists outside the lifetime of a data source or connection, so it has more uses than an `XQResultSequence` – this is reflected in the additional methods defined for `XQCachedSequence`. These include methods to insert, remove, and replace items in the sequence, and to insert whole sequences.

Data Mapping

Now we know that we can use XQJ to execute an XQuery and retrieve XQuery Data Model instances (sequences of items). Since the input to (as well as the output from) an XQuery is always an instance of the XQuery Data Model, this also means we can chain XQueries – use the output from one as the input to another. But to be a useful Java API, XQJ also has to allow us to map these sequences and items to objects and data types that Java can handle natively, and it needs to allow us to pass those sequences and items to some of the already-established Java APIs for manipulating XML data. XQJ does both of those!

XQuery to Java Types

Let's go back to the example we've been building up, and look at some ways to use the result of an XQuery in Java. The simplest way is to take the sequence of titles, which we have in an XQResultSequence object, walk down the sequence using the `next()` method, and apply the `getString()` method to each title in turn.

Example 14-7 *Print Titles*

```
while (ResultSeq.next())
    {
        String outt = "result : " + ResultSeq.getString();
        System.out.println(outt);
    }
```

Now we have enough to show one complete, working example – Example 14-8.

Example 14-8 *Complete, Simple XQuery Using XQJ*

```
package XQJpackage;

//import the XQJ Reference Implementation classes
import javax.xml.xquery.*;
import javax.xml.namespace.QName;
```

```
//import the Oracle XQJ Driver classes
import oracle.xquery.xqj.*;

// simple example of an XQuery using XQJ
// with prepared expression and bind variable
public class XQJCompleteSimpleExample
{
  public static void main(String args[])
  {
  //initialize variables needed for
  //the connection, data source, expression, result
  XQConnection myConnection = null;
  XQPreparedExpression PreparedExpr = null;
  XQResultSequence ResultSeq = null;

  //create a new data source using the Oracle XQJ Driver
  XQDataSource myDatasource = new OXQDataSource();

  try {
    //create a connection
    myConnection = myDatasource.getConnection() ;

    //set up a string to hold the XQuery
    String xqueryDirectors =
      "declare variable $name as xs:string external; " +
      "for $m in doc('movies-we-own.xml')/movies/movie " +
      "where $m/director/familyName = $name " +
      "return string($m/title)";

    //prepare the expression
    PreparedExpr =
        myConnection.prepareExpression(xqueryDirectors) ;

    //bind the string value "Landis" to the variable "name"
    PreparedExpr.bindString(new QName("name"), "Landis") ;

    //run the XQuery, and put the result sequence into ResultSeq
    ResultSeq = PreparedExpr.executeQuery() ;

    //walk down the result sequence, printing each item
    while (ResultSeq.next())
      {
```

```
          String outt = "result : " + ResultSeq.getString();
          System.out.println(outt);
        }

      //close the result sequence
      ResultSeq.close() ;
    }

    //do some error-handling
    catch (Exception e)
      {
          System.out.println("Exception raised");
          e.printStackTrace() ;
        }

      //clean up, free resources
      finally
      {
        try
        {
          if (ResultSeq != null)
            ResultSeq.close();
          if (PreparedExpr != null)
            PreparedExpr.close();
          if (myConnection != null)
            myConnection.close();
          System.out.println("Cleanup done");
        }  catch (Exception e)
        {
          System.out.println("Cleanup exception raised");
          e.printStackTrace() ;
        }
      }
    }
  }
```

Results:

```
result : An American Werewolf in London
result : Animal House
```

In Example 14-8, we effortlessly crossed the boundary from the XQuery data world (where everything is an instance of the XQuery Data Model) to the Java data world (where everything is a Java Object or type). We cheated a little to illustrate the simplest possible data mapping – the XQuery that we ran converted the title nodes (elements) into strings using the `string()` function as part of the return clause. So the query returned a sequence where each member is an item of an atomic type, the XML Schema type "string." XQJ then converted each of those to a Java string, via the `getString()` method.

XQJ defines mappings between the XML Schema atomic types and Java types, in both directions. We don't reproduce that mapping here since, at the time of writing, it is only loosely defined – we'll just point out that such a mapping exists, and is based on the mappings in JAXB and JAXP.

What about the more general case, where an XQuery returns a sequence containing nodes as well as atomic types? XQJ provides a way to deal with those nodes using one of the already-established standards for dealing with XML in Java.

XQuery to XQuery

First, you should be able to deal with a general XQuery sequence (containing nodes and atomic values) by feeding it to another XQuery. Example 14-9 shows that – we first run an XQuery to find all movies where the director is "Landis," then feed the result into another XQuery that pulls out the titles.[24] That's achieved by declaring an external variable in the second XQuery, and binding to it the result sequence from the first XQuery (in the same way we bound a string to a variable in Example 14-8).

Example 14-9 *Chaining XQueries*

```
//select the sequence of movies with director=Landis
String xqueryMovies =
  "for $m in doc('movies-we-own.xml')/movies/movie " +
  "where $m/director/familyName = 'Landis' " +
  "return $m" ;

Expr001 = myConnection.createExpression() ;
```

24 Note that we've gone back to showing an example snippet – we assume the variables for expressions and results have been initialized, and a connection has been created. See Appendix A: The Example for full example listings.

```
ResultSeq001 = Expr001.executeQuery(xqueryMovies) ;

//now query over the sequence of movies
String xqueryTitles = "declare variable $movies xs:string
external; " +
  "for $m in $movies " +
  "return string($m/title)";

Expr002 = myConnection.createExpression() ;

//bind the sequence ResultSeq001 to the variable with QName
//movies
Expr002.bindSequence(new QName("movies"), ResultSeq001) ;
ResultSeq002 = Expr002.executeQuery(xqueryTitles) ;

while (ResultSeq002.next())
  {
    String outt = "result : " + ResultSeq002.getString();
    System.out.println(outt);
  }
```

Now we can chain XQueries, and as long as the last XQuery in the chain returns only atomic values we can map the result to Java values. XQJ also defines ways to handle an XQuery Data Model instance (sequence) in one of the already-established Java standards.

XQuery to DOM, SAX, StAX

We have said (many times) that the input to, and output from, an XQuery are instances of the XQuery Data Model. But any XML document or fragment can be converted to an instance of the XQuery Data Model to be queried, and any Data Model instance can be converted to (serialized as) an XML document or fragment. So it would be nice to be able to take, say, a DOM object and query it with XQuery. It would be equally nice to convert the output from an XQuery into a DOM object for further processing – perhaps you already have some software and tools that can handle DOM objects but not XQuery Data Model instances.

At the time of writing, this area of the XQJ spec is incomplete. The Expert Group seems to recognize the importance of working with DOM, SAX, and StAX – the spec says "The sequence and item interfaces explicitly support XML in [the] form of the DOM data model as specified by org.w3c.dom, the SAX interface, and the StaX interface."

However, these interfaces are not yet defined. Possibly XQJ will also support DOM *input to* an XQuery by defining a `bind`*`xxx`*`()` method (such as `bindDOM()`) to bind a DOM object to an XQuery variable. We await further developments in XQJ with bated breath.

XQuery to Java (Objects)

The XQJ Early Draft Review does mention a general way to handle XQuery output as a Java object, using existing XML-to-Java-object bindings such as JAXB. XQJ provides a pluggable interface called `XQCommonHandler` to achieve this. A vendor or implementation must provide a class that implements the `XQCommonHandler` interface, converting the object returned by the `getObject()` method of the result sequence into, say, a JAXB object. Example 14-10 is adapted from an example in the XQJ Early Draft Review.

Example 14-10 *A Handler for JAXB*

```
...

//run a prepared XQuery, and put the result sequence into ResultSeq
ResultSeq = PreparedExpr.executeQuery() ;

//create a new JAXB context
JAXBContext jaxbContext = JAXBContext.newInstance("com.example.xml") ;

//create a new handler using the JAXB context and a myJAXBHandler class
//(obtained from a vendor, or written as part of the application)
            XQCommonHandler jaxbHandler = new myJAXBHandler(jaxbContext) ;

//walk down the result sequence, processing each item
while (ResultSeq.next())
  {
    //Movie is some JAXB object defined in com.example.xml
    Movie thisMovie = (Movie) ResultSeq.getObject(jaxbHandler) ;

    //process the Movie object
    //e.g. Movie might have a SerializeToString() method
    System.out.println(Movie.SerializeToString() ) ;
  }

...
```

In Example 14-10, the handler is passed to each item in the result sequence. You can also pass a handler to a data source or a connection, as a parameter to the `setCommonHandler()` method of the data source/connection. In addition to JAXB, handlers might be used to deliver nodes and atomic values as DOM4J or JDOM objects.

14.3.4 Static and Dynamic Context

So far, we have described how XQJ executes XQueries and handles XQuery input and output as objects and data types that Java can understand. Another important aspect of an API is to provide a context in which the language executes.

You read in Chapter 10, "Introduction to XQuery 1.0," that XQuery context is split into the *static context* (that which is known before the values of any variables is known) and the *dynamic context* (that which is known at run-time, after variables have been evaluated).

The static context contains useful information that you might expect to "just exist" in your environment, without having to explicitly set it up each time you run a query. This includes the default element namespace, the default function namespace, and the QName and type of all in-scope variables. The `XQStaticContext` interface lets you retrieve static context information, but not to change it. Note that the static context can be changed by an XQuery prolog – `XQStaticContext` only lets you see the static context information *before* any query prolog is processed. `XQConnection` extends `XQStaticContext`, so you can query the static context using methods on the connection, as in Example 14-11.

Example 14-11 *Querying the Static Context*

```
...

//find the name and type of each static in-scope variable
QName[] varNames = myConnection.getStaticInScopeVariableNames();

String typeName = null;

for (int i = 0; i < varNames.length; i++) {
    // Display variable name and type
    typeName =
      myConnection.getStaticInScopeVariableType(varNames[i]).getString();
    System.out.println(varNames[i] + ": " + typeName) ;
}
...
```

The dynamic context contains information that is only known at run-time, as the query is being evaluated. XQJ allows you to retrieve and change the implicit time zone, to bind a value to the context item (the "." in XPaths), and to bind a value to an external variable. We have already seen examples of the latter – using `bindString()` and `bindSequence()` to set the value of a string and a sequence respectively (see Example 14-8 and Example 14-9). The `bind`*`xxx`*`()` methods are part of the `XQExpression` and `XQPreparedEXpression` interfaces, which extend the `XQDynamicContext` interface. We would also expect to be able to retrieve and modify the current date and time, and possibly the list of known documents and collections.

14.3.5 Metadata

The goal of XQJ is to provide access to a wide range of XML data sources – files, SQL databases, XML repositories, plus any XML data source that might be invented in the future. You have seen that XQJ achieves this generality via a driver that can be created (or obtained) for a particular data source and plugged in to XQJ. Since it is impossible to completely standardize the functionality available in all those data sources, we need some way for the application programmer to find out about any particular data source and its contents. XQJ achieves this by defining two kinds of metadata, which we'll call *data source metadata* and *content metadata*.

Data Source Metadata

Data source metadata describes the properties of a data source, such as the product identification (name, version, and so on) and the XQuery features that are supported. An XQJ driver must implement the `XQMetaData` interface, whose methods return this information, so that programs can find out how to interact with the data source.

Content Metadata

Content metadata describes the objects that exist in any particular data source – schemas, modules, collations, functions, collections, documents, and others. An application needs to know which objects exist in order to construct valid XQueries. For those familiar with JDBC, this information is provided in JDBC by the `DatabaseMetaData` interface, with methods such as `getTables()`. XQJ will provide similar functionality using, we predict, similar interfaces.

14.3.6 Summary

In this section, we described the XQJ (XQuery for Java) API. The XQJ Early Draft Review spec is somewhat patchy, and so we have had to gloss over some areas, but we have given an overview of what XQJ provides, and also some of the flavor of the API itself. Though it is still early in the spec's lifetime, we think XQJ will provide an excellent foundation for running XQueries, and manipulating their results, in Java. We also believe that the Early Draft Review spec touches all the areas an API needs, and plays nicely with all existing relevant standards (and therefore tools and implementations) in this area. XQJ provides a way to do the following:

- Connect to any data source via a pluggable driver (following the ODBC/JDBC driver model).
- Run XQueries against a connection, either in a single step or in two steps (static evaluation + dynamic evaluation).
- Bind Java data to XQuery variables, so a Java program can define the input to an XQuery.
- Map XQuery atomic values to Java data, so a Java program can handle the output from an XQuery (as long as that output is a sequence of atomic values).
- Store and copy XQuery output as a Data Model Instance, so a programmer can chain XQueries.
- Use DOM, SAX, and StAX to process input to, and output from, XQueries (though this area of the spec is still under construction).
- Use some supplied handler to convert XQuery output to, say, a DOM or JAXB object.
- Retrieve and, in some cases, change parts of the static and dynamic contexts.
- Retrieve metadata about a data source and its capabilities, so that a program can frame appropriate queries for a wide range of kinds of data sources.

At the time of writing, the JSR 225 Expert Group is meeting regularly and working hard to produce a second draft spec. Oracle is working on an RI (Reference Implementation), and IBM is working on a TCK (Technology Compatibility Kit).[25] For further reading, see:

- The JavaOne 2004 paper "XQuery API for Java™ (XQJ) Technology," by Jim Melton and Andrew Eisenberg[26] (the joint spec leads on JSR 225 / XQJ). Note: some of the examples in this section were adapted from this JavaOne presentation.
- The XQJ online tutorial from DataDirect Technologies that we referenced earlier in this chapter.
- The JSR 225 home page on the Java Community Process website.[27]
- Or, of course, Google for XQJ.

Be forewarned. This chapter presented XQJ as it was defined in mid-2004. The Expert Group has been busy at work and we would be surprised if there were not very significant – even fundamental – changes in XQJ when it is next seen in public.

14.4 SQL/XML

You will read about SQL/XML in Chapter 15, "SQL/XML," so we won't describe it here, but we will take a few lines to describe SQL/XML as an XQuery API. We say in Chapter 15, "SQL/XML" that SQL/XML provides a harness in which to run XQuery in the context of the SQL language, in much the same way as XQJ provides a harness in which to run XQuery in the context of the Java language. Let's compare SQL/XML to XQJ, using the list of features in Section 14.3.6.

- Connect to any data source – SQL/XML provides a data source via the XML Type. The actual data queried is gener-

25 From the JCP (Java Community Process) Process Document, available at: http://www.jcp.org/en/procedures/jcp2
Reference Implementation (RI): The prototype or "proof of concept" implementation of a Specification.
Technology Compatibility Kit (TCK): The suite of tests, tools, and documentation that allows an organization to determine if its implementation is compliant with the Specification.

26 Jim Melton and Andrew Eisenberg, *XQuery API for Java™ (XQJ) Technology* (JavaOne conference, 2004).

27 http://www.jcp.org/en/jsr/detail?id=225.

ally stored in the SQL database, and is available via tables and/or views. There is no need to define any special connection, since there are standard ways to connect to a SQL database (*e.g.*, ODBC).

- Run XQueries — SQL/XML lets you run an XQuery using either `XMLQUERY()` or `XMLTABLE()`.
- Map between XQuery input/output data and data in the native language — SQL/XML provides a native SQL type, XML, which implements the XQuery Data Model. SQL/XML also defines a mapping between SQL names and types to XQuery names and types. This data type mapping is used in the publishing functions (such as `XMLELEMENT()`), which create XML data from SQL data, and in the `XMLQUERY()` function, which allows you to pass in SQL data to an XQuery.
- Context and metadata — SQL/XML statements run in the SQL context, and so all the SQL context information and metadata is available via SQL standard methods.

So which is better, XQJ or SQL/XML? First, SQL/XML is only useful if you want to use XQuery to query XML data stored in a SQL database (or XML *views* of data stored in a SQL database). If some of the data sources you want to query are *not* stored in a SQL database, and you want to use a consistent API across all your data, and your application is written in Java, then you should choose XQJ. If, on the other hand, all your data is stored in a SQL database, then you have a choice between using XQJ and using SQL/XML plus JDBC. Your choice then would probably depend on the tools and skills available to you, and on the relative efficiency of the implementations you are choosing between. It may well be that a particular vendor can execute XQueries more efficiently when they are presented as SQL/XML than when they are presented as XQJ. Then again, XQJ leaves the door open for more flexible query processing — for example, an XQJ driver might operate on both midtier (cached) data and back-end (persistent database) data.

14.5 Looking Ahead

As XQuery becomes more widely accepted, we expect other languages (that is, other than SQL and Java) to have APIs to XQuery, especially Microsoft's .NET. The initial XQJ work provides an excellent template for XQuery APIs in other programming languages. SQL/XML and XQJ have both shown that it's possible to leverage a lot of existing work (in standards and in implementations) when defining XQuery APIs. The future looks bright!

Chapter

15

SQL/XML

15.1 Introduction

For the last several decades, most of the world's critical data has been stored in SQL databases, managed and queried using the SQL language. More recently, people have turned to XML to represent their data in a more natural way, and they need a new language to manage and query that data — a language that takes account of the structure of an XML document as well as its data values. You read in previous chapters how first XPath and then XQuery were defined to do just that. But many experts have asked the question, "why not just use SQL?" — perhaps converting all your data into XML and all your applications into XQuery amounts to throwing the baby out with the bathwater. Relational databases and the SQL language have stood the test of time, evolving and growing to embrace new technologies such as OLAP, data warehousing, and objects. Why not just add XML extensions to SQL? As you will discover in this chapter, it's not quite as simple as that, but that is what the SQLX Group set out to do in 2000. The goal of the SQLX Group was to define a set of extensions to the SQL standard to integrate SQL and XML, supporting bidirectional movement of data and allowing SQL programmers to manage and query XML data. Specifically, they worked to:

- Query SQL data and publish the results as XML

- Store and manage XML natively in a SQL database
- Query XML and publish the results as either XML or as SQL data
- Map SQL data and identifiers to XML, and vice versa

SQLX, SQL/XML, and SQLXML

The SQLX group started as an informal group of companies, including Oracle and IBM, interested in extending the SQL standard to embrace XML. The group's output was blessed by INCITS (the U.S. body chartered with development of standards in IT, including SQL), as "SQL part 14, XML-Related Specifications (SQL/XML)." The SQLX group became formally known as "INCITS Task Group H2.3" (and later an "INCITS H2 ad hoc working group"), but they still maintain a website under the catchier name "SQLX."[1]

We take a moment here to emphasize the difference between SQLX, SQL/XML, and SQLXML (three terms that many people use interchangeably). SQL/XML is the short name for part 14 of the SQL standard, that part that deals with XML. SQLX is the informal name of the group that creates and presents proposals for SQL/XML to INCITS. And SQLXML (*without* a slash)[2] is a Microsoft term for Microsoft's proprietary SQL extensions that do roughly the same thing as the SQL/XML publishing functions.[3]

Chapter Overview

In this chapter, we present an overview of SQL/XML:2003 and SQL/XML:2006, focusing on querying XML, with some simple worked examples. In Section 15.2, we describe the SQL/XML publishing functions, which allow you to query SQL data and produce (or publish) the results as XML, either to send to a customer or partner or, more likely, to display the results as a web page. This is not strictly "Querying XML," rather it is "Querying *to* XML."

In Section 15.3, we describe the XML type — a native SQL data type for XML. This forms the basis for storing, managing, and querying XML natively in a SQL database. Section 15.4 covers the XQuery-

---

1 http://sqlx.org.

2 http://mscn.microsoft.com/sqlxml/.

3 At the time of writing, SQL Server 2000 is Microsoft's latest database offering, and it includes SQLXML. We look forward to seeing the soon-to-be-released SQL Server 2005 database, which is expected to include some XQuery support — see http://msdn.microsoft.com/library/default.asp?url=/library/en-us/dnsql90/html/sql2k5_xqueryintro.asp.

related functions that are part of SQL/XML:2006, including XMLQUERY and XMLTABLE. With these functions you can query XML, stored natively in a SQL database as an XML type, using the power of XQuery in the context of SQL. This is the most detailed section in the chapter, focusing on XMLTABLE.

Section 15.5 talks briefly about managing XML data in a SQL database. And Section 15.6 describes the mappings of character sets, names, types, and values, from SQL to XML and from XML to SQL. Section 15.6 also introduces the casting functions XMLSERIALIZE, XMLPARSE, and XMLCAST.

The SQL and SQL/XML Standards

The SQL/XML Standard, like the XQuery Recommendation, is an ongoing process (that is, it's not yet finished). The first SQL/XML standard to be published was SQL/XML:2003, which was part 14 of the SQL:2003 standard. SQL/XML is currently on a shorter publication schedule tha SQL, so that the next SQL/XML standard, expected to be SQL/XML:2006, will probably be published as an update to SQL:2003. After that, we expect SQL/XML:2007, which may incorporate future XQuery additions such as XQuery Update and XQuery Full Text, to be part of SQL:2007. (All publication dates past 2003 are, at the time of writing, estimates only.)

The SQL/XML Functions

While we refer to "the SQL/XML functions" (*e.g.*, publishing functions and XQuery functions) in the rest of this chapter, the alert reader will notice that they are not actually functions at all. Their syntax looks quite a lot like the syntax of a function, but with extra keywords and clauses thrown in (alternatively, the syntax is keyword-based grammar extensions that use parentheses to look like function). In SQL terms, they are *pseudo-functions*.

The Examples

All the examples in this chapter were tested against a prerelease version of Oracle database 10*g* Release 2. The examples generally conform to the SQL/XML standard – where they are specific to Oracle, or where they illustrate a part of the standard not implemented by our test implementation, we have made an effort to note it.[4]

15.2 SQL/XML Publishing Functions

The first piece of useful query functionality to come out of the SQL/XML effort is the ability to publish the results of a SQL query to XML. Strictly speaking, this is not "Querying XML" – rather, it is "Querying *to* XML." The data to be queried can be any SQL data, and the query can be any SQL query. These SQL extension functions transform the result of the query to XML. Each of the extension functions takes in a SQL thing (part of a SQL tuple, or row), and returns an XML thing (*e.g.*, an element or an attribute). In the rest of this section, we give examples of some of the SQL/XML publishing functions in SQL queries against the movies data.

15.2.1 Examples

The Data

In Figure 15-1, we reproduce the SQL (relational) representation of the movies data from Chapter 1, "XML," for your convenience.

XMLELEMENT

Let's start with a simple case of XML publishing. Suppose you want to want to publish the title of all the movies in your collection, with each title in a separate XML element. Example 15-1 does just that.

Example 15-1 *Simple XMLELEMENT*

```
SELECT
  XMLELEMENT(NAME "title", title) AS "Movie Titles"
  FROM movies

Results:
Movie Titles
--------------------------------------------------
<title>An American Werewolf in London</title>
<title>Animal House</title>

(2 rows in the result)
```

4 For example, in an effort to make the examples conform to the most recent version of the SQL/XML spec available at the time of writing, we have added the mandatory "(NULL | EMPTY) ON EMPTY" clause to the XMLQUERY examples. This is a recent addition to the spec and is not supported in the Oracle implementation we used for testing.

Table MOVIES

ID	title	yearReleased	director	runningTime
42	An American Werewolf in London	1981	78	98
43	Animal House	1978	78	109

Table DIRECTORS

ID	familyName	givenName
78	Landis	John

Table MOVIES_DIRECTORS

MOVIE	DIRECTOR
42	78
43	78

Table PRODUCERS

ID	familyName	givenName	otherNames
44	Folsey	George, Jr.	none
45	Guber	Peter	none
46	Reitman	Ivan	none

Table MOVIES_PRODUCERS

MOVIE	PRODUCER
42	44
42	45
43	46

Table CAST

ID	familyName	givenName	maleOrFemale	character
34	Agutter	Jenny	female	Alex Price
35	Belushi	John	male	John 'Bluto' Blutarsky

Table MOVIES_CAST

MOVIE	CAST
42	34
43	35

Figure 15-1 *movie, SQL Representation (Reproduced from Chapter 1, XML).*

The first argument to XMLELEMENT is the name of the element to be produced (preceded by the keyword "NAME"). This is an *identifier*, in the same way that a table name or column name is an identifier. In Example 15-1, we put quotes around this first argument because we wanted the element name to be lowercase — the same query without quotes around the first argument would result in an element called "TITLE" (since SQL uppercases identifiers by default).

XMLELEMENT takes an optional second argument, a call to the function XMLATTRIBUTES, which defines attributes for the result element. When XMLATTRIBUTES is *not* used, as in Example 15-1, the second argument to XMLELEMENT is an expression that fills in the content of the element. In Example 15-1, it's just the name of the column — `title` — but it could be a function call, or even a subquery.

We added a column alias — `AS "Movie Titles"` — to make the output look nicer. Note that the result is two rows, each of which is a title element (as opposed to a single XML fragment consisting of two elements). That's because the SQL query iterates over each row in the table, returning `XMLELEMENT(NAME "title", title)` for each row. If you want to return one XML fragment that contains all the titles, use XMLAGG (see the next section). There is, of course, a major difference between a set of results (which we get from Example 15-1), and a single result that is an XML fragment. We try to distinguish between the two kinds of results in the rest of this chapter.

Example 15-2 *Less Simple XMLELEMENT*

```
SELECT
  XMLELEMENT(NAME title,
    XMLATTRIBUTES(runningtime AS "RunningTime",
      (select familyName
        from directors AS d
        where d.id=m.director)
        AS "Director"),
      'This movie title is '||m.title)
        AS "Movie Titles"
  FROM movies AS m
```

```
Results:

Movie Titles
------------
```

```
<TITLE RunningTime="98" Director="Landis">This movie title is
An American Werewolf in London</TITLE>
<TITLE RunningTime="109" Director="Landis">This movie title
is Animal House</TITLE>

(2 rows in the result)
```

Example 15-2 illustrates how much you can do with XMLELEMENT. It includes a call to XMLATTRIBUTES to define two attributes, `RunningTime` and `Director`, where `Director` is derived from a query on the `DIRECTORS` table. The third argument, which populates the element body, is a more complex expression than in Example 15-1. It consists of a string literal (this could have been a subquery), a concatenation operator (||), and a column identifier (`m.title`). We have added table aliases `d` and `m` to make the query (somewhat) more readable.

XMLATTRIBUTES is a bit of an oddity. It's not a top-level function — it can only occur as the second argument to XMLELEMENT. This maps nicely to the notion of attributes in the XML InfoSet, since an attribute must always have an element owner. But it's more restrictive than the XQuery Data Model, where the basic unit is the sequence, which may contain attributes without a parent element. Also, the XMLATTRIBUTES argument is optional, which is unusual for the second of three arguments. The arrangement works (does not pose problems for parsers) because this optional second argument can only be a call to XMLATTRIBUTES, and a call to XMLATTRIBUTES is not allowed as any other argument.

15.2.2 XMLAGG

Now you know how to get the result of a SQL query into a set of XML elements. But if you want to publish, say, an XML report summarizing your relational data, you probably want to aggregate all the similar XML elements into a single element. For that, you would use the XMLAGG function. XMLAGG takes an XMLELEMENT function call as its argument, and produces a single result that is the aggregate of all the elements produced by XMLELEMENT. It's an aggregate function in the same way that MIN, MAX, and COUNT are aggregate functions in SQL.

Let's suppose you want to create an XML report that shows the title of each movie in your collection, inside a single element "all-titles." Example 15-3 shows a query that uses only XMLELEMENT. It calls XMLELEMENT to create the element "all-titles," with a second argument that uses XMLELEMENT to fetch a title from the movies table. This query gives the wrong result – since XMLELEMENT is *not* an aggregate function, it gets evaluated once for each row in the table, so we get an all-titles element for each title.

Example 15-3 *Titles of Movies Using XMLELEMENT (WRONG)*

```
SELECT
  XMLELEMENT(NAME "all-titles",
    XMLELEMENT(NAME "title", title)) AS "Movie Titles"
  FROM movies
Results:

Movie Titles
------------
<all-titles>
  <title>An American Werewolf in London</title>
</all-titles>
<all-titles>
  <title>Animal House</title>
</all-titles>

(2 rows in the result)
```

Example 15-4 shows the right way to get a single "all-titles" element containing a "title" element for each title in the table movies. The second argument to XMLELEMENT is now wrapped in the aggregate function XMLAGG, which produces a single result (in the same way that COUNT() produces a single result) containing an element for each row in the `MOVIES` table. Example 15-4 also introduces the `ORDER BY` clause which is part of XMLAGG, to produce titles of movies ordered by the year the movie was released.

Example 15-4 *Titles of Movies Using XMLAGG (RIGHT)*

```
SELECT
  XMLELEMENT(NAME "all-titles",
    XMLAGG(XMLELEMENT(NAME "title", title) ORDER BY yearReleased ASC ) )
      AS "Movie Titles"
  FROM movies
```

```
Results:

Movie Titles
------------
<all-titles>
  <title>Animal House </title>
  <title>An American Werewolf in London </title>
</all-titles>

(1 row selected)
```

15.2.3 XMLFOREST

In Example 15-1 and Example 15-2, we used XMLELEMENT to create XML elements from the values in one column of a SQL table (the `title` column of the `MOVIES` table), and in Example 15-4 we used XMLAGG to aggregate all the values in a column into a single `all-titles` element. Now suppose you want to create XML elements for several columns in a table ("across the row"). You could achieve this by simply calling XMLELEMENT several times, as in Example 15-5.

Example 15-5 *Using XMLELEMENT to Get Values "Across the Row"*

```
SELECT
  XMLELEMENT(NAME "movie-details",
    XMLELEMENT(NAME "title", title) ,
    XMLELEMENT(NAME "yearReleased", yearreleased) ,
    XMLELEMENT(NAME "runningTime", runningtime)
    ) AS "Movie Details"
  FROM movies

Results:

Movie Details
-------------
<movie-details>
  <title>An American Werewolf in London</title>
  <yearReleased>1981</yearReleased>
  <runningTime>98</runningTime>
</movie-details>

<movie-details>
```

```
  <title>Animal House</title>
  <yearReleased>1978</yearReleased>
  <runningTime>109</runningTime>
</movie-details>

(2 rows in the result)
```

Another way to achieve this forest of XML elements is to use XMLFOREST, as in Example 15-6.

Example 15-6 *Using XMLFOREST to Get Values "Across the Row"*

```
SELECT
  XMLELEMENT(NAME "movie-details",
    XMLFOREST(
      title AS "title" ,
      yearreleased AS "yearReleased" ,
      runningtime AS "runningTime")
    ) AS "Movie Details"
  FROM movies
```

```
Results:

Movie Details
-------------
<movie-details>
  <title>An American Werewolf in London</title>
  <yearReleased>1981</yearReleased>
  <runningTime>98</runningTime>
</movie-details>

<movie-details>
  <title>Animal House</title>
  <yearReleased>1978</yearReleased>
  <runningTime>109</runningTime>
</movie-details>

(2 rows in the result)
```

Example 15-6 gives the same results as Example 15-5, but it is more concise and more natural to read and write. XMLFOREST has another advantage over a series of calls to XMLELEMENT – it ignores NULL values in a column. Consider Example 15-7.

Example 15-7 *Producer-Details Using XMLELEMENT*

```
SELECT
  XMLELEMENT(NAME "producer-details",
    XMLELEMENT(NAME "givenName", givenname) ,
    XMLELEMENT(NAME "familyName", familyname) ,
    XMLELEMENT(NAME "otherNames", othernames)
    ) AS "Producer Details"
  FROM producers
Results:

Producer Details
----------------
<producer-details>
  <givenName>George, Jr.</givenName>
  <familyName>Folsey</familyName>
  <otherNames></otherNames>
</producer-details>

<producer-details>
  <givenName>Peter</givenName>
  <familyName>Guber</familyName>
  <otherNames></otherNames>
</producer-details>

<producer-details>
  <givenName>Ivan</givenName>
  <familyName>Reitman</familyName>
  <otherNames></otherNames>
</producer-details>

(3 rows in the result)
```

Example 15-7 yields `producer-details` containing XML elements for given name, family name, and other names. But for NULL values such as the producers' other names, it produces an empty element. You could, of course, filter out these NULL values using SQL (*e.g.*, use a CASE statement), but the SQL gets quite ugly.[5] A better solution is shown in Example 15-8 — XMLFOREST skips NULL values and does not produce empty elements for `otherNames`.

Example 15-8 *Producer-Details Using XMLFOREST*

```
SELECT
  XMLELEMENT(NAME "producer-details",
    XMLFOREST(
      givenname AS "givenName" ,
      familyname AS "familyName" ,
      othernames AS "otherNames"
      )
    ) AS "Producer Details"
  FROM producers

Results:

Producer Details
----------------
<producer-details>
  <givenName>George, Jr.</givenName>
  <familyName>Folsey</familyName>
</producer-details>

<producer-details>
  <givenName>Peter</givenName>
  <familyName>Guber</familyName>
</producer-details>

<producer-details>
  <givenName>Ivan</givenName>
  <familyName>Reitman</familyName>
</producer-details>

(3 rows in the result)
```

While XMLFOREST gives shorter, more natural queries than a series of calls to XMLELEMENT, and eliminates NULL values, it has

5 For a worked example, see *SQL in, XML out*, Jonathan Gennick, Oracle Magazine 2003. Available at: http://www.oracle.com/technology/oramag/oracle/03-may/o33xml.html.

the disadvantage that you cannot add attributes to elements produced by XMLFOREST. If you need attributes on the elements, you have to use XMLELEMENT.

15.2.4 XMLCONCAT

XMLCONCAT takes a list of XML values and concatenates them into a single XML value. In Example 15-9, XMLCONCAT concatenates the first, last, and other names into a single XML value, resulting in one XML value (an XML forest) for each row.

Example 15-9 *XMLCONCAT*

```
SELECT
  XMLCONCAT(
      XMLELEMENT("givenName", givenname) ,
      XMLELEMENT("familyName", familyname) ,
      XMLELEMENT("otherNames", othernames)
      ) AS "Producer Details"
  FROM producers

Results:

Producer Details
----------------
<givenName>George, Jr.</givenName>
<familyName>Folsey</familyName>
<otherNames></otherNames>

<givenName>Peter</givenName>
<familyName>Guber</familyName>
<otherNames></otherNames>

<givenName>Ivan</givenName>
<familyName>Reitman</familyName>
<otherNames></otherNames>

(3 rows in the result)
```

There are three results in Example 15-9, each one an XML value consisting of three elements.

XMLCONCAT and XMLFOREST both take in a list of values, and output an XML forest. Both ignore NULL values (*i.e.*, produce no output for a NULL value). The difference is that the input to XMLCONCAT is a list of XML values, while the input to XMLFOREST is a list of SQL values. Hence in Example 15-8, we passed column names to XMLFOREST, while in Example 15-9, we had to wrap the column names in a call to XMLELEMENT (to create an XML value) before passing them to XMLCONCAT.

15.2.5 Summary

Table 15-1 shows all the publishing functions in SQL:2003.

Table 15-1 *SQL/XML Publishing Functions*

	Input	**Output**	**Notes**
XMLELEMENT	an element-name, optionally a call to XMLATTRIBUTES, and a SQL value expression	an XML element	create an element, optionally with attributes, from a SQL value expression
XMLATTRIBUTES	a list of SQL value expression, attribute-name pairs	attributes	create attributes from SQL value expressions — only valid as the second argument to XMLELEMENT
XMLAGG	a list of XML values, such as the output from a call to XMLELEMENT or XMLCONCAT	a forest of elements	create a forest of elements from SQL value expressions "down the table"*
XMLFOREST	a list of SQL value expression, element-name pairs	a forest of elements	create a forest of elements from column values "across the row"
XMLCONCAT	two or more XML values	a forest of elements	concatenates two or more XML values into a single XML value (a forest)

* XMLAGG aggregates values of a single column over many rows — "down the table" — as opposed to XMLFOREST, which aggregates values of several columns in a single row — "across the row."

As you can see from the examples, the SQL/XML publishing functions are somewhat verbose, and they can be a little tricky to use, but they are extremely powerful. The examples in this section are simple queries, designed to illustrate the functions individually. But these functions can be combined with each other, and with the rest of the SQL language, into arbitrarily complex queries. Of course, we would not expect end users to formulate complicated ad hoc queries – in most cases, *programmers* write SQL queries that include the publishing functions, *e.g.*, to create an XML *view* of the data.

In SQL/XML:2006, there are at least two additional publishing functions – XMLCOMMENT and XMLPI create a comment node and a processing instruction node, respectively. In addition, XMLAGG, XMLCONCAT, XMLELEMENT, and XMLFOREST acquire an optional `RETURNING { CONTENT | SEQUENCE }` clause, so each of these functions can return either an XML content or an XML sequence. This is a direct consequence of the decision in SQL/XML:2006 to upgrade the publishing functions from use of the XML Infoset to the XQuery Data Model.

15.3 XML Data Type

SQL/XML:2003 introduced the notion of a native SQL data type for XML, called "XML." Values of type XML are *XML values*. With the XML type in place, you need no longer restrict yourself to queries against SQL data – now you can manage and query XML data in a SQL database. While the publishing functions take in SQL data and output a serialized form of XML, the functions in the following sections can take in XML values as arguments, and output XML values as results.

SQL/XML:2006 extends the notion of an XML data type in two ways. First, SQL/XML:2006 adopts the XQuery Data Model rather than the XML Infoset,[6] so that any *XML value* (an instance of the XML data type) is now an *XQuery sequence*, as defined in the XQuery Data Model. Second, SQL/XML:2006 defines three subtypes of XML, represented as modifiers to the XML type – XML(DOCUMENT), XML(CONTENT), and XML(SEQUENCE). In the subtype notations, "DOCUMENT" means the XML value is a well-formed XML document, "CONTENT" is an XML fragment (there may be multiple top-level elements or text nodes) wrapped in a document node, and "SEQUENCE" is any sequence of nodes and/or values.

---

6 See Chapter 6, "The XML Information Set (Infoset) and Beyond," and Chapter 10, "Introduction to XQuery 1.0."

Let's look more closely at the definitions of these subtypes. For each *XML value*, there are two properties that may or may not hold. Below, we describe the properties and assign them shorthand names:

- The sequence may consist of a single Document node (*Document node*).
- If the sequence is a single Document node, it may have only the children that are valid for a Document node in a well-formed XML Document — exactly one element node plus zero or more comment nodes, Processing Instruction nodes, *etc.* (*legal Document children*).

Given these properties, we can say that:

- Every *XML value* is an XML(SEQUENCE).
- An XML(SEQUENCE) that is a *Document node* is an XML(CONTENT).
- An XML(SEQUENCE) that is a *Document node* (*i.e.*, an XML(CONTENT)) that has *legal Document children* is an XML(DOCUMENT).

The SQL:2005 XML type forms the structure hierarchy illustrated in Figure 15-2. In the figure, the subtypes of XML are in rectangular boxes and the properties necessary to match the more restrictive types are in ovals. Note that, like all SQL data types, the value of an XML type may be null, and that a null XML value matches all the XML types.

The XML type may have a second modifier, one of UNTYPED, XMLSCHEMA (with some associated Schema information), or ANY.

- "UNTYPED" means there is no associated XML Schema (*i.e.*, every element is of type "`xdt:untypedAny`" and every attribute is of type "`xdt:untypedAtomic`").[7]
- "XMLSCHEMA" means there is an associated XML Schema.

7 "xdt" is the namespace prefix used for XPath (XQuery) data types. This namespace prefix is *predeclared* in XQuery, and is used elsewhere by convention.

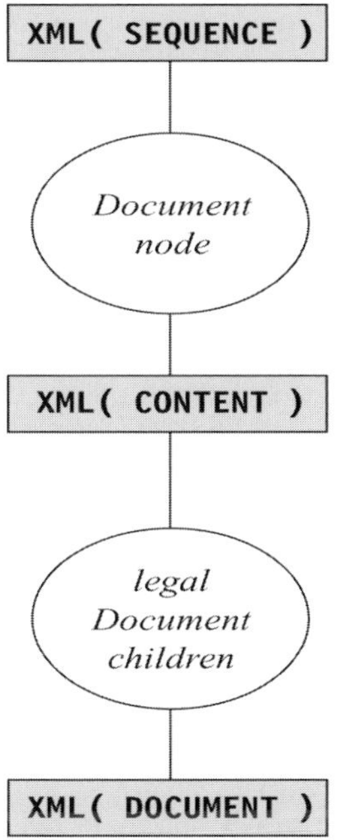

Figure 15-2 *XML Data Type Hierarchy.*

- "ANY" means there may or may not be an XML Schema associated with this *XML value.*

This second (optional) modifier appears in parentheses after the first modifier so that, for example, an untyped document node has the type "XML(DOCUMENT(UNTYPED))."

If the second modifier is "XMLSCHEMA," there are two ways to identify the actual Schema instance. First, you can supply a SQL identifier for some registered Schema (some Schema instance that is "known" to the SQL environment). An example is:

```
XML( DOCUMENT( XMLSCHEMA ID "smith.movies-schema" ) )
```

This form is very SQL-like – "smith" is the SQL schema (owner), and "movies-schema" is a SQL identifier. The second form is more XML-like:

```
XML( DOCUMENT( XMLSCHEMA URI "http://example.com/mm" ELEMENT "movie" ) )
```

This is the type of a document with an XML Schema with the target namespace URI "http://example.com/movies/" and top-level element "movie." The full syntax for the XML type is described in Grammar 15-1.

Grammar 15-1 *XML type*

```
XML [ ( { DOCUMENT | CONTENT | SEQUENCE }
        [ ( {ANY | UNTYPED | XMLSCHEMA schema-details} ) ]
    ) ]
where schema-details is:

URI target-namespace-URI [ LOCATION schema-location ] [ ELEMENT element-name ]
|  NONAMESPACE [ LOCATION schema-location ]  [ ELEMENT element-name ]
|  ID registered-schema-name [ ELEMENT element-name ]
```

The observant reader will notice that everything after "XML" is optional. The spec leaves it up to the implementation to define the meaning of the type "XML" with no modifier, but says it must be XML(SEQUENCE), XML (CONTENT(ANY)), or XML(CONTENT(UNTYPED)).

15.4 XQuery Functions

The SQL/XML publishing functions described in Section 15.2 use XPath (and, in SQL/XML:2006, XQuery) to address parts of an XML value. In SQL/XML:2006, three additional functions are defined — XMLQUERY, XMLTABLE, and XMLEXISTS — which use XQuery. In this section, we describe each new function, with examples, then discuss some of the benefits of these new functions.

For these examples we introduce a new table, `MOVIES_XML`. Many people want to store XML in a database as a single document — *i.e.*, many will store the movies data as a single XML document with top-level element `movies`, containing child elements `movie`. Others want to store each movie in a separate XML document (or file or cell). For the examples in this section, we have chosen the multiple-document approach (though we illustrate the single-document approach when querying a file in Example 15-11). The examples are a little more complex when dealing with multiple XML documents, so the single-document storage choice is a degenerate case of the multiple-document choice.[8]

Table 15-2 *MOVIES_XML*

ID	MOVIE_XML
42	<movie> <title>An American Werewolf in London</title> <yearReleased>1981</yearReleased> . . . </movie>
43	<movie> <title>Animal House</title> <yearReleased>1978</yearReleased> . . . </movie>

Table 15-2 shows part of the MOVIES_XML table, which has two columns — ID, of type INTEGER, and MOVIE_XML, of type XML. Notice that, in this section, we are querying XML stored natively in the database. In Section 15.2, we were querying relational data and representing the output as XML.

15.4.1 XMLQUERY

XMLQUERY is a function that fits naturally in the SQL `SELECT` clause. It takes an XQuery string (*i.e.,* an XQuery expression in a string), plus arguments for XQuery variables and the context item, and returns an XML value (an instance of the XML type). The syntax of XMLQUERY is summarized in Grammar 15-2.

Grammar 15-2 *XMLQUERY Syntax Summary*

```
XMLQUERY (
    XQuery-expression
    [ PASSING { BY REF | BY VALUE }  argument-list ]
    [RETURNING { CONTENT | SEQUENCE } [{ BY REF | BY VALUE }]]
    NULL ON EMPTY | EMPTY ON EMPTY
    )
```

8 This is a matter of some debate in the XML world. Taking the single-document approach to the extreme, all the world's data could be represented in a single XML document, with a top-level element <everything>. We've thought about this approach and have concluded that it may cause performance problems.

```
where argument-list is a comma-separated list of:

    context item | value-expression AS identifier
```

Example 15-10 is a simple SQL query using XMLQUERY. The `XQuery-expression` is the string `"for $m in $col/movie return $m/title"`, and the data to be queried is the data in the column `MOVIE`, passed in to the variable named `col`. The keywords `RETURNING CONTENT` ensure that the result is serialized and returned `BY VALUE` to the SQL engine — `BY REF` or `BY VALUE` can only be specified with `RETURNING SEQUENCE`. This makes sense — the main advantage of using `BY REF` is that you can go "up the tree" (access the parent and ancestors) of the result. Since an XMLTYPE (CONTENT) is an XML value with a single root node, there *is* no parent. The SQL/XML implementation we used does not support `RETURNING SEQUENCE` (and hence does not support `RETURNING BY REF`). We expect this to be the case with most mainstream SQL/XML implementations.

Example 15-10 *Simple XMLQUERY*

```
SELECT
  XMLQUERY(
    'for $m in
      $col/movie
    return
      $m/title'
    PASSING movie AS "col"
    RETURNING CONTENT
    NULL ON EMPTY
  ) AS result
FROM MOVIES_XML
```

Results:

```
RESULT
----------------------------------------------
<title>An American Werewolf in London</title>
<title>Animal House</title>

(2 rows in the result)
```

Note that the query in Example 15-10 returns two results — one for each row in the table — and *not* a single XML value containing all the results. Note also that, given a suitable input function (such as `fn:doc()` or `fn:collection()`) you can use XMLQUERY to query a file as well as a table, subject to the restrictions and security mechanisms in your SQL engine. For example, we could execute the same query in Example 15-10 against an XML file, as in Example 15-11.

Example 15-11 *Simple XMLQUERY over a File*

```
SELECT
  XMLQUERY(
    'for $m in
       doc("/public/movies/movies-we-own.xml")/movies/movie
     return
       $m/title'
    RETURNING CONTENT
    NULL ON EMPTY
  ) AS result
FROM DUAL

Results:

RESULT
-------
<title>The Fifth Element</title>
<title>An American Werewolf in London</title>
<title>American Graffiti</title>
...

(1 row in the result)
```

Example 15-11 returns only a single result — instead of iterating over the column of a table, now we are just querying a single document that contains a `movies` element that wraps all the `movie` elements. Note that we could have queried over many documents using the `fn:collection()` function, just as we could have queried over a single XML document stored in a table cell in Example 15-10.

Example 15-11 really doesn't interact with SQL in any useful way — it queries over a file, and does not use the result as part of a bigger SQL expression. The FROM clause uses FROM DUAL, where DUAL is a dummy, 1-row table available in every Oracle schema, for syntactic convenience. Some SQL implementations allow you to leave out the FROM clause altogether. In this case, XMLQUERY merely provides a convenient harness (a context) for running an XQuery. The real power of XMLQUERY is in its ability to query over data stored in the database and/or to use the result of an XQuery as part of some more complex SQL expression, as in Example 15-12.

Example 15-12 *XMLQUERY and AVG*

```
SELECT
  AVG(
    XMLCAST(
      XMLQUERY(
        'for $m in
          $col/movie
        return
          $m/runningTime/text()'
        PASSING movie AS "col"
        RETURNING CONTENT
        NULL ON EMPTY
        ) AS decimal(8,1)
      )
  ) AS "avgRunningTime"
FROM MOVIES_XML
```

```
Results:

avgRunningTime
--------------
         103.5
```

In Example 15-12, we use XMLQUERY to find the running time of each movie, then we cast the result to decimal[9] and plug the result into the SQL function AVG to get the average running time. While it is possible to do this kind of SQL processing with XMLQUERY, in general it's easier with XMLTABLE (see Section 15.4.2). We expect the most common use for XMLQUERY to be querying XML stored

9 See Section 15.6.3 for a description of XMLCAST. Note that not all implementations will return a zero suppressed result.

in the database and producing XML as a result, possibly for input to XMLTABLE.

Example 15-13 *XMLQUERY, Complete*

```
SELECT
  XMLQUERY(
    'for $m in
      $col/movie
     let $producers := $m/producer
     where $m/yearReleased > 1950
     return
       <output>
         {$m/title}
         {for $p in $producers
            return
              <prodFullName>
                {concat(
                  $p/givenName,
                  " ",
                  $p/familyName
                 )
                }
              </prodFullName>
         }
       </output>'
    PASSING movie AS "col"
    RETURNING CONTENT
    NULL ON EMPTY
  ) AS "Results"
  FROM movies_xml
```

Results:

```
Results
-------
<output>
  <title>An American Werewolf in London</title>
  <prodFullName>George, Jr. Folsey</prodFullName>
  <prodFullName>Peter Guber</prodFullName>
  <prodFullName>Jon Peters</prodFullName>
</output>
```

```
<output>
  <title>Animal House</title>
  <prodFullName>Matty Simmons</prodFullName>
  <prodFullName>Ivan Reitman</prodFullName>
</output>

(2 rows in the result)
```

Example 15-13 shows an XMLQUERY query that:

- Queries across XML data stored in the database — movie data in the `MOVIES_XML` table.
- Restricts the query according to some value in the XML data — in this case, `yearReleased`.
- Concatenates the `givenName` and `FamilyName` of each producer to form a new element, `prodFullName`
- Returns an XML result for each row in the table — Example 15-13 uses element construction to return an XML result in a different form from the input.

15.4.2 XMLTABLE

XMLTABLE uses XQuery to query some XML, and returns the result in the same form as a SQL table. You might think of XMLTABLE as the "opposite" of the publishing functions, which allow you to query SQL tables and return the results as XML. In the examples in this section, we show *queries* that produce *pseudo-tables*. The pseudo-table can be used anywhere you would use a table name — in the `FROM` clause of a `SELECT` statement, for example. You could also create a real, persistent table whose contents are the same as the pseudo-table, by using `CREATE TABLE mytable AS`, or you could create a simple view.

As with XMLQUERY, we start with a syntax summary (Grammar 15-3) and a simple example (Example 15-14).

Grammar 15-3 *XMLTABLE Syntax Summary*

```
XMLTABLE (
    [ namespace-declaration , ]
    XQuery-expression              (: the row pattern :)
```

```
    [ PASSING argument-list ]
    COLUMNS XMLtbl-column-definitions  (: the column definitions :)
```

```
where argument-list is:

    value-expression AS identifier

and XMLtbl-column-definitions is a comma-separated list of column
        definitions, which may contain:

    column-name FOR ORDINALITY

and/or:

    column-name data-type
    [ BY REF | BY VALUE ]
    [ default-clause ]
    [ PATH XQuery-expression ]   (: the column pattern :)
```

The first argument to XMLTABLE is a `namespace-declaration`, which lets you declare namespaces to be used in the evaluation of the function. `XQuery-expression` is a string containing an XQuery expression that expresses the contents of each row. In the rest of this chapter, we refer to this XQuery expression as the *row pattern*. The argument list is the same as for XMLQUERY, except that arguments in the list are always passed by reference. `XMLtbl-column-definitions` defines the name, type, and value of each column. In the rest of this chapter, we refer to the `XMLtbl-column-definitions` clause as the *column definitions*, and to the XQuery expression in the column definitions as the *column pattern*. The column definitions are optional — let's see a simple example without them.

Example 15-14 *Simple XMLTABLE*

```
SELECT result.*
FROM
  movies_xml ,
  XMLTABLE(
    'for $m in
      $col/movie
     return
       $m/title'
```

```
    PASSING movies_xml.movie AS "col"
  ) AS result
```

Results:

```
COLUMN_VALUE
-----------------------------------------
<title>An American Werewolf in London</title>
<title>Animal House</title>

(2 rows in the result)
```

In Example 15-14,[10] we use the same XQuery as in the simple XMLQUERY example at Example 15-10, but instead of using XMLQUERY in the `SELECT` clause, we use XMLTABLE in the `FROM` clause. The `XQuery-expression` string is the same, and we pass in the movie column of the `MOVIES_XML` table as before, except that we cannot rely on a following `FROM` clause to provide the source table — we are already in the `FROM` clause. Instead, we must qualify the column name with its table name — `MOVIES_XML.MOVIE` — and include the `MOVIES_XML` table in the `FROM` clause. The result is a SQL table with a single column of type XML(CONTENT), and one row for each member of the sequence returned by the `XQuery-expression`.[11] The table is called `result` (we used an alias to provide the table name), and the column is called `COLUMN_VALUE` (our implementation provided this column name by default — yours may provide a different default, or insist that you explicitly name the column).

Let's look at this in a bit more detail. For each row in the passed-in table (`MOVIES_XML`), XMLTABLE evaluates the row pattern (the `XQuery-expression`).[12] The row pattern includes a variable, `$col`, whose value is passed in using the `PASSING` keyword. `$col` is an XML sequence, formed by casting the contents of the column `movie` in the table `MOVIES_XML` to XML(CONTENT) (see Section 15.6.3 for more on casting). This sequence is passed in by reference, so the

10 The observant reader will notice this example doesn't quite match the syntax in Grammar 11-5. The standard says the COLUMNS clause is mandatory, while in our test implementation it's optional.

11 In this example, the result has one row for each row that was passed in, but this is coincidental (it's because each movie happens to have only one title).

12 Since the XMLTABLE call includes a column from the xml_movies table, this is a *left correlated join*.

row pattern is free to use reverse axes on the data passed in (to find its parent and ancestors).[13] The result of evaluating an XQuery expression is always a sequence of items,[14] in this example a sequence of two `title` elements. Each item in the sequence becomes a row in the resulting table. This example does not include any column definitions, so the output table has a single column whose name is `COLUMN_VALUE` (the default for our implementation) and whose type is XML(CONTENT) (also the default for our implementation). The output table is called `result`, since we aliased the result of XMLTABLE using "… `AS result`." This allows us to ask for only the columns of `result`, in the SELECT clause ("`SELECT result.*` …"). If we use "`SELECT *` …," the query returns the columns resulting from the join of `MOVIES_XML` with the table created by XMLTABLE (*i.e.*, `id`, `movie`, and `column_value`), which is not what we want.

So far, we have achieved the same result as we achieved with XMLQUERY in Example 15-10. So why do we need both functions, XMLQUERY and XMLTABLE? XMLQUERY lets you query any XML and return XML, while XMLTABLE lets you query any XML and return a SQL table, which you can use as part of any SQL statement. Let's build out our XMLTABLE example, and the difference will become clear.

First, let's take a look at the column definitions. This lets you define columns for the table that XMLTABLE returns, rather than having it return a single column of type XML(CONTENT). For each column that you want to see in this output table, you specify the column name, the SQL data type of the column, and the XQuery expression that addresses the contents for the column (the column pattern). This XQuery expression has as its context the result of the row pattern (the XQuery expression that is the first [nonoptional] argument of XMLTABLE). You can also specify a default value, to be used in case the column would otherwise contain a NULL value, and a passing mechanism (`BY REF` or `BY VALUE`, where the default is `BY VALUE`). In addition, you can specify a column name followed by the keywords `FOR ORDINALITY`, which captures the document order of the results within each sequence passed to the row pattern (*i.e.*, within each row passed in).

13 In the general case — passing in a column, as in this first XMLTABLE example — this is moot, since the column data has no parent.

14 Where an item is either a node or a value.

The alert reader will have noticed that there is an interesting interaction between the row pattern and the column pattern. The query writer can, in many cases, choose to do more of the path processing in the row pattern, leaving the column pattern very simple, or to do more of the path processing in the column pattern, over leaving the row pattern simpler. Also, note that the column pattern is an XPath (or XQuery) expression whose context is the result of the row pattern, and XQuery allows element construction in the return clause. So it's quite reasonable for the row pattern to construct result elements, and "offer them up" to the column pattern (see Example 15-26).

We promised to build out the example – let's do that now. Example 15-15 shows an XMLTABLE call that does include column definitions.

***Example 15-15** XMLTABLE with Column Definitions*

```
SELECT result.*
FROM
  movies_xml ,
  XMLTABLE(
    'for $m in
      $col/movie
     return
       $m'
    PASSING movies_xml.movie AS "col"
    COLUMNS
      "title" VARCHAR(80) PATH 'title' ,
      "runningTime" INTEGER PATH 'runningTime' ,
      "yearReleased" INTEGER PATH 'yearReleased'
  ) AS result
```

Results:

```
title                                    runningTime yearReleased
---------------------------------------- ----------- ------------
An American Werewolf in London                    98         1981
Animal House                                     109         1978

(2 rows in the result)
```

Instead of producing a table with a single column of type XML (CONTENT), in Example 15-15 XMLTABLE produces a table with three columns — the first is a column named `title`, of type `VARCHAR(80)`, which contains the result of evaluating the XPath "`title`" in the context of the result of the row pattern. The column pattern can be any XQuery expression, but in most cases it will be an XPath expression, hence the keyword "PATH."

Variations on Syntax — Column Definitions, PASSING, Examples

In this simple example (Example 15-15), the column name is exactly the same as the column pattern. In such cases, you can leave out the column pattern altogether and just specify the column name and type. In SQL, a column name can contain upper and lowercase characters and special characters such as "/," as long as it is enclosed in double-quotes. So

```
"director[1]/familyName" VARCHAR(80)
```

is a valid column definition, resulting in a column called "`director[1]/familyName`." Just remember that if you do define a column name that is not all-uppercase alphanumerics, then you must quote the `column-name` every time you use it. For example, in Example 15-15, if you want to select only the `title` column, you need to say

```
SELECT "title"
```

since, without the quotes around "title," your SQL processor will look for a column named "`TITLE`."[15]

Some people will find it natural and useful to end up with column names that look like XPath expressions, since the column name will say something about how the data was derived. For others, the column names will be too ugly to live with. You can change the column names by aliasing the columns along with the table, as in Example 15-16.

Example 15-16 *XMLTABLE with Column Definitions, Alternative Syntax*

```
SELECT result.*
FROM
  movies_xml ,
  XMLTABLE(
```

15 In SQL, all nondelimited identifiers are implicitly uppercased.

```
        'for $m in
          $col/movie
         return
           $m'
        PASSING movies_xml.movie AS "col"
        COLUMNS
          "title" VARCHAR(80) ,
          "runningTime" INTEGER ,
          "yearReleased" INTEGER ,
          "producer[1]/familyName" VARCHAR(20)
      ) AS result ("TITLE", "RUNNINGTIME", "YEARRELEASED",
                  "PRODUCER")
```

Results:

```
TITLE                          RUNNINGTIME YEARRELEASED PRODUCER
------------------------------ ----------- ------------ --------
An American Werewolf in London          98         1981 Folsey
Animal House                           109         1978 Simmons

(2 rows in the result)
```

In Example 15-16, the column names in the columns definition double as paths, and then the column names are changed by aliasing them along with the table alias.

Before we leave our simple examples, we should mention that there is a variation on the way you pass in arguments to the row pattern. In our examples so far, we passed in a column as an XQuery variable. You can pass in a list of value expressions (a column is an example of a value expression) as variables, and you can pass in at most one value expression as the context[16] of the row pattern – this value expression is specified on its own, without an "AS" keyword and variable name.

Personally, we prefer the column pattern syntax:

```
column-name data-type PATH XQuery-expression
```

16 See Chapter 9, "XPath 1.0 and XPath 2.0," Chapter 10, "Introduction to XQuery 1.0," and Chapter 11, "XQuery 1.0 Definition," for a description of context.

It seems more natural and straightforward. And we prefer passing in an argument as an XQuery variable, rather than as the context item – it makes it absolutely clear to the reader of the query where and how the column value is used in the row pattern. This is largely a matter of personal taste, but we will continue to use these syntax flavors in the examples in the rest of this chapter.

Dealing with Repeating Elements

One of the major differences between XML and SQL is that an XML element at any level may repeat any number of times. In SQL, a table is made up of rows where typically each cell (row/column intersection) contains only a single value. In the examples so far, we have chosen XML elements that do not repeat – `title`, `runningTime`, `yearReleased` – or, in the case of the `producer` in Example 15-16, we have used a positional predicate (`[1]`) so we only have to deal with the first element. There are a number of other ways to deal with repeating elements in SQL:

1. Denormalize.

   In the SQL representation of the movies data in Figure 15-1, we chose to store all the information about producers in a separate table (`PRODUCERS`). Then, instead of putting producer information directly into the `MOVIE` table, we created a table `MOVIES_PRODUCERS` that maps movies to their producers. This is part of the *normalization*[17] process that many believe is important when designing SQL data stores.

   One way of representing repeating XML elements is to *denormalize* the data – in our example, to insert the information for each producer into the row for each movie. Some consider this bad practice for a couple of reasons. First, it leads to duplication of data – the information for any particular producer appears in many rows in the new table. This may take more disk space and, more importantly, there is no longer a single place to read or update information about a particular producer, so the information may become inconsistent. Second, there may be "holes" in the data. In Example 15-4, we choose to represent producers in three columns in the result table. If some movie has fewer than

---

17 For a full description of normalization, see one of the classic texts on relational database systems, such as: *An Introduction to Database Systems, eighth edition*, C. J. Date (Boston: Addison-Wesley, 2003).

three producers, there will be an empty cell in the table — a "hole." Despite these arguments against denormalizing SQL data, in some cases it will be the simplest and/or best performing way to represent the data.[18]

Example 15-17 *Repeating Elements, Denormalized Result Table*

```
SELECT result.* FROM
  movies_xml ,
  XMLTABLE(
    'for $m in
      $col/movie
    return
      $m'
    PASSING movies_xml.movie AS "col"
    COLUMNS
      "title" VARCHAR(80) PATH 'title' ,
      "producer1" VARCHAR(12) PATH 'producer[1]/familyName' ,
      "producer2" VARCHAR(12) PATH 'producer[2]/familyName' DEFAULT 'none',
      "producer3" VARCHAR(12) PATH 'producer[3]/familyName' DEFAULT 'none'
  ) AS result
```

```
Results:

title                          producer1    producer2    producer3
------------------------------ ------------ ------------ ------------
An American Werewolf in London Folsey       Guber        Peters
Animal House                   Simmons      Reitman      none

(2 rows in the result)
```

In Example 15-17, we represent the repeating XML element `producer` in three separate columns in the `result` table. Then we use the XPath in the column pattern to select the `familyName` of each `producer` in turn. Finally, we introduce the `DEFAULT` clause to define a default value for

18 Note that XML data is, by its nature, highly denormalized, with all the disadvantages this brings. On the other hand, XML is very good at representing data with lots of holes (sparse data).

"holes" in the data – in this case, if there is no second or third producer, then that cell will contain the string "none.[19]

2. Use XML for repeating elements.

   One of the beauties of SQL/XML is that it allows you to "mix'n'match" SQL and XML data. In some cases, the most appropriate way to store repeating XML elements is as XML data right in the table. In Example 15-18, we do just that. Since the result of the column pattern is coerced to the type of the column, and XML is now a SQL type, the result column can be of type XML[20] and the column pattern can return XML.

Example 15-18 *Repeating Elements, XML in the Result Table*

```
SELECT result.* FROM
  movies_xml ,
  XMLTABLE(
    'for $m in
      $col/movie
     return
       $m'
    PASSING movies_xml.movie AS "col"
    COLUMNS
      "title" VARCHAR(80) PATH 'title' ,
      "producers" XMLTYPE PATH 'producer'
  ) AS result
```

Results:

```
title                           producers
------------------------------- ---------------------------------------
An American Werewolf in London <producer>
                                    <familyName>Folsey</familyName>
                                    <givenName>George, Jr.</givenName>
                                    <otherNames/>
                                </producer>
```

19 In Example 15-19, we are *pivoting* the data.

20 The SQL/XML:2006 standard keyword for the XML type is "XML," and not "XMLTYPE." In our test implementation, "XMLTYPE" is used instead of "XML" (more precisely, it is used instead of "XML(CONTENT)"). The examples in this chapter will work in an Oracle SQL/XML context – if they don't work for you, try substituting "XML" or "XML(CONTENT)" for "XMLTYPE."

```
                              <producer>
                                  <familyName>Guber</familyName>
                                  <givenName>Peter</givenName>
                                  <otherNames/>
                              </producer>
                              <producer>
                                  <familyName>Peters</familyName>
                                  <givenName>Jon</givenName>
                                  <otherNames/>
                              </producer>
Animal House                  <producer>
                                  <familyName>Simmons</familyName>
                                  <givenName>Matty</givenName>
                                  <otherNames/>
                              </producer>
                              <producer>
                                  <familyName>Reitman</familyName>
                                  <givenName>Ivan</givenName>
                                  <otherNames/>
                              </producer>

(2 rows in the result)
```

3. Detail Tables.

   We have discussed two ways to represent repeating XML elements as denormalized SQL data. Now let's consider some normalized forms of the same data. One common SQL technique for storing repeating data is to move that data into a separate table, where the data can repeat as multiple rows (rather than multiple columns, as in Example 15-17). This table is known as a *detail table*. A single row in the *master table* — in our example, `MOVIES` — is mapped to multiple rows in the detail table via some key that is unique in the master table. The key is generally some number, made up specifically to be the `ID` of some record (row) in the master table. For the `MOVIES` table, we'll just use the title. So a single movie (row in the master table, `MOVIES`) maps to multiple producers (rows in the detail table) via the title (a column in both tables, which is unique in the master table but not in the detail table). This is known as a *master-detail relationship*, and the key is a *primary key* in the master table and a *foreign key* in the detail table.

Example 15-19 produces a detail table for producers, using two calls to XMLTABLE. Just as we can pass in values from the MOVIES_XML table to the first call to XMLTABLE, so we can also pass in values *from* the result table of the first XMLTABLE call *to* a second XMLTABLE call. In Example 15-19:

- `MOVIES_XML` contains the XML data for each movie.
- `RESULT` (the name we gave to the table that is output from the first XMLTABLE call by aliasing it with "`AS result`") has one row per movie. Each row has a `title` column and a `producers` column.
- `RESULT2` (the name we gave to the table that is output from the second XMLTABLE call) has one row per producer. Each row has a `familyName` column and an `ord` column. This example introduces the *ordinality column definition*. At most one of the column definitions may be a column name followed by the keywords "`FOR ORDINALITY`." This column is populated with the ordinality of the result. Remember, XMLTABLE outputs a row for each member of the sequence that is the result of the row pattern. Each member of the sequence has an *ordinality* – a number that designates its order in the sequence. Using this ordinality column, we can keep track of the order in which producers were represented in the original XML.
- In the `SELECT` clause, we select the `title` (the foreign key) and all the columns from `RESULT2` (`familyName` and `ord`).

The output of this SQL query is a `producers` SQL table – to use the detail table in some other query, simply use this query to create a view.

Example 15-19 *Repeating Elements, Detail Table*

```
SELECT result."title", result2.* FROM
  movies_xml ,
  XMLTABLE(
```

```
      'for $m in
        $col/movie
       return
         $m'
      PASSING movies_xml.movie AS "col"
      COLUMNS
        "title" VARCHAR(80) PATH 'title' ,
        "producers" XMLTYPE PATH 'producer'
    ) AS result ,
    XMLTABLE(
      'for $prod in $p/producer
       return
        $prod'
      PASSING result."producers" AS "p"
      COLUMNS
        "ord" FOR ORDINALITY ,
        "familyName" VARCHAR(20) PATH 'familyName'
    ) AS result2
```

Results:

```
title                                  ord familyName
------------------------------ ---------- ----------------
An American Werewolf in London           1 Folsey
An American Werewolf in London           2 Guber
An American Werewolf in London           3 Peters
Animal House                             1 Simmons
Animal House                             2 Reitman

(5 rows in the result)
```

4. SQL:2003 types.

   We have talked about the SQL/XML contribution to the SQL standard, but it's important to note that the rest of the SQL standard has progressed significantly since SQL-92. The SQL:2003 standard introduced a number of ways of modeling data that is not naturally "table-shaped," notably ARRAYs, nested tables, and objects. It would be natural to model a repeating element as an ARRAY (and a complex element as a nested table). Unfortunately, XMLTABLE does not allow an ARRAY or nested table in the result table —

SQL/XML only allows casting of XML to SQL *predefined* types, and ARRAY and nested table are *constructed* types. Is this a severe limitation? Not really — the SQL ARRAY is useful when you want to iterate over a repeating element. But you can iterate over XML using XMLTABLE (as in Example 15-19), so we don't need to be able to represent result columns as ARRAY.

Dealing with Complex Elements

In the preceding sections, we showed a number of ways of dealing with XML elements that repeat — something that is common ("natural") in XML, but has to be dealt with in a special way in SQL. *Complex elements* also fall into this category — in XML it is common for an element such as `producers` to contain subelements (or *child elements*) such as `familyName` and `givenName` (and for those child elements to contain child elements that contain child elements, and so on). Let's look at how we might represent complex elements in SQL using XMLTABLE. We use the `producers` element again — it is complex as well as repeating.

When looking at repeating elements, our first example (Example 15-17) showed a denormalized table. We could use the same technique to deal with producer as a complex element. This is not useful in the general case (where there are likely to be many levels of child elements) but we show an example of this simple case (with just one level of child elements) in Example 15-20, for completeness.

Example 15-20 *Complex Elements, Denormalized Result Table*

```
SELECT result.* FROM
  movies_xml ,
  XMLTABLE(
    'for $m in
      $col/movie
     return
       $m'
    PASSING movies_xml.movie AS "col"
    COLUMNS
      "title" VARCHAR(80) PATH 'title' ,
      "producerF" VARCHAR(12) PATH 'producer[1]/familyName' ,
      "producerG" VARCHAR(12) PATH 'producer[1]/givenName' ,
     "producerO" VARCHAR(12) PATH 'producer[1]/otherNames' DEFAULT 'none'
  ) AS result
```

Results:

```
title                        producerF    producerG    producerO
---------------------------- ------------ ------------ ------------
An American Werewolf in London Folsey     George, Jr.  none
Animal House                 Simmons      Matty        none

(2 rows in the result)
```

In our second "repeating elements" example, we used XML to represent the repeating elements (Example 15-18). This example also shows `producer` as a complex element — *i.e.*, pulling producers into a column of type XML will solve both "repeating elements" and "complex elements" problems.

That brings us to the SQL storage layout in Figure 15-1. That's the SQL storage we came up with to best represent the `MOVIES_XML` data as (normalized) SQL data. We showed in Section 15.2 that we can use the SQL/XML publishing functions to represent that SQL data as XML. Now, can we go the other way? Can we write a SQL query with XMLTABLE to represent our XML data as the SQL data in Figure 15-1? The answer, of course, is yes. In this section, we show how to produce (a representation of) the producer data as SQL data; we leave it as an exercise for the reader to produce the others.

The producer element is both repeating and complex. In Figure 15-1, we chose to put all the producer-related data into a table called `PRODUCERS`, with some unique key. Then we defined a table `MOVIES_PRODUCERS` that mapped movies to producers. The `PRODUCERS` table allows us to model a complex element — each child element is a column in the `PRODUCERS` table. We now have a hierarchy of depth three (`movie`, `producer`, `familyName`) and, by extension, the hierarchy could be of any depth. If there were only one producer per movie, we could put the `producer_id` in the `movies` table (as we did with `director_id`). Since `producer` is repeating as well as complex, we introduce the `MOVIES_PRODUCERS` table to map movies to producers. This allows us to represent any number of producers per movie.

Example 15-21 *almost* gives us a usable PRODUCERS table.

Example 15-21 *Complex Repeating Elements, PRODUCERS Table (1)*

```
SELECT DISTINCT result.* FROM
  movies_xml ,
  XMLTABLE(
```

```
    'for $m in
      $col/movie
     return
       $m/producer'
    PASSING movies_xml.movie AS "col"
    COLUMNS
      "ID" FOR ORDINALITY ,
      "familyName" VARCHAR(12) PATH 'familyName' ,
      "givenName" VARCHAR(12) PATH 'givenName' DEFAULT 'none' ,
      "otherNames" VARCHAR(12) PATH 'otherNames' DEFAULT 'none'
  ) AS result
```

Results:

```
        ID familyName   givenName    otherNames
---------- ------------ ------------ ------------
         1 Folsey       George, Jr.  none
         1 Simmons      Matty        none
         2 Guber        Peter        none
         2 Reitman      Ivan         none
         3 Peters       Jon          none

(5 rows in the result)
```

Example 15-21 uses XMLTABLE to pull the child elements of `producer` into columns, it uses the SQL `DISTINCT` keyword to make sure we only get each producer once (we could have used the XQuery function `distinct-values` inside the XQuery), and it uses a `FOR ORDINALITY` column to produce a key value for the `ID` column. If our XML table stored just a single `movies` XML document, Example 15-21 would work just fine. Since we chose to store our movies in separate XML documents (separate table rows), one per movie, the ordinality numbering restarts for each row (each movie) — the ID column does *not* hold a unique key! There are a number of ways around this. We chose to use a combination of the ID value in the MOVIES table and the ORDINALITY column in the XMLTABLE result table. Note that we need to multiply the `MOVIES.ID` by some number (the maximum number of producers we ever expect to see in one movie — we chose 10) to avoid collisions. This satisfies all the requirements for the `PRODUCERS.ID` column — it must be a unique number, and it must be derivable from the data (so that we can use it in the `MOVIES_PRODUCERS` table). Of course, it doesn't matter what the actual values are.

Example 15-22 *Complex Repeating Elements, PRODUCERS Table (2)*

```
SELECT
  (10*movies_xml.ID)+result."ord" AS "ID",
  result."familyName",
  result."givenName",
  result."otherNames"
FROM
  movies_xml ,
  XMLTABLE(
    'for $m in
      $col/movie
     return
       $m/producer'
    PASSING movies_xml.movie AS "col"
    COLUMNS
      "ord" FOR ORDINALITY ,
      "familyName" VARCHAR(12) PATH 'familyName' ,
      "givenName" VARCHAR(12) PATH 'givenName' DEFAULT 'none' ,
      "otherNames" VARCHAR(12) PATH 'otherNames' DEFAULT 'none'
  ) AS result
  ORDER BY "ID" ASC
```

Results:

```
        ID familyName   givenName    otherNames
---------- ------------ ------------ ------------
       421 Folsey       George, Jr.  none
       422 Guber        Peter        none
       423 Peters       Jon          none
       431 Simmons      Matty        none
       432 Reitman      Ivan         none

(5 rows in the result)
```

Example 15-22 gives us a usable `PRODUCERS` table. We assume that the order of producers in the XML document is important (perhaps the first producer mentioned in the document is the primary producer), and we retain this ordering information by using "`result."ord"`" as part of the `ID`, and ordering by `ID`.

Now we need a `MOVIES_PRODUCERS` table that maps the `MOVIES.ID` to the `PRODUCERS.ID` that we just created. We produce

MOVIES_PRODUCERS simply by adding MOVIES_XML.ID to the select list of Example 15-22 and removing the producers information, see Example 15-23.

Example 15-23 *Complex Repeating Elements, MOVIES_PRODUCERS Table*

```
SELECT
  movies_xml.id AS "MOVIE",
  (10*movies_xml.ID)+result."ord" AS "PRODUCER"
FROM
  movies_xml ,
  XMLTABLE(
    'for $m in
      $col/movie
     return
       $m/producer'
    PASSING movies_xml.movie AS "col"
    COLUMNS
      "ord" FOR ORDINALITY
  ) AS result
```

```
Results:

     MOVIE   PRODUCER
---------- ----------
        42        421
        42        422
        42        423
        43        431
        43        432

(5 rows in the result)
```

Representing XML as SQL Data

In the preceding sections, we have shown how to represent the movies XML documents as SQL data. This is tremendously useful for two reasons. First, it frees the data administrator from the pressure of having to decide how to store data. If the data is born as XML, he now has the freedom to leave the data as XML and process it as XML, or to convert the data to SQL and physically store it relationally (but still publish it as XML), or to create a set of SQL views that make the XML data look like SQL. There are good reasons for choosing each of these options — the important point here is, SQL/XML makes all those options available.

Second, you can now apply all the power of SQL[21] to your XML data, without necessarily shredding the data and storing it in tables. SQL has evolved far beyond a simple query language that can find and extract items that meet certain criteria. There are many applications of advanced SQL functionality in fields such as Business Intelligence and Data Mining.

Let's look at one small illustration of the power of SQL, the analytic functions *rollup* and *cube*. Analytic functions[22] are generally used to analyze vast amounts of data, so our tiny `movies_xml` table won't do. For these examples, we use a slightly larger table, `movies_xml_big`. Let's suppose you want to know how the running time of movies varies with the director and the year released. You could write a set of queries, each showing one aspect of the data. Or you could use rollup, as illustrated in Example 15-24. This query shows the average running time of all movies directed by each director in each year — *e.g.*, the average running time for movies directed by Besson in 1997 was 126 minutes. This average is then *rolled up* to show the average running time for all movies in each year — *e.g.*, in 1997 the average running time for all movies (all directors) was 123 minutes. And finally, the average running time is *rolled up* to the whole sample — the average running time for all movies in the sample (all directors, all years) is 116.7 minutes.

Example 15-24 *Rollup Function on XML Data*

```
SELECT
  result."yearReleased",
  result."director",
  avg(result."runningTime") AS "length"
FROM
  movies_xml_big ,
  XMLTABLE(
    'for $m in
      $col/movie
```

21 Some say that SQL is a dinosaur — well, maybe it is, but the dinosaurs were tremendously powerful creatures that evolved over more than 165 million years until they were perfectly suited to their environment. Similarly, SQL has evolved over several decades into a hugely powerful language. By comparison, XQuery is still in its infancy — still swimming in the ocean, you might say.

22 Also known as OLAP (online analytic processing) functions.

```
    return
      $m'
  PASSING movies_xml_big.movie AS "col"
  COLUMNS
    "title" VARCHAR(80) PATH 'title' ,
    "yearReleased" NUMBER PATH 'yearReleased' ,
    "producers" XMLTYPE PATH 'producer',
    "runningTime" NUMBER PATH 'runningTime',
    "director" VARCHAR(12) PATH 'director[1]/familyName'
) AS result
WHERE result."yearReleased" IN (1997, 1998, 1999)
GROUP BY
  rollup(result."yearReleased", result."director" )
ORDER BY result."yearReleased" ASC
```

Results:

```
yearReleased director         length
------------ ------------ ----------
        1997 Besson              126
        1997 Duvall              134
        1997 Jeunet              108
        1997 Peterson            124
        1997                     123
        1998 Bay                 151
        1998 Coen                 98
        1998                   124.5
        1999 Mendes              121
        1999 Myrick               87
        1999 Peirce              116
        1999 Wheeler             102
        1999                   106.5
                               116.7

(14 rows in the result)
```

Using the rollup function, you can quickly get a feel for the trends in your data. The cube function takes this one step further, showing more "slices" on the data. For example, the results in Example 15-25 show not only averages rolled up by director and year, but also average running times for each director across all years. Our sample data (`movies`) is not ideally suited to this kind of example — it's difficult to imagine anyone wanting to do this kind of in-depth analysis on running times in movies. But we hope you can imagine the power of this kind of analysis on more structured data, perhaps some data that you deal with.

The rollup and cube functions are widely used to show trends and spot anomalies in data such as sales by product over time, or soil contamination by region over time. The same data could, of course, be gleaned from a *set* of queries, each one showing some aspect of the data, but a single query is much easier to use, manipulate, and optimize.

Example 15-25 *Cube Function on XML Data*

```
SELECT
  result."yearReleased",
  result."director",
  avg(result."runningTime") AS "length"
FROM
  movies_xml_big ,
  XMLTABLE(
    'for $m in
      $col/movie
     return
       $m'
    PASSING movies_xml_big.movie AS "col"
    COLUMNS
      "title" VARCHAR(80) PATH 'title' ,
      "yearReleased" NUMBER PATH 'yearReleased' ,
      "producers" XMLTYPE PATH 'producer',
      "runningTime" NUMBER PATH 'runningTime',
      "director" VARCHAR(12) PATH 'director[1]/familyName'
  ) AS result
  WHERE result."yearReleased" IN (1997, 1998, 1999)
  GROUP BY
    cube(result."yearReleased", result."director" )
  ORDER BY result."yearReleased" ASC
```

Results:

```
yearReleased director      length
------------ ------------ ----------
        1997 Besson              126
        1997 Duvall              134
        1997 Jeunet              108
        1997 Peterson            124
        1997                     123
        1998 Bay                 151
        1998 Coen                 98
        1998                   124.5
        1999 Mendes              121
        1999 Myrick               87
        1999 Peirce              116
        1999 Wheeler             102
        1999                   106.5
             Bay                 151
             Besson              126
             Coen                 98
             Duvall              134
             Jeunet              108
             Mendes              121
             Myrick               87
             Peirce              116
             Peterson            124
             Wheeler             102
                               116.7

(24 rows in the result)
```

Using XMLTABLE

The examples of XMLTABLE in this section have been quite simple. This is deliberate – we wanted to illustrate a number of points with the simplest possible queries. But it would be wrong to end this section without presenting one not-so-simple query. XMLTABLE is a part of the SQL standard, so not only can we combine the features of XMLTABLE in arbitrarily complex ways, but we can combine XMLTABLE with other SQL features. Also, the row pattern can be any arbitrarily complex XQuery expression – it's not limited to the simple XQuery expressions used in the examples thus far.

Example 15-26 *XMLTABLE, Not So Simple*

```
SELECT
  result."title",
  avg(result."rating") AS "average rating",
  count(result."rating") AS "# reviews"
FROM
  movies_xml,
  reviews_xml,
  XMLTABLE(
    'for
       $m in $col/movie,
       $r in $col2/review
     let $rating := $r/rating,
         $title  := $m/title
     where
       $m/title = $r/title and
         $r/medium = "movie" and
         not(contains($r/text, "awful"))
     order by $r/rating
     return
       <output>
         <r>{$rating}</r>
         <t>{$title}</t>
         <p>{$r/medium}</p>
       </output>'
    PASSING movies_xml.movie AS "col",
            reviews_xml.review AS "col2"
    COLUMNS
      "title" VARCHAR(80) PATH 't' ,
      "rating" NUMBER PATH 'r',
      "medium"  VARCHAR(10) PATH 'p'
  ) AS result
  GROUP BY result."title"
```

```
Results:

title                            average rating # reviews
-------------------------------- -------------- ----------
An American Werewolf in London                5          4
Animal House                                  4          3
(2 rows in the result)
```

Some notes on Example 15-26:

- This query joins two data sources, the `MOVIES_XML` table and a new table, `REVIEWS_XML`, containing reviews and a star rating. We do the join in the row pattern XQuery by passing in two data sources, in this case two XML type columns. We could have made two separate calls to XMLTABLE, and joined the results in SQL (outside of XMLTABLE).
- The `let` clause in the row pattern identifies the elements we are interested in.
- The `where` clause in the row pattern applies the join criterion, *i.e.*, it says we are joining the two data sources via the common item "`title`." It also restricts the reviews to movie reviews (we don't want to consider book reviews with the same title), and it excludes reviews with the word "awful" in them (these unnecessarily harsh reviews might bias our sample).
- Note that the `contains` in the where clause is doing a strict substring search and not a full text search. For more on full text search, see Chapter 13, "What's Missing?"
- The row pattern includes an `order by` clause. Note that the order in which the results are displayed is controlled by the SQL statement — the `order by` clause in the row pattern only affects the order within each row. If the XML were stored in a single `movies` document, the `order by` in the row pattern would affect the result, but could still be overridden by a SQL `order by` clause.
- The `return` clause uses element construction to create elements that are pulled out by the column patterns. In this way, you can use an arbitrarily complex XQuery expression — including a complete FLWOR expression — to express each cell in the result table. In this example, the row pattern returns a single element called output, with a child element containing the value to be used in each of the column patterns. In the general case, the row pattern returns a *sequence* (not a *document*). The column pattern is evaluated with its context set to each member of the sequence in turn, and the results merged to form a new sequence. In Example 15-26, the sequence has only one member — the element called `output`. Why is this distinction (between sequence and document) important? Since

the context of the column pattern is the output element, the column pattern for, *e.g.*, `title` is "`./t`," or simply "`t`" for short. If the row pattern returned a document, then the context of the column pattern would have been the document node, and the path would have been "`output/t`."

- Finally, the SQL query groups the results by title and, for each title, reports the average rating and the number of ratings considered.

15.4.3 XMLEXISTS

XMLEXISTS[23] is the last XQuery function in SQL/XML that we discuss in this section. While XMLQUERY fits naturally into the `SELECT` clause of a SQL query, and XMLTABLE fits naturally into the `FROM` clause, XMLEXISTS sits comfortably in the `WHERE` clause. XMLEXISTS is defined as part of the definition of XMLTABLE, and is surfaced as a callable function in the SQL/XML standard. (By contrast, XMLIterate is also defined as part of the definition of XMLTABLE, but it is *not* exposed as a callable function — it exists solely to support the definition of XMLTABLE.)

XMLEXISTS has just about the same syntax as XMLQUERY. It returns `false` if the result of the XQuery expression is the empty sequence, otherwise it returns `true`.

In our `movies` sample data, some of the movies have a `studio` element telling us which studio produced the movie, others do not. Example 15-27 finds the `ID` of the movies that do have a `studio` element (there are none in our small test table).

Example 15-27 *XMLEXISTS*

```
SELECT
  ID
  FROM movies_xml
  WHERE XMLEXISTS('/movie/studio' PASSING BY VALUE movie)
```

```
Results:

no rows selected
```

23 Our test implementation does not currently support XMLEXISTS. Instead, Oracle supports a similar function, existsNode(), as a proprietary extension.

The XQuery expression in Example 15-27 is a simple XPath, but it could be any XQuery expression. In Example 15-28, the XPath includes a simple `contains` predicate (again, this is the substring `contains`, not a full text `contains`).

Example 15-28 *XMLEXISTS with Predicate*

```
SELECT
  ID
  FROM movies_xml
  WHERE
    XMLEXISTS('/movie/title[contains(.,"Werewolf")]'
      PASSING BY VALUE movie)
```

Results:

```
  ID
----
  42

(1 row in the result)
```

XMLEXISTS does not add new functionality – *i.e.*, any query written with XMLEXISTS could be written with XMLQUERY and/or XMLTABLE. The XMLTABLE justifies the inclusion of XMLEXISTS in the standard by comparing it to the SQL predicate EXISTS, which could similarly be displaced by COUNT. The additional convenience that comes with XMLEXISTS, as with EXISTS, justifies its inclusion as part of the standard.

A Note on Proprietary Extensions

Many vendors have released proprietary extensions to SQL to achieve the same goals as the SQL/XML functions – the ability to publish SQL data to XML, and to query XML data using SQL. Often, this is simply a matter of timing – a vendor's customers ask for some functionality, and it must be released in a product before the standard is finished (or, in some cases, before the standardization effort has begun). We have already mentioned Microsoft's SQLXML, a proprietary extension with roughly the same functionality as the SQL/XML publishing functions. Oracle also has proprietary extensions in this area, including functions to extract data from inside an XML value using XPath (extract, extractValue), a function to test for node existence using XPath (existsNode), and an XML native type (XMLTYPE), as well as the standard functions XMLQUERY, XMLTABLE, and the publishing functions. Oracle's proprietary functions map quite well to the functions that are emerging in the standard (this is, of course, by design and not by accident). Over time, we expect Oracle and other vendors to (re)implement this functionality using the standard's syntax.

15.5 Managing XML in the Database

The XML native SQL type allows us to store XML in a SQL database. Since it is a native type, data of type XML can be inserted, updated, and deleted in a SQL statement just like a date or an integer. This is necessary, but not sufficient for many users. Values of most data types can only reasonably be managed as a whole — you would not try to insert, update, or delete a part of an integer, for example. While you might want to insert/update/delete a part of a string or a LOB (Large OBject), in general it's acceptable to insert a whole string, or to replace a whole string with a slightly-modified copy. With XML, this approach is cumbersome for the user and inefficient for the database engine.

In Example 15-27, you saw that some of the movies in our sample data include a studio element, but not all. Suppose you just found out that one of the movies — *An American Werewolf in London* — was released by Universal Studios. Using SQL with the functions we have already described (XMLQUERY and XMLTABLE), you could find the entry for *An American Werewolf in London*, pull out the XML data, do something with it to add the studio information, then update the `movie` column in `MOVIES_XML` with the new version. But SQL/XML does not help you with that "do something with it" in the middle, and neither does XQuery — they do not provide any way for you to express "add an element called studio, as a child of movie, immediately after runningTime, and give it the value 'Universal Studios'." You would need to use some other tool, perhaps a Java application that built and modified a DOM. Having to do this makes the operation very cumbersome for the user.

What about efficiency? Pulling out all the data about one movie, and then replacing it all using a SQL update statement, is inefficient. It would be much worse if all the movies were stored in a single `movies` document — you could be updating many megabytes of data, plus any associated indexes, just to add one tiny string.

What we need is the ability to express a piecewise insert, update, or delete of the XML as part of the SQL statement. This would be simple and intuitive for the user, and could be efficiently implemented by the database engine. At the time of writing, efforts are under way within the W3C XML Query Working Group (which has spawned an Update Task Force) to produce the language for piecewise updates of XML. See Chapter 13, "What's Missing?" for more details.

15.6 Talking the Same Language — Mappings

So far in this chapter we have talked about publishing SQL data to XML, and querying XML data in SQL to produce either SQL data (XMLTABLE) or XML data (XMLQUERY) or a Boolean result (XMLEXISTS). We have assumed that the two languages – SQL and XQuery/XPath – have the same context, or at least that there is an obvious mapping from the SQL context to the XQuery/XPath context and vice versa. In fact, these mappings are neither obvious nor trivial, and a great deal of the early work of the SQLX group involved defining these mappings. In this section we look a bit more closely at the way character sets, names, data types, and values are mapped.

15.6.1 Character Sets

SQL data can be stored and managed in a database using one or more named character sets. For example, you might choose to store data in US7ASCII plus ISO-8859-1. XML data, on the other hand, is Unicode – the W3C XML specification[24] says that "All XML processors MUST accept the UTF-8 and UTF-16 encodings of Unicode 3.1." To address this possible inconsistency between character sets (the most basic building blocks of language and data exchange), the SQL/XML standard insists that any SQL/XML implementation provides a mapping from strings of each character set supported in its database to strings in Unicode, and vice versa.

---

24 See *Extensible Markup Language (XML) 1.0, third edition*, Section 2.2 (Cambridge, MA: World Wide Web Consortium, 2004). Available at: http://w3.org/TR/2004/REC-xml-20040204/#charsets.

15.6.2 Names

When using SQL/XML, we need to be able to map SQL identifiers to XML Names. The simplest example is where we map a SQL column name to an XML element name, *e.g.*, in XMLATTRIBUTES and XMLFOREST. Many people who use SQL use only uppercase alphabetic characters and numbers in their identifiers but, as we saw in some of the XMLTABLE examples, a SQL identifier can contain almost any character if you enclose the identifier in double-quotes. We were careful to double-quote the column names in some of our examples in this chapter, so they would be read by the SQL engine as lowercase identifiers and not converted to uppercase. We also saw that a SQL identifier can look like an XPath expression — "`producer[1]/familyName`" — as long as you double-quote it.

How do you map an arbitrary SQL identifier to an XML name, which can only contain letters, digits, hyphens, underscores, colons, or full stops?[25] First you map the SQL identifier characters to Unicode. Then, for each character, apply the following rules:

- If it is a valid XML Name character, leave it unchanged.[26]
- If it is not a valid XML Name character, convert it to a hexadecimal number (derived from its Unicode encoding), consisting of either four or six uppercase hexadecimal digits. Add a prefix of "_x" (underscore-x) and a suffix of "_" (underscore) to this number.
- Map a leading colon in the SQL identifier to "_x003A_."

---

25 The W3C XML 1.0 Recommendation defines a Name thusly: "A **Name** is a token beginning with a letter or one of a few punctuation characters, and continuing with letters, digits, hyphens, underscores, colons, or full stops, together known as name characters. Names beginning with the string "`xml`", or with any string which would match `(('X'|'x') ('M'|'m') ('L'|'l'))`, are reserved for standardization in this or future versions of this specification."

26 There is an exception to this rule. "_" (underscore) is a valid character in a SQL identifier and in an XML Name. But what if the SQL identifier contains a sequence of characters that looks just like an escape sequence, *e.g.*, "_x003A_"? Applying the mappings rules, this would be mapped to "_x003A_" in the XML Name. Then if you wanted to reverse the mapping (map the XML Name back into a SQL identifier), "_x003A_" would be mapped to a ":" (colon). To address this problem, there is an extra rule that says that an underscore character that is immediately followed by an "x" is escaped (mapped to "_x005F_"), so that the SQL identifier mapping to XML Name is fully reversible.

This set of rules comprises the *partially escaped mapping*.[27] SQL/XML also defines a fully escaped mapping — in addition to the rules in the partially escaped mapping, apply these rules:

- Map all colons in the SQL identifier to "_x003A_" (not just a leading colon).
- If the SQL identifier begins with "XML," in any combination of cases, then prefix the XML Name with "_xFFFF_."

So, for example, the SQL identifier "`title`" maps to the XML Name "`title`," while the SQL identifier "`Running Time`" maps to the XML Name "`Running_x0020_Time`."

SQL/XML also defines the rules to map from an XML Name to a SQL identifier — essentially, apply the rules above in reverse. When you map a SQL identifier to an XML Name and back, you are guaranteed to get the same SQL identifier (*i.e.*, the operation is fully reversible). When you start with an XML Name and map to a SQL identifier, the operation is *not* fully reversible (in the case where the XML Name contains a sequence of characters that looks like an escape sequence, *e.g.*, "_x003A_").

15.6.3 Types and Values

For any meaningful exchange of data between two languages (in this case, SQL and XQuery/XPath), there must be a bidirectional mapping between the typed values of those languages. If this were not the case, then a string, say, passed from SQL to XQuery would not have a clearly defined value in XQuery. SQL/XML defines a mapping from each of SQL's scalar data types to an XML Schema data type, possibly with facets and annotations. This type mapping determines the mapping of SQL values to typed XML values. In the other direction, SQL/XML defines a mapping from XQuery atomic types to SQL types, and hence a mapping from XML typed atomic values to SQL values.

Mapping SQL Data Types to XML Schema Data Types

SQL/XML defines a mapping from each of SQL's scalar data types to its closest analog in the XML Schema data types. In general, the XML Schema data type will be less restrictive than the SQL data type, so

27 At the time of writing, there is a proposal to eliminate the partially escaped mapping from SQL/XML:2006 and to keep only the fully escaped mapping.

XML Schema *facets* are used to further restrict the type. Where there are distinctions between SQL data types that have no corresponding distinctions in XML Schema, SQL/XML defines XML Schema annotations in the sqlxml namespace. The following mappings are defined, with an optional annotation to indicate the exact SQL type.

- The SQL character string types are mapped to `xs:string`, with either the facet `xs:length` (for SQL type fixed-length `CHARACTER` in which the character set mapping from SQL character set to Unicode is homomorphic), or the facet `xs:maxLength` (for `CHARACTER VARYING` and `CHARACTER LARGE OBJECT`, as well as `CHARACTER` where the character set mapping is not homomorphic). There are optional annotations to show the character set and default collation.
- The SQL binary string type (BLOB) is mapped to `xs:hexBinary` or `xs:base64Binary`, with the facet `xs:maxLength` to indicate the maximum length in octets.
- The SQL exact numeric types `NUMERIC` and `DECIMAL` are mapped to `xs:decimal`, with the facets `xs:totalDigits` and `xs:fractionDigits`. `INTEGER`, `SMALLINT`, and `BIGINT` are mapped to *either* `xs:integer`, with the facets `xs:maxInclusive` and `xs:minInclusive`, *or* to a subtype of `xs:integer`, possibly with the facets `xs:maxInclusive` and `xs:minInclusive`. There are optional annotations to show the precision (`NUMERIC`), user-specified precision (`DECIMAL`), and scale (`NUMERIC` and `DECIMAL`).
- The SQL approximate numeric types `REAL`, `DOUBLE PRECISION`, and `FLOAT` are mapped to *either* `xs:float` (if the binary precision is less than or equal to 24 binary digits and the range of the binary exponent lies between –149 and 104), *or* `xs:double`. There are optional annotations to show the binary precision, the minimum and maximum values of the range of binary exponents, and the user-specified binary precision (`FLOAT`).
- The SQL type `BOOLEAN` is mapped to `xs:boolean`.
- The SQL type `DATE` is mapped to `xs:date`, with the `xs:pattern` facet.
- The SQL `TIME` types are mapped to `xs:dateTime` and `xs:time`, with the `xs:pattern` facet.

- The SQL interval types are mapped to `xdt:yearMonthDuration` and `xdt:day-TimeDuration`, with the `xs:pattern` facet.

Mapping XML Schema Atomic Values to SQL Values

The rules for mapping XML Schema values with atomic data types to SQL values are approximately the reverse of the rules in the previous section:

- A value with XML Schema type `xs:string`[28] maps to a Unicode string.
- A value with XML Schema types `xs:hexBinary` and `xs:base64Binary` map to a binary string.
- A value with XML Schema type `xs:decimal` maps to an exact numeric value.
- A value with XML Schema type `xs:float` or `xs:double` maps to an approximate numeric value.
- A value with XML Schema type `xs:time` maps to a value of SQL type `TIME`.
- A value with XML Schema type `xs:dateTime` maps to a value of SQL type `TIMESTAMP`.
- A value with XML Schema type `xs:date` maps to a value of SQL type `DATE`.
- A value with XML Schema type `xs:boolean` maps to a value of SQL type `BOOLEAN`.

The Casting Functions — XMLSERIALIZE, XMLPARSE, XMLCAST

SQL/XML:2003 includes two functions to cast an XML value to a SQL character string and vice versa. XMLSERIALIZE takes an XML value and serializes it to some SQL character string type, while XML-PARSE takes some SQL character string type and converts it to an XML value.

Example 15-29 shows how to convert movies from the `MOVIES_XML` table, of type XML, to CLOB (Character Large OBject) type.[29] The first keyword inside the parentheses may be "`DOCUMENT`" (an XML document) or "`CONTENT`" (and XML forest, or fragment).

28 "xs" is the namespace prefix used for XML Schema data types. This namespace prefix is *predeclared* in XQuery, and is used elsewhere by convention.

Example 15-29 *XMLSERIALIZE*

```
SELECT
  XMLSERIALIZE( DOCUMENT movie AS CLOB ) AS "CLOB data"
  FROM movies_xml

Results:

CLOB data
----------------------------------------------------
<movie>
  <title>An American Werewolf in London</title>
  <yearReleased>1981</yearReleased>
  <director>
    <familyName>Landis</familyName>
    <givenName>John</givenName>
...
```

Example 15-30 shows the reverse – converting from a string value to an XML type, in this case to insert into a column of type XML.

Example 15-30 *XMLPARSE*

```
INSERT INTO movies_xml (ID, movie)
  VALUES (
    77,
    XMLPARSE( DOCUMENT '<movie>...</movie>' )
  )
```

SQL/XML:2006 introduces a more general-purpose function for casting between XML values and any SQL type (actually, any SQL *predefined* type). XMLCAST takes two arguments, an operand and a target type. Either the operand's type or the target type must be XML, so XMLCAST will convert both to and from XML. *Both* the operand *and* the target type may be XML, so XMLCAST can also be used to cast from one flavor of the XML type to another. You have

29 A cautionary note: when storing XML data in a CLOB, you need to be aware that CLOB data is stored in the character set of the database (as opposed to a Binary LOB, which stores data in raw form). Most databases will attempt to do character set conversion on data inserted into a CLOB. Depending on your database and the way it is installed and configured, Unicode text may fail to insert correctly.

already seen an example of XMLCAST – Example 15-12 casts the result of a call to XMLQUERY to a decimal, so it can be fed into the SQL function `AVG`.

Mapping SQL Tables, Schemas, Catalogs to XML

In addition to defining mappings for data types and atomic values, SQL/XML defines a structure mapping, from a SQL table or schema or catalog to an XML document. The idea is that you should be able to take any SQL table and represent it as XML in a standard way. That involves not just mapping the values of the individual cells to XML atomic values, but also mapping the structure of that table to an XML Schema.

Let's take as an example the `MOVIES` table in Figure 15-1. The SQL/XML table mapping would produce a root element whose name is the name of the table ("`MOVIES`"), with a child element called "`row`" representing each row in the table. The row element in turn has a child element representing each column in the table, as in Figure 15-4.

Figure 15-4 *XML Representation Of MOVIES Table.*

```
<MOVIES>
  <row>
    <ID>42</ID>
    <title>An American Werewolf in London</title>
    <yearReleased>1981</yearReleased>
    <director>78</director>
    <runningTime>98</runningTime>
  </row>
  <row>
    <ID>43</ID>
    <title>Animal House</title>
    <yearReleased>1978</yearReleased>
    <director>78</director>
    <runningTime>109</runningTime>
  </row>
</MOVIES>
```

Somewhat mysteriously, though SQL/XML spells out exactly how to produce an XML document and an XML Schema from any SQL table, it stops short of defining a table function to actually implement this mapping, *i.e.*, a SQL/XML function to produce an XML document from a SQL table. At the time of writing, such a function is under discussion in both the XQuery and the SQL/XML Working Groups. (One vendor, Oracle, already has a proprietary extension, `ora:view`, to produce an XML document from a SQL table.)

Once you know how to map a SQL table to an XML document, you can easily map a schema or collection, by wrapping a sequence of table elements with a schema or collection element.

15.7 Chapter Summary

We have covered a lot of ground in this chapter, but we have only scratched the surface of SQL/XML. First, we described the SQL/XML publishing functions, which let you query SQL data using the SQL query language and publish the results as XML. Then we discussed the XML type, which allows you to store XML as SQL data in a native SQL data type. The SQL/XML:2006 XQuery functions (XMLQUERY, XMLTABLE, and XMLEXISTS) were then described in some detail, especially XMLTABLE. XMLQUERY lets you query any XML, including XML stored in SQL's XML data type, using the XQuery language, and produces results in XML. XMLTABLE, on the other hand, queries XML and produces results as a SQL table. This opens up your XML data to the full power of SQL – we illustrated this with some examples of the OLAP rollup and cube functions applied to our XML sample data. We talked briefly about managing XML in a SQL database, then described mappings between SQL and XML character sets, names, types, and values. This description included the XML-to-string function XMLSERIALIZE and the string-to-XML function XMLPARSE, and the more general-purpose XML-to-SQL/SQL-to-XML/XML-to-XML casting function, XMLCast.

SQL/XML is still a relatively new part of the SQL standard, but we believe it provides a powerful basis for storing, managing, and querying XML data, leveraging both the power and robustness of SQL and the XML-centric capabilities of XPath and XQuery. If this chapter has whetted your appetite – and we hope it has – we suggest the following follow-up reading:

- ISO/IEC FCD 9075-14, *Information Technology – Database Languages – SQL – Part 14: XML-Related Specifications, (SQL/XML)*. Available from your country's standards body; in the United States, that body is ANSI (http://www.ansi.org).

- Andrew Eisenberg and Jim Melton, SQL/XML and the SQLX Informal Group of Companies, *ACM SIGMOD Record*, Vol. 30 No. 3, September 2001. Available at: http://www.acm.org/sigmod/record/issues/0109/standards.pdf.
- Andrew Eisenberg and Jim Melton, SQL/XML Is Making Good Progress, *ACM SIGMOD Record*, Vol. 31, No. 2, June 2002. Available at: http://www.acm.org/sigmod/record/issues/0206/standard.pdf .
- Andrew Eisenberg and Jim Melton, Advancements in SQL/XML, *ACM SIGMOD Record*, Vol. 33, No. 3, September 2004. Available at: http://www.sigmod.org/sigmod/record/issues/0409/11.JimMelton.pdf.
- Stephen Buxton, *Querying XML – XQuery, SQL/XML, and SQL in Context*, XML 2004 Conference. Available at: http://www.idealliance.org/proceedings/xml04/abstracts/paper218.html.

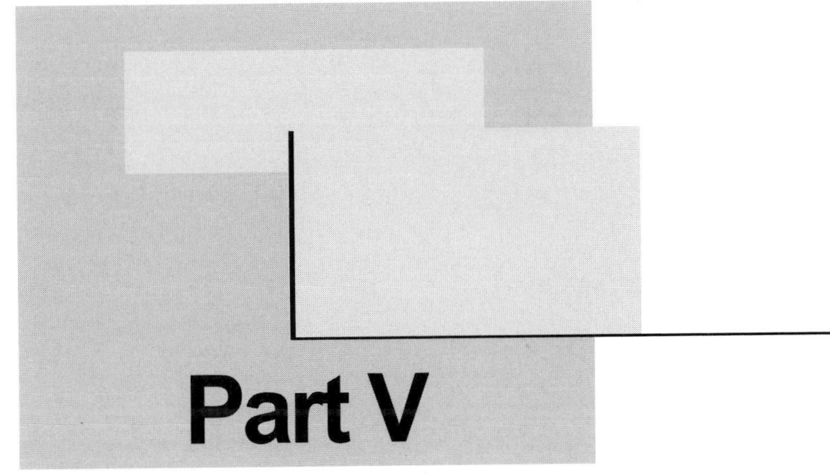

Part V

Querying and The World Wide Web

Chapter 16

XML-Derived Markup Languages

16.1 Introduction

Throughout this book so far, we've discussed XML itself, the more common ways in which XML vocabularies are defined, and – predominately – how you can query XML documents using a variety of approaches, including XPath, XQuery, and SQL/XML.

In this chapter, we take a look at a number of specialized XML languages[1] and express a few thoughts about the ways in which documents built using those vocabularies might be queried. In particular, we'll see that at least some of these vocabularies might be more appropriately queried using languages other than those we've featured in this book.

We also look at the subject of how to discover things – such as web services, businesses from which you can purchase or to which you can sell, and the like – on the web, using XML vocabularies, exploring how you can query that information to get what you need.

1 As you read in Chapter 1, "XML," we use the term *markup language* to mean both the definition (normally done using an XML Schema) of the elements and attributes that are used to mark up information *and* the description of what each of those components mean. By contrast, we use the term *markup vocabulary* to mean only the element and attribute definitions, exclusive of explicit semantic definition of their meanings.

16.2 Markup Languages

XML, being the *extensible* markup language, serves as the definitional paradigm for a large set of specialized markup languages (many of which are no more than vocabularies). Many different industries, scientific disciplines, individual organizations, and even individuals have designed and published the specifications for XML vocabularies suitable for specific needs. In Chapter 1, "XML," we speculated that we could create an XML-based markup language called MDL (Movie Definition Language) for managing our movie collections. In fact, the XML Schema published in Appendix A describes the XML document containing our movie data. That could quite reasonably be called the definition of MDL's vocabulary. Almost any DTD or XML Schema falls into the same category, whether or not the authors of the DTD or Schema make that claim.

There are undoubtedly hundreds – probably thousands – of specialized XML languages that have been defined for one purpose or another. In this section, we take a look at only a few of the markup languages (MathML, SMIL, SVG) that have achieved some level of standardization *and* acceptance. Our choices are not actually random, but they do represent a variety of communities. In fact, this section looks at some relatively esoteric markup languages specifically because many of the more commonly used languages have been discussed elsewhere in this book.

We illustrate in this chapter that general-purpose query languages (*e.g.*, XQuery) readily query documents of any XML vocabulary, but that the query authors must apply the semantics of the markup language. Special-purpose query languages could be defined for each markup language in which the semantics of those languages are recognized in the query languages themselves; however, this is rarely done.

One such markup language (not further discussed in this chapter) is XBRL, the Extended Business Reporting Language.[2] The United States Securities and Exchange Commission announced[3] in late 2004 a new program encouraging businesses to voluntarily submit supplemental financial information marked up using XBRL for posting

---

2 *Extensible Business Reporting Language (XBRL) 2.1, XBRL Recommendation* (New York: XBRL International, 2005). Available at: http://www.xbrl.org/Specification/XBRL-RECOMMENDATION-2003-12-31+Corrected-Errata-2005-04-25.htm.

3 *XBRL Voluntary Reporting Program on the EDGAR System*, http://www.sec.gov/rules/final/33-8529.htm.

on EDGAR, the Commission's Electronic Data Gathering, Analysis, and Retrieval System (an online financial information database accessible to the public). We believe that the U.S. Government will eventually require reporting of such information in an XML-based vocabulary, probably XBRL or some derivative vocabulary. Naturally, there will be significant interest in querying financial data reported using XBRL!

16.2.1 MathML

MathML[4] is, according to the specification's abstract, "an XML application for describing mathematical notation and capturing both its structure and content" and its goal is "to enable mathematics to be served, received, and processed on the World Wide Web, just as HTML has enabled this functionality for text." It is quite beyond the scope of this book to give a detailed description of MathML, so we've limited ourselves to a bit of introduction and a couple of examples of MathML use.

Until MathML was defined, the principal system used for formatting mathematical notations was Donald Knuth's TeX.[5] Put charitably, although TeX probably produces the best-looking computer-generated mathematical notations in print, the language is rather difficult for most people to use. MathML has not taken the lead from TeX, but it certainly represents a major step forward both in the use of computers to typeset mathematical notations and in the generation and accessibility of marked-up material.

MathML is intended to be used both for mathematical notation and mathematical content in web (or hardcopy) documents. The specification defines about 180 different elements, some 30 of which are used to describe "abstract notational structures" and the rest to "unambiguously [specify] the intended meaning of an expression."

There are three broad categories of MathML elements. One, presentation markup, is used to describe the two-dimensional layout and presentation of mathematical expressions. A second, content markup, provides access to the semantics of those expressions; there is clearly a relationship between mathematical notation and the underlying semantics, but there are also obvious differences. For

4 *Mathematical Markup Language (MathML) Version 2.0, second edition, W3C Recommendation* (Cambridge, MA: World Wide Web Consortium, 2003). Available at: http://www/w3.org/TR/MathML2/.

5 Donald Knuth, *The TeXbook* (New York: Addison-Wesley Professional, 1984).

example, stating that a digit is to be set as a superscript immediately following a letter is significantly different from specifying that the value represented by that letter is to be raised to the power indicated by the digit. The third category of MathML elements provides the MathML interface — these are used primarily when MathML expressions are embedded into other markup languages, such as HTML, and we do not discuss them further.

Example 16-1 and Example 16-2 illustrate two different ways of marking up the equation seen in Equation 16-1.

Equation 16-1 *Example Equation*

$$(a + b)^2$$

Example 16-1 *Equation Marked Up Using MathML Presentation Markup*

```
<mrow>
  <msup>
    <mfenced>
      <mrow>
        <mi>a</mi>
        <mo>+</mo>
        <mi>b</mi>
      </mrow>
    </mfenced>
    <mn>2</mn>
  </msup>
</mrow>
```

The `<mrow>` element indicates that its content is intended to be a single horizontal "row" (in this context, a *row* is nothing more than a horizontally related group of objects), `<msup>` signals a superscripted expression, `<fenced>` surrounds the expression it contains with parentheses, and `<mi>`, `<mn>`, and `<mo>` encapsulate identifiers, numbers, and operators, respectively.

Example 16-2 *Equation Marked Up Using MathML Content Markup*

```
<mrow>
  <apply>
    <power/>
    <apply>
      <plus/>
      <ci>a</ci>
```

```
      <ci>b</ci>
    </apply>
    <cn>2</cn>
  </apply>
</mrow>
```

As before, the <mrow> element indicates that its content is intended to be a single horizontal "row," but that's where the similarities end. <apply> represents an operation to be applied to an expression, <power> and <plus> specify the operations to be applied, and <ci> and <cn> represent identifiers and numbers, respectively.

MathML processors are allowed to use either of these markup conventions (presentation or content), and might generate the same visual results for both. In general, however, the content markup approach makes it easier for other applications to consume the marked up expressions and act on them semantically. For example, a calculator application could consume the content markup of that equation, request values for the two variables a and b, and then perform the appropriate calculations.

It's also possible to combine the two forms of markup for a single mathematical expression, as indicated in Example 16-3. This sort of combination allows you to specify the form in which you'd like the expression to be presented, while providing the semantics of the expression as an annotation that doesn't affect the presentation.

Example 16-3 *Equation Marked Up with Both Presentation and Content Markup*

```
<mrow>
  <semantics>
    <mrow>
      <msup>
        <mfenced>
          <mrow>
            <mi>a</mi>
            <mo>+</mo>
            <mi>b</mi>
          </mrow>
        </mfenced>
        <mn>2</mn>
      </msup>
    </mrow>
```

```
      <annotation-xml encoding="MathML-Content">
        <apply>
          <power/>
          <apply>
            <plus/>
            <ci>a</ci>
            <ci>b</ci>
          </apply>
          <cn>2</cn>
        </apply>
      </annotation-xml>
    </semantics>
  </mrow>
```

Now, as you have seen from these examples, MathML is obviously "just another" form of XML. As such, it's certainly easy to imagine querying it using XPath or XQuery. For example, if we wanted to find whether there are any square (or cube or higher-order) expressions in Example 16-2 and, if so, what the operands of those expressions are, we might write the XPath expression found in Example 16-4.

Example 16-4 *An XPath Expression Applied to a MathML Expression*

```
//power/following-sibling::*

Result:
<apply>
  <plus/>
  <ci>a</ci>
  <ci>b</ci>
</apply>
<cn>2</cn>
```

The value returned by that expression contains any and all following siblings of any and all `power` elements in the XPath context. Of course, if there were no `power` elements, the expression would return the empty sequence. But, if there were multiple `power` elements, the expression would return the following siblings of all of them without any obvious way of determining which elements were associated with which `power` element (other than the fact that they'd be in document order, that is).

Note that the simple XPath expression in Example 16-4 didn't really have anything to do with the fact that the `power` element is used to represent mathematical squares, nor that the values returned indicate that the result is indeed the square (and not the cube) of another expression. Sure, XPath (and XQuery) can be used to query MathML expressions of this sort, but there is no mathematical *knowledge* implied by such queries.

It might be nice to design some sort of special-purpose MathML-inspired query language that would allow us to ask a question such as "`for each power(2), return MathML-query(contents)`" or (more generally) questions such as "what formulae in this document make use of both cube roots and integration?" Would such a language be useful? Probably not too often, but it might sometimes be helpful to mathematicians working with collections of documents marked up in MathML. Although the MathML specification refers to the importance of "automatic searching and indexing" of mathematical documents, it does not otherwise mention ways (or languages) by which such searching might be done. We doubt that there is sufficient demand to justify design and implementation of a special-purpose query language just for this purpose. If ever created, such a language might be represented simply as an application built using XQuery as its foundation, transforming the kinds of questions we've asked into XQuery (or XPath) expressions.

16.2.2 SMIL

SMIL[6] (Synchronized Multimedia Integration Language) is a markup language published by the W3C to integrate "a set of independent multimedia objects into a synchronized multimedia presentation." Such presentations might include animations, audio, video, text, and other forms of information. The language allows the specification of a presentation's temporal behavior (that is, what events happen when), the layout of a presentation (meaning what information appears where on a visual display), and hyperlinks to various media objects (such as a video file published by another author).

The syntax of SMIL is defined *normatively* by means of a series of DTDs. It is also defined (but not normatively) by means of a series of SMIL Schemas. There is more than one DTD (and more than one

6 *Synchronized Multimedia Integration Language (SMIL 2.0), second edition, W3C Recommendation* (Cambridge, MA: World Wide Web Consortium, 2005). Available at: http://www.w3.org/TR/SMIL/.

Schema) because the SMIL specification defines the language in a very modular way, allowing implementations to choose which of various modules to implement. Each module is defined by a single XML Schema or DTD. At least one SMIL *profile* (precise identification of a set of features specified in a standard) appears normatively as a DTD — and informatively as an XML Schema — in the SMIL Recommendation.

A SMIL "document" is a single `<smil>` element that contains either a `<head>` element, a `<body>` element, or both. The `<head>` element contains any layout specifications and may use either the SMIL-defined `<layout>` element or the facilities of CSS2,[7] it may also contain information about the presentation (such as the title, creation date, keywords, and so forth).

The `<layout>` element "determines how the elements in the document's body are positioned on an abstract rendering surface (either visual or acoustic)." If the element is omitted, then the layout is determined by the SMIL implementation. SMIL's `<layout>` element is used only to control the layout of the media object elements that are identified in the `<body>` element (the layout of all other `<layout>` elements must be specified using CSS2). For example, a `<layout>` element may contain a `<region>` element that defines a part of the "rendering surface" by name, giving that region an absolute position relative to the position of the `<smil>` element itself. The `<region>` element has a number of attributes, all optional. These attributes allow the specification of such characteristics as background color, scaling (or fit) of an object within the region, and the position of the region.

The `<body>` element is the heart of SMIL. It provides "information that is related to the temporal and linking behavior of the document" and can contain any of 11 kinds of child element. Among these are a `<par>` element whose children identify objects that are allowed to overlap in time (we suspect that "`par`" is intended to evoke "parallel"), and a `<seq>` element whose children identify objects that form a temporal sequence.

Those `<par>` and `<seq>` elements have precisely the same possible child elements as the `<body>` element. This implies, of course, that objects participating in an overlapping presentation can themselves be overlapping or sequential presentations of other objects.

---

7 *Cascading Style Sheets Level 2, CSS2 Specification, W3C Recommendation* (Cambridge, MA: World Wide Web Consortium, 1998). Available at: http://www.w3.org/TR/REC-CSS2/.

Other children of the `<body>` element (as well as the `<par>` and `<seq>` elements) include `<animation>`, `<audio>`, `<img>`, `<text>`, `<textstream>`, and `<video>`. Some of those elements (`<animation>`, `<audio>`, and `<video>`) specify objects, called *continuous media,* that have an inherent duration. Others (`<img>`, `<text>`, and `<textstream>`) specify objects without an intrinsic duration; these are called *discrete media*. The attributes of the media elements allow specification of such characteristics as: the length of time after the object's container is activated before the object itself is activated, the length of time during which the object is activated, the name of the region in which the object is to be activated, and captions associated with the object.

Every SMIL object appears in a four-dimensional space: horizontal, vertical, depth (the z-axis, representing depth, is supported to govern physically overlapping objects), and time. The elements representing those objects can be given attributes that determine whether or not the object appears at all, based on various tests: for example, if the SMIL implementation can determine that the environment has no sound facilities, then no `<audio>` elements should cause sound presentations to be emitted from the implementation. It might be reasonable for applications dealing with SMIL presentations to ask questions such as "Are there any images that are partially obscured by text while the theme song from *Shaft* is playing?" "What physically adjacent objects visible at the same time (wholly or partly) have complementary background colors?" "Does the video of President Kennedy terminate before or after the map of Vietnam appears on the screen?" or "Where on the display can I add my Easter bunny animation, starting seven minutes into the presentation and lasting for 30 seconds, without covering up the photograph of my youngest child?"

SMIL is a language designed explicitly for multimedia authors and is rapidly gaining acceptance within that community. Authoring tools for SMIL-based media are already emerging, but the need for broad, flexible search capabilities has not yet been recognized by most of the community using SMIL. But the reason that multimedia productions would be represented in SMIL is so that they can be processed by a variety of processors, all of which interpret the SMIL vocabulary, including manipulation (editing, for example) of the productions and searching (querying) productions.

We are not surprised that we've found no evidence of a special-purpose query language designed to support queries that answer questions such as these. Writing XPath or XQuery expressions to answer them is certainly possible, but would undoubtedly be tedious because of the level of detailed knowledge of a SMIL document's structure that would be required. On the other hand, defining XQuery and XPath function libraries that support queries on SMIL documents seems like a reasonable approach to providing the capabilities of a purpose-built SMIL query language. We would expect that, for something as complex as multimedia documents, end users would have to be provided with some sort of visual (GUI) tool that would generate the XQuery expressions and function invocations.

16.2.3 SVG

SVG[8] (Scalable Vector Graphics) is an XML markup language, used for representing graphics that can be displayed over the web, in print, *etc.*, with whatever resolution the destination medium can support (that's the "scalable" part of the name). The graphics that are created with SVG are inherently "two-dimensional vector and mixed vector/raster graphics" in nature. The vocabulary supports three types of objects: vector graphic shapes (that is, line drawings), images (also known as raster graphics), and text. The graphics can be interactive (responding to an event like a mouse click) and dynamic (changing the image as time passes), the latter implying animation.

The value in having an XML vocabulary to represent such graphics lies in the ability to abstract the specification of the graphics from the sequences of bits used to draw them onto some medium, whether paper or video monitor. Earlier ways of encoding this sort of graphic tended to depend on much less flexible notations, often binary notations that were difficult to interpret in the absence of an explicitly provided processor for each specific kind of graphic. SVG, on the other hand, can be "read" by humans who can get at least a sense of the graphic.

SVG shares a number of characteristics with, and even incorporates a few features from, SMIL (see Section 16.2.2). For example, SVG takes SMIL's animation feature and extends it. Furthermore, SVG was designed to be used to create both dynamic and static objects for SMIL.

An SVG image can be used "stand-alone" as a web page by itself, it can be linked (or referenced) from an XHTML or other XML

---

8 *Scalable Vector Graphics (SVG) 1.1 Specification, W3C Recommendation* (Cambridge, MA: World Wide Web Consortium, 2003). Available at: http://www/w3.org/TR/SVG11/.

document, and it can be embedded in another SVG image. Although the SVG specification defines a large number of elements and attributes, the language has a simplicity to it that makes it relatively easy to grasp. For example, consider the first shape specified in Example 16-5.

Example 16-5 *Simple SVG Images*

```
<svg width="5cm" height="4cm" version="1.1"
     xmlns="http://www.w3.org/2000/svg">
  <desc>Four separate rectangles</desc>
  <rect x="0.5cm" y="0.5cm" width="2cm" height="1cm"/>
  <rect x="0.5cm" y="2cm" width="1cm" height="1.5cm"/>
  <rect x="3cm" y="0.5cm" width="1.5cm" height="2cm"/>
  <rect x="3.5cm" y="3cm" width="1cm" height="0.5cm"/>
  <!-- Show outline of canvas using 'rect' element -->
  <rect x=".01cm" y=".01cm" width="4.98cm" height="3.98cm"
        fill="none" stroke="blue" stroke-width=".02cm" />
</svg>

<svg width="10cm" height="3cm" viewBox="0 0 100 30"
     xmlns="http://www.w3.org/2000/svg" version="1.1">
  <rect x=".1" y=".1" width="99.8" height="29.8"
        fill="none" stroke="blue" stroke-width=".2" />
  <g transform="translate(45, 10)" >
    <svg width="10" height="10"
         viewBox="0 0 20 20">
      <rect x="1" y="1" width="8" height="8"/>
      <rect x="11" y="1" width="8" height="8"/>
      <rect x="1" y="11" width="8" height="8"/>
      <rect x="11" y="11" width="8" height="8"/>
    </svg>
  </g>
</svg>

<svg width="10cm" height="3cm" viewBox="0 0 100 30" version="1.1">
  <rect x=".1" y=".1" width="99.8" height="29.8"
        fill="none" stroke="red" stroke-width=".2" />
  <g transform="translate(20,2.5) rotate(-10)">
    <rect x="0" y="0" fill="blue" width="60" height="10"/>
  </g>
</svg>
```

The first shape includes four different rectangles, of different sizes, with another rectangle drawn as a narrow blue line at the borders of the image area.

We observed above that one SVG graphic can be embedded within another one. The second shape in Example 16-5 illustrates that possibility (but observe that the nested graphic is enclosed in a `<g>` element). Figure 16-1 shows the results of evaluating the first two SVG drawings in Example 16-5.

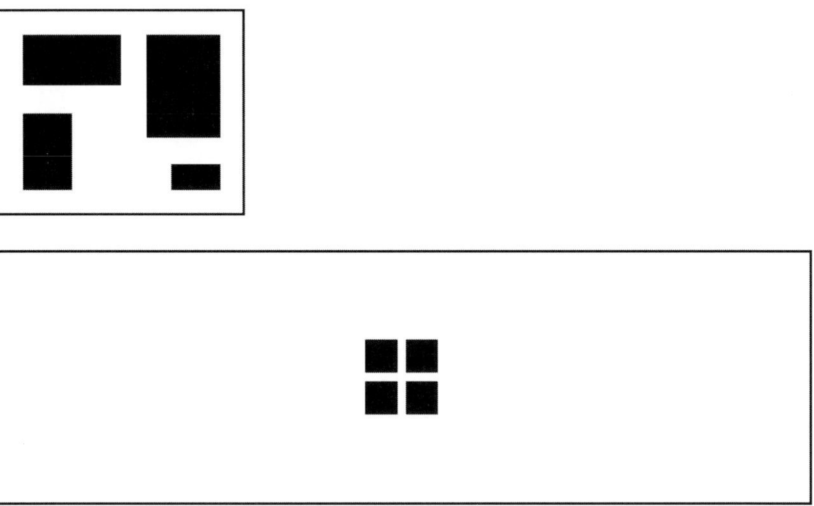

Figure 16-1 *The Visual Results: Two SVG Images.*

What sorts of questions might one want to ask about SVG graphics? In some ways, they are likely to be similar to those asked about SMIL documents. Due to the greater imaging power of SVG, the questions might ask about characteristics not directly available in SMIL. For example, we might want to know the width of every blue rectangle resting at an angle with the right end higher than the left, whose longer dimension is the dimension closest to horizontal. Or we might need to learn whether there are any raster images that would ever partly or wholly obscure a vector image such that both images are located within an animation that slides images around in the viewing area.

Overall, the questions are sufficiently similar to those we might ask in a SMIL context, so we believe that the situation is likely to be the same: No special-purpose query language exists to support queries that answer questions such as these; and writing XPath or XQuery expressions to answer them is possible, but probably tedious.

A possible XPath expression to answer the question about the blue rectangle (whose SVG expression is the third example in Example 16-5 and whose visual representation is in Figure 16-2) can be found in Example 16-6. (Because of production limitations, we regret that the viewport outline and rectangle cannot be in glorious color.)

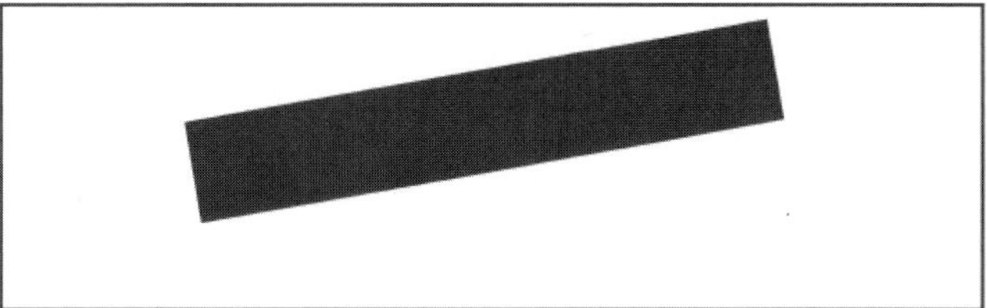

Figure 16-2 *The Visual Result: A Slanted Blue Rectangle.*

Example 16-6 *Finding the Width of the Blue Rectangle*

```
//rect[@width>@height][@fill="blue"]
      [parent::g[contains (@transform, "rotate(-")]]/@width
```

```
Result:
60
```

Not exactly obvious, perhaps, but it is usable — at least as long as the questions don't get too complex. Would a specialized query language for SVG be useful? Perhaps, but (as for SMIL) we are unaware of any efforts to produce one.

Through examples like the ones we've provided in Section 16.2, we have concluded that there is great value in defining specialized markup languages for specific domains, but that the cost of defining special-purpose query languages for most of those markup languages would exceed the value they'd provide. XQuery and XPath, on the other hand, can be used to perform meaningful queries on all of them — even though the expressions required to express such queries are likely to be cumbersome in many cases.

16.3 Discovery on the World Wide Web

The World Wide Web is — well, big. Estimates of its size range to billions of pages. In all those pages, we wouldn't be surprised if most of human knowledge were captured —somewhere. Finding the knowledge in which we're interested at any given moment is a challenge that is addressed by search engines such as Google, AltaVista, Yahoo, and AskJeeves, as well as metasearch engines like Dogpile and Mamma. (In Chapter 18, "Finding Stuff," you'll read more about querying and search engine technology.)

Search engines, which seem to improve almost daily, work pretty well for use by humans sitting in front of a computer, formulating queries that the search engines evaluate. (We don't address such queries in this book, largely because they are directed toward HTML and text rather than XML, but also because the syntaxes they use are generally engine-specific.)

But when application software is the initiator of a search on the web, ordinary search engine technology is rarely appropriate. This is due at least in part because applications are rather unlikely to be curious about the latest football scores, catching up on celebrity gossip, researching SVG for inclusion in a book, or tracking down a support group for a rare disease. Instead, applications are more likely to be looking for purveyors of services — often called *web services* — required by the application doing the search. (Of course, the *purpose* of some of those web services may well be the offering of sports scores, titillation, and self-help!)

In fact, many web publishers, especially in the news business, are already seeing a shift in the use of their sites from eyeballs to applications. Such publishers are beginning to redesign their sites to cater directly to applications' use of the data they provide — or, in some cases, to fend off such applications' direct consumption of their data! Offering content as a web service (something already being done by Google and others) is the logical extension of this trend, and a potentially important business model for such publishers.

The organization or individual offering a web service obviously has to somehow publish the information about that service. For the service to be most accessible, the published information should be available directly to applications and not require the intervention of a person. This implies that the information for all web services should be published in a standardized format — and that quickly suggests a standardized XML language.

In fact, the term *web service* is defined by a W3C architecture document[9] this way:

9 *Web Services Architecture, W3C Note* (Cambridge, MA: World Wide Web Consortium, 2004). Available at: http://www.w3.org/TR/ws-arch/.

> A Web service is a software system designed to support interoperable machine-to-machine interaction over a network. It has an interface described in a machine-processable format (specifically WSDL). Other systems interact with the Web service in a manner prescribed by its description using SOAP messages, typically conveyed using HTTP with an XML serialization in conjunction with other Web-related standards.

Of course, merely having a standardized vocabulary used for publishing information about your web service doesn't solve the entire problem – you've also got to ensure that applications that might be interested in your web service know how to find that information you've published. We should note that publication of a web service doesn't necessarily mean that it can be found only through searches; indeed, businesses may simply exchange their web service publications and use the information for prearranged business-to-business activities. This section focuses primarily on the standardized XML vocabulary for web services (discussed at greater length in Chapter 18, "Finding Stuff"), but we also glance briefly at the way in which that information about your service can be located.

There are several approaches to publishing standardized information about web services either in use today or being designed for use in the near future. Two of the most important are the W3C's WSDL (Web Services Description Language) and UDDI[10] (Universal Description Discovery & Integration) from Oasis. WSDL is currently specified in four parts: a Primer,[11] a Core language specification,[12] some predefined extensions,[13] and specifications for binding WSDL[14]

---

10 *UDDI Version 3.0.2, UDDI Spec Technical Committee Draft* (OASIS Open, 2004). Available at: http://uddi.org/pubs/uddi_v3.htm.

11 *Web Services Description Language (WSDL) Version 2.0 Part 0: Primer, W3C Working Draft* (Cambridge, MA: World Wide Web Consortium, 2004). Available at: http://www.w3.org/TR/wsdl20-primer.

12 *Web Services Description Language (WSDL) Version 2.0 Part 1: Core Language, W3C Working Draft* (Cambridge, MA: World Wide Web Consortium, 2004). Available at: http://www.w3.org/TR/wsdl20.

13 *Web Services Description Language (WSDL) Version 2.0 Part 2: Predefined Extensions, W3C Working Draft* (Cambridge, MA: World Wide Web Consortium, 2004). Available at: http://www.w3.org/TR/wsdl20-extensions.

14 *Web Services Description Language (WSDL) Version 2.0 Part 3: Bindings, W3C Working Draft* (Cambridge, MA: World Wide Web Consortium, 2004). Available at: http://www.w3.org/TR/wsdl20-binding.

to SOAP[15] (SOAP, the Simple Object Access Protocol, is a W3C specification[16] for "XML-based information which can be used for exchanging structured and typed information between peers in a decentralized, distributed environment") and HTTP.[17] In addition, the WSDL suite of documents include specifications of XML Schemas for WSDL itself, for the binding with SOAP, and for the HTTP binding.

As you may have inferred from the names of the various WSDL documents, not all of them deal with an XML vocabulary. Because WSDL is all about defining web services, we have to understand what it takes to define such a service. It's beyond the scope of this book to cover all of the details, so we'll just mention the highlights: message formats, data types, transport protocols, transport serialization formats, and perhaps some information about the message exchange pattern that is expected when the service is used.

Perhaps more importantly, web services involve a specification of the service or services that are offered, the resources involved in providing those services, the policies governing the use of the resources, and the messages through which a service communicates with its clients. All of these aspects are represented in XML using a specialized vocabulary.

WSDL provides vocabularies to specify the kinds of messages that a web service can send and receive, to describe the functionality that the service provides, to describe how to access the service, and to indicate where the service can be found on the web. For example, WSDL defines an XML element called `<types>` in which a web service definer specifies the various kinds of messages that the service consumes or emits. It also provides an `<interface>` element that is used to describe the services provided; each specific service is described by an `<operation>` child element.

WSDL is fairly complex, defining a large number of elements and attributes, and specifying the relationships between them. The complexity is, of course, due to the fact that it must be able to describe a very wide variety of services with all of the different aspects they present. Of course, the descriptions are pretty regular, and are in any

---

15 *SOAP Version 1.2 Part 1: Messaging Framework, W3C Recommendation* (Cambridge, MA: World Wide Web Consortium, 2003). Available at: http://www.w3.org/TR/soap12-part1/.

16 *SOAP Version 1.2 Primer, W3C Recommendation* (Cambridge, MA: World Wide Web Consortium, 2003). Available at: http://www.w3.org/TR/soap12-part0/.

17 *RFC 2616, Hypertext Transfer Protocol – HTTP/1.1* (The Internet Society, 1999). Available at: http://www.ietf.org/rfc/rfc2616.txt.

case described by XML Schemas. Nonetheless, finding information about a web service described using WSDL requires some thought. As we've seen in earlier sections of this chapter, XPath and, by extension, XQuery can be used for that purpose, but neither language has any particular knowledge of what a WSDL document *means*. Surely, you might ask, it is desirable for applications to be able to use searching facilities that understand the meaning of WSDL descriptions. As we discuss below, that isn't necessarily true.

UDDI, as its name implies, focuses on assisting applications in locating web services having particular characteristics – such as offering particular services, perhaps at a specific price or within a required time frame. UDDI provides "the definition of a set of services supporting the description and discovery of (1) businesses, organizations, and other Web services providers, (2) the Web services they make available, and (3) the technical interfaces which may be used to access those services."

Sounds a lot like WSDL, doesn't it? The difference between WSDL and UDDI, however, is that WSDL focuses on describing the services themselves, while UDDI focuses on publication of the services for automatic discovery. UDDI defines its own specialized vocabulary, oriented toward the creation, automatic maintenance, and automatic use of *registries* of services (that is, collections of descriptions of services, which might be represented in WSDL, as well as in other languages). UDDI registries capture business entities (the providers of web services), business services, templates for describing the information required to use a service, the relationship between one business entity and another (relative to the service), and requests by business entities to be kept informed of changes to the service.

UDDI does not provide a specific query language that consumers of web services use to locate services. It does, however, provide an API, the UDDI Inquiry API, that "provides the ability to issue precise searches based on the different classification schemes." The Inquiry API accepts XML fragments whose elements and attributes describe the business, service, or access detail that is required. It is through those elements and attributes that the details of a query are specified.

XQuery, as you read in Chapter 12, has both a "human-readable" syntax and an XML syntax. The language used to query UDDI registries has only an XML syntax. We are not aware of any interest in providing a syntax more comfortable to human users. In our opinion, such a syntax would be of little use, as machine generation of an XML fragment to describe search criteria is at least as easy as generation of an expression in the kind of less regular language that humans use more readily.

But what about searching the WSDL-expressed information that a UDDI registry might contain? Since UDDI is not limited to a registry of web services that are described in WSDL, its inquiry APIs have been designed without specific WSDL syntax in mind. Instead, UDDI's APIs express search conditions in an abstract form that the UDDI registries' engines can adapt to the specific syntax and vocabularies of the web service description languages that they support.

(On a less positive note, there are in fact two "flavors" of WSDL and two competing UDDI registries – one from Microsoft and one from IBM.)

16.4 Customized Query Languages

As we've seen throughout this chapter, the specialized markup languages are not generally accompanied by an associated, specialized query language. XPath and XQuery can always be used to query documents expressed in such vocabularies, but those two languages have the weakness that they are unaware of the underlying meaning of the documents being searched.

As you will read in Chapter 18, "Finding Stuff," the effort to apply meaning to the information available on the web involves specification of a model known as RDF (Resource Description Framework) that can be used to represent the semantics of data in ways that can be used automatically. RDF is not inherently represented in XML, but XML is certainly going to be one of the more popular ways of representing RDF. But, represented in XML or not, RDF has certain specific characteristics that both simplify and complicate the process of uncovering the information that it captures. A query language named SPARQL has been designed by the W3C specifically to query information represented as RDF.

So, there we have it. At least one important specialized (not necessarily XML) vocabulary has been given a specialized query language to accompany it. But, one should ask, why would XQuery (or XPath) not be adequate for querying RDF information? Surely, if MathML, SMIL, or SVG, or even WSDL do not deserve a special-purpose query language, then RDF cannot justify it either. We confess to having asked exactly these questions when we first learned of SPARQL.

But we subsequently realized that XPath and XQuery are purpose-built to query data represented in the XPath 2.0 and XQuery

2.0 Data Model (described in Chapter 10, "Introduction to XQuery 1.0," and other chapters of this book) and can certainly be used to query data represented in an Infoset (see Chapter 6, "The XML Information Set (Infoset) and Beyond"), while RDF uses quite a different data model. It is, of course, *possible* to use XPath and XQuery to find information in RDF (when it's represented in XML, at least), but SPARQL is designed explicitly for querying data represented in the RDF data model.

That doesn't mean that the two data models, nor the two languages, are intended to be competitors. They have quite different sets of goals and requirements, and they serve quite different needs. At the time of writing, neither SPARQL nor XQuery 1.0 (nor XPath 2.0) had reached the final Recommendation stage of processing within the W3C. That leaves opportunity for interested parties to attempt to rationalize the situation and perhaps bring both the models and the languages into harmony with one another.

Much the same sort of debate could be had regarding the suitability of XQuery (and XPath) for querying documents defined using specialized XML vocabularies, such as RSS[18] documents and specifications of ontologies.[19] In our opinion, XQuery is usable for such purposes, but – as for other specialized vocabularies discussed in this chapter – not ideal for them. Within the W3C, we expect that SPARQL will be chosen as the most appropriate language for querying ontologies. We do not know of any effort to define a query language specifically oriented toward RSS, although we are aware of a language called RQL (RDF Query Language) that can be used to query RSS in its RDF form.

---

18 The name "RSS" has been variously claimed to be an acronym for "Rich Site Summary," "RDF Site Summary," and "Real Simple Syndication" (and probably other phrases as well). RSS provides a "publish/subscribe" mechanism for sharing content from one website with other websites. It is being increasingly used to publish news headlines, weblogs ("blobs"), and the like. RSS is normally specified in an XML format, initially (but no longer) as an RDF document.

19 An *ontology* is "an explicit formal specification of how to represent the objects, concepts, and other entities that are assumed to exist in some area of interest and the relationships that hold among them" (taken from http://dli.grainger.uiuc.edu/glossary.htm). In the W3C, ontologies are specified using OWL (see http://www.w3.org/2004/OWL/ for additional information about this RDF-based, and thus XML-based, vocabulary).

16.5 Chapter Summary

In this chapter, we've seen that XML is used for more than merely exchanging data and documents, or storing them. It is the foundation for a very large number of specialized XML vocabularies, some of which have very large communities of users and some of which are narrowly focused. We explored a small number of specialized XML vocabularies and considered whether they would benefit from having a custom query language that could be used by their user communities; we concluded that, in most cases, either there was no great motivation to query the marked-up data (at least not enough to support development, standardization, and implementation of specialized query languages), or the obvious solution was to query the data using XQuery (or an application based on XQuery).

Does this mean that we believe that XQuery and XPath are sufficient to address all of the world's XML querying problems? For the most part, XQuery and XPath are sufficient (if not entirely ideal) for querying data represented in XML, whether in specialized vocabularies or not. But, of course, XQuery/XPath are not satisfactory for "all of the world's querying problems," since not all of the world's data is (or should be) represented in XML. We (the collective "we") have to consider a number of factors when considering special-purpose query languages. Among the factors are the size of the potential user community for a given XML vocabulary, the difficulties of using existing tools (*e.g.*, XPath, XQuery, DOM), the added benefits of a purpose-built query language, the costs of trying to define and standardize that language, and the probability that there will be useful implementations of it. When all factors are taken into account, we think that it's not surprising that a few specialized query languages, supplemented by a small number of powerful general purpose languages, do a sufficiently good job of meeting market requirements.

Again, XQuery is a good (maybe even the best possible?) base for querying anything that is represented as XML. Specialized XML languages may motivate specialized query languages, but we suspect that they would probably be based on XQuery. RDF is an exception – because RDF is *not* an XML language, even though it can be represented in an XML form.

Chapter 17

Internationalization: Putting the "W" in "WWW"

17.1 Introduction

The organization that developed the XML standard,[1] the namespaces standard, XML Schema, XSLT, and XQuery is named "World Wide Web Consortium." A great deal of emphasis has been, and continues to be, given to the first words: World Wide. The Director of the W3C, Tim Berners-Lee, is adamant, as is the entire staff, that the scope of the web must be world wide. As a result, the policies and practices of the W3C demand that the Recommendations developed by its Working Groups be written in a way that serves the entire world, not merely Americans and Western Europeans.

One of the most important consequences of those policies and practices is that the specifications written by the various Working Groups have to carefully consider implications of many cultures, some of which might not even be recognized when the specs are under development. In this chapter, we'll explore some of the ways in which the work of the W3C is affected by the desire to serve the entire world, particularly as it applies to the subject of this book: querying XML.

---

1 *Extensible Markup Language (XML) 1.0, third edition, W3C Recommendation* (Cambridge, MA: World Wide Web Consortium, 2004). Available at: http://www.w3.org/TR/REC-xml.

17.2 What Is Internationalization?

The process of ensuring that a specification or a product can be used by any culture, using any script (writing system) or language, is commonly called *internationalization*, often abbreviated as "I18n" (that is, the letter *i* followed by 18 letters, followed by the letter *n*). (By contrast, the process of customizing a specification or product to be optimal in a specific culture, set of cultures, geographic regions, languages, and so forth is known as *localization*, or "L10n.")

The concept of internationalization is sometimes difficult for "westerners" (by which we mean members of cultures established primarily by people whose family origins lie in western Europe) to fully grasp. In fact, the computer industry has struggled with the many components of that concept for many years. A number of different factors are involved in any culture's world view, and most of those are necessarily involved in making computer systems, communications systems, *etc.* Here's a list of some of the more obvious items (and some not-so-obvious ones):

- The language(s) spoken.
- The script(s), or writing system(s), used to represent the language(s), including the character set(s) and writing direction(s).
- The rules for comparing and ordering sequences of characters.
- The conventions for "spelling" written forms of the language(s).
- The notation(s) used to write dates and times.
- The time zone(s) in use and the rules for adjusting them by season.
- The notations used to write numbers (*e.g.*, decimal marker, thousands separator).
- The conventions for writing words, sentences, and paragraphs (including, for example, whether white space is used to separate words and whether the first lines of paragraphs are indented).
- The ways in which currency ("money") is represented in writing.
- Units used for measures (*e.g.*, metric *vs.* "Imperial").

Obviously, that list is far from complete, but it should be sufficient to give you a sense of the scope of the problems involved in making computer systems and languages equally accessible to all cultures. Over the decades, a great deal of work has been done in pursuit of internationalization of hardware and software products, of specifications and standards, of applications, and of operating systems. Different (computer industry) communities have taken many different approaches, sometimes leveraging concurrent or preceding work and sometimes conflicting with it.

To make matters worse, software in particular is often developed under severe time and scope pressures, leaving developers insufficient resources to think about and address aspects for which they have relatively little appreciation. For example, the average American software engineer in the 1980s had little knowledge of languages and scripts used in the Far East (such as China, Japan, Korea, and Vietnam)[2] or the problems with representing text in languages where vowels and consonants are treated differently (such as Semitic, Sanskrit, and Dravidian languages). Consequently, systems developed at that time tended to have a strong English, or at least Latin script-based, orientation.

Even today, a significant amount of discipline is required by developers to keep in mind the needs of unfamiliar cultures. A particular problem is that commercial, proprietary software tends to be written to support only those cultures that are sufficiently important economically — that is, where the software will return enough revenue to pay for the process of making the software useful in those cultures.[3]

17.3 Internationalization and the World Wide Web

The W3C has established a Working Group, appropriately called the Internationalization WG, to monitor the work of the W3C — especially the development of Recommendation-track specifications — to ensure that the work truly addresses the needs of the world. It's illustrative to read the mission statement[4] of the I18n WG:

---

2 Software developers who are concerned with these languages may be interested in this book: Kend Lunde, *CJKV Information Processing* (Sebastopol, CA: O'Reilly, 1998).

3 While we don't have a problem with such decisions, we do believe that virtually all software should be internationalized. After all, one never knows what countries will be the next economic giants!

4 W3C Internationalization Core Working Group home page, available at: http://www.w3.org/International/core/.

> To enable universal access to the World Wide Web by proposing and coordinating the adoption by the W3C of techniques, conventions, technologies, and designs that enable and enhance the use of W3C technology and the Web worldwide, with and between the various different languages, scripts, regions, and cultures.

Of course, concepts such as "universal access" can be interpreted more or less broadly. Clearly, neither the W3C nor its I18n WG has any significant influence on the availability of computer systems, networking facilities, or educational systems throughout the world. A more reasonable interpretation of that mission statement is easy to attain after reading a bit further: "by proposing . . . techniques, conventions, technologies, and designs" that help those different regions and cultures to use the web.

Not surprisingly, the W3C is not the only — perhaps not even the principal — organization with a strong commitment to internationalization. For example, the Unicode Consortium[5] (about which you'll read more in Section 17.3.1) is devoted entirely to creation of specifications that encourage the production of software that supports cultural conventions in the areas of writing. ISO, the International Organization for Standardization, does not have explicit policies that require careful internationalization of its standards, but publishes many standards in support of internationalization as well as many other standards that include internationalization components.

In this section, we discuss the two most important (in our opinions) specifications that drive internationalization today. The first of these (Unicode) defines a character set intended to cover every writing system and culture of any importance at any time in human history, as well as a number of other factors that a computer system must address in order to properly support those writing systems and cultures. The other (the W3C Character Model for the World Wide Web) defines a model for the transmission and manipulation of character data on the web.

5 The Unicode Consortium's website is found at http://www.unicode.org.

17.3.1 Unicode

Unicode is a character set defined by The Unicode Consortium and published as The Unicode Standard.[6] The goal of Unicode is "to remedy two serious problems common to most multilingual computer programs. The first problem was the overloading of the font mechanism[7] when encoding characters . . . [the] second major problem was the use of multiple, inconsistent character codes because of conflicting national and industry character standards."

Unicode is, for all practical purposes, identical to an international standard known as the Universal Character Set (or UCS).[8] UCS (which, interestingly enough, is more popularly called by its number: 10646) evolved from a simple, elegant model in which a complete 32-bit space was dedicated to character encoding, allowing over 4 billion characters – slight overkill, in the estimation of many observers!

The space was partitioned into 256 "groups" of 256 "planes" each; each plane provided 65,536 (that is, 256 × 256) positions in which characters could be encoded. Group 0, plane 0 was designated to be the *multilingual plane,* in which the characters most widely used in the most widely-used languages would be encoded, while the remaining 255 planes in group 0 would be used for encoding less common characters. Limiting the character encoding space to group 0 provided 16,777,216 positions in which characters could be encoded – even that number was thought to be a bit much.

Concurrently with the initial development of UCS, the Unicode Consortium was established under the premise (some thought it a dubious premise) that only the multilingual plane was required for practical use in information technology applications and that the advantages to programmers of having "fixed-width" character

---

6 The Unicode Consortium. The Unicode Standard, Version 4.1.0, defined by: *The Unicode Standard, Version 4.0* (Boston, MA: Addison-Wesley, 2003), as amended by *Unicode 4.0.1* (http://www.unicode.org/versions/Unicode4.0.1) and by *Unicode 4.1.0* (http://www.unicode.org/versions/Unicode4.1.0).

7 For many years, it was the practice of font publishers to build fonts for different languages using the same character codes. For example, a font intended for use in western Europe or the Americas would probably be based on Latin 1 (aka ISO/IEC 8859-1). But a font for use in Israel would use the same character codes (that is, the numbers that identify each character) for Hebrew characters.

8 ISO/IEC 10646:2003, *Information Technology – Universal Multi-Octet Coded Character Set (UCS) – Part 1: Architecture and Basic Multilingual Plane* (Geneva, Switzerland: International Organization for Standardization, 2003).

encodings whose number of bytes was a power of two (*e.g.*, $2^1 = 2$ or $2^2 = 4$) were considerable.

Over time, both standards development groups realized that their basic premises were flawed. The Unicode Consortium recognized that the world's current languages (not to mention historical languages and scripts) could not be satisfied with only 65,536 characters, while the ISO committees realized that their (arguably more pure) 32-bit model was unnecessarily large. The groups decided to form a coalition in which supporters of the *de jure* process (such as national governments) would be presented with an international standard whose development was guided by an organization with full-time staff dedicated to continued evolution of the underlying character set and associated concepts.

The coalition of the two groups incorporated a formal agreement that the character set standard being published by each of the groups would be identical (at least to the degree that they contained exactly the same set of characters that are encoded at identical positions) and that the groups would work together to ensure that the standards remained identical. There are, however, slight differences between the two standards; for example, ISO/IEC 10646 defines an encoding form (UCS2) that is not part of The Unicode Standard.

In the end, the Unicode Consortium allocated a total of 16 planes beyond the multilingual plane for encoding characters. That space provides a total of 17 × 65,536 (that is, 1,114,112) positions. Of those positions, a small number have been set aside as "not a character."

Figure 17-1 illustrates the original ISO/IEC 10646 character encoding space, a variation reduced to a single group of 256 planes, and the final Unicode encoding space (adopted by the definers of ISO/IEC 10646) of 17 planes.

Unicode (and, by extension, UCS) undertook to create a repertoire of characters for every known script and language. Of course, it can never be proven is that work is complete, because new scripts and even new languages are discovered every now and then. While it might seem straightforward to create such a repertoire, reserving lots of space for characters yet to be discovered, there are complications.

One of these is the fact that a great many scripts depend on "decorations" being associated with certain characters. For example, Semitic languages are written primarily with characters representing consonants while the vowels are usually omitted, but represented as decorations printed "near" the consonants with which they are associated. Similarly, languages such as French and German depend on

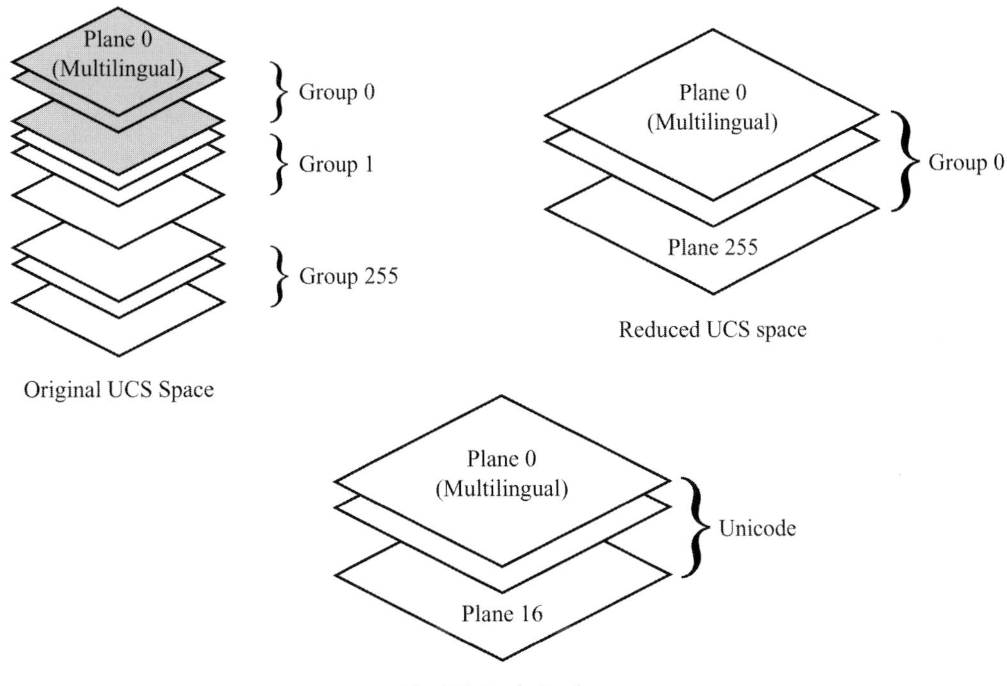

Figure 17-1 *UCS and Unicode character encoding space.*

marks, often called "accents" that (when displayed or printed) appear above the characters they modify. As one can easily imagine, the number of possible combinations of characters and related marks is very large indeed. Not all of those combinations are in actual use, but languages such as Vietnamese depend on the ability to place several such marks on individual characters.

The "obvious" solution to this issue was to encode "base characters" and their decorations separately. Therefore, the German character u-umlaut (ü) would be encoded as two separate characters, the letter "u" and a "nonspacing" umlaut. While that might be considered an elegant solution, it failed to account for the ability that most Westerners were used to encoding common characters in their languages using just one code position. For example, a very common character encoding standard used in Germany, known as Latin 1,[9] includes u-umlaut as a single character.

9 ISO/IEC 8859-1:1998, *Information Technology – 8-bit Single-byte Coded Graphic Character Sets – Part 1: Latin Alphabet No. 1* (Geneva, Switzerland: International Organization for Standardization, 1998).

Consequently, a guiding principle of Unicode was to incorporate existing widely-used character coding standards into Unicode as completely as possible. Thus, Latin 1 appears in Unicode as a contiguous sequence of characters in the same sequence that they appeared in the Latin 1 standard. Characters that are a base character plus an accent or other decoration, such as "ü," encoded at a single position, are known as *composed* (sometimes called "*precomposed*") characters. Unicode also permits such characters to be encoded as two separate characters (the "u" and the umlaut); when they are encoded in that manner, they are called *decomposed* characters.

The Unicode Standard defines several forms of normalization, including *canonical composition*, in which every character that can be composed into a single codepoint is represented that way, and *canonical decomposition*, in which all characters are decomposed into their base character and separate decorations.

In addition to normalization, the Unicode Standard defines several ways to encode Unicode into a sequence of bytes. Two of these are in such wide use that we briefly describe them here. We must emphasize this: Unicode is a character set, the formats we describe next are still Unicode — they're just ways to represent Unicode in byte sequences.

The first, called UTF-8 (Unicode Transformation Format, 8-bit form), is a *variable-width encoding*, meaning that the encoding of different Unicode characters might require a different number of octets. UTF-8 was designed so that all of the original ASCII[10] characters are encoded in one octet (byte). However, characters other than 7-bit ASCII characters require more than octet, up to four octets for characters used in Japanese, Chinese, and Korean scripts.

The other widely used encoding form is called UTF-16 (Unicode Transformation Format for 16 Planes of Group 00). In UTF-16, all characters that are encoded on the multilingual plane are represented in exactly 16 bits, or two octets. In addition, a total of 2048 positions of the multilingual plane are reserved for *surrogates*. Surrogates, which are valid only in UTF-16, are used to represent the 1024 × 1024 (1,048,576) character positions that are not part of the multilingual plane — in other words, the positions on the additional 16 planes. Those characters are represented in four octets: two octets that iden-

10 ANSI/INCITS 4-1986(R1997), *Coded Character Sets — 7-bit American National Standard Code for Information Interchange (7-bit ASCII)* (New York: American National Standards Institute, 1986).

tify one surrogate value and two that identify a second surrogate value. Surrogates are also not characters.

It is not always obvious which of these encoding formats, UTF-8 or UTF-16, should be used for any particular situation. There's a definite trade-off in terms of the amount of space required to represent any given character string.

If your data uses only ASCII characters, then UTF-8 is most certainly the right choice, since every character is encoded in a single byte. However, if your data contains characters other than those in ASCII, UTF-8 begins to require more space: A great many nonideographic characters are represented in UTF by two bytes, all characters of the multilingual plane are represented in no more than three bytes, and all characters from the other 16 planes are represented in four bytes. If your data contains only those ASCII characters and those that can be represented in two bytes, then the average number of bytes required for any given text string will be somewhere between one and two bytes, inclusive. When you start using the less-common characters, especially those encoded outside the multilingual plane, the average number of bytes per character grows, increasing the space required to store the data and the time required to transmit it.

If your data comprises characters on the multilingual plane beyond those represented in ASCII, UTF-16 is a good choice. While UTF-8 is a varying-length encoding (that is, the number of bytes to represent a character varies depending on the specific character), UTF-16 is a fixed-length encoding — as long as you stick to the multilingual plane, every character occupies exactly two bytes. If your data includes some characters from the 16 supplementary planes, those characters are represented in UTF-16 by two consecutive 16-bit surrogates, four bytes in all — thus making UTF-16 a varying-length encoding in this situation. Consequently, the average number of bytes per character needed to represent text strings in UTF-16 ranges between two and four, inclusive.

Which is better for your environment? The answer to that question depends entirely on the nature of your data. If it is primarily data used in the English-speaking world, then UTF-8 may well be the best choice. But if your data includes a great many characters from non-English speaking cultures, particularly ideographic characters, then UTF-16 is likely to be more efficient.

One more thing about encoding forms: ISO/IEC 10646 defines two encoding forms of its own, both of them fixed-length. The first,

UCS2, represents every character in exactly two bytes. That obviously limits its repertoire of characters to those encoded on the multilingual plane. UCS2 has no mechanism for representing characters on the 16 supplementary planes, because it does not support the concept of surrogates. (That is the only difference between UCS2 and UTF-16, but it's an important difference.) The other encoding form is UCS4, which represents every character in exactly four bytes; Unicode defines an encoding form called UTF-32 that is identical to UCS4.

The Unicode Consortium has, of course, not rested on its laurels. It continues to release versions of The Unicode Standard, adding new scripts and new characters for existing scripts, refining the designated characteristics of existing and new characters, and specifying elegant mechanisms for defining collations,[11] defining normalized forms of character strings that maximize communication between processes, and so forth. Some of these additional mechanisms are published as Unicode Technical Reports (UTR), others are published as Unicode Technical Standards (UTS), and others are incorporated directly in The Unicode Standard as Unicode Standard Annexes (UAX).

Unicode (and UCS) is a resounding success and has proven to be one of the more important underpinnings of the World Wide Web. In particular, the character set on which both HTML and XML are defined is Unicode. Consequently, specifications that are based on, or depend on, XML are also defined in terms of Unicode. This includes W3C specifications discussed in this book, such as XML Schema, XSLT, and XQuery. In Section 17.4, we discuss some of the implications of these relationships.

We think it's worth noting that, in addition to Unicode's use in XML-related specifications, the Java Programming Language uses Unicode in the UCS2 encoding form mentioned above as its character set, and a number of Microsoft's data management and web-related products do the same. While UCS2 is not a precise match for UTF-16, the two encoding forms represent characters on the multilingual plane identically. Java's and Microsoft's use of Unicode in UCS2 makes them just that much more useful in developing your XML queries.

11 A *collation* is a mechanism for defining comparison and ordering of character strings. A common example of collations is "use the numeric value of the characters to compare characters." Many examples of culturally sensitive collations exist that allow sorting according to the rules of French, German, Arabic, or Japanese.

17.3.2 W3C Character Model for the World Wide Web

In early 1999, the W3C began development of a *character model* for the World Wide Web.[12] The development process was unusually painful, in large part because of the difficulties in getting "buy-in" from all interested parties. The character model was intended to provide definitions and specifications related to character sets and character strings that can be referenced by other specifications. In particular, the model defined the concept of *character string normalization* and proposes rules for comparing character strings and identifying specific characters in a string by their position, as well as conventions for representation of URIs.

For almost five years, the Character Model specification went through several Working Draft iterations, during which time the Internationalization Working Group responded to comments from other W3C Working Groups and from the general public. When it became apparent that some parts of the Character Model were so controversial that still more delays would be incurred in its publication, the Internationalization WG decided in early 2004 to split the specification into two documents: Fundamentals and Normalization. Shortly thereafter, a third document was split off from the other two. The three documents that exist at the time of writing are the Fundamentals,[13] Normalization,[14] and Resource Identifiers.[15] Additional documents related to the Character Model may be created in the future.

Fundamentals states:

> . . . the goal of the Character Model for the World Wide Web is to facilitate use of the Web by all people, regardless of their language, script, writing system, and cultural conven-

12 *Character Model for the World Wide Web, W3C Working Draft* (Cambridge, MA: World Wide Web Consortium, 1999). Available at: http://www.w3.org/TR/1999/WD-charmod-19990225.

13 *Character Model for the World Wide Web 1.0: Fundamentals, W3C Recommendation* (Cambridge, MA: World Wide Web Consortium, 2005). Available at: http://www.w3.org/TR/charmod/.

14 *Character Model for the World Wide Web 1.0: Normalization, W3C Working Draft* (Cambridge, MA: World Wide Web Consortium, 2005). Available at: http://www.w3.org/TR/charmod-norm/.

15 *Character Model for the World Wide Web 1.0: Resource Identifiers, W3C Candidate Recommendation* (Cambridge, MA: World Wide Web Consortium, 2004). Available at: http://www.w3.org/TR/charmod-resid/.

> tions, in accordance with the *W3C goal of universal access.* One basic prerequisite to achieve this goal is to be able to transmit and process the characters used around the world in a well-defined and well-understood way.

Perhaps the most important requirement specified in the Fundamentals is that all specifications adhering to the Character Model must define text in terms of Unicode characters and *not* in terms of the glyphs (shapes) that might appear on a screen or on paper. This requirement applies even when the text is originally represented in some (possibly proprietary, possibly standardized) character encoding that is *visually oriented* (that is, encoded based on the sequence of glyphs that a human reads on paper or on a screen).

Another important specification in Fundamentals are the rules for *string indexing* — that is, for determining the index, or the number of the position, of a given character in a character string. For example, in the character string "XML is popular," the character in the third position is "L."

While the other two documents have — at the time of writing — achieved Recommendation and Proposed Recommendation status, respectively, the Normalization document is still at the Working Draft stage. The controversy that caused the development of the Character Model to take so long is apparently related to normalization of character strings.

The Normalization spec defines two facilities: *character normalization* and *string identity matching*. Character normalization is described as bringing the characters in a string into a well-defined canonical encoding, such as canonically composed or canonically decomposed. Normalization is important because of problems associated with comparison of character strings. Virtually all computer systems compare two character strings in a byte-by-byte style, in which the corresponding bytes in the strings are compared (usually "from left to right," more properly described as "from most significant to least significant").

Consider two character strings being compared, in which one contains the German word "stück" in which the "ü" character is represented as a single code position and the other contains the same word, but with the "ü" represented as two code positions (the letter and the umlaut). The first string is encoded as five characters, while the second is encoded as six. The comparison of the strings would initially compare the first characters, which would compare equal ("s" = "s"). The second characters would also compare equal ("t" = "t"). But the third characters would not compare equal ("ü" is not the same as "u"!), nor would the fourth characters ("c" is not the same as a combining umlaut).

In order to reliably compare two character strings, they must be represented in the same character encoding scheme, but they must also be represented in the same normalization form. This requirement often means that one character string must be converted to the normalization form of the other; to be certain, it is often desirable to convert both strings to the chosen normalization form (this ensures against some characters in a single string being represented in their composed form and others in their decomposed form).

Now, here's where the controversy arose: The Character Model Normalization draft specifies that normalization is to be performed "early" — that is, by the producers of data, and prohibits the consumers of that data from performing the normalization. In order for comparisons to be dependable, all data producers on the World Wide Web would have to normalize the character strings they produce, and do so in exactly the same normalization form (the Character Model specifies the canonically composed form named NFC by Unicode). Many participants in other W3C Working Groups agreed that, in an ideal world, that would be how things worked. But, they argued, the world is far from ideal and the web is filled with documents of uncertain normalization; it was thus more effective for the consumers of character string data to perform normalization when (and only when!) normalization was required. Because normalization (to a given normalization form, such as NFC) is idempotent, it never causes problems to renormalize a string that has already been normalized.

The controversy rages on, with a lot of creativity being used to attempt to find solutions (sometimes in the form of rather clever definitions) that will allow all parties' requirements to be satisfied.

The other facility defined in the Normalization spec is string identity matching. The spec defined the term to mean that two strings being matched for string identity have no user-identifiable distinctions. For example, the strings "The Thing" and "The thing" have a user-identifiable distinction: the first contains a capital "T," while the second has a lowercase "t" in the corresponding position. The spec defines the concept such that strings do not match when they differ in case or accentuation, but do match when they differ only in nonsemantically significant ways, such as character encoding, use of character escapes (of potentially different kinds), or use of precomposed *vs.* decomposed character sequences.

We are personally quite impressed with the Character Model (even though we disagree with the Normalization draft's specification that normalization is to be performed early). The Character Model provides some perspectives, definitions, guidelines, and policies that are proving very helpful in making the World Wide Web truly universal.

17.4 Internationalization Implications: XPath, XQuery, and SQL/XML

At the end of Section 17.3.1, we told you that the choice of using Unicode as the character set for XML would have implications on all specifications and products that use or depend on XML. That certainly applies to the technologies we've discussed in this book for querying XML, obviously including XPath[16] and XQuery;[17] perhaps a little less obviously, SQL/XML[18] is also affected. In this section, we look at some of those implications.

The first, and most obvious, implication is that XPaths and XQuery expressions must be able to specify data used for comparisons and matching in XML. For example, in the XPath `/movies/movie[title="Starship Troopers"]`, the `title` element child of each `movie` element is, of course, XML and thus encoded in Unicode. Consequently, the comparison of the value of that title element with the literal `"Starship Troopers"` is done using Unicode comparison rules. As a result, the literal itself should also be encoded in Unicode. The W3C Working Groups responsible for XPath and XQuery made the obvious decision that the character set for both XPath and XQuery is Unicode. (Note that, in specifications for all Unicode-based languages, including XML, the specific Unicode encoding form – *e.g.*, UFT-8, UTF-16, or anything else – is irrele-

16 *XML Path Language (XPath) 2.0, W3C Candidate Recommendation* (Cambridge, MA: World Wide Web Consortium, 2005). Available at: http://www.w3.org/TR/xpath20/.

17 *XQuery 1.0: An XML Query Language, W3C Candidate Recommendation* (Cambridge, MA: World Wide Web Consortium, 2005). Available at: http://www.w3.org/TR/xquery/.

18 ISO/IEC 9075-14:2006 (planned), *Information Technology – Database Languages – SQL – Part 14: XML-Related Specifications (SQL/XML)* (Geneva, Switzerland: International Organization for Standardization, 2006).

vant.[19] Implementations of those languages must, of course, deal with the actual encoding forms.)

A second, rather more subtle, implication relates to a few of the functions described in the Functions and Operators spec.[20] The functions in question (`fn:matches`, `fn:replace`, and `fn:tokenize`) perform matching operations using *regular expressions*. The Unicode Consortium has published a UTS[21] that describes the issues related to regular expression mapping when the character set in use is Unicode. This UTS is primarily concerned with regular expression matching implementations, so one of the principal issues is the very large number of characters encoded by Unicode (especially compared with a standard like ASCII, which defines fewer than 100 characters).

UTS #18 defines three levels of Unicode support:

- Level 1: Basic Unicode Support requires that the regular expression (regex) engine recognize and process Unicode characters instead of bytes (which, because it works fine with ASCII, is the — inappropriate — technique used by some regex engines).
- Level 2: Extended Unicode Support requires that the regex engine recognize *grapheme clusters* (that is, it recognizes Unicode character sequences that have been defined to correspond to the marks that appear on paper or on a screen that most human readers would think of as a character).
- Level 3: Tailored Support is provided by regex engines that provide application-specific treatment of characters, such as that assumed by specific countries, languages, or scripts.

---

19 The specific Unicode encoding form used by an instance XML document being searched and literals used in queries on that document is irrelevant because both the XML document and the query literals are represented as XQuery Data Model instances. The Data Model represents character data in "Unicode," but not in a specified encoding form. A common implementation technique is to transform all such character data into UTF-32 (equivalently, to UCS4) as the most generalized encoding form.

20 *XQuery 1.0 and XPath 2.0 Functions and Operators, W3C Candidate Recommendation,* (Cambridge, MA: World Wide Web Consortium, 2005). Available at: http://www.w3.org/TR/xpath-functions/.

21 *Unicode Technical Standard #18, Unicode Regular Expressions,* The Unicode Consortium (2005). Available at: http://www.unicode.org/reports/tr18/.

Among the requirements placed on regular expression engines by UTS #18 are the following.

- Some mechanism for specifying arbitrary Unicode characters must be provided (such as the notation used by XML: "`㉯`").
- The engine must provide a way to reference whole categories of characters using the Unicode character properties (*e.g.*, "letter," "digit," or "whitespace"). Minimally, the engine must support at least these properties: General_Category, Script, Alphabetic, Uppercase, Lowercase, White_Space, Noncharacter_Code_Point, Default_Ignorable_Code_Point, ANY, ASCII, and ASSIGNED. There are 40 General_Category properties, including things such as Letter, Mark, Decimal Digit Number, Final Punctuation, and Surrogate.

A third implication of Unicode on XPath and XQuery is the definition of functions and operations either focused on Unicode semantics or influenced by Unicode semantics. The XQuery Functions and Operators specification defines a number of such functions: fn:codepoints-to-string, fn:string-to-codepoints, fn:codepoint-equal, fn:normalize-unicode, fn:upper-case, fn:lower-case, fn:contains, fn:starts-with, fn:ends-with, fn:substring-before, fn:substring-after, fn:matches, fn:replace, and fn:tokenize. In addition, all string comparison and ordering operations are dependent on the Unicode Collation Algorithm.[22]

The effects of Unicode on SQL/XML exist in part because of the relationship between SQL/XML and XQuery (see Chapter 16, "XML-Derived Markup Languages," for more information). There is a second source of those effects, though, and that is the recent dependence on Unicode in SQL itself. SQL has been "internationalized" since its 1992 edition,[23] at least in its recognition that ASCII (or even Latin 1) was not the only character set in use by database system customers and that culturally-appropriate collations were required by those customers. At that time, however, the first version of Unicode had just been published and it was far from certain that it would gather sufficient support from the computer industry. Consequently, SQL-

22 *Unicode Technical Standard #10, Unicode Collation Algorithm* (The Unicode Consortium, 2005). Available at: http://www.unicode.org/reports/tr10/.

23 ISO/IEC 9075:1992, *Information Technology – Database Languages – SQL* (Geneva, Switzerland: International Organization for Standardization, 1992).

92 did not explicitly recognize Unicode as a source of a model for character processing.

Later versions of SQL increasingly took notice of Unicode. Finally, in SQL:2003,[24] Unicode was adopted as the model by which the SQL specifications talked about characters. Many SQL implementations explicitly use Unicode as the foundation for supporting databases using characters beyond the range included in the familiar Latin 1 character set.

17.5 Chapter Summary

In this chapter, we've introduced the subject of internationalization and the W3C's support for the concept. We wrote at some length about the universal character set known as Unicode (and its *de jure* standard twin, ISO 10646), its success in the marketplace, and its use as the foundation for the computer industry's efforts to become friendlier to users all over the world.

You also read about the W3C's Internationalization Working Group's still-emerging Character Model for the World Wide Web, including both the two component documents that have reached (or nearly reached) Recommendation status and the third document that is still at Working Draft stage, in part because of lingering controversy over its requirements. And, finally, we gave you a peek at several of the ways in which Unicode (and, by extension, the Character Model) have influenced XPath, XQuery, and even SQL/XML.

---

24 ISO/IEC 9075-*:2003, *Information Technology – Database Languages – SQL (all parts)* (Geneva, Switzerland: International Organization for Standardization, 2003).

Chapter

18

Finding Stuff

18.1 Introduction

For this last chapter in the book, we wanted to take a step back – actually, to take several giant leaps back – and consider what "querying XML" is intended to achieve. In the bigger picture, the technologies we have discussed for querying XML, such as SQL/XML and XQuery, provide some useful infrastructure to achieve universal, intelligent search over all information. Most people don't care in the slightest whether the underlying technology to achieve this involves SQL or XQuery or XML – all they care about is *finding stuff.*

We break "finding stuff" down into the various kinds of stuff that you might want to find. We start with structured data, which is the simplest and, currently, the most useful and widely used kind of search. It includes all database search – tables and XML. Then we look at finding stuff on the web – we start by discussing the Google phenomenon, then describe and discuss the Semantic Web. Web search also includes the "deep web" – information that is available on the web, but is not necessarily available as individual web *pages* (*e.g.,* catalog information that is available via a web form).

After that, we move to finding stuff at work, describing Enterprise Search. This is currently a hot area, with advances in technology (and in perceptions and practices) that promise to make many of us more productive and less stressed at work. We discuss federated search (finding other people's stuff) and finding services (another hot area), before briefly discussing how people might do all these searches in a more natural way.

Finally, we summarize the chapter and make some predictions for the future of search.

18.2 Finding Structured Data — Databases

So far in this book, we have talked mostly about how to query structured data — dates, numbers, short strings — using query languages such as SQL and XQuery. Finding structured data has been the mainstay of the computer industry for several decades. It's at the heart of most computer applications, from banking to airline reservations to payroll accounting. What is changing is that this information is shared and exchanged more and more. That means we need standard ways to *express* the data (to transfer the data from party to party), and standard ways to *query* the data (so that each party can query any other's). (A *party* here may be an application, a data store, a corporation, or a person.)

XML is the obvious choice for a standard way to express structured data. We predict that more and more structured data will be expressed — stored, represented, and/or published — as XML over the next few years. As the amount of structured-data-as-XML grows, the importance of being able to find and extract parts of that XML easily and accurately, in a standard way, will grow too. XQuery is the obvious choice here — it is a rich, expressive language designed specifically to find and extract parts of an XML collection. XQuery has been crafted by some of the computer industry's leading experts in XML and query languages, and the W3C process (though time-consuming) is thorough and it guarantees participation from a host of experts and users.

Where structured data is stored in a database, SQL/XML is the obvious harness for XQuery, allowing the richness and versatility of XQuery expressions over either XML or relational data, and returning results in either XML or relational form. SQL/XML also forms a bridge between the mature, proven world of relational data and the more flexible, sharable XML data. As the major database vendors roll out SQL/XML with XQuery as standard functionality in the latest versions of their databases, SQL/XML will represent the mainstream adoption of XQuery over the next few years.

18.3 Finding Stuff on the Web — Web Search

18.3.1 The Google Phenomenon

One cannot discuss web search without mentioning Google. Google has been phenomenally successful in a number of dimensions — everyone, it seems, uses Google, whether doing academic or business research, finding out about the latest hot band, or just shopping for T-shirts. The word *Google* has entered the English language as a verb — "Just Google it." And then there's the money — at the time of writing, Google shares are trading at around $350 each, up from an initial public offering price of $85 in August 2005, and Google's founders, Larry Page and Sergey Brin, are among the top 50 richest men in the world.

But Google were not the first to search the World Wide Web. Alta Vista did a creditable job of making the world's web pages searchable as far back as 1995, and there have been a whole slew of other web search sites in the past decade (Lycos, Inktomi, Excite, Hotbot, Dogpile, AskJeeves, *etc.*). Some of these are still in operation, though most have been acquired by larger outfits such as Yahoo or Microsoft.

So, if Google wasn't the first web search site, what has made it so successful? Quite simply, Google did it better. The Google site is simple and easy to use, performance is crisp, and, above all, the pages you are looking for appear in the top few hits most of the time.[1] This accuracy can be attributed (in part) to Google's use of *link analysis* to figure out which web pages are more authoritative. In brief, here's how it works: When the Google spider goes out and crawls web pages, it starts at a number of seed pages. For each page crawled, the crawler adds index information for that page, follows each link on the page, and adds index information for those pages too. Given the interconnectedness of the web, a spider can crawl most of the world's web pages with relatively few seed sites.[2] What you end up with is an index to web pages. What *link analysis* adds is

1 This is deliberately vague. There has been a lot of work done to define objective measurements for the results of this kind of search — see, *e.g.*, the TREC (Text REtrieval Conference) home page at: http://trec.nist.gov/. Also, some people would argue that "the pages you are looking for appear in the top few hits" is misleading — since Google is searching so many pages, it's more accurate to say "the top few hits are acceptable results," since there may be many pages that would satisfy your search.

2 But see also Section 18.3.4, "The Deep Web."

a catalog of information about which pages link to other pages. The idea is that if lots of people create links to some page, then that page must be authoritative, and so it should appear toward the top of the results page, all other factors being equal.

Let's look at a simple example. Each year, Idealliance presents an XML conference, which is sponsored by some of the major players in the XML world. The home page for this conference (currently showing notes and presentations from XML 2005) is http://www.xmlconference.org/xmlusa/. This page obviously mentions the word "XML" a lot, and the page is very much *about* XML. Not only does Google count the links to this page, but they are also kind enough to share that information, via the "link" keyword — a Google search for "link: http://www.xmlconference.org/xmlusa/" reveals that around 820 other pages link to the Idealliance (XML 2005) page.[3] That's quite a lot, and it makes the Idealliance page fairly authoritative. But if you do a Google search for "XML," the Idealliance page does not appear first in the list of results — you have to go the third page of results to find that. The top result is http://www.xml.com/, which has around 19,400 other pages linking to it.

This example is rather simplistic — there is a lot more going on than a simple link count. The authority of a page is calculated based on the number *and authority* of the pages that link to it — that is, if a page that links to your target page has itself got a large number of pages linking to it, that counts for more. And of course there's the whole machinery of keyword search affecting the results and their order (relevancy ranking). For more details, see the original paper on link analysis and relevancy ranking, by Page and Brin (Google's founders).[4]

The important point here is that the whole Google phenomenon — a huge leap forward in the utility of the web, a new verb in the English language, and at least two very rich guys — came about because of one incremental advance in search quality, *i.e.*, link analysis (the PageRank algorithm). Web search still has a long way to go, and there are a number of techniques waiting in the wings to be the next PageRank. For the rest of this section, we examine a few of them — metadata, the semantic web, and the deep web.

---

3 Those nice people at Google even show you *which* pages link to the target page.

4 Sergey Brin and Lawrence Page, *The Anatomy of a Large-Scale Hypertextual Web Search Engine* (Stanford, CA: Computer Science Department, Stanford University, 1997). Available at: http://www-db.stanford.edu/pub/papers/google.pdf.

18.3.2 Metadata

In Part II, "Metadata and XML," we discussed the importance of metadata. On the web, metadata is found in the `title` and `meta` elements of an HTML or XHTML[5] document. The web address (URL), too, can be considered metadata — it's clear that http://www.xml.com/ is about XML without looking into the page at all. A sophisticated web search takes into account not just the existence and number of occurrences of a search term on a page, but also the existence of the keyword (or similar terms) in the URL, `title`, and `meta` elements. In this way, web page authors can collaborate with search engines to help ensure that a page is found whenever the page is truly *about* the search term(s).[6] Existence of search terms in metadata can also help with page ranking (ordering hits in a results list to accurately reflect their relevance to the search). For example, if you search for the term "XML," you would prefer to see pages with "XML" in the URL or in the `title` element rather than pages that happen to mention XML in passing.

Moving on to the contents of the page itself, the first few lines, headings, and emphasized terms could all be considered as metadata. And there are a growing number of engines that can do entity extraction — pulling out the names of entities (such as people's names, place names, company names, *etc.*) from plain, unmarked-up text, by a combination of context recognition and dictionary lookup.

Link text might also be considered part of the metadata of a web page, even though it is not a part of the document itself. The link text is the text of the `<a>` element that includes the `href` attribute that points to a page — the text that is (generally) underlined and highlighted in blue, which you click to get to another page. This text is often very descriptive, and can give good clues about the meaning of

---

5 Of course, XHTML allows the inclusion of metadata from other namespaces, so an author can include any metadata, including RDF, as part of her web page. We believe this is rare today, but growing. Of particular interest are some experiments allowing web users to add metadata to pages they view — Adam Bosworth (http://www.adambosworth.net/) is a proponent of this sort of "sloppy" data on the web.

6 Ideally, this would be an honest attempt by authors to make sure that their page shows up in the results of appropriate searches. It is well known, however, that some authors try to trick search engines into showing their pages on *any* results list, whether or not they belong there. This practice is sometimes called *search engine spoofing*.

the page. Google and other search engines make use of this text as if it were metadata as part of the page.[7]

But this is still just keyword metadata — we are looking for keyword matches, we are just looking for them in metadata as well as in the text of the page. *Semantic metadata* (see also Chapter 4, "Metadata — An Overview") takes us one step on from keyword search, toward a semantic search, by providing pointers to what the data *mean*.

18.3.3 The Semantic Web — The Search for Meaning

The term *semantic web* was coined by Tim Berners-Lee,[8] who described it as "data on the Web in a form that machines can naturally understand . . . a web of data that can be processed directly or indirectly by machines." The key here is that machines must be able to *understand* the data. Keyword search (or, in structured data, number or date or string search), does not involve any understanding of the meaning (semantics) of the search terms or of the data being searched.

When you search across text, a search term may have many meanings. If you search for the word "bat," are you looking for a flying mammal, or an instrument with which to play baseball (or cricket)? When you type "bat" into Google, it does only a keyword search, and returns pages that include "bat" in all its meanings.[9] When you search for a number or a date, there is generally only one possible meaning for the search term.[10] If you search in an Excel spreadsheet, for example, for the number 42, you would not expect to get results that include the number 24 (which is similar to 42 in many ways — both are numbers, both are integers, both are even, both have the digits 4 and 2, *etc.*). But number search would also improve if you could search on the meaning of the number, in the sense that you could search for "the number 42 where it is an employee number at Beeswax Corporation," or "the number 42 where it is the price in dollars of a medium red T-shirt." This is the essence of the semantic web — to be able to search for documents

---

7 Yet another reason — if one were needed — to ***not*** use "Click here" for link text.

8 Tim Berners-Lee, *Weaving the Web: The Original Design and Ultimate Destiny of the World Wide Web* (New York: HarperCollins, 2000).

9 We were surprised to find the first result from Google to a search for "bat" was none of these — it was "British American Tobacco."

10 There are, of course, differences due to type — the integer 42 and the string 42 are different.

(and other stuff) as if you were asking a librarian. The librarian understands the subject matter that exists in the library, and understands your description of what you are looking for, and so can come up with the book or article or paper that meets your needs. Imagine approaching the help desk at the Library of Congress and saying just "bat," and you can see just how much distance there is between even the smartest keyword-based search and a search that involves meaning.

To search for meaning, we need two things. First, we need the ability to describe real-world things in a way that is machine-*understandable*, in the same way that XML is machine-*readable*. (Once this is achieved, computers can *process* and *integrate* data in an intelligent way. By contrast, the current World Wide Web demonstrates only how good computers are at *presenting* data to people.) Second, we need to be able to describe a meaning search as easily as we can describe a keyword search (to, say, Google). In the rest of this section, we describe the contribution that RDF, RDF-S, OWL, and SPARQL have made to this "search for meaning," and assess how close we are to the goals of the semantic web.

URL, URI, URIRef

Anyone who has used a browser has used a *URL* — it's the string you type into the browser to get to a web page, also known as a *web address*. URL stands for Uniform Resource Locator — a standard way to *locate* a web resource, usually a web page.

RDF (see next subsection) uses the notion of a *URI*[11] — a Uniform Resource *Identifier*. This is an ambitious extension to the notion of a URL. A URI is a string that can identify anything in the universe, including things that can be located on the web (web pages, documents, services) and things that cannot (a person, a corporation, a physical copy of a book, even a concept). A *URIRef* is a URI with an optional fragment identifier.[12]

---

11 Tim Berners-Lee, *Uniform Resource Identifiers (URI): Generic Syntax* (August 1988). Available at: http://www.isi.edu/in-notes/rfc2396.txt.

12 The role of fragment identifiers (which often appear at the end of a URL, beginning with a "#" character, to denote a position within the page) has been a matter of hot debate within the W3C and the XML community. Some believe the fragment identifier should be considered a part of the URL, others that the fragment identifier is an addition to the URL. The RDF specs talk about a *URIRef* as their basic building block, where a URIRef is a URI with an optional fragment identifier at the end.

RDF Statements

Once we can identify a thing, we can describe its properties. RDF — the Resource Description Framework — defines a framework for describing things (resources) in a machine-readable format. Using RDF, we can make *statements* about resources, where each statement has a subject, a predicate, and an object.

For example, "An American Werewolf in London was directed by John Landis" is a statement that describes one of our sample movies. "An American Werewolf in London" is the subject, "directed by" is the predicate, "John Landis" is the object. More precisely, *the movie with the title* "An American Werewolf in London" is the subject, and *the person whose name is* "John Landis" is the object.

We can express this as an RDF statement. First, we need to know (or assign) a URI for each of the resources.[13] Let's say that the movie is denoted by the URI "http://example.org/movie/42," the predicate is denoted by "http://example.org/predicates/isDirectedBy," and the subject is denoted by "http://example.org/people/Landis/John/001." Note that none of these URIs is a URL — *i.e.*, none of them is a web address that resolves to an actual page or document. Each URI is used to identify some specific thing, *not* to point to its location (hence it's a URI and not a URL). Of course, these URIs might also point to a physical location that contains a description of the resource (where the resource is a person, it might contain a biography of that person), but that's not its primary purpose.[14]

Serializing RDF Statements

RDF gives us a way to formulate a statement about a resource. But how do we express that statement? The RDF Primer describes three ways — a graph, a triple, and an XML fragment.

Figure 18-1 shows a graph representation of our example statement, saying that the movie "An American Werewolf in London" was directed by the person whose name is "John Landis" (we have invented, for these examples, a person-id scheme where each person is identified by first name and last name, plus a number to distinguish between people with the same name). We have added a second statement to the graph, which says that the title of the movie is "An American Werewolf in London." Note that the value of the title is a

13 Note that RDF does not provide a vocabulary (valid set of terms), even for predicates.

14 This is similar to the use of a URI as a *namespace name* or a *schema location hint*.

literal string, not a URI — in RDF, any object (but not subject or predicate) may be either a URI or a literal. Literals can be typed, and the type of a literal may be an XML Schema type or some implementation-defined type.

The same statements could be expressed as tuples (more specifically, triples), as in Example 18-1. The RDF Primer describes a shorthand form of this fairly verbose serialization, with no angle brackets, and with part or all of the URI represented by a predefined prefix.

A third way to represent an RDF statement is as an XML document. Example 18-2 shows one possible XML representation of the RDF statements described in the previous section. The XML document starts with an `rdf:RDF` tag, with three namespace definitions. The first is the namespace associated with the `rdf` prefix, and the second is the namespace we invented for RDF predicates that we define, such as `isDirectedBy`. The third is the namespace for Dublin Core metadata definitions (see Chapter 5, "Structural Metadata"). Dublin Core already has a definition for "title," so we reused that definition for our XML example. The `rdf:RDF` tag has a child element `rdf:Description`, which encloses an RDF statement. The `rdf:about` attribute gives the subject of the statement. The child of `rdf:Description` gives the predicate and object of the statement — the predicate is represented by the element name (`pred:isDirectedBy`), and the object is given by the content of the element. The `rdf:Description` element has a second child, showing how several statements about the same subject can be represented in the same `rdf:Description`.

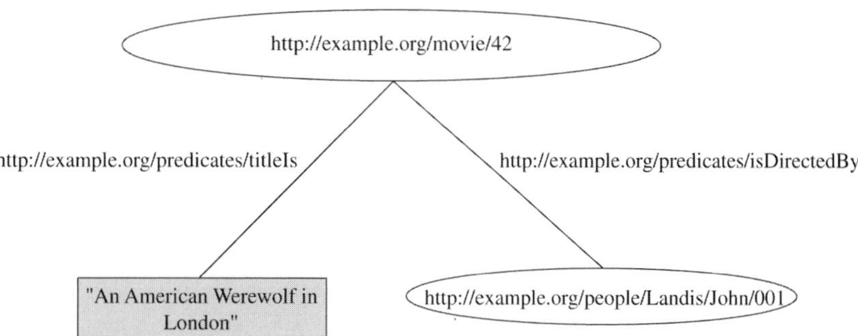

Figure 18-1 *RDF Graph.*

Example 18-1 *RDF triples*

```
<http://example.org/movie/42>
<http://example.org/predicates/isDirectedBy>
<http://example.org/people/Landis/John/001> .

<http://example.org/movie/42>
<http://example.org/predicates/title>
"An American Werewolf in London" .
```

Example 18-2 *RDF/XML*

```
<?xml version="1.0"?>
<rdf:RDF
    xmlns:rdf="http://www.w3.org/1999/02/22-rdf-syntax-ns#"
    xmlns:pred="http://example.org/predicates/"
    xmlns:dc="http://purl.org/dc/elements/1.1/" >
    <rdf:Description rdf:about="http://example.org/movie/42">
        <pred:isDirectedBy>http://example.org/people/Landis/John/001
        </pred:isDirectedBy>
        <dc:title>An American Werewolf in London</dc:title>
    </rdf:Description>
</rdf:RDF>
```

At this point we need to emphasize that RDF is *not* XML. RDF is a framework for describing resources using statements containing subjects, predicates, and objects. RDF/XML describes a possible XML serialization of those statements.

Toward Meaning — RDF-S, OWL

The semantic web is all about describing (and searching for) meaning rather than keywords, semantics rather than syntax. But RDF is just one step on from metadata tags in this respect. Two more standards efforts – RDF-S and OWL – push us further along the spectrum toward meaning.

RDF-S,[15] or RDF Schema, lets you define a *vocabulary* for use in RDF statements. The vocabulary sets out:

15 *RDF Vocabulary Description Language 1.0: RDF Schema* (Cambridge, MA: World Wide Web Consortium, 2004). Available at: http://www.w3.org/TR/rdf-schema/. See also Chapter 5 of the RDF Primer, at: http://www.w3.org/TR/2004/REC-rdf-primer-20040210/#rdfschema.

- Classes of resources to be described.
- Properties to be used in describing resources.
- Which properties can be used with which classes.

This gives additional meaning to RDF statements by restricting the vocabulary, in the same way that a data type system adds meaning to unstructured data ("the integer 42" or "the string 42" carry more meaning than "the untyped 42"). RDF-S also allows the definition of a resource class hierarchy, which gives information about how resources relate to each other. The RDF-S vocabulary and class hierarchy constitute a *taxonomy*.

At this point we need to take a side-trip to discuss the meaning of the terms *taxonomy* and *ontology*. There is some debate in the knowledge management and linguistics communities over the precise definitions of these terms, and the differences between them. We describe here our preferred definitions, but warn the reader that she may find the terms used in slightly different ways in different texts.[16] A *taxonomy* is a hierarchical ordering of *terms*. One obvious example of a taxonomy occurs in biology — a Sheltie is a dog is a mammal is an animal. A taxonomy is generally drawn as a tree with a single root.[17] An *ontology* is a (not necessarily hierarchical)[18] representation of *concepts* and the relationships between them. At first glance, an ontology might look exactly the same as a taxonomy — a Sheltie is a dog is a mammal is an animal. But the ontology node is not "the term Sheltie," rather it is "the *concept* which is a breed of dog that is quite small and has long hair and . . . and is referred to in English by the term Sheltie." An ontology represents *concepts* rather than *terms*. It is language-independent (the term for a concept in some language is one of the properties of that concept), and it implies that we know something about each concept. The relationships between nodes in an ontology tend to be meaning-based (rather than subset/superset-based), so that an ontology is often referred to as a knowledge representation (as opposed to a classification hierarchy).[19]

---

16 The OWL definition of an ontology is given in *OWL Web Ontology Language Use Cases and Requirements* (Cambridge, MA: World Wide Web Consortium, 2004). Avaliable at http://www.w3.org/TR/webont-req/#onto-def.

17 Probably the most well-known example of a taxonomy is the scientific classification of living things, the *Linnaean taxonomy*. A taxonomy often describes a system of classification.

18 The relationships between concepts in an ontology often form a network rather than a tree.

Now that we have taken our side trip, we can say that RDF lets you describe the properties of resources; RDF-S lets you define which properties are appropriate for describing which resources, and also lets you define a *taxonomy* of resources. OWL,[20] the Web Ontology Language, takes you one step further on the path to meaning by letting you define an *ontology* of resources. This ontology describes the meaning of both resources and properties in RDF statements.

Querying RDF Statements — SPARQL

The RDF Data Access Working Group (DAWG)[21] was tasked with defining how to query over RDF statements. They came up with SPARQL,[22] defined as the SPARQL Protocol And RDF Query Language.[23] SPARQL queries across an *RDF Dataset*, which is a set of one or more RDF graphs (as described above). We give two examples of SPARQL, just to give the reader a general flavor of the language.

Example 18-3 *SPARQL, Simple SELECT*

```
SELECT ?movie
WHERE
  ( ?movie <http://example.org/predicates/isDirectedBy>
           <http://example.org/people/Landis/John/001> )

Returns:

<http://example.org/movie/42>
```

Example 18-3 shows the basic structure of a SPARQL SELECT statement. The WHERE clause is a single triple with a variable (`?movie`) in place of the subject. This statement returns the value of the variable `?movie`, where the triple exists in the RDF Dataset, for any value of ?movie; *i.e.*, the statement returns all movies directed by

---

19 The even more subtle distinction between a taxonomy — a hierarchy of terms — and a thesaurus — a hierarchy of words — is left as an exercise for the reader.

20 *OWL Web Ontology Language Overview* (Cambridge, MA: World Wide Web Consortium, 2004). Avaliable at: http://www.w3.org/TR/owl-features/.

21 http://www.w3.org/2001/sw/DataAccess/.

22 *SPARQL Query Language for RDF* (Cambridge, MA: World Wide Web Consortium, 2005). Available at: http://www.w3.org/TR/rdf-sparql-query/.

23 SQL veterans will recognize this recursive acronym as a nod to the SQL acronym, originally expanded to Structured Query Language or Standard Query Language, and now accepted to be SQL Query Language.

John Landis. Note the superficial resemblance to the SQL `SELECT` statement.

Example 18-4 *Less Simple SELECT*

```
PREFIX pred: <http://example.org/predicates/>
PREFIX dc: < http://purl.org/dc/elements/1.1/>
SELECT ?title
WHERE
  ( ?movie pred:isDirectedBy> <http://example.org/people/Landis/John/001> )
  ( ?movie dc:title ?title )
```

Returns:

```
"An American Werewolf in London"
```

Example 18-4 extends Example 18-3 to return the title of each movie directed by John Landis. Note that the two instances of `?movie` in the two triples in the `WHERE` clause must bind to the same value for the match to happen, effectively giving us a "join" across RDF statements.

In addition to `SELECT`, SPARQL has three other query forms. `CONSTRUCT` returns an RDF graph given a query or a set of triple templates, `DESCRIBE` returns an RDF graph that describes the resources returned by a query, and `ASK` returns yes or no according to whether some statement exists that satisfies the query. Example 18-5 is an `ASK` query that asks whether or not there is some movie directed by John Landis.

Example 18-5 *ASK*

```
PREFIX pred: <http://example.org/predicates/>
PREFIX dc: < http://purl.org/dc/elements/1.1/>
ASK
  ( ?movie <pred:isDirectedBy> <http://example.org/people/Landis/John/001>)
```

Returns:

```
yes
```

SPARQL — YAXQL?

Is SPARQL "Yet Another XML Query Language"? It could be argued that RDF statements can be expressed as XML, and XQuery is a language designed specifically for querying XML, so we should not reinvent the wheel by coming up with a brand new language. There are some practical difficulties in this approach – for example, any given RDF statement can be serialized as XML in many different forms. However, Jonathan Robie showed in his 2001 paper, "The Syntactic Web,"[24] that RDF could be serialized in a *normalized* XML form, allowing us to query it using XQuery. Nonetheless, the Semantic Web people have insisted that what is needed is a comprehensive language that can query over, and return results as, the RDF graphs that underly the XML serialization, just as XQuery queries over, and returns results as, instances of the XQuery Data Model. The answer is left for the reader to ponder – we lean toward the opinion that inventing another query language is a necessary evil.

The Search for Meaning — Still a Long Way to Go

We have only briefly touched on the semantic web here. The efforts to express meaning rather than just data are in their infancy, and while the goals are laudable, the barriers to adoption of the standards described in this section are enormous.[25] People already have a way of expressing meaning to any level of precision and detail that they choose – via human language – and they are generally unwilling to learn a complicated new syntax and vocabulary just to make that meaning machine-understandable. We believe the only way that the semantic web can achieve mass adoption is for machines to be able to translate human language automatically (or perhaps with some human feedback) into machine-understandable form.[26] Once computers can codify meaning from human language, it's a small step to codifying questions and searches into something that will search over that machine-understandable data. RDF, RDF-S, and OWL are a welcome step in the right direction, but we still have a long way to go.

---

24 Jonathan Robie, *The Syntactic Web* (XML 2001 Conference). Available at: http://www.idealliance.org/papers/xml2001/papers/html/03-01-04.html.

25 We should point out that the semantic web folks claim a small but growing number of real-world implementations: see *Testimonials for W3C's Semantic Web Recommendations – RDF and OWL* (Cambridge, MA: World Wide Web Consortium, 2004). Available at: http://www.w3.org/2004/01/sws-testimonial.

26 Codifying meaning in a machine-understandable form, and translating from human language to and from that form, has been a goal of the AI community for many years: see, *e.g.*, Terry Winograd, *Understanding Natural Language* (San Diego, CA: Academic Press, 1972).

18.3.4 The Deep Web — Feel the Width

The title of this section borrows from a 1960s British sitcom about tailors, "Never Mind the Quality, Feel the Width."[27] The title of this sitcom shows the two important dimensions of web search — *quality* (getting the right results, in the right order, for each search), and *width* (searching across all possible web pages). In Section 18.3.1, we suggested that a web spider or crawler can index most of the pages on the web by following the links on a set of seed pages, then following those links to get more "seed" pages, and so on. But this method of crawling misses any page that cannot be reached directly from some link on another page — it misses the so-called *deep web*. As an example of deep web information, the United Airlines website — at http://www.united.com/ — allows you to type in start and end points for a trip, and find available flights and prices. We typed in a round-trip from SFO to BOS, and found that United Airlines 176 services the first leg, for 366.90 USD. Now try finding that same information on Google — *e.g.*, search for "United Airlines 176." It cannot be found! The page showing details of United Airlines flight 176 is not a part of the surface or shallow web, it's part of the deep web.

The deep web consists of all the information that is available on the web, but cannot be found using (most) search engines. Typically, this information is stored in a database, and is available via some database search on the web page — the result is displayed on a dynamic page (a web page created on the fly), and there is no link to that dynamic page from any other page. Some estimates place the amount of information in the deep web at 500 to 1,000 times as much as on the surface web. If we are to achieve universal search, we must be able to search and present this deep web content.

At the time of writing, deep web search is in the research stage.[28] There are two obvious ways to make the deep web available. First, a website administrator can make deep web content available in static pages, and offer it up to search engines via a hidden link — one that the web page user cannot see, but which can be seen and followed by a crawler. This is done most often when the dynamic content in the deep web is really a set of textual web pages that have been stored in a database and retrieved dynamically to support a particular look and feel on the site, or perhaps to maximize reuse of the text. Where

27 http://www.bbc.co.uk/comedy/guide/articles/n/nevermindthequal_1299002290.shtml.

28 http://www.deepwebresearch.info/ is a website that tracks deep web research.

the information is more structured – as in our United Airlines example – this is more difficult and expensive, but still possible. Of course, this requires a development effort to set up, and a maintenance effort to keep the static data in sync with the dynamic data, not to mention additional disk space.

Second, the search engine can mine the deep web using a mixture of heuristics and manual input. Bright Planet[29] and Deep Web Technologies[30] are two companies offering to make deep web content searchable. The techniques include identifying pages with form fields, allowing search administrators to set up stored queries for each form page, and cataloging existing deep websites with useful queries. There is no silver bullet here – there is room for huge improvement, probably involving standards for a web page to identify itself as a deep web portal, and to give hints to the crawler on how to extract the deep web content behind that portal.

18.4 Finding Stuff at Work — Enterprise Search

The Google phenomenon has had a knock-on effect in other areas where people who are not necessarily technically minded need to search for documents (and structured data). Everyone, it seems, has used Google to search the web and wants (and expects) all their search experiences to be just as simple, fast, and accurate as their web search experience. This applies especially to anyone who needs to be able to find documents and data in an enterprise (everyone, it seems, is a "knowledge worker" nowadays).

This expectation seems reasonable enough – if Google can find what I'm looking for out of the bazillion pages on the web, why can't my enterprise search find the competitive analysis whitepaper a colleague wrote last year? But there are a number of qualitative differences between web search and enterprise search.

- Some searches are easier, not harder, when you have a bazillion documents to choose from. When you go to the web and search for "javascript," there is a wealth of good information out there to help you dash off a piece of javascript to

29 Michael K. Bergman, *The Deep Web: Surfacing Hidden Value* (Sioux Falls, SD: Bright Planet, 2001). Available at: http://www.brightplanet.com/technology/deepweb.asp.

30 http://www.deepwebtech.com/.

liven up your web page. There may be thousands of results that would all work equally well for your particular needs. But in an enterprise search, you are often looking for a particular document, and that's the only result that will work for you.

- Link analysis, described briefly in Section 18.3.1, rarely applies in enterprise search. Most enterprise documents are stored in file systems or databases, where there is no URL to examine, no links to count, no link text to read.
- In enterprise search, there is some kind of access restriction (security) on most documents. In web search, there is no concept of security — you search only across publicly available information. In an enterprise, users want to see all the documents they have access to (personally, or by virtue of membership of a group or a role) show up in their search results.

On the other hand, enterprise search is bounded, and the enterprise has (at least in theory) complete control over location, format, and metadata of every document.[31] There is huge potential here for an enterprise search solution that combines the "automatic" high-quality search of Google with the metadata available to an enterprise. The successful enterprise search solution must also be able to search all the different sources in an enterprise — file systems, document repositories, e-mail servers, calendars, applications, *etc.* (the deep enterprise web), and it must respect the various styles and levels of security in the enterprise.

Two companies that have already declared ambitions in this area are Google and Oracle, interesting because they represent opposite starting points. Google are trying to leverage their brand name and technology in web search by selling the Google search appliance.[32] And Oracle is trying to leverage their reputation and expertise in databases and document archives with a product called, at the time of writing, Oracle Enterprise Search.[33]

---

31 Anyone who has been involved in an enterprise search or content management project knows how difficult it is to get authors to add a name and date to each document, let alone enforce a long list of required metadata.

32 http://www.google.com/enterprise/.

33 http://www.oracle.com/technology/products/text/files/trydoingthiswithgoogleowsf04.zip.

18.5 Finding Other People's Stuff — Federated Search

Another area with potential for enormous impact over the next few years is that of federated search. If you want to search data from lots of different sources – websites, databases, document repositories, *etc.* – you can crawl each of those sources in turn, creating one large index, and build a global search. Alternatively, you can take advantage of the fact that many of those sources already have a local search capability, and "federate out" the search to those sources in parallel, merging the results into a final results set. This last step is famously difficult if the search involves full-text retrieval, for there is no way to merge the relevance of results from multiple sources even when the search at each source is executed using the same search engine. When different search engines are used, even results from the *same* source are not comparable. (See Chapter 13, "What's Missing?")

This is an area of enormous potential – imagine moving from a world where every search engine needs to crawl and index every source, to a world where each source is indexed locally. In this federated world, searches across many sources are done in parallel, each source searching itself on behalf of each searcher. A number of attempts were made in the 1990s to get this kind of collaborative search off the ground, the most famous being the Harvester project. For now, the single universal index approach has won out on the web; in the enterprise, federated search is hampered by the lack of standards. But the benefits are enormous:

- Parallel query across any number of sources – degree of parallelization = the number of sources.
- No duplication of effort – each source is "crawled" and indexed only once, which leads to cost savings across an enterprise.
- All data is accessible – each source can crawl and index in the way most appropriate to that source. Deep web data can be made accessible *by* (rather than *from*) the source.

To make this work, we need standards in:

- Query language (of course) – XQuery 1.0 is a good first pass at a standardized definition of the syntax and semantics of a query language that can query (the XML representation of) any data.

- Full-text query – as you read in Chapter 13, XQuery 1.0 does not have any full-text capability (though work on XQuery Full-Text is well under way, with several Public Working Drafts already published, so there is hope here). The queries that are passed from federator to source *must* be full-text queries.
- Result sets – the result passed back from source to query federator must be in a standard format. The syntax (probably an XML schema) and semantics need to be standardized.
- Relevance – the relevance of results should be comparable across sources, so that the federator can merge and order the results correctly. This is hard!

18.6 Finding Services — WSDL, UDDI, WSIL, RDDL

So far we have discussed a number of different kinds of *data* that you might want to find. The web also offers the possibility of finding *services*.

A *web service* is a service provided over the web. Let's say we want to make our movies database available to anyone with a website – we could define a web service that allows anyone to query for information (director, producer, rating, *etc.*) about any movie. The vision is that web services will proliferate in the same way as web pages, so that every operation you might want to perform – finding information about movies, calculating the current time in some city, converting from one currency (or language) to another, *etc.* – could be done by some web service somewhere. When creating a website, or even a web service, you would have access to thousands of existing web services on which to build. Let's look at an example, then review what's available today to help achieve this vision.

First, let's suppose that *we* have built a web service that takes in a movie title and gives back the director, producer, rating, and reviews for that movie (*movie search*). Next, let's suppose that *you* want to build a website selling books and movies and CDs. To attract people to your site (and to encourage them to buy stuff once they get there), you offer a host of information around everything you sell. Your customer types in the title of a movie, and you display a page with links to director, producer, rating, and reviews. When the customer clicks any of these links, the software behind your website merely finds the cheapest available web service that will deliver that information. It could also plug web services together – if your customer is browsing in French, it could use one web service to get movie reviews, and another to translate those reviews into French. During the ordering process, your website might use other web services to calculate currency exchange rates, shipping costs, local applicable taxes, *etc.* This is the dream of reusable (open source) software – that any piece of functionality needs to be written only once – but applied in real time.

Now let's look at the standards that need to be in place to make this all work. First, let's assume that you know that the movie search service exists. Your website software needs to know how to invoke the movie search, what to send it, and what to expect back. WSDL[34] (the Web Services Definition Language) describes exactly that – a standard way to describe, in XML, the API to a web service. If we publish a WSDL document for movie search, you know everything you need to know to use that service.

So how would you find out that the movie search web service exists? There are several possible ways to discover a web service. First, you could look in a web services directory (a sort of yellow pages, or an LDAP[35] server, for web services). UDDI,[36] Universal Description Discovery and Integration, describes a standard way to publish a directory of web services, again as XML. The standard includes an XML Schema for such directories. Both IBM[37] and Microsoft[38] have created UDDI *business registry nodes*. They both have simple user interfaces (UIs) allowing a search for a web service. Using Microsoft's search we found a web service that claims to "Search web services using all UDDI registries." This looks promising! Since both the UDDI entries and the web services they refer to are stored in XML, we would expect XQuery to be used in implementing services search.

An alternative to this centralized, directory lookup method is for each website to "publish" its web services, and make details available upon request. The specification of WSIL (Web Services Inspec-

---

34 *Web Services Description Language (WSDL) 1.1, W3C Note* (Cambridge, MA: World Wide Web Consortium, 2001). Available at: http://www.w3.org/TR/wsdl.

35 Lightweight Directory Access Protocol – see http://rfc.net/rfc1777.html.

36 UDDI Version 3.0.2, UDDI Spec Technical Committee Draft, Dated 20041019. Available at: http://uddi.org/pubs/uddi-v3.0.2-20041019.htm.

37 https://uddi.ibm.com/ubr/registry.html.

38 http://uddi.microsoft.com/default.aspx.

tion Language),[39] which "complements UDDI by facilitating the discovery of services available on Web sites, but which may not be listed yet in a UDDI registry,"[40] came out of a collaboration between IBM and Microsoft.[41]

While UDDI is a centralized directory for web services, and WSIL (and DISCO) operate at the web *server* (site) level, RDDL (Resource Directory Description Language)[42] has been touted as a way of publishing a link to a web service inside a web *page*. RDDL provides a way of adding information about a link on a web page by adding attributes to the XHTML `<a>` element, such as `nature`, `purpose`, and `resource`. So you could do a web search and find a page with a reference to a web service in some `<a>` element.

Publishing and finding (discovering) web services is a problem that, at the the time of writing, does not have a complete solution, though all three areas discussed in this section show promise. UDDI seems an obvious way to publish and find web services. It is seen by many as overly complex, while others think it does not go far enough and would like to see UDDI grow into a full-blown directory service (on the lines of LDAP), capable of holding information such as legal disclaimers, privacy policy, *etc.* Uptake of UDDI has been slow, partly because there are two "central" repositories (at IBM and Microsoft). DISCO and WSIL (at the web server level) and RDDL (at the page level) also show promise, but have seen little uptake. What is needed is a universal search that will find web services programmatically, searching all these forms of web service publishing.

---

39 Specification: Web Services Inspection Language (WS-Inspection) 1.0, IBM, Microsoft (November 2001). Available at: http://www-106.ibm.com/developerworks/webservices/library/ws-wsilspec.html.

40 Peter Brittenham, *An Overview of the Web Services Inspection Language* (June 2002). Available at: http://www-106.ibm.com/developerworks/library/ws-wsilover/index.html.

41 Microsoft also has its own technology for publishing and discovering web services as part of the .NET framework — DISCO. See http://msdn.microsoft.com/msdnmag/issues/02/02/xml/.

42 Jonathan Borden and Tim Bray, *Resource Directory Description Language (RDDL)* (March 2001). Available at: http://www.rddl.org/. See also Jonathan Borden and Tim Bray, *Resource Directory Description Language (RDDL)* (September 2003). Available at: http://www.tbray.org/tag/rddl4.html.

18.7 Finding Stuff in a More Natural Way

So far in this chapter we have discussed *what* is searched (web pages, applications and database data, services) but not *how* it is searched. We have already alluded to the limitations of keyword-based web search. Languages such as XQuery provide rich tools to programmers who build user interfaces, but there is much work to be done on the human interface side of search. Tim Bray provides some motivation for better user interfaces in his "On Search" blog.[43] Certainly the Google paradigm – type in a few keywords and get a long list of URLs to click – is severely limited.[44] Here are some of the search–user interface technologies that are entering the mainstream.

- Smart browsing – lets the user select from a number of different views of the data, presenting each view as a hierarchy. Lets the user "drill down" into a hierarchy, "drill across" to related hierarchies, and combine browsing and searching.
- Classification and categorization – shows search results (or all available data) categorized according to some ontology. Dynamic categorization of search results allows a combination of searching plus browsing your own custom hierarchy.
- Visualization – shows results in a number of ways, not just a flat list. Result sets can be visualized as hyperbolic trees, heat maps, topographic maps, and so on.[45]
- Personalization – when you do a search on the web, the search engine gives you the same result it gives everybody else. But that is changing, as search applications gather more data about you – starting with what you search for and which results you look at.
- Context – search applications are beginning to take notice of the context of the search. If you are currently building a spreadsheet that shows sales of database software by region, then when you look for "California" the search

---

43 Tim Bray, *On Search: UI Archeology* (2003). Available at: http://tbray.org/ongoing/When/200x/2003/07/04/PatMotif.

44 Think Tom Cruise in the movie *Minority Report*.

45 For an overview of visualization of search results, see: Information Visualization with Oracle 10*g* Text, January 2004. Available at: http://www.oracle.com/technology/products/text/pdf/10g_infovis_v1_0.pdf.

engine should show you the latest database software sales for California, not restaurants or airline seats.

The next big challenge in search is to move the burden of expressing a search (and dredging through possible results) from the user to the computer. Instead of asking the user to formulate and run the query that will return precisely the right results, the user should be able to press a button that says "show me something that I would find useful or interesting," or just "Help." The result should be an easily-navigable map of information related to the user's current task.

18.8 Putting It All Together — The Semantic Web+

In this chapter we have indulged in some visioning, imagining what the ultimate search engine might be able to do. It is already a cliché that search has changed most people's daily lives, and enhanced the experiences of the World Wide Web. Efficient, accurate, reliable search is now changing the way many of us do our jobs — from Google's gmail,[46] which rejects the concept of message foldering in favor of a single folder plus search, to the rise of enterprise search software that will allow us to do the same for all the information we consume (mail, files, calendar appointments, database data, news, websites). But search still has a long way to go — most search is still based on either a highly-structured language such as SQL or XQuery, or on keywords plus a small amount of intelligence. We expect that, in the future, you will be able to find information, goods, and services without having to think about how or where to ask for it. The world will host a true semantic web — a web of rich, meaningful content that you can find and consume without asking for it. But we will not predict *when*.

46 http://gmail.com.

Appendix A

The Example

A.1 Introduction

Throughout this book there are examples — XML data, relational data, XQueries, SQL queries, and so on — based on data about a collection of movies. The examples in the chapters of this book are not entirely consistent, since they were produced to illustrate specific points made in the text, and they are not always complete, due to space considerations. The purpose of this appendix is to set out in one place a more complete, consistent set of example data, metadata, and queries. Many of the examples are copied directly from previous chapters, some have been changed only slightly, and some are completely new. An appendix provides more space to lay out more data and queries, but even here we have made some tradeoffs between completeness and trees — some queries, for example, have somewhat arbitrary predicates to reduce the number of results.

We begin by reproducing the movies XML data, showing complete contents for 10 movies. Then we present metadata for the movies data — a possible XML Schema and a DTD. That's followed by the XML data, XML Schema, and DTD for reviews. Then we look at some SQL/XML queries to convert the XML data into relational data and back again. These queries exercise SQL/XML to address a specific task (converting data), and they constitute substantial examples. After the data we present example queries — first XQueries and then

SQL/XML queries. We finish with a complete web application written in XQuery.

The SQL/XML queries in this appendix were tested against an Oracle database, version 10.2.0.1. A fully functional trial copy of the Oracle database can be downloaded for free (after registration) from Oracle's website. We encourage anyone interested in trying the examples for themselves to visit http://www.oracle.com/technology/index.html and download and install Oracle.

The XQueries and the web application were tested against MarkLogic Server version 3.0-3. Mark Logic also offers a fully functional trial copy of its software, with registration. We encourage anyone interested in trying the XQuery examples in this appendix to visit http://marklogic.com/ and download and install the MarkLogic Server. We also used "Altova XMLSpy 2006 Enterprise Edition" and "Stylus Studio 6, XML Enterprise Edition, Release 3" to produce the XML data, metadata, and queries.

Some queries in this appendix have been changed slightly to use vendor-specific syntax or extensions so that they will run in our test environment. The downside is that the examples in this appendix do not exactly match similar examples in the chapters, and they do not all conform to the latest standard syntax. The upside is that they all actually run and yield results against a stated software configuration.

The data and queries in this appendix, plus additional examples and explanations, are available for download from the website for this book's examples, http://xqzone.marklogic.com/queryingxmlbook/.

A.2 Example Data

Throughout the book we have used movie data and review data. In this section we present the data in a number of forms, along with some metadata.

A.2.1 Movies We Own

Most of the examples in this book are based on the data in Data A-1, which might be stored in a file called "movies-we-own.xml." In the interests of saving trees, the data don't include every movie we own, but we have managed to squeeze in all four "Alien" movies, "Animal House," and "An American Werewolf in London" – not a bad selection.

"Movies We Own" XML

Data A—1 *movies-we-own.xml*

```
<?xml version="1.0" encoding="UTF-8"?>
<movies xmlns:xsi="http://www.w3.org/2001/XMLSchema-instance"
xsi:noNamespaceSchemaLocation="movies.xsd">
 <movie myStars="3">
   <title>The Fifth Element</title>
   <yearReleased>1997</yearReleased>
   <director>
     <familyName>Besson</familyName>
     <givenName>Luc</givenName>
   </director>p
   <producer>
     <familyName>Amicarella</familyName>
     <givenName>John</givenName>
     <otherNames>C.</otherNames>
   </producer>
   <producer>
     <familyName>Ledoux</familyName>
     <givenName>Patrice</givenName>
   </producer>
   <producer>
     <familyName>Smith</familyName>
     <givenName>Iain</givenName>
   </producer>
   <runningTime>126</runningTime>
   <studio>Gaument</studio>
   <cast>
     <familyName>Willis</familyName>
     <givenName>Bruce</givenName>
     <maleOrFemale>male</maleOrFemale>
     <character>Korben Dallas</character>
   </cast>
   <cast>
     <familyName>Oldman</familyName>
     <givenName>Gary</givenName>
     <maleOrFemale>male</maleOrFemale>
     <character>Jean-Baptiste Emanuel Zorg</character>
   </cast>
   <cast>
```

```
      <familyName>Holm</familyName>
      <givenName>Ian</givenName>
      <maleOrFemale>male</maleOrFemale>
      <character>Vito Cornelius</character>
    </cast>
    <cast>
      <familyName>Jovovich</familyName>
      <givenName>Milla</givenName>
      <maleOrFemale>female</maleOrFemale>
      <character>Leeloo</character>
    </cast>
    <cast>
      <familyName>Tucker</familyName>
      <givenName>Chris</givenName>
      <maleOrFemale>male</maleOrFemale>
      <character>Ruby Rhod</character>
    </cast>
    <sound>
      <dolbyDigital5.1>true</dolbyDigital5.1>
      <DTS5.1>true</DTS5.1>
      <THX>true</THX>
      <otherSound>English 2-channel, Spanish</otherSound>
    </sound>
    <aspectRatio>2.35:1</aspectRatio>
    <writer>
      <familyName>Besson</familyName>
      <givenName>Luc</givenName>
      <storyOrScreenplay>story</storyOrScreenplay>
    </writer>
    <writer>
      <familyName>Besson</familyName>
      <givenName>Luc</givenName>
      <storyOrScreenplay>screenplay</storyOrScreenplay>
    </writer>
    <writer>
      <familyName>Kamen</familyName>
      <givenName>Robert</givenName>
      <otherNames>Mark</otherNames>
      <storyOrScreenplay>screenplay</storyOrScreenplay>
    </writer>
    <tagLine>It must be found</tagLine>
```

```
  <plotSummary>Two hundred and fifty years in the future, life as we know it is
   threatened by the arrival of Evil. Only the fifth element (played by Milla
   Jovovich) can stop the Evil from extinguishing life, as it tries to do every
   five thousand years. She is helped by ex-soldier, current-cab-driver, Corben
   Dallas (played by Bruce Willis), who is, in turn, helped by Prince/Arsenio
   clone, Ruby Rhod. Unfortunately, Evil is being assisted by Mr. Zorg (Gary
   Oldman), who seeks to profit from the chaos that Evil will bring, and his
   alien mercenaries. </plotSummary>
  <MPAArating>PG-13</MPAArating>
</movie>
<movie myStars="5">
  <title>An American Werewolf in London</title>
  <yearReleased>1981</yearReleased>
  <director>
    <familyName>Landis</familyName>
    <givenName>John</givenName>
  </director>
  <producer>
    <familyName>Folsey</familyName>
    <givenName>George, Jr.</givenName>
    <otherNames/>
  </producer>
  <producer>
    <familyName>Guber</familyName>
    <givenName>Peter</givenName>
    <otherNames/>
  </producer>
  <producer>
    <familyName>Peters</familyName>
    <givenName>Jon</givenName>
    <otherNames/>
  </producer>
  <runningTime>98</runningTime>
  <cast>
    <familyName>Naughton</familyName>
    <givenName>David</givenName>
    <maleOrFemale>male</maleOrFemale>
    <character>David Kessler</character>
  </cast>
  <cast>
    <familyName>Agutter</familyName>
    <givenName>Jenny</givenName>
```

```
      <maleOrFemale>female</maleOrFemale>
      <character>Alex Price</character>
    </cast>
    <cast>
      <familyName>Dunne</familyName>
      <givenName>Griffin</givenName>
      <maleOrFemale>male</maleOrFemale>
      <character>Jack Goodman</character>
    </cast>
    <cast>
      <familyName>Woodvine</familyName>
      <givenName>John</givenName>
      <maleOrFemale>male</maleOrFemale>
      <character>Dr. Hirsch</character>
    </cast>
    <sound>
      <dolbyDigital5.1>true</dolbyDigital5.1>
      <DTS5.1>true</DTS5.1>
      <THX>false</THX>
      <otherSound>Mono</otherSound>
    </sound>
    <aspectRatio>1.85:1</aspectRatio>
    <writer>
      <familyName>Landis</familyName>
      <givenName>John</givenName>
      <storyOrScreenplay>Screenplay</storyOrScreenplay>
    </writer>
    <tagLine>From the director of Animal House - - a different kind of animal. </
     tagLine>
   <plotSummary>It's a rainy night on the Welsh moors.  Two American students on a
     walking tour of Europe trudge on to the next town, when suddenly the air is
     pierced by an unearthly howl... Three weeks later, one is dead, the other is
     in the hospital and the nightmare begins for An American Werewolf in London.
    </plotSummary>
    <MPAArating>R</MPAArating>
</movie>
<movie myStars="3">
    <title>American Graffiti</title>
    <yearReleased>1973</yearReleased>
    <director>
      <familyName>Lucas</familyName>
      <givenName>George</givenName>
```

```
</director>
<producer>
  <familyName>Coppola</familyName>
  <givenName>Francis Ford</givenName>
  <otherNames/>
</producer>
<producer>
  <familyName>Kurtz</familyName>
  <givenName>Gary</givenName>
  <otherNames/>
</producer>
<runningTime>110</runningTime>
<cast>
  <familyName>Dreyfuss</familyName>
  <givenName>Richard</givenName>
  <maleOrFemale>male</maleOrFemale>
  <character>Curt Henderson</character>
</cast>
<cast>
  <familyName>Howard</familyName>
  <givenName>Ronny</givenName>
  <maleOrFemale>male</maleOrFemale>
  <character>Steve Bolander</character>
</cast>
<cast>
  <familyName>Le Mat</familyName>
  <givenName>Paul</givenName>
  <maleOrFemale>male</maleOrFemale>
  <character>John Milner</character>
</cast>
<cast>
  <familyName>Smith</familyName>
  <givenName>Charlie Martin</givenName>
  <maleOrFemale>male</maleOrFemale>
  <character>Terry "The Toad" Fields</character>
</cast>
<sound>
  <dolbyDigital5.1>false</dolbyDigital5.1>
  <DTS5.1>false</DTS5.1>
  <THX>true</THX>
  <otherSound>Dolby Surround, French 2-channel</otherSound>
```

```
    </sound>
    <aspectRatio>2.35:1</aspectRatio>
    <writer>
      <familyName>Lucas</familyName>
      <givenName>George</givenName>
      <storyOrScreenplay>Screenplay</storyOrScreenplay>
    </writer>
    <writer>
      <familyName>Katz</familyName>
      <givenName>Gloria</givenName>
      <storyOrScreenplay>Screenplay</storyOrScreenplay>
    </writer>
    <writer>
      <familyName>Huyck</familyName>
      <givenName>Willard</givenName>
      <storyOrScreenplay>Screenplay</storyOrScreenplay>
    </writer>
    <tagLine>Where were you in '62?</tagLine>
    <plotSummary>The coming of age of four teenagers on their last summer night
     before college.</plotSummary>
    <MPAArating>PG</MPAArating>
  </movie>
  <movie myStars="5">
    <title>American Beauty</title>
    <yearReleased>1999</yearReleased>
    <director>
      <familyName>Mendes</familyName>
      <givenName>Sam</givenName>
    </director>
    <producer>
      <familyName>Cohen</familyName>
      <givenName>Bruce</givenName>
      <otherNames/>
    </producer>
    <producer>
      <familyName>Jinks</familyName>
      <givenName>Dan</givenName>
      <otherNames/>
    </producer>
    <runningTime>121</runningTime>
    <cast>
      <familyName>Spacey</familyName>
```

```
    <givenName>Kevin</givenName>
    <maleOrFemale>male</maleOrFemale>
    <character>Lester Burnham</character>
  </cast>
  <cast>
    <familyName>Bening</familyName>
    <givenName>Annette</givenName>
    <maleOrFemale>female</maleOrFemale>
    <character>Carolyn Burnham</character>
  </cast>
  <cast>
    <familyName>Birch</familyName>
    <givenName>Thora</givenName>
    <maleOrFemale>female</maleOrFemale>
    <character>Jane Burnham</character>
  </cast>
  <cast>
    <familyName>Suvari</familyName>
    <givenName>Mena</givenName>
    <maleOrFemale>female</maleOrFemale>
    <character>Angela Hayes</character>
  </cast>
  <cast>
    <familyName>Bentley</familyName>
    <givenName>Wes</givenName>
    <maleOrFemale>male</maleOrFemale>
    <character>Ricky Fitts</character>
  </cast>
  <sound>
    <dolbyDigital5.1>true</dolbyDigital5.1>
    <DTS5.1>true</DTS5.1>
    <THX>false</THX>
    <otherSound>Dolby Surround</otherSound>
  </sound>
  <aspectRatio>2.35:1</aspectRatio>
  <writer>
    <familyName>Ball</familyName>
    <givenName>Alan</givenName>
    <storyOrScreenplay>Screenplay</storyOrScreenplay>
  </writer>
  <tagLine>...look closer</tagLine>
```

```
  <plotSummary>A man tells his tale of how he turned his miserable life around
   and turned everyone else's upside down as a result.</plotSummary>
  <MPAArating>R</MPAArating>
</movie>
<movie myStars="2">
  <title>Air Force One</title>
  <yearReleased>1997</yearReleased>
  <director>
    <familyName>Peterson</familyName>
    <givenName>Wolfgang</givenName>
  </director>
  <producer>
    <familyName>Bernstein</familyName>
    <givenName>Armyan</givenName>
    <otherNames/>
  </producer>
  <producer>
    <familyName>Peterson</familyName>
    <givenName>Wolfgang</givenName>
    <otherNames/>
  </producer>
  <producer>
    <familyName>Katz</familyName>
    <givenName>Gail</givenName>
    <otherNames/>
  </producer>
  <producer>
    <familyName>Shestack</familyName>
    <givenName>Jon</givenName>
    <otherNames/>
  </producer>
  <runningTime>124</runningTime>
  <cast>
    <familyName>Ford</familyName>
    <givenName>Harrison</givenName>
    <maleOrFemale>male</maleOrFemale>
    <character>James Marshall</character>
  </cast>
  <cast>
    <familyName>Oldman</familyName>
    <givenName>Gary</givenName>
    <maleOrFemale>male</maleOrFemale>
```

```
    <character>Egor Korshunov </character>
  </cast>
  <cast>
    <familyName>Close</familyName>
    <givenName>Glenn</givenName>
    <maleOrFemale>female</maleOrFemale>
    <character>Kathryn Bennett</character>
  </cast>
  <cast>
    <familyName>Macy</familyName>
    <givenName>William H.</givenName>
    <maleOrFemale>male</maleOrFemale>
    <character>Major Caldwell</character>
  </cast>
  <cast>
    <familyName>Matthews</familyName>
    <givenName>Liesel</givenName>
    <maleOrFemale>female</maleOrFemale>
    <character>Alice Marshall</character>
  </cast>
  <cast>
    <familyName>Crewson</familyName>
    <givenName>Wendy</givenName>
    <maleOrFemale>female</maleOrFemale>
    <character>Grace Marshall</character>
  </cast>
  <sound>
    <dolbyDigital5.1>true</dolbyDigital5.1>
    <DTS5.1>false</DTS5.1>
    <THX>false</THX>
    <otherSound>English 2-channel, French, Spanish</otherSound>
  </sound>
  <aspectRatio>2.35:1</aspectRatio>
  <writer>
    <familyName>Marlowe</familyName>
    <givenName>Andrew W.</givenName>
    <storyOrScreenplay>Screenplay</storyOrScreenplay>
  </writer>
  <tagLine>The fate of the nation rests on the courage of one man.</tagLine>
  <plotSummary>A gripping thriller about a steadfast U.S. President who has just
   told the world he will not negotiate with terrorists.  Now, Russian neo-
   nationalists have hijacked Air Force One, and the President is faced with a
```

```
    nearly impossible decision - give in to the terrorists demands or sacrifice
    not only the country's dignity, but the lives of his wife and daughter.
  </plotSummary>
  <MPAArating>R</MPAArating>
</movie>
<movie myStars="4">
  <title>Alien</title>
  <yearReleased>1979</yearReleased>
  <director>
    <familyName>Scott</familyName>
    <givenName>Ridley</givenName>
  </director>
  <producer>
    <familyName>Carroll</familyName>
    <givenName>Gordon</givenName>
    <otherNames/>
  </producer>
  <producer>
    <familyName>Giler</familyName>
    <givenName>David</givenName>
    <otherNames/>
  </producer>
  <runningTime>117</runningTime>
  <cast>
    <familyName>Weaver</familyName>
    <givenName>Sigourney</givenName>
    <maleOrFemale>female</maleOrFemale>
    <character>Ellen Ripley</character>
  </cast>
  <cast>
    <familyName>Skerritt</familyName>
    <givenName>Tom</givenName>
    <maleOrFemale>male</maleOrFemale>
    <character>A. Dallas</character>
  </cast>
  <cast>
    <familyName>Cartwright</familyName>
    <givenName>Veronica</givenName>
    <maleOrFemale>female</maleOrFemale>
    <character>J. Lambert</character>
  </cast>
  <cast>
```

```
    <familyName>Stanton</familyName>
    <givenName>Harry Dean</givenName>
    <maleOrFemale>male</maleOrFemale>
    <character>S. E. Brett</character>
  </cast>
  <cast>
    <familyName>Hurt</familyName>
    <givenName>John</givenName>
    <maleOrFemale>male</maleOrFemale>
    <character>G. E. Kanet</character>
  </cast>
  <sound>
    <dolbyDigital5.1>true</dolbyDigital5.1>
    <DTS5.1>false</DTS5.1>
    <THX>true</THX>
    <otherSound>Dolby Surround, French Surround</otherSound>
  </sound>
  <aspectRatio>2.35:1</aspectRatio>
  <writer>
    <familyName>O'Bannon</familyName>
    <givenName>Dan</givenName>
    <storyOrScreenplay>Story</storyOrScreenplay>
  </writer>
  <writer>
    <familyName>Shusett</familyName>
    <givenName>Ronald</givenName>
    <storyOrScreenplay>Story</storyOrScreenplay>
  </writer>
  <tagLine>In space no one can hear you scream.</tagLine>
  <plotSummary>The terror begins when the crew of the spaceship Nostromo
   investigates a transmission from a desolate planet and makes a horrifying
   discovery - a life form that breeds within a human host.  Now the crew must
   fight not only for its own survival, but for the survival of all mankind.
  </plotSummary>
  <MPAArating>R</MPAArating>
</movie>
<movie myStars="4">
  <title>Aliens</title>
  <yearReleased>1986</yearReleased>
  <director>
    <familyName>Cameron</familyName>
    <givenName>James</givenName>
```

```
  </director>
  <producer>
    <familyName>Hurd</familyName>
    <givenName>Gale Ann</givenName>
    <otherNames/>
  </producer>
  <runningTime>154</runningTime>
  <cast>
    <familyName>Weaver</familyName>
    <givenName>Sigorney</givenName>
    <maleOrFemale>female</maleOrFemale>
    <character>Ellen Ripley</character>
  </cast>
  <cast>
    <familyName>Biehn</familyName>
    <givenName>Micheal</givenName>
    <maleOrFemale>male</maleOrFemale>
    <character>Dwayne Hicks</character>
  </cast>
  <cast>
    <familyName>Reiser</familyName>
    <givenName>Paul</givenName>
    <maleOrFemale>male</maleOrFemale>
    <character>Carter J. Burke</character>
  </cast>
  <sound>
    <dolbyDigital5.1>true</dolbyDigital5.1>
    <DTS5.1>false</DTS5.1>
    <THX>true</THX>
    <otherSound>Dolby Surround</otherSound>
  </sound>
  <aspectRatio>1.85:1</aspectRatio>
  <writer>
    <familyName>Cameron</familyName>
    <givenName>James</givenName>
    <storyOrScreenplay>Story</storyOrScreenplay>
  </writer>
  <writer>
    <familyName>Giler</familyName>
    <givenName>David</givenName>
    <storyOrScreenplay>Story</storyOrScreenplay>
```

```
  </writer>
  <writer>
    <familyName>Hill</familyName>
    <givenName>Walter</givenName>
    <storyOrScreenplay>Story</storyOrScreenplay>
  </writer>
  <tagLine>This time it's war.</tagLine>
  <plotSummary>As the only survivor from mankind's first encounter with the
   monstrous Alien, Ripley's account of the Alien and the fate of her crew are
   received with skepticism - until the mysterious disappearance of colonists on
   LV-426 lead her to join a team of high-tech colonial marines sent in to
   investigate.  </plotSummary>
  <MPAArating>R</MPAArating>
</movie>
<movie myStars="4">
  <title>Alien 3</title>
  <yearReleased>1992</yearReleased>
  <director>
    <familyName>Fincher</familyName>
    <givenName>David</givenName>
  </director>
  <producer>
    <familyName>Carroll</familyName>
    <givenName>Gordon</givenName>
    <otherNames/>
  </producer>
  <producer>
    <familyName>Giler</familyName>
    <givenName>David</givenName>
    <otherNames/>
  </producer>
  <producer>
    <familyName>Hill</familyName>
    <givenName>Walter</givenName>
    <otherNames/>
  </producer>
  <runningTime>115</runningTime>
  <cast>
    <familyName>Weaver</familyName>
    <givenName>Sigourney</givenName>
    <maleOrFemale>female</maleOrFemale>
    <character>Ellen Ripley</character>
```

```
  </cast>
  <cast>
    <familyName>Henriksen</familyName>
    <givenName>Lance</givenName>
    <maleOrFemale>male</maleOrFemale>
    <character>Bishop II</character>
  </cast>
  <cast>
    <familyName>Dutton</familyName>
    <givenName>Charles S.</givenName>
    <maleOrFemale>male</maleOrFemale>
    <character>Dillon</character>
  </cast>
  <sound>
    <dolbyDigital5.1>true</dolbyDigital5.1>
    <DTS5.1>false</DTS5.1>
    <THX>true</THX>
    <otherSound>Dolby Surround, French</otherSound>
  </sound>
  <aspectRatio>2.35:1</aspectRatio>
  <writer>
    <familyName>Ward</familyName>
    <givenName>Vincent</givenName>
    <storyOrScreenplay>Story</storyOrScreenplay>
  </writer>
  <writer>
    <familyName>Giler</familyName>
    <givenName>David</givenName>
    <storyOrScreenplay>Screenplay</storyOrScreenplay>
  </writer>
  <tagLine>The bitch is back</tagLine>
  <plotSummary>Lt. Ripley is the lone survivor when her crippled spaceship crash
   lands on Fiorina 161, a bleak wasteland inhabited by former inmates of the
   planet's maximum security prison.  Ripley's fears that an Alien was aboard her
   craft are confirmed when the mutilated bodies of ex-cons begin to mount.
   Without weapons or modern technology of any kind, Ripley must lead the men
   into battle against the terrifying creature.  And soon she discovers a
   horrifying fact about her link with the Alien, a realization that may compel
   Ripley to try destroying not only the horrific creature, but herself as
   well.</plotSummary>
  <MPAArating>R</MPAArating>
</movie>
<movie myStars="3">
```

```
<title>Alien Resurrection</title>
<yearReleased>1997</yearReleased>
<director>
  <familyName>Jeunet</familyName>
  <givenName>Jean-Pierre</givenName>
</director>
<producer>
  <familyName>Badalato</familyName>
  <givenName>Bill</givenName>
  <otherNames/>
</producer>
<producer>
  <familyName>Carroll</familyName>
  <givenName>Gordon</givenName>
  <otherNames/>
</producer>
<producer>
  <familyName>Giler</familyName>
  <givenName>David</givenName>
  <otherNames/>
</producer>
<producer>
  <familyName>Hill</familyName>
  <givenName>Walter</givenName>
  <otherNames/>
</producer>
<runningTime>108</runningTime>
<cast>
  <familyName>Weaver</familyName>
  <givenName>Sigorney</givenName>
  <maleOrFemale>female</maleOrFemale>
  <character>Ellen Ripley</character>
</cast>
<cast>
  <familyName>Ryder</familyName>
  <givenName>Winona</givenName>
  <maleOrFemale>female</maleOrFemale>
  <character>Annalee Call</character>
</cast>
<cast>
  <familyName>Perlman</familyName>
```

```
    <givenName>Ron</givenName>
    <maleOrFemale>male</maleOrFemale>
    <character>Johner</character>
  </cast>
  <sound>
    <dolbyDigital5.1>true</dolbyDigital5.1>
    <DTS5.1>false</DTS5.1>
    <THX>true</THX>
    <otherSound>Dolby Surround, French</otherSound>
  </sound>
  <aspectRatio>2.35:1</aspectRatio>
  <writer>
    <familyName>Whedon</familyName>
    <givenName>Joss</givenName>
    <storyOrScreenplay>Screenplay</storyOrScreenplay>
  </writer>
  <tagLine>Witness the resurrection</tagLine>
  <plotSummary>Ellen Ripley died fighting the perfect predator.  Two hundred
   years and eight horrific experiments later, she's back.  A group of scientists
   has cloned her - along with the alien queen inside her - hoping to breed the
   ultimate weapon.  But the resurrected Ripley is full of surprises for her
   "creators," as are the aliens.  And soon, a lot more than "all hell" breaks
   loose!   To combat the creatures, Ripley must team up with a band of
   smugglers, including a mechanic named Call, who holds more than a few
   surprises of her own.</plotSummary>
  <MPAArating>R</MPAArating>
</movie>
<movie myStars="5">
  <title>Animal House</title>
  <yearReleased>1978</yearReleased>
  <director>
    <familyName>Landis</familyName>
    <givenName>John</givenName>
  </director>
  <producer>
    <familyName>Simmons</familyName>
    <givenName>Matty</givenName>
    <otherNames/>
  </producer>
  <producer>
    <familyName>Reitman</familyName>
    <givenName>Ivan</givenName>
```

```
  <otherNames/>
</producer>
<runningTime>109</runningTime>
<cast>
  <familyName>Belushi</familyName>
  <givenName>John</givenName>
  <maleOrFemale>male</maleOrFemale>
  <character>John 'Bluto' Blutarsky </character>
</cast>
<cast>
  <familyName>Matheson</familyName>
  <givenName>Tim</givenName>
  <maleOrFemale>male</maleOrFemale>
  <character>Eric 'Otter' Stratton</character>
</cast>
<cast>
  <familyName>Vernon</familyName>
  <givenName>John</givenName>
  <maleOrFemale>male</maleOrFemale>
  <character>Vernon Wormer </character>
</cast>
<sound>
  <dolbyDigital5.1>false</dolbyDigital5.1>
  <DTS5.1>false</DTS5.1>
  <THX>false</THX>
  <otherSound>English 2-channel mono, French 2-channel mono, Spanish 2-channel
 mono </otherSound>
</sound>
<aspectRatio>1.85:1</aspectRatio>
<writer>
  <familyName>Kenney</familyName>
  <givenName>Douglas</givenName>
  <storyOrScreenplay>Screenplay</storyOrScreenplay>
</writer>
<writer>
  <familyName>Ramis</familyName>
  <givenName>Harold</givenName>
  <storyOrScreenplay>Screenplay</storyOrScreenplay>
</writer>
<writer>
  <familyName>Miller</familyName>
  <givenName>Chris</givenName>
```

```
    <storyOrScreenplay>Screenplay</storyOrScreenplay>
   </writer>
   <tagLine>It was the Deltas against the rules... the rules lost!</tagLine>
   <plotSummary>At a 1962 College, Dean Vernon Wormer is determined to expel the
    Delta House Fraternity, but those roughhousers have other plans for him.
   </plotSummary>
   <MPAArating>R</MPAArating>
  </movie>
</movies>
```

"Movies We Own" Schema

Data A-2 is one possible XML Schema for the data in Data A-1.

There are a number of decisions to be made when creating an XML Schema. Some have an effect on the variations in data that can be "caught" by schema validation, others are largely a question of style. For example, in Example 1-6, we defined an element for each of `givenName` and `familyName` and referenced those elements in `producer`, `director`, `writer`, and `cast`. In Data A-2, on the other hand, we chose to create a type for `person` and then to define `producer`, `director`, `writer`, and `cast` to be of type `person` (sometimes with extensions).

We have included a liberal sprinkling of comments in the schema. There are two possible styles of comment in a schema – either you can use the schema style (add an annotation element with a documentation child) or, since the schema is an XML document, you can use XML comments (`<!-- like this -->`). The annotation element lends itself to easier querying (if you want to do XQueries against comments in your schema), and its contents show up in the *schema design view* in XMLSpy. But the XML comments are simpler and less verbose, so we chose the XML comment style. Note that comments are very necessary in a schema – the schema supplies lots of information about syntax, but the schema author still needs to document syntax and style choices, and the semantics underlying the data.

When writing and testing the schema, we were reminded just how useful a schema is – in the original movies data, there was a near-even split between "Male" and "male," "Female" and "female," "Story" and "story," "Screenplay" and "screenplay." The enumeration in the schema caught that inconsistency. If there were no schema and the inconsistency had not been caught, queries would not fail but they would silently give "wrong" answers.

Of course, there are a number of ways that the same data can be represented in a schema. We have already mentioned that we abstracted out `persons`, for example. Similarly, there are a number of ways to represent the same data in an XML document. As one example, in movies-we-own `storyOrScreenplay` is a child of `writer`. We could have decided to make `story` and `screenplay` children of `movie`, each with a `writer` child.

Finally, take a look at the schema definition of `plotSummary`. Here is an example of presentation markup — a `plotSummary` contains text with an arbitrary number of `emph` tags bracketing parts of the text.

Data A—2 *movies-we-own.xsd*

```
<?xml version="1.0" encoding="UTF-8"?>
<xs:schema xmlns:xs="http://www.w3.org/2001/XMLSchema"
  elementFormDefault="qualified" attributeFormDefault="unqualified">
 <!-- Define a complexType "person" to be used for director, producer, etc.
      Defining the type once here saves typing and ensures consistency. -->
 <xs:complexType name="person">
   <xs:sequence>
     <xs:element name="familyName" type="xs:string"/>
     <!-- Every person is known by at least one name. If only a single name
          is used, then it appears as the familyName (even if the single
          name is derived from the person's given name). -->
     <xs:element name="givenName" type="xs:string" nillable="true"/>
     <!-- givenName is always present, but might be specified as
          xsi:nil="true". -->
     <xs:element name="otherNames" type="xs:string" nillable="true"
       minOccurs="0"/>
     <!-- otherNames might include middle names, or might be absent
          entirely. -->
   </xs:sequence>
 </xs:complexType>
 <xs:element name="movies">
   <!-- Root of a movies "database" -->
   <xs:complexType>
     <xs:sequence>
       <xs:element name="movie" maxOccurs="unbounded">
         <!-- Individual movie -->
         <xs:complexType>
           <xs:sequence>
```

```
<xs:element name="title" type="xs:string">
  <!-- The title of a movie; title and yearReleased together
       form a key -->
</xs:element>
<xs:element name="yearReleased">
<!-- The year in which a movie was first released in the USA;
     title and yearReleased together form a key -->
<!-- We want to guard against faulty data for this element,
     but do not want to enumerate every possible value, so we
     use a range of integers. Note: type xs:gYear (Gregorian
     Year) would work too, but for this range xs:integer is
     just as good. -->
  <xs:simpleType>
    <xs:restriction base="xs:integer">
      <xs:minInclusive value="1900"/>
      <xs:maxInclusive value="2100"/>
    </xs:restriction>
  </xs:simpleType>
</xs:element>
<xs:element name="alternateTitle" type="xs:string"
  minOccurs="0" maxOccurs="unbounded"/>
<!-- Some films, but not all, have alternate titles. -->
<xs:element name="director" type="person"
  maxOccurs="unbounded"/>
<!-- A director is a person. Using the type attribute saves
     having to describe a person (givenName, familyName,
     otherNames) again here -->
<!-- All movies have at least one director. -->
<xs:element name="producer" type="person"
  maxOccurs="unbounded"/>
<!-- All films have at least one producer; all variations of
     producer (e.g., Executive Procedure) are included in this
     element. -->
<xs:element name="runningTime" type="xs:positiveInteger"
  nillable="true"/>
<!-- Running time of the film in minutes, based on the USA
     release. If the running time is not known, then this
     element specifies xsi:nil="true".  -->
<xs:element name="studio" type="xs:string" minOccurs="0"
  maxOccurs="unbounded"/>
<!-- Every film is produced by a studio or is an independent
```

```
     film. There may be multiple studios specified, or this
     element may be absent.  -->
<!-- this element is a candidate for enumeration, if we know
     up-front all possible studio names. Enumeration protects
     against spelling mistakes, typos, and variations
     ("Warner Bros." vs. "Warner" vs. "Warner Brothers"). -->
<xs:element name="cast" id="id" maxOccurs="unbounded">
  <!-- The cast includes all actors and actresses, may include
       animals or even other entities such as robots. -->
  <!-- A cast member is a person, but with some additional
       information -->
  <xs:complexType>
    <xs:complexContent>
      <xs:extension base="person">
        <xs:sequence>
          <xs:element name="maleOrFemale">
            <!-- This element indicates the cast member's sex:
                 male, female, none, or unknown -->
            <xs:simpleType>
              <xs:restriction base="xs:string">
                <xs:enumeration value="male"/>
                <xs:enumeration value="female"/>
                <xs:enumeration value="none"/>
                <xs:enumeration value="unknown"/>
              </xs:restriction>
            </xs:simpleType>
          </xs:element>
          <xs:element name="character" type="xs:string"
            maxOccurs="unbounded"/>
          <!-- The name of the character (or, if there are
               multiple copies, characters played by this cast
               member). -->
          <!-- This element might work better as type
               "person", but that would rule out "second tough
               guy in bar" -->
        </xs:sequence>
      </xs:extension>
    </xs:complexContent>
  </xs:complexType>
</xs:element>
<xs:element name="sound">
```

```
        <xs:complexType>
          <xs:sequence>
            <xs:element name="dolbyDigital5.1" type="xs:boolean"/>
            <xs:element name="DTS5.1" type="xs:boolean"/>
            <xs:element name="THX" type="xs:boolean"/>
            <xs:element name="otherSound" type="xs:string"
              minOccurs="0" maxOccurs="unbounded"/>
          </xs:sequence>
        </xs:complexType>
      </xs:element>
      <xs:element name="aspectRatio" type="xs:string"
        default="4:3"/>
      <!-- The aspectRatio element identifies the aspect ratio in
           which the movie was originally produced; this might be
           4:3 for ordinary television framing, or it might be
           2.35:1 or some other widescreen framing. -->
      <xs:element name="writer" maxOccurs="unbounded">
        <!-- Every movie has at least one writer, frequently more
             than one. -->
        <!-- A writer is a "person", with some additional
             information -->
        <xs:complexType>
          <xs:complexContent>
            <xs:extension base="person">
              <xs:sequence>
                <xs:element name="storyOrScreenplay">
                  <!-- This element should be "story" if the writer
                       is credited for the story or a novel on which
                       the movie is based; otherwise, it should be
                       "screenplay". -->
                  <xs:simpleType>
                    <xs:restriction base="xs:string">
                      <xs:enumeration value="story"/>
                      <xs:enumeration value="screenplay"/>
                    </xs:restriction>
                  </xs:simpleType>
                </xs:element>
              </xs:sequence>
            </xs:extension>
          </xs:complexContent>
        </xs:complexType>
```

```
            </xs:element>
            <xs:element name="tagLine" type="xs:string"
              maxOccurs="unbounded"/>
            <!-- The "tag line" by which the movie has been advertised;
                 often a "sound bit" that is used in television ads. -->
            <xs:element name="plotSummary">
              <!-- The plot summary for the movie, taken from a source
                   such as iMDB.com or the box in which a DVD or VHS tape
                   is stored. -->
              <xs:complexType mixed="true">
                <xs:sequence minOccurs="0">
                  <xs:element name="emph" maxOccurs="unbounded">
                    <xs:annotation>
                      <xs:documentation>Used for italics within the
                        content of a plotSummary</xs:documentation>
                    </xs:annotation>
                  </xs:element>
                </xs:sequence>
              </xs:complexType>
            </xs:element>
            <xs:element name="MPAArating" nillable="true">
              <!-- The MPAA rating. If the film has not been rated by the
                   MPAA, then xsi:nil="true". -->
              <xs:simpleType>
                <xs:restriction base="xs:string">
                  <xs:enumeration value="G"/>
                  <xs:enumeration value="PG"/>
                  <xs:enumeration value="PG-13"/>
                  <xs:enumeration value="R"/>
                  <xs:enumeration value="NC-17"/>
                  <xs:enumeration value="X"/>
                </xs:restriction>
              </xs:simpleType>
            </xs:element>
          </xs:sequence>
          <xs:attribute name="myStars" type="xs:integer" use="optional"/>
        </xs:complexType>
      </xs:element>
    </xs:sequence>
  </xs:complexType>
 </xs:element>
</xs:schema>
```

"Movies We Own" DTD

The DTD in Data A-3 is based on the DTD produced from Data A-2 by XMLSpy. Note how much richness is lost when going from XML Schema to DTD.

Data A—3 *movies-we-own.dtd*

```
<?xml version="1.0" encoding="UTF-8"?>
<!ELEMENT familyName (#PCDATA)>
<!ELEMENT givenName (#PCDATA)>
<!ELEMENT otherNames (#PCDATA)>
<!ELEMENT movies (movie+)>
<!ELEMENT movie (title, yearReleased, alternateTitle*, director+,
  producer+, runningTime, studio*, cast+, sound, aspectRatio, writer+,
  tagLine+, plotSummary, MPAArating)>
<!ATTLIST movie
 myStars NMTOKEN #IMPLIED>
<!ELEMENT title (#PCDATA)>
<!ELEMENT yearReleased (#PCDATA)>
<!ELEMENT alternateTitle (#PCDATA)>
<!ELEMENT director (familyName, givenName, otherNames?)>
<!ELEMENT producer (familyName, givenName, otherNames?)>
<!ELEMENT runningTime (#PCDATA)>
<!ELEMENT studio (#PCDATA)>
<!ELEMENT cast ((familyName, givenName, otherNames?), (maleOrFemale,
  character+))>
<!ELEMENT maleOrFemale (#PCDATA)>
<!ELEMENT character (#PCDATA)>
<!ELEMENT sound (dolbyDigital5.1, DTS5.1, THX, otherSound*)>
<!ELEMENT dolbyDigital5.1 (#PCDATA)>
<!ELEMENT DTS5.1 (#PCDATA)>
<!ELEMENT THX (#PCDATA)>
<!ELEMENT otherSound (#PCDATA)>
<!ELEMENT aspectRatio (#PCDATA)>
<!ELEMENT writer ((familyName, givenName, otherNames?),
  (storyOrScreenplay))>
<!ELEMENT storyOrScreenplay (#PCDATA)>
<!ELEMENT tagLine (#PCDATA)>
<!ELEMENT plotSummary (#PCDATA | emph)*>
<!ELEMENT emph ANY>
<!ELEMENT MPAArating (#PCDATA)>
```

"Movies We Own" SQL Tables for XML Data

When considering a storage/representation strategy for XML data, you need to consider what constitutes a *document*. There are two obvious strategies for the movies data — a document could be all the movies wrapped in a single `<movies>` tag, or it could be a set of documents, each representing a single movie. These two options are illustrated by the `ALL_MOVIES_XML` table (Data A-4) and the `MOVIES_XML` table (Data A-5) respectively. In both examples, we create a SQL table and store the data *natively* in a column of type `XMLType`. Again, the syntax throughout this appendix is vendor-specific (the SQL standard calls the special XML type "XML," for example).

Data A—4 *movies-we-own XML Table (1): ALL_MOVIES_XML*

```
CREATE TABLE all_movies_xml (
  ID                  INT ,
  ALL_MOVIES          XMLType
)
/
-- requires CREATE DIRECTORY privilege
CREATE DIRECTORY xmldir AS 'C:\stage'
/
INSERT INTO all_movies_xml (
  ID ,
  ALL_MOVIES
  )
VALUES (
  1 ,
  XMLType( bfilename('XMLDIR', 'movies-we-own.xml'),
           nls_charset_id('AL32UTF8') )
  )
/
```

Data A—5 *movies-we-own XML Table (2): MOVIES_XML*

```
Table Description:

 Name                                       Type
 ----------------------------------------- ---------------
 ID                                         NUMBER
 MOVIE                                      SYS.XMLTYPE
```

Create and populate the table:

```
CREATE SEQUENCE movies_id_seq
/
CREATE TABLE movies_xml AS (
  SELECT
    movies_id_seq.nextval as id,
    result.column_value AS movie
  FROM
    all_movies_xml ,
    XMLTABLE(
      'for $m in
        $col/movies/movie
      return
        $m'
      PASSING all_movies_xml.all_movies AS "col"
    ) AS result
  )
/
```

"Movies We Own" SQL Tables for Relational Data

The data in Data A-1 could be stored as relational data (as well as, or instead of, XML data) in SQL tables. In this section we present one possible representation. For each table we show a `CREATE TABLE` statement followed by a listing of the data in that table. For the largest table (`MOVIES`) we have split the data into three separate listings. Note that the `CREATE TABLE` statements use Oracle, rather than standard SQL, syntax. For example, some columns are of type `VARCHAR2` rather than `CHARACTER VARYING`. There is some other proprietary syntax (such as `CREATE DIRECTORY` and `CREATE SEQUENCE`) — if you want to run these samples on a database from some vendor other than Oracle, you'll need to work around these differences.

The main table, `MOVIES`, has a column for each property of a movie, minus repeating properties. Data A-6 shows how to create `MOVIES` and populate it from the data in the `MOVIES_XML` table. Note that `MOVIES`, and the other SQL tables we present, could be created as a view instead of a table.

***Data A—6** MOVIES Table*

Table Description:

```
Name                                      Type
----------------------------------------- -----------------
ID                                        NUMBER
TITLE                                     VARCHAR2(40)
MY_STARS                                  NUMBER
YEAR_RELEASED                             NUMBER
RUNNING_TIME                              NUMBER
STUDIO                                    VARCHAR2(60)
TAGLINE                                   VARCHAR2(200)
PLOT_SUMMARY                              VARCHAR2(1000)
MPAA_RATING                               VARCHAR2(5)
ASPECT_RATIO                              VARCHAR2(8)
```

Create and populate the table:

```
DROP SEQUENCE movies_seq
/
CREATE SEQUENCE movies_seq
/
DROP TABLE movies
/
CREATE TABLE movies AS (
SELECT
  movies_seq.nextval AS id,
  m.*
FROM dual d,
(
  SELECT
    result.*
  FROM
    movies_xml ,
    XMLTABLE(
      '$col/movie'
      PASSING movies_xml.movie AS "col"
      COLUMNS
        "TITLE"            VARCHAR(40)   PATH 'title' ,
        "MY_STARS"         INTEGER       PATH '@myStars' ,
        "YEAR_RELEASED"    INTEGER       PATH 'yearReleased' ,
```

```
        "RUNNING_TIME"      INTEGER        PATH 'runningTime' ,
        "STUDIO"            VARCHAR(60)    PATH 'studio' ,
        "TAGLINE"           VARCHAR(200)   PATH 'tagLine' ,
        "PLOT_SUMMARY"      VARCHAR(1000)  PATH 'plotSummary' ,
        "MPAA_RATING"       VARCHAR(5)     PATH 'MPAARating' ,
        "ASPECT_RATIO"      VARCHAR(8)     PATH 'aspectRatio' ,
        "DOLBY_DIGITAL_51"  VARCHAR(5)     PATH 'sound/dolbyDigital5.1' ,
        "DTS_51"            VARCHAR(5)     PATH 'sound/DTS5.1' ,
        "THX"               VARCHAR(5)     PATH 'sound/THX' ,
        "OTHER_SOUND"       VARCHAR(80)    PATH 'sound/otherSound'
    ) AS result
  ORDER BY
    result.title
  ) m
)
/
```

```
 Name                                      Type
 ----------------------------------------- --------------------
 ID                                        NUMBER
 TITLE                                     VARCHAR2(40)
 MY_STARS                                  NUMBER
 YEAR_RELEASED                             NUMBER
 RUNNING_TIME                              NUMBER
 STUDIO                                    VARCHAR2(60)
 TAGLINE                                   VARCHAR2(200)
 PLOT_SUMMARY                              VARCHAR2(1000)
 MPAA_RATING                               VARCHAR2(5)
 ASPECT_RATIO                              VARCHAR2(8)
 DOLBY_DIGITAL_51                          VARCHAR2(5)
 DTS_51                                    VARCHAR2(5)
 THX                                       VARCHAR2(5)
 OTHER_SOUND                               VARCHAR2(80)
```

Table contents (shown as 3 tables to fit the page):

```
ID  TITLE                 MY_STARS YEAR_RELEASED RUNNING_TIME MPAA_ ASPECT
--- -------------------- -------- ------------- ------------ ----- ------
  1 Air Force One               2          1997          124 R     2.35:1
  2 Alien                       4          1979          117 R     2.35:1
  3 Alien 3                     4          1992          115 R     2.35:1
```

```
  4 Alien Resurrection           3          1997         108 R      2.35:1
  5 Aliens                       4          1986         154 R      1.85:1
  6 American Beauty              5          1999         121 R      2.35:1
  7 American Graffiti            3          1973         110 PG     2.35:1
  8 An American Werewolf         5          1981          98 R      1.85:1
     in London
  9 Animal House                 5          1978         109 R      1.85:1
 10 The Fifth Element            3          1997         126 PG-13 2.35:1

ID  STUDIO            DOLBY DTS_5 THX   OTHER_SOUND
--- ----------------- ----- ----- ----- ----------------------------------
  1                   true  false false English 2-channel, French, Spanish
  2 20th Century Fox  true  false true  Dolby Surround, French Surround
  3 20th Century Fox  true  false true  Dolby Surround, French
  4 20th Century Fox  true  false true  Dolby Surround, French
  5 20th Century Fox  true  false true  Dolby Surround
  6                   true  true  false Dolby Surround
  7 Universal Studios false false true  Dolby Surround, French 2-channel
  8 Universal Studios true  true  false Mono
  9                   false false false English 2-channel mono, French 2-ch
                                        annel mono, Spanish 2-channel mono

 10 Tristar Studios   true  true  true  English 2-channel, Spanish


ID  TAGLINE                        PLOT_SUMMARY
--- ------------------------------ ----------------------------------------
  1 It must be found               Two hundred and fifty years in the futur
                                   e, life as ...

  2 From the director of Animal Ho Its a rainy night on the Welsh moors.  T
    use - - a different kind of an wo America ...
    imal.

  3 Where were you in 62?          The coming of age of four teenagers on t
                                   heir last  ...

  4 ...look closer                 A man tells his tale of how he turned hi
                                   s miserabl ...

  5 The fate of the nation rests o A gripping thriller about a steadfast U.
```

```
   n the courage of one man.        S. Preside ...

 6 In space no one can hear you s  The terror begins when the crew of the s
   cream.                          paceship N ...

 7 This time its war.              As the only survivor from mankinds first
                                    encounter ...

 8 The bitch is back               Lt. Ripley is the lone survivor when her
                                    crippled  ...

 9 Witness the resurrection        Ellen Ripley died fighting the perfect p
                                   redator.    ...

10 It was the Deltas against the   At a 1962 College, Dean Vernon Wormer is
   rules... the rules lost!         determine ...
```

Of course, you could split the `MOVIES` table into any number of tables — for example, it might be useful to split the sound fields into their own table.

In the body of the book, we created tables for producers and directors. In this appendix, we decided to abstract out all the persons into a single table, and then to create tracking tables to link producers with movies, directors with movies, writers with movies, and cast with movies. SQL readers will be familiar with this notion of *normalizing* data so that common facts (such as a person's names) are stored only once, no matter how many roles and movies he is associated with. Data A-7 through Data A-11 create and populate these tables from the data in the `MOVIES_XML` table.

***Data A—7** PERSONS Table*

```
Table Description:

Name                                      Type
----------------------------------------- ---------------
ID                                        NUMBER
FAMILY_NAME                               VARCHAR2(12)
GIVEN_NAME                                VARCHAR2(12)
OTHER_NAMES                               VARCHAR2(12)
```

Create and populate the table:

```
DROP SEQUENCE persons_seq
/
CREATE SEQUENCE persons_seq
/
DROP TABLE persons
/
CREATE TABLE persons AS (
SELECT persons_seq.nextval AS id, p.*
FROM dual d,
(
  SELECT DISTINCT
    result.family_name,
    result.given_name,
    result.other_Names
  FROM
    movies_xml ,
    XMLTABLE(
      '($col//producer, $col//director, $col//cast, $col//writer)'
      PASSING movies_xml.movie AS "col"
      COLUMNS
        "FAMILY_NAME" VARCHAR(12) PATH 'familyName' ,
        "GIVEN_NAME"  VARCHAR(12) PATH 'givenName' DEFAULT '' ,
        "OTHER_NAMES" VARCHAR(12) PATH 'otherNames' DEFAULT ''
    ) AS result
  ORDER BY
    result.family_name
  ) p
)
/
```

Table contents:

```
ID FAMILY_NAME  GIVEN_NAME   OTHER_NAMES
--- ------------ ------------ ------------
  1 Agutter      Jenny
  2 Amicarella   John         C.
  3 Badalato     Bill
  4 Ball         Alan
  5 Belushi      John
```

```
 6 Bening       Annette
 7 Bentley      Wes
 8 Bernstein    Armyan
 9 Besson       Luc
10 Biehn        Michael
11 Birch        Thora
12 Cameron      James
13 Carroll      Gordon
14 Cartwright   Veronica
15 Close        Glenn
16 Cohen        Bruce
17 Coppola      Francis Ford
18 Crewson      Wendy
19 Dreyfuss     Richard
20 Dunne        Griffin
21 Dutton       Charles S.
22 Fincher      David
23 Folsey       George, Jr.
24 Ford         Harrison
25 Giler        David
26 Guber        Peter
27 Henriksen    Lance
28 Hill         Walter
29 Holm         Ian
30 Howard       Ronny
31 Hurd         Gale Ann
32 Hurt         John
33 Huyck        Willard
34 Jeunet       Jean-Pierre
35 Jinks        Dan
36 Jovovich     Milla
37 Kamen        Robert        Mark
38 Katz         Gail
39 Katz         Gloria
40 Kenney       Douglas
41 Kurtz        Gary
42 Landis       John
43 Le Mat       Paul
44 Ledoux       Patrice
45 Lucas        George
46 Macy         William H.
```

```
47 Marlowe      Andrew W.
48 Matheson     Tim
49 Matthews     Liesel
50 Mendes       Sam
51 Miller       Chris
52 Naughton     David
53 O'Bannon     Dan
54 Oldman       Gary
55 Perlman      Ron
56 Peters       Jon
57 Peterson     Wolfgang
58 Ramis        Harold
59 Reiser       Paul
60 Reitman      Ivan
61 Ryder        Winona
62 Scott        Ridley
63 Shestack     Jon
64 Shusett      Ronald
65 Simmons      Matty
66 Skerritt     Tom
67 Smith        Charlie Mart
68 Smith        Iain
69 Spacey       Kevin
70 Stanton      Harry Dean
71 Suvari       Mena
72 Tucker       Chris
73 Vernon       John
74 Ward         Vincent
75 Weaver       Sigourney
76 Whedon       Joss
77 Willis       Bruce
78 Woodvine     John
```

Data A—8 *movies-we-own Tables: MOVIES_PRODUCERS*

```
Table Description:

Name                                       Type
------------------------------------------ --------
MOVIE_ID                                   NUMBER
PRODUCER_ID                                NUMBER
```

Create and populate the table:

```
DROP TABLE movies_producers
/
CREATE TABLE movies_producers AS (
SELECT
  movies.id AS movie_id ,
  persons.id AS producer_id
FROM
  persons ,
  movies ,
  movies_xml ,
    XMLTABLE(
      'for $p in $col/movie/producer
       return
         <producer-info>
           <movie-title>{ $p/../title }</movie-title>
           <movie-year-released>{
               $p/../yearReleased }</movie-year-released>
           <family>{ $p/familyName }</family>
           <given>{ $p/givenName }</given>
           <other>{ $p/otherNames }</other>
         </producer-info>'
      PASSING movies_xml.movie AS "col"
      COLUMNS
        "TITLE" VARCHAR(100) PATH '/producer-info/movie-title' ,
        "YEAR_RELEASED" VARCHAR(100) PATH '/producer-info/movie-year-released' ,
        "FAMILY_NAME" VARCHAR(100) PATH '/producer-info/family' ,
        "GIVEN_NAME" VARCHAR(100) PATH '/producer-info/given' DEFAULT '' ,
        "OTHER_NAMES" VARCHAR(100) PATH '/producer-info/other' DEFAULT ''
    ) AS result
WHERE
  result.title = movies.title and
  result.year_released = movies.year_released and
  result.family_name = persons.family_name and
  result.given_name = persons.given_name
)
/
```

Table contents:

```
  MOVIE_ID PRODUCER_ID
---------- -----------
         1          63
         1          38
         1          57
         1           8
         2          25
         2          13
         3          28
         3          25
         3          13
         4          25
         4           3
         4          28
         4          13
         5          31
         6          16
         6          35
         7          41
         7          17
         8          23
         8          26
         8          56
         9          65
         9          60
        10           2
        10          44
        10          68
```

Data A—9 *movies-we-own Tables: MOVIES_DIRECTORS*

Table Description:

```
Name                                      Type
----------------------------------------- ---------
MOVIE_ID                                  NUMBER
DIRECTOR_ID                               NUMBER
```

Create and populate the table:

```
DROP TABLE movies_directors
/
CREATE TABLE movies_directors AS (
SELECT
  movies.id AS movie_id ,
  persons.id AS director_id
FROM
  persons ,
  movies ,
  movies_xml ,
    XMLTABLE(
      'for $d in $col/movie/director
       return
         <director-info>
           <movie-title>{ $d/../title }</movie-title>
           <movie-year-released>{ $d/../yearReleased }</movie-year-released>
           <family>{ $d/familyName }</family>
           <given>{ $d/givenName }</given>
           <other>{ $d/otherNames }</other>
         </director-info>'
      PASSING movies_xml.movie AS "col"
      COLUMNS
        "TITLE" VARCHAR(100) PATH '/director-info/movie-title' ,
        "YEAR_RELEASED" VARCHAR(100) PATH '/director-info/movie-year-released' ,
        "FAMILY_NAME" VARCHAR(100) PATH '/director-info/family' ,
        "GIVEN_NAME" VARCHAR(100) PATH '/director-info/given' DEFAULT '' ,
        "OTHER_NAMES" VARCHAR(100) PATH '/director-info/other' DEFAULT ''
    ) AS result
WHERE
  result.title = movies.title and
  result.year_released = movies.year_released and
  result.family_name = persons.family_name and
  result.given_name = persons.given_name
)
/
```

Table contents:

```
  MOVIE_ID DIRECTOR_ID
---------- -----------
         1          57
         2          62
         3          22
         4          34
         5          12
         6          50
         7          45
         8          42
         9          42
        10           9
```

Data A—10 *movies-we-own Tables: MOVIES_CAST*

Table Description:

```
 Name                                      Type
 ----------------------------------------- --------------------
 MOVIE_ID                                  NUMBER
 CAST_ID                                   NUMBER
 MF                                        VARCHAR2(6)
 CHARACTER                                 VARCHAR2(100)
```

Create and populate the table:

```
DROP TABLE movies_cast
/
DROP TABLE movies_cast
/
CREATE TABLE movies_cast AS (
SELECT
  movies.id AS movie_id ,
  persons.id AS cast_id ,
  result.mf AS mf ,
  result.character AS character
FROM
  persons ,
  movies ,
```

```
  movies_xml ,
    XMLTABLE(
      'for $c in $col/movie/cast
       return
         <cast-info>
           <movie-title>{ $c/../title }</movie-title>
           <movie-year-released>{$c/../yearReleased}</movie-year-released>
           <family>{ $c/familyName }</family>
           <given>{ $c/givenName }</given>
           <other>{ $c/otherNames }</other>
           <maleOrFemale>{ $c/maleOrFemale }</maleOrFemale>
           <character>{ $c/character }</character>
         </cast-info>'
      PASSING movies_xml.movie AS "col"
      COLUMNS
        "TITLE" VARCHAR(100) PATH '/cast-info/movie-title' ,
        "YEAR_RELEASED" VARCHAR(100) PATH '/cast-info/movie-year-released',
        "FAMILY_NAME" VARCHAR(100) PATH '/cast-info/family' ,
        "GIVEN_NAME" VARCHAR(100) PATH '/cast-info/given' DEFAULT '' ,
        "OTHER_NAMES" VARCHAR(100) PATH '/cast-info/other' DEFAULT '' ,
        "MF"  VARCHAR(6) PATH '/cast-info/maleOrFemale' ,
        "CHARACTER"  VARCHAR(100) PATH '/cast-info/character'
    ) AS result
WHERE
  result.title         = movies.title and
  result.year_released = movies.year_released and
  result.family_name   = persons.family_name and
  result.given_name    = persons.given_name
)
/
```

Table contents:

```
  MOVIE_ID    CAST_ID MF     CHARACTER
---------- ---------- ------ -----------------------------
         1         15 female Kathryn Bennett
         1         54 male   Egor Korshunov
         1         46 male   Major Caldwell
         1         49 female Alice Marshall
         1         18 female Grace Marshall
         1         24 male   James Marshall
```

```
 2          70 male   S. E. Brett
 2          32 male   G. E. Kanet
 2          14 female J. Lambert
 2          75 female Ellen Ripley
 2          66 male   A. Dallas
 3          27 male   Bishop II
 3          21 male   Dillon
 3          75 female Ellen Ripley
 4          75 female Ellen Ripley
 4          55 male   Johner
 4          61 female Annalee Call
 5          59 male   Carter J. Burke
 5          10 male   Dwayne Hicks
 5          75 female Ellen Ripley
 6          71 female Angela Hayes
 6          11 female Jane Burnham
 6           7 male   Ricky Fitts
 6           6 female Carolyn Burnham
 6          69 male   Lester Burnham
 7          43 male   John Milner
 7          30 male   Steve Bolander
 7          19 male   Curt Henderson
 8          52 male   David Kessler
 8           1 female Alex Price
 8          20 male   Jack Goodman
 8          78 male   Dr. Hirsch
 9          48 male   Eric 'Otter' Stratton
 9          73 male   Vernon Wormer
 9           5 male   John 'Bluto' Blutarsky
10          54 male   Jean-Baptiste Emanuel Zorg
10          77 male   Korben Dallas
10          29 male   Vito Cornelius
10          36 female Leeloo
10          72 male   Ruby Rhod
```

***Data A—11** movies-we-own Tables: MOVIES_WRITERS*

```
Table Description:

 Name                                      Type
 ----------------------------------------- ---------------
 MOVIE_ID                                  NUMBER
 WRITER_ID                                 NUMBER
 STORY_OR_SCREENPLAY                       VARCHAR2(100)
```

Create and populate the table:

```
DROP TABLE movies_writers
/
CREATE TABLE movies_writers AS (
SELECT
  movies.id AS movie_id ,
  persons.id AS writer_id ,
  result.story_or_screenplay AS story_or_screenplay
FROM
  persons ,
  movies ,
  movies_xml ,
    XMLTABLE(
      'for $w in $col/movie/writer
       return
         <writer-info>
           <movie-title>{ $w/../title }</movie-title>
           <movie-year-released>{$w/../yearReleased}</movie-year-released>
           <family>{ $w/familyName }</family>
           <given>{ $w/givenName }</given>
           <other>{ $w/otherNames }</other>
           <st>{if ($w/storyOrScreenplay="story") then "ST" else "SC"}</st>
         </writer-info>'
      PASSING movies_xml.movie AS "col"
      COLUMNS
        "TITLE" VARCHAR(100) PATH '/writer-info/movie-title' ,
        "YEAR_RELEASED" VARCHAR(100) PATH '/writer-info/movie-year-released' ,
        "FAMILY_NAME" VARCHAR(100) PATH '/writer-info/family' ,
        "GIVEN_NAME" VARCHAR(100) PATH '/writer-info/given' DEFAULT '' ,
        "OTHER_NAMES" VARCHAR(100) PATH '/writer-info/other' DEFAULT '' ,
        "STORY_OR_SCREENPLAY"  VARCHAR(100) PATH '/writer-info/st'
```

```
    ) AS result
WHERE
  result.title         = movies.title and
  result.year_released = movies.year_released and
  result.family_name   = persons.family_name and
  result.given_name    = persons.given_name
)
/
```

Table contents:

```
  MOVIE_ID  WRITER_ID STORY_OR_SCREENPLAY
---------- ---------- -------------------
         1         47 SC
         2         64 ST
         2         53 ST
         3         74 ST
         3         25 SC
         4         76 SC
         5         28 ST
         5         12 ST
         5         25 ST
         6          4 SC
         7         39 SC
         7         45 SC
         7         33 SC
         8         42 SC
         9         58 SC
         9         51 SC
         9         40 SC
        10          9 ST
        10          9 SC
        10         37 SC
```

Check on Relational Tables

We now have a couple of tables that store the `movies-we-own.xml` data *in XML columns* in relational tables, and we have a set of purely relational tables (with no XML columns) built from the XML data in the `MOVIES_XML` table. Now let's turn this relational data back into XML, and check the result against the original XML file.

We assume that the order of repeating elements is not significant. The movies were inserted into the relational tables in title order, though we could have done that in document order, in which case we could have used `ORDER BY id` to get them back in the same order. If we'd gone with a movies_producer table instead of normalizing to persons, we could have done the same with producers (and directors and writers and cast). Note that if the order of any of these fields were important, you could add an "order" column to the table to preserve the original document order.

Data A—12 *Translate Relational Data Into XML: Check*

```
SELECT
XMLELEMENT(NAME "movies",
XMLAGG(
  XMLELEMENT(NAME "movie",
    XMLATTRIBUTES(my_stars AS "myStars") ,
    XMLELEMENT(NAME "title", title) ,
    XMLELEMENT(NAME "yearReleased", year_released) ,
      (SELECT
        XMLAGG(
          XMLELEMENT( "director" ,
            XMLFOREST(
              persons.family_name AS "familyName" ,
              persons.given_name AS "givenName" ,
              persons.other_names AS "otherNames"
              )
            )
          )
        FROM
          persons, movies_directors
        WHERE
          movies.id = movies_directors.movie_id and
          persons.id = movies_directors.director_id
        ) ,
      (SELECT
        XMLAGG(
          XMLELEMENT( "producer" ,
            XMLFOREST(
              persons.family_name AS "familyName" ,
              persons.given_name AS "givenName" ,
              persons.other_names AS "otherNames"
```

```
          )
        )
      )
    FROM
      persons, movies_producers
    WHERE
      movies.id = movies_producers.movie_id and
      persons.id = movies_producers.producer_id
    ) ,
XMLELEMENT(NAME "runningTime", running_time) ,
XMLELEMENT(NAME "studio", studio) ,
  (SELECT
    XMLAGG(
      XMLELEMENT( "cast" ,
        XMLFOREST(
          persons.family_name AS "familyName" ,
          persons.given_name AS "givenName" ,
          persons.other_names AS "otherNames" ,
          movies_cast.mf AS "maleOrFemale" ,
          movies_cast.character AS "character"
          )
        )
      )
    FROM
      persons, movies_cast
    WHERE
      movies.id = movies_cast.movie_id and
      persons.id = movies_cast.cast_id
    ) ,
  XMLELEMENT( "sound" ,
    XMLFOREST(
      dolby_digital_51 AS "dolbyDigital5.1" ,
      DTS_51 AS "DTS5.1" ,
      THX AS "THX" ,
      other_sound AS "otherSound"
      )
    ) ,
XMLELEMENT(NAME "aspectRatio", aspect_ratio) ,
  (SELECT
    XMLAGG(
      XMLELEMENT( "writer" ,
```

```
            XMLFOREST(
              persons.family_name AS "familyName" ,
              persons.given_name AS "givenName" ,
              persons.other_names AS "otherNames" ,
              replace(
                replace(movies_writers.story_or_screenplay, 'ST', 'story'),
                'SC',
                'screenplay'
                )
              AS "storyOrScreenplay"
              )
            )
          )
        FROM
          persons, movies_writers
        WHERE
          movies.id = movies_writers.movie_id and
          persons.id = movies_writers.writer_id
        ) ,
    XMLELEMENT(NAME "tagLine", tagline) ,
    XMLELEMENT(NAME "plotSummary", plot_summary) ,
    XMLELEMENT(NAME "MPAArating", mpaa_rating)
    )
  )
) AS "movies-we-own"
FROM
  movies
```

The output from Data A-12 does indeed match `movies-we-own.xml`, modulo ordering of repeating properties (see http://xqzone.marklogic.com/queryingxmlbook/ for a listing of the output). As we explained earlier, in our example the ordering is not significant, but the ordering could be captured if it were important.

"Movie Reviews" XML

In this section, we present `movie-reviews.xml` and its associated metadata and SQL tables. The movie reviews data are a small sample of ratings and reviews of some of the movies. They are presented here so that we can illustrate queries across more than one data source (XML file or table).

Data A—13 *movie-reviews.xml*

```
<reviews xsi:noNamespaceSchemaLocation="reviews.xsd"
    xmlns:xsi="http://www.w3.org/2001/XMLSchema-instance">
 <review>
   <medium>movie</medium>
   <title>An American Werewolf in London</title>
   <yearReleased>1981</yearReleased>
   <rating>5</rating>
   <text>Great cast, great movie.</text>
 </review>
 <review>
   <medium>movie</medium>
   <title>An American Werewolf in London</title>
   <yearReleased>1981</yearReleased>
   <rating>5</rating>
   <text>An excellent movie.</text>
 </review>
 <review>
   <medium>movie</medium>
   <title>An American Werewolf in London</title>
   <yearReleased>1981</yearReleased>
   <rating>5</rating>
   <text>Jenny Agutter should have won an Oscar.</text>
 </review>
 <review>
   <medium>movie</medium>
   <title>An American Werewolf in London</title>
   <yearReleased>1981</yearReleased>
   <rating>5</rating>
   <text>One of my favorites.</text>
 </review>
 <review>
   <medium>movie</medium>
   <title>Animal House</title>
   <yearReleased>1978</yearReleased>
  <rating>5</rating>
   <text>Excellent cult movie.</text>
 </review>
 <review>
   <medium>movie</medium>
   <title>Animal House</title>
```

```
      <yearReleased>1978</yearReleased>
      <rating>3</rating>
      <text>Pretty good.</text>
    </review>
    <review>
      <medium>movie</medium>
      <title>Animal House</title>
      <yearReleased>1978</yearReleased>
      <rating>4</rating>
      <text>John Belushi at his best.</text>
    </review>
    <review>
      <medium>movie</medium>
      <title>Animal House</title>
      <yearReleased>1978</yearReleased>
      <rating>2</rating>
      <text>This movie is awful.</text>
    </review>
  </reviews>
```

"Movie Reviews" Schema

Just for fun, we use a slightly different style for defining elements in Data A-14. Instead of defining a set of complex types, as in Data A-2, we define a set of elements up front and reference them in the definition of the `reviews` element. Neither style is particularly appropriate for our rather simple data set; we just used them to show some variations in schema styles.

Data A—14 *reviews.xsd*

```
<?xml version="1.0" encoding="UTF-8" standalone="yes"?>
<xs:schema xmlns:xs="http://www.w3.org/2001/XMLSchema"
    elementFormDefault="qualified">
 <!-- This Schema is written in a different style, it uses element refs
    instead of types -->
 <xs:element name="medium">
   <!-- Start by defining each element to be refed later on. -->
   <!-- medium can be movie, book, or play -->
   <xs:simpleType>
     <xs:restriction base="xs:string">
       <xs:enumeration value="movie"/>
       <xs:enumeration value="book"/>
```

```
        <xs:enumeration value="play"/>
      </xs:restriction>
    </xs:simpleType>
  </xs:element>
  <xs:element name="title">
    <!-- limit the title to 80 characters -->
    <xs:simpleType>
      <xs:restriction base="xs:string">
        <xs:maxLength value="80"/>
      </xs:restriction>
    </xs:simpleType>
  </xs:element>
<xs:element name="yearReleased" type="xs:integer"/>
  <xs:element name="rating">
    <!-- the rating is an int from 0 to 5 inclusive -->
    <xs:simpleType>
      <xs:restriction base="xs:int">
        <xs:minInclusive value="0"/>
        <xs:maxInclusive value="5"/>
      </xs:restriction>
    </xs:simpleType>
  </xs:element>
  <xs:element name="text" type="xs:string"/>
  <!-- the text of the review -->
  <xs:element name="review">
    <!-- here is the actual review element. Each child is a ref to an element
defined above. -->
    <xs:complexType>
      <xs:sequence>
        <xs:element ref="medium"/>
        <xs:element ref="title"/>
        <xs:element ref="yearReleased"/>
        <xs:element ref="rating"/>
        <xs:element ref="text"/>
      </xs:sequence>
    </xs:complexType>
  </xs:element>
  <xs:element name="reviews">
    <!-- Here at the end is the root element, reviews -->
    <xs:complexType>
      <xs:sequence>
        <xs:element ref="review" maxOccurs="unbounded"/>
```

```
    </xs:sequence>
  </xs:complexType>
 </xs:element>
</xs:schema>
```

"Movie Reviews" DTD

Data A—15 *reviews.dtd*

```
<?xml version="1.0" encoding="UTF-8"?>
<!ELEMENT medium (#PCDATA)>
<!ELEMENT title (#PCDATA)>
<!ELEMENT yearReleased (#PCDATA)>
<!ELEMENT rating (#PCDATA)>
<!ELEMENT text (#PCDATA)>
<!ELEMENT review (medium, title, yearReleased, rating, text)>
<!ELEMENT reviews (review+)>
```

"Movie Reviews" XML Table

Instead of using SQL/XML to populate the `REVIEWS` table from `reviews.xml` (as we did with movies), we created an XSLT stylesheet that, when run over `reviews.xml`, outputs a SQL script to create and populate the `REVIEWS` table. (Our first pass at creating the movies tables was to write XQueries that output SQL scripts — see the examples website).

Data A—16 *REVIEWS*

```
Table Description:

Name                                        Type
 ----------------------------------------- ---------
 ID                                         NUMBER
 REVIEW                                     XMLTYPE
```

Create and populate the table:

```
<?xml version="1.0" encoding="UTF-8"?>
<xsl:stylesheet version="1.0"
    xmlns:xsl="http://www.w3.org/1999/XSL/Transform">
 <xsl:template match="reviews">
   <!-- start the SQL script -->
   <xsl:text>-- SQL script to populate reviews table from reviews.xml
```

```
    </xsl:text>
    <xsl:call-template name="newline"/>
    <xsl:text>-- produced magically with cre_table_reviews.xsl</xsl:text>
    <xsl:call-template name="newline"/>
    <xsl:text>spool ins_reviews.log</xsl:text>
    <xsl:call-template name="newline"/>
    <xsl:text>set echo on</xsl:text>
    <xsl:call-template name="newline"/>
    <xsl:text>DROP SEQUENCE reviews_xml_seq;
    CREATE SEQUENCE reviews_xml_seq;
    DROP TABLE reviews_xml;
    CREATE TABLE reviews_xml(ID number, review XMLType);
    </xsl:text>
    <!-- create an insert statement for each element (review) -->
    <xsl:apply-templates/>
    <!-- end the SQL script -->
    <xsl:text>COMMIT</xsl:text>
    <xsl:call-template name="newline"/>
    <xsl:text>/</xsl:text>
    <xsl:call-template name="newline"/>
    <xsl:text>spool off</xsl:text>
    <xsl:call-template name="newline"/>
  </xsl:template>
  <!-- -->
  <xsl:template match="review">
    <xsl:text>INSERT INTO reviews_xml (ID, review) VALUES (reviews_xml_seq.nextval,
'</xsl:text>
    <xsl:copy-of select="."/>
    <xsl:text>');</xsl:text>
    <xsl:call-template name="newline"/>
  </xsl:template>
  <!-- add a newline character -->
  <xsl:template name="newline">
    <xsl:text>&#xa;</xsl:text>
  </xsl:template>
</xsl:stylesheet>
```

Table contents:

```
ID  REVIEW
--- -----------------------------------------------------------
  1 <review><medium>movie</medium><title>An American Werewolf in
```

```
  London</title><yearReleased>1981</yearReleased><rating>5</r
ating><text>Great cast, great movie.</text></review>

2 <review><medium>movie</medium><title>An American Werewolf in
  London</title><yearReleased>1981</yearReleased><rating>5</r
ating><text>An excellent movie.</text></review>

3 <review><medium>movie</medium><title>An American Werewolf in
  London</title><yearReleased>1981</yearReleased><rating>5</r
ating><text>Jenny Agutter should have won an Oscar.</text></
review>

4 <review><medium>movie</medium><title>An American Werewolf in
  London</title><yearReleased>1981</yearReleased><rating>5</r
ating><text>One of my favorites.</text></review>

5 <review><medium>movie</medium><title>Animal House</title><ye
arReleased>1978</yearReleased><rating>5</rating><text>Excell
ent cult movie.</text></review>

6 <review><medium>movie</medium><title>Animal House</title><ye
arReleased>1978</yearReleased><rating>3</rating><text>Pretty
  good.</text></review>

7 <review><medium>movie</medium><title>Animal House</title><ye
arReleased>1978</yearReleased><rating>4</rating><text>John B
elushi at his best.</text></review>

8 <review><medium>movie</medium><title>Animal House</title><ye
arReleased>1978</yearReleased><rating>2</rating><text>This m
ovie is awful.</text></review>
```

A.3 Some Examples from the Book

Most of the examples in this section are from the body of the book. Some have been changed slightly to make the examples or the results fit on the page, or to make the example queries and data consistent throughout this appendix. Some of the XPath expressions assume that a context has been established.

A.3.1 XQuery Examples

Example A—1 *Some Simple Expressions*

Simple Expression	Result
42	42
1 + 1	2
1 + 3.14159	4.14159
3.14159 + "22"	Error
"American Werewolf in London"	"American Werewolf in London"
43 div 12	3.58333333333333333
43 idiv 12	3
true()	true

Example A—2 *Comparisons*

Comparison Expression	Result
1 gt 3	false
1 > 3	false
"abc" ne 5	error (incompatible operands)
<a>Shogun</a> lt "Titanic"	true
(1, 2) eq (1, 2)	error (sequence longer than one)
(1, 2) = (1, 2)	true
(1, 2) = (2, 1)	true
(1, 2, 3) = 2.0	true
(1, 2, 'The Magnificent Seven', 3) > (2, 12, xs:date('2005-02-27'))	either true or error

Example A—3 *Node Comparisons*

Comparison Expression	Result
`<a>42</a> is <a>42</a>`	`false (not the same node)`

`let $a := <a>42</a>`
`let $b := <a>42</a>`
`$a is $b`
	`false`

`let $a := <a>42</a>`
`let $b := $a`
`$a is $b`
	`true`

`<a>Shogun</a> lt "Titanic"`	`true`
`( 1, 2 ) eq ( 1, 2 )`	`error (sequence longer than 1)`
`( 1, 2 ) = ( 1, 2 )`	`true`
`( 1, 2 ) = ( 2, 1 )`	`true`
`( 1, 2, 3 ) = 2.0`	`true`

`( 1, 2, 'The Magnificent Seven', 3)`
`>`
`( 2, 12, xs:date('2005-02-27') )`
	`either true or error`

Example A—4 *Quantified Expressions*

Quantified Expression	Result
`some $x in (1, 2, 3) satisfies $x>2`	`true`
`every $x in (1, 2, 3) satisfies $x>2`	`false`
`some $x in (1, 2, 3), $y in (2, 3, 5) satisfies $x = $y idiv 2`	`true`
`some $m in /movies/movie/yearReleased satisfies $m < 1980`	`true`

Example A—5 *Find the Titles of All Movies*

```
/movies/movie/title
```

Result:

```
<title>The Fifth Element</title>
<title>An American Werewolf in London</title>
<title>American Graffiti</title>
<title>American Beauty</title>
<title>Air Force One</title>
<title>Alien</title>
<title>Aliens</title>
<title>Alien 3</title>
<title>Alien Resurrection</title>
<title>Animal House</title>
```

Example A—6 *Find the Titles of All 5-star Movies*

```
/movies/movie[@myStars=5]/title
```

Result:

```
<title>An American Werewolf in London</title>
<title>American Beauty</title>
<title>Animal House</title>
```

Example A—7 *Find the Title of the 5th Movie*

```
/movies/movie[5]/title
```

Result:

```
<title>Air Force One</title>
```

Example A—8 *Find the Title of the 5th Movie Using Structure*

```
/movies/*[5]/*[1]
```

Result:

```
<title>Air Force One</title>
```

Example A—9 *Find the Titles of Movies That Contain the String Werewolf*

```
/movies/movie/title[contains(., "Werewolf")]
```

Result:

```
<title>An American Werewolf in London</title>
```

Example A—10 *Find the Running Times of Movies Where the Title Contains the String Werewolf*

```
/movies/movie/runningTime[contains(../title, "Werewolf")]
or:
/movies/movie[contains(title, "Werewolf")]/runningTime

Result:
<runningTime>98</runningTime>
```

Example A—11 *Find the Titles of All Movies Where the Director Is Also the Producer*

```
/movies/movie/title[../director/familyName=../producer/familyName]
or:
/movies/movie[director/familyName=producer/familyName]/title


Result:
<title>Air Force One</title>
```

Example A-12 is an XPath expression that calculates the average star ratings for movies directed by John Landis. Of course, we could use the function avg() instead of sum(), div, and count(). Although most of our XPath examples are shown on a single line, XPaths can include whitespace as in Example A-12.

Example A—12 *Average myStars Rating of Movies Directed by John Landis*

```
sum( /movies/movie
      [
        director/givenName="John"
      ]
      [
        director/familyName="Landis"
      ]/@myStars)
div
count( /movies/movie[
        director/givenName="John"
      ]
      [
        director/familyName="Landis"
      ]/@myStars)
```

```
Result:
5
```

Example A—13 *Using the* `for` *Expression*

```
for $m in //movie[yearReleased > 1998]
return $m/title/text()
```

```
Result:
American Beauty
```

Example A-13 introduces `for` to iterate over a sequence, such as the sequence produced by an XPath. If there is more than one title in the result then you probably want to format the results – Example A–14 formats results with a direct constructor.

Example A—14 *Using a Direct Constructor to Format Results*

```
<results>{
for $m in doc("/example/movies-we-own.xml")/movies/movie
  where $m/yearReleased < 1979
  return (
  <result>{
    ($m/title, $m/director)
  }</result>
  )
}</results>
```

```
Result:
<results>
  <result>
    <title>American Graffiti</title>
    <director>
      <familyName>Lucas</familyName>
      <givenName>George</givenName>
    </director>
  </result>
  <result>
    <title>Animal House</title>
    <director>
      <familyName>Landis</familyName>
      <givenName>John</givenName>
    </director>
```

```
  </result>
</results>
```

Example A—15 *Using a Computed Constructor to Format Results*

```
element results {
  for $m in doc("/example/movies-we-own.xml")/movies/movie
  where $m/yearReleased < 1979
  return (
    element result {
      ($m/title, $m/director)
      } (: end result :)
    ) (: end return :)
  } (: end results :)
```

```
Result:
<results>
  <result>
    <title>American Graffiti</title>
    <director>
      <familyName>Lucas</familyName>
      <givenName>George</givenName>
    </director>
  </result>
  <result>
    <title>Animal House</title>
    <director>
      <familyName>Landis</familyName>
      <givenName>John</givenName>
    </director>
  </result>
</results>
```

Example A-16 and Example A-17 illustrate the composability of XQuery expressions. Example A-16 is an expression that evaluates to the newer of two movies. Because XQuery expressions are composable, this expression can be used as part of another expression – Example A-17 uses this expression on the right-hand side of a comparison.

Example A—16 if Expression: Find the Newer Alien Movie

```
if ( /movies/movie[title="Aliens"]/yearReleased gt
     /movies/movie[title="Alien Resurrection"]/yearReleased )
  then "Aliens"
  else "Alien Resurrection"
```

Result:

```
Alien Resurrection
```

Example A—17 if Expression: Find Movies Newer Than the Newest Alien Movie

```
/movies/movie[
  yearReleased gt (
    if (
      /movies/movie[title="Aliens"]/yearReleased gt
      /movies/movie[title="Alien Resurrection"]/yearReleased
      )
    then
      /movies/movie[title="Aliens"]/yearReleased
    else
      /movies/movie[title="Alien Resurrection"]/yearReleased
    ) (: end yearReleased gt :)
  ]/title
```

Result:

```
<title>American Beauty</title>
```

It's common to want to query across data from more than one source, joining the data according to some common criterion (or key). Example A-18 shows one way to do a join in XQuery, using two expressions in the `for` clause.

Example A—18 Query Across movies and reviews, join

```
<reviewDetails>{
for $m in doc("/example/movies-we-own.xml")/movies/movie ,
    $r in doc("/example/reviews.xml")/reviews/review
where
  $m/title = $r/title and
  $m/yearReleased = $r/yearReleased and
  $r/rating < 4
order by
```

```
  $m/title ,
  $m/yearReleased
return
<reviewDetail>
  { $m/title }
  { $r/rating }
  <director>{
    concat( $m/director[1]/givenName, " ", $m/director[1]/familyName )
    }
  </director>
  <producers>{ string-join( $m/producer/familyName, " and " )
    }
  </producers>
  { $r/text }
</reviewDetail>
}
</reviewDetails>
```

```
Result:
<reviewDetails>
 <reviewDetail>
   <title>Animal House</title>
   <rating>3</rating>
   <director>John Landis</director>
   <producers>Simmons and Reitman</producers>
   <text>Pretty good.</text>
 </reviewDetail>
 <reviewDetail>
   <title>Animal House</title>
   <rating>2</rating>
   <director>John Landis</director>
   <producers>Simmons and Reitman</producers>
   <text>This movie is awful.</text>
 </reviewDetail>
</reviewDetails>
```

Example A–19 also joins data from movies and reviews, but it uses an inner `for` loop (or *subquery*), this time with movies in the outer loop and reviews in the inner loop. In addition, Example A–19 uses `if` to insert a different element if there are no reviews available.

Example A—19 *Query Across movies and reviews, join (2)*

```
<movieDetails>{
(: for each movie :)
for $m in doc("/example/movies-we-own.xml")/movies/movie
(: where the average review is more than 4 :)
where
  avg(
    (: this expression returns a sequence of ratings for this movie :)
    for $review in doc("/example/reviews.xml")/reviews/review
    where
      $review/title = $m/title and
      $review/yearReleased = $m/yearReleased
    return
      $review/rating
    ) > 4
order by
  $m/title ,
  $m/yearReleased
return
<movieDetail>
  { $m/title }
  { $m/yearReleased }
  <reviews>{
    if (
      some $x in doc("/example/reviews.xml")/reviews/review satisfies
        $x/title = $m/title and
        $x/yearReleased = $m/yearReleased
      ) (: end if :)
    then (
      for $r in doc("/example/reviews.xml")/reviews/review
      where
        $r/title = $m/title and
        $r/yearReleased = $m/yearReleased
      order by
        $r/rating descending
      return
        <review>{
          ( $r/rating, $r/text, $m/title )
          }</review>
      ) (: end then :)
    else (
```

```
      <none/>
      ) (: end else :)
    }</reviews>
</movieDetail>
}
</movieDetails>
```

Result:

```
<movieDetails>
 <movieDetail>
   <title>An American Werewolf in London</title>
   <yearReleased>1981</yearReleased>
   <reviews>
     <review>
       <rating>5</rating>
       <text>Great cast, great movie.</text>
       <title>An American Werewolf in London</title>
     </review>
     <review>
       <rating>5</rating>
       <text>An excellent movie.</text>
       <title>An American Werewolf in London</title>
     </review>
     <review>
       <rating>5</rating>
       <text>Jenny Agutter should have won an Oscar.</text>
       <title>An American Werewolf in London</title>
     </review>
     <review>
       <rating>5</rating>
       <text>One of my favorites.</text>
       <title>An American Werewolf in London</title>
     </review>
   </reviews>
 </movieDetail>
</movieDetails>
```

A.3.2 SQL/XML Examples

Most of the examples in this section are from the body of the book, modified to make them consistent with the other examples and the data in this appendix.

Publishing Functions — Representing SQL Data as XML

Example A—20 *Find Movie Titles and Represent Them as XML Elements*

```
SELECT
  XMLELEMENT(NAME "title", title) AS "Movie Titles"
  FROM movies
```

```
Result:
Movie Titles
------------------------------------------------------------------------
<title>The Fifth Element</title>
<title>An American Werewolf in London</title>
<title>American Graffiti</title>
<title>American Beauty</title>
<title>Air Force One</title>
<title>Alien</title>
<title>Aliens</title>
<title>Alien 3</title>
<title>Alien Resurrection</title>
<title>Animal House</title>

(10 rows in the result)
```

Example A—21 *Find Movie Titles and Represent Them as XML Elements With a RunningTime Attribute*

```
SELECT
  XMLELEMENT(NAME title,
    XMLATTRIBUTES(running_time AS "RunningTime"),
      'This movie title is '||m.title)
        AS "Movie Titles"
  FROM movies m
```

```
Result:
Movie Titles
------------------------------------------------------------------------
<TITLE RunningTime="126">This movie title is The Fifth Element</TITLE>
```

```
<TITLE RunningTime="98">This movie title is An American Werewolf in London</TITLE>
<TITLE RunningTime="110">This movie title is American Graffiti</TITLE>
<TITLE RunningTime="121">This movie title is American Beauty</TITLE>
<TITLE RunningTime="124">This movie title is Air Force One</TITLE>
<TITLE RunningTime="117">This movie title is Alien</TITLE>
<TITLE RunningTime="154">This movie title is Aliens</TITLE>
<TITLE RunningTime="115">This movie title is Alien 3</TITLE>
<TITLE RunningTime="108">This movie title is Alien Resurrection</TITLE>
<TITLE RunningTime="109">This movie title is Animal House</TITLE>

(10 rows in the result)
```

Example A—22 *Titles of Movies Using XMLAGG*

```
SELECT
  XMLELEMENT(NAME "all-titles",
    XMLAGG(XMLELEMENT(NAME "title", title) ORDER BY year_released ASC ) )
      AS "Movie Titles"
  FROM movies
```

```
Result:
Movie Titles
----------------------------------------------------------------------------
<all-titles>
  <title>The Fifth Element</title>
  <title>An American Werewolf in London</title>
  <title>American Graffiti</title>
  <title>American Beauty</title>
  <title>Air Force One</title>
  <title>Alien</title>
  <title>Aliens</title>
  <title>Alien 3</title>
  <title>Alien Resurrection</title>
  <title>Animal House</title>
</all-titles>

(1 row in the result)
```

Example A—23 *Using XMLELEMENT to Get Values Across the Row*

```
SELECT
  XMLELEMENT(NAME "movie-details",
    XMLFOREST(
```

```
      title AS "title" ,
      year_released AS "yearReleased" ,
      running_time AS "runningTime")
    ) AS "Movie Details"
  FROM movies
  WHERE
    year_released = 1997
```

Result:

```
Movie Details
-----------------------------------------------------------------------
 <movie-details>
   <title>Alien Resurrection</title>
   <yearReleased>1997</yearReleased>
   <runningTime>108</runningTime>
 </movie-details>
 <movie-details>
   <title>The Fifth Element</title>
   <yearReleased>1997</yearReleased>
   <runningTime>126</runningTime>
 </movie-details>
 <movie-details>
   <title>Air Force One</title>
   <yearReleased>1997</yearReleased>
   <runningTime>124</runningTime>
 </movie-details>

(3 rows in the result)
```

In Example A–24 and some following examples, we introduced a spurious condition to keep the results size down (to save some paper).

Example A–24 and Example A–25 give similar results, but Example A–25 uses `XMLFOREST` to skip null values (for otherNames).

***Example A—24** Producer-Details Using XMLELEMENT*

```
SELECT
  XMLELEMENT(NAME "producer-details",
    XMLELEMENT(NAME "givenName", given_name) ,
    XMLELEMENT(NAME "familyName", family_name) ,
    XMLELEMENT(NAME "otherNames", other_names)
```

```
    ) AS "Producer Details"
  FROM persons
  WHERE
    id IN (
      SELECT distinct(producer_id) FROM movies_producers
      WHERE movie_id IN (
        SELECT id FROM movies WHERE running_time > 125
        )
      )
```

```
Result:
Producer Details
----------------------------------------------------------------------
 <producer-details>
   <givenName>John</givenName>
   <familyName>Amicarella</familyName>
   <otherNames>C.</otherNames>
 </producer-details>
 <producer-details>
   <givenName>Patrice</givenName>
   <familyName>Ledoux</familyName>
   <otherNames></otherNames>
 </producer-details>
 <producer-details>
   <givenName>Iain</givenName>
   <familyName>Smith</familyName>
   <otherNames></otherNames>
 </producer-details>
 <producer-details>
   <givenName>Gale Ann</givenName>
   <familyName>Hurd</familyName>
   <otherNames></otherNames>
 </producer-details>

(4 rows in the result)
```

Example A—25 *Producer-Details Using XMLFOREST*

```
SELECT
  XMLELEMENT(NAME "producer-details",
    XMLFOREST(
      given_name AS "givenName" ,
```

```
      family_name AS "familyName" ,
      other_names AS "otherNames"
      )
    ) AS "Producer Details"
  FROM persons
  WHERE
    id IN (
      SELECT distinct(producer_id) FROM movies_producers
      WHERE movie_id IN (
        SELECT id FROM movies WHERE running_time > 125
        )
      )
```

```
Result:
Producer Details
---------------------------------------------------------------------
 <producer-details>
   <givenName>John</givenName>
   <familyName>Amicarella</familyName>
   <otherNames>C.</otherNames>
 </producer-details>
 <producer-details>
   <givenName>Patrice</givenName>
   <familyName>Ledoux</familyName>
</producer-details>
 <producer-details>
   <givenName>Iain</givenName>
   <familyName>Smith</familyName>
</producer-details>
 <producer-details>
   <givenName>Gale Ann</givenName>
   <familyName>Hurd</familyName>
</producer-details>

(4 rows in the result)
```

Example A—26 *XMLCONCAT*

```
SELECT
  XMLCONCAT(
      XMLELEMENT("givenName", given_name) ,
      XMLELEMENT("familyName", family_name) ,
```

```
      XMLELEMENT("otherNames", other_names)
      ) AS "Producer Details"
  FROM persons
  WHERE
    id IN (
      SELECT distinct(producer_id) FROM movies_producers
      WHERE movie_id IN (
        SELECT id FROM movies WHERE running_time > 125
        )
      )
```

```
Result:
Producer Details
----------------------------------------------------------------------
 <givenName>John</givenName>
 <familyName>Amicarella</familyName>
 <otherNames>C.</otherNames>

 <givenName>Patrice</givenName>
 <familyName>Ledoux</familyName>
 <otherNames></otherNames>

 <givenName>Iain</givenName>
 <familyName>Smith</familyName>
 <otherNames></otherNames>

 <givenName>Gale Ann</givenName>
 <familyName>Hurd</familyName>
 <otherNames></otherNames>

(4 rows in the result)
```

XMLQUERY and XMLTABLE — Manipulating XML in SQL

Example A—27 *Simple XMLQUERY over all_movies_xml*

```
SELECT
  XMLQUERY(
    'for $m in
      $col/movies/movie
    return
      $m/title'
    PASSING all_movies AS "col"
```

```
    RETURNING CONTENT
  ) AS result
FROM all_movies_xml
```

Result:

```
Movie Titles
-------------------------------------------------
<title>The Fifth Element</title>
<title>An American Werewolf in London</title>
<title>American Graffiti</title>
<title>American Beauty</title>
<title>Air Force One</title>
<title>Alien</title>
<title>Aliens</title>
<title>Alien 3</title>
<title>Alien Resurrection</title>
<title>Animal House</title>

(1 row in the result)
```

Example A—28 *Simple XMLQUERY over movies_xml*

```
SELECT
  XMLQUERY(
    'for $m in
      $col/movie
    return
      $m/title'
    PASSING movie AS "col"
    RETURNING CONTENT
  ) AS "Movie Titles"
FROM movies_xml
```

Result:

```
Movie Titles
-------------------------------------------------
<title>The Fifth Element</title>
<title>An American Werewolf in London</title>
<title>American Graffiti</title>
<title>American Beauty</title>
<title>Air Force One</title>
<title>Alien</title>
```

```
<title>Aliens</title>
<title>Alien 3</title>
<title>Alien Resurrection</title>
<title>Animal House</title>

(10 rows in the result)
```

Of course, you could use XMLTABLE to create MOVIES_XML from ALL_MOVIES_XML; see Example A-29.

Example A—29 *Create Table all_movies_xml Using XMLTABLE*

```
CREATE TABLE movies_xml AS (
  SELECT id, result.column_value AS movie
  FROM
    all_movies_xml ,
    XMLTABLE(
      'for $m in
        $col/movies/movie
      return
        $m'
      PASSING all_movies_xml.all_movies AS "col"
    ) AS result
  )
```

Example A—30 *XMLQUERY and AVG*

```
SELECT
  AVG(
    XMLCAST(
      XMLQUERY(
        'for $m in
          $col/movie
        return
          $m/runningTime/text()'
        PASSING movie AS "col"
        RETURNING CONTENT
        ) AS decimal(8,1)
      )
  ) AS "avgRunningTime"
FROM MOVIES_XML
```

```
Result:
avgRunningTime
--------------
         118.2

(1 row in the result)
```

Example A—31 *XMLQUERY, Complete*

```
SELECT
  XMLQUERY(
    'for $m in
      $col/movie
     let $producers := $m/producer
     where $m/yearReleased < 1980
    return
      <output>
        {$m/title}
        {for $p in $producers
           return
             <prodFullName>
               {concat(
                 $p/givenName,
                 " ",
                 $p/familyName
                )
               }
             </prodFullName>
        }
      </output>'
    PASSING movie AS "col"
    RETURNING CONTENT
  ) AS "Producers"
  FROM movies_xml
```

```
Result:
Producers
----------------------------------------


<output>
   <title>American Graffiti</title>
```

```
    <prodFullName>Francis Ford Coppola</prodFullName>
    <prodFullName>Gary Kurtz</prodFullName>
</output>


<output>
    <title>Alien</title>
    <prodFullName>Gordon Carroll</prodFullName>
    <prodFullName>David Giler</prodFullName>
</output>



<output>
    <title>Animal House</title>
    <prodFullName>Matty Simmons</prodFullName>
    <prodFullName>Ivan Reitman</prodFullName>
</output>

(10 rows in the result)
```

Note that in Example A-31, there are 10 rows in the result, since we are iterating over all 10 rows in the table.

Example A—32 *Simple XMLTABLE*

```
SELECT result.*
FROM
  movies_xml ,
  XMLTABLE(
    'for $m in
      $col/movie
    return
      $m/title'
    PASSING movies_xml.movie AS "col"
  ) AS result
```

```
Results:
COLUMN_VALUE
-----------------------------------------------
<title>The Fifth Element</title>
<title>An American Werewolf in London</title>
```

```
<title>American Graffiti</title>
<title>American Beauty</title>
<title>Air Force One</title>
<title>Alien</title>
<title>Aliens</title>
<title>Alien 3</title>
<title>Alien Resurrection</title>
<title>Animal House</title>

(10 rows in the result)
```

Example A—33 *XMLTABLE with Column Definitions*

```
SELECT result.*
FROM
  movies_xml ,
  XMLTABLE(
    'for $m in
      $col/movie
    return
      $m'
    PASSING movies_xml.movie AS "col"
    COLUMNS
      "title" VARCHAR(80) PATH 'title' ,
      "runningTime" INTEGER PATH 'runningTime' ,
      "yearReleased" INTEGER PATH 'yearReleased'
  ) AS result
ORDER BY
  result."runningTime"
```

Results:

```
title                          runningTime yearReleased
------------------------------ ----------- ------------
An American Werewolf in London          98         1981
Alien Resurrection                     108         1997
Animal House                           109         1978
American Graffiti                      110         1973
Alien 3                                115         1992
Alien                                  117         1979
American Beauty                        121         1999
Air Force One                          124         1997
```

```
The Fifth Element                        126          1997
Aliens                                   154          1986

(10 rows in the result)
```

***Example A—34** XMLTABLE with Column Definitions, Alternative Syntax*

```
SELECT result.*
FROM
  movies_xml ,
  XMLTABLE(
    'for $m in
      $col/movie
    return
      $m'
    PASSING movies_xml.movie AS "col"
    COLUMNS
      "title" VARCHAR(80) ,
      "runningTime" INTEGER ,
      "yearReleased" INTEGER ,
      "producer[1]/familyName" VARCHAR(20)
  ) AS result ("TITLE", "RUNNINGTIME", "YEARRELEASED", "PRODUCER")
ORDER BY
  result."RUNNINGTIME"
```

Results:

```
TITLE                          RUNNINGTIME YEARRELEASED PRODUCER
------------------------------ ----------- ------------ ------------
An American Werewolf in London          98         1981 Folsey
Alien Resurrection                     108         1997 Badalato
Animal House                           109         1978 Simmons
American Graffiti                      110         1973 Coppola
Alien 3                                115         1992 Carroll
Alien                                  117         1979 Carroll
American Beauty                        121         1999 Cohen
Air Force One                          124         1997 Bernstein
The Fifth Element                      126         1997 Amicarella
Aliens                                 154         1986 Hurd

(10 rows in the result)
```

Example A—35 *Repeating Elements, Denormalized Result Table*

```
SELECT result.*
FROM
  movies_xml ,
  XMLTABLE(
    'for $m in
      $col/movie
    return
      $m'
    PASSING movies_xml.movie AS "col"
    COLUMNS
      "title" VARCHAR(80) PATH 'title' ,
      "producer1" VARCHAR(12) PATH 'producer[1]/familyName' ,
      "producer2" VARCHAR(12) PATH 'producer[2]/familyName' DEFAULT 'none',
      "producer3" VARCHAR(12) PATH 'producer[3]/familyName' DEFAULT 'none'
  ) AS result
ORDER BY
  result."producer1"
```

Results:

```
title                          producer1    producer2    producer3
------------------------------ ------------ ------------ ----------
The Fifth Element              Amicarella   Ledoux       Smith
Alien Resurrection             Badalato     Carroll      Giler
Air Force One                  Bernstein    Peterson     Katz
Alien                          Carroll      Giler        none
Alien 3                        Carroll      Giler        Hill
American Beauty                Cohen        Jinks        none
American Graffiti              Coppola      Kurtz        none
An American Werewolf in London Folsey       Guber        Peters
Aliens                         Hurd         none         none
Animal House                   Simmons      Reitman      none

(10 rows in the result)
```

Example A—36 *Repeating Elements, XML in the Result Table*

```
SELECT result.*
FROM
  movies_xml ,
  XMLTABLE(
```

```
    'for $m in
      $col/movie
    where $m/yearReleased < 1980
    return
      $m'
    PASSING movies_xml.movie AS "col"
    COLUMNS
      "title" VARCHAR(80) PATH 'title' ,
      "producers" XMLTYPE PATH 'producer'
  ) AS result
```

Results:

```
title                          producers
------------------------------ ----------------------------------------
American Graffiti              <producer>
                                 <familyName>Coppola</familyName>
                                 <givenName>Francis Ford</givenName>
                                 <otherNames/>
                               </producer>
                               <producer>
                                 <familyName>Kurtz</familyName>
                                 <givenName>Gary</givenName>
                                 <otherNames/>
                               </producer>

Alien                          <producer>
                                 <familyName>Carroll</familyName>
                                 <givenName>Gordon</givenName>
                                 <otherNames/>
                               </producer>
                               <producer>
                                 <familyName>Giler</familyName>
                                 <givenName>David</givenName>
                                 <otherNames/>
                               </producer>

Animal House                   <producer>
                                 <familyName>Simmons</familyName>
                                 <givenName>Matty</givenName>
                                 <otherNames/>
                               </producer>
```

```
                    <producer>
                      <familyName>Reitman</familyName>
                      <givenName>Ivan</givenName>
                      <otherNames/>
                    </producer>

(3 rows in the result)
```

Example A—37 *Repeating Elements, Detail Table*

```
SELECT result."title", result2.* FROM
  movies_xml ,
  XMLTABLE(
    'for $m in
      $col/movie
    where
      contains($m/title, "Alien")
    return
      $m'
    PASSING movies_xml.movie AS "col"
    COLUMNS
      "title" VARCHAR(80) PATH 'title' ,
      "producers" XMLTYPE PATH 'producer'
  ) AS result ,
  XMLTABLE(
    'for $prod in $p/producer
     return
      $prod'
    PASSING result."producers" AS "p"
    COLUMNS
      "ord" FOR ORDINALITY ,
      "familyName" VARCHAR(20) PATH 'familyName'
  ) AS result2
```

Results:

```
title                                     ord familyName
------------------------------ ---------- --------------------
Alien                                       1 Carroll
Alien                                       2 Giler
Aliens                                      1 Hurd
Alien 3                                     1 Carroll
Alien 3                                     2 Giler
```

```
Alien 3                                    3 Hill
Alien Resurrection                         1 Badalato
Alien Resurrection                         2 Carroll
Alien Resurrection                         3 Giler
Alien Resurrection                         4 Hill

(10 rows in the result)
```

***Example A—38** Complex Elements, Denormalized Result Table*

```
SELECT result.* FROM
  movies_xml ,
  XMLTABLE(
    'for $m in
      $col/movie
    return
      $m'
    PASSING movies_xml.movie AS "col"
    COLUMNS
      "title" VARCHAR(80) PATH 'title' ,
      "producerF" VARCHAR(12) PATH 'producer[1]/familyName' ,
      "producerG" VARCHAR(12) PATH 'producer[1]/givenName' ,
      "producerO" VARCHAR(12) PATH 'producer[1]/otherNames' DEFAULT 'none'
  ) AS result
```

Results:

```
title                          producerF    producerG    producerO
------------------------------ ------------ ------------ ------------
The Fifth Element              Amicarella   John         C.
An American Werewolf in London Folsey       George, Jr.
American Graffiti              Coppola      Francis Ford
American Beauty                Cohen        Bruce
Air Force One                  Bernstein    Armyan
Alien                          Carroll      Gordon
Aliens                         Hurd         Gale Ann
Alien 3                        Carroll      Gordon
Alien Resurrection             Badalato     Bill
Animal House                   Simmons      Matty

(10 rows in the result)
```

In Example A–39, we use a sequence to yield an ID. Any unique, increasing number would serve. Note that Example A–39 uses the SQL `DISTINCT` keyword to ensure that producer details are distinct (each producer is represented only once in the table, no matter how many movies he produced).

Example A—39 *Complex Repeating Elements, PRODUCERS*

```
CREATE SEQUENCE producers_seq
/
SELECT producers_seq.nextval AS id, p.*
from dual d,
(
  SELECT DISTINCT
    result."familyName",
    result."givenName",
    result."otherNames"
  FROM
    movies_xml ,
    XMLTABLE(
      'for $m in
        $col/movie
      return
        $m/producer'
      PASSING movies_xml.movie AS "col"
      COLUMNS
        "familyName" VARCHAR(12) PATH 'familyName' ,
        "givenName" VARCHAR(12) PATH 'givenName' DEFAULT 'none' ,
        "otherNames" VARCHAR(12) PATH 'otherNames' DEFAULT 'none'
    ) AS result
  ) p
/
```

```
Results:
        ID familyName   givenName    otherNames
---------- ------------ ------------ ------------
         1 Hill         Walter
         2 Hurd         Gale Ann
         3 Katz         Gail
         4 Cohen        Bruce
         5 Giler        David
         6 Guber        Peter
```

```
  7 Jinks        Dan
  8 Kurtz        Gary
  9 Smith        Iain         none
 10 Folsey       George, Jr.
 11 Ledoux       Patrice      none
 12 Peters       Jon
 13 Carroll      Gordon
 14 Coppola      Francis Ford
 15 Reitman      Ivan
 16 Simmons      Matty
 17 Badalato     Bill
 18 Peterson     Wolfgang
 19 Shestack     Jon
 20 Bernstein    Armyan
 21 Amicarella   John         C.

(21 rows in the result)
```

Example A—40 *Complex Repeating Elements, MOVIES_PRODUCERS Table*

```
SELECT
  movies_xml.id AS "MOVIE",
  producers.id AS "PRODUCER"
FROM
  movies_xml ,
  producers ,
  XMLTABLE(
    'for $m in
      $col/movie
    return
      $m/producer'
    PASSING movies_xml.movie AS "col"
    COLUMNS
      "familyName" VARCHAR(12),
      "givenName" VARCHAR(12) ,
      "otherNames" VARCHAR(12)
  ) AS result
WHERE
  result."familyName" = producers."familyName" AND
  result."givenName" = producers."givenName"
/
```

```
Results:

     MOVIE   PRODUCER
---------- ----------
         1         21
         1         11
         1          9
         2         10
         2          6
         2         12
         3         14
         3          8
         4          4
         4          7
         5         20
         5         18
         5          3
         5         19
         6         13
         6          5
         7          2
         8         13
         8          5
         8          1
         9         17
         9         13
         9          5
         9          1
        10         16
        10         15

(26 rows in the result)
```

To end this section, we present two analytic functions, *rollup* and *cube*, in Example A–41 and Example A–42, respectively. These examples illustrate the power of SQL/XML, providing the ability to perform sophisticated functions on XML data.

Example A—41 *Rollup Function on XML Data*

```
SELECT
  result."yearReleased",
```

```
  result."director",
  avg(result."runningTime") AS "length"
FROM
  movies_xml ,
  XMLTABLE(
    'for $m in
      $col/movie
    return
      $m'
    PASSING movies_xml.movie AS "col"
    COLUMNS
      "title" VARCHAR(80) PATH 'title' ,
      "yearReleased" NUMBER PATH 'yearReleased' ,
      "producers" XMLTYPE PATH 'producer',
      "runningTime" NUMBER PATH 'runningTime',
      "director" VARCHAR(12) PATH 'director[1]/familyName'
  ) AS result
  WHERE result."yearReleased" IN (1997, 1998, 1999)
  GROUP BY
    rollup(result."yearReleased", result."director" )
  ORDER BY result."yearReleased" ASC
```

Results:

```
yearReleased director         length
------------ ------------ ----------
        1997 Besson              126
        1997 Jeunet              108
        1997 Peterson            124
        1997                  119.33
        1999 Mendes              121
        1999                     121
                              119.75
(7 rows in the result)
```

Example A—42 *Cube Function on XML Data*

```
SELECT
  result."yearReleased",
  result."director",
  avg(result."runningTime") AS "length"
FROM
```

```
movies_xml ,
XMLTABLE(
  'for $m in
    $col/movie
  return
    $m'
  PASSING movies_xml.movie AS "col"
  COLUMNS
    "title" VARCHAR(80) PATH 'title' ,
    "yearReleased" NUMBER PATH 'yearReleased' ,
    "producers" XMLTYPE PATH 'producer',
    "runningTime" NUMBER PATH 'runningTime',
    "director" VARCHAR(12) PATH 'director[1]/familyName'
) AS result
WHERE result."yearReleased" IN (1997, 1998, 1999)
GROUP BY
  cube(result."yearReleased", result."director" )
ORDER BY result."yearReleased" ASC
```

Results:

```
yearReleased director         length
------------ ------------ ----------
        1997 Besson              126
        1997 Jeunet              108
        1997 Peterson            124
        1997              119.333333
        1999 Mendes              121
        1999                     121
             Besson              126
             Jeunet              108
             Mendes              121
             Peterson            124
                              119.75

(11 rows in the result)
```

A.4 A Simple Web Application

XQuery is a powerful query language for expressing precise queries against XML data. It is also (with a few extensions) a powerful programming language for querying, storing, managing, manipulating, and publishing XML content. This section presents a complete web application written in XQuery. All the code needed to run the application is included, and of course the application runs against the movies and reviews data reproduced at the beginning of this appendix.

The application runs on the MarkLogic application server. The application server, which is a part of the MarkLogic Content Server, executes XQuery modules (.xqy files) stored in the file system or in MarkLogic, and it outputs html or xhtml to be displayed in a browser (there are also Java and .NET APIs). The data were loaded into MarkLogic via the built-in WebDAV server — we simply dragged `movies-we-own.xml` and `reviews.xml` from the desktop into a WebDAV folder, and they became available for querying.

The application code is not meant to be particularly efficient, it just needs to work. We've picked up the coding style from several people/examples; for tips on XQuery coding style, see http://xqdoc.org/xquery-style.pdf.

The example application runs in a browser, see Figure A–1.

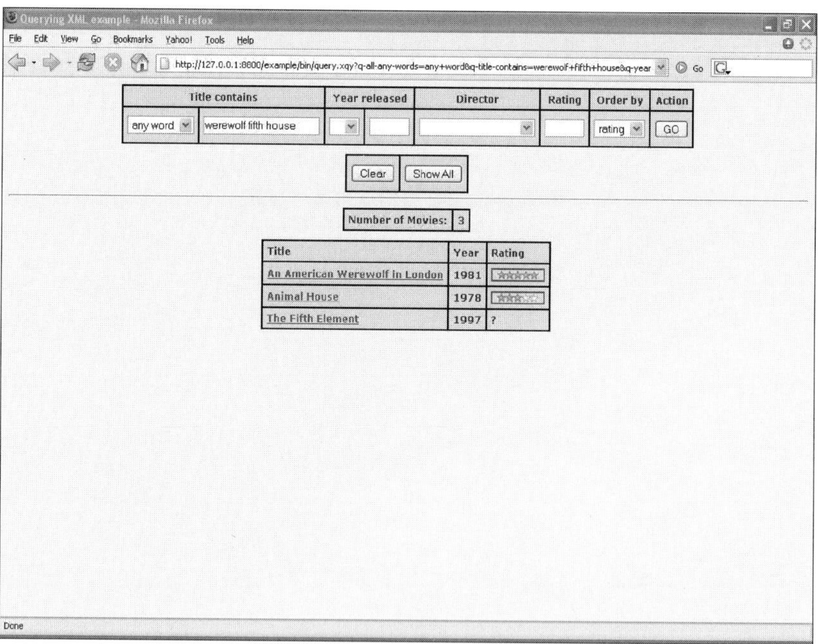

Figure A-1 Screenshot of the Example Application

The general idea of the application is to query movies and reviews. Looking at the form fields in Figure A–1 from left to right, you can do full-text search on words in the title ("all words" or "any word"), you can query by year released ("<", ">", or "="), by director (from a pull-down list of values), or by the average rating over all available reviews. In addition, you can choose to order the results either by title or by rating.

The results of the query are shown in the bottom section of the screen. The application counts the results and shows the title, year released, and star rating of each movie found. The title is a hot link to a listing of the movie data. The star rating is an image of a number of stars, hot-linked to a dynamically produced listing of all the reviews for that movie.

The application consists of a main module and two library modules, one to handle generic processing and the other to handle display-specific processing. Example A–43 is the main module – it simply imports the two libraries, picks up any parameters that have been passed in, and calls functions to paint the query and results.

Example A—43 *Main Module query.xqy*

```
(: No special namespaces here, so that we don't need a namespace prefix for
   XPaths or for (x)html tags or for function names.
:)

(: import the movies-lib library module, for general-purpose movies
   functions
:)
import module "http://www.w3.org/2003/05/xpath-functions"
  at "movies-lib.xqy"

(: import the movies-display-lib library, for display functions :)
import module "http://www.w3.org/2003/05/xpath-functions"
  at "movies-display-lib.xqy"

(: This is the main body of the query app.
   Display a form for the query, remember fields if they have already been
   filled in.
   xdmp:get-request-field() is a Mark Logic extension that gets the form
   parameter.
:)
let $stylesheet := get-stylesheet()
```

```
(: get the input parameters, if any :)
let $q-all-any-words    := xdmp:get-request-field("q-all-any-words")
let $q-title-contains   := xdmp:get-request-field("q-title-contains")
let $q-year-op          := xdmp:get-request-field("q-year-op")
let $q-year             := xdmp:get-request-field("q-year")
let $q-director         := xdmp:get-request-field("q-director")
let $q-rating           := xdmp:get-request-field("q-rating")
let $q-orderby          := xdmp:get-request-field("q-orderby")
let $all                := xdmp:get-request-field("all")

(: default to all words :)
let $q-all-any-words    := if ($q-all-any-words) then $q-all-any-words
                              else "all"
return
(
(: return a sequence.
   The first member of the sequence is a call to
   xdmp:set-response-content-type().
   The second is an html element, produced using direct element
   construction with embedded expressions.
:)
xdmp:set-response-content-type("text/html") ,
<html xmlspace="preserve">
  <head>{
    (: link to a stylesheet if there is one in the config file :)
    if ( $stylesheet="none" ) then ()
    else  <link rel="stylesheet" type="text/css" href="{$stylesheet}" />
    }
    <title>Querying XML example</title>
  </head>
  <body>{
    (: print the query part of the page :)
    print-query(
      $q-all-any-words, $q-title-contains, $q-year-op, $q-year,
      $q-director, $q-rating, $q-orderby, $all
      )
      }<hr/>
    <p>{
      (: print the results part of the page, if there is one :)
      print-results(
        $q-all-any-words, $q-title-contains, $q-year-op, $q-year,
```

```
        $q-director, $q-rating, $q-orderby, $all
        )
      }</p>
  </body>
</html>
) (: end return :)
```

Example A–44 is the display library. It returns a bunch of xhtml, with values inserted dynamically by XQuery calls. It uses XQuery to determine what xhtml to return, and calls functions in movies-lib.xqy for any generic processing (such as querying).

***Example A—44** Display Library Module movies-display-lib.xqy*

```
module "http://www.w3.org/2003/05/xpath-functions"

import module "http://www.w3.org/2003/05/xpath-functions"
  at "movies-lib.xqy"

(: ============================================================== :)

(: print the query boxes.
   Parameters $q-xxx are of type xs:string? because the first time around,
   there are no query parameters.
   Return type is element(query) -- the query tag will be ignored by
   browsers.
:)
define function print-query
(
  $q-all-any-words     as xs:string? ,
  $q-title-contains    as xs:string? ,
  $q-year-op           as xs:string? ,
  $q-year              as xs:string? ,
  $q-director          as xs:string? ,
  $q-rating            as xs:string? ,
  $q-orderby           as xs:string? ,
  $all                 as xs:string?
) as element(query)
{
(
<query>
  <form action="query.xqy" class="query-box">
```

```
<table class="query">
  <tbody>
    <tr class="topRow">
      <td colspan="2">Title contains</td>
      <td colspan="2">Year released</td>
      <td>Director</td>
      <td>Rating</td>
      <td>Order by</td>
      <td>Action</td>
    </tr>
    <tr>
      <td>
        <select name="q-all-any-words">{
          element option {
            if ( $q-all-any-words = "all words" )
            then
              attribute selected {}
            else (),
            "all words"
            } ,
          element option {
            if ( $q-all-any-words = "any word" )
            then
              attribute selected {}
            else (),
            "any word"
            }
          } (: end select expression :)
        </select>
      </td>
      <td>
        <input type="text" name="q-title-contains"
          size="20" value="{$q-title-contains}"/>
      </td>
      <td>
      <!-- pull-down list of year operators.
           Add the "selected" attribute if this operator is "current"
           (was passed into the last query)
      -->
        <select name="q-year-op">{
          element option {
```

```
          if ( not($q-year-op) )
          then
            attribute selected {}
          else ()
        } ,
        for $op in ( ">", "<", "=" )
        return (
          element option {
            if ($op = $q-year-op)
            then
              attribute selected {}
            else () ,
            $op
            } (: end element option :)
          ) (: end return :)
        } (: end select expression :)
      </select>
    </td>
    <td>
      <input type="text" name="q-year" size="4" value="{$q-year}"/>
    </td>
    <td>
      <select name="q-director">{
        element option {
          if ( not($q-director) )
          then
            attribute selected {}
          else ()
          } ,
        for $director in get-all-directors()
        return (
          element option {
            if ($director = $q-director)
            then
              attribute selected {}
            else () ,
            $director
            } (: end element option :)
          ) (: end return :)
        } (: end select expression :)
      </select>
```

```
          </td>
          <td>
            <input type="text" name="q-rating" size="4"
              value="{$q-rating}"/>
          </td>
          <td>
            <select name="q-orderby">{
              element option {
                if ( not($q-orderby) )
                then
                  attribute selected {}
                else ()
                } ,
              (: the next for makes it easy to expand the choices later :)
              for $orderby in ("title", "rating")
              return (
                element option {
                  if ($orderby = $q-orderby)
                  then
                    attribute selected {}
                  else () ,
                  $orderby
                  } (: end element option :)
                ) (: end return :)
              } (: end select expression :)
            </select>
          </td>
          <td>
            <input type="submit" value="GO"/>
          </td>
        </tr>
      </tbody>
    </table>
  </form>
  <table class="buttons">
    <tbody>
      <tr>
        <td>
          <form action="query.xqy" class="buttons">
            <input type="submit" value="Clear"/>
          </form>
```

```
        </td>
        <td>
          <form action="query.xqy" class="buttons">
            <input type="hidden" name="all" value="Y"/>
            <input type="submit" value="Show All"/>
          </form>
        </td>
      </tr>
    </tbody>
  </table>
</query>
)
} (: end print-query :)

(: ================================================================ :)

(: print results of a query.  :)
define function print-results
(
  $q-all-any-words     as xs:string? ,
  $q-title-contains    as xs:string? ,
  $q-year-op           as xs:string? ,
  $q-year              as xs:string? ,
  $q-director          as xs:string? ,
  $q-rating            as xs:string? ,
  $q-orderby           as xs:string? ,
  $all                 as xs:string?
) as element(results)?
{
(: if $all is empty and all query fields are empty, do nothing :)
if ( not( $q-title-contains or ($q-year-op and $q-year) or $q-director
  or $q-rating or $q-orderby or $all  ) )
then ()
else (
  (: we got something in parameters.
     Get the movies that are in the result set
   :)
  let $movies := get-movies( $q-all-any-words, $q-title-contains,
                   $q-year-op, $q-year, $q-director, $q-rating, $q-orderby,
                   $all )
  return (
```

```
<results>
  <table class="count">
    <tbody>
      <tr>
        <td>Number of Movies:</td>
        <td>{ count($movies) }</td>
      </tr>
    </tbody>
  </table>
  <p/>{
    if ( count($movies) > 0 )
    then (
      <table class="results">
        <tbody>
          <tr>
            <td>Title</td>
            <td>Year</td>
            <td>Rating</td>
          </tr>
          { (: for each movie :)
            for $movie in $movies
            (: order by is a bit of a stretch.
               It's hard to express because you want order by title
               ascending, but order by rating descending.
               The ascending/descending is a keyword and not an
               expression.
               This code relies on the fact that "... order by ()
               ascending, rating descending ..." will order by
               rating descending. If the order specified is rating, we
               then order by title within rating.
            :)
            order by
              if ( $q-orderby = "title" )
              then $movie/title
              else ()
              ascending ,
              if ( $q-orderby = "rating" )
              then
                get-avg-rating( $movie/title, $movie/yearReleased )
              else ()
              descending ,
```

```
                if ( $q-orderby = "rating" )
                then $movie/title
                else ()
                ascending
              return
                print-one-movie( $movie )
              }
          </tbody>
        </table>
        ) (: end then :)
      else ()
      }
    </results>
    ) (: end return :)
  ) (: end else :)
} (: end print-results :)

(: =============================================================== :)

(: print a single movie result, as a table row :)

define function print-one-movie
(
  $movie                as element(movie)
)  as element(tr)
{
<tr>
  <td>
    <a target="new_window" href="print-movie.xqy
      ?p-title={ $movie/title/text() }
      &p-yearReleased={ $movie/yearReleased/text() }">
      { $movie/title/text() }
    </a>
  </td>
  <td>{ $movie/yearReleased }</td>
  <td>{
    let $rating := get-avg-rating( $movie/title, $movie/yearReleased )
    return (
      if ($rating)
      then (
        if ( ($rating >= 0) and ($rating < 1) )
```

```
then
  <a target="new_window" href="print-reviews.xqy
    ?p-title={$movie/title}
    &p-yearReleased={$movie/yearReleased}">
    <img src="../../image/stars-0-0.gif"/>
  </a>
else (
  if ( ($rating >= 1) and ($rating < 2) )
  then
    <a target="new_window" href="print-reviews.xqy
      ?p-title={$movie/title}
      &p-yearReleased={$movie/yearReleased}">
    <img src="../../image/stars-1-0.gif"/>
  </a>
  else (
    if ( ($rating >= 2) and ($rating < 3) )
    then
      <a target="new_window" href="print-reviews.xqy
        ?p-title={$movie/title}
        &p-yearReleased={$movie/yearReleased}">
      <img src="../../image/stars-2-0.gif"/>
      </a>
    else (
      if ( ($rating >= 3) and ($rating < 4) )
      then
        <a target="new_window" href="print-reviews.xqy
          ?p-title={$movie/title}
          &p-yearReleased={$movie/yearReleased}">
        <img src="../../image/stars-3-0.gif"/>
        </a>
      else (
        if ( ($rating >= 4) and ($rating < 5) )
        then
          <a target="new_window" href="print-reviews.xqy
            ?p-title={$movie/title}
            &p-yearReleased={$movie/yearReleased}">
          <img src="../../image/stars-4-0.gif"/>
          </a>
        else (
          if ( $rating = 5 )
          then
```

```
                    <a target="new_window" href="print-reviews.xqy
                      ?p-title={$movie/title}
                      &p-yearReleased={$movie/yearReleased}">
                    <img src="../../image/stars-5-0.gif"/>
                    </a>
                  else () (: error condition -- rating is out of range :)
                  )
                )
              )
            )
          )
        )
      else (<b>?</b>)
    ) (: end return :)
    }</td>
</tr>
} (: end print-one-movie :)
```

Example A-45 does any generic processing the application needs. Keeping the display functions and generic functions separate means we could write a similar application with a completely different user interface quite easily.

Example A—45 *Movies Library movies-lib.xqy*

```
module "http://www.w3.org/2003/05/xpath-functions"

(: ============================================================ :)

(: get all movies. Do this in one place only, in case the location changes
:)
define function get-all-movies() as element(movie)*
{
  doc("/example/movies-we-own.xml")/movies/movie
}

(: ============================================================ :)

(: get a sequence of movies, given some search and ordering criteria.
   Written as a restriction of get-all-movies() so we only mention the
   document in one place
:)
```

```
define function get-movies(
  $q-all-any-words     as xs:string? ,
  $q-title-contains    as xs:string? ,
  $q-year-op           as xs:string? ,
  $q-year              as xs:string? ,
  $q-director          as xs:string? ,
  $q-rating            as xs:string? ,
  $q-orderby           as xs:string? ,
  $all                 as xs:string?
) as element(movie)*
{
if ($all)
then
  get-all-movies()
else (
  (: for each possible predicate, check to see if we have a parameter,
     then apply the predicate or true().
     Note that the next 50+ lines of code are a single XPath expression.
  :)
  get-all-movies()
    [ (: start title words condition :)
      (: This is a bit brittle - it assumes users type a single space
         between words
       :)
      if ( tokenize($q-title-contains, " ") )
      then (
        if ( $q-all-any-words = "all words" )
        then
          cts:contains(title,
            cts:and-query( tokenize($q-title-contains, " "), "unordered"))
        else
          cts:contains(title,
            cts:or-query( tokenize($q-title-contains, " ")))
          )
      else
        true()
      ] (: end title words condition :)
      [ (: start year condition :)
        if ($q-year-op = "=")
        then
          (data(yearReleased) = $q-year)
```

```
        else (
          if ($q-year-op = "<")
          then
            (data(yearReleased) < $q-year)
          else (
            if ($q-year-op = ">")
            then
              (data(yearReleased) > $q-year)
            else (
              true()
              (: if $q-year-op doesn't match one of the expected operators,
                 condition is true :)
              )
            )
          )
        ] (: end year condition :)
        [ (: start director condition :)
          if ( $q-director )
          then (
            director/givenName = get-name( $q-director, "given" ) and
            director/familyName = get-name( $q-director, "family" )
            )
          else ( true() ) (: no director condition :)
        ] (: end director condition :)
        [ (: start rating condition :)
          (: if $q-rating is NOT castable as xs:double,
             ignore it (should be an error condition) :)
          if ( $q-rating and ($q-rating castable as xs:double) )
          then (
            get-avg-rating( title, yearReleased ) > xs:double($q-rating)
            ) (: end then :)
          else ( true() )
         (: no rating condition, or it's not castable as xs:decimal,
            or there are no reviews for this movie :)
        ] (: end rating condition :)
  ) (: end else :)
} (: end get-movies :)

(: ============================================================ :)

(: get all directors, in a convenient "first-name space last-name" string
```

```
:)
define function get-all-directors() as xs:string*
{
for $director in get-all-movies()/director
return
  (: concat() takes a sequence of strings, so e.g. givenName will yield the
     string value. Perhaps this is a bit sloppy, and we should use, e.g.,
     givenName/text()
  :)
  concat( $director/givenName, " ", $director/familyName )
} (: end get-all-directors :)

(: ================================================================ :)

(: get given or family name from a "first-name space last-name" string
   (as created by get-all-directors)
:)

define function get-name
(
  $stringName          as xs:string ,
  $whichName           as xs:string
) as xs:string
{
let $names := tokenize( $stringName, " ")
return
  if ( $whichName = "given" )
  then $names[1]
  else (
    if ( $whichName = "family" )
    then $names[2]
    else ( ) (: this is an error condition -- bad whichName parameter :)
    ) (: end else :)
} (: end get-name :)

(: ================================================================ :)

(: get the average rating for a given movie (keyed on title and
   yearReleased). If there are no reviews for this movie, return
   the empty sequence.
:)
```

```
define function get-avg-rating (
  $title              as xs:string ,
  $yearReleased       as xs:string
) as xs:double?
{
avg (
  for $review in doc("/example/reviews.xml")/reviews/review
  where
    $review/title = $title and
    $review/yearReleased = $yearReleased
  return
    $review/rating
  )

} (: end get-avg-rating :)

(: ============================================================== :)

(: get config details from the config file. :)
define function get-config() as element(config)
{
  doc("/example/bin/config.xml")/config
}

(: ============================================================== :)


(: get the name of the stylesheet to use, from the config file.
   If there is no stylesheet info in the config file, or if the stylesheet
   info is "none", then return "none", else return the name of the
   stylesheet
:)
define function get-stylesheet() as xs:string
{
  if ( get-config()/stylesheet = "none" or not( get-config()/stylesheet) )
  then "none"
  else string( get-config()/stylesheet )

} (: end get-stylesheet :)

(: ============================================================== :)
```

Example A-46 and Example A-47 are main modules that print a single movie and print all reviews for a single movie, respectively. These modules are called when you click on the movie title or the star rating in the results list.

***Example A—46** Standalone Module to Display a Movie print-movie.xqy*

```
import module "http://www.w3.org/2003/05/xpath-functions"
  at "movies-lib.xqy"

(: ================================================================ :)

(: This is a stand-alone XQuery module to print a single movie, keyed on
   title and yearReleased.
   We could do fancy things with the display.
   For now, just print the XML version of the movie.
:)

let $p-title            := xdmp:get-request-field("p-title")
let $p-yearReleased     := xdmp:get-request-field("p-yearReleased")
let $movie              := get-all-movies()
                              [ title = $p-title ]
                              [ yearReleased = $p-yearReleased ]

let $stylesheet         := get-stylesheet()

return (
  xdmp:set-response-content-type("text/html") ,
  (
<html xmlspace="preserve">
  <head>{
    if ( $stylesheet="none" )
    then ()
    else
      <link rel="stylesheet" type="text/css" href="{$stylesheet}" />
  }<title>{
  concat( "Movie: ", $p-title, ", ", $p-yearReleased )
  }</title>
  </head>
  <body>
    <hr/>{
    (: show the movie XML -- quote the tags so they show in the browser,
```

```
        but use pre to keep formatting :)
     }<pre>{
       xdmp:quote($movie)
     }</pre>
     <hr/>
   </body>
</html>
   )
) (: end print-movie.xqy :)
```

Example A—47 *Standalone Module to Display Reviews of a Movie print-reviews.xqy*

```
import module "http://www.w3.org/2003/05/xpath-functions"
  at "movies-lib.xqy"

(: ============================================================= :)

(: This is a stand-alone XQuery module to print reviews of a single movie,
   keyed on title and yearReleased.
   We could do fancy things with the display.
   For now, just print the XML version of all reviews.
:)

let $p-title           := xdmp:get-request-field("p-title")
let $p-yearReleased    := xdmp:get-request-field("p-yearReleased")
let $reviews           := doc("/example/reviews.xml")/reviews/review
                              [ title = $p-title ]
                              [ yearReleased = $p-yearReleased ]

let $stylesheet        := get-stylesheet()

return (
  xdmp:set-response-content-type("text/html") ,
  (
<html xmlspace="preserve">
  <head>{
    if ( $stylesheet="none" )
    then ()
    else
      <link rel="stylesheet" type="text/css" href="{$stylesheet}" />
  }<title>{
  concat( "Reviews for Movie: ", $p-title, ", ", $p-yearReleased )
```

```
  }</title>
  </head>
  <body>
    <hr/>{
    (: show the reviews XML -- quote the tags so they show in the browser,
       but use pre to keep formatting. Separate reviews with <p/>
    :) }
      { for $review in $reviews
        return
          <pre>{xdmp:quote($review)}</pre>, <p/>
      }
    <hr/>
  </body>
</html>
  )
) (: end print-reviews.xqy :)
```

Finally, Example A–48 is the configuration file. Currently, it only contains the designation of the CSS stylesheet to be used, but it could contain a collection of defaults, preferences, and other settings, such as the location of the movies data or the maximum number of results to display.

Example A—48 *Simple Configuration File config.xml*

```
<!–
  configuration file config.xml
  Defines a stylesheet, could contain other preferences,
  defaults, etc.
-->
<config>
  <stylesheet>style001.css</stylesheet>
</config>
```

That's it! The only file not reproduced here is the CSS stylesheet we used to get the appearance in Figure A–1. That's left as an exercise for the reader (or, of course, it's available for download at the example website).

A.5 Summary

In this appendix we presented some sample data for movies and reviews in an XML format, along with their metadata (an XML Schema and a DTD for each file). We showed you how to load these data into a SQL table with an XML column and how to query them using SQL/XML. You also saw how to store the data in a set of normalized SQL tables (or *represent* the data in a set of SQL *views*). We reviewed some of the SQL/XML examples from the body of the book, and we added some new ones, exercising the publishing functions and the newer `XMLTABLE` and `XMLQUERY`. We also reviewed some of the XPath and XQuery examples from earlier in the book, and we added some new ones. While the examples throughout this book are *somewhat* consistent, each example was presented to echo a particular point in the text. The examples and data in this appendix, on the other hand, are all completely consistent and can be run from the scripts on the example website (though some examples necessarily have vendor-specific syntax and extensions).

Appendix B

Standards Processes

B.1 Introduction

The standards that we've discussed in this book have been developed under the auspices of several different organizations. Some of those organizations, such as the World Wide Web Consortium, disavow the word *standard* in favor of the less imperative-sounding word, *recommendation*. Nonetheless, the specifications they publish are viewed by the general community as standards. The specifications developed by consortia and other, sometimes less formal organizations may become widely used and respected, in which case they become *de facto* standards — standards in fact. For that matter, some entirely proprietary specifications developed by commercial organizations (including software companies like Oracle, IBM, and Microsoft) may become *de facto* standards simply because they become widely adopted. Of course, many specifications developed by consortia or companies are not widely accepted and do not become *de facto* standards at all.

Other organizations, such as the American National Standards Institute (ANSI)[1] and the International Organization for Standardization (ISO),[2] are explicitly charged with developing and publishing

1 http://www.ansi.org.
2 http://www.iso.org.

more formal standards. Such standards are called *de jure* standards, meaning "standards in law." The term doesn't mean that the law is called into play to enforce adherence to those standards, only that they were developed in accordance with the rules of legally constituted standards development organizations. A *de jure* standard may or may not achieve the status of a "real" (*de facto*) standard, based entirely on whether it appeals to a wide enough audience to be adopted, implemented, and followed.

Regardless of its origins, no standard should be adopted based entirely on the status of the organization that developed it. Each standard must be evaluated on its own merits.

But what are the merits of standards? Why should a business select products that are built in conformance to certain standards? Why should a business create products that implement certain standards? Consider the problem of the sort of electrical plugs and outlets used for hair dryers, computer power supplies, stereo equipment, *etc.* Within the United States and Canada, there is a common *standard* for the plugs and outlets. That standard allows residents of those countries to be confident that their equipment will be able to connect to electrical power anywhere within that geographical area. That's the beauty of having a standard. Of course, even in this geographical region, there are multiple standards for electrical power connection, generally for safety reasons (*e.g.*, 15-amp connections *vs* 50-amp connections, older ungrounded two-blade plugs *vs* modern plugs that add a grounding pin).

However, just travel to another continent and see the trouble you'll have using electrical power. A quick look at the website of a company (Europlugs, Inc.[3]) that sells products to deal with this situation will quickly convince you that a standard with a much broader reach would be nice to have. (Of course, that same website brings to mind a well-known quotation attributed to Andrew Tanenburg: "The nice thing about standards is that there are so many of them to choose from.")

In the rest of this appendix, we discuss four well-known organizations that publish *de facto* and *de jure* standards. We chose these organizations because they have responsibility for the technologies discussed throughout this book.

---

3 A chart illustrating the problem is located at http://www.europlugs.com/wonpro%20universal%20receptacle%20map.htm.

B.2 World Wide Web Consortium (W3C)

B.2.1 What Is the W3C?

The World Wide Web Consortium (W3C) is a "public consortium" in the sense that it is open to membership by anybody with the resources (financial and otherwise) to participate. At press time, there were over 350 member organizations. According to the W3C's website,[4] the mission of the consortium is "to lead the World Wide Web to its full potential by developing protocols and guidelines that ensure long-term growth for the Web."

In practice, this has meant publishing specifications based on HTML and XML technologies. Among the W3C's success stories are several of the publications discussed in this book. Some of the principal specifications published by the W3C are:

- HTML (HyperText Markup Language)
- CSS (Cascading Style Sheets)
- XML (eXtensible Markup Language)
- XHTML (eXtensible HyperText Markup Language)
- The Information Set (Infoset)
- XML Schema
- SOAP (Simple Object Access Protocol)
- P3P (Platform for Privacy Preferences)
- XSLT (eXtensible Stylesheet Language: Transformations)

The W3C publications most relevant to this book, of course, include the entire XPath 2.0 and XQuery 1.0 suite of documents (including the Data Model, Functions and Operators, Formal Semantics, Serialization, and XQueryX), XSLT 1.0 and XSLT 2.0, XPath 1.0, Infoset, and XML Schema (parts 1 and 2).

The W3C was founded by Tim Berners-Lee, who invented the World Wide Web, along with the first web browser, the first web server, HTML, and the HTTP (HyperText Transfer Protocol), while working at CERN (European Organization for Nuclear Research). Sir Tim, as he is sometimes known, remains the Director of the W3C

4 http://www.w3.org.

today and takes a very active part in establishing new work and approving the progression of completed work. Berners-Lee spends much of his time working on technology related to the Semantic Web, an effort to add meaning to the web itself to make it more useable and useful to people and to automatic systems.

The W3C, founded in 1994, has published nearly a hundred Recommendations, as its completed specifications are known, ranging from protocols such as HTTP and SOAP, through markup languages such as XML and PNG (Portable Network Graphics), through higher-level specifications such as XML Schema and XQuery. One of the consortium's most important goals is to make the web accessible to all people, regardless of the language they speak and read or whatever disabilities they might have. Consequently, the Internationalization and Accessibility activities are given significant authority to review and propose changes to the content of specifications before they are advanced to Recommendation status.

B.2.2 The W3C Process Document

The W3C is governed primarily by its Process Document,[5] which "describes the organizational structure of the W3C and the processes related to the responsibilities and functions they exercise to enable W3C to accomplish its mission." Among other things, the Process Document sets up the structure of the consortium, including the rights and responsibilities of its members as well as the existence and duties of:

- An Advisory Board (AB) comprising nine members chosen from the W3C membership and a chair (usually the W3C chair). The duties of the AB are to provide "ongoing guidance to the Team on issues of strategy, management, legal matters, process, and conflict resolution."
- An Advisory Committee (AC) composed of one representative from each W3C member organization. Its duties are not spelled out particularly well in the Process Document, but it is clear that the AC should be kept informed of the W3C's financial status, budget information, including deployment of Team members, and the status of each W3C activity.

5 http://www.w3.org/2004/02/Process-20040205/.

- The W3C Team, including paid staff, unpaid interns, and W3C Fellows. The Team "provides technical leadership about Web technologies, organizes and manages W3C Activities to reach goals within practical constraints (such as resources available), and communicates with the Members and the public about the Web and W3C technologies."
- A Technical Architecture Group (TAG), which includes a chair (usually the Director), three members appointed by the Director, and five additional members elected by the AC.

The process document also spells out how W3C Activities (the formal term includes very broad topics, such as "XML," "Internationalization," and "Multimodal Interaction") are created and managed, how Working Groups are established, chartered, managed, and terminated, and how coordination between Working Groups within an Activity is maintained.

Perhaps most importantly, the document establishes the criteria by which *Recommendation Track* documents are initiated and progressed. We discuss this further in Section B.2.3.

B.2.3 The W3C Stages of Progression

In the context of the W3C, there are two broad types of document to consider. One of these, the Note, has very little official standing and correspondingly has very little process associated with it. A Note can be developed by a Working Group (a Working Group Note), by an Interest Group (Interest Group note), or by a Coordinating Group (Coordinating Group Note). Notes sometimes identify a *best practice,* and they sometimes describe a specific technology or technique that, while interesting to the web community, doesn't have enough support to become a more formal Recommendation.

The other type of document is described as "Recommendation Track." It is this kind that receives significant attention from the Process Document and from the W3C administration.

A Recommendation Track (REC-track) document is one intended to be published eventually as a W3C Recommendation. Most REC-track documents are eventually published as Recommendations, but not all. Some stall during development because of the inability of the responsible Working Group to achieve consensus, while others are overtaken by events and become irrelevant or unneeded. The Recommendation Track process is responsible for advancing specifications from early Working Drafts to Recommendation, for terminating work on a specification before it reaches Recommendation status, for modifying approved Recommendations, and for rescinding approved Recommendations.

There are four "maturity levels" (often called "steps") along the path toward Recommendation status:

- Working Draft (WD): A document that the W3C has published for review by the web community. Most REC-track documents are published more than once – frequently much more – in WD form. All REC-track documents must undergo a Last Call Working Draft comment period (often called "Last Call," as though it were a separate maturity level) before advancing further.
- Candidate Recommendation (CR): A document that the W3C believes has been properly reviewed by the WG, by related WGs, and by the community at large and that satisfies its stated technical requirements; Candidate Recommendations are published specifically to gather information about implementation experience. Before a spec can progress beyond CR stage, it must have been implemented at least once (most CR documents require two or more implementations). The intent of this requirement is to ensure not only that the spec is implementable, but also that there is sufficient interest in it to attract implementers.
- Proposed Recommendation (PR): A specification that has received wide review for technical soundness and implementability that is then sent to the W3C AC for final endorsement.
- Recommendation (REC): A specification that has achieved significant consensus and has received the endorsement of W3C members and of the Director. The W3C "recommends the wide deployment" of its Recommendations. Recommendations correspond reasonably well to *standards* published by other organizations.

There are well-defined criteria specified for advancing from one maturity level to the next. The entire process, from first draft to Recommendation, might take as little as several months, for very small, very mature specs, and might take as long as six or eight years, for large, complex sets of specifications involving the invention of new technology. Those readers interested in the details are encouraged to read the W3C Process Document.

B.3 Java Community Process (JCP)

B.3.1 What Is the JCP?

The Java Community Process (JCP)[6] is described as "the open, participative process to develop and revise the Java™ technology specifications, reference implementations, and test suites." Its goal is to allow Java developers worldwide to participate in the ongoing evolution of the Java platform.

The day-to-day management of the JCP is handled by the Process Management Office (PMO), which is a group within Sun Microsystems. The PMO is responsible for the JCP website, for administering the membership program, for handling press releases, and other such activities. In our view, the PMO is the organ through which Sun exercises its control of the Java Community Process. Sun does this in order to ensure that the Java language and platform are not "hijacked" by entities that do not necessarily have the best interests of the Java community at heart. A cynic might add that Sun may want to be certain that the Java platform evolves in directions that support Sun's corporate goals. We hasten to note, however, that the JCP is a *process*, not a consortium or an incorporated entity of any sort.

Participation in the JCP is open to any individual who, or organization that, signs the Java Specification Agreement (JSPA).[7] The JSPA is a contract (which must be renewed annually) between the JCP member and Sun, setting out the rights and responsibilities of each. Once a JSPA has been sent to Sun and Sun has "executed" it, the new member has the rights to:

- Review and comment on each Java Specification Request (JSR) – after it has been approved by the Expert Group (EG) that developed it – before the public has a change to see it. (We discuss JSRs and EGs in Section B.3.2.)

---

6 http://www.jcp.org.

7 There are multiple JSPAs, each with a different purpose (corporate member, individual member, *etc.*). They are linked from the JCP membership page, located at http://www.jcp.org/en/participation/membership.

- Submit proposals for new JSRs.
- Participate in and lead Expert Groups.
- Vote in Executive Committee (EC) elections.
- Attend JCP member events.

There are, in fact, two Executive Committees, one covering Standard and Enterprise Java matters and the other covering Micro Edition Java issues. Each Executive Committee is a body comprising a non-voting chair staffed by the PMO, 10 "ratified seats," five elected seats, and a permanent seat for Sun. (A ratified seat is one filled by a JCP member nominated by the PMO and elected by the JCP membership. An elected seat is one filled by a JCP member nominated by and elected by the JCP membership.) The responsibilities of each EC include selection of proposed JSRs for inclusion in the JCP, approving draft specifications for review, giving final approval to completed specifications and their supporting material, and providing guidance to the PMO.

(By now, you may well feel as though you are drowning in alphabet soup. It's unfortunate, but the TLAs[8] are part of the jargon in many activities and organizations, especially those dominated by us computer software types. With our apologies, we unavoidably use them throughout this appendix.)

B.3.2 JSRs and Expert Groups: Formation and Operation

The term *Java Specification Request* reminds us of the term *"Request For Comment"* (RFC) used by the Internet Engineering Task Force (IETF).[9] Those two terms mean somewhat more than a "request" for anything. They also might refer to the resulting document and to the process by which the document is developed.

The formal process of developing Java specifications is spelled out in the JCP Process Document.[10] In Section B.2.3, you'll read about the various stages through which a JSR goes from proposal to final specification. In this section, we are concerned with how a JSR comes into being and is set into motion, and with the nature of Expert Groups.

8 Three-Letter Acronyms, some of which have two or four letters. Droll, *n'est ce pas?*
9 http://www.ietf.org.
10 http://www.jcp.org/en/procedures/jcp2.

The Process Document defines a Java Specification Request as "the document submitted to the PMO by one or more Members to propose the development of a new Specification or significant revision to an existing Specification." This definition clearly establishes the "request" aspect of the term.

A JSR is submitted to the PMO by one or more JCP members. The submission identifies the submitters, the person — less frequently, persons — who will be the Spec Leads (that is, the chairs) of the Expert Group that is intended to develop the specification, the initial members of the Expert Group, the reasons for the submission, and an estimated development schedule. Once the PMO approves the format of the submission and establishes that the submission is not redundant with existing or other newly proposed JSRs, the JSR is given to the appropriate EC for its consideration. The EC can reject the JSR or approve it; it can also reject it without prejudice and suggest changes that are likely to result in an approval in a future vote.

When approved by the EC, the JSR is given a number (*e.g.*, JSR 225 is the 225th JSR approved by an EC). The JSR then transforms from a request into a process. The EG is constituted and the Spec Lead sets the development process in motion. In addition to acting as the chair of the EG, a Spec Lead is responsible for ensuring that there is a Reference Implementation (RI) of the specification being developed, as well as a Technology Compatibility Kit (TCK) — essentially a test suite to ensure that the RI actually conforms to the specification. If there are multiple Spec Leads, they may divide the responsibilities for the specification, the RI, and the TCK among themselves.

In practice, EG members frequently have little control over the JSR's development. They essentially act as advisors to the Spec Leads, who are given complete authority over the JSR's development. We know of some JSRs in which the Spec Leads have already-completed specifications, RIs, and TCKs when the JSR is submitted; in those JSRs, the EG is little more than a façade to give the appearance of an open process. Other JSRs are run by Spec Leads who are genuinely interested in an open, community-driven process and give EG members considerable ability to guide the specification's development.

Ultimately, the Spec Lead has the responsibility to deliver — according to the planned schedule — the specification, the RI, and the TCK identified in the JSR's initial submission, and to ensure that the specification has achieved a consensus from the overall Java community.

B.3.3 The JSR Stages of Progression

As you learned in Section B.3.2, a JSR is established, after submission to the PMO by one or more JCP members, by a vote of the appropriate EC.[11] A Spec Lead is named (in the submission), an Expert Group is constituted (starting with the initial members named in the submission), and the development process begins.

The current version of the JCP identifies four steps in the development of a Java specification:

1. Initiation – Submission and approval of the JSR as described in Section B.3.2.
2. Early Draft – The Spec Lead, with assistance from the EG, develops a "preliminary draft" of the specification and posts it on the JCP website to allow both the JCP members and the general public to review it. The Spec Lead and the EG use feedback from the review to revise and refine the draft.
3. Public Draft – When the Spec Lead and the EG believe that the draft is "done," it is again released for review by the general public. Feedback received during this review may be used to further revise the specification. After the review (and possible revision) is complete, the EC determines whether the draft should be progressed. If the EC votes for progression, the Spec Lead ensures that the RI and TCK are finished, after which the specification is sent back to the EC for final approval.
4. Maintenance – The completed spec, RI, and TCK may be updated as a result of requests for clarification, interpretation, enhancements, and revisions. The EC reviews proposed changes to the spec and determines which can be implemented immediately and which require the creation of an EG to develop a revised specification. Any of the tests in a TCK can be challenged (meaning that the challenger believes that they do not accurately reflect the intent of the specification). Such challenges, if they can't be resolved

11 Yes, we're being a bit cruel by using so many acronyms in one sentence, but there's really no other way to express the process without taking much more space.

easily, are decided by the EC and may result in changes to the TCK.

Significant revisions to existing specifications aren't handled by simple maintenance activities. Instead, they require a new JSR that goes through the entire process described in this section.

B.4 *De Jure* Standards: ANSI and ISO

B.4.1 The De Jure Process and Organizations

A *de jure* standard is a specification that has been approved by a "recognized standardization body." *De Jure* standards differ from specifications published by consortia and corporations principally because they are entirely public and are meant to be used freely by literally anybody. Although users may find themselves required to pay for copies of these standards, there is no cost associated with *using* the standard.

By contrast, specifications published by a consortium or corporation remain the property of the publisher, who may place restrictions or licensing obligations on their use. Not all such specifications come with such encumbrances. Increasingly, consortia that develop specifications they wish to become *de facto* standards are minimizing the restrictions they place on users of those specs. In many ways, the lines between this sort of standard and those published by *de jure* standards bodies have begun to blur.

One way in which the lines do not blur at all is the cost of participation. The *de jure* standards organizations commonly make it very easy for members of the general public to participate in their standards development activities. This often means that relatively low fees are charged for participation and that the documents under development have wide public visibility to permit public review, comment, and contribution.

By contrast, it is common for consortia to charge thousands, even tens or hundreds of thousands, of dollars for membership — and membership is always required for participation in the development of the specifications. Thus, even though the specifications might be made readily available for review and comment during their development cycles, only those who have paid for membership actively control the specifications.

There is a wide perception that *de jure* standards organizations have such burdensome rules and processes that development of their standards takes far too long in today's fast-paced world. (The words *glacial time* have been sardonically applied to describe this situation.) We are convinced, however, that this is nothing more than a myth, an urban legend. Because of our extensive participation, spanning decades, in both sorts of organizations, we have good insights into the perceptions.

The standards developed by *de jure* standards bodies are always done very publicly, from their inception. The processes that seem so cumbersome and impractical have been put in place to ensure that all stakeholders, even those who are not active participants in the development of those standards, are served by due process — that is, they and their opinions are not excluded from affecting the content of the specification. Consequently, a very public development process that takes, say, three years from inception to final approval is all that exists.

Consortia and similar organizations, on the other hand, frequently (not universally) begin development of a specification long before the general public is made aware of the activity. Once the specification has been developed sufficiently, it is announced and often made visible for public review. By that time, however, the spec is usually far along the path toward publication. In addition, voting is done very quickly among the relatively small number of members of the organization — because the larger public isn't involved. The result is that public perception of the time it takes to publish this sort of specification is shorter than the actual development period.

In the United States, the principle *de jure* standards organization is ANSI. According to the Wikipedia, ANSI is a "private, nonprofit standards organization that serves as a facilitator for the standardization work of its members in the United States. ANSI accredits standards developing organizations (SDOs) that meet a set of requirements and criteria governing the management of consensus standards development."[12] ANSI is also the "National Body" that represents the United States in a number of international standards bodies, including ISO, IEC,[13] and ITU.[14] The standards published by ANSI are American National Standards.

12 http://en.wikipedia.org/wiki/Ansi.

13 International Electrotechnical Commission, http://www.iec.ch.

14 International Telecommunications Union, http://www.itu.org.

ANSI does not develop standards itself. Instead, it delegates that job to SDOs that it accredits; those SDOs must adopt policies approved by ANSI that ensure complete openness of the standards development process. Examples of SDOs operating under the auspices of ANSI, of which there are scores, are the Acoustical Society of America, the American Boat and Yacht Council, the Clinical and Laboratory Standards Institute, the National Electrical Contractors Association, the Steel Shipping Container Institute, and the U.S. Department of Agriculture. For the purposes of this book, the most relevant ANSI SDO is INCITS, the InterNational Committee for Information Technology Standards.[15] INCITS is responsible for development of and U.S. participation in the development of the great majority of IT (information technology) standards.

INCITS obviously has very broad responsibilities, so it delegates the IT standards development activities to its technical committees (TCs), which range from INCITS B10 (Identification Cards and Related Devices) to INCITS W1 (Office Equipment). It is INCITS H2 (Database) that is responsible for the development of the SQL standard. INCITS H2 is also the United States Technical Advisory Group (TAG) for participation in the corresponding ISO activities discussed in Section B.4.2. INCITS prescribes the procedures under which its TCs operate, initiates and manages public review of proposed American National Standards that it develops, and handles final approval of such standards.

Other countries (including all of the developed countries as well as many developing countries) have their own standards bodies, for example, BSI (the British Standards Institute) in the UK, AFNOR (Association Française de Normalization) in France, and DIN (Deutsches Institut für Normung) in Germany. They develop many standards that are used both nationally and internationally. BSI process management and evaluations standards are particularly well known, as are German safety standards.

Internationally, ISO is the principal standards development organization. ISO's members are not individuals or commercial organizations. Instead, its members are the National Bodies of countries, such as ANSI from the United States. There are other international standards development organizations, many of them working closely with ISO. Because of space limitations, we focus these paragraphs on ISO alone.

15 http://www.incits.org.

ISO publishes standards on an extremely wide range of subjects, ranging from screw threads to processes for measuring the quality of steel in a furnace to algorithms for recognizing human faces automatically. Analogously to ANSI, ISO does not develop standards itself; instead, it delegates that responsibility to its Technical Committees (TCs). ISO TC 97 was responsible for most IT standardization until the late 1990s, when it joined forces with IEC to form Joint Technical Committee 1 (JTC 1), Information technology. The U.S. TAG for all of JTC 1's activities is INCITS.

Many ISO TCs develop standards directly. However, like INCITS, JTC 1's brief is far too broad for it to actually develop standards. It delegates those responsibilities to subcommittees (SCs). SC 32, Data Management and Interchange, is the JTC 1 subcommittee responsible for a number of standards activities related to databases, data management, and metadata management, including SQL. Often, an SC's responsibilities are too great for standards to be developed directly by the SC, in which case, the SC may further delegate that job to one or more working groups (WGs). SC 32 is in that position, and it has delegated responsibility for all parts of the SQL standard to its WG 3, Database Languages.

B.4.2 The SQL/XML Standardization Environment

ISO/IEC JTC 1/SC 32/WG 3 is, as you learned in Section B.4.1, the international organization responsible for SQL standards activities. You also learned that U.S. SQL-related activities are handled in INCITS H2. In this section, we compare and contrast the ways in which these two organizations go about their jobs.

INCITS H2 came into existence in 1978 as X3H2 (X3 being the original name of INCITS). Its members are organizations, such as corporations and even consortia, as well as individual persons. For years, H2 held approximately six meetings every year, at locations selected largely by the individual willing to act as host. (Interesting factoid: H2 is the only INCITS TC to have met in all 50 of the United States.) Membership of H2 has ranged as high as 50 or 60 members at its peak during the development of the 1992 edition of the SQL standard. In recent years, membership has dropped off to the low double digits (between 10 and 20, currently closer to 10) and meetings are held both at some physical location (about one-third of each year's meetings) and by telephone and Internet (about two-thirds of the meetings each year).

WG 3 meets once each year concurrently, and collocated, with the rest of SC 32 (which includes three other working groups). In addition, it meets one or two additional times per year in order to increase the speed of development. After a ballot has completed, WG 3 meets with the authority of SC 32 in a *ballot resolution meeting* (often called an *editing meeting*).

During the development of SQL:1999, WG 3 had nine consecutive meetings of three weeks each! ("Consecutive" in this case does not imply that the start of one meeting began immediately following the end of the preceding meeting. The consecutive meetings were typically spaced about four months apart.) That was an extreme situation, happily, and WG 3 currently meets for only one or two weeks at a time.

One of us (Jim) has been a leading participant in, and editor for, both H2 and WG 3 for nearly 20 years. During that time, the *de jure* standards development landscape has changed dramatically. Some of those changes are definitely good — for example, WG 3 is able to publish a new standard (a new part of SQL) or to revise an existing standard in only two years. In the "good old days," the process was more likely to take three to four years. (Some of us believe that the time can be shortened to 18 months, but only if no glitches in the process or in timing of meetings comes into play.)

Both H2 and WG 3 require that all changes to an emerging standard be provided as formal, detailed change proposals that give the editor specific instructions for adding, deleting, or modifying text in the document. By contrast, most standards-developing consortia and even many INCITS and ISO organizations accept conceptual changes and give the documents' editors broad discretion to make appropriate changes. With a standard as large as SQL, however, the editor (that would be Jim) has declined that authority.

One important consideration of any standards effort is the impact of intellectual property rights, or IPR. IPR includes patents, copyrights, and even trade secrets. Most *de jure* standards organizations, including JTC 1 and INCITS, require that all participants declare the existence of any IPR concerning the technology that is being proposed for inclusion in a standard — regardless of whether that technology is being proposed by the owner of the IPR or by someone else. This policy avoids the potential disaster of adopting and publishing a standard that contains some organization's IPR, after which the owner of that IPR can make almost any demand on implementers and users of the standard. Neither INCITS nor JTC 1 prohibits the use of patented or otherwise protected material in standards, as long as the facts – and the terms of its inclusion – are disclosed in advance. In virtually all cases, these *de jure* standards organizations require that the IPR be made available on reasonable and nondiscriminatory (RAND) terms;[16] some such organizations go a step further and require that the IPR be made royalty-free (RF) as well.

SQL/XML is currently receiving more attention in both H2 and WG3 than any other aspect of the SQL standard. The first edition of SQL/XML was published as part of the 2003 edition of the SQL standard (commonly known as SQL:2003). A second edition was completed very late in 2005, and the third edition is planned for late 2007. The specification was very heavily revised and extended between the first and second editions – as you read in Chapter 15, "SQL/XML," the 2003 edition was based on the XML Information Set, while the 2005 edition is based on the XQuery 1.0 and XPath 2.0 Data Model. Plans for the 2007 edition include the addition of Full-Text support and the ability to update XML data (see Chapter 13, "What's Missing?").

B.4.3 Stages of Progression

Aside from such details as meeting frequency and what sort of members they allow, the ANSI/INCITS and ISO/JTC 1 standards development processes are significantly different in many ways. We discuss first the U.S. process and then the international one.

Development of an American National Standard involves 8 "milestones":

1. Approval of a project proposal – Project proposals are sent to the INCITS secretariat; they are often submitted by an existing INCITS TC, but may come from the general public (in which case, when they are approved either they are assigned to a TC or a new TC is established).
2. Notification to the public – INCITS issues a press release focused on publications most relevant to the proposal.
3. Technical development – This is usually the longest stage, sometimes taking several years. During this stage, the responsible TC develops a specification according to certain

16 Consult your own legal advisor. While we have seen actors play lawyers on television, we ourselves are not lawyers. We should not, and do not, pretend to have the ability to properly define these terms.

practices and formats. It is in this phase that all IPR must be declared.

4. Initial public review – This stage comprises a 45-day review period initiated by an announcement published in *ANSI Standards Action* and additional press releases.
5. Management review – During this phase, a second public review may be held, depending on various factors. The INCITS secretariat reviews several aspects of the standard's development to ensure that all ANSI and INCITS policies were followed and that due process was provided to every commenter. At this point, the specification becomes known as a *draft proposed American National Standard*, or *dpANS*.
6. Executive Board approval – The final specification is reviewed by the INCITS Executive Board, which votes either to accept the specification for consideration as an American National Standard or to reject it.
7. ANSI approval – If the Executive Board accepts the specification, it is forwarded to ANSI for final approval. ANSI reviews both the form of the specification and the documentation of the process used in its development (again, to ensure openness).
8. Publication – If ANSI approves the specification, it is published as an American National Standard.

Slight variations of the milestones exist to accommodate publication of an International Standard as an American National Standard and for "fast-tracking" a standard or specification developed outside of the ANSI/INCITS procedures as an American National Standard.

INCITS' procedures have been fine-tuned to the point that a standard can be published in as little as 18 months following initial submission of a project proposal.

The JTC 1 process comprises more steps than the ANSI/INCITS one. There are many possible variations, depending on the exact type of document being processed, but the following is typical for processing a specification intended to become an International Standard (IS).

- Project proposal, also known as New Work Item (NWI) proposal – A project proposal is submitted to an ISO TC,

ISO/IEC JTC, or SC. For example, proposals can be submitted to ISO/IEC JTC 1/SC 32. An NWI is balloted at the TC or JTC level by member National Bodies.

- Working Draft — This is the actual development stage. Small, simple specifications might be published as a WD only once or twice before advancing to the next stage. Larger, more complex standards are published more times. For example, during its development process, there were at least 15 WD publications of the spec that became SQL:1999. WDs are normally made visible to the public at large for review and comment, although there are rarely press releases associated with their publication.
- Committee Draft (CD) — This optional step allows the development group, such as WG 3, to force a review of a specification by National Bodies to determine problems that would inhibit its advancement to a subsequent stage. A specification is published as a CD if the development group expects the result of the review to result in significant changes to the document. CD ballots last for three months. A ballot resolution meeting almost always results from a CD ballot.
- Final Committee Draft (FCD) — No specification is allowed to progress to subsequent stages until it has undergone a successful FCD ballot. The purpose of this ballot is not so much to discover serious problems in its content as much as to determine whether there is sufficient National Body support to advance the document to a subsequent stage. The result of a successful FCD ballot may still be the subject of a ballot resolution meeting before the document is further advanced. FCD ballots last for four months.
- Draft International Standard (DIS) — This is another optional step that forces National Bodies to give the specification one last serious review before it is considered for advancement to International Standard status. If a document receives approval at the DIS stage, it may still be the subject of a ballot resolution meeting, but only to correct very minor problems (such as typographical errors). Significant technical changes are severely discouraged at this stage. DIS ballots last for three months.
- Final Draft International Standard (FDIS) — This is sometimes called "once more with feeling." It is at this stage that

the National Bodies give their final approval for the document to be published as an International Standard. The result of a successful FDIS ballot is never returned to the development group and cannot be changed in any way (except for the cover, frontmatter, and page headers and footers that ISO and JTC 1 prescribe). FDIS ballots last for two months.

- International Standard (IS) – This is, of course, final publication of the specification.

When a specification is intended for publication as both an International Standard and an American National Standard – which is the case with SQL/XML and the other parts of the SQL standard – these two disparate processes must be synchronized to whatever degree possible. That poses some interesting management challenges, but there are formal policies in place (at least within INCITS) to help keep them aligned.

B.5 Summary

In this appendix, we have described several standards processes, including those of one consortium, those of one company-managed effort, and those of two *de jure* standards organizations.

Even though the processes themselves differ very significantly, the goals are quite the same: to produce high-quality, timely, and relevant specifications that are adopted by the appropriate community as a practical and useful standard.

During our years of experience in various standards bodies, we have observed that it takes a special kind of person to pursue standards participation. (Some people have even said that we tend to be "special," in a noncomplimentary way.) Characteristics of successful standards participants include reasonably good people skills, a high tolerance for ambiguity and frustration, the ability to express one's self clearly both in writing and in speaking, attention to detail, the ability to understand technical arguments both conceptual and detailed (while weighing such details as general usefulness, completeness, the odds of gaining a consensus, and perhaps even the benefit to one's employer) – and a sturdy bottom (for sitting in all those interminable meetings and on all those plane rides).

Standards people are sometimes academics, implementers, project or product managers, and even managers. A very few lucky ones participate in standards organizations as a full-time professional activity.

Grammars

C.1 Introduction

In this appendix, we provide the grammar of SQL/XML and of XQuery. Both are presented in a variation of Backus-Naur Form (BNF) and both of these variations are called "extended BNF" (which XQuery calls EBNF). In each section, we summarize the meanings of the notations used in the grammar. We do not present the grammar for XPath 2.0, largely because it is a subset of the XQuery grammar.

C.2 XQuery Grammar

The XQuery grammar[1] (which is used by all W3C specifications) involves a variation of EBNF that uses a notation derived from regular expressions. For example, in the XQuery grammar, the BNF non-terminal symbol `digits` is defined to be any sequence of one or more instances of the characters 0, 1, 2, 3, 4, 5, 6, 7, 8, and 9:

```
digits ::= [0-9]+
```

1 The grammar presented here is taken from the XQuery Last Call Working Draft published on 4 April 2005 at http://www.w3.org/TR/2005/WD-xquery-20050404/.

In this production, the notation `[0-9]` means "every character in the range starting with 0 and ending with 9," and the plus sign + means "one or more."

As in almost all uses of BNF, the notation `A ::= B C` is a *production* that is equivalent to the statement "the nonterminal symbol A is defined to be the nonterminal symbol B followed by the nonterminal symbol C." *Nonterminal* symbols are those that are defined by an EBNF production, while *terminal* symbols are those that are not defined in EBNF productions (except for a few that are defined in special productions used to specify the internal syntax of some terminal symbols).

The rules associated with matching strings of one or more characters in a terminal symbol are provided in Table C–1.

***Table C—1** Rules for Matching Terminal Symbols*

Notation	Meaning
`#xN` (`"N" is a hexadecimal integer`)	Matches the character in ISO 10646 whose canonical (UCS-4) code value has the specified value
`[a-zA-Z]`	Matches any Char with a value in the range(s) indicated (inclusive)
`[abc]`	Matches any Char with a value among the characters enumerated
`[^a-z]`	Matches any Char with a value outside the range indicated
`[^abc]`	Matches any Char with a value not among the characters given
`"string"` or `'string'`	Matches the sequence of characters that appear inside the double quotes or single quotes, respectively

Table C–2 gives the rules for interpreting the notations used to define nonterminal symbols in this variation of EBNF.

Table C—2 Rules for Matching Nonterminal Symbols

Notation	Meaning
`(A)`	A is treated as a unit and may be combined as described in this list.
`A?`	Matches A or nothing; equivalent to saying that A is *optional*.
`A B`	Matches A followed by B. In this variation of EBNF, this operator has higher precedence than alternation; thus A B | C D is identical to (A B) | (C D).
`A | B`	Matches either A or B but not both.
`A - B`	Matches any string that matches A but does not match B.
`A+`	Matches *one or more* occurrences of A. Concatenation has higher precedence than alternation; thus A+ | B+ is identical to (A+) | (B+).
`A*`	Matches *zero or more* occurrences of A. Concatenation has higher precedence than alternation; thus A* | B* is identical to (A*) | (B*).
`"(", "comment"`	Matches a literal open parenthesis or a literal example of the word "comment," respectively.

Note that, in this variation of EBNF, nonterminal symbols are not delineated by any special characters, while terminal symbols are always enclosed in double quotes.

XQuery's EBNF notation that defines all nonterminal symbols other than single-character nonterminals and keywords appears in Grammar C-1.

Grammar C—1 XQuery Terminal Symbol EBNF

```
IntegerLiteral ::= Digits
DecimalLiteral ::= ("." Digits) | (Digits "." [0-9]*)
DoubleLiteral ::= (("." Digits) | (Digits ("." [0-9]*)?)) [eE] [+-]? Digits
StringLiteral ::= ('"' (PredefinedEntityRef | CharRef | EscapeQuot |
                  [^"&])* '"') | ("'" (PredefinedEntityRef | CharRef |
```

```
                    EscapeApos | [^'&])* "'")
PredefinedEntityRef ::= "&" ("lt" | "gt" | "amp" | "quot" | "apos") ";"
EscapeQuot ::= '""'
EscapeApos ::= "''"
ElementContentChar ::= Char - [{}<&]
QuotAttrContentChar ::= Char - ["{}<&]
AposAttrContentChar ::= Char - ['{}<&]
Comment ::= "(:" (CommentContents | Comment)* ":)"
PITarget ::= (See the XML Recommendation)
CharRef ::= (See the XML Recommendation)
QName ::= (See the XML Namespaces Recommendation)
NCName ::= (See the XML Namespaces Recommendation)
S ::= (See the XML Recommendation)
Char ::= (See the XML Recommendation)
Digits ::= [0-9]+
CommentContents ::= (Char+ - (Char* ('(:' | ':)') Char*))
```

XQuery's EBNF notation for all of the nonterminal symbol productions of the XQuery language appears in Grammar C–2.

Grammar C—2 *XQuery Nonterminal Symbol EBNF*

```
Module ::= VersionDecl? (MainModule | LibraryModule)
VersionDecl ::= "xquery" "version" StringLiteral
                ("encoding" StringLiteral)? Separator
MainModule ::= Prolog QueryBody
LibraryModule ::= ModuleDecl Prolog
ModuleDecl ::= "module" "namespace" NCName "=" URILiteral Separator
Prolog ::= ((Setter | Import | NamespaceDecl | DefaultNamespaceDecl)
             Separator)* ((VarDecl | FunctionDecl | OptionDecl) Separator)*
Setter ::= BoundarySpaceDecl | DefaultCollationDecl | BaseURIDecl |
           ConstructionDecl | OrderingModeDecl | EmptyOrderDecl |
           CopyNamespacesDecl
Import ::= SchemaImport | ModuleImport
Separator ::= ";"
NamespaceDecl ::= <"declare" "namespace"> NCName "=" URILiteral
BoundarySpaceDecl ::= <"declare" "boundary-space"> ("preserve" | "strip")
DefaultNamespaceDecl ::= (<"declare" "default" "element"> |
                          <"declare" "default" "function">)
                         "namespace" URILiteral
OptionDecl ::= <"declare" "option"> QName StringLiteral
OrderingModeDecl ::= <"declare" "ordering"> ("ordered" | "unordered")
```

```
EmptyOrderDecl ::= "declare" "default" "order"
                   ("empty" "greatest" | "empty" "least")
CopyNamespacesDecl ::= "declare" "copy-namespaces" PreserveMode
                       "," InheritMode
PreserveMode ::= "preserve" | "no-preserve"
InheritMode ::= "inherit" | "no-inherit"
DefaultCollationDecl ::= "declare" "default" "collation" URILiteral
BaseURIDecl ::= "declare" "base-uri" URILiteral
SchemaImport ::= "import" "schema" SchemaPrefix? URILiteral
                 ("at" URILiteral ("," URILiteral)*)?
SchemaPrefix ::= ("namespace" NCName "=") |
                 ("default" "element" "namespace")
ModuleImport ::= "import" "module" ("namespace" NCName "=")?
                 URILiteral ("at" URILiteral ("," URILiteral)*)?
VarDecl ::= "declare" "variable" "$" QName TypeDeclaration?
            ((":=" ExprSingle) | "external")
ConstructionDecl ::= "declare" "construction" ("strip" | "preserve")
FunctionDecl ::= "declare" "function" QName "(" ParamList? ")"
                 ("as" SequenceType)? (EnclosedExpr | "external")
ParamList ::= Param ("," Param)*
Param ::= "$" QName TypeDeclaration?
EnclosedExpr ::= "{" Expr "}"
QueryBody ::= Expr
Expr ::= ExprSingle ("," ExprSingle)*
ExprSingle ::= FLWORExpr | QuantifiedExpr | TypeswitchExpr |
               IfExpr | OrExpr
FLWORExpr ::= (ForClause | LetClause)+ WhereClause? OrderByClause?
              "return" ExprSingle
ForClause ::= "for" "$" VarName TypeDeclaration? PositionalVar?
              "in" ExprSingle ("," "$" VarName TypeDeclaration?
              PositionalVar? "in" ExprSingle)*
PositionalVar ::= "at" "$" VarName
LetClause ::= "let" "$" VarName TypeDeclaration? ":=" ExprSingle
              ("," "$" VarName TypeDeclaration? ":=" ExprSingle)*
WhereClause ::= "where" ExprSingle
OrderByClause ::= ("order" "by" | "stable" "order" "by") OrderSpecList
OrderSpecList ::= OrderSpec ("," OrderSpec)*
OrderSpec ::= ExprSingle OrderModifier
OrderModifier ::= ("ascending" | "descending")?
                  ("empty" "greatest" | "empty" "least")?
                  ("collation" URILiteral)?
QuantifiedExpr ::= ("some" "$" | "every" "$") VarName TypeDeclaration?
                   "in" ExprSingle
```

```
                  ("," "$" VarName TypeDeclaration? "in" ExprSingle)*
                  "satisfies" ExprSingle
TypeswitchExpr ::= "typeswitch" "(" Expr ")" CaseClause+
                  "default" ("$" VarName)? "return" ExprSingle
CaseClause ::= "case" ("$" VarName "as")? SequenceType "return" ExprSingle
IfExpr ::= "if" "(" Expr ")" "then" ExprSingle "else" ExprSingle
OrExpr ::= AndExpr ( "or" AndExpr )*
AndExpr ::= ComparisonExpr ( "and" ComparisonExpr )*
ComparisonExpr ::= RangeExpr ( (ValueComp
                              | GeneralComp
                              | NodeComp) RangeExpr )?
RangeExpr ::= AdditiveExpr ( "to" AdditiveExpr )?
AdditiveExpr ::= MultiplicativeExpr ( ("+" | "-") MultiplicativeExpr )*
MultiplicativeExpr ::= UnionExpr ( ("*" | "div" | "idiv" | "mod")
                       UnionExpr )*
UnionExpr ::= IntersectExceptExpr ( ("union" | "|") IntersectExceptExpr )*
IntersectExceptExpr ::= InstanceofExpr ( ("intersect" | "except")
                        InstanceofExpr )*
InstanceofExpr ::= TreatExpr ( "instance" "of" SequenceType )?
TreatExpr ::= CastableExpr ( "treat" "as" SequenceType )?
CastableExpr ::= CastExpr ( "castable" "as" SingleType )?
CastExpr ::= UnaryExpr ( "cast" "as" SingleType )?
UnaryExpr ::= ("-" | "+")* ValueExpr
ValueExpr ::= ValidateExpr | PathExpr | ExtensionExpr
GeneralComp ::= "=" | "!=" | "<" | "<=" | ">" | ">="
ValueComp ::= "eq" | "ne" | "lt" | "le" | "gt" | "ge"
NodeComp ::= "is" | "<<" | ">>"
ValidateExpr ::= ("validate" "{" | ("validate" ValidationMode "{"))
                Expr "}"
ValidationMode ::= "lax" | "strict"
ExtensionExpr ::= Pragma+ "{" Expr? "}"
Pragma ::= "(#" S? QName PragmaContents "#)"
PragmaContents ::= (Char* - (Char* '#)' Char*))
PathExpr ::= ("/" RelativePathExpr?) | ("//" RelativePathExpr)
            | RelativePathExpr
RelativePathExpr ::= StepExpr (("/" | "//") StepExpr)*
StepExpr ::= AxisStep | FilterExpr
AxisStep ::= (ForwardStep | ReverseStep) PredicateList
ForwardStep ::= (ForwardAxis NodeTest) | AbbrevForwardStep
ForwardAxis ::= "child" "::" | "descendant" "::" | "attribute" "::"
              | "self" "::" | "descendant-or-self" "::"
              | "following-sibling" "::" | "following" "::"
```

```
AbbrevForwardStep ::= "@"? NodeTest
ReverseStep ::= (ReverseAxis NodeTest) | AbbrevReverseStep
ReverseAxis ::= "parent" "::" | "ancestor" "::" | "preceding-sibling" "::"
                | "preceding" "::" | "ancestor-or-self" "::"
AbbrevReverseStep ::= ".."
NodeTest ::= KindTest | NameTest
NameTest ::= QName | Wildcard
Wildcard ::= "*" | NCName ":" "*" | "*" ":" NCName
FilterExpr ::= PrimaryExpr PredicateList
PredicateList ::= Predicate*
Predicate ::= "[" Expr "]"
PrimaryExpr ::= Literal | VarRef | ParenthesizedExpr | ContextItemExpr |
                FunctionCall | Constructor | OrderedExpr | UnorderedExpr
Literal ::= NumericLiteral | StringLiteral
NumericLiteral ::= IntegerLiteral | DecimalLiteral | DoubleLiteral
VarRef ::= "$" VarName
VarName ::= QName
ParenthesizedExpr ::= "(" Expr? ")"
ContextItemExpr ::= "."
OrderedExpr ::= <"ordered" "{"> Expr "}"
UnorderedExpr ::= "unordered" "{" Expr "}"
FunctionCall ::= QName "(" (ExprSingle ("," ExprSingle)*)? ")"
Constructor ::= DirectConstructor | ComputedConstructor
DirectConstructor ::= DirElemConstructor | DirCommentConstructor
                      | DirPIConstructor
DirElemConstructor ::= "<" QName DirAttributeList ("/>" |
                       (">" DirElemContent* "</" QName S? ">"))
DirAttributeList ::= (S (QName S? "=" S? DirAttributeValue)?)*
DirAttributeValue ::= ('"' (EscapeQuot | QuotAttrValueContent)* '"') |
                      ("'" (EscapeApos | AposAttrValueContent)* "'")
QuotAttrValueContent ::= QuotAttrContentChar | CommonContent
AposAttrValueContent ::= AposAttrContentChar | CommonContent
DirElemContent ::= DirectConstructor | ElementContentChar |
                   CdataSection | CommonContent
CommonContent ::= PredefinedEntityRef | CharRef | "{{" | "}}" |
                  EnclosedExpr
DirCommentConstructor ::= "<!--" DirCommentContents "-->"
DirCommentContents ::= ((Char - '-') | '-' (Char - '-'))*
DirPIConstructor ::= "<?" PITarget (S DirPIContents)? "?>"
DirPIContents ::= (Char* - (Char* '?>' Char*))
CDataSection ::= "<![CDATA[" CDataSectionContents "]]>"
CDataSectionContents ::= (Char* - (Char* ']]>' Char*))
```

```
ComputedConstructor ::= CompDocConstructor | CompElemConstructor
                        | CompAttrConstructor | CompTextConstructor
                        | CompCommentConstructor | CompPIConstructor
CompDocConstructor ::= "document" "{" Expr "}"
CompElemConstructor ::= ("element" QName "{" |
                         ("element" "{" Expr "}" "{"))
                        ContentExpr? "}"
ContentExpr ::= Expr
CompAttrConstructor ::= ("attribute" QName "{" |
                         ("attribute" "{" Expr "}" "{")) Expr? "}"
CompTextConstructor ::= "text" "{" Expr "}"
CompCommentConstructor ::= "comment" "{" Expr "}"
CompPIConstructor ::= ("processing-instruction" NCName "{" |
                      ("processing-instruction" "{" Expr "}" "{"))
                      Expr? "}"
SingleType ::= AtomicType "?"?
TypeDeclaration ::= "as" SequenceType
SequenceType ::= (ItemType OccurrenceIndicator?) |
                 "empty-sequence" "(" ")"
OccurrenceIndicator ::= "?" | "*" | "+"
ItemType ::= AtomicType | KindTest | "item" "(" ")"
AtomicType ::= QName
KindTest ::= DocumentTest | ElementTest | AttributeTest |
             SchemaElementTest | SchemaAttributeTest | PITest |
             CommentTest | TextTest | AnyKindTest
AnyKindTest ::= "node" "(" ")"
DocumentTest ::= "document-node" "(" (ElementTest | SchemaElementTest)? ")"
TextTest ::= "text" "(" ")"
CommentTest ::= "comment" "(" ")"
PITest ::= "processing-instruction" "(" (NCName | StringLiteral)? ")"
AttributeTest ::= "attribute"
                  "(" (AttribNameOrWildcard ("," TypeName)?)? ")"
AttribNameOrWildcard ::= AttributeName | "*"
SchemaAttributeTest ::= "schema-attribute" "(" AttributeDeclaration ")"
AttributeDeclaration ::= AttributeName
ElementTest ::= "element" "(" (ElementNameOrWildcard
                ("," TypeName "?"?)?)? ")"
ElementNameOrWildcard ::= ElementName | "*"
SchemaElementTest ::= "schema-element" "(" ElementDeclaration ")"
ElementDeclaration ::= ElementName
AttributeName ::= QName
ElementName ::= QName
TypeName ::= QName
URILiteral ::= StringLiteral
```

C.3 SQL/XML Grammar

The version of EBNF used to specify SQL/XML[2] is significantly different from that used by XQuery. For one thing, it does not use any regular expression notation. For another, nonterminal symbols are delineated by leading left angle brackets and trailing right angle brackets <...>, while terminal symbols in general stand for themselves – the exceptions are those characters specified in Table C-3. The SQL/XML EBNF includes a few productions for nonterminal symbols that stand for terminal symbols that are the same characters as the characters in this table. (Many of this sort of production appear in SQL/Foundation[3] instead of in SQL/XML; we repeat them in this appendix only if required for comprehension.)

***Table C—3** Symbols Used in SQL/XML EBNF*

Symbol	Meaning
< >	A character string enclosed in angle brackets is the name of a BNF nonterminal symbol.
::=	The nonterminal symbol appears to the left of the operator, and the formula that defines the element appears to the right.
[ ]	Square brackets indicate optional elements in a formula. The material within the brackets may be omitted or it may be specified explicitly.
{ }	Braces group elements in a formula.
|	The vertical bar indicates that the material to the left of the bar and the material to the right of the bar are alternatives; either one, but not both, can be used.
...	The ellipsis indicates that the element to which it applies in a formula may be repeated any number of times.
!!	Introduces normal English text, used when the definition of a syntactic element is not expressed in BNF.

2 The SQL/XML grammar presented here is taken from SQL/XML:2005.

3 ISO/IEC 9075-2:2003, *Information technology – Database languages – SQL – Part 2: Foundation (SQL/Foundation)*, International Organization for Standardization (Geneva, Switzerland: 2003).

Grammar C–3 contains the essential parts of the SQL/XML grammar. Some productions have been omitted because they are not necessary for comprehension. A number of the productions define nonterminal symbols that are originally defined in SQL/Foundation but are augmented in SQL/XML. Such productions begin with an alternative that indicates that there are alternatives that are defined in SQL/Foundation:

!! All alternatives from ISO/IEC 9075-2

A few other productions in SQL/XML completely replace a production for the same nonterminal symbol that appears in SQL/Foundation; the replacement is done to add new syntax on the right-hand side of the production in some form other than a new alternative. Such productions are not specially noted in Grammar C–3 because their replacement is all that is needed for understanding SQL/XML. In this grammar, we have omitted the grammar associated with embedding SQL statements, including those that use SQL/XML, into various host programming languages.

Grammar C—3 *SQL/XML EBNF*

```
<predefined type> ::=
    !! All alternatives from ISO/IEC 9075-2
  | <XML type>
<XML type> ::=
    XML [ <left paren> <XML type modifier> <right paren> ]
<XML type modifier> ::=
    <primary XML type modifier>
    [ <left paren> <secondary XML type modifier> <right paren> ]
<primary XML type modifier> ::=
    DOCUMENT
  | CONTENT
  | SEQUENCE
<secondary XML type modifier> ::=
    ANY
  | UNTYPED
  | XMLSCHEMA <XML valid according to what> [ <XML valid element clause> ]
<nonparenthesized value expression primary> ::=
    !! All alternatives from ISO/IEC 9075-2
  | <XML cast specification>
<cast specification> ::=
    CAST <left paren> <cast operand> AS <cast target>
```

```
    [ <XML passing mechanism> ]
    <right paren>
<XML cast specification> ::=
    XMLCAST <left paren> <XML cast operand> AS
    <XML cast target> [ <XML passing mechanism> ] <right paren>
<XML cast operand> ::=
    <value expression>
  | <implicitly typed value specification>
<XML cast target> ::=
    <domain name>
  | <data type>
<common value expression> ::=
    !! All alternatives from ISO/IEC 9075-2
  | <XML value expression>
<character value function> ::=
    !! All alternatives from ISO/IEC 9075-2
  | <XML character string serialization>
<XML character string serialization> ::=
    XMLSERIALIZE <left paren> [ <document or content> ]
    <XML value expression> AS <data type>
    [ <XML serialize version> ]
    [ <XML declaration option> ] <right paren>
<XML declaration option> ::=
    INCLUDING XMLDECLARATION
  | EXCLUDING XMLDECLARATION
<document or content> ::=
    DOCUMENT
  | CONTENT
<XML serialize version> ::=
    VERSION <character string literal>
<blob value function> ::=
    !! All alternatives from ISO/IEC 9075-2
  | <XML binary string serialization>
<XML binary string serialization> ::=
    XMLSERIALIZE <left paren> [ <document or content> ]
    <XML value expression> AS <data type>
    [ ENCODING <XML encoding specification> ]
    [ <XML serialize version> ]
    [ <XML declaration option> ] <right paren>
<XML encoding specification> ::= <XML encoding name>
<XML encoding name> ::= <SQL language identifier>
<XML value expression> ::= <XML primary>
<XML primary> ::=
    <value expression primary>
  | <XML value function>
```

```
<XML value function> ::=
    <XML comment>
  | <XML concatenation>
  | <XML document>
  | <XML element>
  | <XML forest>
  | <XML parse>
  | <XML PI>
  | <XML query>
  | <XML text>
  | <XML validate>
<XML comment> ::=
    XMLCOMMENT <left paren> <string value expression>
    [ <XML returning clause> ] <right paren>
<XML concatenation> ::=
    XMLCONCAT <left paren> <XML value expression>
    { <comma> <XML value expression> }...
    [ <XML returning clause> ] <right paren>
<XML document> ::=
    XMLDOCUMENT <left paren> <XML value expression>
    [ <XML returning clause> ] <right paren>
<XML element> ::=
    XMLELEMENT <left paren> NAME <XML element name>
    [ <comma> <XML namespace declaration> ] [ <comma> <XML attributes> ]
    [ { <comma> <XML element content> }...
    [ OPTION <XML content option> ] ]
    [ <XML returning clause> ] <right paren>
<XML element name> ::= <identifier>
<XML attributes> ::=
    XMLATTRIBUTES <left paren> <XML attribute list> <right paren>
<XML attribute list> ::=
    <XML attribute> [ { <comma> <XML attribute> }... ]
<XML attribute> ::=
    <XML attribute value> [ AS <XML attribute name> ]
<XML attribute value> ::= <value expression>
<XML attribute name> ::= <identifier>
<XML element content> ::= <value expression>
<XML content option> ::=
    NULL ON NULL
  | EMPTY ON NULL
  | ABSENT ON NULL
  | NIL ON NULL
  | NIL ON NO CONTENT
<XML forest> ::=
    XMLFOREST <left paren> [ <XML namespace declaration> <comma> ]
    <forest element list>
```

```
    [ OPTION <XML content option> ]
    [ <XML returning clause> ]
    <right paren>
<forest element list> ::=
    <forest element> [ { <comma> <forest element> }... ]
<forest element> ::=
    <forest element value> [ AS <forest element name> ]
<forest element value> ::= <value expression>
<forest element name> ::= <identifier>
<XML parse> ::=
    XMLPARSE <left paren> <document or content> <string value expression>
    <XML whitespace option> <right paren>
<XML whitespace option> ::=
    { PRESERVE | STRIP } WHITESPACE
<XML PI> ::=
    XMLPI <left paren> NAME <XML PI target>
    [ <comma> <string value expression> ]
    [ <XML returning clause> ]
    <right paren>
<XML PI target> ::= <identifier>
<XML query> ::=
    XMLQUERY <left paren>
    <XQuery expression>
    [ <XML query argument list> ]
    [ <XML returning clause>
    [ <XML query returning mechanism> ] ]
    <XML query empty handling option>
    <right paren>
<XQuery expression> ::= <character string literal>
<XML query argument list> ::=
    PASSING <XML query default passing mechanism>
    <XML query argument>
    [ { <comma> <XML query argument> }... ]
<XML query default passing mechanism> ::=
<XML passing mechanism>
<XML query argument> ::=
<XML query context item>
| <XML query variable>
<XML query context item> ::=
    <value expression> [ <XML passing mechanism> ]
<XML query variable> ::=
    <value expression> AS <identifier>
    [ <XML passing mechanism> ]
<XML query returning mechanism> ::=
    <XML passing mechanism>
```

```
<XML query empty handling option> ::=
    NULL ON EMPTY
  | EMPTY ON EMPTY
<XML text> ::=
    XMLTEXT <left paren> <string value expression>
    [ <XML returning clause> ] <right paren>
<XML validate> ::=
    XMLVALIDATE <left paren>
    <document or content or sequence>
    <XML value expression>
    [ <XML valid according to clause> ]
    <right paren>
<document or content or sequence> ::=
    <document or content>
  | SEQUENCE
<table primary> ::=
    !! All alternatives from ISO/IEC 9075-2
  | <XML iterate> [ AS ] <correlation name>
    <left paren> <derived column list> <right paren>
  | <XML table> [ AS ] <correlation name>
    [ <left paren> <derived column list> <right paren> ]
<XML iterate> ::=
    XMLITERATE <left paren> <XML value expression> <right paren>
<XML table> ::=
    XMLTABLE <left paren>
    [ <XML namespace declaration> <comma> ]
    <XML table row pattern>
    [ <XML table argument list> ]
    COLUMNS <XML table column definitions> <right paren>
<XML table row pattern> ::=
    <character string literal>
<XML table argument list> ::=
    PASSING <XML table argument passing mechanism>
    <XML query argument>
    [ { <comma> <XML query argument> }... ]
<XML table argument passing mechanism> ::=
    <XML passing mechanism>
<XML table column definitions> ::=
    <XML table column definition>
    [ { <comma> <XML table column definition> }... ]
<XML table column definition> ::=
    <XML table ordinality column definition>
  | <XML table regular column definition>
<XML table ordinality column definition> ::=
    <column name> FOR ORDINALITY
```

```
<XML table regular column definition> ::=
    <column name> <data type> [ <XML passing mechanism> ]
    [ <default clause> ]
    [ PATH <XML table column pattern> ]
<XML table column pattern> ::=
    <character string literal>
<with clause> ::=
    WITH [ <XML lexically scoped options> ]
    [ <comma> ] [ [ RECURSIVE ] <with list> ]
<predicate> ::=
    !! All alternatives from ISO/IEC 9075-2
  | <XML content predicate>
  | <XML document predicate>
  | <XML exists predicate>
  | <XML valid predicate>
<XML content predicate> ::=
    <XML value expression> IS [ NOT ] CONTENT
<XML document predicate> ::=
    <XML value expression> IS [ NOT ] DOCUMENT
<XML exists predicate> ::=
    XMLEXISTS <left paren> <XQuery expression>
    [ <XML query argument list> ]<right paren>
<XML valid predicate> ::=
    <XML value expression> IS [ NOT ] VALID
<document or content or sequence>
    [ <XML valid according to clause> ]
<uppercase hexit> ::=
    <digit> | A | B | C | D | E | F
<aggregate function> ::=
    !! All alternatives from ISO/IEC 9075-2
  | <XML aggregate>
<XML aggregate> ::=
    XMLAGG <left paren> <XML value expression>
    [ ORDER BY <sort specification list> ]
    [ <XML returning clause> ]
    <right paren>
<XML lexically scoped options> ::=
    <XML lexically scoped option> [ <comma> <XML lexically scoped option> ]
<XML lexically scoped option> ::=
    <XML namespace declaration>
  | <XML binary encoding>
<XML namespace declaration> ::=
    XMLNAMESPACES <left paren> <XML namespace declaration item>
    [ { <comma> <XML namespace declaration item> }... ] <right paren>
```

```
<XML namespace declaration item> ::=
    <XML regular namespace declaration item>
  | <XML default namespace declaration item>
<XML namespace prefix> ::= <identifier>
<XML namespace URI> ::= <character string literal>
<XML regular namespace declaration item> ::=
    <XML namespace URI> AS <XML namespace prefix>
<XML default namespace declaration item> ::=
    DEFAULT <XML namespace URI>
  | NO DEFAULT
<XML binary encoding> ::=
    XMLBINARY [ USING ] { BASE64 | HEX }
<XML returning clause> ::=
    RETURNING { CONTENT | SEQUENCE }
<XML passing mechanism> ::=
    BY REF
  | BY VALUE
<XML valid according to clause> ::=
    ACCORDING TO XMLSCHEMA <XML valid according to what>
    [ <XML valid element clause> ]
<XML valid according to what> ::=
    <XML valid according to URI>
  | <XML valid according to identifier>
<XML valid according to URI> ::=
    URI <XML valid target namespace URI> [ <XML valid schema location> ]
  | NO NAMESPACE [ <XML valid schema location> ]
<XML valid target namespace URI> ::=
    <XML URI>
<XML URI> ::= <character string literal>
<XML valid schema location> ::=
    LOCATION <XML valid schema location URI>
<XML valid schema location URI> ::= <XML URI>
<XML valid according to identifier> ::=
    ID <registered XML Schema name>
<XML valid element clause> ::=
    <XML valid element name specification>
  | <XML valid element namespace specification>
    [ <XML valid element name specification> ]
<XML valid element name specification> ::=
    ELEMENT <XML valid element name>
<XML valid element namespace specification> ::=
    NO NAMESPACE
  | NAMESPACE <XML valid element namespace URI>
<XML valid element namespace URI> ::= <XML URI>
<XML valid element name> ::= <identifier>
```

```
<generation expression> ::=
    <left paren> [ WITH <XML lexically scoped options> ]
    <value expression> <right paren>
<check constraint definition> ::=
    CHECK <left paren> [ WITH <XML lexically scoped options> ]
    <search condition> <right paren>
<assertion definition> ::=
    CREATE ASSERTION <constraint name> CHECK
    <left paren> [ WITH <XML lexically scoped options> ]
    <search condition> <right paren>
<SQL parameter declaration> ::=
    [ <parameter mode> ]
    [ <SQL parameter name> ]
    <parameter type>
    [ RESULT ]
    [ <XML passing mechanism> ]
<parameter type> ::=
    <data type> [ <locator indication> ]
    [ <document or content> ] [ <string type option> ]
<returns clause> ::=
    RETURNS <returns type> [ <XML passing mechanism> ]
<returns data type> ::=
    <data type> [ <locator indication> ]
    [ <document or content> ] [ <string type option> ]
<string type option> ::=
    AS <character string type>
<SQL session statement> ::=
    !! All alternatives from ISO/IEC 9075-2
  | <set XML option statement>
<fetch target list> ::=
    <target specification 1> [ { <comma> <target specification 1> }... ]
<target specification 1> ::=
    <target specification> [ <XML passing mechanism> ]
<select target list> ::=
    <target specification 1> [ { <comma> <target specification 1> }... ]
<delete statement: searched> ::=
    DELETE [ WITH <XML lexically scoped options> ] FROM <target table>
    [ WHERE <search condition> ]
<insert statement> ::=
    INSERT [ WITH <XML lexically scoped options> ] INTO <insertion target>
    <insert columns and source>
<merge statement> ::=
    MERGE [ WITH <XML lexically scoped options> ] INTO <target table>
    [ [ AS ] <correlation name> ]
    USING <table reference> ON <search condition>
    <merge operation specification>
```

```
<update statement: positioned> ::=
    UPDATE [ WITH <XML lexically scoped options> ] <target table>
    SET <set clause list> WHERE CURRENT OF <cursor name>
<update statement: searched> ::=
    UPDATE [ WITH <XML lexically scoped options> ] <target table>
    SET <set clause list> [ WHERE <search condition> ]
<compound statement> ::=
    [ <beginning label> <colon> ]
    BEGIN [ [ NOT ] ATOMIC ]
    [ DECLARE <XML lexically scoped options> <semicolon> ]
    [ <local declaration list> ]
    [ <local cursor declaration list> ]
    [ <local handler declaration list> ]
    [ <SQL statement list> ]
    END [ <ending label> ]
<singleton variable assignment> ::=
    SET <assignment target> <equals operator> <assignment source>
    [ <XML passing mechanism> ]
<set XML option statement> ::=
    SET XML OPTION <document or content>
```

C.4 Chapter Summary

In this appendix, we have presented the grammar for XQuery and the grammar for SQL/XML. These two languages are defined using different versions of EBNF, but it's reasonably easy to mentally map between the two notations.

Index

D

F

G

H

I

Q

R

V

W

X

About the Authors

Jim Melton is editor of all parts of ISO/IEC 9075 (SQL) and is a representative for database standards at Oracle Corporation. Since 1986, he has been his company's representative to ANSI INCITS Technical Committee H2 for Database and a US representative to ISO/IEC JTC1/SC32/WG3 (Database Languages). In addition, Jim has participated in the W3C's XML Query Working Group since 1998 and is currently co-Chair of that Working Group. He is also Chair of the WG's Full-Text Task Force, co-Chair of the Update Language Task Force, and co-editor of two XQuery-related specifications. He is the author of several SQL books.

Stephen Buxton is Director of Product Management at Mark Logic Corporation. Stephen is a member of the W3C XQuery Working Group and a founder/member of the XQuery Full-Text Task Force. Stephen has written a number of papers and articles on XQuery and SQL/XML, and is an editor of several W3C XQuery Full-Text specs. Before joining Mark Logic, Stephen was Director of Product Management for Text and XML at Oracle Corporation.